Manhattan Phoenix

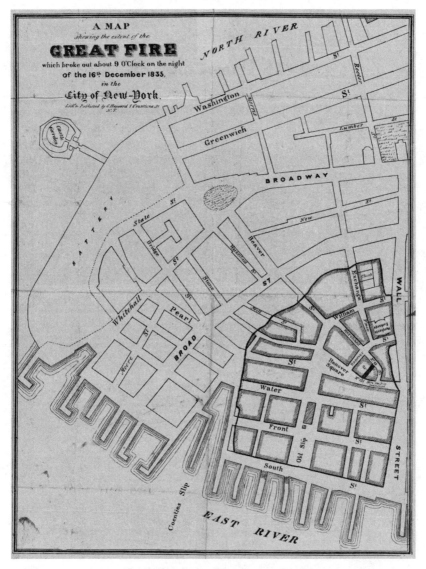

The Great Fire of 1835 devastated Lower Manhattan, but the clearing away of the older sections of New York accelerated the city's unparalleled northward growth.

Manhattan Phoenix

The Great Fire of 1835 and the Emergence of Modern New York

DANIEL S. LEVY

OXFORD

UNIVERSITY PRESS

Oxford University Press is a department of the University of Oxford. It furthers
the University's objective of excellence in research, scholarship, and education
by publishing worldwide. Oxford is a registered trade mark of Oxford University
Press in the UK and certain other countries.

Published in the United States of America by Oxford University Press
198 Madison Avenue, New York, NY 10016, United States of America.

CIP data is on file at the Library of Congress
ISBN 978-0-19-538237-2

DOI: 10.1093/oso/9780195382372.001.0001

1 3 5 7 9 8 6 4 2

Printed by LSC Communications, United States of America

For my Three Muses
Lillie, Clara, and Emma

"Silence? What can New York—noisy, roaring, rumbling, tumbling bustling, stormy, turbulent New York—have to do with *silence*? Amid the universal clatter, the incessant din of business, the all swallowing vortex of the great money whirlpool, the strife and the warfare, and the fever and the trembling—who has any, even distant, idea, of the profound repose, the hushed lethargy of silence?"

Walt Whitman, *New York Aurora*, March 19, 1842

Contents

Acknowledgments

As long as I can remember, I have been fascinated by my hometown, and in the fall of my sophomore year at New York University I took a class called Exploring Architecture in New York. The course was taught by Professor Carol Krinsky. For our final assignment she had us study a stretch of the city, and I diligently catalogued all the buildings along Sixth Avenue from 20th Street through 54th Street. As I prepared my paper, I went to see Professor Krinsky. While she was impressed that I had described all the structures, she then asked me to think about why, for instance, Richard Upjohn's Gothic Revival Church of the Holy Communion stood on 20th Street, what brought about Bryant Park alongside 42nd, and what was the reason for the series of post–World War II towers that march up the avenue in the 40s and 50s? Professor Krinsky made me realize that I needed to not only look at what was there, but to try and understand what went into the creation of an intricate urban area like New York.

I continued to study the city's history, explored the town with my high school friend Danny Luey, did research on the streams and waterways of Manhattan for South Street Seaport Museum's *Seaport* magazine, and earned a master's degree in architectural preservation at Columbia University, where my thesis dealt with a firemen's monument set in the shadow of Trinity Church, Upjohn's first great creation.

Manhattan Phoenix is the result of years of thought and research on New York, and how and why it transformed from a large urban center to a world metropolis. There are numerous people along with Professor Krinsky and Danny Luey whom I would like to thank for helping me understand and explore the city I love. My agents Michael Carlisle and Ethan Bassoff at InkWell Management long knew of my interest in New York and encouraged me to put together the proposal. They then brought it by Oxford University Press, where Timothy Bent and Niko Pfund accepted the idea. Throughout the writing of this book, Tim has been a very, very patient editor who suggested insightful points, both large and small, for the volume you now hold.

I was fortunate to have three sharp-eyed readers. My old friend and *Time* magazine colleague David Bjerklie—who also read the manuscript for my previous book, *Two-Gun Cohen*—diligently went through the pages and offered helpful thoughts, as did historians Marika Plater and Nicholas Sage.

Needless to say, as I worked on this volume I spent a lot of time in libraries and archives reading through old newspapers, letters, diaries, and planning records. One of my main homes away from home was the New-York Historical Society, that treasure trove of the city's past on Central Park West, and am grateful for the help of much of the staff, especially Edward O'Reilly, Mariam Touba, and Jean Ashton. Another hangout of mine was Columbia University's libraries, where I passed many months searching the stacks. Some of the other librarians who have assisted me over the years include Helen Beckert at the Glen Ridge Public Library, Lori Chien at the Jervis Public Library, Laura Ruttum at the New York Public Library, Marissa Maggs at Trinity Church's archives, John Zarrillo at New York University's archives, Michelle Kennedy at South Street Seaport Museum, D.A. Levy at the Maritime Heritage Project, as well as those at the Library of Congress, the National Archives, the New York City Municipal Archives, Harvard University's Baker and Houghton Libraries, Yale University's Beinecke Rare Book & Manuscript Library, the Hagley Museum and Library, the Museum of the City of New York, the National Canal Museum Archives, the American Antiquarian Society, the Oberlin College Archives, and not to forget the digital libraries created and maintained by those at the Internet Archive, HathiTrust Digital Library, Google Books, and Newspapers.com.

Joseph Pierro helped me appreciate the forces at play in pre–Civil War America, and others whom I want to acknowledge include Peter-Christian Aigner, Anne Brown, William "Liam" Dickson, David Gary, Koko T.G.O. Levy, Lisa and Michael Luey, Jonathan Petropoulos, and Mike Wallace.

This book took a long time to write, and there was a running joke in my home where I would say to my wife, Lillie, and my daughters, Clara and Emma, "Did you know that I am writing a book on pre–Civil War New York?" They would without fail look surprised, smile, and say, "Really! We didn't know that." Throughout, they encouraged my exploration of New York and embraced the volume's presence in our house with humor, patience, and love.

Preface: The Bowery Theatre Burns

The fire that started at the Chambers' livery stable spread quickly. Fueled by bales of hay, and whipped up by heavy winds from the west on that May evening in 1828, the blaze on Bayard Street between the Bowery and Elizabeth Street hopped to nearby buildings, so that by the time firemen like Morris Franklin of the Brass Back Engine Company arrived, a reporter for the *New York American* noted how "the horizon was lighted up with bursts of flames, which . . . were visible from various parts of the city."

The Bowery Theatre stood nearby. Manager Charles Antonio Gilfert had been busy finalizing plans for a festive benefit for his wife, the British actress Agnes Holman Gilfert, who was to appear in the tragedy *Thirty Years, or the Life of a Gambler*. Yet as the cast and crew learned of the fire, they fled the building and, along with those living and working in the area, huddled outside as the firemen set up their engines and searched for water to stop the flames.

Manhattan lacked a reliable source of fresh water, and the men first found some in a nearby family's cistern. It proved too little, though, to save Chambers' livery and its horses. As other fire companies raced to the scene, one of the companies' engineers directed the crews. "A line was formed . . . stretching from the foot of Catherine Street to the burning building, and engaging the services of six hundred and eighty men," recalled fireman Charles Forrester. No fewer than 19 companies snaked their hoses half a mile to the East River. Householders also joined in the work by "passing the buckets from hand to hand" to fill the engines as the firemen frantically pumped the long-handled brakes to build up pressure to spray the water.

While the engine companies drenched the buildings, some of the firemen helped homeowners save their belongings, and those from two hook-and-ladder companies—which brought the equipment to reach the upper floors, punch holes in walls to vent heat and smoke, and if necessary pull down walls and nearby houses—tried to prevent the blaze from spreading further. As the men worked, wind blew the flames closer to the Bowery Theatre. Fearing for the building, the firemen leaned a ladder up against it and started to soak the top of the structure. Designed by the prominent architect and civil engineer Ithiel Town, the theater boasted four-foot-thick fireproof brick sidewalls and iron window shutters. This made the actors and crews believe their wardrobes and sets would be safe. They therefore watched in horror as the flames raced up to the pediment and melted the tarred-paper-and-zinc roof, turning the top of the theater into what the *New York Evening Post* called "a pyramid of flame."[1]

By then, Franklin had made it up to the Bowery's third tier to supervise his men. Someone yelled, "All out!" and they fled. Franklin couldn't find a quick exit and was forced to jump from the balcony to the orchestra level. Bruised and stunned, he groped his way out as firemen pulled the doors shut. The roof and the chimneys then crashed in, collapsing the western wall and killing a fireman.

Colleagues carried Franklin to a nearby house, but once the foreman caught his breath he returned to the scene. After three hours battling the blaze, the crews finally got it under control. Even so, the once stately Bowery with its towering Doric columns stood a scorched shell, its front cracked and warped. And some 20 other buildings, such as Chambers' livery, Thomas Swift's porterhouse, a barbershop, Givin's Stagehouse and tavern, Benjamin Scribner's Shakespeare tavern, and a confectionary shop all lay in ruins.

Afterward, many heaped praise on the firemen. The *American* noted how "In no part of the world is there a body of men, of more zeal, intelligence in their calling, or courage, than the New-York firemen." Former mayor Philip Hone, who had officiated at the theater's 1826 groundbreaking, came by the following day to look at the site, and wrote in his diary: "The conclusion is irresistible that it might have been saved if certain smaller buildings adjoining to it, which were utterly destroyed, had been pulled down in time." Some pointedly criticized the firemen, saying they should have hosed the building more thoroughly before the roof ignited, and called for an inspection of the companies' equipment, noting how their elaborately painted engines with the shiny brass hardware seemed to be made more for show than for actual use.

The New York Association, a consortium of businessmen, owned the Bowery Theatre. Association members, a Who's Who of prominent New Yorkers in the 1820s, including Henry Astor and James Alexander Hamilton—Alexander Hamilton's fourth child—met the day after the blaze. They "resolved" that the theater immediately be rebuilt. Gilfert had the site cleared and hired architect Joseph Sera. Peale's Museum & Gallery of the Fine Arts near City Hall, meanwhile, lost no time immortalizing the fire, commissioning two artists to create a mammoth canvas of the scene, which visitors could view for 25¢.[2]

By August 1828, less than three months after the fire, workers completed Sera's redesign, which the press pronounced to be grand and plush. A former Bowery scene painter, Sera based the new theater on the Temple of Theseus, a sanctuary the Athenians dedicated to the gods Hephaestus and Athena, mythological patrons of the arts and crafts. The *New York Mirror* wrote that with its faux-marble stucco exterior, the structure had a "simplicity and grandeur." The marble steps at the entrance led to a portico fronted by six Doric columns and offered access to a theater profuse with ancient Greek motifs. Some 600 gas burners spaced throughout the house lit up its crimson-cushioned seats, and boxes embossed with golden griffins, eagles, and wreaths; the balconies were gilded, the balustrades made from mahogany. The light-blue, white, and golden doors were designed to swing both ways to lessen panic in the event of another fire. The Bowery possessed the largest stage in America, and its proscenium arch was painted to look like Parian marble and sported images of Apollo as well as the muses Thalia and Melpomene. Overhead stretched a dome on which was painted a sweeping scene of a woman scattering flowers.

The day of the theater's reopening, Philip Hone, who had served as New York's mayor from 1826 to 1827 and kept a diary that is one of the major chronicles of the period, marveled that the "immense Edifice has been built in the short span of 86 days." To calm its fire-fearing potential patrons, local architects and builders had put an item in the *New York Gazette & General Advertiser* letting all know that they had inspected the building and could "certify without hesitation that the materials used for the walls, the roof, the support of boxes, the gallery, and every other part of the Theatre . . . render the building in all respects perfectly safe." Then, at the grand opening, the popular Shakespearean actor Edwin Forrest who had debuted at the theater two years earlier and whose feud with the British star William Macready would lead to the deadly 1849 Astor Place Riot, recited a poem. Afterward, the audience enjoyed a performance of the prolific British playwright Frederick Reynolds' comedy *The Dramatist*, and the English-born tightrope walker known as Herr Cline, who was scheduled to perform the day of the fire, displayed his amazing "Elastic Cord" show.[3]

While the city now had four playhouses—the Bowery, Park, Chatham, and Lafayette—Frances Trollope, mother of British novelist Anthony Trollope, singled out the Bowery "as pretty a theatre as I ever entered, perfect as to size and proportion, elegantly decorated, and the scenery and machinery equal to any in London." Owning a theater, however, even one as stylish as the Bowery, could be a brutal business. Jacksonian-era audiences demanded a constantly changing offering of entertainment and were notorious for hurling food and other objects at the actors, as well as fighting amongst themselves. They also regularly trashed theaters.[4]

Running a theater was also expensive. Gilfert suffered from regular financial woes, and died on July 30, 1829, a day after his lease on the Bowery ran out. The New York–born comedian James Hackett briefly oversaw the place. Actor Thomas Hamblin then received a lease and started staging shows in August 1830. Hamblin, who got his start in London playhouses and had arrived in the city five years earlier, knew how to cater to a general audience. He put on elaborate melodramas and lively spectacles, including horse-and-dog exhibitions and shows with elephants. Over the course of the next two decades during which he owned the Bowery, the British manager bestowed upon his theater a decidedly democratic American tone. Yet, the theater burned three more times during his time there.

This too proved the fate of Manhattan. For most of the 19th century, the city suffered regular and catastrophic fires. Its lack of a reliable water source, a dearth of construction codes, and at times unruly volunteer fire companies only exacerbated the problem. The threat of fire was especially evident with the outbreak of the Great Fire of 1835, which consumed 674 buildings in the Wall Street district. While destructive, it and other conflagrations allowed for new construction. The city then flourished in the decades leading through the end of the Civil War, as builders pushed the settled community northward. As they did, Manhattan metamorphosed from an island of ponds and streams, winding roads, small homes, and local markets, to one with wide avenues, lavish mansions, booming industries, and a sprawling Central Park. While its population soared, immigrants streamed in, developers subdivided the land, and buildings like the Bowery, along with thousands of businesses and row houses rose, then were razed or burned down, only to be quickly replaced by newer, grander ones. Many of the changes to the city came so fast that the city government was unable to handle such basic issues as sanitation, which contributed to the pandemics that periodically ravaged families in crowded tenements and wealthy homes. The arrival of a fresh water supply from Westchester in 1842 did help ameliorate some of this—and also proved essential to combat the fires—but the city's expansion also stoked the power of gangs, and those politicians who called on criminals to help them seize public offices and coffers.

Such a grand, whiplash-like transformation should have crippled New York. Residents, though, refused to let turmoil and loss hobble their town. They constantly sought to renew and improve the community, just like the citizens of London would after their great fire in 1666, and those in San Francisco following their devastating earthquake in 1906. While those catastrophes were clearly more destructive than anything that happened in New York, Manhattanites refused to let misfortune stop them. For during these crucial decades as they quenched blazes, fought over the issues of slavery and what it meant to be a New Yorker and an American, the city's inhabitants—both rich and poor, native-born and newly arrived—turned their island city into the nation's commercial, financial, and cultural center. For like the phoenix, a mythical bird which consumes itself in flames and from its ashes springs anew, Manhattan would each time emerge refreshed and stronger following its fires, its plagues, its riots, as its development pushed farther up the island.

And more importantly, the changes that took place in those years set the stage for even bigger ones a half century later. It made possible the 1898 consolidation of Manhattan, the Bronx, Brooklyn, Queens, and Staten Island, and the creation of what we today know as Greater New York.

Manhattan Phoenix is the story of New York during the first half of the 1800s. It explores the Great Fire of 1835 and its effect on the city, told through a number of subjects such as fire, land development, culture, water, abolitionism, and politics, that will progress chronologically through the book. At the same it will follow the lives of New Yorkers who help tell the story—those like Philip Hone, the lawyer George Templeton Strong, the restaurateur Thomas Downing, Mayor Fernando Wood, and Central Park designer Frederick Law Olmsted, along with the impresario Thomas Hamblin, his Bowery Theatre, and its proud and often unruly audience.

Nineteenth-century New York is a city that both embodied America and, in some ways, transcended it, a place unlike anything else in the United States. This is a tale of how the famous as well as the forgotten inhabitants of this once provincial center on the Eastern Seaboard turned their restive community into a dynamic world metropolis.

Introduction

1825–1835: "One of the Greatest Commercial Towns in the World"

On January 7, 1825, three years before the Bowery Theatre fire and just over a decade before the fire that began New York's renaissance, investors gathered around the fireplace at the Tontine Coffee House, located on the northwest corner of Wall Street and Water Street. They gazed at the glowing firebox and saw firsthand the advantages of the anthracite coal shipped in from northeast Pennsylvania, about which they had read in such papers as the *New York American*. The press had lauded the "rich mines," and promoters were trying to interest those gathered in their product, explaining how they planned to ship the slow-burning and low-smoking coal to Manhattan by way of a new canal, one that would run from Pennsylvania to the Hudson River. Most of all, they stressed the vast profits investors could make.

Maurice and William Wurts, the promoters in question, had long dreamed of this stock-offering day. The dry goods merchants laid the groundwork for their Delaware & Hudson Canal Company, garnering the support of DeWitt Clinton, the canal-advocating New York governor whose Erie Canal was nearing completion. In the early 1820s the brothers had also convinced Philip Hone of the wisdom of their scheme, and the retired auctioneer and well-connected future mayor helped form the firm. In March 1823 the Pennsylvania legislature approved the Wurts' proposal to canalize the Lackawaxen River, and the following month, New York's legislature incorporated the Delaware & Hudson.

The advertisements and the articles by the press moved things along. People quickly scooped up the $100 shares for what was to be the first privately built canal in the United States. Hone himself handed over $3,360 as first payment on 672 shares of stock. In just a few hours on the 7th, investors had bought all $1.5 million worth of shares. In March, officers gathered again at Tontine and made Hone president. They had convinced Benjamin Wright to take the position of principal engineer. The Connecticut-born

Wright was then completing the Erie Canal. In March, he dispatched John Bloomfield Jervis, who had worked on the Erie Canal, to survey the area near their mine, and then planned a 32-foot-wide canal to run along the banks of the Delaware and the Lackawaxen Rivers and then to the Hudson River. At the July 13 groundbreaking, which took place in the Catskills town of Mamakating, located in the southeast part of Sullivan County, Hone turned the first shovel full of dirt, telling the crowd that while the canal might be small compared to the Erie Canal, it would benefit "the products of your own farms, and the timber of your own forests."

As with the stock, things moved fast. In December 1828, ten canal boats filled with coal left the newly founded community of Honesdale—named in Hone's honor and today the county seat of Wayne County, Pennsylvania—for a 108-mile ride to New York City. The coal sold well, the company prospered, and Hone, whose opinion was highly respected around town, helped promote the product, lending his name to an ad for Pierce's Kitchen Range and Cooking Apparatus, which had been adapted to use Lackawanna coal and was now installed in his own kitchen, "which I approve of very highly, and recommend to public patronage."[1]

The canal was part of the burgeoning of trade that followed the end of the War of 1812, a time called the Era of Good Feelings when the new republic was entering a period of domestic tranquility that saw an expanding international trade. Canals as well as ports, steamboats, and roads were seen as essential for the growth of the nation, which in 1816 only had 100 miles of manmade waterways. Canals rapidly became big business. Besides the Delaware & Hudson and the Erie, numerous others, such as the Champlain (1823) and Morris (1831), crisscrossed the land. By 1840, the nation could claim 3,000 miles of canals.

None of those waterways, though, could compete with the audacious scale of the Erie Canal. Early on, Clinton seized on the idea of a grand path to the west that would turn New York into the world's greatest commercial emporium. When the 338-mile-long canal opened in 1825, Hone, along with Alderman Henry Wyckoff. headed to Albany to invite dignitaries to Manhattan for a gala celebration. As part of the festivities, Clinton and others boarded the *Seneca Chief* for a trip down the canal to the Hudson River. When the boat arrived downriver in New York on November 4, they came upon a three-mile-wide flotilla made up of steamboats, visiting British war ships, and vessels filled with dignitaries and ordinary citizens. Guns fired salutes; those on the shore and rooftops cheered. At the Narrows—the mile-wide waterway that leads from New York harbor into the Atlantic Ocean—Clinton sanctified the "Wedding of the Waters" by pouring in two casks of Lake Erie water while others added waters from the Mississippi, the Amazon, and the Danube. The group then headed back to the Battery, a park located at the tip of Manhattan, for a grand parade. One hundred thousand people in a city of 166,000 came out for the occasion. That night, thousands feasted at a dinner at the Lafayette Theatre and gazed at the fireworks lighting up the sky.

The Erie Canal's success proved Clinton's prescience. Within a year of the Wedding of the Waters, shipping costs from Lake Erie to the city dropped from $100 a ton to $9. Five hundred trade and commercial businesses opened in the city in 1825, including textile factories, sawmills, and iron works. Soon the annual value of material passing through hit $15 million. Businessmen were flocking to New York.[2] New York was well on its way to establishing a transportation network that gave it both access and financial dominance over the nation. Besides canals allowing trade with states as far away as western Ohio, roads connected it to the hinterlands, railroad lines were laid and trains started to roll into town, and sloops and steamboats slipped up and down the East Coast, along the Hudson and East Rivers as well as through an intricate network of rivers, inlets, and bays. The city's manufactured goods headed west and south, while southern and western farm produce flowed to Manhattan. Dock workers meanwhile kept busy transferring southern cotton and wheat to Europe-bound ships. The vessels came back with finished British and Continental goods.

The city had already taken the lead in the China trade, with merchants like John Jacob Astor making a fortune by sending ships with furs and opium to Asia, then returning with silk, porcelain, tea, and ivory. There was likewise a growing trade with Central and South America, as shippers packed outbound vessels with flour, textiles, and machinery, and brought back coffee and hides. Not surprisingly, the city had become the nation's center of shipbuilding. Shipwrights, blacksmiths, and caulkers turned out barques, fishing schooners, and whitehalls, with shipyards launching 19 percent of the nation's ships, barks, and brigs in 1831.[3]

* * *

New York's location made all this possible. In the 1820s the city was just on Manhattan Island. The settled part of town stretched up to around 14th Street. To the north were hamlets, villages, and communities such as Bloomingdale, Harlem, Harsenville, Manhattanville, and Yorkville. With its sprawling harbor and river system, it was developing in just the right spot on the Eastern Seaboard. When novelist James Fenimore Cooper moved down from upstate New York to New York in 1822, he noted how "It is only necessary to sit down with a minute map of the country before you, to perceive, at a glance, that Nature herself has intended the island of Manhattan for the site of one of the greatest commercial towns in the world." He announced that "the hour of this supremacy has arrived."[4]

With so much arriving on ships, one arena in which fortunes could be made was in auctioning. As stevedores unloaded goods, auctioneers took out ads, displayed the merchandise, and held sales. Auctions handled 10 percent of goods in 1818; the number more than doubled and reached 26 percent in 1826.

The auction business had turned Hone into a wealthy man and allowed him to become an active leader in the social and political life of his hometown. Born on October 25, 1780, Hone came from modest German-French stock. His father, Philip Sr., and mother, Hester, owned a small wooden house on Dutch and John Streets. Philip Sr. worked as a carpenter, advertising in the *New York Gazette* and the *Weekly Mercury*, "All kinds of Albany boards and planck, oak and Jersey pine timber of all sorts, the best three feet or long shingles, lath, &c." The couple had 12 children, though just four—Judith, John, Samuel, and Philip Jr. —lived into adulthood.[5]

By age 17, Philip joined his older brother John's new auction house, which initially stood on Pearl Street, and soon moved to Wall Street. Hone learned fast and soon became a consummate auctioneer. A tall, spare man, with a shock of curly hair, a strong jaw, and a commanding voice, he handled whatever the auction house needed him to do. He inspected consignments, filled out invoices, and sold everything from India lute strings, satins, beaver pelts, British textiles, and French paintings, to Hyson green tea from China, New Jersey cornmeal, stretches of land in Onondaga County, and even a 150-ton brig called *Anna Maria*. At the start of 1800, Hone became a partner of the newly christened John and Philip Hone auction house. In October 1801, the 21-year-old merchant married 23-year-old Catharine Dunscomb, the daughter of Daniel and Margaret Dunscomb.

Their business enjoyed a large clientele, and among them was Astor, with whom Hone formed a lifelong friendship. In 1815 the house netted $159,007 in profits, with Hone receiving $55,652. The prominent merchant Nathaniel T. Hubbard recalled how Hone's firm became "widely known throughout this city for their honesty, industry, and integrity."[6] As New York grew, Hone joined numerous business ventures. He sat on the first board of directors of the Bank of America and served as a director of the National Insurance Company. He became a director of the Eagle Fire Company of New York in 1811, an early fire insurance firm. In 1818 he dabbled in the ferrying business, running horse-powered team-boats to Hoboken, NJ. He helped found the Bank for Savings. Along with his brother John and an associate named Peter Schenck, he formed a company to build the Matteawan and Glenham companies in Dutchess County to make woolen goods. The venture was joined by Astor and others.

By the time Hone retired from the auction business in 1821, his net worth was $500,000—a staggering sum at the time. He decided to travel, heading out for a grand tour of Europe. He attended the July 1821 coronation of George IV in London, visited cathedrals and museums throughout the continent, and started to collect art. When Hone returned home, he bought a four-story Federal style home at 235 Broadway that stood opposite the nine-acre spot simply known by New Yorkers as the Park. This open space around City Hall stretched from St. Paul's Chapel to Chambers Street, and at its southern end rose a marble gateway; the area contained a massive fountain. Hone's was one of the city's finest row houses, with a slant roof and dormers and a cistern in the yard for rainwater. The home was outfitted with wainscoting, sliding mahogany doors, large sideboards, and huge mirrors, and Hone filled it with art, statues, cut glass, porcelain, and other collectables. Merchant John Pintard observed how the home allowed Hone to live "in the genteelest style of any man in our city."[7]

While Hone stopped working, he kept busy. He doted on Catharine and their large family—three sons, John, Robert, and Philip Jr., and three daughters, Catharine, Mary, and Margaret. His wife, Catharine, was a homebody who rarely went out, but Hone took his children to openings, dinner parties, the theater, and events around town, and set up his sons in assorted business. He also belonged to and founded a slew of social entities—such civic organizations as the Mercantile Library—served as a vestryman for Trinity Church, and stayed active with the New York Hospital, Bloomingdale Asylum, Columbia College, the Merchants' Exchange, the New-York Historical Society, and the Union Club. Hone had always regretted his meager education. To make up for it he read voraciously, consuming everything from Homer and Shakespeare to histories and fiction, and amassed a library with some 2,000 books. This desire to improve on his humble origins stayed with Hone his whole life, leading him to cultivate a patrician, imperious manner.

And while he loved the opera and dance and classical music, and fervently promoted American artists and writers, he also enjoyed Irish songs and Negro spirituals.

New York didn't have popular elections for mayor until 1834. The city was divided into wards—individual political districts—and in January 1826, the Common Council, in which the heads of all the wards sat, voted for the mayor and chose Hone.[8] As the city's chief, Hone took his responsibilities seriously, and his time as mayor proved active, perhaps more so than most mayors to that point. Besides attending meetings and civic functions, he reviewed troops and even officiated at weddings. The city's growth in the mid-1820s brought lots of new buildings. Additional ones were being called for. There were three theaters—the Park, the Chatham, and the Lafayette. Some felt there should be more, and the New York Association set out to build one that catered more to the average city dweller. In October 1825 the association bought the Bull's Head Tavern from John Jacob Astor's brother, Henry. The tavern and adjoining cattle market sat on the Bowery and served as a popular spot where butchers, drovers, and dealers met. It had 16 lots, eight on Bowery and eight on Elizabeth Street. In April 1826, the association unanimously chose a building plan by architect Ithiel Town for what was initially called the New York Theatre, though it would soon be called the Bowery Theatre.

Hone oversaw the June 17, 1826, cornerstone-laying. He reminded the large crowd that "this spot which a few years since was surrounded by cultivated fields, where the husbandman was employed in reaping the generous harvest, and cattle grazed for the use of the city, then afar off, has now become the centre of a compact population." Afterward, the gathered made their way to the Morse Hotel for champagne, local and tropical fruits, and many toasts, including one to theater manager Charles Gilfert, who modestly responded that "The path of a manager is not strewed with roses—he commences with cares, and frequently finishes in sorrow." Town's grand Greek Revival Bowery Theatre opened on October 23. Gilfert's first performance included Thomas Holcroft's ominously named comedy *The Road to Ruin* and James Kenney's farce *Raising the Wind*. Hone attended a performance soon after of Richard Sheridan's *The School for Scandal*, and the *New York Mirror* wrote that he "appeared in a most excellent humour with the actors."[9]

Hone served as mayor for one year, until January 1827, when the council chose former mayor William Paulding Jr. to replace him. The *Commercial Advertiser* called Hone "incomparably the best Mayor we have had for years." Hone's friends teased him about his loss, with his friend, the author Anthony Bleecker penning a poem, "Unsuspecting Phil Is King No More." They hosted a lavish dinner for him, to celebrate, as they put it, his "dignified, impartial and enlightened administration of our municipal concerns." Hone never held office again. Even so, he kept active politically, dutifully working for the advancement of the Whigs, a major political party that had evolved from the National Republicans and was embraced by bankers, merchants, and the well-to-do, and promoted large-scale development. Hone served as chairman of its general committee, organized rallies, worked to smooth out differences between competing Whig factions, and was an indefatigable booster of the party's positions.

Throughout his life, Hone continued to be a major advocate for New York, feeling a sense of guardianship and even personal responsibility for its expansion. He proved to be a consummate promoter of the city. In the spring of 1828 he purchased a series of blank books from Pearl Street stationer T.A. Ronalds and started work on his diary. "I have occasionally introduced matters of trifling importance, and have omitted others which were entitled to a place," he admitted in an entry. Nonetheless Hone's diary, which grew to 28 volumes, remains an invaluable guide to the period. Over the course of the next few decades, Hone wrote about his family, high and low society, local and national politics, the growing art scene, real estate, trade, fires, parties, plagues, and wars, along with his musings on the business of the city, the state of the Union, detailed thoughts on the latest plays and meetings, and dinners with such notables as Astor, Senator Daniel Webster, former presidents John Quincy Adams and Martin Van Buren, and authors Washington Irving and Charles Dickens. In the process he created an invaluable chronicle of his time, and a reflection of New York's seemingly unstoppable growth.[10]

* * *

There was expansion, but there was also accompanying unrest in the city. Hone himself was distressed by what he saw as the unbridled growth of democracy, fearing that it would bring about the downfall of America. Tensions percolated in New York. It was much on display on the streets and perhaps especially in theaters like the Bowery. In early 19th-century New York, theaters became flash points, a haven and rallying place for populist resentment. In October 1831, for example, the British actor Joshua Anderson was about to star in the opera *Guy Mannering* at the Park Theatre. He was accused of making anti-American comments on the way to the States. When word spread of the rumored insult, a mob swarmed the theater and destroyed windows and lamps, thus prompting the managers to hang red-white-and-blue bunting to appease the crowd. Capitalizing on his competitor's woes, Thomas Hamblin, who had recently taken over the running of the Bowery, announced that from then on his theater "will hereafter be called 'American Theatre, Bowery.'" To stress the point, in mid-November he set a large American eagle on the theater's pediment and staged Mordecai Noah's patriotic play, *She Would Be a Soldier*.[11]

In the late 1820s Broadway served as New York's main road, lined with some of the city's most prominent churches and finest hotels. Broadway dominated, but other streets including Greenwich, Washington, Hudson, Canal, and the Bowery featured a number of businesses. One of the most important commercial sections was Pearl Street, a crescent-shape stretch along the East Side lined with stores, counting houses, warehouses, and dry goods businesses. The city was growing in every direction, and commerce beckoned. The silk merchant Arthur Tappan hailed from Northampton, Massachusetts, and set up shop in New York in 1815. By 1827 Tappan was the country's largest silk importer. The Irish-born Alexander Turney Stewart opened his first dry goods shop in 1823, and would quickly become one of the most successful merchants of his age. Thomas Downing, a free Black man from Virginia, came to New York in 1819 and set up a restaurant on Broad Street. Downing's establishment would become legendary, and he was known as the "oyster king of New York" and one of the city's wealthier citizens. Richard Tweed ran his chair-making business on Cherry Street, where in April 1823 his son William, the future Tammany Hall boss, was born. Alexander Jackson Davis, who later would become one of the era's greatest architects, began drafting and prepared detailed illustrations of buildings. Swiss ship captain Giovanni Del-Monico and his brother Pietro settled in New York. They Anglicized their names to John and Peter Delmonico and in 1827 opened a café on William Street.

The town had a number of attorneys, and among the most prominent was George Washington Strong. Strong joined the bar in 1805. Three years later he became a counselor at law, and in 1818 formed a firm with John Wells. The partners handled commercial and maritime cases, wills, and real estate transactions. Strong, whom banker John Stewart described as "not at all effusive," would have other colleagues over the next few decades, and successfully developed a clientele that included Alexander Hamilton's widow Elizabeth, as well as Aaron Burr. In 1809, Strong married his second cousin Angelina

Lloyd. They lived on Sugar Loaf Street, which was soon renamed Franklin Street, and had two daughters. Angelina died in 1814, and five years later Strong married Eliza Catharine Templeton. On January 26, 1820, Eliza gave birth to George Templeton. George Templeton proved to be a precocious child. He read early, and played the piano and organ. He attended Columbia Grammar School and soon headed to Columbia College, where he, along with Hone's son Philip, were part of the class of 1838.

In October 1835, at the age of 15, George Templeton began a journal focused mainly on the minutia of school life and his interest in book- and coin collecting. Later Strong would develop into a sharp-eyed critic of political, social, and artistic events of the city and the nation, which, along with Hone's writings, offers historians an intimate glimpse of 19th-century New York. Ultimately filling more than 2,250 pages, Strong's journal reflected his fascination with music, politics, fires, and riots. As with Hone, he was a wealthy, civically engaged, and generous citizen with decidedly conservative views, which shifted as the city expanded, the nation changed, and the stresses of immigration, the growth of democracy, and the fight over slavery increased. Also like Hone's diary, it is a record of the city's expansion and growing tensions.[12]

* * *

Columbia students like Strong mostly hailed from the city's professional and commercial families. In 1835 the school had some 100 students. New York, meanwhile, had a population of 268,089 people, a number that had more than doubled since 1820. Each ship that arrived seemed to have as many people as could be crammed below deck. By 1825 a fifth of New York's population claimed foreign birth, and Timothy Dwight, the former president of Yale College, was amazed by "The bustle in the streets," as well as "the perpetual activity of the carts; the noise and hurry at the docks." Milkmen with horse-drawn carts delivered large kettles to houses, and the streets filled with peddlers loudly hawking watermelons, strawberries, baked pears, buttermilk, clams, oysters, root beer, and boiled husks of corn.

All the growth created a market for those eagerly seeking the latest news—and business trends—and by 1830, New York was awash in papers. William Leete Stone and others started running the *Commercial Advertiser* in 1820. One of the city's most important publications was the *Morning Courier and New-York Enquirer*, edited by James Watson Webb, who started it as a Jacksonian-supporting publication, and by the early 1830s would switch its allegiance to the Whig Party, which he helped found. Tappan the silk importer jumped into the newspaper business in 1827, starting the *Journal of Commerce* in order to create a publication "that would exert a wholesome moral influence." Charles King, whose father, Rufus, was a signer of the U.S. Constitution, bought the *New York American* in 1819. The poet and Massachusetts native William Cullen Bryant joined the *New York Evening Post* in 1826, and soon became editor in chief. In 1833, the *New York Sun* appeared. Edited by Benjamin H. Day, and hawked by newsboys, it sold for 1¢ and became the first successful "penny paper," offering up light pieces about local life, fires, theater performances, fiction, and the popular police reports. That same year, the playwright Mordecai Noah founded the *Evening Star*, and the following year the bookseller and novelist Asa Greene began publishing the *New York Transcript*, with its working-class slant. Then in May 1835, the Scotsman James Gordon Bennett launched the penny paper the *New York Herald*. In 1841, Horace Greeley founded the *New York Tribune*. The following decade, Henry Raymond started the *New York Daily Times*, which he renamed the *New York Times* in September 1857.[13]

Editors competed for readership and battled it out in print. When Bennett founded the *Herald*, he initially worked out of a cellar lit by tallow candles with a plank desk supported by flour barrels. He promised in his first edition: "We shall endeavor to record facts, on every public and proper subject, stripped of verbiage and coloring, with comments when suitable, just independent, fearless, and good tempered." Bennett's startup offered readers reliable news on Wall Street—already a major power in the financial world—and the markets, while also presenting both serious news and entertainment. Even so, the editor proved to be far from "good tempered." "The days of Webb and his impotent paper are numbered," he boasted defiantly. Bennett branded the *Sun*'s editors a "brace of blockheads." A fervent anti-Semite, Bennett personally disliked Noah, writing how he believed him to be "a descendant, very likely of the family of Judas Iscariot." Bennett also took a quick and long-lasting dislike of Hamblin, the Bowery Theatre's manager, regularly attacking him in his paper, and likewise enjoyed flinging barbs at Hone, perhaps one of the most popular New Yorker of his day.

There were more than just fighting words. While shaving one morning in 1831, Hone noted in his journal that the *Evening Post*'s Bryant had struck the *Commercial Advertiser*'s Stone "over the head with a cowskin." Reports varied, but one stated that Stone hit back with a bamboo cane, which shattered and revealed a sword. Onlookers separated the editors before Stone could use it.[14]

* * *

In the 1820s, a few hundred buildings dating from before the American Revolution still stood, and of course fewer from the Dutch era, which ended in the mid-17th century. The north of current-day 14th Street was still undeveloped. Much of it was held by families of Dutch heritage, like the Stuyvesants, or well-to-do merchants and artisans who had built homes and estates there, mainly to get away from the crowded downtown. In the 1820s and 1830s, New York was still a small, walkable place. Perhaps most notable were its churches, such as the South Reformed Dutch Church on Garden Street, a solid stone structure that went up in 1807 and boasted of a fine-toned organ.

Nearly a quarter of the city's wealthiest 500 people—some of whom have been introduced—resided in the lower Broadway area, many in compact but elegant Georgian and Federal style structures. Merchants often lived near the wharves or had stores and businesses around Wall Street. Trades concentrated in specific areas. Shipping-related workers made their homes in or near Corlear's Hook on the East River. Many of those who settled northeast of City Hall in the Five Points neighborhood—so called because at its heart stood an intersection of three roads—worked at nearby sugar and confectionary manufacturers, ironworks, tobacco, pottery, and brewery industries. In addition to its famous theater, the Bowery neighborhood meanwhile had residents who worked at slaughterhouses and tanneries.

As people moved to the city, new streets were settled and buildings went up—more than 1,200 in 1825 alone. Bryant and congressman Gulian Verplanck observed five years later in the literary journal, the *Talisman*, how buildings now stood where they had once hunted quails and woodcocks, and had once been covered by "hills, hollows, marshes, and rivulets." When the Irish actor Tyrone Power arrived in New York three years later, he found it filled with tree-lined streets and stooped houses with colored fronts and "gaily painted" shutters, and along Broadway "showy shops, and numerous hotels." Yet many noted that the city still lacked grand buildings. Partly this was due to the lack of professional architects, since structures at the time were largely put up by builders and contractors who relied on reference guidebooks.

But that was about to change, particularly as a new and grand style was becoming popular. The Greeks' revolution against the Ottoman Empire during the 1820s had sparked interest in the United States in the proverbial "cradle of democracy." Soon banks and offices emulating the Parthenon and other classical structures were appearing all along the streets of Manhattan.[15] People embraced the symbolism of Greek design, which enshrined a noble democratic purpose. A temple to finance was thus what city merchants desired to conduct their own sacred business. In the early 1820s, Astor's son William, along with the merchant Stephen Whitney, set out to build such a place on Wall Street. Designed by the architect-builders Martin Euclid Thompson and Josiah Brady, and partly inspired by the Temple of Minerva Polias in Priene, Greece, the new Merchants' Exchange opened in the spring of 1827 and immediately became, according to the *Mirror*, "an honour and ornament to the city." It was one of the largest buildings built in New York, stretching 115 feet in front and extending 150 feet deep. Visitors entering the gleaming marble structure passed through a screen of four columns, opening to a grand cupola-topped rotunda. They could then reach the 75-foot-long exchange room by means of a broad flight of marble steps.

All temples need a resident god, or a statue of one, and in December 1830, Hone took part in a committee that included the painter Colonel John Trumbull and Dr. David Hosack, the physician who tended to Alexander Hamilton following his fatal 1804 duel with Aaron Burr. The group approved the commissioning of a model of a statue of Hamilton by the British artist Robert Ball Hughes. By the spring of 1835, the sculptor had completed a towering likeness of Hamilton, looking pensive, clothed in a partial toga, and holding a scroll in his hand. The merchants set the marble statue in the Exchange Room, and at its April 18 unveiling Trumbull noted, "there are very few pieces of statuary in Europe superior to this."[16]

Like Hughes, architect Davis hoped to make it big in the city. In February 1829, he teamed up with Ithiel Town. Soon their firm was designing churches and houses across lower Manhattan, many (though not all) in the Greek Revival mode. Arthur Tappan sought a new store on Hanover Square for his growing silk business. Town designed a building, more modest than the Exchange, with spare granite piers and lintels. Others copied Town's style, which became the standard in the city for commercial buildings.

One of the appeals of the new buildings was that they were constructed from more durable and permanent stone. Wooden structures, though, still dominated New York, and despite the dangers, profits trumped fire safety for many builders with a focus on constructing quickly. As a result, fire was a constant problem. In the early 1820s the city could boast of having 1,215 volunteer firemen. A chief engineer oversaw the companies—baker and alderman Jamieson Cox heading the department from 1824 to 1828, Uzziah Wenman serving from 1828 to 1831, and the widely popular James Gulick taking over in 1831. The latter, Gulick, was a particularly impressive figure—tall and charismatic. Companies, though, did more than just battle blazes. Firehouses served as fraternal orders. Fireman marched at parades in their red shirts and wide suspenders. For young working-class New Yorkers, the life of a fireman seemed glamorous. Young Bill Tweed raced to blazes to watch, and hoped to lend a hand.[17]

* * *

As the city grew it also became wealthier, at least for some. In the late 1820s, New York's richest 4 percent possessed nearly half of the city's wealth, and those in the top 1 percent held just under a third. By then the Second Bank of the United States—which replaced the first created by Alexander Hamilton and served as the nation's central bank—had become the country's most powerful financial institution. It was where the U.S. Treasury parked its funds. The financier and lawyer Nicholas Biddle had taken over as president in 1823, and through his efforts the bank soon controlled a third of the country's bank deposits, increased credit, steadied the economy, and issued an occasional loan. There were 29 branches around the country. Whigs viewed the Second Bank as a stabilizing force in the nation's economy. Westerners and southerners, who voted as Democrats and favored states' rights, disliked the bank and opposed its tight credit stance. The bank's most powerful opponent was Andrew Jackson, who was elected president in 1828. Jackson viewed it as a corrupted, hydra-headed monster, dominated by elitist northern easterners like Astor. Believing that the bank's existence harmed local institutions, "King Jackson," as his detractors called him, vetoed its re-charter and withdrew government deposits.

The rise of Jackson and his years as president fueled internal turmoil. In 1834, a year that became known as the Year of the Riots, upheaval broke out across the land—in New Orleans, Charlestown, Massachusetts, Baltimore, and Philadelphia. Much of it had economic roots, for as industries grew, many workers felt they had lost control over their trades and feared that immigrants and African Americans would take away their jobs.

New York was not exempt. That April, the city held its first general election for mayor. The vote followed a change to the state's constitution in the previous decade, which removed property qualifications for white men to cast ballots. In 1825 the city had 18,283 eligible voters; the number reached 43,091 in 1835. Most welcomed this opportunity to flex their new political muscle, and the mayoral election became a struggle over Jackson's policies. Whigs put forward Congressman Verplanck. The Democrats, with their working-class following, stood behind the merchant and congressman Cornelius Van Wyck Lawrence.[18]

To get out the vote and to antagonize their opponents, the Whigs rolled out a miniature frigate called the *Constitution* on a float with wheels. Webb, the editor of the *Courier and Enquirer*, stood at the helm of the ship, which was accompanied by two bands and a thousand followers. The procession marched along Broadway, the Bowery, Wall Street, and to the wharves, and then over to the polls in the Sixth Ward, where they fought Democrats. In response, Lawrence's supporters rigged up their own vessel, a rolling boat called the *Veto*. One group set out to destroy Webb's paper. In preparation for the attack, the editor and his supporters armed themselves and hauled six loads of paving stones to the roof of his office. They then waited for the mob, which wisely stayed away. The *Constitution* meanwhile continued to cruise the streets. When Hone saw it docked on Broadway in front of the Masonic Hall, he entered the building. All seemed quiet, as he wrote in his journal, "when suddenly the alarm was given, and a band of Irishmen of the lowest class came out of Duane Street from the Sixth Ward poll, armed with clubs, and commenced a savage attack upon all about the ship and the hall."

Throughout the streets, people fought with brickbats, clubs, and stones. Some sacked City Hall just below Chambers Street. The police, constables, and members of the watch—an early version of the police whose tasks included looking out for fires and patrolling the potter's fields—tried to control the unrest. Hundreds of Whigs rushed to gun shops for weapons. When they learned that their Democratic opponents were headed to the arsenal on Elm and Franklin Streets, they tried to get there first, with some yelling, "Let us fly to the arsenal and arm ourselves!" Rioting Whigs indeed got there first and forced open the doors, climbed through windows, grabbed guns, mounted bayonets, and waited. Meanwhile some 20,000 Democrats—laborers, merchants, cartmen, and others—gathered outside. The tension was palpable. Mayor Gideon Lee rushed to the building, yelling, "Stop, for the love of heaven, stop. . . . Do not cause the streets of our city to be dyed in blood!" The group calmed down, and troops from Governors Island and the Navy Yard, as well as a local militia, took control of the streets. After all that, the election was close, with the Democrat Lawrence winning by 181 votes—17,576 to 17,395—and the Whigs securing the Common Council.[19]

* * *

At the start of the year that would end with the Great Fire of 1835, the *Evening Post* reported that 843 buildings had gone up the previous year. Thomas Hamblin bought 71 Bowery for $14,000. The home of former mayor Stephen Allen and his wife boasted 14 rooms—ten with fireplaces and Italian marble mantle pieces. And there were unions to celebrate. On February 18, James and Mary Hamilton's daughter Eliza, for example, married George Lee Schuyler, the grandson of Revolutionary War general Philip Schuyler and her first cousin once removed, further linking two of the nation's most prominent families. Halley's Comet passed by, and for six cents, visitors could gaze at it through a large telescope set in the City Hall Park. The architect Davis took a room for most of the year, invested in a hair mattress, and bought half a ton of Schuylkill coal for $4.25. In November he moved into a back room at the Merchants' Exchange. That year, 16-year-old Walt Whitman decided to make his fortune as a journeyman compositor in New York.[20]

Yet throughout, the specter of fire loomed, and building owners sought to protect their investments. There had been fire insurance companies in New York since the 1787 founding of the Mutual Assurance Company for Insuring Houses from Loss by Fire in New-York. In 1801 the Columbian Insurance Company of New York started. Then on April 4, 1806, Hone's Eagle Fire Company began offering insurance policies. Many such firms only handled local coverage and were founded by wealthy businessmen like Hone. Firms from outside the state, disparagingly referred to as "foreign," were discouraged. Starting in 1824, those representing out-of-state businesses needed to not only post a $1,000 bond but also earned a 10 percent tax on premiums. Because of this, New York City—which had more than 100 reported fires a year—had mostly small, local firms such as City Fire, Eighth Ward Fire, Farmers Fire & Loan, Franklin Fire, New York Bowery, New York Contributionship, and United States Fire. Among the few from outside the state offering insurance were the Connecticut-based Ætna Insurance Company and the Hartford Fire Insurance Company. By 1835 there were some two dozen fire insurance companies covering the city, and that year Hone's Eagle Fire Company was expanding and constructing a Greek Revival building on Wall Street. To help speed up responses to fires, that April the Fire Department installed a 24-hour watchman in the City Hall cupola to keep an eye out and ring the bell. That same month, citizens voted to build the Croton Aqueduct to bring a reliable source of water to the city from upstate.

The fires still came, of course. Early on the morning of June 8, 1835, a fire broke out at a stable near the original St. Patrick's Cathedral on Mulberry Street. It quickly spread and destroyed some 20 houses, taking with it a number of porterhouses and groceries and leaving 200 Irish American and African American families homeless. The firemen under Chief Gulick's command, though, prevented it from harming the cathedral.[21]

On August 12 a blaze started in a bookbinder office on Fulton Street. It spread along Fulton and Ann Street, destroying boarding houses, cabinet warehouses, residences, a millinery, a weapons manufacturer, and a ten-pin bowling alley, along with the offices of such publications as the *Transcript* and the *New-Yorker*. Several people died, the financial loss came to some $2 million, and at least 1,000 people, including the young compositor Whitman, lost their jobs.

Despite the devastation, on the 20th the *Sun* reported that William and Henry Hanington, artists known for creating popular grand-canvas dioramas, had completed a new work. Displayed at the City Saloon, a local exhibition hall on Broadway, this one featured the biblical flood, and like their other works was slowly unwound to reveal scenes, accompanied by sound effects. The following day the *Sun* published what would later be revealed to be an elaborate hoax, involving a British astronomer who used an immense telescope to discover on the moon winged man-bats, unicorns, temples, lakes, and waterfalls. Readers lapped it up. Hamblin sought to profit from the hoax, staging at the Bowery an extravaganza called *Moonshine, or Lunar Discoveries*.

The national discussion continued to focus around slavery. Earlier that year, abolitionists had initiated a postal campaign, flooding the South with anti-slavery writings and producing handkerchiefs, chocolate wrappers, medals, and emblems emblazoned with images attesting to the brutality of the institution. The movement infuriated southerners and unsettled many northerners, including Hone, who took part in a public meeting in the City Hall Park at the end of August 1835, which he wrote was for "citizens opposed to the abolition society, and the interference of individuals between the masters and the slaves in the Southern States."

In October William Astor sold Hamblin 40 shares of the Bowery Theatre stock. That same month, a young man who worked at Wanzer & Harrison on Pearl Street set fire to the business in an attempt to cover up his embezzlement. After the police arrested him it was discovered that the scuttles—where the coal was stored—in his office as well as in a dozen adjoining stores had been left open. Some saw this as an omen, and Comstock & Andrews, a dry goods jobber on Merchant Street, made sure their building was secured from cellar to garret so no one could break in. The following month, the New York Vigilance Committee, which set out to protect African Americans from kidnapping, held their first meeting.

In early December, a frost gripped the city. It was so cold out that the Erie Canal shut down. Business and life, though, continued. On the 7th, a ship auction at the Merchants' Exchange sold the *Constellation* for $13,900 and the *Constitution* for $10,000. On the evening of the 10th, Tappan, an abolitionist, and other members of the American Anti-Slavery Society met at the Third Free Church on Houston and Thompson Streets and prayed for the end of the institution.[22]

The nearly two-week-long cold snap would not let up. George Templeton Strong wrote on the 12th how the city suffered from "Diabolical weather," and the *Commercial Advertiser* reported that during the previous 11 days the temperatures ranged between 12° and 24° Fahrenheit, during which there was "a rough penetrating wind." Hone called it "the coldest and most tempestuous of this season." Trade continued despite the cold. On the 15th someone offered $60,000 profit for a cargo of Cantonese tea that arrived onboard the *Paris*. The chests were stored on South Street, but the firm decided not to accept the offer after one of the ship's officers advised that, "You can by keeping it a month make $200,000."

A fire started at about 11 that evening in the four-story iron, spike, and nail store of Fullerton & Pickering on Water Street. "The bells were ringing nearly the whole night," wrote Hone. The weather made it hard to battle the fire. The men finally got it under control, but the flames broke out again at three in the morning, taking with them five or six adjoining houses and stores. Fireman John Finch fought that blaze, and was exhausted when he returned to his home on Chrystie Street. Then at four, his wife woke him to tell him that a fire was burning on their block. He headed out to fight the blaze, which consumed several dwelling houses and workshops. It quickly spread to Finch's own apartment, and the *American* noted that he "had barely time to extricate his family, by the flaming stairs," and they got away "with only the clothes on their backs."[23]

It had been a long night for the firemen. As the 16th dawned, their engine hoses lay frozen stiff on the ground, and the city's limited water reservoir supply was drained. Readers of the *Commercial Advertiser* came across an ad by Charles J. Gayler offering double fire-proof iron chests and book safes, and letting them know that the safes were good for keeping merchant and bank records. That morning, a shipment of Indian silk goods arrived at Tappan's store. A porter was told to hoist the merchandise to one of the lofts, but he didn't get around to doing it, so the goods remained in the basement. A large invoice of French goods likewise had been purchased, and a Tappan clerk stayed till after dark to make sure the goods were sent off.

The weather stayed bad, and ice shut down traffic on the Hudson River. Hone wrote how "the thermometer on my back stoop ranges from 6 to 10 degrees, and has been to-day in situation more exposed down to zero." As Hone warmed himself in his home, Bennett's *Herald* set the paper for the next day, taking Hone and others to task: "We pity the poor. They are suffering terribly. Is it not time to call meetings in every ward for the relief of the poor? Come—bustle, bustle, ye men of wealth. Philip Hone, John Lang, Cornelius W. Lawrence,—fathers, grand-fathers, and great-grand-fathers of the city,—be stirring for the poor. No muffling up in your princely sables—forgetting the houseless, unfed poor."[24]

While it was painfully cold for the poor, those the *Herald* criticized could afford to enjoy the city's offerings. That Wednesday evening, the British actor Junius Brutus Booth—father of John Wilkes Booth—appeared at the Bowery as Pescara opposite Hamblin as Hemeya in Richard Lalor Sheil's 1817 tragedy *The Apostate*, a play the younger Booth would appear in at Washington's Ford's Theatre less than a month before he would assassinate President Abraham Lincoln. At the Euterpian Hall on Broadway, patrons beheld the celebrated mechanical Panorama, an elaborate device touted for its thousand moving figures, and Peale's Museum & Gallery of the Fine Arts on Broadway between Warren and Murray Streets presented "Mr. Hart, the celebrated English Fire King, or Salamander" who performed "a variety of the most extraordinary feats with red hot bars of iron, such as passing it over his bare tongue, bending and straightening out with his bare feet, biting a piece off with his teeth."

By late that evening Hone sat snugly in his library overlooking the park. Across town, 12-year-old Bill Tweed and his friends Adolphus Borst,

William Drew, and John Garsight tried to stay warm at Knickerbocker Engine Company No. 12's house. Tweed suggested they head out and look for some coal, and he and his friends grabbed buckets and went over to the coal yard at Dover and Pearl Streets. There Tweed hopped the fence, and the group scooped up a supply of coal, then headed back to the firehouse to start a small fire and stay warm.[25]

1

Ten Hours

All day on December 16, 1835, a gale blanketed Manhattan with snow. The merchant Gabriel Disosway remembered when night fell it was "the coldest one we had had for thirty-six years." At about 9 PM, officers Peter Holmes and William B. Hays smelled smoke as they made their rounds. The men called over other members of the City Watch—which was tasked with keeping an eye out for fires—and they discovered a fire burning at Comstock & Andrews, a brick dry goods store on Merchant Street. Hays recalled that they managed to open the doors to the store. "We found the whole interior of the building in flames from cellar to roof, and I can tell you we shut the door mighty quick. Almost immediately the flames broke through the roof."

A watchman stationed in the City Hall cupola to spot fires saw the blaze and tolled the bell. As the warning spread, others took note. "I was writing in the library when the alarm was given," wrote Philip Hone. The teenager Catherine Wynkoop was having tea with friends. "We were all sitting quietly around the fire, enjoying ourselves in peace and safety." Then at about nine, "we heard the cry of 'fire' directly under our window." The commission merchant Nathaniel Hubbard was attending a lecture at the Mercantile Library on Beekman Street. Arthur Tappan was overseeing an anti-slavery society meeting on Spruce Street. The gathering was discussing President Andrew Jackson's attack on their Postal Campaign, which was flooding the South with anti-slavery literature. Mary Sturges had already put her children to bed, and her husband, Jonathan, was playing the flute when the sound of the bell reached them. A relative of the Philadelphia financier John Watson heard the cry of fire, but paid it no mind, and he and his wife and their servants turned in for the night. And on Greenwich Street, George Washington Strong heard the bells, but he, too, went to sleep.[1]

While Hone had as yet no idea of the extent of the fire, his son John had a store on Pearl Street, and Hone headed "immediately down" from his Broadway home to see what was happening, as did Tappan and the flute-playing Jonathan Sturges. Disosway left his house on Vandewater Street and rushed to his Pearl Street business, Disosway & Brothers. He met with his clerks, told them to watch over the building, and then made his way to Merchant Street, just south of Wall Street. The chief clerk at Rogers & Co. hadn't yet left the firm's Exchange Place counting rooms. When he realized the danger, he stowed the firm's cashbooks as well as their "portfolio" inside the vault, which contained nearly $1 million worth of notes, bills of exchange, bills receivable, and $250,000 in insurance policies.

Meanwhile, at the Bowery Theatre, the audience was enjoying a performance of *The Apostate* when they heard the City Hall bell. " 'Fire! Fire!' echoed around and within the theatre," wrote one in attendance. "We were all, in an instant, rushing out of the slamming doors, and onward toward the scene of the conflagration, which was 'glaring on night's startled eye' away down town."[2]

Chief Engineer James Gulick and fire crews raced to Merchant Street from throughout Manhattan. Uzziah Wenman, Gulick's predecessor and now the city's water surveyor, headed down on the sound of the first bell. Cornelius V. Anderson, foreman of Engine Company No. 1, which was housed on Duane Street, got there 10 minutes after the blaze broke out. William Macy, who served with the Supply Engine Company on Franklin Street, showed up with his uniform pulled over his business suit. And the 12-year-old Bill Tweed and his friends ran out of Engine Company No. 12's firehouse on Rose Street to see if they could lend a hand.

On Merchant Street, Disosway and some others entered the Comstock & Andrews building. "Those few of us present had time to remove a considerable quantity of light fancy silk articles," he recalled. But as the men carried out the fabric, the group was horrified to witness how "a strong current of air sweeping through the adjoining lane" ignited the goods, and how the fire "burst from the doors and windows on both streets."

Firemen tapped the nearby hydrants for water. In search of more water, crews headed east to the foot of Wall Street to break through the ice on the East River. "We got the engine on the deck of a vessel, and got to work in about twenty minutes," said foreman John Cox from Engine No. 26. Since their hoses could not reach Merchant Street, the companies formed a hose line. The men poured brandy on the machines to prevent them from freezing. Soon water flowed, and they sprayed the flames. But the strong winds made controlling the fire especially difficult, and the driving gale slapped the water back into their faces.

Merchant Street and the crooked streets of lower Manhattan generally were a maze, hard to navigate under the best of circumstances. And the fire made it harder. Disosway noted, "a burning wall of fire now intervened, and increased every moment." The northern end of Merchant Street curved into Pearl Street, and Zophar Mills and his men from Engine Company No. 13 worked on Pearl to try and "stop the fire from crossing that street. Five or six stores were then blazing in Pearl Street. Our one stream of water seemed almost useless to contend with such a conflagration."[3]

Despite their best efforts, within 15 minutes of the alarm, Watchman Hays realized that "fully fifty buildings were blazing." No one had ever known a fire to spread that quickly. As the *New York Evening Post* reported, "Never was there a more rapid extension of the flames. The stores on Pearl street and on each side of Merchant street, were soon enveloped in the devouring element." Mills recalled how the fire hopped to the other side of Pearl, and "in a few minutes twenty windows of the upper stories of the high buildings on the east side of Pearl Street were in a blaze." Wenman and some others managed to pull out more than two cart-loads worth of goods from one building when things turned bad. "Everything we took out was on fire in a few minutes. The fire burned so rapidly, that the people inside got alarmed least [*sic*] they could not get out." He and the others pried apart some iron bars on the windows in the back and managed to get out.

As the fire spread, Rensselaer Havens, who was president of the Howard Insurance Company on Wall Street, went to alert George Washington Strong, whose office stood nearby, that the fire also threatened his building. By the time he arrived at Strong's home, the glow of the fire illuminated the house. "The fire is evidently an extensive one and shines splendidly on the shipping and houses in the rear," his son George Templeton wrote. "Mr. Havens has just come to call Papa up, as the office is in danger. It is a tremendous fire, by his account." When the elder Strong made it to his office, he got to work. "We immediately removed everything valuable, and then suspended operations for two or three hours, supposing our office would not be burnt." This, as he would soon learn, turned out to be a mistake.

Hone made his way down Broadway, and was appalled by what he discovered. "When I arrived at the spot the scene exceeded all description; the progress of the flames, like flashes of lightning, communicated in every direction, and a few minutes sufficed to level the lofty edifices on every side." Determined to get to his son's store, he found a way through. Hubbard, for his part, made it to his business; he saw that the fire hadn't reached there yet. He sensed that it soon would, and immediately got men ready to remove his stock of goods.[4]

Most who streamed downtown, though, stood paralyzed, mesmerized by the sight of flames engulfing building after building. More people came by Strong's house to let the younger Strong know what was happening: "Mr. Lambert has just come in. He thinks the office out of danger, but the fire is still raging in Exchange, Pearl, Front Streets, etc. It is very cold—mercury at zero." Hone also noted that a few places were "considered out of reach of danger," as merchants hurriedly carted over merchandise to new storage locations. One was Reverend James Mathews' South Reformed Dutch Church on Garden Street, near which Exchange Place merchant Caleb O. Halsted had his business. Many spent more than an hour bringing over goods. "The church was built of stone," Halsted recalled. "The walls were from 2 to 3 feet thick; and it was thought that it would be a safe place for goods."[5]

Disosway had rushed over and helped the staff at Burns, Halliburton & Company move bales of calicoes, muslin, and flannels to the church. He was working in the firm's William Street building and climbed to the building's roof to get a sense of the extent of the blaze. "What a sight now presented itself!" Disosway exclaimed, nearly incredulous: "An ocean of fire, as it were, with roaring, rolling, burning waves, surging onward and upward, and spreading certain universal destruction; tottering walls and falling chimneys, with black smoke, hissing, crashing sounds on every side." It turned so exceedingly bright out that Wynkoop and her younger sister Henrietta, who had retired for the night at their home on Greenwich Street to the west of the fire, could barely "close our eyes, the lights of the fire was so great in our room."

Though cold, the season had been dry. And the city's buildings, which were largely built out of wood, proved to be tinder. As a result, the fire racing through the city's First Ward met little resistance and "went on a straight line to the river," recalled Company No. 1's Anderson. "Then it chopped round, and made its way back to the south side of Tappan's store." By the time Arthur Tappan, his brother Lewis and their associates had reached their Hanover Square businesses to the south of Wall Street, the flames "were devouring the adjacent store," wrote Lewis. Ithiel Town had designed Tappan's store, a few years earlier, and the brothers hoped their granite-clad structure with its iron-shuttered windows would withstand the flames. The partners discussed whether they should remove $500,000 in promissory notes. Prudence won over hope. Arthur rushed in, took the papers, and handed them to his clerks to spirit away.[6]

Meanwhile, Tappan's partners and employees carried out all they could, as did some African Americans who had heard that fire threatened the business of their progressive benefactor, a man who was seeking the end of slavery. According to the *New York Evangelist*, "it was with difficulty they were restrained from rushing in after the flames had burst out at the door." By then the fire turned the place into "an oven," reported the *New York Sun*. Some of Tappan's crew ran down to the basement and took out the India silks that the porter hadn't hoisted into the loft that morning. At first, like those from neighboring businesses, they dumped their goods in a pile at the center of Hanover Square. But sensing the speed and strength of the moving fire, Tappan directed that the remaining stock be taken to a friend's nearby shop. "All hands were thus engaged until the flames burst into the store, and several persevered until they were driven away by the scorching heat," wrote Lewis. All told, workers rescued about two-thirds of Tappan's stock—some $100,000 worth—and "in a short time the store, and a considerable part of the goods, were destroyed."

On the north side of Hanover Square stood the storehouse of Peter Remsen & Company, one of the largest East India firms. Disosway and others heaved merchandise from the upper windows into the square. When Disosway finished carrying out goods he "put on an old warm overcoat and an old hat, for active service" and got to work with his former fire company. A hydrant stood in the square, and Samuel Swartwout, who held the government position of Collector of the Port of New York, also started battling the blaze: "I went to work at the engine, as a good citizen should." Many others did all they could. Hone's Eagle Fire Company had been constructing a three-story brick structure at 59 Wall Street. The building featured a new copper roof and a number of the insurance firm's directors went in and poured water from pails onto window casements and interior woodwork to stop it from igniting.[7]

Throughout downtown Manhattan—for a third of a mile from Broad to South Streets and a similar distance down to Coenties Slip—piles of marble-topped mahogany tables, sideboards, sofas, silks, satins, broadcloths, fine muslins, boxes of cutlery, and crates of expensive French wine littered the streets. A prominent spot was the triangular-shaped Hanover Square where Tappan's store had stood, and according to the *New York Commercial Advertiser* it "filled with piece goods promiscuously piled together, and much of this property was of the most valuable kind." In 1835, the square, through which Pearl Street ran, was a large open area, covering "some seventy-five or eighty feet in width, and tapering to thirty or forty," recalled merchant

Prosper Wetmore. So much had been brought there that Wetmore called it "a pyramid of goods . . . one or two hundred cart-loads." It seemed the safe place to be, and soon, "there was accumulated from the stock of all the French stores, a mass of silks, satins, laces, cartons of dresses, gloves, capes, Cashmere, shawls, and the richest kinds of fancy articles, forming a pile of 60 feet wide and 25 feet in height," reported the *New York Star*. Hone helped his son John move his stock of dry goods from his Pearl Street store and deposit them there. But as merchandise piled up, and people streamed through, they trampled silks and muslins into the snow and mud, broke furniture, splintered boxes, and scattered bottles.[8]

While merchants tried to save their goods, others, inevitably, made off with all they could. "Nearly a hundred scoundrels were seized in the very act of stealing valuable articles, even when the alarm and danger were at the highest," wrote the *Commercial Advertiser*. When a crowd saw a man attempting to burn a building at Broad and Stone Streets, enraged citizens grabbed him and, to the horror of some onlookers, immediately hanged him from a tree.

But while at least some New Yorkers enacted vengeance on those trying to take advantage of the chaos, they could not stop the wind and the flames whipping through Hanover Square. Then, according to the *Sun*, "a gust of flame, like a streak of lightning," came from the northeast corner building, and it shot "across the square, blown by the strong wind, and set fire to the entire mass, which it in a few moments consumed to cinders, and then communicated to the houses opposite." Disosway watched in disbelief as the goods he helped to rescue "dissolved and mingled in the common and increasing ruin."[9]

By 10 PM, everything seemed to be engulfed: "The bells ringing—the fire engines rolling—the foremen bawling—the wind blowing—the snow driving—the whole heavens above illuminated, formed altogether a terrific spectacle," reported the *New York Herald*. The crews could not slow the flames. As the fire swept in the direction of the store where Tappan had moved his goods, he hired a shop on Beaver Street and had the goods shifted again.

The Tontine Coffee House's wooden cornice caught fire. Many feared that the destruction of the Wall Street building—where a decade before investors had marveled at the new coal brought to town by Hone's Delaware & Hudson Canal Company—would allow the fire to spread even further. Oliver Hull told the volunteers he would donate $100 to the Firemen's Fund "if they would extinguish that blaze." Eagle Engine Company No. 13 worked there, and Zophar Mills pulled over a counter from a nearby store. On top of it the men stacked boxes, casks, barrels, and other items, and placed the hose high up on top. As they fought that blaze, William Macy held a nozzle so close to the building's steps that he later recalled, "the heat was so intense that my great coat was burnt through and the leather on the inside of my cap was crisped." Disosway was relieved to note that the "stream reached the spot and quickly put out the alarming flame."

Despite the searing heat, the *Star* reported, the frigid weather meant "that the firemen were compelled to take the fine blankets saved, and cutting a hole through them, convert them into temporary cloaks." Many of the firemen were still exhausted from fighting the Water and Chrystie Street blazes from the night before. To compound matters, those fires had largely drained the city's reservoir, and made it impossible to get enough pressure to shoot the water high enough.[10]

River water also proved insufficient. The Black Joke Engine Company No. 33, which was named for a ship that fought in the War of 1812, worked from the deck of a brig at the foot of Wall Street trying to get water, but they found the low tide made water difficult to pump up. Foreman Charles Forrester recalled how his men had to regularly leave off pumping their cumbersome engine brakes to warm themselves in the ship's cabin. When those on deck felt that they deserved a turn to thaw out, they would put a hat over the stove-pipe and literally smoke them out. Soon, though, the cold made it especially difficult for the various companies to use the water since engines, pipes, hoses, and valves iced over. John Cox sent men off "for salt, to put into the engine, to keep it from freezing." And what water did shoot out of their hoses rained "down like hail," recalled retired general Joseph Gardner Swift of the Army Corps of Engineers, who had been in town surveying routes for various railroads.

Some firemen laid wet blankets on building windows and cornices. Cornelius Anderson meanwhile entered a house near South William Street. He headed to the top of the building to prevent it from catching on fire. But after just ten minutes, Chief Gulick realized that the structure could not be saved and warned the crew to evacuate. "I heard a great cry in the street, and immediately ordered the men to get the hose out of the building," Anderson recalled. They then rushed with his men to the corner of South William and Stone Streets to tap a hydrant. When they arrived, however, they found the street littered with merchants' goods, which had caught on fire and burned their hose. The naval engineer Charles Haswell recalled how "the hose attached to the hydrants was so frozen that the water did not flow." And there was an added danger from frozen hoses, which "lay like bars of iron in the streets."

As the city burned, George Templeton Strong sat at home on Greenwich Street and waited anxiously. "Papa has not returned," he wrote in his journal at midnight. "I would give a good deal to be there. I shall turn in, notwith-standing, as my anxiety for the office cannot prevent me from feeling very sleepy." By then, fire had engulfed his father's business. The fate of his "of-fice became inevitable," remembered the senior Strong, adding how soon "it was too late to remove what was left, consisting of empty paper cases, tables, chairs, boxes, some old papers of not great value, &c."[11]

Gulick and his men had never fought anything like this. By then "there seemed to be a general panic among the firemen," said Swartwout. The men, Hone noted, found themselves "almost incapable of performing their usual services." Since there seemed to be little Gulick could do, he ordered his men to assist businessmen and others in rescuing goods. At 11:30 Swartwout went to his office in the Custom House, where the papers were carried out.

When not fighting fires, foreman Cox worked as a banker, and the day before the blaze had purchased $1,500 worth of goods on Water Street. He told his crew that he needed help saving the merchandise, and with his brothers, William and Henry, and the two dozen men from Engine Company No. 26, set to work. "They commenced removing the goods, and by the time I thought I had my proportion of goods out, the fire was falling down the hatchway," Cox recalled. As they then wended their way south to Old Slip and then west through Hanover Square, Stone, Broad, and Garden Streets, they helped others rescue goods and safes and piled the merchandise on carts. "There were some trucks such as they use in stores; and once in a while they would get a case of goods on a truck, but not often, on account of the ice. Sometimes we broke open cases, and carried goods away in our arms."[12]

The location of the fire had made those who made a living carting goods in great demand, heaping goods onto carts and hauling them away. Alexander Jackson Davis, who had moved his architect's office into a back room at the Merchants' Exchange the previous month, paid a mere $3 to save his books and papers. Others were not so fortunate. "Some crossed their arms, as they leaned against their carts, and refused to stir a step, unless twenty dollars a load were paid them on the spot," the British essayist Harriet Martineau wrote. A few businessmen even handed over more. One French merchant couldn't get anyone to help, and finally asked, "For what sum will you sell your horse and cart?" The man insisted on the outrageous amount of $500 for his hack and vehicle, and the merchant immediately paid it and saved $100,000 worth of goods. Others used barrows and coaches to take away all they could. Mary Sturges recalled listening to the "noise of wagons conveying goods to places of safety."[13]

* * *

The clerk from Rogers & Co. on Exchange Place was determined to find his boss, Charles Sagory, and around midnight headed uptown to look for him. The lower part of the city, below Pine Street, might have been a furious oven, but he found that "as he passed along the silent streets he was surprised at the apparent indifference of people uptown to the burning city." The clerk couldn't find Sagory, so he returned to Exchange Place, gathered the firm's portfolio, and spirited them away. He wasn't the only one surprised at the obliviousness of those living outside range of the fire. Some of John Watson's friends were attending a wedding party at Houston and Broadway. Yet while they heard the distant bells and saw the glow, it was only after one of the celebrants, a merchant, headed south of Houston that he realized what was happening. "There in his gala dress and dancing pumps, he had to set to work earnestly to pack up his store goods."

New York American editor Charles King lived to the north in Greenwich Village and slept through the early part of the fire, only to be wakened by a relative. When he reached his Wall Street office, he recalled, he found his printers and workers trying to save as much as they could. "I went in, and worked until the roof of my building took fire." As was apparent to everyone, this was the fastest-moving fire in memory. "In a quarter of an hour, it was all consumed. I looked on with exceeding terror, I confess, I never saw anything so formidable."[14]

Merchant Caleb Halsted saw flames advancing toward the South Reformed Dutch Church on Garden Street, and within half an hour of getting there had his goods shifted to a grocery store on New Street and Exchange Place a few blocks away. It proved to be a wise move, for before long even the sanctuary caught on fire. "The venerable pile was but sport to flames," wrote *Journal of Commerce* editor Gerald Hallock. As the church burned, organ music wafted out with the billowing smoke. The organist, wrote Disosway, had "commenced performing upon it its own funeral dirge." For nearly half an hour the church withstood the flames, and then, reported the *Star*, "The bright gold ball and star above it on the highest point of the spire, gleamed brilliantly." The organ music only stopped when the ceiling took fire. Then the steeple "gave one surge and fell in all their glory into the heap of chaos beneath them."

The *Journal's* office stood near the Dutch church. Seeing what happened to the sanctuary, Hallock felt it "prepared us fully to expect a similar fate with hundreds of our fellow-citizens." He and his staff emptied the office as best they could, and, by luck, Thomas Downing, whose oyster house stood to the west on Broad Street, noticed a few hogsheads of white-wine vinegar in a shed at the rear of the *Journal's* lot. The cold had not frozen the liquid. Hallock and Downing and others carried around pails of liquid and splashed the *Journal* and the oyster house, and, as Hallock noted, "by this one feat with waterpails and dippers, we have no doubt that at least a million dollars was saved from destruction." For if his printing office was destroyed, Hallock believed that nothing would have "arrested the progress of the flames until they had reached Broad street."[15]

While most in the businesses tried to empty their stores, others stayed inside. John Benson, a coppersmith on 83 Water Street, refused to leave his business and stayed behind its wooden cellar doors. "He got water, and a hand engine, and wherever fire appeared, he put it out," recalled Wetmore. Another was John A. Moore, who had a successful iron trade on Water Street near Old Slip. He watched from inside his store, one of the city's few fire-proof buildings, as "the rapid flames seemed, as it were, to overleap the building, destroying all others," wrote Disosway.

One perceived safe spot for the salvaged merchandise was the cavernous Merchants' Exchange, which in addition to offices was home to New York's central post office. As Samuel L. Gouverneur, the city's postmaster, and Swift surveyed the scene, Gouverneur determined that the fire wouldn't reach the Wall Street building, which was, he said, "solid." He didn't therefore think it necessary to remove the mail. Others agreed with his assessment, and merchants stacked bulky silks and other goods in the rotunda, a 75-foot-long, 55-foot-wide, and 45-foot-high room that was used as the main exchange room, and elsewhere in the structure. But the building caught on fire at about 11:30. Uzziah Wenman and others put out the flames, yet, at about 12:30, smoke could be seen pouring from the back. "I went up, and was going over the dome, when I found the fire had got to the roof," Wenman said. "I ordered every thing to be taken out as quickly as possible." The banknote engravers Rawdon, Wright & Hatch carried out their dies and banknote plates for various banks.

As the grand building burned, a reporter from the *New York Mirror* slipped inside, despite the danger. "We mounted the steps of the Exchange and entered the building," he wrote. "Its top was already in flames. The ample walls rose silently around, scarcely visible to the ceiling, through the dense and slowly wreathing smoke that filled the apartment." And in the midst of all this, "tall, erect, proud and beautiful" loomed Robert Ball Hughes' marble statue of Alexander Hamilton.[16]

Postmaster Gouverneur now tried to remove the mail, but with the fire out of control he had to focus on small articles. They brought the mail to the City Bank on the other side of Wall Street, yet the fires continued advancing, and, like Tappan's crew, he had to move it all again. Flames rushed across the Exchange's roof, and "the public gaze evidently centered most upon its cupola," wrote Disosway, as the flames reached higher and higher. Columns of flames shot from the dome. Everyone wondered how they might save the statue of Hamilton. James Hamilton had run over from the City Hotel on Broadway just north of Trinity Church at about midnight, but he and the others could only watch helplessly as the building with his father's statue became unreachable, surrounded by what the *Herald* called a "blazing light—a transient flood of awful glory." A young officer from the Navy Yard, along with four or five sailors, rushed inside to save the piece. They succeeded in getting the statue off of the pedestal, but when they were warned that the ceiling was about to give way, they, too, had to flee. The sailors just made it out as the dome fell "with a tremendous crash," burying the statue. A shout then rang out as a man ran through the street yelling, "Is there a surgeon among you, gentlemen? For God's sake, is there a surgeon?" and onlookers heard a rumor that many people had been trapped inside.[17]

* * *

The blaze indiscriminately destroyed homes, churches, banks, and stores. Fire bells rang out so feverishly that the hammer of the City Hall bell broke. Watchman Hays called it "the most awful night I ever saw." And journalist Asa Greene commented that "people on all sides were in the utmost consternation. Terror and dismay sat on every face. Despair was in all men's words and actions."[18]

While the main area affected by the fire consisted of businesses, a few people also lived in this part of town. Midshipman Louis Wilkins was on the street when he heard "the agonizing cries of a female," reported the *Commercial Advertiser*. She told the sailor that her infant was in the upper floors of a house. Wilkins ran upstairs and found the baby on the bed of a burning room. He grabbed the child and brought it to the mother, who threw her arms around him, exclaiming, "My God! My God! Thou hast not forsaken me."[19]

The heat from the fire proved so intense that Disosway warned the fire crews of melting iron shutters, doors, copper roofs, and gutters, and he watched as "the burning liquid ran off in great drops." As Disosway helped take the last load of goods out of S. B. Harper & Sons on Front Street near the East River, "a terrible explosion occurred near by with the noise of a cannon. The earth shook. We ran for safety, not knowing what might follow." Then "a second explosion took place, then another and another." The blasts were produced by bags of saltpeter stored in a warehouse, and continued for about half an hour. The explosions were "accompanied with the darkest, thickest clouds of smoke imaginable," and "out leaped the flaming streams of these neutral salts in their own peculiar colors, from every door and window."

Liquor casks exploded, as did barrels of gunpowder. Along Manhattan's docks, storehouses filled with barrels of sperm and other oils ignited. Disosway recalled that as a four-story building on Old Slip and South Street blazed, it "fired hogshead after hogshead, and over the spacious edifice resembled a vast bonfire or giant beacon, casting its bright beams far and wide on the river and surrounding region." Then "the confined inflammable mass, from eaves to cellar, shot out with tremendous force through every window and opening, and soon all disappeared except the cracked, tottering, and falling walls. The blazing, flying timbers were carried across the East River." The wind whipped "flakes of fire" and showered Brooklyn homes with burning items. In Flatbush pieces of burning silk, woolens, paper, and wood littered the streets. The sails of the ship *Alonzo,* sitting at bay at a wharf in Brooklyn, burned. Naval storehouses also caught on fire, though the flames were quickly put out.[20]

The wharves, being made of wood, were especially vulnerable. Barrels of turpentine spilled from their containers, and the *Evening Post* reported that the contents "poured down into the slip like a steam of burning lava, and spread out over the surface of the river for several hundred yards, sending up a bright flame, and giving the appearance of the river being on fire." The brig *Powhatan* burned, though the crew managed to put out the flames. Desperate captains slipped their crafts into the stream. Because of the low tide, however, some found it hard to pull away. A ship rigger named Michael

Kelly was working to haul the *Roscoe* into the river when he fell from the fore-yard and was killed.

As the skies above Manhattan glowed and pulsed, people throughout New Jersey, and up in New Haven, wondered what was going on. Philadelphia firemen rushed from their firehouses thinking a blaze had ignited in one of their nearby communities.

It was a surreal combination of comedy and tragedy. Baskets of champagne floated in the docks, and cheese and provisions were scattered there and about the slips. The *Star* reported that most of the tops of champagne bottles had been unceremoniously knocked off and the contents drunk by the crowds surrounding the fire. James Hamilton recalled how by then, "The ladders were frozen; the firemen were exhausted and demoralized." One company adorned their caps with wreaths and bunches of flowers taken from the wreckage, the decorations contrasting with their begrimed appearances. And Postmaster Gouverneur observed how some of the men "were incapable of acting, some from drinking liquor, which they were obliged to take to keep themselves from freezing."[21]

* * *

At one in the morning, all the hoses used to put out the fire laid frozen, and soon after Anderson realized that "no means existed to stop the fire." After Mathews' Dutch church steeple fell, Mayor Cornelius Lawrence, Gulick, Hamilton, Alderman Morgan Smith, Swift, Colonel James Monroe, King, Wenman, and others started to discuss which building to blow up to staunch the flames. "I entertained and expressed the opinion, that the only way to keep back the fire from that part of the city that was not burned, was by powder," recalled Hamilton. Lawrence asked Wenman if he had ever detonated a structure. He said he hadn't but that he could if necessary. Lawrence turned to Swift for advice, and the retired general agreed that explosions could stop the flames. Lawrence then told Hamilton and Swift to figure out which would be the best buildings to destroy. The two men raced to different points in the city. When they returned they met the mayor and a few aldermen and decided that they should focus on Exchange Place.[22]

A few meanwhile set out in search of explosives, unaware that a schooner anchored in the river had 2,000 casks of gunpowder in its hold. Hamilton, Lawrence, and Smith scoured six or seven grocery stores along Broad Street to see what they could use. Hamilton and Smith then started the "long and tedious" job of emptying cartridges and canisters into a casket. When they filled it about half way they brought it to Exchange Place. General Henry Arcularius of the Army Corps of Engineers sent two boxes with cartridges and loose powder to Wall and Nassau Streets, a block north of Exchange Place.

But they didn't have enough explosives. Lawrence asked Arcularius for more, while Hamilton discussed with Alderman Lawrence P. Jordan about approaching Commodore Charles G. Ridgely at the Brooklyn Navy Yard for powder. Charles King set off for Brooklyn: "I went immediately to the foot of Fulton-street, East River, as fast as I could; where I found a boatman who knew me, and who rowed me up to the Navy Yard, about a mile distant," the journalist recalled. "I wished to go there direct, and I believe the state of the tide allowed it. There was much ice in the river." Once across, he bordered the frigate *Hudson*. The commodore had his lieutenant "get ready all the marines." They gathered what they had there and also sent for powder from Red Hook, Brooklyn.[23]

While King headed to Brooklyn, Army Lieutenant Robert Temple, who was stationed in the city as the naval commissary, searched elsewhere. He went to the tip of Whitehall Street where he "found a stray boat, got two men, and started for Governors Island." Reaching the island a half-mile south of the city involved a rough crossing, particularly since the boat he was in was a "crazy little thing, unsafe to cross in. I thought several times, we should be swamped as we were rowing over." On Governors Island they found three or four 100-pound kegs of powder and headed back with a number of men in a "better boat than the one I crossed in." They landed on Manhattan after 3 AM, and Temple delivered the powder.

Wenman went to Nassau Street to get explosives. "There was a cart, with a barrel of powder on it. A board was laid on the top of the barrel," he later wrote. "The sparks were flying in every direction, like a snow storm." The group filled the barrel about half way. "I got a piece of muslin, and covered the top of the barrel with the muslin. I asked a watchman to assist us, in carrying it. He put his club under the barrel, and Mr. Cox took hold of one end of the club. The policeman held the other end; while I held up the bottom of the barrel." As they passed south along Broad Street, Wenman noticed powder leaking out of the container. Just then he saw a man with a blanket. He cried out to him to stop. The man insisted that he had not stolen the blanket. They told him that they didn't care as long as he gave them the blanket. With it they covered the barrel, stopped the leak, and continued on their way.[24]

Forty-Eight Exchange Place had been chosen as the building to blow up. It stood just east of Broad Street and across the street from the remains of the

Dutch church. Cox and his crew had been busy inside helping Henry Stone and John P. Marsh and the rest of the staff at Stone, Swan & Mason remove goods from the upper loft. Fire was falling through the hatchway as Wenman and the others carried a cask into the cellar. A piece of calico was attached to the upper rim of the cask along with loose papers. "I fastened one end of it with my penknife on the top of the cask; the other was passed into the street," said Hamilton of how he prepared a fuse while Wenman and Haswell spread a train of powder across the floor. Haswell then went out to clear the street. "All present retired to near Broad Street, except General Swift and myself," wrote Hamilton. "I said, 'Who is to fire this?—General, as I got the powder, I must have the first shot.' The General, laughing, and said, 'Well, Hamilton, you shall,' and retired." Hamilton lit the fuse. There was a tremendous explosion and "the whole building," recalled Wenman, "seemed to rise up and quiver."[25]

Nonetheless, the blast did not go exactly as planned. "It threw down the front of the building, a part of the adjoining one—threw off the roof, but did not destroy all the floors," wrote Hamilton. "The fire carried up by the floors endangered the next building, and thus rendered it necessary to blow up that building also." Wenman went into 50 Exchange Place to see what effect the blast had on the building. "I saw that the wall was completely cracked; the rear was on fire; and . . . the fire was approaching more rapidly than in front," he recalled. By then it was five in the morning, and they had to blow up Number 52. Lawrence told James Griswold, a bookkeeper at Lee, Savage & Company, who had been working since 10 PM, that they could continue removing goods from the four-story building until the powder arrived.

King, Captain Mix, Lieutenant Nicholas, and Lieutenant John De Camp, as well as the marines and sailors, had made it ashore with the powder. The cold proved intense. De Camp recalled how "The men's fingers became so numb, they could hardly carry it." Along the way the officer found a handcart. "I was concerned, for the ground was frozen and covered with ice," said King, "and it was raining fire." In order to protect their cargo, "The sailors took off their jackets, and covered the kegs . . . to prevent them from exploding."[26]

As the men neared, Cox called out, "Clear the street, the marines are coming!" Hamilton recalled that "It was consequently so hot, and there were sparks and fire-brands flying everywhere, as to render the approach to the store extremely hazardous. This was, however, unheeded by the gallant tars, who carried the barrel of powder on their shoulders, passed over the gangway, and placed the barrel in the cellar." It only took the men two or three minutes to set up the charges in the basement. "I stood looking on to see how it would be blown up, by experienced men," recalled Cox. "They did it pretty much as we green-hands did,—with this exception:—the officer, after touching off the train, put his hands into his pockets, and walked off, as if nothing was to happen."[27]

The explosion slowed the fire. Mayor Lawrence, Alderman Smith, King, Hamilton, Mix, De Camp, and others looked to see if other buildings needed to be destroyed. They decided to blow up a 12-foot-wide wooden crockery store at the corner of Coenties Alley and Slip. A 200-pound barrel of powder was brought into the building. Hamilton, once again, prepared the charge. A sailor meanwhile held a lit candle in his left hand for light while he used his right one to knock in the head of the barrel. As he did this, powder swirled around the candle, and Hamilton later commented that "seeing that this would be inevitable destruction, I took him by the arm in which he held the light, drew him over before he struck a second blow, and drove him out of the cellar." Hamilton then knocked in the head of the cask, inserted the muslin, and ran a fuse from the cellar to the sidewalk.[28]

A bright moonlight illuminated the crowd standing by the water as Hamilton ascended the stairs. "After setting fire to the mass of combustibles, I walked deliberately toward the spectators, they crying out, 'Run! Run! why don't you run?' This was a little affectation of fearlessness on my part; well knowing that it could not burn down the train of powder before I could get away." When the explosion then took place it "blew the whole house and all its contents into atoms, making thus a vacant space of many feet from the next burning house and the store." Not only did they preserve the block, but Catherine Wynkoop noted how "by blowing up with powder, a store on the corner of Coenties Slip and Pearl Street, the whole block from that to Broad & probably lower down toward the Battery, was saved."

By early morning of December 17, the seemingly relentless march of the fire had been stopped. Crews continued to put out sporadic blazes, and stunned-looking merchants started to sift through the remains of their businesses. Firemen dragged home their engines, with the *Star* reporting how "many of them [were] so exhausted by fatigue that they were asleep as they walked." Firefighter William Macy made his way back to his house on Pike Street. When he undressed, he couldn't help but notice that his fire clothes "actually stood up stiff when I took them off." Hamilton returned to his family at the City Hotel on Broadway and recalled, "My work was done. My cloak was stiff with frozen water. I was so worn down by the excitement that when I got to my parlor I fainted."[29]

2

"Like a Phoenix from Her Ashes"

At precisely 9 AM on December 17, 1835, James Gordon Bennett headed out to look at what quickly became known as the "Burnt District." What he found was "heart rending in the extreme." The *New York Herald* publisher wasn't alone. Others made their way there, many wearing heavy coats to protect them from the piercing cold. "On approaching the corner of Wall and William Streets, the smoking ruins were awful," Bennett wrote. Not only were buildings destroyed, but boxes, bales, desks, safes, and dry goods, as well as the remains of frozen fire hoses were scattered everywhere. Bennett found it difficult to get around, since "both sides were burned down and the streets were filled up with hot bricks, burning goods and heaps of rubbish."

As Bennett made it down Wall Street, he passed the ruins of various brokers' offices and "the splendid marble columns" of the Merchants' Exchange, noting how "The front walls of the Exchange were in part remaining—covered with smoke, and exhibiting the effects of the fire." Throughout, facades lined the streets. Behind them were gaping voids. When he arrived at the corner of Wall and Pearl Streets he looked southward, toward Hanover Square. He saw only one crumbling building. He proceeded, making his way over the hot bricks, along what he thought was Pearl Street— he couldn't be sure— "till I got to the single solitary wall that reared its head as if it was in mockery of the elemental war." Bennett made his way over, and "on approaching, I read on the mutilated granite wall, 'ARTH—TAP—N, 122 PE—L STREET.'" This was all that remained of Arthur Tappan's silk emporium. "These were all the characters I could distinguish on the column. Two stories of this great wall were standing—the rest entirely in ruins. It was the only portion of a wall standing from the corner of Wall street to Hanover Square—far beyond that there are nothing but smoke, and fire, and dust."[1]

For citizens it seemed as if the apocalypse had "opened upon New-York with a scene of devastation around, sufficient to dismay the stoutest heart," wrote the writer C. Foster in his account of the Great Fire of 1835. "The fine range of buildings and splendid stores in Exchange Place, Merchant street, and all the adjoining streets down to the river, lay, literally leveled to the earth." For those viewing the destruction, it seemed to defy belief. When Philip Hone surveyed the wreckage south of his home, he felt "fatigued in body, disturbed in mind." The city had 16 wards at the time, and Hone calculated that the flames turned nearly half of the First Ward, which was located at the southern tip of the city, into ash. All told, the fire destroyed 674 buildings, a swath of New York stretching just east of Broad Street to the East River and from Wall Street south to Coenties Slip. The property loss from the fire was later estimated at about $20 million (about $600 million today). That was three times the cost of building the Erie Canal.[2]

In human terms, the damage was comparatively light. Because the area served primarily as the city's business sector, only two people died. However, that ignores the actual cost. On the morning of the 18th, Dr. David Hosack had breakfast and made some calls. He felt ill when he returned home. As Philip and Catharine Hone walked around the Burnt District, they learned that Hosack "had been seized a few minutes previous with a fit of apoplexy." The stroke prevented him from moving his right arm and made it difficult for him to speak. To treat him, Hosack's son Alexander—carrying out an accepted medical practice—bled him of 18 ounces of blood, only worsening his condition. John Lang, editor of the *New York Gazette & General Advertiser*, had been suffering from paralysis and apoplexy before the fire, and Gabriel Disosway wrote that his death soon after "was hastened by the excitement and devastation of this great public calamity."[3]

To many New Yorkers, it felt like the wrath of a merciless God had been visited upon them, and in an editorial Bennett openly implored a higher power. "Forgive us our sins as we forgive those that sin against us?" Yet amid all the destruction, some places miraculously survived. Zophar Mills' crews successfully stopped the flames from consuming the Tontine Coffee House. Hone's recently built Eagle Fire Company building was the only one on the south side of the street that remained intact. And an old sycamore tree near the corner of Beaver and William Streets still stood.[4]

Bennett continued his tour of the devastation. As he walked, he passed a long line of porters, merchants, brokers, bankers, women, children, and others who came to gawk. George Templeton Strong visited with his Columbia classmate Richard Henry Douglass, whose father's store had burned. Strong felt the destruction "presents a splendid spectacle."[5]

To others it offered a pitiful sight. The cold was unrelenting, and women and children who had lost homes around Broad and Beaver Streets wrapped themselves in blankets and "were seen shivering near the heaps of furniture."

On Pearl Street, Bennett saw men and boys digging in the hot bricks and dust. "What are they doing?" he asked one of the group. "'Damn them,' said he, 'They are looking for money. Some of them have found gold pieces.'" As Bennett chatted, one of the boys cried out, "Hello!" and exulted, "I have got something!"

Near the water's edge between Water and Front Streets, Bennett made his way through a thick crowd of spectators and came across a large group of men stirring up a fire. Bennett moved close to warm himself and saw in the embers the rich merchandise and fine furniture from some of the area's counting rooms. On Front Street he nearly suffocated from smoke that poured from the piles of goods. "From the corner of Front and Wall I proceeded southwardly—for I cannot now talk of streets—all their sites are buried in ruins and smoking bricks. . . . I went down the wharf—the basin was floating with calicos, silks, teas, packing cases, and other valuable merchandise."[6]

Bennett's account of his survey appeared in the *Herald* on the 18th. It was ground-breaking. In some 4,400 words he presented a form of on-the-scene reportage that most readers had not experienced before. He described how he had continued his investigation of the Burnt District, and his inability to make his way to the wharf at the foot of Broad Street. Looking in the direction of Williamsburg, he wrote, he had seen "nothing but flames ascending to heaven, and prodigious clouds of smoke curling after it as if from a volcano." The fire from the previous night had not been fully extinguished, for at Front and Coenties Slip, Bennett watched "the most awful scenes burst upon my eyes. I beheld the several blocks of seven story stores, full of rich merchandise, on the northern side of the slip, in one bright, burning, horrible flame."

All along the streets Bennett watched, he reported, as "boys, men and women, of all colors, were stealing and pilfering as fast as they could." For some New Yorkers, the aftermath of the fire offered a harvest of opportunity. One poor old woman filled her basket from a pile of burning sugar. "No doubt she had a sweet cup of tea" that night, commented Bennett. Rag gatherers stuffed sacks with scorched fragments of cotton and silk, and at a former jeweler's store, Philadelphia financier John Watson noted how boys and girls searched "for sundry trinkets." Boats meanwhile streamed in from Long Island in search of booty. That first day, the police arrested some 200 people. They then simply discharged most of them, since they could not identify where the stolen goods came from.[7]

* * *

The day after the fire, while Bennett was taking his tour, Mayor Cornelius Lawrence summoned the Common Council to figure out how to safeguard the exposed property. He called for a doubling of the watch. Regiments and volunteer infantry patrolled the Burnt District. Citizens also organized volunteer patrols. Sixteen-year-old Cyrus Field, who worked as an errand boy for the dry goods merchant Alexander Stewart, took his turn "as a guard to prevent people from going to the ruins to steal property." Troops braving the freezing cold as well as sleet and rain found respite in taverns, which served the men bread and cheese. William Dumont on Water Street brought out a "liberal supply of refreshments" for members of the Lady Washington Fire Company. Thomas Downing meanwhile supplied "refreshments, consisting of tea, coffee oysters, &'c. to at least 571 persons."

Catherine Wynkoop's father's shop escaped destruction. "It seems almost a miracle that our store did not go with the rest," she wrote. Yet many who had gone to bed well-off now faced severe losses as they frantically sifted through the charred remains of years of work. Hone found among those who had suffered "most of my nearest friends and of my family; my son John, my son-in-law Schermerhorn, and my nephew Isaac S. Hone, and Samuel S. Howland."[8]

When Charles Sagory from Rogers & Co.—the merchant whose clerk had gone in search of him during the fire—reached Exchange Place he found his store in ruins. Yet his clerk's efforts the night before had thankfully saved the firm's books along with the business' "portfolio." According to Hone, the $300,000 cargo of Cantonese tea that arrived right before the fire "lies in a state not worth picking up." Other merchants who had been uptown during the blaze came down and found themselves unable to locate their stores, nor even the streets on which they had stood. Lothrop Sturges, whose business Doane, Sturges & Co. handled cotton, flour, and tobacco imports, walked there in the bitter cold, and as he passed "down William Street, he thought that the city had a strange, lonesome look," wrote his sister-in-law Mary Sturges, "and as he went farther down, to his astonishment, he saw the masts of vessels, and reaching the corner of Wall Street, found everything gone to the water's edge." When Sturges got to the spot where his store once stood, there was nothing there.[9]

People dug through burning ruins to salvage all they could. The *New York Commercial Advertiser* observed how some pulled out "blankets, silks, linens, calicoes—every thing—some ruined by water, some by fire, some by being trampled in the mud—some half burnt, and many yet on fire." When Bennett visited the Custom House, which now housed the post office, he found the clerks "in an awful state of confusion. They scarcely knew what they had lost or saved." Newspapers traditionally filled columns with lists of fire damages and losses, and the press was packed with notices about those who had suffered. One merchant lost $300,000 in silks alone, another $200,000 in teas and brandies. Of the 27 merchants who imported French goods, 23 were literally burned out. Ten crockery stores were destroyed, along with some 10 hardware stores. I. & A. Brown, an importer of Irish linen on Merchants Street, lost $40,000. Stephen Whitney had just built 24 stores and the fire leveled all of them. The Ohio Hotel was destroyed. Moses Taylor on South Street lost coffee, sugar, and other goods worth $300,000. The list of losses went on and on: 12,000 bags of coffee; 2,500 to 3,000 boxes of Cuban sugar; 40,000 gallons of saltpeter; several thousand bags of pimentos; large quantities of brandy and indigo.[10]

Those who salvaged goods looked for places to store them. To play it safe, Jonathan Sturges moved his merchandise onto vessels and had them backed away from the shore. "Carmen and porters were heaping goods upon carts, barrows, in coaches and omnibuses; the Battery and Bowling Green are thickly studded with piles of goods," reported the *Commercial Advertiser*. In Bowling Green, as he wrote in his piece, Bennett had come across nervous clerks tending to $500,000 worth of goods. Whitehall Slip also filled with goods, and Castle Garden, a former fort off the tip of the island that had been turned into a restaurant and entertainment center, was tasked as a depot for unclaimed goods. Shanties went up along South Street. Assistant aldermen had a shed built for butchers who had lost their stalls at the Franklin Market on Old Slip between Front and Water Streets.[11]

* * *

The Stock Exchange, founded only 18 years earlier in 1817, suspended business until the 21st. The Board of Assistant Aldermen meanwhile set aside the Superior Court Room in City Hall as a temporary Merchants' Exchange. But with businesses shuttered, jobs vanished. The *Herald* estimated that as many as 8,000 clerks, warehousemen, porters, cartmen, and others had lost their work. The fire worsened the state of publishing and printing, which had already been hit hard by the August 12 Fulton Street blaze. Many of the town's newspapers, such as the *New York American* and the *New York Daily Advertiser*, were either damaged or destroyed, as were smaller publications like the *Knickerbocker*. Some papers set up temporary offices. With no work, young Walt Whitman soon headed back across the East River to his family on Long Island.

Readers eagerly followed the news, avidly reading the morning edition of the *New York Sun*. Prior to the fire, the paper had a daily circulation of 15,000. It now had its presses running around the clock to produce an extra 30,000 copies. On the 21st, Bennett printed—at great expense—an illustration of the ruins of the Merchants' Exchange.

Fire companies from Brooklyn, Newark, and other surrounding communities came to help the exhausted New York City firemen, with crews arriving from Philadelphia. "This is truly a brotherly kindness and charity," noted Hone approvingly. New York's firemen needed the assistance, for blazes continued. Some of them were intentionally set. On the morning of the 17th, someone torched the third floor of the First Ward Hotel on Broad Street. On the morning of the 18th, a shanty in Greenwich Lane caught fire. The following day someone tried to burn down a building on Pearl Street that housed the *New York Transcript*. The frozen body of the arsonist, lynched the night of the fire, was soon cut down.[12]

At noon on the 19th, with the city still in shock, Mayor Lawrence chaired a public meeting at City Hall at which was formed a sort of fire committee. Among its many members (125 in all) were such civic leaders as Albert Gallatin, Samuel Swartwout, Mangle Quackenbos, Prosper M. Wetmore, John Pintard, Samuel B. Ruggles, William B. Astor, John Coster, Charles King, Hone, as well as Preserved Fish, a prominent merchant with a Quaker name, which means "preserved from sin" or "preserved in a state of grace."

There were to be inquiries to determine the cause of the fire and suggestions as to what alterations should be made to city streets and what modifications need to be carried out for building construction. The committee would investigate how the fire department should be improved, and to come up with ways to help those affected by the blaze. Lawrence, Gallatin, Fish, and others joined a separate committee, one whose task would be to ask Congress for an extension of credit on duty bonds. Hone, meanwhile, belonged to yet another committee that planned to appeal to the Albany legislature for financial aid. Disosway and John Hone's son, Isaac, were given the job of finding out from businessmen about the extent of their losses.

Merchants and bankers entreated the Second Bank of the United States for help. Nicholas Biddle, the third and final president of the Second Bank, arrived on the 19th. The following day he toured the Burnt District. Afterward, he let it be known that he had asked the bank's directors to advance to the insurance companies up to $2 million so they could pay off claims, which within days of the fire threatened to bankrupt them. These were extraordinary times, and the Treasury Department instructed the Customs Department to extend time on bonds for those who had suffered losses. Hone's and the others' visit to Albany also paid off, as New York State authorized a $6 million loan, equal to about $180 million today. The heads of the city's banks meanwhile met and resolved "to extend every possible facility to the merchants and traders, and the public generally, in the present emergency."[13]

While Biddle's pledge seemed like a blessing, many saw the fire as more than a financial crisis. Abolitionists were among the first to sense divine retribution. Lewis Tappan wrote Gerrit Smith that the destruction was a "rebuke to our covetousness & other sins." People flocked to churches, which were packed on the first Sunday after the fire. In his sermon, Reverend William Muhlenberg, an Episcopalian who became an early disciple of what became known as the Social Gospel, warned his congregation in Flushing that the fire had resulted from "that *inordinate spirit of money making*, which marks our country in general, and its commercial cities in particular." Catherine Wynkoop was devastated when she visited the South Reformed Dutch Church on Garden Street. "It almost made me cry to see the place where we used to worship, laid waste, a mere mass of smoking ruins." The congregation gathered in the church's lecture room, which, miraculously, survived the blaze, aside from the windows, "the great heat from the church having shattered that."

The city had never experienced anything on this scale, and private citizens began to raise money for the afflicted. The Bowery Theatre's Thomas Hamblin published a letter on the 18th, announcing that given he had "derived all that I am worth from the American public" he felt the need to return the favor. He offered $500 toward a public subscription for those suffering from the fire, an act of charity that won him the admiration of even the misanthropic Bennett, a man who took a dislike to many in New York society and had been happily lambasting the theater owner over his extramarital activities and his divorce from his wife, the actress Elizabeth Walker Blanchard Hamblin: "He has acted so liberally, so gentlemanly, so much like a man at this lamentable crisis, that we most cheerfully forget and forgive everything." People in other cities raised money and collected clothes for survivors. Montreal, for example, sent $2,000, equal to about $60,000 today.[14]

Unsurprisingly and inevitably, the losses sorely taxed insurance companies. Twenty-year-old Samuel Tilden, future New York governor and

Democratic candidate for president in 1876, was a student and observed how, "The whole insurance capital of the city will scarce exceed one-half the amount of property consumed in one night!" For the city's 25 insurance firms, the fire proved devastating. Altogether, companies were on the hook for claims amounting to as much as $7 million, about $210 million today. Fourteen of them, over half, immediately became insolvent. George Washington Strong's older brother Joseph served as secretary of New York Equitable Insurance, and on January 1 the firm canceled all policies and offered to refund a portion of the premiums. "Brother Joseph's occupation is gone," Strong wrote. Strong noted that there were others in a similar situation. Eagle insurance company, for example, held policies amounting to $1.6 million in coverage, yet only had $631,172 in assets. Its board met on the morning of the 18th and determined to pay out no more nor to enter any new contracts until they figured out what to do. Hone owned $11,000 worth of stock. "I suffer directly, and in others indirectly," he wrote ruefully in his diary, "to a large amount." The suffering wasn't limited to businesses. The insurance companies' failures especially hurt the aged, widows, orphans, and others who depended on the stock dividends "who had invested their funds in insurance stock with a view to get a large income," as Strong noted.

One insurance company that did honor its policies was the Hartford Fire Insurance Company. When word of the fire arrived in Connecticut, its president, Eliphalet Terry, and the firm's directors immediately went to the Hartford Bank and itemized their policies. Terry pledged his own property as security. He and the company's secretary, James Bolles, then took copies of their New York policies and raced south by sleigh. When they arrived in New York, they took space on Wall Street to meet with clients and settle their claims. The lack of stability in the industry would cause New York State to soon slash the tax imposed on out-of-state firms from 10 percent to 2 percent.[15]

Also strapped for cash were banks and their depositors. Hone reported that crowds rushed to the Bank for Savings and sought to withdraw their money, even if that meant taking it out before the 31st and thus losing six months' worth of interest. "There was an evident run upon the bank by a gang of low Irishmen, who demanded their money in a peremptory and threatening manner," he wrote disapprovingly and revealing his anti-Irish prejudice. When they realized that their withdrawal amounts did not include the dividends, many were bitterly disappointed and angry. Lawyers seemed to be the only group to benefit from the fire. Strong's firm, for example, handled the affairs of numerous insurance companies. As he wrote three months after the Great Fire, "more than half of my professional business has been attributable in one way or other to that event. I am employed in the winding up of the business of six of the insolvent Insurance Companies."[16]

Christmas was nearing. Hone, like many others, knew that it was not going to be a merry one. "The recent calamity bears so hard upon the whole community, that it seems unfeeling to be joyful." Dr. Hosack's condition had worsened following his stroke, and he died on the 22nd at age 66. His funeral was held at Grace Church on Christmas Day. At the service, which was officiated by Bishop Benjamin Onderdonk and Dr. Henry Ducachet, Hone observed how Ducachet "was so much affected that his tears and sobs almost prevented his utterance."

Business had been suspended for the holiday, and yet despite the pall hovering over the city—and exhortations issuing from pulpits warning of the existence of "evil in a city, and the Lord hath not done it"—there was at least some seasonal gaiety. The actor Joseph Jefferson was six years old at the time and went to the Burnt District with his father. He later recalled watching how "two Indians in theatrical costumes began dancing a war dance which they terminated by tomahawking each other in the most friendly way, and then bowing to the people, who applauded them." On the 21st, Junius Brutus Booth performed *King Lear* at the Bowery "to a very crowded house, with vast power and effect," noted the *Sun*, with Hamblin as Edgar, who "gave to that difficult and ill-understood part a highly original and impressive character."[17] Then on Christmas Day, so many people headed to the Bowery that hundreds had to be turned away. The Franklin Theatre was similarly packed, and on the 28th Niblo's Garden held a fair for the New York Institute for the Blind. William and Henry Hanington's diorama at the City Saloon drew many people who came to see "these splendid exhibitions of ingenuity" that included scenes from Arabian Nights, the Deluge, and the 1812 burning of Moscow following Napoleon's capture of the city. The brothers donated the proceeds from two nights to the relief of sufferers.[18]

* * *

Arthur Tappan had managed to gather up the firm's papers before the fire destroyed his building, and the morning after the Great Fire ran a notice:

Arthur Tappan & Co. acknowledges with gratitude the efficient exertions of their friends and fellow-citizens in saving (by the blessing of God) the largest portion of their goods, all their books of account, and most of their papers. They give notice that they have taken the new and commodious warehouse, No. 25 Beaver-street, into which their goods are moved, and where they will be arranged in a short time; and where they will be happy to see their friends and customers, until their store in Pearl-street shall be rebuilt, for which they have made arrangements.

That same morning, the Tappan brothers, their partners, and clerks gathered for an early breakfast to discuss matters. Arthur Tappan had a simple solution: "Rebuild immediately," and on the same spot. A clerk went to find Samuel Thompson, who constructed the original store, and within two hours they had signed a contract for a new building, one that they wanted erected "with all possible despatch." On the 19th the *Herald* reported, with some amazement, that "The solitary front wall of Arthur Tappan's store is removed and the excavations of the foundation begun." The new shop opened in early 1836, made from the same Maine granite as the destroyed building. The firm also spent a few thousand dollars on iron shutters and "other fastenings" to protect from future fires as well as potential anti-abolitionist mob violence.[19]

Some businesses started to set up offices in new locations. The banknote engravers Rawdon, Wright and Hatch, who had also been at the Exchange and saved their dies and banknote plates, moved to Broadway and Cedar Street. David Comstock and Robert Andrews moved their luxury goods firm to Liberty Street. In March 1836, Hone helped his son Robert establish a new dry goods firm with John B. Fleming. "It is gratifying to witness the spirit and firmness with which the merchants meet this calamity," wrote Hone. "There is no despondency; every man is determined to go to work to redeem his loss, and all are ready to assist their more unfortunate neighbors." Signs started to pop up among the smoldering ruins, advising customers and associates where the firms had relocated to. Alexander Jackson Davis, who had just lost $60 worth of furniture, paid a painter 50¢ to make a sign for him. Those looking to capitalize on the destruction—brokers, lawyers, building firms, sign-makers—took out newspaper ads. While safe-maker Charles Gayler's building on Water Street had been destroyed, he continued to tout Gayler's Patent Double Fire Proof Chests, writing how "not one of Gayler's Double Chests, has at any time proved insecure against Fire or Burglars." The civil engineer Timothy Dewey ran an ad letting all know that he had "Wrought Iron Roofs" for sale.[20]

As we've seen, the southern end of Manhattan contained many narrow and winding streets dating to the Dutch era. Their tightness had increased the level of destruction by the fire and impeded the work of the fire companies. Almost immediately after the blaze, the Board of Aldermen and Board of Assistants met to discuss the need "to alter the route and width of the streets." The Common Council asked landowners for help improving roads, and the city got to work straightening crooked alleys in the Burnt District, standardizing streets and regulating building construction. On January 25, the Street Committee proposed widening Pearl and William Streets and Exchange Place, among other places. Three days later, Ithiel Town wrote up his own proposal, calling on the council to widen and straighten Wall Street, fill in Coenties Slip and Old Slip, and use the slips and Hanover Square to widen other streets, thus "producing regular blocks of stores." Town also called for changing building practices, getting rid of double party walls and using buttresses to strengthen structures and as a protection against fire.

The city made its plans, and municipal and private reconstruction progressed quickly. All along Wall Street firms got to work. In January 1836, the *American Monthly Magazine* reported that "the click of trowels is already heard among the half-cooled bricks, and the dust of mortar is even now mingling with the smoke from the still smouldering ruins." This was continuing work that had begun in earnest right after the fire, when merchants resolved to rebuild the Merchants' Exchange "with all convenient dispatch." Soon they hired the architect Isaiah Rogers, who had recently built Boston's Tremont House Hotel, the nation's first true luxury hotel, and was finishing work north of the Burnt District on what would become a grand hotel on Broadway for John Jacob Astor. By February 1836, a million dollars had been raised for the construction. Work started in April on the site, and to protect it from fire, the blue-granite Greek Revival structure with its Ionic-columned facade did not contain any structural wood.[21]

* * *

New York quickly got back to business. The city became "like a Phoenix from her ashes," wrote Mary Sturges. Soon the post office opened full time at the Rotunda in City Hall Park. Within two months of the fire, the Hartford covered all of their policies and paid out $84,973.34. While insurance firms like the American, Franklin Fire, and the Globe went under, some 20 others soon revived, and in March the Eagle issued $500,000 worth of new stock.

Even in the Burnt District, whose devastation had seemed so complete, life started to return to normal. One sign of this was when newspaper editors resumed attacking each other. The *Sun* noted how *Journal of Commerce* editors had used vinegar to put out their fire and now filled their inkstands with the same liquid in order to write scathing articles. And in May, Bennett's *Herald* ran a piece implicating the *Morning Courier and New York Enquirer's* James Watson Webb in shady stock dealings. Soon after, Webb retaliated, literally, and assaulted Bennett, knocking him down on Wall Street and striking him with a stick. The next day Bennett responded to the attack by running a piece in which he proclaimed, "hereafter I shall be obliged to carry weapons to defend my person, *and if he gets killed in the street, the blood be upon his own head.*"

In March the Hanington brothers premiered their new grand moving diorama, *Awful and Devastating Conflagration of a Large Part of the City of New York*, advertising the work in the *Herald* with an illustration that ran across two columns—a huge investment. They set their massive canvas at Scudder's American Museum on Park Row. Alongside it they hung a painting of Robert Ball Hughes' statue of Alexander Hamilton rising from the ruins and had "fragments of the real statue lying round it as they have been discovered since the fire." Music accompanied the unrolling of the work, and a neighbor recalled it as quite an extravaganza: "The ringing of the bells—the rattling of the engines—the sudden flashes of light—the roar of the flames—the cries and shouts of the distracted citizens—are given, as the bills have it, 'with appalling effect!'"[22]

Businesses scrambled for space. By March, more than 600 firms had found temporary spots, causing a huge spike in rents. George Washington Strong wrote in February how "Rents have advanced most enormously. It is no uncommon event for a store to rent for $6,000 a year. We have taken our offices after May next in Broadway on the corner of Exchange Place, (late Garden Street). The house in which our offices are taken last year rented for $1200; now it is let on a lease for $2500 a year."[23]

Real estate values likewise shot up. Astor, who had moved his office north of Broadway and Prince Street about a year before the fire, bought up properties. The real estate firm of James Bleecker & Sons quickly opened a new sales room on Broad Street. At a sale on February 23, the firm sold lots from an estate, bringing in $765,100, an amount that Hone noted was "greater than they would have brought before the fire, when covered with valuable buildings." This was a sizable sum for New York real estate, and indeed among the highest in the city's history. "In a comparatively short time the debris of the burnt district was removed," wrote merchant Nathaniel Hubbard, "and new stores immediately erected; and in many locations property advanced more than to cover the cost of erecting new buildings."[24]

In June 1836, six months after the fire, the land where Dr. Mathews' Dutch church had stood sold for an astounding $285,400. Commerce was the new religion. The *Mirror* also reported how the area around Bowling Green, which once served as an enclave for the city's "wealthiest and oldest families," was quickly changing to a place filled with commercial enterprises, public hotels, and boarding houses. Banker Nathaniel Prime owned 1 Broadway and planned to build a hotel there to rival one being erected by Astor farther up the street. The home of the prominent merchant Asa Fitch at 30 Broadway was being converted for commercial use. The home at 36 was being turned into a silk store, as was the house next door. The dry goods merchants Bailey, Keller & Remsen leased carpenter Richard Carman's nearby home for another silk store, and the building was about to be demolished for a larger one, as was the home at 52. Meanwhile Elizabeth Mann's boarding house was about to become a restaurant.

The nature of the Pearl Street area, home to New York's dry goods industry, also started to change in the aftermath of the fire as shops shifted their locations north along Broadway. At the same time, the Wall Street area became more purely financial. Gone were the small stores and businesses, replaced by gleaming Greek Revival buildings, housing, banks, and insurance companies. Each one was a temple to commerce and trade, featuring iron shutters and foot-thick brick walls for added protection. Many of the older buildings were enlarged and converted, with their first-floor brick facades replaced with granite piers. Delmonico's William Street restaurant had been destroyed in the fire. In early 1836, the brothers purchased two parcels of land at the intersection of Beaver, William, and South William Streets for a new restaurant. By December they began setting up equipment, getting carpentry work, and in March 1837 installed silver mounting for the stairs and gas fixtures. In September the Delmonicos invited the press in to show off their new restaurant complete with ancient marble columns on the porch that they brought in from a villa in Pompeii, Italy.[25]

* * *

The return to business as usual made New Yorkers appreciate that while the Great Fire had devastated part of their city—and was larger than anything the city had ever endured—it could have been worse. It was also a chance to size up the heroes and the villains. New Yorkers praised firemen for their work, with the *New York Evening Post* proclaiming, "No exertion on their part has ever been wanting to stay publick calamity, and in their endeavours they have held their own lives more cheap than the property of others." On the villainy side, a fight brewed over whom to blame for the destruction. Just two days after the blaze, the Board of Assistant Aldermen criticized Chief James Gulick and the department. An investigation into the blaze had begun on December 21, five days after the blaze. Gulick called a public meeting at the Firemen's Hall on the 24th at which the group sought to refute the "many slanderous and illiberal remarks which have been made" against the department.[26]

When a chimney caught fire on Duane Street on the evening of New Year's Day, Alderman Samuel Purdy immediately made his way there. The fire was quickly extinguished, and as he left he saw Engine No. 10 racing by. Purdy was among the fire company's critics, believing that they could have done more during the Great Fire and needed to improve their operations. He called out to the men that the blaze had been put out. One of the members yelled back, "Stand aside, damn your eyes, or we will run you down." Purdy demanded to know the man's name. "I won't tell you my name," he responded, "damn you, you have insulted the Fire Department; you have treated them lately like damned dogs." The man then hit and kicked Purdy. The Common Council condemned the attack, and suspended as well as expelled a number of the firemen.

Purdy was not alone. There were calls to reorganize the department. At a May 3 meeting, the Common Council's Fire and Water Committee reprimanded Gulick, and the following day they removed him and made John Riker the new fire chief. Word of their action arrived as Gulick was battling a blaze opposite the Union Market. When Gulick heard what happened, he turned his cap around, and handed control over to an assistant. "In less than five minutes, almost every fireman's cap was turned, in token of their displeasure, and their determination to make no farther efforts to arrest the progress of the flames," reported the *Commercial Advertiser*. Mayor Lawrence heard what was happening and rushed there to implore the crews to get back to work. Yet for two hours the men stood idly by as the buildings burned. When Gulick returned, the crowds cheered him, and the firemen resumed their work. By then, however, 20 houses, the market house, a dry goods store, and a cabinetmaker's shop were destroyed. Gulick's and the firemen's actions incurred the wrath of the papers. The *Herald* noted that, "in such a city as this, the refusal of the regular firemen to work . . . is too gross—too bad—too alarming an outrage to be at all tolerated."[27]

The recriminations abated, however, and by the end of June the *Evening Post* observed, "The part of the city consumed last winter by fire, now presents a curious and animated spectacle." The author of the piece struggled for a historical analogy, but it reminded him of what he had read "concerning cities built up suddenly in waste places—Carthage on the African shore, Tadmor in the wilderness, and St. Petersburg on the morasses of the Baltic." In the middle of the month, engineers finished maps to build the Croton Aqueduct to bring a reliable source of water to the city. As we'll see, this was a revolutionary improvement. Two weeks later, Gabriel Furman recalled walking through the City Hall Park the day before Independence Day. It was a warm evening, and he was amazed to find, "The streets were literally thronged with people, so much so, that it was difficult either to walk on the side walks, or in the centre of the street."[28]

With the city renewed, news could turn to other topics, or so it seemed. Bennett, for one, turned his sneering attention back to Thomas Hamblin, writing at the end of August how a theater manager in Philadelphia had been busy signing up all the great acting talent in England, thus making it harder for Hamblin to find needed actors: "The Bowery may as well put out its lights, or be rented for a loafers' alms house establishment." In September Hamblin signed the Boston-born actress Charlotte Cushman for a three-year contract. On the 12th, she made her New York debut as Lady Macbeth.

Then early on the 22nd, a fire broke out at the theater, possibly ignited by smoldering gun waddings used the night before during a performance of *Lafitte: The Pirate of The Gulf*. The blaze was already going strong when the firemen arrived. Because Hamblin long feared that the scripts for the Bowery's plays would be stolen, he did not make copies of the works. As the Bowery burned, Hamblin rushed in to try and save the scripts and whatever else he could. But the smoke triggered an asthma attack and he hurt his left hand. With the fire raging, his popular and prolific European-born playwright Louisa Medina could only helplessly watch the burning of the building and the destruction of her work.[29]

Despite the firemen's efforts, nothing could be done to save the theater. "The mighty tongues of fire rushed exulting upwards in a direct line, as if disdaining to be fed on any grosser fuel," wrote the *New York Spirit of the Times*. "For a length of time the solid pediment resisted their terrible embrace, and the American Eagle, that magnificent piece of gilded carving full 25 feet from wing to wing, which was presented to Mr. Hamblin by an association of gentlemen, seemed soaring, phoenix like, above a bed of fire and flame. At last it fell with a tremendous crash, and as an instance of the interest felt for the concern, it was cut into a thousand bits and showered as a relic among the spectators." Hamblin himself couldn't have scripted a more dramatic scenario. Medina reportedly lost $20,000 in the blaze. And to make matters worse, Hamblin had not reinsured the building, which he'd had a chance to do two days earlier, thus losing as much as $100,000.

Unbowed, Hamblin vowed to rebuild with "greater splendor and magnificence." He sought to form a new association, selling 100 shares for $1,000 each to rebuild the theater and buy scenery, wardrobe, and supplies. Other theater owners—Edmund Simpson at the Park Theatre and William Dinneford at the Franklin Theatre—held benefits at their theaters for sufferers of the fire. They also helped collect money for reconstruction. While the men did not tally up what he had hoped—they raised barely $2,000—Hamblin used the cash to buy up the remaining shares of the theater from the New York Association. The manager now fully owned the theater, yet still had a mortgage held by Astor.[30]

Bennett didn't let up on Hamblin and had been tarring the Bowery as "the worst and wickedest that ever stood a month in any city under heaven." He likewise attacked Hamblin and his reputation, claiming that he had a hidden stockpile of cash, had turned the theater into a brothel, and accused him of being a wanton womanizer. Despondent over the failure to raise funds, Hamblin went out for drinks with some associates on November 11 and decided to seek revenge on the editor. They made their way to the *Herald*'s office. Once there, Hamblin demanded a retraction, and the men attacked Bennett, yelling, "Kill him—kill him!" They fought until the police came. The publisher pressed changes for assault and battery, and accused the men of stealing $500. On the 24th Hamblin sailed for England, not returning until the following June.[31]

By the fall of 1836 the Great Fire was becoming a memory for many. In November the *Evening Post* reported that "Eleven months have hardly elapsed since the great fire . . . and the district embraced by it is nearly all rebuilt with fine and commodious stores, much improved in their appearance and construction. The Exchange is fast going up, the foundation being laid and all things in progress; and . . . our city has not been materially interrupted in her onward career of commercial prosperity."

But while the Great Fire's destruction was being swept away, it was also being memorialized and transformed into a cultural touchstone about the resilience of New Yorkers. Many saw the Great Fire as an opportunity to profit, not only from the rebuilding, but also by referencing and even mythologizing the blaze and the efforts of those who fought it. The penny presses, which had started only a few years earlier, had increased the public's appetite for sensationalism with their reports of fires, crimes, and scandals. Nathaniel Currier, a 22-year-old lithographer from Roxbury, Massachusetts, who had recently set up shop on Wall Street, started making prints of the fire that citizens avidly bought. The Naples-born artist Nicolino Calyo produced a series of gouaches and aquatints that included the burning of the Merchants' Exchange, views of the flames from Brooklyn, and illustrations of the subsequent devastation. For the steep price of $5, the publisher Lewis Clover sold copperplate engravings by William James Bennett, marketing them as *A Brief History Intended to Accompany the Beautifully Colored Views of the Destructive Fire in New-York, December 16 and 17, 1835.* From the English county of Staffordshire, an unknown potter produced a series of plates with transferware images of the burning of a warehouse on Coenties Slip, along with the streets on fire and the Exchange in ruins, all done up in blues, greens, pink, black, and brown, with the rims displaying city fire engines. And it is possible that the painter Thomas Cole, who lived on Laight Street, took inspiration from the fire to create "Destruction," the fourth part of his "The Course of Empire" series about the rise and fall of a civilization.

On the first anniversary of the fire, Hone reported that the city was a changed place. "It is just a year since the desolating calamity took place," wrote Hone. "To the honor of the merchants, and as an evidence of the prosperity of the city, the whole is rebuilt with more splendor than before." Nearly two weeks later, he observed that 500 stores had been built in the past year, noting approvingly that the aggregate rent "will be between a million and a million and a half." And despite all the turmoil of the past year, Hone wrote on New Year's Day, "I have great reason to be thankful for the blessings I enjoy. My health is good, my family happy, and my position in society respectable. I am not too old to have a taste for the enjoyments of life, and my circumstances admit of a reasonable indulgence in them." Hone's improving sentiments, just like his reborn city, had returned.[32]

3

Overturning Manhattan

New York in 1836 might have been rebuilding from the ashes of the Great Fire, but by then it had already gone from being a provincial city to a global center. As it rose from the ruins, it attracted visitors and tourists, curious about the extent of the fire's damage and equally intrigued by the new construction. So many arrived in the spring of 1836 that the city's taverns and boarding houses couldn't accommodate all those coming to town to attend its theaters, shop in its stores, see its sights, and eat in its restaurants and oyster cellars. There was a shortage even before the fire. In 1818, the city had a mere eight hotels. By 1835, the year of the Great Fire, New York could boast of 28 hotels for the 70,000 tourists visiting each year. But it still proved too few. The City Hotel on Broadway, the biggest of them all, was designed by John McComb Jr., who was one of New York's most prolific architects, and featured 137 rooms, carpeted parlors, a bar, and coffee rooms. The four-story Pearl Street House could accommodate 300 guests, with the *New York Evening Post* raving about its large dining room. Most places, though, proved far from grand. William Sykes' New-York Coffee House offered "boarding by the week or month."[1]

The lack of accommodation convinced John Jacob Astor, who by then had started to move away from his fortune-making fur trade, that he could make money housing out-of-towners. He had first dabbled in the hospitality business in 1828 when he snapped up the City Hotel. As noted earlier, he then decided to build a grand hotel. Astor needed an architect, and having admired Isaiah Rogers' design for Boston's Tremont House, hired him. Four stories tall and sheathed in granite, the Tremont had opened in 1829 and was the nation's first luxury hotel, featuring a majestic Doric portico, a rotunda with a stained-glass dome, and 170 rooms.

Astor directed Rogers to top the Tremont. Since the developer realized the center of commercial and residential New York had been shifting uptown, he decided to build on the site of his home at 223 Broadway, across from the City Hall Park. He bought up the adjoining properties from John and Catherine Coster, David Lydig, and others, and then sailed off to Europe to see his daughter Eliza, who was living in Paris. Astor returned in April 1834, intent on getting back to work. But when he landed on the 4th, both his son William and Philip Hone met him at the dock to give him the sad news of his wife Sarah's death the week before. Her passing—which came nearly two years after their daughter Magdalen died—came as a huge shock to Astor. Hone observed that he "looks poorly and is much thinner than he was when he went to Europe."[2]

Despite the tragedy, Astor persevered. At the start of July 1834, a hundred spectators gathered for the laying of the cornerstone. It took two years to build Astor's dream hotel. In May 1836, five months after the Great Fire, the building that Hone predicted would be "an ornament to the city" opened its doors. It was unlike anything seen before in the town. The *New York Mirror* noted how it "imparts a most lordly air to the city." Massachusetts granite as well as marble shipped down the Hudson from Ossining covered the six-story Greek Revival structure, its Doric entrance portico topped by a florid anthemion crest. The lobby had marble pillars and a blue and white inlaid floor. Guests could sit on the parlor's satin couches, buy dresses and clocks at shops, and visit Rabineau's Baths for a soothing soak (hot or cold). The hotel featured a gentlemen's reading room, a "conversation room," and a ladies' drawing room. For the dining room, a French chef and a dozen cooks whipped up dishes served by 60 waiters. The hotel contained more than 300 spacious rooms filled with black walnut furniture, grand mirrors, fireplaces, and Brussels carpets.[3]

While many felt that Astor was taking a chance building a mile north of Wall Street, the hotel proved to be an immediate success. According to Scottish publisher William Chambers, "The whole house swarms like a hive." Lots of people would stay there, from Charles Dickens in 1842 to presidential hopeful Abraham Lincoln in 1860. Senator Daniel Webster was a favored guest, and when he came to town the hotel flew "the Webster Flag," a large white banner emblazoned with "Liberty and Union." The Astor House Hotel became the place to see and be seen, so popular that James Gordon Bennett told his *New York Herald* staff, "Anyone who can pay two dollars a day for a room must be important."[4]

* * *

The hotel was a dream for Astor in part because it seemed so far from the New York he stepped into when he arrived from Germany in the spring of 1784. Manhattan was still a wild place until the beginning of the 19th century. The original inhabitants, the Munsee-speaking Lenapes, called the spit of land either "Island of Many Hills" or "the place where we get bows." Forests and marshes blanketed the surface. The woods were dense with red maple, American chestnuts, beech, Atlantic cedar, thorn apples, hickory, oak, birches, sweet gum, white pines, hickories, tulip trees, eastern hemlock, white ash, and hornbeam. Thick bushes of blackberries, raspberries, huckleberries, teaberries, snowberries, partridgeberries, chokeberries, and gooseberries covered the ground. Deer, elk, cougars, bears, and wolves lived in the woods. Beaver proliferated in the marshes. Wood ducks splashed around the ponds, and passenger pigeons crowded the sky. Water lapped against the jagged shoreline, while 66 miles' worth of streams flowed over the island, and hundreds of springs dotted the surface.

The Lenape name for Manhattan was entirely appropriate. Five hundred and seventy-three hills stretched across the island. Some, like Bayard's Mount—also known as Bunker's Hill—loomed north of current-day Foley Square. Lawyer William Duer remembered that it "rose gradually from its margin to the height of one hundred feet." And further uptown stood a string of sand hills, which the 17th-century Dutch settlers called Zandtberg, that ran down the center of the island. Harlem boasted of fertile meadows and plains.

Manhattan was water-logged. Pearl Street was but a swampy meadow filled with trees, bushes, and blackberries. Partridges and heath hens were plentiful. In 1625 the Dutch engineer and surveyor Cryn Fredericksz laid out a rough grid for the city's first street plan. And attracted by the inlets and streams downtown, the Dutch created canals similar to those found in Holland. Present-day Broad Street was once a small stream that ran through a marshy area, and the Dutch turned it into *Heere Gracht*, Gentleman Canal. An inlet inhabited by beavers that is now called Beaver Street became known as *Bever Gracht* as well as *Prince Gracht*, Prince Canal. Maiden's Lane, or Maiden's Path, *Maagde Paatje*, was a pebbly stream with a steep southern bank that flowed eastward to the East River. It was so named because women brought clothes to wash there.

This stretch of the city contained *Bestevaer's Kripplebush*, what became known as Beekman's Swamp. It was filled with woods, crossed by streams, and dotted with the farms and the country homes of the wealthy. Near it Richard Sackett had a cherry garden whose name would survive as Cherry Street. George and Martha Washington lived on that street for a year when New York served as the nation's capital, which it did from 1785 to 1790.

Manhattan had 21 ponds and salt pannes, and alongside Bayard's Mount stretched the Collect, a kettle pond created by glacial melt water. Claimed to be bottomless, the Collect got its name from a corruption of the *Kalch Hoek*, Dutch for lime point, which was bestowed on the spot after the Dutch discovered large mounds of oyster shells left by the natives who harvested them in the rivers. Alongside it lay the Little Collect.[5]

The Collect's water, with its killifishes and yellow-bellied cobblers, was a popular fishing hole. Daniel Tiemann, who would later become mayor of New York, fondly recalled, "We used to catch perch, sunfish, and eels in this lake in Summer." Two streams flowed from the Collect. Lispenard's Creek meandered westerly to the Hudson River through Lispenard's Meadow, a marsh with pools and swamps, bulrushes and brambles, and filled with water snakes and bullfrogs that attracted sportsmen and hunters. The Old Wreck Brook, also known as Wolfert's Creek, wandered easterly through a swampy area called Wolfert's Marsh. When the tide rose, water flowed in and it reportedly linked the Hudson and East Rivers. Others places like the Stuyvesant's Meadows, in the current-day East Village, were lined with cattails, bladderworts, duckweed, water lilies, and pondweeds, and filled with pumpkinseed and American eel.[6]

In his 1809 *A History of New York*, the celebrated writer Washington Irving described how at the center of the island stretched "a sweet and rural valley, beautified with many a bright wild flower, refreshed by many a pure streamlet." Two streams, the first starting at what would become Fifth Avenue and 21st Street and the other at Sixth Avenue and 16th Street, met up around 12th Street. The Dutch called it *Bestevaer's Killetje*, and the English Minetta Brook. The stream flowed through a marsh inhabited by muskrats, an area that would eventually become known as Washington Square Park. Trout coursed through the waterway that then made its way southwesterly to the Hudson and passed alongside Aaron Burr's home on Richmond Hill, which was located on current-day Charlton Street east of Varick Street. There the third vice president formed what became known as Burr's Pond, where his beloved daughter Theodosia learned to ice skate.[7]

A stream started around Fifth Avenue and 46th Street and ran southeast into Kip's Bay at 36th Street and the East River, the site where British troops landed on September 15, 1776, during the American Revolution and routed American militias, who then hurriedly retreated north to Harlem Heights. Another one began at Broadway and 44th Street and expanded at Madison Avenue in the lower 30s into Sun Fish Pond. It proved popular for fishermen;

children collected hickory nuts from the trees along its edges. To the north in the 40s lay Turtle Bay, named for a turtle-filled cove, which sat on the edge of the East River, a tidal estuary with porpoises, seals, and whales. Further up the island, there were such water sources as the Kill of Schepmoes, Unquenchable Spring, Montayne's Rivulet, and Sherman Creek.

The seven-year-long British occupation of New York during the American Revolution slowed development. The British added very little and turned the city into an armed camp, building military earthworks along side streets and using some churches for stables and jails. Also, two fires ripped through Manhattan, one in 1776 and the other in 1778, both of which did enormous damage, with the former scorching nearly a mile from the tip of the island up the West Side and destroying more than 500 buildings, while the latter took out more than 60 houses and businesses. Once the British surrendered New York in 1783, the town's planners started pushing north and straightening out and widening the paths into the rural parts of the island.

This reclaiming of the land went on for decades. In the process, property owners filled in streams, marshes, and ponds. There had been attempts over the years to stem the progress. For example, in order to preserve the Collect as a popular fishing hole, the city in 1734 banned the use of "Hoop-Net, Draw-net, Purse-net, Casting-net, Cod-net, Bley-net, or any Other Net or Nets," only allowing "Angling, with Angle Rod, Hook and Line only." Yet as businesses moved north, tanners, breweries, furnaces, and others set up alongside the water and dumped in carcasses and trash. By the early 19th century the city had cut down the bordering trees and filled the despoiled body of water and nearby marsh. Both Bayard's Mount and Powder-House knoll were leveled and pushed into the Collect, and Lispenard's Meadow dried out.

As the pond and meadow vanished, stagnant pools formed, which was a genuine public danger. The waters bred mosquitoes, which helped spread Yellow Fever, a disease that ravaged the population in 1795, 1798, 1805, and 1822. Water from the submerged springs continued to percolate into the area. Engineers lined a drainage channel to the Hudson, erected a railing along its side, and planted shade trees on what became known as Canal Street. Trinity Church owned some of the land on the West Side, and at the turn of the century started to develop St. John's Park, a haven for the wealthy. The city also began selling the reclaimed parcels of land that it owned, even though the presence of below-grade water and decomposing vegetation released noxious vapors. As a result, only the poor would settle the area on the East Side, which in the early 19th century evolved into the notorious Five Points slum.[8]

* * *

By the time Astor arrived in the mid-1780s, a number of streets in lower Manhattan were paved. In a few years, a field in what was then the northern part of the city—to the south of the Collect where City Hall and its park now stands—had become a popular spot for holding public rallies. It became known simply as "the Park." Even so, traveling around the island could be rough going, since much of it was covered in rocky outcroppings. Until the 19th century, most assumed that there would never be much growth to the north. When in the early 1800s the new City Hall was built at the north end of the Park, only the southern, western, and eastern facades were sheathed with white marble; the northern side featured less expensive brownstone, since it was assumed that no one would go around to the back.

A prime location or not, land was money. Good land brought wealth, and the island had lots of open space. Peter Warren, a British naval officer who had settled in New York prior to the American Revolution, made his fortune capturing enemy vessels and built a Georgian style home that commanded 300 acres on what is now Perry and Bleecker Streets in Greenwich Village. The area above what would become 14th Street was sparsely settled. A census taken in 1840 determined that 33,811 of the city's 312,710 people lived there in homes and farms, as well as estates. To give a sense of the residents, there was Petersfield on First Avenue and 15th Street, built prior to the American Revolution by the Stuyvesant family, descendants of Petrus Stuyvesant, the last Dutch director general of New Amsterdam. The Tiemann family, which manufactured paint, lived in a wood-framed house on 23rd east of Broadway. Isaac Varian, who served as mayor from 1839 to 1841, had a home at Broadway and 26th Street. James Beekman, whose family dated from the Dutch era, built his Mount Pleasant mansion in 1763 near First Avenue and 51st Street. Peter Schermerhorn, whose family ran a ship chandlery, had a house on 64th Street, just off of York Avenue on Manhattan's eastern edge. Colonel William Smith and his wife, Abigail, daughter of President John Adams, had started to build an estate on 61st Street overlooking the East River that they called Mount Vernon. When they ran out of money they sold it to merchant William Robinson. Commodore Isaac Chauncey, who helped capture current-day Toronto, Canada, during the War of 1812, had a place in Yorkville. Former district attorney Richard Riker's Arch Brook home was at 75th Street, and Major Joseph Delafield's mansion loomed on 77th Street.

Along the West Side, in 1840 the poet Clement Clarke Moore—the presumed author of "A Visit from Saint Nicholas," better known as "The Night before Christmas"—lived in Chelsea House on a 94-acre estate in the 20s that his grandfather, Major Thomas Clarke, a retired British officer, had settled in 1750. At 53rd Street and the Hudson stood Gerrit Striker's mansion. The Havemeyer family, which made its money in sugar refining, had a place at Eighth Avenue and 58th Street. Jacob Harsen had a homestead at Tenth Avenue and 70th Street. James Boggs' Chevilly home sat on 16 acres in the lower 70s. The Somerindyck family's farmhouse stood at what is now Broadway and 75th Street. Merchant Pelatiah Perit had a home on 75th Street and the Hudson waterfront. All the way uptown, on a 34-acre spread, former Secretary of the Treasury Alexander Hamilton's John McComb–designed home stood at 143rd and Amsterdam Avenue. Colonel James Monroe—nephew of the former president—built Fanwood on 37.5 acres in Washington Heights. The naturalist John James Audubon had his estate with a two-story frame home on 155th Street, facing the Hudson River. He called it Minnie's Land, after a Scottish term for "mother" that the Audubon children called Lucy Audubon during their time in the United Kingdom. The Morris-Jumel Mansion, where Washington briefly set up his Revolutionary War headquarters, sat (as it sits still) on 161st Street and Edgecombe Avenue. And near the top of the island stood the Dyckman family house at Broadway and 204th Street, which farmer William Dyckman built in the mid 1780s after the British burned the family's previous home.

Some of the estates had laid-out grounds. The prominent newspaper publisher Horace Greeley and his wife, Mary, kept house in a large wooden home in Turtle Bay, situated on eight acres with a wooded ravine and extensive gardens. Astor had a home at 88th Street on an 11-acre East Side spread overlooking Hell Gate. Washington Irving had spent some time there in 1835, writing his nephew Pierre, "I cannot tell you how sweet and delightful I have found this retreat; pure air, agreeable scenery, a spacious house, profound quiet, and perfect command of my time and self." James Gordon Bennett owned a large estate in Washington Heights. A belvedere sat atop the main house, offering commanding views of the Hudson River and the Palisades.[9]

* * *

Those living to the north soon started to sense the coming encroachment of their land as development pushed irresistibly and haphazardly in their direction. Into the 19th century, New York had been poorly planned, making it, according to the *Mirror,* "an ill-laid out and commercial city." As space become more of a premium, efforts began to level and regulate the island. On April 3, 1807, the state legislature formed a special commission and appointed Gouverneur Morris, Simeon De Witt, and John Rutherfurd, three of its most distinguished citizens, as commissioners. The trio set out to decide the street patterns above Houston Street and were granted the authority "to lay out streets, roads and public squares of such width, extent and direction as to them shall seem most conducive to public good." De Witt had trained as a surveyor and served as geographer and surveyor of the Continental Army, and following the Revolution became New York State's surveyor general. Morris had been the American minister to Paris and helped write the final draft of the US Constitution. The Manhattan-born Rutherfurd served as a senator from New Jersey and married Morris' niece. To map out the land, they hired the surveyor John Randel Jr., whose family knew De Witt's and had completed surveys upstate. Randel started trekking across the island, making his way around the ponds, through meadows and marshes, and over outcroppings. Some did not care for his staking out and mapping their land. Historian Martha Lamb wrote how on one occasion, homeowners drove him and his crew away. They were drawing the line of an avenue directly through the kitchen of "an estimable old woman, who had sold vegetables for a living upwards of twenty years" and as a result "were pelted with cabbages and artichokes until they were compelled to retreat."

Undaunted, Randel finished his survey in 1810. His plan for the city included the suggestion that the varied topography be taken into consideration for a number of streets. The commissioners, though, ignored any such concessions. And instead of creating a civic design with ovals and diagonal layouts—like that laid out by Pierre Charles L'Enfant in Washington, D.C., in 1791—the Commissioners' Plan of 1811 set up a scheme that focused entirely on growth. To do that, they imposed upon the land a rigid grid of streets and avenues. As the commissioners noted, "a city is to be composed principally of the habitations of men, and that straight-sided, and right-angled houses are the most cheap to build and the most convenient to live in."[10]

All these perpendicular roads ran regardless of the location of streams, hills, and outcroppings. This regular system of roads included a dozen 100-foot-wide, north–south avenues. The streets began at Houston Street, with

155 east–west roadways set 200 feet apart; Since the city relied so heavily on the rivers for trade, the traffic naturally flowed toward the water. Broadway was the only existing road allowed to continue its meandering path. The idea that the whole island would be developed seemed chimerical at the time, and the commissioners saw no reason to plan above 155th Street. As they commented, "It may be a subject of merriment, that the Commissioners have provided space for a greater population than is collected at any spot on this side of China."

Theirs proved an unloved plan. In the *New York Sunday Dispatch* in 1849, Walt Whitman noted that "streets cutting each other at right angles, are certainly the last things in the world consistent with beauty of situation." Yet the plan standardized expansion and—as a side benefit—made responding to fires easier. The commissioners had a single-minded focus on growth, setting aside merely 470 acres for parks, squares, and public spaces. The plan therefore quickly sealed the city's position as the ultimate real estate boomtown.[11]

However, even after the land had been marked and planned, and streets mapped for orderly growth, the city had no grand scheme to bring it all to fruition. Individual streets were generally completed river to river in one shot, while the longer avenues were done a part at a time. To open streets, the city needed to first acquire the land, which they did through condemnation. Once a landowner received reimbursement, the city graded and paved the roadway, recouping some of the expense through assessments levied on those whose property it ran through.

The taking of land proved to be a long and tortuous process. Not surprisingly, a good many landowners objected to the plan, claiming that the surveyors, commissioners, and assessors arbitrarily described their property and undervalued its worth. Clement Moore, for one, did not like the city taxing him for streets he didn't want. After workers cut Ninth Avenue through his Chelsea estate in 1818, Moore published *A Plain Statement, Addressed to the Proprietors of Real Estate in the City and County of New York.* In it he derided how "The great principle which appears to govern these plans is, to reduce the surface of the earth as nearly as possible to a dead level." The following year, Astor and others similarly sent a petition to the Common Council objecting to the commissioners' street plans.[12]

In 1827 writers William Cullen Bryant and Gulian Verplanck founded the publication *The Talisman* and created a fictitious character—a "New Yorker." The resident channeled the Book of Isaiah and bemoaned how "every high hill has been brought low, and every valley exalted." Everything was being regimented to the grid, even the seating in churches. Other New Yorkers embraced the plan, particularly developers. At first, these builders preferred the East Side, with its low and flat land, while the West Side's hills and valleys took longer to entice people. They directed laborers to use shovels, picks, and mules to level hills and fill in ponds and marshes. Much of the rocks, roots, and boulders were then dumped in valleys and swamps to raise that ground. In the process they brought about what seemed like a state of constant change. In 1847 Hone and his children went to Mrs. Robert Ray's home "away up at the corner of 28th Street and Ninth Avenue." He referred to the house as "one of those palaces which have lately sprung up in places where a few years since cattle grazed, and orchards dropped their ripened fruits."[13]

* * *

In the early part of the 19th century, many speculators and developers made money on land, yet none as much as John Jacob Astor. His early years, though, made him seem like the least likely to become one of the world's richest men, nor to become one of the individuals who so profoundly shaped not only New York City but also the early Republic. Born on July 17, 1763, in the village of Walldorf, in what is today the state of Baden-Württemberg, John Jacob was one of six children born to Johann Jacob and Maria Magdalena Astor. Maria died when John Jacob was just three. Johann Jacob remarried and had six more children. Johann Jacob hoped that John Jacob would follow him in the family's butcher business. But while his son learned the trade, John Jacob had no interest in doing that for the rest of his life. The young Astor still needed a profession. The family could not afford an apprenticeship for him, and he decided to try his luck elsewhere. In 1779, the teenager bundled together a small pack of clothes and a little money and headed off. "Soon after I left the village, I sat down beneath a tree to rest," he recalled later in life. "There I made three resolutions: to be honest, to be industrious, and not to gamble."[14]

John Jacob wasn't the only one of Johann Jacob Astor's sons to strike out on his own. Henry, John Jacob's older brother, worked as a butcher in New York. Another brother, George, was a partner in Astor & Broadwood, their uncle's London musical instrument firm. In fact, John Jacob decided to head to England first to work at the firm. There he learned the musical instrument trade and mastered English, though he would always retain his thick German accent. Soon John Jacob and George started a music business of their own. Throughout, Astor scrupulously saved his money, and when the 1783 Treaty of Paris officially ended the American Revolution, John Jacob, then just 20, packed a good suit of clothes and seven German flutes, and headed to America to join his brother Henry.

Astor traveled steerage across the Atlantic. The hard, cold passage ended up being life-changing, for while on board he struck up a friendship with a fellow German who regaled him with tales of fur trading. Astor found the business intriguing. When he landed, he made his way to New York to Henry's home, arriving in the spring of 1784. His brother ran a butcher's stall in the Fly Market at Maiden Lane and the East River. Rather than work with his brother, John Jacob decided to go into the fur trade. He took to his new profession, and with financial help from Henry started his own business. He would head to Montreal in search of beaver, raccoon, muskrat, otter, and other pelts, along the way negotiating with settlers, farmers, trappers, and Indians. He also traveled to London to sell the furs, and established contacts there.

Astor set up a small shop on Water Street, and in 1785 married Sarah Todd, the daughter of Adam and Sarah Todd. Sarah not only had a sharp eye for furs, her relation on her mother's side to the well-connected Brevoort family brought with her a $300 dowry. During their first few years together, Sarah and John Jacob lived simply and squirreled away their profits as he expanded his territory. They also started having children, many of whom survived childhood. Magdalen was born first, in 1788, John Jacob II in 1790, William Backhouse in 1792, Dorothea in 1795, and Eliza in 1801.

During Astor's travels he met Peter Smith, a fur trader who had a general store in Utica, and the two men formed a partnership. As his business grew, Astor spent time with other rising and ambitious New Yorkers at the Tontine Coffee House, got to know the city's elite, and became a Freemason. While he made a living in fur and assorted items, Astor of course also bought land, purchasing his first property, located on Bowery Lane, in 1789. He initially focused on uncultivated land in New York State, as well as in Lower Canada. But these lands were distant from his home and became hard to manage, so he started to concentrate on local acquisitions. His New York City investments were fueled by money from his 1808 founding of the American Fur Company. Two years later he started a subsidiary of American Fur called the Pacific Fur Company.[15]

Astor likewise became involved in the China trade starting in the 1790s, and soon had numerous ships, such as the appropriately christened *Beaver*, along with the *Enterprise*, *Fox*, *Magdalen*, *Severn*, and *Sylph*. By the early 19th century, his ships were taking North American furs and Turkish opium to China and returning with porcelain, tea, fans, satins, silks, instruments, and spices, which he sold in England. From there he brought back finished goods to sell in Manhattan. This triangular trade proved wildly profitable. He made about $30,000—a fortune—per trip. Philip and John Hone auctioned off many of his cargoes, and Philip found in Mr. Astor "a valuable customer." This was an understatement, since Astor surpassed them all in wealth and power. In fact, Astor turned out to be a formidable businessman. Within 15 years of arriving with a bag containing all his belongings and some flutes, the man Hone called a "modern Croesus" had an estate worth a quarter of a million dollars. As he grew richer, Astor eyed the palatial houses that were beginning to rise uptown. In 1803 he paid Rufus King—one of the signers of the US Constitution—and his wife, Mary, for their house, located at 223 Broadway across from City Hall Park. It was an elegant mansion with drawing rooms and a paneled dining room. Nearly two decades later, Hone paid $25,000 for his own mansion, situated just a block to the north.[16]

By the early 19th century, New York had become a prime investment for wealthy men like Astor. The city was fast-changing, and the island's original topography was being transformed. The Collect was gone. Streams like the Minetta, which flowed through what is now Washington Square, were paved over. Sun Fish Pond in the lower 30s, where New Yorkers once fished for eels and sunfish and in the winter ice-skated, was drained and filled in 1839. Land value in Manhattan totaled $58.4 million in 1825, $87.6 million in 1830, and stood at $143 million in 1835, the year of the Great Fire. Businesses, stores, stables, churches, and circuses sprouted everywhere. In 1834, 877 buildings and 654 dwellings were built. In the year of the Great Fire, the number of new constructions included 1,259 buildings and 865 dwellings. By the end of 1836, 1,826 new buildings and 868 dwellings rose, and land values reached $233.7 million. Construction and destruction took place at a dizzying rate. Hone observed that four banks were torn down in mid-1839 to make way for new buildings, noting that "it looks like the ruins occasioned by an earthquake." During the 1830s, New York was the nation's fastest-growing city and the largest in the New World. Not only were more buildings rising, their size increased. By 1834 two-thirds of the new stores stood at three or more stories.[17]

Besides being keen observers of the city's real estate market, Philip Hone and his wife, Catharine, actively participated in the buying and selling of land. Prominent families such as the Livingstons, Roosevelts, and

Schermerhorns—the core of New York's aristocracy—also joined in the land frenzy, selling off inherited estates. The Stuyvesants developed their property around current-day Tompkins Square in the East Village. Swamps were drained, and in the mid-1830s the city created a small park, whose presence only further caused the area to boom. The Brevoort family still had an 11-acre farm near Washington Square in the early years of the century. As the journalist Moses Beach observed, "this little farm, then of comparative little value, has now risen to be of immense value." By selling his land for townhouses, Henry Brevoort Jr. became worth $1 million.[18]

Astor bought and traded more than anyone else, having an early sense of the value of buying many of the island's larger properties. On the East Side, for example, he acquired a farm for about $20,000 in 1803. Other lands Astor bought included the Medcef Eden farm along the Hudson in the 40s, which he and William Cutting acquired in 1803. Two years later Astor paid $75,000 for a half interest in former governor George Clinton's land in Greenwich Village. These were very high prices for their time, and many thought that Astor was crazy to be paying them. But they were soon worth many times their original value. Astor's approach was to acquire land on the edge of the city, which few expected to be developed soon. He had a simple motto: "Buy and hold." Actually, however, he did not cling to everything, and when he sold he generally got market price and used it to purchase something else. In 1810, for example, Astor sold a lot in the Wall Street area for $8,000. The price appeared low, and as James Parton wrote in his *Famous Americans of Recent Times*, the purchaser asked Astor why he had offered him such a bargain:

> "Why, Mr. Astor, in a few years this lot will be worth twelve thousand dollars."
>
> "Very true," Astor replied. "But now you shall see what I will do with this money. With eight thousand dollars I buy eighty lots above Canal Street. By the time your lot is worth twelve thousand dollars, my eighty lots will be worth eighty thousand dollars."

Landowners like Astor often offered leases on property for periods that could cover decades. Such long-term contracts let workers and artisans build homes and set up business. As the number of single-family homes grew, builders and developers laid out new neighborhoods for those who wanted some distance from business districts, the docks, factories, and the poor. But the latter were not ignored as a source of income. As the needs of the working class grew, owners and developers started to subdivide homes and businesses in the older areas, rent out basements, and even construct structures out back.[19] Leasing could be profitable. At the turn of the 19th century, for example, Astor bought a large farm near what is now called, appropriately, Astor Place. He let some of the land to Joseph Delacroix. There Delacroix laid out Vauxhall Gardens, a landscaped pleasure ground, one of the amusement sites that businessmen set up that catered to citizens. The city soon extended up to there. When Vauxhall's lease expired in 1825, Astor cut Lafayette Place through the amusement complex and laid out lots. His son William even built a home there.

One of Astor's best investments was a lease he picked up from Aaron Burr. In 1797 Burr obtained from Trinity Church a long-term ground lease to 241 lots around Spring and Varick Streets. Burr's lifestyle, though, proved way beyond his means, and his duel with Alexander Hamilton forced him to become a fugitive. Astor took full advantage and bought the leases from Burr. In 1820, Astor moved Burr's Richmond Hill house to Charlton and Varick Streets. The public was invited to witness the move, which averaged 55 feet in 45 minutes, with the *New York Daily Advertiser* reporting how the transfer was completed "with chimnies standing and without the slightest injury to the house or fixture." Literally moving houses was fairly common, as the old dwellings had to be made to fit on the city's new grid. *Architectural Magazine* noted in 1838 how "Many of the old houses were found to interfere with the new lines of street, but, instead of taking down and rebuilding those tenements, the ingenious inhabitants have recourse to the more simple method of moving the whole, *en masse,* to a new site."

With Burr's old home out of the way, Astor leveled the hill on which it was built, cut though streets, and put up houses and dug wells. But Astor didn't outright own the property. He only held the Trinity lease that Burr had held. So, he offered leases, which could be secured for a lump sum ranging from $375 to $700. Short-term leases might go for $45 to as much as $100. None ran to the end of his Trinity lease period in the 1860s, since by ensuring that the lease would revert to him, Astor retained the right of renewal. Astor likewise acted as a financer, selling other land on bond and mortgage contracts. At the end of the loan, the purchaser received title to property.[20]

As we've seen, Astor had his fingers in many pies. He and John Beekman had bought the Park Theater in 1806. Astor served as a director of the Second Bank of the United States' New York branch, and had stock in the Bank of New York, the Bank of Manhattan Company, the Bank of Oswego, and the Bank of America. He invested heavily in Ohio State Canal Bonds, the New York State Canal, and the Delaware and Raritan Canal, along with Hone's Matteawan and Glenham companies. He became active in the Mohawk & Hudson Railroad Company and invested in the Trenton Railroad Company and the Camden and Amboy Railroad. He also placed money in city and state improvement bonds as well as public debt issues.

But his heart remained in property, which was easier to manage than ships, captains, trappers, and foreign governments. He left the China and fur trades and between 1820 and 1834 bought $445,000 in land. His son William, whom he schooled in the family business, helped run the shop.[21]

New York was in constant motion, and this helped developers like Astor command higher rents. February 1 was traditionally the day landlords and tenants discussed rents for the coming year. If they couldn't come to an agreement, the tenant needed to vacate on May 1. Moving Day, as it became known, was a 24-hour stretch of civic insanity. British novelist Frances Trollope said the day had "the appearance of sending off a population flying from the plague." In 1839, the *Mirror* estimated that more than 200,000 people, nearly two-thirds of the population, moved that day. In 1844, George Templeton Strong observed, "Never knew the city in such a chaotic state. Every other house seems to be disgorging itself into the street; all the sidewalks are lumbered with bureaus and bedsteads to the utter destruction of their character as thoroughfares, and all the space between the sidewalks is occupied by long processions of carts and wagons and vehicles omnigenous laden with perilous piles of moveables."

Mobility only heightened the city's reputation as a place of continuous building and rebuilding. Citizens, the *Mirror* observed, "pull down their houses regularly every twelve calendar months. . . . While we write, the work of devastation is still raging with insatiable fury. In short, the city is topsy-turvy; every street is laid in ruins." For some, like Hone, who lived in the midst of it all, "the pulling down of houses and stores in the lower parts is awful. Brickbats, rafters, and slates are showering down in every direction. There is no safety on the sidewalks, and the head must be saved at the expense of dirtying the boots." "Overturn, overturn, overturn! is the maxim of New York," added Hone a few years later, "and one generation of men seem studious to remove all relics of those which preceded them."[22]

4

"I Would Buy Every Foot of Land on the Island of Manhattan"

In April 1835, eight months before the Great Fire, Philip Hone marveled how William Bayard's country place—which had sold two or three years earlier for about $50,000—went for the colossal sum of $225,000. Soon after, Hone noted that a group of investors who paid top price for an "ancient house and grounds" on Court Street, along with another house, "pulled down the houses, leveled a hill sixty feet in height, and made fifty or sixty building lots, of which they will make maps and sell the whole at auction." Hone couldn't resist getting involved in the market. At that time, Elijah Boardman had offered him $55,000 for his home at 235 Broadway. Hone refused. Yet there was so much to be made in land in the booming city, and in March 1836, three months after the fire and two months before the Astor House opened, Hone sold his house to Boardman for $60,000.

With the sale, Hone agonized, "where to go I know not." He noted that lots even two miles from City Hall were going for as much as $10,000, and that on the East River—even farther from City Hall, which was the epicenter of his life—they were going for as much as $5,000. He soon found property on the southeast corner of Broadway and Great Jones Street, paying Samuel Ward $15,000 for a 29-by-130-foot corner lot. Then in May 1836, he started the arduous task of packing up his books and other belongings. On the 21st of May, the Hones settled into a temporary home, one of the Colonnade Houses on Broadway built by hat manufacturer Elisha Bloomer. Work progressed on what Hone predicted would be "one of the best and most commodious houses in the city." He eventually found himself snugly settled in his new home, writing at the start of 1838 that, "I would not, if I could, have it altered in a single particular." He was blissfully content to have his children around him, and his favorite, Mary, who was ill, was gaining strength, while daughter "Catharine is happy as the day is long, and enjoys the gayety of a first season in society, with a light heart and excellent disposition."

Boardman had wanted Hone's home so that it could become part of the neighboring American Hotel, and soon after the sale, the hotel opened elegant rooms in the house. Yet nothing lasted for long in New York, and in May 1839 as Hone's former home was slated to be razed, he bemoaned that, "in a few weeks the home of my happy days will be incontinently swept from the earth." His wasn't the only one falling. Hone noted other demolitions going on nearby. "Farther up, at the corner of Chambers Street, a row of low buildings has been removed to make way for one of those mighty edifices called hotels—eating, drinking, and lodging above, and gay shops below; and so all the way up."[1]

Some residents, like Hone, moved early, meaning the mid-1830s. Others, like George Washington Strong, at first ignored what was happening—despite pleas from his son—only moving in the 1840s. As those like the Hones and the Strongs migrated from downtown areas, former residential sections became solidly business and were relatively empty at night. In 1836 the New York Mirror was already talking about the enormous transformation seen in the city. "In one year," it reported, "there will be scarcely a private residence or a boarding-house below Wall-street." Three years later that paper predicted that, "from present appearances, there will not be a private residence in Broadway, ten years hence." Soon the area around Astor House, near where Hone's old house had stood—which many had not long before believed lay far uptown—buzzed with ice-cream palaces, barrooms, oyster cellars, P.T. Barnum's American Museum, and Mathew Brady's photo studio.[2]

Growth became a self-fulfilling prophecy, for as the city streets stretched out, houses followed. All this real estate activity was a boon for lawyers like Strong, who raked in 1 to 2 percent of the value of each deal. His office, unsurprisingly, prospered. In early 1836 the elder Strong was offered a spot uptown as a law professor at the newly opened New York University. But George Templeton, his son, was still at Columbia College. And, realizing that "There is no more idle class in this community than law students," the elder Strong decided it was his "imperative duty" to make sure that his son got a spot in a lawyer's office. He thus decided that, "should I continue in business till he is licensed, I shall then be able to assist him, both as to business and clients."[3]

Strong need not have worried about his son. In 1838, the younger Strong graduated from Columbia at the top of his class, earning silver medals in Political Economy, Greek Language, Grecian Literature, Greek and Latin Composition, Theoretic Mechanics, and Physical Astronomy. He then began a three-year clerkship in his father's office. "Clear and very glorious. Walked into the office. A new act of my life is just beginning," he wrote brightly of his first day there. In 1841 he gained admission to the common law bar, and soon became a counselor in law, a junior partner, and then a partner, handling deeds, mortgages, probate cases, subpoenas, and depositions. As the younger Strong worked, he could not help but note the changes to the city as he helped congregations purchase land for churches as they settled farther north. Old places were closing and tumbling down, and he was dismayed to note that parts of his beloved Columbia College were being divided into city lots: "Goths are they, and vandals and a horde, or board, of barbarous blackguards. If they think of cutting down those trees, I'll assassinate 'em in detail or blow up the president's room at their next meeting."[4]

But there was nothing he or anyone could do to stop it. And while growth could be volatile and the economy buffeted by booms and busts, many took advantage of the benefits of land ownership. "From 1825, when I purchased eighty lots of ground," James Hamilton wrote in his *Reminiscences*, "I devoted my attention to making money by dealing in real estate in New York and Brooklyn, and building houses, with very marked success." From the mid-1830s through the end of the 1840s, Bowery Theatre manager Thomas Hamblin bought and sold some 20 lots. Around that time, the father and uncle of future mayor Daniel Tiemann sold for $27,000 land on Broadway and 19th Street that they had picked up two decades earlier for $250. In 1848, merchant and future mayor Fernando Wood got into the real estate business, making a down payment on 150 acres of the uptown Somerindyck estate. As the city continued its northward expansion, fewer and fewer such large parcels remained.

Knowing that there was money to be made in land, and more particularly that if African Americans had at least $250 in property they could earn the right to vote, the widely read *Colored American* advised its readers in July 1837 to "take a survey of the whole city," figure out what improvements were being done, invest near the harbor or growing business section, and "buy several acres at once." The following week the paper instructed its readers not to build too close to the property line: "Every foot spared for a yard, with shrubbery, plants or grass, give an air of neatness and taste, and the greater value to the property." Some African American residents did very well by investing in real estate. Restaurateur Thomas Downing and his wife, Rebecca, bought and sold land. By March 1859, two years before the outbreak of the Civil War, the *New York Tribune* reported that 1,000 African American residents were taxed on $1.5 million in real estate.[5]

While the 1811 Commissioners' Plan gave short shrift to park creation, some saw the advantages of including them in their private developments. One example is offered by the lawyer Samuel Ruggles, who started buying land in the mid-1820s. Ruggles, a good friend of Hone's, gave up the law to focus on his properties and by 1833 owned more than 500 lots. Part of his investment was in the hilly and marshy area of the former Gramercy Farm, whose name came from a corruption of *krom moerasje*, "crooked little swamp," for the watercourse that flowed to the East River and became known as Cedar Creek. Ruggles spent a fortune to level the land and fill the deep gully—some 40 feet—in the middle of it. He then opened his "Gramercy Park" development, conveyed the central land to the surrounding property owners for a square, and petitioned for the creation a north–south road to the park, bounded by Irving Place and Lexington Avenue. Gramercy Park remains one of the most coveted private parks in Manhattan, and a key to it is considered a particular draw for those living in the area.

As land values rose, rents did as well. Hone still owned the home he had built in 1813 at 44 Cortlandt Street. It was at this spot that a few of his children were born "and in which the happiest days of my life were passed." In the early 1830s he leased it to merchant Nathaniel Hubbard, and his family moved in. The Hubbards stayed for a few years and paid Hone $1,000 a year. By the early 1850s the rent had risen to $3,000. Such increasing living expenses hit the working class especially hard. The Irish-born Democratic politician Michael Walsh, who was a champion of the poor and the working man, complained in 1847 how, "Of all the curses with which this city is infested, that of high rents is probably the most frightful. Thousands of hard-working people are driven up town to get a place for their wives and families to reside in, 3 or 4 miles from their places."[6]

* * *

As homes rose and the city stretched out in the 1830s and 1840s, those settling in the northern edges needed a way to get to and from work, as well as to stores and theaters. Savvy businessmen launched public transportation lines. Omnibuses, which carried about a dozen passengers and were pulled by two or four horses, began running along Broadway in 1829. Within four years the city had 80 omnibuses. By 1837 the number reached 108. In the mid-1840s the Empire Line ran 20 stages with 140 horses that transported people from South Ferry to 14th Street. The Ninth Avenue Chelsea Line claimed 22 stages and 206 horses, while the Knickerbocker Line—which went from 23rd Street down to South Ferry—had 38 stages and 222 horses. With their hard benches and poor ventilation, though, omnibuses proved both slow and uncomfortable. One reader of the *New York Gazette & General Advertiser* stated outright in March 1835, "They are unfit to ride in." The more reliable horsecars had started running in 1832. These lines were superior to omnibuses, since the cars rolled on rails. By the start of the 1860s, horsecars followed 142 miles of track that reached up to Central Park, which had opened only a few years earlier.[7]

Steam railroads began running in the city prior to the Civil War. The New York & Harlem Railroad started traveling down the eastern side of the city in the 1830s. In 1846 the Hudson River Railroad Company began on the West Side. People feared their arrival in town. In February 1833, Hone chaired a meeting at Tammany Hall at which the steam engines were denounced as "dangerous to the personal safety of our families and ourselves." Citizens perceived a real threat, such as when the New York & Harlem Railroad on July 4, 1839, barreled off its rails at Union Square and the steam engine exploded, killing the chief engineer and injuring others. Because of the fear of the technology and the smoke, trains were banned below 14th Street, and passengers needed to transfer to horsecars when heading farther south in the city.

New York's uneven and rough streets were also slowly improving. In 1835 the city experimented with paving made from octagonal blocks of hemlock. Hone noted the first use of the new pavement, and said that "the multitudinous train of omnibuses, carriages, carts, and wagons which infest Broadway appeared to pass over the new Appian Way 'pretty tolerably slick.'" Other attempts were made to upgrade the roadbeds. In 1846 the city started installing pavement fashioned from blocks of stones resting on a layer of concrete and a foundation of granite chips. It offered a smooth surface ride for carriages. In 1853 the city started laying down what were called "Belgian blocks," which were even sturdier.[8]

Booming as their city was in the 1830s and 1840s—extending relentlessly northward with footpaths transforming into streets and avenues—some New Yorkers began to bemoan that the town they grew up in was disappearing almost before their eyes. Hone found himself saddened when he read in the paper in May 1844 that workers were demolishing a small downtown house. "It occurred to me that this must be my father's house," he wrote of the home that Philip and Hester had bought six decades earlier at the corner of John and Dutch Streets. "So I went that way . . . and sure enough, the old house in which my youthful days were passed was no more to be seen, and a shapeless mass of ruins marked the spot." One year later, Walt Whitman decried in the *American Review* how builders looked at land that meant so much to some people and proclaimed, "Let us level to the earth all the houses that were not built within the last ten years; let us raise the devil and break things!" Whitman especially mourned the loss of such landmarks as the Old Sugar-House on Liberty Street, in which the British jailed American prisoners of war during the Revolution. He therefore implored builders, "Stay your hand, leveler!" In 1846 John F. Watson wrote that at the time, only four or five Dutch homes remained in Manhattan. In 1856, the Cherry Street home where George and Martha Washington had lived came down. As *Harper's* magazine pointed out, mournfully at that time, "the fatal enemy of the picturesqueness of New York is the constant demolition and erection of important structures. No house remains long enough to become hallowed and interesting from association."[9]

Even houses of worship fell before the rush of new building. "Nothing is respected in New York by the onward march of trade, not even the churches," wrote businessman Richard Lathers, "and the elaborate exercises of laying their corner stones and the sacred ceremonies of their dedication to the worship of Almighty God, should include this proviso: 'till the property becomes more valuable for trade than for Christian worship.'" In June 1845 Dr. Thomas House Taylor preached his last sermon at Grace Church on Broadway and Rector Street. The church, which had been consecrated in 1809, was sold to be converted into stores and the Chinese Museum, with its artwork and curiosities. The congregation then headed north to a new location at Broadway and 10th Street. Others soon leapfrogged as churches rushed uptown, with author Isaac Kendall noting how "Church spires are the milestones of the city's progress."[10]

As homes and churches tumbled, new ones rose. Edgar Allan Poe, writing in the *Columbia Spy* in 1844, noted how the old estates of the island "are doomed.... In some thirty years every noble cliff will be a pier, and the whole island will be densely desecrated by buildings of brick, with portentous *facades* of brown-stone, or brown-*stonn*, as the Gothamites have it." Two years later, the *New York Evening Post* reported that Clement Moore's neighborhood of Chelsea was "rapidly covering itself with new buildings." And despite Moore's earlier objection to development, even he had been bitten by the real estate bug. To make sure his land developed into an elegant area, he placed restrictions on buildings. Anyone constructing there had to plant trees and couldn't put up stables or rear buildings. Nothing could be built, he announced, "for any purpose which will make the neighborhood disagreeable." Even with his covenants, Moore's development horrified the editors of *The Knickerbocker*. "Hack men" were "destroying in half an hour what GOD himself, in the 'course of nature,' could not create in seventy years!" In 1849, Moore's own Chelsea House was demolished.[11]

Greater New York was also growing. Such surrounding areas as Jersey City, Hoboken, Queens, and Westchester underwent their own booms. In 1814 the Brooklyn *Star* noted that Manhattan's cross-river neighbor "must necessarily become a favorite residence for gentlemen of taste and fortune, for merchants and shopkeepers of every description, for artists, artisans, mechanics, laborers, and persons of every trade in society." As developers subdivided Brooklyn farms, that city's population, which stood at 15,394 in 1830, rose to 96,838 by 1850, effectively increasing by six-fold in just 20 years. Brooklyn Heights, with its elegant homes and favorable sea breezes, enticed many, Lewis Tappan among them. Whitman's family developed property in Brooklyn, and he pointed out that one of the main reasons for living in that city "is to be found in the fact that here men of moderate means may find homes at a moderate rent, whereas in New York there is no medium between the palatial mansion and a dilapidated hovel."

Ferries made commuting to Manhattan for work or pleasure possible. Hoboken got regular ferry service in 1821. By the early 1850s, ferries—costing 3¢ a ride—left Jersey City at least four times an hour. Williamsburg had numerous boats departing throughout the day. Author Isabella Bird marveled a few years later that she made a trip from Brooklyn to Manhattan "in one of those palace ferry-boats, where the spacious rooms for passengers are heated by steam-pipes, and the charge is only one cent."[12]

* * *

Throughout, John Jacob Astor was at the center of much that was happening in New York in the 1830s and 1840s, and particularly the post–Great Fire years. He ran his businesses—and they were many—out of a temple-fronted place on Prince Street just off Broadway, with large masonry walls, iron doors, and window grates, giving it the appearance of a bank. Author Matthew Hale Smith referred to the sparsely furnished interior as having "the general air of a house of detention." There Astor and son William supervised their staff of lawyers, estate managers, rental agents, contractors, as well as a "small army of painters, carpenters, and other mechanics, in order to keep up suitable repairs" to the properties. Accountants and bookkeepers meanwhile maintained Astor's sacred "Rent Rolls," lined ledger books that listed each renter's name, street, and yearly rent. The "House and Land Book" contained the costs of everything so that Astor could monitor his earnings. These volumes, according to historian James McCabe, had become Astor's "Bible." "He scanned it fondly, and saw, with quiet but deep delight, the catalogue of his property lengthening from month to month." As the largest landowner in New York, Astor had a lot to keep in order. His real estate empire ranged "from the dwelling at three hundred dollars per annum to the magnificent warehouse or hotel at thirty thousand dollars," observed *The Continental Monthly*.

All the continued growth only drove Astor to buy and lease more. From 1835 until his death in March 1848 (at the age of 84), he invested an additional $832,000 in land. From 1840 to 1841, Astor had 355 tenants and made $128,767, and from 1847 to 1848 he had 450 tenants and brought in $194,000. The Astors owned hundreds of undeveloped lots in the upper part of the city. Generally, they would sell the middle lots on a block but hold on to the corner ones, knowing that buildings constructed next door would only increase the land's value.[13]

Much of the business transferred to Astor's son William, who was not the genial sort. Poet Julia Ward Howe (author of "The Battle Hymn of the Republic") viewed William as "a rather shy and silent man" well suited to the dry and droll world of business and "the management of the great Astor estate." Fortunately, William inherited his father's ability for acquiring property. Married in 1818 to Margaret Armstrong, the daughter of Secretary of War John Armstrong Jr., William rose early and walked to the firm's office. Like his father, William had a great memory. He knew the family's holdings well, and could even recite the rental rolls. Smith wrote that he knew "every inch of real estate that stands in his name, every bond, contract, and lease. He knows what is due when leases expire, and attends personally to all this matter. No tenant can expend a dollar, or put in a pane of glass, without his personal inspection."[14]

With his wife Sarah's death in 1834, John Jacob Astor was watched over by his favorite grandson, Charles Astor Bristed, and friends like the poet and writer—and member of the so-called Knickerbocker Group—Fitz-Greene Halleck, who served as Astor's confidential secretary, a position later taken over by the educator and librarian Joseph Green Cogswell. After decades of work, success brought leisure. Astor enjoyed smoking a pipe, drinking a glass of beer, riding his horse, and going to the theater. To avoid the crowded downtown, he spent time at his sprawling uptown home.

The Astor family delighted in throwing and attending parties. In 1838 Howe served as the first bridesmaid when her brother Samuel married William's daughter Emily. Howe also enjoyed her visits to John Jacob's house at 585 Broadway, a home that brimmed with servants and attendants and was filled with artwork, including celebrated artist Gilbert Stuart's portrait of Astor. "He was very fond of music, and sometimes engaged the services of a professional pianist," wrote Howe. "I remember that he was much pleased at recognizing, one evening, the strains of a brilliant waltz, of which he said: 'I heard it at a fair in Switzerland years ago.'" At another get-together the group sang "Am Rhein," "and Mr. Astor, who was very stout and infirm of person, rose and stood beside the piano, joining with the singers."[15]

The land baron had become a legend in the nation's development, renowned for his business insight, work ethic, and of course for his wealth. By 1830 he had numerous grandchildren. Hone enjoyed the December 1846 wedding of William's son John to Charlotte Augusta Gibbes. The party at William's Lafayette Place home was quite extravagant, with its "splendid crowd of charming women, pretty girls, and well-dressed beaux," wrote Hone. "The spacious mansion . . . was open from cellar to garret, blazing with a thousand lights. The crowd was excessive; the ladies . . . elegantly and tastefully attired, with a display of rich jewelry enough to pay one day's expense of the Mexican war." That latter of course referred to the Mexican American War, which was fought from April 1846 to February 1848.

Astor proved generous with friends. The watchmaker Emmet T. Pell stopped by the office to see if he could buy out the last three years of his lease on Hudson Street between Vandam and Spring Streets, which would allow him the right to renew it directly from Trinity Church. William refused the request. But as Pell was leaving, someone told him to return the next day and to see the elder Astor. Pell duly came back the following day. "It was very cold, and he took a seat by the fire in the outer office," according to an account by Smith in his book, *Sunshine and Shadow in New York*. Soon Astor arrived. "He walked very slowly, doubled up, leaning on the head of his cane in a stooping posture, taking short steps, so that he rather scuffled along than walked." Smith wrote how Astor asked what Pell wanted, and when Pell told him what he hoped for, Astor immediately replied, "We don't wish to sell those reversions, young man." He apparently asked Pell his name, and when

Pell told him, Astor realized that the young man was the son of the down-town coach maker on Wall and Broad Streets whom Astor was friendly with when he was younger. "Why, he used to give me rides in his coaches. How I should like to see him!" Astor then said to the junior Pell, "You shall have the lease, young man. Go home, have the papers drawn, come here at eleven o'clock precisely, on Thursday, and I'll sign them."[16]

Nonetheless, Astor viewed poverty as nothing other than a personal failing, though it was said that he had an alley at the back of his home by which the poor could head to the kitchen for food. He also had little time for organized charities. Once, according to one account, when a group came to see him for a donation, he gave them $50. The committee members had hoped for much more: "Your son gave us a hundred dollars." Astor replied quite dryly, "Ah! William has a rich father. Mine was very poor." There was an occasional exception. In November 1835, a mere month before the Great Fire, Astor made a $5,000 donation to the Society for the Relief of Aged Indigent Females. A few years later he was talking to Cogswell, and his secretary—who had worked at Harvard's library—suggested the idea of building a library in New York. At the time there were no such public institutions in the United States, and Astor decided to set aside $400,000 in his will for the project.[17]

As he looked back on his remarkable life, Astor would recall that the hardest thing had been the accumulation of the first thousand dollars. Near the end of his life, he and William made an accounting of their vast holdings in Manhattan and elsewhere, revealing their full range, from undeveloped land to homes, stores, hotels, and businesses. Yet when someone asked if he had too much real estate, Astor wistfully responded, "Could I begin life again, knowing what I now know, and had money to invest, I would buy every foot of land on the Island of Manhattan."

While Astor's money could buy him all he wanted, it couldn't buy him more time. In the early 1840s he commented to Gerrit Smith, the son of his former fur-trading partner Peter, "I am broken up. It is time for me to be out of the way." One evening in October 1844, Hone had dinner and played billiards at the lawyer Richard Blatchford's Hell Gate home on the upper east side with Astor, Cogswell, Daniel Webster, and others, including the celebrated Norwegian violinist Ole Bull. Hone stayed the night, and found himself saddened by Astor's state of health. "He sat at the dinner table with his head down upon his breast, saying very little, and in a voice almost unintelligible; the saliva dropping from his mouth, and a servant behind him to guide the victuals which he was eating, and to watch him as an infant is watched." Despite the fact that Astor was still sharp, "the machinery," as Hone put it, "is all broken up."[18]

Astor's last real estate deal occurred on February 26, 1848. He died at nine in the morning of March 29, 1848. Three days later, William set his father's casket with a rich black velvet cloth and a plate of glass on the top in his Lafayette Place home. "The doors thrown open, that every one might have an opportunity to see him, and thousands rushed in, until the hall was crowded almost to suffocation," reported the *New York Herald*. Six Episcopal clergymen officiated at the funeral, and Hone, Washington Irving, politician Sylvanus Miller, banker James Gallatin, financier James King, shipping merchants Isaac Bell and David Ogden, Superior Court chief judge Thomas J. Oakley, fur trader Ramsay Crooks, and Astor agent Jacob Taylor, who assisted with real estate purchases, carried the tycoon's coffin as several thousand followed. Astor was then placed in the family vault at the back of St. Thomas Episcopal Church on Broadway and Houston Street.

That day, the popular writer James Fenimore Cooper wrote his wife: "It is said that he sent checks of $100,000 each to several grandchildren a few days before he died, in order to place them at their ease from the start." The *Herald* published Astor's will a week after his death. Most of his money went to his children and grandchildren, with the lion's share of the estate and business going to William. His grandson, Charles Bristed, got the Hell Gate estate. Daughter Dorothea received 100 lots below 14th Street. His son, John Jacob II, was mentally incapacitated, and Astor set him with a $10,000-a-year allowance. Astor also gave $50,000 for an institution for the poor and sick in Walldorf, Germany, and $20,000 for the German Society of New York to help immigrants.[19]

Astor's main charitable bequeath was the $400,000 for the planned Astor Library. Executors were directed to erect "a suitable building" with "furnishing and supplying the same from time to time with books, maps, charts, models, drawings, paintings, engravings, casts, statues, furniture and other things." George Washington Strong incorporated the institution, and William added an additional $200,000 in land, books, and money. William also set aside a generous-sized plot on Lafayette Place for a building. William, Irving, Cogswell, Halleck, King, Ruggles, banker Samuel Ward, and others served as trustees. They held a design competition with a $300 prize for the winner. Not surprisingly, given the library's namesake, they chose a German

Rundbogenstil—round-arched—style building designed by the German-born architect Alexander Saeltzer, a three-story-high structure with a brick and rusticated brownstone façade and arched windows. In September 1849, workers began cutting down the shrubberies and trees from the site of the former Vauxhall Gardens, which was opened in 1803.[20]

Cogswell started seriously amassing the library's collection. He made numerous buying visits to Europe. By the time the library opened in early 1854, it held some 90,000 volumes, along with American and foreign periodicals and journals. The *Evening Post* reported how during the opening, "the whole day the beautiful hall was filled with a constantly changing throng, who looked with delight upon the magnificent facilities there afforded for the pursuit of knowledge." Visitors ascended the marble stairs to the second floor and entered the main room, which was 100 feet long and 64 feet wide. In the middle, beneath a broad skylight, was a bust of Astor as well as one of Washington Irving, the institution's first president. There, the *United States Magazine* noted, "the pauper from the street may sit beside the merchant prince, if he will; may read just as many, and the same sort of books, and is just as promptly waited upon."

Astor left the city a very different place than the one he found when he arrived in the late 18th century. The sleepy town that he had entered in the spring of 1784 at age 20 was now booming. British editor Charles Mackay noted that Broadway "in its details, surpasses any single street that England or the British Isles can show," and that from Trinity on Wall Street to Grace Church on 10th Street "a distance in a straight line of nearly three miles, and thence on to Union Square, and the statue of Washington, Broadway offers one grand succession of commercial palaces." These were all the fruit of the unrelenting development spearheaded by the man who wished he had bought every foot of land in Manhattan.[21]

And the "pull-down-and-build-over-again spirit" that Whitman, for one, bemoaned, only accelerated. A decade after Astor's death, the city was solidly built up to 42nd Street. In the late 1850s, when the Astor Library was enlarged by St. Nicholas and Fifth Avenue Hotels' architect Griffith Thomas, George Templeton Strong wrote how Third Avenue and 79th Street had "newly excavated trenches (that will be streets hereafters) . . . which will result in city lots and leases and a rent-roll." At that time, Mayor Tiemann started marking lampposts and displaying the names of streets. "This was done as a matter of necessity," he recalled, "for the city was expanding at such a rapid rate that many of the inhabitants were getting lost on their way to their homes, or to places of amusement every night."

Manhattan was no longer the small town of some 30,000 souls with plentiful ponds and streams that it had been in 1784. By 1860, New York's population had soared to 813,669, and the place the Lenapes once called the "Island of Many Hills" was leveled out and expanding.[22]

5

London on the Hudson

By the time he and his wife arrived in Boston on January 22, 1842, Charles Dickens was revered on both sides of the Atlantic. Though only 29 years old, he had already written *Nicholas Nickleby* and *Oliver Twist* and felt it the right time to visit America, where his books were enormously popular. Boston fêted the man known as the Boz, and New Yorkers snickered at how their northern rivals comported themselves. George Templeton Strong wrote, "The Bostonians are making horrid asses of themselves with Mr. Charles Dickens, poor man."

Hoping to lure him to visit, New York's elite formed a Dickens committee that included Mayor Robert Morris, Philip Hone, General Charles Sandford, merchant Prosper Wetmore, banker James King, the lawyer John Duer, William B. Astor, and Fitz-Greene Halleck. Hone prepared the invitation to Dickens, flattering him by noting that the genius "with which you have been so signally gifted . . . has secured to you a passport to all hearts." Dickens wrote back that, "I need not tell you that I accept with inexpressible pride and pleasure the invitation with which you have honored me."[1]

Now all New York, which in 1840 had 312,710 residents, needed to do was best Boston (with its 93,383 citizens). "One thing we are certain," observed Philadelphia's *Public Ledger*, "for the Gothamites, who outnumber them and outdollar them by a very large difference, will thoroughly outshine them." But what should New York do? Some wanted an all-male dinner, such as the ones held in Boston. Others believed that that they should throw a grand ball, since excluding women would offend Dickens's wife Catherine. After much discussion, Hone noted approvingly that the "ballites" beat the "dinnerites."

With plans in place, the New York elite set out to create an impressive welcome. Needing an appropriate venue to hold their celebration, they chose the Park Theatre. The Boz Committee—as it was informally called—offered $5 tickets for the upcoming Valentine's Day love fest. The 3,000 passes sold quickly, and to make sure they threw a proper and respectful affair, Hone—as chairman of the reception committee—along with others reviewed the guest list to make sure that only the better sorts showed up.[2] In preparation for the festivities, dressmakers prepared gowns, and advertisements touted such products as Gouraud's Poudres Subtiles, a powder that promised discreetly to remove "unsightly" facial hair. Meanwhile, organizers transformed the Park. Inside they crafted a ballroom by extending the stage over the theater pit. Flowers, draperies, and bunting filled the place. Gilded ropes snaked around chandelier cords, and painted scenes from Dickens' stories adorned the walls. One hundred forty chefs, food preparers, and kitchen staff spent more than three days and nights putting together the feast that included 50 hams and 50 tongues, as well as champagne, tea, and chocolate. Restaurateur Thomas Downing oversaw all the work. Hone called him "the great man of oysters," and he lived up to his name, piling tables with no fewer than 28,000 stewed and 10,000 pickled oysters. Margaret Armstrong Salter, the wife of Commodore William Salter, correctly observed afterwards that, "I am afraid at this rate, oysters will become very scarce."[3]

On the night of February 14, carriages snaked along a line of a quarter mile to the Park Theatre. When Charles and Catherine Dickens made their entrance, there were "cheers, then the waving of handkerchiefs from floor to boxes, and all the tiers," wrote the journalist Thomas Nichols. As the couple moved around the hall, musicians played "God Save the Queen," "Hail Columbia," "Happy Land," and "Yankee Doodle." Mayor Morris greeted them, and Hone seized Dickens's hand. "My dear sir, here is a handful of our people—right glad—bright eyes—rejoice—heartfelt welcome—can't express—overpowered—feelings." Dickens bowed and placed his hand on his heart. Hone then called out "nine cheers," and the crowd shouted out their welcome.

The party proved a huge success. Hone unabashedly called it "the greatest affair in modern times." Unsurprisingly, Thomas Hamblin tried to capitalize on the Dickenses' arrival. He touted his own "Benefit of the American Giant," staging *Pickwick Club!* and *Nicholas Nickleby* at the Bowery Theatre on the same night as the Boz Ball. Yet, according to the *Dramatic Mirror*, "his tickets of admission were more plentiful than the applicants." Even so, Hamblin soon lured Dickens to the Bowery, where he watched two comedies—James Sheridan Knowles' *The Love Chase* and James Rodwell's *The Young Widow*.[4]

The celebrating continued with dinners and parties. On the 18th, Hone and a crowd of 230 gathered at the City Hotel and feasted with Dickens at a meal organized by Washington Irving. Then in early June, James King and his wife, Sarah, served strawberries and cream at a breakfast party for Dickens at their Weehawken, New Jersey, country house. Hone went to say good-bye to Dickens when he headed back to England. At the wharf of Sandy Hook in New Jersey, he boarded the *George Washington* with "a large party of gentlemen." The group then dined on some "cold collation" and champagne.

Following Dickens' whirlwind visit and all the work that went into it, Hone was therefore understandably aghast to read a published letter that made its way into Walt Whitman's *New York Evening Tattler* purportedly penned by Dickens, attacking what he saw as the pernicious "money making" nature of Americans. "Every good desire, every refined wish, every aspiration for the lofty, and the pure, and the holy, is swallowed up in the whirlpool of avarice." Hone wrote to Dickens about the letter, and the author responded by calling it "a most wicked and nefarious Forgery." He promised to send Hone a copy of his *American Notes for General Circulation* when it came out. Hone was pleased when he read the book, writing in his diary that, "Mr. Dickens has written a very fair and impartial book about this country." Strong meanwhile found it "clever, light stuff, with some good things in it, in his best style."[5]

* * *

For all their sense of superiority over Bostonians, New Yorkers worried keenly how others viewed them. They wanted to be seen as the leaders of American society, sought to be taken seriously, and wondered how their city was viewed by places like London, which in 1840 had nearly two million people. That wasn't an unrealistic aspiration. By the 1840s the city had become the cultural center of the nation, attracting writers, musicians, architects, and artists, and aspired for their creations to be seen on par with those of their European contemporaries. They wrote, they fêted, they referenced each other, as Clement Clarke Moore did in verse when he sent the following stanza with a bunch of flowers to Hone. He then included it and Hone's response in his book *Poems*, which contained "A Visit from St. Nicholas":

> THERE is a language giv'n to flowers,
>   By which a lover may impart
> The bitter anguish that devours,
>   Or extacy that swells his heart.
>
> And all the feelings of the breast,
>   Between the extremes of bliss and wo,
> By tender flow'rets are exprest,
>   Or plants that in the wild wood grow.

Hone thanked his friend in return:

> Come as thou wilt, my warm regard
> And welcome, shall thy steps attend;
> Scholar, musician, florist, bard—
> More dear to me than all, as friend.
> Bring flow'rs and poesy, a goodly store,
> Like Dickens' Oliver. I ask for Moore.[6]

Much of New York's self-celebration involved its expansion, the boom that followed the 1825 opening of the Erie Canal. Banks rose along Wall Street, and stores went up on Broadway. After the Great Fire, development stretched farther and farther uptown; townhouses lined newly opened avenues and side streets. But to really take its place among the great cities of the world, New York needed architects. Yet while the city had some talented designers and craftsmen, most were essentially builders and contractors. Lacking schools of architecture to attend to develop their craft, those eager to learn did so through watching, making drawings, and picking up techniques from construction sites. There were some reference guides, starting in the late 18th century, such as William Pain's *The Practical House Carpenter*. In 1797, the Boston architect Asher Benjamin published *The Country Builder's Assistant*, containing useful plans and elevations. And in 1818, John Haviland—who would go on to build Philadelphia's Eastern State Penitentiary, with its radical design containing isolated cells and prison yards that was believed to help reform prisoners—brought out his *The Builders' Assistant*.

At the start of the 19th century, John McComb Jr. produced the City Hall, which he designed with French architect Joseph François Mangin, who would soon design the original St. Patrick's Cathedral on Mulberry Street. McComb also created Alexander Hamilton's uptown home, the Grange, as well as Castle Garden, and was named street commissioner—an influential job in a growing city—in 1813. As New York grew, other master builders set up shop, such as Samuel Thomson, Josiah Brady, Martin Euclid Thompson, and Minard Lafever.[7]

The presence of these designers coincided with an interest in classical architecture, as we've seen with the Greek Revival style that became popular in the 1820s and 1830s. And while few Americans had actually seen the temples and ruins of the Aegean or Italy, they got to know them from such illustrated books as Julien-David LeRoy's *Les Ruines des plus beaux monuments de la Grèce*. Thomas Jefferson first came across architecture books while studying at William & Mary College. His love of classical architecture grew when he served as United States minister to France in the 1780s and visited many European ruins. He used Roman elements when designing his own home, Monticello. As president, Jefferson appointed the British-trained architect Benjamin Henry Latrobe surveyor of public buildings. The Classical style appeared in New York with Thompson's Phenix Bank—a small Doric-fronted temple that rose on Wall Street in the early 1820s—and with his United States Branch Bank, one of the earliest buildings to feature a marble facade. Thompson and Brady worked together on the original Merchants' Exchange, which opened in 1827. The interest in the Aegean only increased because of sympathy for the Greeks in their war of independence from the Ottoman Turks. The style offered ordinary citizens in this Age of Jackson a tangible link to the birthplace of democracy.

New York's path to architectural distinction began with the success of Brady and Thompson, and particularly with the arrival of Ithiel Town. Born in Connecticut in October 1784, Town would prove to be a new and visionary type of architect. He had worked and studied in Boston under Asher Benjamin, and was well versed in classical styles. In 1820 he also patented his "improvement in the construction of wood and iron bridges." His so-called Town Truss would prove an ingenious way to build spans, and to be highly profitable.

In the fall of 1825, Town made his way to New York. He placed an ad in the *New York Evening Post* offering "his services in the profession of an Architect, to gentlemen improving real estate by buildings." He told potential clients how the new "Grecian Architecture, which from its simplicity, elegance, and grandeur," could be used for both "public and private buildings." Commissions arrived, and his style started to adorn places like his Bowery Theatre. At the same time, he designed Arthur Tappan's Pearl Street store, adorning it with square granite piers and a thick horizontal lintel, and defining a style that quickly became *de rigueur* for commercial buildings.[8]

Another key figure was Alexander Jackson Davis. The eldest of four, Davis was born on July 24, 1803, on Peck's Slip on Manhattan's East Side. His father edited the *New York Theological Magazine*, sold religious books, and taught at the African Free School, which was established in 1787 by the New-York Manumission Society as a place to educate the children of the city's growing free Black population. When Davis was young, the family moved to Utica and Auburn. Both those central New York communities were growing, and

Davis recalled how his "mind [became] formed for Architecture." It was an appreciation that blossomed after he moved to Alexandria, Virginia, in 1818, where he worked at the *Gazette*. However, Davis grew bored by newspaper work and took refuge exploring the town as well as the neighboring District of Columbia, which was being rebuilt following its destruction by the British during the War of 1812. There he immersed himself in drawing, passing his time studying plans for romantic-looking castles, and reading poetry.

Davis returned to New York in 1823 and studied at the American Academy of the Fine Arts, the Antique School at the Philosophical Society, and the New-York Drawing Association. Soon he opened an office on Wall Street, advertising himself as an architectural draftsman. He walked around town, drawing the city's buildings, making plans and perspectives, and did drafting work for Brady and sketches for Thompson.

But Davis aspired to be more than just a draftsman. Not surprisingly, he gravitated into Town's orbit. He made drawings for Town, and the architect let him use his library, which was the largest and best such collection in the country, containing 11,000 art books and more than 20,000 engravings, paintings, and architectural models. James Stuart and Nicholas Revett's *The Antiquities of Athens* in particular mesmerized Davis. On March 15, 1828, he noted in his diary, "First study of Stuart's Athens, from which I date Professional Practice."[9]

Town and Davis formed a partnership in February 1829, and their work dovetailed with the Greek Revival wave sweeping America. All things Aegean became popular. Schoolchildren collected coins for foreign freedom fighters, and citizens constructed a 20-foot Grecian cross in Brooklyn Heights. Town and Davis kept busy turning out designs, such as the one for the 1831 Carmine Street Church in Greenwich Village, with its recessed porch and Doric columns, and in 1832 the Church of the French Protestants (Eglise Français du Saint Esprit) on Church and Franklin Streets, with its Ionic portico and tall dome, all topped by a cylindrical-shaped lantern.

Other builders and architects climbed aboard the Greek Revival bandwagon, and the city's pitched-roofed homes gave way to temple-fronted banks, offices, warehouses, and houses. The style, it was decided, bestowed upon New York a stately and noble look. One writer commented how "every thing is a Greek temple, from the privies in the back court, through the various grades of prison, theatre, church, custom-house, and state-house." Congregation Shearith Israel built an austere Greek-style building on Crosby Street. Thomson based his Doric-style 13th Street Presbyterian Church on the Theseum temple in Athens. Lafever created a temple-like complex of buildings for Sailors' Snug Harbor, a charitable organization for indigent seamen on Staten Island. Isaiah Rogers, who we remember had built John Jacob Astor's Astor House Hotel, designed the Middle Collegiate Church on Lafayette Place, crowning it with a soaring wooden steeple. As we've also seen, following the Great Fire, Rogers was tasked with creating the new Merchants' Exchange, which Hone called a "superb edifice." The granite building opened in 1841. With its colossal Ionic colonnade and 80-foot-wide rotunda, the rebuilt Exchange became one of the grandest buildings of its age.[10]

Despite the growing competition for clients, Town and Davis dominated the field. *Brother Jonathan* newspaper noted, "A large proportion of this improvement, so observable throughout our city and State, has been brought about by the unceasing exertions of ITHIEL TOWN and ALEXANDER J. DAVIS." The partners kept busy, building homes for the city's elite. Yet the men did not restrict their building to New York, turning out designs for public and private buildings—as well as gates and birdbaths—from New England to New Orleans, and creating the state houses in Connecticut and North Carolina. Town and Davis likewise sought federal jobs, and in 1833 received the commission for the new United States Custom House. The building on Wall and Broad Streets, on the site where George Washington had taken the presidential oath of office in April 1789, was one of the main government buildings to go up prior to the Civil War. Their marble temple rose from above a towering flight of stairs that called to mind Athens' Parthenon. Inside, a 60-foot-wide central rotunda was topped by a dome inspired by Rome's Pantheon and supported by 16 Corinthian columns. The partners believed that to make a civilizing mark on their nation's architecture, they needed to nurture young talent, turning their office into a modern atelier filled with student draftsmen. Probably the best known of their protégés was the New York–born draftsman turned architect James Dakin, who worked on plans for the Custom House.[11]

The idea of urban living fascinated many architects and builders, who sought to emulate such London developments as Bloomsbury. The British started building homes with uniform fronts following London's Great Fire of 1666. Elaborate ones were created first in the city's Grosvenor Square and to the west of London in Bath on Queen Square. Builders and developers constructed rows of homes at a time, with some of the finest examples in London designed by architects John Nash and Thomas Cubitt. The form gave a stateliness and regimented elegance to an area, and proved ideal for

New York with its grid system. In 1827 developer Isaac Pearson constructed two rows of homes with front yards on Bleecker Street, calling it LeRoy Place in honor of the merchant Jacob LeRoy. It was followed by Depau Row, also on Bleecker, consisting of six brick buildings with second-floor verandas and Italian marble–lined halls. And there was the Carroll Place development, which ran on Bleecker from Thompson Street to current-day LaGuardia Place. James Fenimore Cooper moved in there, and his wife, Susan, wrote that it was "too magnificent for our simple French tastes."

Town and Davis led the way with their work, with Davis creating what were widely considered the best of these row houses for the builder Seth Geer on the site of the former Vauxhall Gardens. La Grange Terrace on Lafayette Place was named after the Marquis de Lafayette's country house. With its towering marble Corinthian columns, rising from a formidably proportioned base and containing spacious dining rooms and nurseries, La Grange soon became known as Colonnade Row. Then in 1835, Town received a patent for his improved bridge design. He and Davis amicably ended their partnership, with Town returning to the lucrative span-building practice he had been running in parallel. They would, though, continue to work on and off with each other over the next few years.[12]

* * *

The uptown migration created new streets and therefore new buildings, most of it in the northern areas. The area that would become Washington Square had been used as a potter's field—the final resting place of plague victims and destitute residents—and contained tens of thousands of bodies. The city bought up the land, even purchasing part of the Scotch Presbyterian Church's burial ground. On July 4, 1826, Mayor Hone oversaw its christening as the Washington Military Parade Ground. Two years later, the city filled and graded the area. Workmen meanwhile erected "a handsome fence" and prepared the turf and gravel foot walks, with the *Evening Post* noting that shade trees and shrubbery would soon be planted.

Soon a row of buildings rose along Washington Square, and New York's wealthier citizens—Henry James' grandmother Elizabeth Walsh, the commission merchant Nathaniel Hubbard, and others—moved into the opulent Greek Revival homes with high stoops and such classical touches as Doric and Ionic columns and entablatures. Inside were spiraling staircases, mahogany pocket doors, gilt, marble, and molding. In 1839–1840, William and Mary Rhinelander, whose family had extensive land holdings in the city, had architect Richard Upjohn design a home on the north side of the square. A matching house went up next door for the merchant Gardiner Greene Howland. By the early 1850s, buildings entirely ringed the Square.[13]

The development of Washington Square spurred the growth of the surrounding area, and those, like the Brevoort family, who had farms and estates there, divided and sold off their land. Just to the north of the square on Fifth Avenue and 9th Street, Davis reportedly designed Henry Brevoort Jr.'s house. Houses also went up for such prominent families as the Lenoxes, Belmonts, and Grinnells. "The fashionable end of town is now decidedly at Washington Square," reported the *New York Herald*, "and the surrounding neighborhood from Bleecker street to Albion Place." Bond Street to the park's southeast was the most desirable spot from 1820 to 1850s. It was the area to which Hone had moved in the late 1830s. Julia Ward Howe's father, the banker Samuel Ward, commissioned Town and Davis to create a home for him on the corner of Bond and Broadway. Nearby on Astor Place and Lafayette Place, Astor built a house for his daughter Dorothea Langdon.[14]

The changes to Washington Square seemed to represent the pace and style of development. Some, however, didn't see the haphazard expansion as a good thing. Back in August 1833, the *Evening Post* bemoaned the lack of uniformity of building heights, and called for the use of stone instead of brick. Even so, there was general agreement that while uneven, development was bringing with it some beautiful and grand structures. Samuel Ruggles helped ensure the exclusivity of his Gramercy Park by defining its tone through the imposition of deeds and covenants. Homes needed to be at least three stories tall, constructed of brick or stone, and he forbade the presence of such businesses as slaughterhouses and circuses. Soon a large number of wealthy citizens, like James Harper and Albert Gallatin, settled on his square in richly decorated homes. Tompkins Square to the south opened in 1834 and became a residential neighborhood. Union Square on 14th Street opened in 1839, and Madison Square on 23rd in 1847.

George Templeton Strong first roamed up to Gramercy Park in 1842 to take a look at the development and determined that he would look into living there. In 1848, he started building a house there at 74 East 21st Street alongside homes going up for his parents, and his aunt Olivia Templeton. On May 15, 1848, he married Samuel and Mary Ruggles' daughter, Ellen, at Grace Church, noting that "one era of my life is ending" and a happy new one starting.[15] Work went on apace at Strong's house, though in May 1849 he complained of the "[m]ost reckless expenditure of plaster in the hall, a grand frieze runs around it like that of the Parthenon."

As people like Strong settled uptown, more buildings went up. *The Knickerbocker* noted in 1848 how "the Great Metropolis" that the city was becoming was "itself stretching into the distance, with its domes and spires, its towers, cupolas and 'steepled chimnnies,' rising through a canopy of smoke, in the gray dawn of a cloudless September morning."[16]

* * *

Homes were being built for growing families, but education was still in its infancy. By 1829, three times as many of the city's children went to private schools than attended public schools. Some went to church schools, Sunday schools, and charity schools, and Black children attended the African Free Schools. The wealthy meanwhile sent their sons and daughters to day or boarding schools. Mozart's librettist, Lorenzo Da Ponte, had established the Manhattan Academy for Young Gentlemen and the Manhattan Academy for Young Ladies, where the children of prominent families learned Italian dancing, music, and Latin. Mary Okill ran one of the top female finishing schools in the city, assuring New York's leading families that "every attention will be paid to the ordinary and ornamental branches of a finished female education, the department of *religious instruction* will receive particular care." There were regular ads for classes and tutors. The *Freedom's Journal* ran a notice in 1828 offering, at the New-York African Mutual Instruction Society on Centre Street, six months of evening classes in reading, writing, and arithmetic for men and women for $1.50. Bowery Theatre architect Joseph Sera opened a school for drawing and painting.[17]

A few sought out higher education. Columbia College, founded in 1754, was the town's most prominent institution. Set to the west of City Hall Park between Murray and Barclay Streets, College Place and Church Street, its sycamore trees shaded the college green with its three-and-a-half-story-tall building where Alexander Hamilton had studied and his son James had graduated in 1805. By the 1830s it taught classics to the sons of the well-to-do, such as George Templeton Strong and Philip Hone Jr. The College of Physicians and Surgeons was founded in 1807. Given all the city's growth, it is not surprising that the idea would come up, of building a new college that might be open not just to the wealthy but a wider demographic. In December 1829, Gallatin, Isaac Hone, Valentine Mott, and other civic leaders met at the home of Reverend James Mathews to discuss the issue. Before long they had raised $100,000 for the University of the City of New-York. Gallatin was made its first president, and Mathews the chancellor. Classes began in October 1832 in space at Clinton Hall on Nassau and Beekman Streets.

It was soon clear that a more permanent home was needed for the school, which would become known as New York University (NYU), and in November, property was purchased on the east side of Washington Square. The university fathers tapped Davis, Town, and Dakin to create the school's main hall, and the architects decided on English Gothic—somewhat a break from the Greek Revival style. Brady's St. Thomas Episcopal Church building on Broadway and Houston had been built in this style in 1826, but NYU put Gothic on the city's architectural map. During the summer of 1833, a procession of students and teachers held a ceremony for the laying of the cornerstone. Work did not proceed as smoothly as planned. When stone cutters learned that contractor Elisha Bloomer had hired prisoners to do the work, they marched up Broadway and attacked his shop. Work was completed in May 1837, and NYU's grand marble structure, with its winged parapeted towers, now lorded over Washington Square.[18]

Other institutions began to eye the Square. Reverend Mathews' Dutch church congregation had split after losing their Garden Street sanctuary during the Great Fire. One faction constructed the South Reformed Dutch Church on Murray and Church Streets, while Mathews' group relocated to the Square. The congregation commissioned Minard Lafever, who designed for them the Washington Square Reformed Dutch Church, a dark granite Gothic sanctuary with two tall towers and red stone trim. The building opened in 1840, meshing nicely with NYU's neighboring university building, and imparted a medieval feel to the square's eastern side.

Meanwhile, the area around Washington Square would quickly evolve over the next few decades into what was called the "Athenian Quarter of the city." In addition to New York University, there was Alexander Saeltzer's Astor Library and his Academy of Music; Roger's Astor Place Opera House; Charles Mettam and Edmund A. Burke's New-York Historical Society; Frederick A. Peterson's Cooper Union for the Advancement of Science and Art; Peter B. Wight's National Academy of Design, along with the New York Society Library.

Washington Square's development shifted New York's development northward, and it moved fast. Fifth Avenue had opened up to 13th Street in 1824, to 21st Street in 1830, and to 42nd Street in 1837. From 1836 through 1840, 8,267 buildings and dwellings went up, and between 1841 and 1845 an additional 11,286. So much was being built that the city's assessed land value, which stood at $233.7 million in 1836, reached $398.5 million in 1860. By the 1850s Fifth Avenue possessed the city's most elegant houses and took pride in being the city's most fashionable thoroughfare.[19]

To cope with the wildly different styles and approaches, and hoping to offer design guidance, in 1836 Davis had started work on his *Rural Residences*, a grand architectural series that would expand appreciation for country homes and picturesque architecture. Town, for his part, fervently believed that an organization should be founded to promote the best of design and to make architecture recognized as a fine art. In December 1836, along with Davis, Rogers, Haviland, Lafever, Benjamin, William Strickland, and others, he called a meeting at the Astor House to form an architects association. Unfortunately, the organization's launching coincided with the Panic of 1837, which for a number of years brought development to a standstill. It would thus take until 1857 for a band of architects to meet at Upjohn's office to establish the American Institute of Architects.

The economic downturn similarly affected Davis' grand architectural opus, and only two volumes of his *Rural Residences* came out. Even so, in 1839 he started working with Andrew Jackson Downing, who was perhaps the preeminent architecture and landscape critic of the age. Like Davis, Downing had clear ideas of what made for good design and wanted to educate the public. He used Davis's illustrations in quite a few of his books and publications. Since readers relied on such works for their homes, it helped to spread widely an appreciation for the picturesque styles.

In 1842, Davis moved into the new Merchants' Exchange and briefly reentered into a partnership with Town, who died in June 1844. Davis continued designing at a furious pace. He had an unlimited imagination, creating inventive designs for urban homes, businesses, and governmental buildings that mixed the classical and the quaint. He built libraries, public buildings, and asylums. He especially liked to focus on domestic spaces, creating homes and villas, many of which had asymmetrical layouts that were wild like nature yet perfectly suited to their surroundings.

Davis designed some of New York's most notable houses. His monumental Greek Revival home in lower Manhattan for John Cox Stevens, the first commodore of the New York Yacht Club, had an imposing semicircular portico supported by two-story Corinthian columns, a great domed central hall, lush parlors, and landscaped gardens. Hone commented that the house, known as "Stevens' Palace," "is, indeed, a palace." Another of

Davis' buildings was for William Coventry Henry Waddell, who served as US marshal in New York. When Davis and Waddell first went to look over the property, an orchard sat on the spot at Fifth Avenue between 37th and 38th Streets, and Waddell's wife, Charlotte, sat under a tree eating fruit. Davis created a yellowish-gray stuccoed Gothic villa with brownstone trim that sported a riot of towers and gables, along with a conservatory. His most over-the-top design appeared in the late 1850s just up the avenue opposite the Murray Hill Distributing Reservoir. Called the House of Mansions, it was made up of a collection of 11 attached English Gothic Collegiate style row homes.[20]

Realizing that the United States lacked its own indigenous architectural vernacular, architects like Davis experimented with a plethora of styles. Many of the wealthy wanted houses emulating the Italian Renaissance, a style deemed more cheerful than the more austere Greek Revival. "Greece has fallen a victim to Italy," wrote an editor in *Putnam's*. Davis helped lead the trend and was the first in the city to adopt the style, creating an elevation for an 1835 exhibition. The success of architects Joseph Trench and John Butler Snook's Marble Palace for the merchant Alexander Stewart in 1846 made the "palazzo" design a favorite for houses and mansions. At that time, the partners designed an Italianate home for Colonel Herman Thorne on 16th Street, featuring a brownstone Tuscan portico with an imposing enframed front doorway. One critic wrote that it "has an air of unostentatious magnificence that no town house in the Union can pretend to." Soon, hulking Italianate homes lined the city's streets, with their thick rusticated basements, high stoops, spirited lintels, sills, and cornices looming over their brownstone facades.[21]

The design boom was further fueled by the arrival of professional architects from other parts of the country and abroad. It seemed as if a floodgate had been pulled wide apart, and the architects who poured into New York transformed the city into a global center of architectural style. In the 1820s and '30s there were the British architects Frederick Diaper, Upjohn, and Joseph C. Wells. In the 1840s and '50s came Henry Dudley, Jacob Wrey Mould, Calvert Vaux, and Frederick Withers. Numerous architects arrived from German states in the 1840s and '50s, including Detlef Lienau, Peterson, and Saeltzer. With them came a range of architectural styles and variations, from now-standard Greek Revival, Gothic, and Italianate, to Romanesque, Tudor, French Empire, Tuscan, Swiss, Egyptian Revival, and what was termed "Oriental." Some of their creations, commented Scottish publisher

William Chambers in his book *Things As They Are in America*, "are more like the palaces of kings than places for the transaction of business."

As the city pushed northward, more and more opportunities appeared for architects, particularly those who worked on religious structures. In 1834, a year before the Great Fire, the *New York Mirror* commented how "few of our churches are grand and imposing." Things quickly changed with the arrival of Upjohn, the British architect who had come to America in 1829, making his way to New York in 1839. Upjohn was hired to repair Trinity Church, one of the city's most prominent structures, on Broadway and Wall Street. Built in 1790, the sanctuary had become so dilapidated that it needed to be demolished, and Upjohn designed an entirely new church. Dedicated on Ascension Day in May 1846, the 284-foot-tall Gothic spire soared above everything else in the city, both revolutionizing church architecture and cementing Upjohn's stature. Whitman found the building "beautiful,—and majestic and chaste." With his success at Trinity, other commissions flowed Upjohn's way. His English Gothic Church of the Ascension opened on 10th Street in 1841. A decade later, in 1855, his Trinity Chapel was consecrated on 25th Street just west of Broadway.[22]

Sanctuaries sprouted everywhere. Grace Church, which originally stood across from Trinity Church, was sold in 1843. Strong's Columbia classmate James Renwick won the competition to build the church's new home at 10th Street, where Broadway veers slightly to the west, a placement that allowed his glistening marble English–French Gothic building to command a place of prominence. Grace quickly earned the reputation as the preferred place for funerals, weddings, and baptisms. As Hone noted, its aisles were filled "with gay parties of ladies in feathers and *mousseline-de-laine* dresses, and dandies with mustaches and high-heeled boots." The success of that commission brought Renwick other clients. In 1846, he started work on Union Square West on the city's first Romanesque house of worship—the Congregational Church of the Puritans. In 1848 his Calvary Church opened on East 21st Street. In 1853 he was tapped to design the new St. Patrick's Cathedral on Fifth Avenue and 50th Street, one of the city's most prominent churches. And in 1854 his Romanesque-style St. Stephen's was consecrated on East 28th Street.

Meanwhile, the First Presbyterian Church, which had been down on Wall Street, moved into a Wells-designed Gothic building on 11th Street in 1846. That year, Leopold Eidlitz and Karl Otto Blesch laid the cornerstone for their Romanesque Revival St. George's Church on Stuyvesant Square. At the start of the next decade, B'nai Jeshurun moved out of their synagogue on Elm Street and into a new Gothic-style structure designed by William Field and John Correja on Greene Street. Then, in the early 1850s Eidlitz's Victorian Gothic style Fifth Avenue Presbyterian Church opened on 19th Street. At the end of the decade, his Broadway United Church of Christ appeared on Sixth Avenue and 34th Street. Jacob Mould, who described himself as "hell on color," brought eye-popping polychrome, creating in 1855 the All Souls' Unitarian Church, a grand Lombard-Romanesque style building sheathed with stripes of yellow Caen limestone and red Philadelphia brick. It was a combination he felt went well with the blue American sky. While Strong, for one, viewed Mould as a "universal Genius," many others found his striped building garish, earning All Souls the nickname "Church of the Holy Zebra."[23]

Styles evolved, church spires grew taller, homes became grander. All of this was made possible by advances in technology. New steam-cutting equipment meant that brownstone and marble could now be prepared at modest cost. Meanwhile, plate glass prices dropped, allowing homes to feature larger windows. Into these bigger and lofty rooms, architects set solid mahogany and black walnut doors and stained-glass windows. Houses boasted numerous bathrooms, made possible by the arrival of water from upstate in 1842 that spurred the installation of bathroom fixtures.

* * *

Unsurprisingly, the wealthy fixated on where they lived, vying for the top spot and choice location. In 1848, the *Tribune* observed, "Every man who builds a new house seems ambitious to have the roof a foot or two higher, the marble steps a few inches broader, or the cornice and entablatures a little richer than his neighbors." Probably no house more embodied this competition than the one built on East 17th Street for merchant and banker Henry Parish in 1848. The dwelling had half a dozen reception rooms—each done up in a different style, such as Medieval, Elizabethan, and Persian—and featuring elaborate fountains, Old Masters paintings, cameos by Benvenuto Cellini, Gobelin tapestry, and tables fashioned out of malachite and agate.[24]

John Jacob Astor's grandson Charles Astor Bristed wrote in 1852 how many a new millionaire "occasionally half ruins himself by building and furnishing to make a new lion for the town." Whitman, who grew up far from that social order, noted in *Life Illustrated* in 1856, "It may be stated, as a general principle, that in New York city, among all ranks, except the poorest, there is a habit of occupying houses outrageously and absurdly too expensive." The middle class meanwhile bought or rented smaller brick or brownstone homes in Greenwich Village and Chelsea, and on side streets. Some moved to growing areas in the Bronx, such as Fordham, Mott Haven, and Morrisania. Many likewise migrated to Brooklyn, settling in Brooklyn Heights and Cobble Hill. And as Whitman—a proud Brooklynite—wrote, those who couldn't afford a place took to living in boarding houses, a home that is "Simply a place to keep a man's trunk and his wife while he is at work, and where he has breakfast, tea, and sleeping-room."

A house and furnishings were only part of the look. "The first thing, as a general rule, that a young Gothamite does is to get a horse; the second, to get a wife," observed Bristed in mock seriousness. Both meant setting out in elaborate carriages, as well as sleighs in the winter, to see and be seen. And when out in a carriage or on foot, they made sure to dress resplendently, men sporting stovepipe hats and women wearing the latest French fashions and adorning themselves with fine jewelry from stores like Tiffany & Young, which opened in 1837.

They likewise courted within their social sets. When Strong first mentioned Ellen Ruggles by name in his diary in January 1848, he noted that, "Miss Ellen Ruggles is *rather* worth cultivating." Others similarly sought out their equals, and intermarriage among the wealthy was commonplace. John Hone's daughter Elizabeth, for example, married the businessman and politician Myndert Van Schaick; his daughter Ann married Reverend Mathews; and Joanna Esther married Samuel Howland. When John Jones Schermerhorn—the son of Sarah and Peter Schermerhorn—became engaged in 1832 to Philip Hone's daughter Mary, Hone wrote in his diary that she "could not have made a choice more pleasing to me." In November 1842, Hone's son Robert married Eliza Rodman Russell, whose father Charles served as director of the Bank of Commerce and lived across from Hone on Great Jones Street. Charles in 1850 would then marry Hone's grandniece, Caroline Howland. In 1870 lawyer Richard Blatchford would marry Hone's daughter Catharine.[25]

They all of course socialized among themselves. Isabella Bird noted how "On New Year's Day, in accordance of an old Dutch custom, the ladies remain at home, and all the gentlemen of their acquaintance make a point of calling upon them." For such occasions, Thomas Downing—our Oyster King— offered "a choice lot of Oysters, which I am pickling in a superior manner for the New Year day congratulating table." Catherine Elizabeth Havens wrote at the start of January 1850 about all their visitors: "We had 139 callers, and I have an ivory tablet and I write all their names down in it."

Soirees proved especially popular. Hone noted how people regularly invited small circles of friends to their houses. The former mayor had dozens of people over at his home, entertaining notables like Washington Irving, Senator Daniel Webster, and President John Quincy Adams. Isabella Bird in 1856 was amazed at the gatherings at people's homes: "Poets, historians, and men of science are to be met with frequently at these receptions; but they do not go as lions, but to please and be pleased; and such men as Longfellow, Prescott, or Washington Irving may be seen mixing with the general throng with so much *bonhommie* and simplicity."[26]

The gathering that became the talk of the town was the masked ball that Henry and Laura Brevoort threw in their home in February 1840. Some 600 masked guests flitted through the Red Room, the Green Room, and others, admiring the paintings by Raphael and others on the walls. Hone was pleased with how his family turned out. "My family contributed a large number of actors in the gay scene. I went as Cardinal Wolsey, in a grand robe of new scarlet merino, with an exceedingly well-contrived cap of the same material; a cape of real ermine, which I borrowed from Mrs. Thomas W. Ludlow, gold chain and cross, scarlet stockings, etc."[27]

The grandest party of the following decade was the 1854 costumed ball given by Ann Schermerhorn on Lafayette Place. This was a Louis XV–themed party, and her home had been decorated to look like the Palace of Versailles. Like the Brevoort party, hundreds came, and Strong was stunned by the variety of costumes: "The chaos of nuns and devils, Ivanhoe and Harlequin, Loyola, Paul Pry, the cavalier and the Swiss peasant, presented by a ball on any other principle, or rather without principle of any sort, is so incoherent and insane that a thoughtful spectator would certainly be qualified for the Bloomingdale Asylum after some assignable period of inspection."

Papers covered the social scene, assiduously noting births, marriages, scandals, and deaths of the rich. Just after the Brevoort party, the papers were a-twitter with news that Matilda Barclay—the daughter of the British consul in New York—had run off with T. Pollock Burgwyne, a gentleman from North Carolina. Given the large number of eligible rich young ladies about town, there were of course plenty of those ready to take advantage. The *Herald* warned in 1839 that with 88 young New York women, each worth from $100,000 to $1.5 million, there were "several fashionable fortune hunters, with the requisite quantity of mustachios, imperials and whiskers, (little brains required), from France, England, and other foreign parts."[28]

Throughout, there were the ever-popular organizations to which the upper class—"Uppertendom," as one writer called it—belonged. People started such groups to be with those with whom they shared interests or pastimes, for a sense of exclusivity, to burnish their social status, and to emulate what was going on in Europe. Starting in the early 1820s, James Fenimore Cooper hosted a small gathering that evolved into the Bread and Cheese Club. Those attending included the Hudson River School painter Thomas Cole, the inventor Samuel F.B. Morse, Washington Irving, Hone, and painter Henry Inman. In 1824 Cooper, along with Irving, Dr. David Hosack, and others established the New York Athenaeum, intended *"for the advancement of literature and science,"* on Broadway and Pine Street. It featured a science and literature library and lecture rooms, and joined with the New York Society Library in 1840. In 1828, John Jacob Astor, Hone, and others formed the Clinton Hall Association and two years later opened Clinton Hall on Nassau and Beekman Streets. There, the association held lectures and classes in French, German, and Spanish, as well as lessons in drawing and business arithmetic for the Mercantile Library Association. Irving helped start the St. Nicholas Society in 1835, its purpose to celebrate New York history, with a who's-who membership. Food proved very important at these gatherings, with hosts striving to be noticed for creating elaborate spreads. Sometimes, though, there could be too much of a good thing. In 1847, Strong noted how one St. Nicholas Society meal included oysters, soup, fish, turkey, venison, canvasback duck, along with white wine, champagne, and sherry, all of which "gave me a shocking sick headache, which I deserved."[29]

Old-money merchants and lawyers formed the Union Club in 1836, a society to promote social intercourse—and generate business opportunities. The Kent Club was named for the lawyer James Kent. While open to lawyers, it also welcomed non-lawyers like Hone. In 1844 a group of gentlemen met on John Cox Stevens's schooner *Gimcrack* and formed the New York Yacht Club. In 1846 Hone joined the Racket Club—intended to promote the increasingly popular game of indoor court tennis—and the following year saw the creation of the Century Club to cultivate the arts. Hone seemed central to them all, and he loved to give toasts. He adjusted them to the setting and occasion, reflecting the tenor of the clubs themselves. Some were serious-minded, some heartfelt, and some openly frivolous. In April 1835 at the St. Nicholas Society inaugural dinner at the City Hotel, Hone raised a toast to

"The Beaver—The first freeman of New-York; who laid out streets where he pleased, and built his house without caring a *dam* for the Assessors."[30]

One club that touched Hone's heart—while also expressing the belief in the city's great destiny—was formed on October 22, 1838. A large group of worthies gathered at John Ward's Bond Street home where they founded the Hone Club. Members agreed to gather at a different home each time, at which that evening's host could invite four people, with gatherings including such personalities as Governor William Seward and Senator Webster. The club bought a portrait of Webster by George Healy and hung it in Hone's dining room. Naturally, the members were especially interested in their meals, and the food included a choice of soup, fish, four types of meat, oysters, fruit desert, jellies, and ice creams. And of course there was wine. Loud singing was likewise encouraged. "A Devonshire duke might have been astonished at the amplitude of the repast, and the richness and style of the entertainment," wrote Dr. John Francis. The first December after it started, Hone wrote an "Ode for the Hone Club," which included the verse:

> Shall Truth, Love, and Friendship our club still unite,
> And the cares of the day ne'er extend to the night?
> Shall innocent mirth and good-humour abound,
> And our bosom beat high as each Monday comes 'round?
>> Gentlemen of the jury, are you all agreed?
>> President: Agreed.
>> Chorus. Agreed, agreed; we are all of one mind,
>> For Truth, Love, and Friendship, our verdict we find.[31]

6

The City and the Arts

On Saturday nights, culture-seeking New Yorkers followed a well-worn path to the home of Anne Charlotte Lynch. Her soirees at 116 Waverly Place, just off Washington Square, had become the proverbial talk of the town, attracting authors Washington Irving, Ralph Waldo Emerson, and Herman Melville; journalists William Cullen Bryant, Horace Greeley, Margaret Fuller, and Nathaniel Parker Willis; the poet George Morris; the Norwegian violinist Ole Bull; along with assorted phrenologists and mesmerists (reflecting fascination with these pseudo sciences). Lynch, a teacher from Bennington, Vermont, started hosting the gatherings in 1845, and they transformed her into a leader of the city's literary and artistic life. One evening in 1846, author Catharine Sedgwick stopped by to see what she had heard so much about. As Sedgwick entered, she found Lynch's two parlors "filled with guests, in a high state of social enjoyment." All there happily snacked on sandwiches, wafers, cakes, lemonade, and tea made by Lynch's mother and her students from the Brooklyn Female Academy. The audience listened to poetry and music, took part in dancing, and discussed the latest plays, music, and exhibitions. Some guests prepared tableaux vivants to entertain their fellow celebrants, while others gave readings of their works. Edgar Allan Poe lived on nearby 3rd Street and regularly attended Lynch's soirees. He was a favorite of the women, who clustered around him. It was there that the poet supposedly first recited his poem "The Raven."[1]

Lynch was herself a poet, her work appearing in newspapers like the *New York Tribune* alongside those of Emerson. She believed that the arts could elevate society, and New Yorkers were eager to be a part of their city's burgeoning cultural life as they created works and celebrated their home-grown and adopted writers and artists. Washington Irving was among the earliest. Born in the city in 1783, he went on to write such classics as *Letters of Jonathan Oldstyle Gent.*, *A History of New-York from the Beginning of the World to the End of the Dutch Dynasty*, *Rip Van Winkle*, and *The Legend of Sleepy Hollow*. And for his friend, John Jacob Astor, in 1836 he wrote *Astoria, or, Anecdotes of an Enterprise Beyond the Rocky Mountains*, on the businessman's ill-fated attempts to start a fur-trading post on the Columbia River.

The Melville family settled in New York, and Herman arrived in 1819. In 1841 he crewed aboard the *Acushnet*, a whale-hunting ship, deserting when he arrived in the Marquesas Islands in Polynesia. He would write of his captivity there at the hands of the reportedly cannibal natives in his 1846 book *Typee*. The volume became an immediate success, and the following year Melville married Elizabeth Knapp Shaw. The couple settled in a New York brownstone on Fourth Avenue, where he wrote such books as *Redburn* and *White-Jacket*. In 1850 he bought a farm in Pittsfield, Massachusetts, brought out *Moby-Dick*, and soon after that, his short story "Bartleby, the Scrivener" about a Manhattan clerk who prefers not to work.

James Fenimore Cooper arrived in New York in 1822 at the age of 33. He had already written his novel *The Spy*, and in the city began his Leatherstocking tales, bringing out *The Pioneers* in 1823, *The Last of the Mohicans* in 1826, and *The Prairie* in 1827. After spending time in Europe, he returned to the United States in 1833 and then settled in Cooperstown, having started on his *New York, or the Towns of Manhattan* before his death in 1851.

Walt Whitman's family moved from West Hills, Long Island, to Brooklyn in 1823 just before he turned four. As we've seen, he first came to Manhattan in 1835 as a printer and set type. An August 1835 fire destroyed the paper where he was working. When, four months later, the Great Fire swept away not only buildings but jobs, he headed back to Long Island. Whitman returned to the city in 1841. He worked at the *New World, Aurora, Democratic Review, Evening Tattler*, the *New York Mirror*, and *Brother Jonathan*, and moved back to Brooklyn in 1845 to work and run such publications as the Brooklyn *Evening Star*—and, most famously, the Brooklyn *Daily Eagle*. He regularly tramped around the city for inspiration, writing about everything he saw, from high and low society to the theater and the fires that regularly ripped through the city. In 1855 he came out with *Leaves of Grass*.

Boston-born Edgar Allan Poe first arrived in New York in 1837, before heading to Philadelphia, only to return to the city in 1844 with his wife, Virginia—who was also his cousin—and her mother, Maria. He saw the city as a spot "where I intend living for the future." Besides enjoying Lynch's evenings, Poe also attended New York University programs held by the Philomathean and Eucleian Societies. It turned out to be a prolific time for the writer. He had already published "The Murders in the Rue Morgue" and "The Mystery of Marie Rogêt," and would see the publication of his "Balloon

Hoax" in the *New York Sun* in April 1844, and "The Raven" in the *New York Evening Mirror* in January 1845. A number of Poe's literary characters were New Yorkers. Ernest Valdemar in the December 1845 story "The Facts in the Case of M. Valdemar" resides in Harlem, and the character in "The Sphinx," published a year later, escapes the city during a cholera epidemic. Poe served as the New York correspondent for the *Columbia Spy* and wrote for the *Democratic Review*. In 1845 he took over ownership of the *Broadway Journal*. Whitman recalled him as "very cordial . . . very kindly and human."[2]

New York drew artists and inventors. NYU's new building became a popular place for them to live and work, since the school rented out space. Its architect, Alexander Jackson Davis, set up his office and library in the northwest tower. Other tenants at the school included Samuel Colt, who was designing his revolver. In the 1850s, the architect Richard Morris Hunt took a space in the building, along with such organizations as the New-York Historical Society, the New York Academy of Medicine, and the American Geographical Society.

Samuel F.B. Morse, who taught at the school and worked there on his telegraph, happened to be in Paris in 1839. There he met with Louis-Jacques-Mandé Daguerre, who, along with Nicéphore Niépce, created the Daguerreotype, the first widespread form of photography. Daguerre showed Morse how to create clear, sharp, and highly polished-looking images by coating silver-plated copper sheets with iodine, exposing them in the camera, fuming the plate with mercury vapor, and then fixing it with salt. When Morse returned to the States, he brought with him a camera—one of the first in the nation—and started to teach others how to use it.

Photo studios soon flourished throughout the city, and by the mid-1840s New York had more of them than any other city in the nation. In 1846, Edward Ruggles' city guide listed Plumbe's Studio as the most extensive, noting that "Mr. Plumbe is esteemed one of the very best Daguerreotypists in the world." Philip Hone and others sat for photographers, and in 1852 the South Carolinian William Bobo observed that, "There is hardly a block in New-York that has not one or more of these concerns upon it."

One of the city's most successful photographers was Mathew Brady. The young Brady arrived in New York from upstate in the late 1830s. He studied photography with Morse and opened his Daguerrian Miniature Gallery on Broadway, across from Barnum's American Museum. Like the neighboring showman, Brady knew the advantages of promotion. He photographed celebrities and ran ads inviting the public to see "the very fine specimens of

Daguerreotype Likenesses on exhibition at his establishment." Many hoped to have their images captured by the new medium, and prominent members of society flocked to his studio.[3]

* * *

As New Yorkers vied to be cultural leaders on par with those in Europe, the city's more sophisticated and socially conscious citizens actively supported both new and older art forms. The Park Theatre, which stood opposite the City Hall Park, first opened in 1798. Astor and John Beekman bought it in 1806, then rebuilt it after a fire in 1820. According to Whitman, the Park "held a large part in my boyhood's and young manhood's life." Other theaters included the Bowery, which has been much discussed in these pages, the Chatham, the Broadway, the Franklin, and the National. Some of them had box seats for the wealthy—Hone had one at the Park. And despite the wishes of those who saw theater as an uplifting and civilizing experience, many proved to be unruly places. Patrons drank, spat tobacco juice, and threw food on the stage. There were regular exchanges—sometimes devolving into shouting matches—between the audience and the actors, accompanied by either cheering or hissing and the hurling of objects. In 1802 Irving, following a visit to the Park, commented on the sudden "discharge of apples, nuts, and gingerbread, on the heads of the honest folks in the pit, who had no possibility of retreating from this new kind of thunderbolts." He offered this simple advice: "sit down quietly and bend your back to it."[4]

With the growth of theaters and concert halls, actors and musicians flocked to town. Junius Brutus Booth, perhaps the most famous of his generation, arrived in the United States in 1821. The Shakespearean actor embraced his new home, and his American audience similarly cherished him. During a November 1832 performance of *Richard III* at the Bowery, the stage became jammed with audience members who thrilled at the Battle of Bosworth scene. The crowd pressed close around Booth's Richard and George Jones's Henry, Earl of Richmond. As they did, they fervently encouraged the fencing, thus extending the sword fight for 15 minutes.

The Philadelphia-born Edwin Forrest debuted in New York at the Park in *Othello* in June 1826. The tall, strapping actor earned the nickname the "Mastodon of the Drama" and the "Ferocious Tragedian" and attracted a rabid following among the regulars at places like the Bowery. Four months after Forrest's first appearance, the British actor William Macready arrived in the States. George Templeton Strong saw Macready in *Macbeth* in October

1848, a performance that he considered "Very finished and forcible." He soon after caught him in *Julius Caesar*, where Macready played Brutus, and Strong found his "conception of his part was very beautiful."[5]

Much of the artistic life of the city did not consist of Shakespeare plays, but what were deemed lower forms of entertaining. The Bowery—with its dance halls, oyster houses, billiard halls, brothels, taverns, gambling dens, bowling alleys, dime museums, boxing matches, and cock fights—was the center of the common man's entertainment world. The wide, mile-long, north–south running street was a popular haunt for young, aggressive, tobacco-chewing B'hoys, whose names reflect the common Irish pronunciation in the area. The men saw themselves as true democrats, lovers of their firehouses, and of course their G'hals, their fairer halves with whom they frequented saloons, music halls, and theaters.[6] The Bowery Theatre developed into a natural entertainment center for the B'hoys and G'hals. In its early days, when the theater impresario Charles Gilfert ran the place, he focused on comedy, recruited British actors, and catered to the upper class. Unfortunately, the theater failed to draw enough patrons, and when Gilfert died in 1829 the New York comedian James Hackett took over. Hackett soon subleased the theater to Thomas Souness Hamblin, who in August 1830 staged his first performance, Richard Sheridan's *The School for Scandal,* and the farces *Teddy the Tiler* by George Rodwell and Samuel Beazley's *Lottery Ticket.*

Born in London in May 1800, Hamblin had trained in local theaters. Tall and handsome, with deep-set hazel eyes, dark curly hair, Roman nose, and husky voice, he was, according to Whitman, "a large, shapely, imposing presence, and dark and flashing eyes." He married the actress Elizabeth Walker Blanchard in 1821. Along with their baby daughter, the family sailed for America, arriving in New York in 1825. Hamblin first appeared at the Bowery in December 1826 as Virginius in the James Sheridan Knowles tragedy of the same name. A few nights later he performed with Edwin Forrest in Thomas Otway's *Venice Preserved.*[7]

While Hamblin employed at the Bowery famous performers like his friend Booth, he generally avoided the so-called star system and downplayed his highbrow Shakespearean roots. Instead, the actor-turned-manager enthusiastically pitched his theater to the masses. Rather than making the Bowery a place that exalted British plays and culture, he joyfully wrapped himself in the Stars and Stripes. To do this he catered to national-pride tastes, promoting the Bowery as a home for all things American. To make this possible, Hamblin developed a stock company filled with what he called "Native Talent." He hired and pro-moted American-born actors and playwrights such as Josephine Clifton, Charlotte Cushman, and Lester Wallack. He also renamed the house the American Theatre, Bowery.

Most of all, Hamblin popularized grand melodramas, popularly known as "Blood and Thunder" theater, earning the Bowery the nickname "The Slaughterhouse"—playing not only on its offerings but on the fact that the site on which the theater stood had once been a stockyard and abattoir. Hamblin aggressively advertised the Bowery, seizing every chance to tout the differences between his house and those of his competitors, especially if they featured foreign actors. When the British father–daughter combo, Charles and Fanny Kemble, performed at the Park in Shakespeare's *Romeo and Juliet* and Henry Milman's *Fazio*, Hamblin staged the same plays with American talent.

People took notice. In August 1836, eight months after the Great Fire and a month before the Bowery's second fire, the *New York Mirror* wrote that Hamblin had transformed the theater into the "handsomest in the city . . . and quite a formidable rival to the Park." What brought the change was "Not English money . . . for it has profited wholly by the native genius of our soil."

Unsurprisingly, polite New York society with their European sensibilities viewed the Bowery as filled with all the wrong sorts, with one denouncing it as "the home of Satan. . . . A plague spot to be avoided." The *Tribune* dis-paragingly called the theater "the realm of orange-peel and peanuts—the legitimate home of unadulterated, undiluted sanguinary drama . . . where adolescent 'shoulder-hitters' and politicians in futuro take their first lessons in rowdyism." And the *Mirror* ran one poet's couplet, which seemed quite ap-plicable to the theater: "Throw not the pearl of Shakespeare's wit / Before the swine of the Bowery pit." Hone especially regretted having laid the theater's cornerstone in 1826, commenting in 1838, "No act of my public life cost me so many friends."[8]

Audience members, though, loved the Bowery and its mix of comedies, tragedies, Shakespeare, dramas, French dances, minstrelsy, and circuses. For just 25¢, crowds jammed into the gallery. The lawyer and journalist Matthew Hale Smith commented on the mass assembled there as "News-boys, street-sweepers, rag-pickers, begging girls, collectors of cinders," along with its journeymen butchers, mechanics, artisans, firemen, folding-girls and seamstresses, milliners' apprentices and shop-girls. As the *New York Spirit of the Times* noted in 1847, they would all "vent in a perfect tornado and maelstrom united, of 'hi hi's!' cat-calls, screamings, whistling and stampings," all the while "chanking pea nuts and squirting tobacco juice upon the stage."

To feed the appetites and raise the volume, Hamblin featured the work of such playwrights as Louïsine Honor De Medina. Known as Louisa Medina, the European-born writer created many plays that kept the audience coming back to the Bowery, including *Wacousta: or, the Curse, Norman Leslie,* and *Rienzi, the Last of the Roman Tribunes.* The *Mirror* noted how her work embraces "a wider range of subjects than has been attempted by any other modern dramatist." Many of Medina's staged pieces included virtuous women who bested villainous men, and she gladly gave the audiences the grand spectacles they craved. Her tempestuous adaptation of Edward Bulwer-Lytton's novel *The Last Days of Pompeii* featured an ash-spewing volcano. It took in $10,000 in its first week.[9]

Other of Hamblin's productions were similarly extravagant. Thomas Holcroft's *Lady of the Rock* was staged with a sea storm. *The Pirates' Signal* presented a tank drama with a boat. *The Spectre King, and His Phantom Steed* involved 200 soldiers attacking a fortress; and *The Robbers* featured a decapitated yet talking head. Hamblin's over-the-top shows paid off. According to the author and abolitionist Lydia Maria Child, "gorgeous decorations, fantastic tricks, terrific ascensions, and performances full of fire, blood, and thunder" filled the Bowery, not to forget its "vaunting drama, and boastful song," which "works up the patriotism of the audience, till they feel a comfortable assurance that every American can 'whip his weight in wild cats.'"

Hamblin also liked to use animals in his shows. When he staged *The Elephant of Siam and the Fire-Fiend!* in 1831, he included an elephant brought in from London. In 1840, *The Battle of Waterloo* called for 50 horses. And lion tamer Herr Jacob Driesbach—who, despite his German honorific, was born in Sharon, New York—first appeared with his trained tigers and lions in 1842. Exotic animals not only proved expensive to obtain, but Hamblin's spectacles called for larger and more realistic sets as well as bigger casts and staff. A shrewd businessman, he managed to make it all work. To ensure that he had control of what he did, in June 1834 he bought his first six shares from the New York Association. Avoiding the star system also kept costs down. And, in order to popularize his theater and its offerings, he held regular benefits, such as one in 1830 to help families of those in debtor's prison, and another in 1836 raising money for the Texas Revolution.[10] Hamblin likewise was a tough negotiator, as especially evident in his long and tortured friendship with Booth. In November 1832, Booth entered into a contract with Hamblin, who paid him $120 for each night he performed. But when cholera struck Booth's family, the actor left for his home in Maryland. When he arrived, Booth became so distraught that he even exhumed the body of daughter Mary in the hope of reviving her. He then begged Hamblin to release him from his contract. Hamblin reluctantly agreed, but demanded that he return soon.

Hamblin similarly had a fraught relationship with his wife, Elizabeth. She divorced him in 1834, and the court forbade him from remarrying during her lifetime. James Gordon Bennett used the marriage split to tar the manager in the *New York Herald*. Hamblin was in fact an utterly self-engrossed philanderer and made an easy target for Bennett's dislike. The theatrical manager Joseph Tooker noted that, "He fancied that every woman that once looked upon his manly form was fascinated." Hamblin's indiscretions were widely known, and they included a series of questionable relationships with young actresses including Josephine Clifton, and her half-sister Louisa Missouri Miller, who was known as Louisa Missouri. Both were the daughters of Adeline Miller, who ran a brothel that Hamblin regularly visited. Another young actress was Naomi Vincent, the daughter of Mary Gallagher, whose brothel Hamblin also frequented. Vincent died in July 1835 giving birth to Hamblin's child. Despite being forbidden to remarry while his ex-wife lived, Hamblin said that he and Medina soon after exchanged vows, and the couple named Vincent's newborn Louisa.[11]

* * *

For entertainment aside from that offered by the theater, New Yorkers in the 1830s and 1840s could go to the New York Zoological Institute, located on the Bowery, to see its menagerie of animals. The taxidermist and collector John Scudder's American Museum stood on Park Row and featured not fewer than 150,000 curiosities, from live mud turtles to the bed curtains said to have belonged to Mary, Queen of Scots. Phineas Taylor Barnum bought the museum's contents in 1841 and the following year opened his Barnum's American Museum on Broadway and Ann Street. He soon added the collection from Rubens Peale's Museum & Gallery of the Fine Arts, which was located near City Hall, and in 1850 leased the Chinese Museum on Broadway and Rector Street.

A supreme self-promoter, P.T. Barnum placed ads in papers, and dispatched along the streets his "bulletin wagons," carts covered with signs. He likewise hung posters, flew colorful flags, set up a roof garden on which he sold ice cream, featured an oyster bar, launched fireworks, and installed a fountain that shot water 100 feet into the air. "Barnumizing," making the mundane extraordinary, was what Barnum did best, boasting that he presented everything from "educated" dogs, industrious fleas, and automatons, to giants, dwarfs, rope-dancers, and instrumental music. Audiences of the post–Great Fire period loved Barnum's offbeat menagerie, from a bearded lady and magicians to a "mammoth crocodile" and an orangutan named Mademoiselle Fanny. One of Barnum's most famous performers was Charles Stratton, a 25-inch-tall distant relative of the showman. Stratton would eventually grow to 40 inches, and the 6-foot-2-inch-tall Barnum introduced him to viewers as "General" Tom Thumb. Hone took his daughter Margaret to see Stratton in July 1843, and found the General to be "lively, agreeable, sprightly, and talkative."[12]

New Yorkers could find assorted entertainment throughout town. In 1824, the Southwest Battery, a fort built the previous decade and located on a man-made island off the tip of the southern edge of Manhattan, was transformed into Castle Garden, a roofed public resort with a restaurant and entertainment. Concerts were performed there, as were operas, circuses, minstrel shows, equestrian acts, acrobats, dancing girls, and fireworks. The city also offered smaller venues with a mix of dance, magic, ventriloquism, comedy, and music. Small hotels and taverns sometimes offered free entertainment to attract cart-men, butchers, firemen, domestics, and tradesmen, and to sell drinks. General Charles Sandford, who would become Hamblin's lawyer, opened the 3,500-seat Mount Pitt Circus on Broome Street in November 1826. Not all the entertainment required a permanent structure. In 1843 Herr Driesbach set up under an enormous tent at the corner of Broadway and 13th Street, in which were displayed four elephants, two camels, two llamas, an alpaca, tigers, lions, hyenas, leopards, panthers, and a boa constrictor.

In European capitals, opera was already popular, and New York was willing to try. In 1825 at the Park Theatre, Lorenzo Da Ponte arranged for a visiting Italian opera company to stage performances of Gioachino Rossini's 1816 *The Barber of Seville*, which had been enthusiastically performed throughout Europe. In November 1833, he opened the Italian Opera House in the Richmond Hill Theatre, with tier boxes and a domed ceiling painted by the Italian artists Giuseppe Guidicini, Mario Bragaldi, and Gioachino Albe, featuring images of the nine muses and Apollo. Hone went to the opening performance of Rossini's *La Gazza Ladra*, but wondered, "Will this splendid and refined amusement be supported in New York? I am doubtful." He was right.

It closed in 1836. In 1844, Signor Ferdinand Palmo, who owned the Café des Mille Colonnes restaurant, made a go at an opera house on Chambers Street between Broadway and Centre Street, but it also soon folded.

Undaunted, others tried bringing opera and classical music to New York. Among the most upscale venues was the Astor Place Opera House. Designed by Isaiah Rogers and opened in November 1847, it attracted the cream of New York society. German-born Alexander Saeltzer's Academy of Music opened a few blocks to the north at Irving Place and 14th Street in 1854. The academy's main hall seated 4,000. Whitman observed in 1855 in *Life Illustrated* how the city's elite arrived there in carriages pulled by "beautiful, proud, fat, pampered horses!"[13]

The Philharmonic Society of New York premiered in December 1842. Its first concert included Beethoven's Fifth Symphony, with Strong calling the performers "most perfectly drilled." Strong loved music. He played the organ—he commissioned Henry Erben to build one for his Gramercy Park home—and his wife, Ellen, sang. The couple regularly attended concerts around town, and he proved to be a discriminating critic. In June 1851 at Castle Garden, he and Ellen heard Giuseppe Verdi's *Ernani*, and he afterward wrote that "The music is vile, and no living or possible company of performers can make it other than vile. But it's pleasant." In September he headed back to Castle Garden for Vincenzo Bellini's *Norma*, where the Dutch soprano Rose de Vries played the heroine, and "the louder this lady screamed, the more uproariously they applauded." Yet, after attending Mozart's *The Marriage of Figaro* in 1858, he was moved to report, "I'm still tingling and nervous from undergoing that most intense and exquisite music."[14]

Smaller performances similarly went on around town. The Prague Company performed at the City Hotel in February 1837. In February 1840, Mary Okill, who ran a finishing school for women, threw open her 12-room house on Clinton Place, hosted a Grand Musical Soiree with music and French vaudeville, and offered cakes, wine, and lemonade. The German Musical Society held a concert at City Hotel in February 1840. May 1841 found the pianist L. Rakeman and the violinist Leopold Herwig staging a concert at the New York Society Library. The Harmoneons' Grand Musical Soiree played at Palmo's in January 1846.

Musically, the event of the post–Great Fire era was the arrival of Jenny Lind. Barnum, though he had never previously heard the Swedish soprano sing, arranged for Lind to visit the United States. He then spent six months whipping up interest in her tour, announcing with his customary hyperbole that she was "the greatest musical wonder in the world." The woman who was touted as "the Swedish Nightingale," "the Siren," "the Tenth Muse," and "the Angel," arrived in New York on September 1, 1850. Not since Charles Dickens' visit had an arrival so stirred the population. The city turned out in droves to see her. Barnum escorted Lind in his carriage to the Irving House Hotel as onlookers tossed flowers. That evening, numerous musical societies serenaded her with such numbers as "Hail Columbia" and "Yankee Doodle." Strong marveled at the "spontaneous outbreak of rushing, and crowding, and hurrahing, and serenading."[15]

For Lind's September 11 show, Barnum had the bridge to Castle Garden covered with canvas and lighted to look like a triumphal arch. Six thousand people jammed into the theater, while others rented rowboats and floated nearby. When Lind appeared, the audience showered the stage with flowers. She sang the prelude to Bellini's cavatina from *Norma,* and with baritone Giovanni Belletti did a duet from Rossini's *Il Turco in Italia.* She also played the piano and performed the Swedish melody the *Herdsman's Song.* New York diarist Catherine Elizabeth Havens commented how, when her father heard her sing, "tears ran down his face."

The first show was a grand success, financially. Lind proved quite generous with her earnings, and, according to Hone, "has secured the affection as well as the admiration of the mass of the people by an act of munificence" by donating thousands of dollars to various groups, such as the Firemen's Fund for widows and orphans. When Lind went to Brady's studio for a daguerreotype, such a large crowd gathered that she had to sneak out on the Fulton Street side. But the fans learned of Lind's ruse and surrounded the carriage before she could finally get away.[16]

* * *

While New York brimmed with cultural life, much of the city's entertainment was restricted to white audiences. The majority of residents wanted nothing to do with Blacks. African Americans were demeaned, feared, hated, and attacked, and individuals and businesses routinely barred their access to most places. Journalist Thomas Nichols commented that, "The negro, though he might come to the theatre in his private carriage, and have money enough in [the] bank to buy the theater, could not get admission to boxes, or pit, not even to the third tier, set apart for fallen women." The Park Theatre segregated African American audiences, forcing them sit in "an obscure portion of a highest gallery"—a spot where, the New York–born Black actor Ira

Aldridge wrote, respectable Black citizens "are expected to herd with sweeps and pickpockets." The New York Zoological Institute went further, posting a sign, "The proprietors wish it to be understood, that PEOPLE OF COLOR are *not permitted to enter*, EXCEPT WHEN IN ATTENDANCE UPON CHILDREN AND FAMILIES." And Vauxhall Gardens simply wouldn't allow Blacks admittance.[17]

New York society was awash with unflattering characterizations of African Americans. And while in 1852, Purdy's National Theatre on the Bowery staged New York's first performance of *Uncle Tom's Cabin*—the novel that exposed the cruelty inflicted on Blacks and galvanized the abolition movement around the country—racist stereotypes were embraced. Barnum even presented a version of Harriet Beecher Stowe's novel with the abolitionist message removed and minstrel characters playing Blacks, causing the *Tribune* to note, "The effort of the dramatist has evidently been to destroy the point and moral of the story of Uncle Tom, and to make a play to which no apologist for Slavery could object."[18]

Although banned from trains, ferries, dance halls, billiard rooms, bowling alleys, and museums, Blacks found themselves regularly targeted. The performer who seared the negative image of Blacks into the public's consciousness was Thomas Dartmouth "Daddy" Rice. Born in New York, Rice was working in Louisville, Kentucky, when he heard a disabled Black stable hand singing "Jump Jim Crow." Rice "listened with delight to the negro's singing for several days," recalled the theatrical manager Noah Miller Ludlow, "and finally went to him and paid him to sing the song over to him until he had learned it." Rice started to perform the tune, and Hamblin booked him for the Bowery. There he appeared on November 12, 1832, and sang the song that included the lines:

> Weel about and turn about
> And do jis so,
> Eb'ry time I weel about
> I jump Jim Crow

Rice presented the tune complete with awkward movements which mimicked the Louisville man's gait. Rice's skit became so popular that whenever he appeared, audience members asked him to sing it, some even pressing onto the stage to get a closer look. Composer Stephen Foster noted how Jim Crow "was on everybody's tongue," a fact that annoyed Hone, who

complained how it "is made to repeat nightly, almost *ad infinitum*, his bal-
derdash song."[19]

"Jump Jim Crow" was far from the only such demeaning musical and theatrical presentation of African Americans. Dan Emmett—the composer of
"Dixie"—performed with the Virginia Minstrels and gaited across the stage
in what they called the Virginia Jungle Dance. George Stevens' 1834 play
The Patriot contained the character Sambo, who was a servant of George
Washington and did a Jim Crow–like dance. Performances by troupes such
as the Christy's Original Minstrels and the Ethiopian Serenaders were the
rage, all brimming with degrading references, cliché pantomiming, jokes,
and folklore, along with banjo and fiddle music and dancing. To prepare for
their parts, white actors darkened their faces, donned curly wigs, and spoke
in a cartoonish dialect.

Minstrels began to appear everywhere—at Barnum's Museum, Niblo's
Garden, the Park, Mitchell's Olympic Theatre, the Astor Place Opera House,
as well as in circuses. New Yorkers could see blackface versions of operas
such as at Buckley's Ethiopian Opera House, where they staged Bellini's *La
Sonnambula*, Gaetano Donizetti's *Lucia di Lammermoor*, and Daniel Auber's
Fra Diavolo. Future mayor Fernando Wood's brother Henry ran some of the
most successful minstrel shows. He and Jerome Fellowe started Wood and
Fellowe's Minstrels in 1851, and Wood afterward continued with Wood's
Minstrels. In 1852 the *New York Atlas* called Wood's "company of Ethiopian
delineators . . . the best musicians and combine the best comic talent ever
concentrated in one company." Wood soon joined his minstrels with George
Christy's, becoming Wood and Christy's Minstrels. There was so much of it
that Hone bemoaned, "The good is mixed up with the bad, Shakespeare and
Jim Crow come in equally for their share of condemnation, and the stage
is indiscriminately voted immoral, irreligious, and, what is much worse,
unfashionable."[20]

At the same time, one of the less obviously derogatory depictions of a Black
proved to be a sham. Barnum served as a perfect barometer for society's
views on race. For while he had started the abolitionist newspaper *Herald
of Freedom* in 1831, his thoughts on African Americans were not dissimilar
to those of his fellow citizens. In 1835 the 25-year-old Barnum learned of a
showman who owned a woman named Joice Heth, who he claimed was the
161-year-old nursemaid of young Washington. Barnum bought Heth and
ran ads, distributed pamphlets, and put up posters touting Heth as "the most
astonishing and interesting curiosity in the world!" To back up his claim,

he displayed a 1727 bill of sale for her. And while Heth could not see, had no teeth, and suffered from a paralyzed arm and legs, Barnum boasted how despite her frailty and shriveled frame, "She retains her faculties in an unparalleled degree, converses freely, sings numerous hymns, relates many interesting anecdotes of the boy Washington." Six hundred people attended the August 10 opening show at Niblo's, with some audience members touching Heth, and even taking her pulse.

And while people might have treated Heth, whom they saw as a link to the Founding Fathers with a degree of reverence, she received little dignity in death. Barnum used her February 1836 passing as a money-making venture. He invited physicians, clergy, the press, and the public to the City Saloon to witness Heth's autopsy. Fifteen hundred people paid the 50¢ entrance fee. At the end, the doctors determined that Heth was actually half her stated age. Barnum simply shrugged off the determination of the *Sun*, which called the hoax "one of the most precious humbugs that ever was imposed upon a credulous community." The revelation, though, gave the showman a chance to con Bennett. After the autopsy, Barnum and his assistant Levi Lyman visited the *Herald*'s office, where they convinced Bennett that Heth was still alive and living in Hebron, Connecticut. Figuring he had one-upped his competition, Bennett crowed that he had the true story, proudly reporting "*Joice Heth is not dead.*" He was therefore furious when he learned that he had been the one taken.[21]

Yet despite their treatment, music and dance were one of the few ways that African Americans could express themselves. The first introduction of "negro dancing" in the city took place at Catharine Market on the East River. Blacks, mainly slaves from Long Island, danced there on a board called a Shingle, while one of them made the music by "patting juba," keeping time and producing rhythms by clapping, beating his hands against his legs, and stamping his heels. The audience cheered on the best dancers, and performers collected donations and won eels or fish. African American fiddlers were popular at dances, and at the turn of the 19th century, dancing cellars appeared around town. Many, grouped around Bancker Street—current-day Duane Street—were run by Blacks and accommodated 30 to 40 customers, who came to eat, gamble, drink, and dance. One popular spot was the Black-owned Almack's Dance Hall on Orange Street, current-day Baxter Street, northeast of City Hall. Club owner Pete Williams ran the well-lit place, with its sanded whitewashed walls, simple stage, and waitresses who sang and danced. Charles Dickens ventured to Almack's in 1842. There he marveled at

William Henry Lane, also known as "Master Juba" and sometimes called "the greatest dancer known." The spot then became known as "Dickens' Place."

More serious fare could be found on Thomas Street starting in 1816, where William Brown—who had previously worked as a ship steward—opened a popular Black-only pleasure garden. In 1821 he set up the African Grove Theatre on Mercer Street. There Brown staged Shakespeare, and served liquor and ice cream. The theater had its detractors. While the house presented two of Mordecai Noah's plays, the *National Advocate* editor mocked the theater in his paper. And the theater's success bothered its white neighbors. The performers endured regular abuse. In August 1822, members of a circus attacked the actor James Hewlett and others and destroyed their furniture and scenery. The police then arrested the African American cast members. Soon after, the city shut it down, claiming that it caused civil disorder.[22]

* * *

While popular entertainments attracted massive crowds, there were few places to promote the fine arts. The American Academy of Fine Arts was founded in 1802, and was headed by the painter John Trumbull. John Vanderlyn's Rotunda on Chambers Street opened in 1818, and below its pantheon-shaped ceiling he exhibited his 3,000-square-foot panoramic views of the palace and gardens of Versailles. In October 1825, Rubens Peale opened his Peale's Museum & Gallery of the Fine Arts. In 1825, a group of artists and architects, which included Thomas Cole, Rembrandt Peale, Ithiel Town, and painter Asher B. Durand formed the New-York Drawing Association in order to promote the fine arts in America. They later changed its name to the National Academy of Design. Samuel Morse served as president, and the Academy's spring show became a major cultural event. In 1847, many flocked there to see Hiram Powers' marble sculpture, *The Greek Slave*. The provocative piece of art showed a nude white woman at a slave market at the time of the Greek Revolution from the Ottoman Empire in the 1820s and early '30s. Besides becoming one of the most famous sculptures of its day, it was also seen as quite scandalous. Men and women were admitted to separate viewings, and abolitionists would latch onto its symbolism in their fight to abolish slavery.

Other places started to display work. The artist George Catlin first headed out west in 1830 to paint the Native American tribes, and in 1837 exhibited his portraits and landscapes in New York. In 1838 the engraver and portraitist James Herring established the Apollo Gallery on Broadway near

Canal Street, charging 25¢ for admission. In December 1839, Hone viewed on Broadway a collection of daguerreotype images being shown by the Frenchman François Gouraud. He found them to be "one of the wonders of modern times." By 1846, Edward Ruggles reported how the city could boast of more than 300 artists doing portrait, miniature, landscape, and historical paintings. When the Hudson River School painter Frederic Church exhibited his grand painting *Niagara* in 1857, more than 100,000 people came to see it.

The town had numerous galleries where the wealthy could buy new works as well as older pieces. German émigré Michael Paff opened the city's first art gallery and ran his business for a number of years across from the City Hall Park, offering paintings, etchings, engravings, and medals, including works claimed to be by Rembrandt, Titian, and Michelangelo. Those who couldn't afford original artworks could pick up Nathaniel Currier and James Merritt Ives' hand-colored lithographs of images of everything from Broadway streetscapes to important buildings around town.[23]

Others sought to support the arts and offered commissions to painters and sculptors. Artists and architects traveled to Europe to look and learn. Morse sailed over in 1829 with the financial help of wealthy patrons (including Hone). Robert Ball Hughes was asked to make a sculpture of Governor DeWitt Clinton for the front of Clinton Hall, and a few years later completed his ill-fated sculpture of Alexander Hamilton for the Merchants' Exchange. Many made a living on commissions. William Sidney Mount painted a portrait of George Washington Strong. Thomas Crawford created a bust of Hone's daughter Mary. So did John T. Battin, of which Hone commented, "the likeness is so striking that I could spend half my time in gazing upon it." Daniel Huntington painted Hone, as did John Wesley Jarvis. John Henri Isaac Browere fashioned a plaster sculpture of him. And William Astor, James King, Moses Grinnell, and others had Shobal Vail Clevenger—who had started his career as a stone mason in Ohio and was encouraged by Hiram Powers to become a professional sculptor—create a bust of Hone for the Mercantile Library, which Powers then completed after Clevenger's 1843 death.[24]

Hone started to form his own art collection in the early 1820s, with the *New York Evening Post* commenting how, "Mr. Hone is no collector of old pictures . . . . He encourages painters, by employing the meritorious." Banker Samuel Ward collected paintings, including Thomas Cole's "The Voyage of Life" series, and the architect Alexander Jackson Davis created for him a marble-clad art gallery to the side of his Bond Street home.

Produce merchant Luman Reed began collecting around 1830, and set his paintings in a gallery on the third floor of his house so people could visit. It included Cole's monumental painting cycle "The Course of Empire," as well as works from Flemish, Dutch, Italian, German, Scottish, and English artists. Importer and commission merchant William Aspinwall amassed works purported to be by Leonardo, Titian, and Pontormo, and also had pieces by Thomas Gainsborough, Thomas Lawrence, and Gilbert Stuart. Architect James Renwick designed a gallery for him to show it off.[25]

To make art more accessible, the Apollo Association for the Promotion of the Fine Arts in the United States began a subscription system in 1839 to purchase artwork which people could then acquire. Called the American Art-Union, it was run by Hone and others, and by the late 1840s numbered 19,000 subscribers and had become a main market for portrait painting. The Apollo's lottery, which awarded a lucky winner a work of art, raised a lot of money, though the association shut down soon after a ban on lotteries went into effect.

Large-scale paintings, as with Vanderlyn's views of Versailles at the Rotunda, were very popular in the early 19th century, and Henry and William Hanington, who did the rendition of the Great Fire at Scudder's American Museum in March 1836, attracted crowds with their massive paintings. In 1837 their Dioramic Institute at the City Saloon offered a "faithful representation" of the "Shipwreck of the Mexico," as well as an animated view near Plymouth, England, an East Indian Scene, Fall of the Angels, the Celestial Regions, a Naval Battle, a Storm and Shipwreck, and the cathedral of Cologne. Two years later their new Grand Moving Dioramas depicted the Israelites fleeing Egypt, along with views of the pyramids.[26]

While New York was keenly aware of its rising stature, it was equally aware of cultural goings-on in Europe. City fathers enviously watched the success of London's Great Exhibition of 1851—the first world's fair—with its glass-and-iron miracle, the Crystal Palace pavilion. Determined not to be outdone and to tout its own cultural arrival, New York State chartered the Association for the Exhibition of the Industry of All Nations to create their own pavilion, indeed their own Crystal Palace, and chose a design by architects Charles Gildemeister and Georg J.B. Carstensen. The structure, with its 365-foot-long galleries, was shaped like a Greek Cross and topped by a 123-feet-high dome. Made up of 1,800 tons of iron with 15,000 panes of glass, it rose on Reservoir Square on 42nd Street behind the Murray Hill Distributing Reservoir (and what is today the New York Public Library). President Franklin Pierce opened it in July 1853.

A grand equestrian statue of Washington stood below the dome, and like its British counterpart, which was packed with such innovations as hydraulic presses, adding machines, cotton spinning machines, and steam engines, there were displays of both American and foreign products. Americans, and New Yorkers in particular, flocked to see the gathered marvels of modern engineering, industry, and society, and men, women, children, militia, and fire companies roamed though halls filled with fountains, clocks, carriages, quilts, giant squashes, pianos, diamonds, pickles, steam engines, vases, Japanese pottery, terra cotta statues, marble busts, and paintings. That summer, Samuel Clemens, who would become famous as Mark Twain, visited and pronounced it to be "a perfect fairy palace—beautiful beyond description." Ellen and George Templeton Strong went in September, and Strong reported, "The interior lit up is undeniably very imposing and splendid." Whitman visited so often that the suspicious staff had detectives follow him.[27]

Other attractions popped up in the area of the Crystal Palace, from saloons, galleries with mechanized wax figures, and a merry-go-round, to a show displaying a moving panorama of Mount Vesuvius. George Foster commented how the neighborhood had an "accumulation of coffee houses, grog-shops, 'saloons,' peep-shows of living alligators, model-artists and three-headed calves." Waring Latting's Observatory—a 315-foot-tall wooden tower on 42nd Street next to the fairgrounds—contained an art gallery and ice cream parlor, and had a "Heaven-kissing peak" at the top.

While the Crystal Palace was grand and awe-inspiring—Barnum even had a go at running it—the fair failed financially. Then on October 5, 1858, while 3,000 people milled around inside, a fire broke out. Despite the building having eight hydrants, its pitch pine flooring and framework allowed the flames to spread quickly and fill the space with hot, suffocating smoke. Strong, who ran up to see the blaze, said it "burned up like a pile of shavings." As panicked visitors fled, those overseeing displays, like the clerks at Tiffany's, gathered up what they could, and others grabbed all they could pilfer. Twenty-five minutes after it started, the dome collapsed, and within 40 minutes all that remained of the building was a twisted mass of iron and melted glass.[28]

Panic and Promise

Following the Bowery Theatre's second fire in late 1836, and having to contend with the criminal case against him for attacking *New York Herald* editor James Gordon Bennett, Thomas Hamblin leased the theater to William Dinneford and then sailed to England. Dinneford hired Calvin Pollard to design a new structure. The builder-turned-architect, who a year earlier had won the commission to create the Brooklyn City Hall, fashioned a theater eight feet taller than the one designed in 1828 by Joseph Sera. And because of the Bowery's flammable history, he outfitted it with water tanks. This theater had a grand stair to the entry and four fluted Corinthian columns. Inside were Italianate ornamental paintings, which, as with the previous theater, included images of Apollo and the Muses.

The new Bowery reopened on January 2, 1837, with performances of *Rent Day*, *The Waterman*, and *Charles II*. Two weeks later, playwright Louisa Medina's timely new play, *The Burning of the Bowery*, premiered. Hamblin quite possibly had ended his relationship with Medina at this point, having her write for the recently widowed Dinneford. She likely felt abandoned by the theater owner and portrayed him in her play as drunk. Bennett, for one, agreed that it was good to do a play on Hamblin, though he felt that Medina's script should have delved into all Hamblin's faults and presented him "in his own, real, unadulterated character . . . Represent him breaking asunder all the sacred ties of social life." Hamblin didn't return for the new theater's unveiling, Medina's new play, or Bennett's latest attack. He also blithely skipped his trial. Though in late February the court found him guilty of assault, battery, and riot, it fined him only court costs. Bennett immediately announced a $10,000 suit "against the Hamblin gang."[1]

At the time of the Bowery's opening, the city and the nation seemed just as unsettled as the disaster-prone theater. The economy was overheating and buffeted by a combination of President Andrew Jackson's war on the Second Bank of the United States, rabid speculation, an unfettered economic boom, and wildly expanding trade. Jackson had opposed the idea of easy credit, and had tried in 1833 to rein in growth by transferring federal funds from the Second Bank to state institutions. The nation lacked a uniform currency, and local and state-chartered banks could print their own bills. With limited regulations, loans increased, and banks raised the number of notes in circulation, nearly tripling the amount from $48 million in 1828 to $149 million in 1836. At the same time, the sale of government lands grew from $2.5 million in 1832 to $25 million in 1836, much of the property bought by speculators with borrowed cash. Even congressmen and cabinet officers took part in the speculation. Some went further. Samuel Swartwout, Jackson's collector of customs at New York, absconded with $1,225,000 in government funds— a colossal amount of money—left for England, and was never prosecuted. Then, while Congress was on recess, Jackson issued his Specie Circular, directing government land offices to only accept silver or gold in the hope of stopping the spread of paper money.

This helped send the economy into a tailspin. Because of this turmoil, Philip Hone welcomed the end of Jackson's administration, which he called, "the most disastrous in the annals of the country." While he differed with the politics of new president Martin Van Buren, Hone considered the upstate New York politician and Jackson vice-president a friend, and someone who "is too much of a gentleman to be governed by the rabble who surrounded his predecessor and administered to his bad passions."[2]

Despite the good will of Hone and others toward Van Buren, ill tidings about the economy greeted his presidency just as it was about to begin. In early 1837, rumors swirled in New York that local flour merchants had been hoarding goods and raising prices. In response, a notice appeared around town:

> Bread, Meat, Rent, Fuel!
> Their Prices Must Come Down!
> The Voice of the People shall be Heard, and Will Prevail!

Then, on February 13, more than 10,000 people braved freezing gales to listen to speakers in City Hall Park denounce landlords and the high cost of fuel, food, and rent. The crowd railed against merchants like Eli Hart, with one of the speakers provoking them to action: "Fellow-citizens! Mr. Hart has now fifty-three thousand barrels of flour in his store: let us go and offer him eight dollars a barrel." A cry went out, "To Hart's flour store!" The crowd, which George Templeton Strong wrote had "the usual discretion of all mobs," swarmed to Eli Hart and Company. They ripped off one door and used it to batter in the others. Once inside, they tossed out hundreds of barrels of flour. Protesters then smashed those barrels that didn't break from the fall. Flour swirled in the air, and mixed with the wheat blanketing Washington Street. Women filled baskets while boys shoveled the powder into sacks. When the police arrived, the mob stoned the officers and chanted, "bread, bread, bread." The crowd then moved en masse to Meech & Co. on Coenties Slip, first stopping at S.H. Herrick & Son's store, where they heaved brickbats through windows and rolled out 20 to 30 barrels. When the police and militia arrived, they arrested 30 to 40 protesters.[3]

The city remained tense, a mood that was not helped when on the morning of March 13 a row of new brick warehouses on Fulton Street collapsed. The builder Seth Geer had subcontracted the masonry, and the work done in the cold weather did not hold. Then the following morning, a building under construction on Wall Street and Exchange Place for the banking house of J. L. & S. Joseph & Co. "came down with a crash like that of an earthquake," wrote Hone. As with the Fulton Street buildings, it had been badly constructed, and its brick arches couldn't support the floors, pushing out the thin exterior walls and bringing the structure down.

In all this economic uncertainty, the Bank of England—the world's most powerful financial institution—decided to raise its discount rate. Credit contracted, and British merchants cut back on cotton purchases. The price of cotton dropped by nearly half. News then arrived that several New Orleans commercial cotton houses had defaulted on millions in loans. By the morning of March 17, "word was passed from street to street, and from counting room to counting room, that the firm of J. L. & S. Joseph & Co. had stopped payment, in consequence of the failures in New Orleans," reported the New York *Commercial Advertiser*. Hone feared that "the great crisis is near at hand."

The shock from the collapse of the cotton market rippled through New York's economy. The flow of capital slackened, and European creditors demanded that American businesses pay what they owed. Like J. L. & S. Joseph's ill-fated building, the United States economy possessed weak supports. Panic spread, with the *Morning Courier and New-York Enquirer* observing that, "The distress is rapidly extending itself from the merchant to the *laborer*." Strong wrote on April 12, "Terrible lot of failures today, Mr. Hull and Abraham Ogden among them. Awful bad times. The merchants going to the devil *en masse*."[4]

In hindsight, signs of the looming crash and the arrival of a depression called the Panic of 1837 were clear, with Hone writing how "the business of the last six months has been perfect madness." The time leading up to the Panic had been hard for Hone, and saw the start of personal financial problems that would plague him until his death. Rumors circulated that he was insolvent. On April 22, Strong reported on Hone's financial turmoil, writing, "Philip Hone has gone to the d---l, figuratively speaking, having lost pretty much everything by his son, by Schenck & Co. (of Matteawan factory) and by some speculation moreover, all of which have eased him out of not much below $200,000."

Hone was not alone. Credit contraction brought financial terror for many, further fueled by years of crop failures. As the panic spread, Strong noted on April 27, "Ruin here, and on the other side of the Atlantic." Concerned that the whole system might come apart, the heads of such firms as Snelling, Strong & Co., Arthur L. Levy, J.D. Disosway & Brothers, and William Delano attended a meeting of merchants at the Masonic Hall to discuss the faltering economy. Hone chaired the gathering, with the *Courier and Enquirer* reporting that "a petition was presented from a large number of operators asking employment, and declaring that they are without the *common necessaries of life!*"[5]

Petitions did little to quell the panic. Banks called in loans, as crowds swarmed there to demand money. On May 6 Strong wrote of a run on his uncle Benjamin's Dry Dock Bank, and feared "utter ruin" for him. By the 9th, customers emptied Manhattan banks of $652,000 in gold and silver coins. Hone served as a trustee for the Bank for Savings and witnessed one such bank run: "The press was awful," he wrote. So many people demanded their money that cashiers ran out of cash. The day after the run, banks stopped redeeming paper for gold or silver. Forty percent of U.S. banks closed. The stock market plummeted.[6]

The economic shock destroyed the small and the big. Hone's son John's firm, Brown & Hone, did not last. It could no longer cover payments, thus making Hone personally accountable, since he had underwritten the business and stood liable "to a fearful amount." Despite weathering the Great Fire two years earlier, Arthur Tappan's business had been severely affected. He had also lost southern business because of his anti-slavery stance. Then, on May 1, the silk merchant couldn't meet his British creditors' demands, causing Strong to exclaim, "Arthur Tappan has failed!" The merchant suspended payments, and it soon came out that his silk business owed more than $1 million. While the *Commercial Advertiser* reported 260 "heavy suspensions" since March, not including the demise of smaller business, the fall of the House of Tappan rattled New York's business community, and made clear the truly precarious state of the economy.

Because of his good financial reputation, Tappan's creditors allowed him to keep working, though they charged him an exorbitant 25 percent to 30 percent interest. To deal with the downturn, Tappan slashed expenses, moved into a boarding house, and cut his aid to worthy causes. That spring his brother Lewis headed to Philadelphia to see Nicholas Biddle of the Second Bank of the United States, who offered the firm a $150,000 loan. It took Arthur Tappan 18 months to repay all his outstanding debts. His silk business, though, never flourished again.[7]

* * *

With the Panic of 1837, a decade of prosperity came to an abrupt standstill. "A deadly calm pervades this lately flourishing city," wrote Hone in late May. "No goods are selling, no business stirring, no boxes encumber the sidewalks of Pearl Street." The real estate boom ended. Development ceased. Land, which was valued at $233.7 million in 1836, dropped to $196.5 million in 1837 and $104.5 million in 1838. In 1838 a bargain-hunting John Jacob Astor went on a buying spree. Others also saw opportunities in the turmoil. August Belmont, who worked for the House of Rothschild, happened to be passing through New York on his way to check on the firm's interests in Cuba. The Rothschild's American agents were not in town, and Belmont seized the opportunity and formed August Belmont and Company. Then, with his bosses' approval and credit, he started picking up banknotes and commodities as well as inexpensive building lots. Jacob Little, who would earn the nickname "the Great Bear of Wall Street," also did well during the Panic, and Cornelius Van Shaack Roosevelt snapped up land all over Manhattan.[8]

The crash hit workers especially hard. That spring of 1837, a third of all New Yorkers lacked work, and more than half struggled. Some who lost their homes camped on the streets and panhandled outside of oyster houses. Money proved dear, so businesses handed out chits in place of cash. "Go to the theatres and places of public amusement, and, instead of change, you receive an I.O.U.," observed the visiting English novelist Frederick Marryat. "At the hotels and oyster-cellars it is the same thing. Call for a glass of brandy and water and the change is fifteen tickets, each 'good for one glass of brandy and water.' At an oyster-shop, eat a plate of oysters and you have in return seven tickets, good for one plate of oysters each. It is the same every where." The *Courier and Enquirer* commented sarcastically on "humble endeavors" to provide a better currency, listing assorted notes in circulation, pointing out that restaurateur Thomas Downing "has on the reverse, drawn with a pen— we supposed to prevent counterfeits—a likeness of Gen. Jackson, a ship, and something else which we were not able exactly to make out, though we believe it is a hog." Other notes included: "The bearer will be entitled to 50 cents value in refreshments at the Auction Hotel."[9]

Hone was stunned at how, despite the dire state of the economy, people continued to flock to the theater, commenting in September how "It is almost incredible that in these times of distress, when the study of economy is so great an object, there should be nine of these money drains in operation." Even so, places like the Bowery still struggled. Hamblin returned to the United States in June 1837, reassumed control of the theater, heavily promoted the house, and soon after paid Bennett $1,150 to settle his lawsuit. He also reunited with Medina and premiered her *Nick of the Woods* at the beginning of February 1838. The show was a success. Then on the 18th, a fire broke out in the carpenter's shop and destroyed the theater a third time, taking with it nearby homes, a porterhouse, oyster restaurant, and tailor shop. It also shot cinders across the street to Hamblin's stable, setting it ablaze and killing Thomas Francis, an African American who worked there, as well as five horses.

Unbowed, Hamblin rebuilt yet again, using Calvin Pollard's Greek design for the previous structure. Containing four tiers, the new theater had ornamental paintings by Henry Liebenau, the theater's scene painter. The house reopened on May 6, 1839. Walt Whitman called the theater "one of the best looking buildings in the city." Hamblin worked hard to attract famous theatergoers. That July, President Van Buren visited and watched *The Honeymoon* and *The Lion King*.

Despite the house's success, Hamblin's personal life was still a mess, and Bennett continued to needle him in his paper, with the editor writing in August 1837 how "Poor Tom Hamblin is incorrigible," and that any "wholesome instruction" has had "no more effect upon him than the wasting of so much seed in a desert." Then, Louisa Missouri died in Boston in June 1838. Medina was rumored to have poisoned her. A coroner's jury, though, determined that the actress's death resulted from "an inflammation of the brain, caused by great mental excitement," which could have been meningitis. To repair his image, Hamblin became an American citizen that July. Medina then died of apoplexy that November at age 25. In 1840, the actress Eliza Mary Ann Trewar Shaw moved in with Hamblin. Edgar Allan Poe called her "the best actress in America." The couple would have five children. And after Hamblin's ex-wife Elizabeth died in 1849, Shaw would take to the stage as "Mrs. Hamblin."[10]

It was tough going for Hamblin and the Bowery, just as it was for all Americans and the national economy. Congress repealed Jackson's Specie Circular in May 1838. While public land could now be bought with paper money, the damage had been done. During the depression, canal building plummeted by 90 percent, and the construction of railroads dropped by two-thirds. While still worth $150,000, Hone felt overwhelmed by debt. He soon saw a slight betterment of his own finances, mainly thanks to good mortgage rates. A brief recovery began, then a second Panic set in in 1839. More contraction followed, resulting in a long and painful four-year depression during which Hone noted that "money [was] uncome-at-able, and confidence at an end."[11]

A barometer of the economy was, of course, real estate. While land values had risen back to $196.9 million in 1839, they dropped to $187.2 the following year. That March the Bowling Green mansion of Mrs. E. White went for a mere $15,000, a sale that Hone called "the saddest proof of the fall in real estate." Then in November 1840, Nathaniel Prime, a pillar of moneyed New York and one of the founders of the house of Prime, Ward & Co., committed suicide. The Second Bank of the United States ceased operations during the summer of 1841, with the New York Evening Post writing that it "Departed this life . . . after a lingering illness." And "as the deceased is known never to have had a soul, no clergyman will be in attendance." While the new Merchants' Exchange opened at this time, it soon defaulted on interest payments. Hone unfortunately had invested $2,500 in it. Thankfully, English bankers saved the place.

While financial woes beset Hone, many appreciated his desire to properly pay his debts. Long a friend and political advisor to many city, state, and federal leaders—from John Quincy Adams and Henry Clay to Daniel Webster—Hone hoped for a federal posting. In 1841, talk spread around New York that President William Henry Harrison would give him a spot in the office of postmaster of the city. Harrison died just a month after taking office, however, and the position never materialized. Then that June, one of Hone's Matteawan mills in Dutchess County burned, destroying a new building and thousands of dollars in machinery as well as throwing 300 people out of work. In July, Hone thankfully secured the position as president of the Bank for Savings. But it was still tough going. As the recession stretched on, Hone made less on rents, writing how in February 1843, "Rents are fifty per cent lower and taxes fifty per cent higher."[12]

* * *

Seeing the state of the economy, Lewis Tappan sought to exit his brother's silk business. As a businessman, he had long understood the importance of knowing about a customer's finances before extending credit. Jobbers and merchants trusted his opinion, and routinely sought his and Arthur's opinions on various businessmen. Stores required visiting merchants to supply letters from lawyers, bankers, and others attesting to their financial worthiness. Yet it was often difficult to figure out who would pay their bills. To solve the problem, Tappan came up with the idea of a central credit-checking service linked to a network of informants who gathered background information. Businessmen, he figured, would pay for such reliable intelligence. "In prosperous times they will feel able to pay for the information," he wrote, "and in bad times they feel they must have it."

In 1841, Tappan founded the Mercantile Agency, the nation's first credit-rating service. He set up his office opposite the Merchants' Exchange and hired people to gather the findings, often those he felt more comfortable with who conformed to his views. Yet the sluggishness of the economy initially made it difficult to attract customers. And since the business proved quite novel, many did not understand let alone trust such a company, with some merchants believing that the agency simply conspired against them.[13]

Tappan's reputation for inflexibility and intolerance didn't help, and he had trouble doing business with those who objected to his religious and social stands. His position on slavery was well known, making it especially hard to find southern clients. Edward Dunbar, an early colleague, noted of "the great prejudice, which existed against him in all directions, on account of his abolitionism." Not surprisingly, years of expounding on unpopular social causes brought powerful enemies. Local papers showed little sympathy for Tappan's venture. *Courier and Enquirer* editor James Watson Webb reprinted a piece from Norfolk, Virginia, claiming that an attorney there had publicly declined an offer from Tappan "to act as a spy." Webb called Tappan's new agency a "new clap-trap of notoriety . . . carrying on the business of a secret inquiry into the private affairs and personal standing of every body buying goods in New York." Tappan had become used to such attacks, having weathered the backlash during the Postal Campaign in 1835, when he and other abolitionists flooded the South with anti-slavery material.[14]

By August 1841, Tappan claimed 133 clients. Most ran dry goods, grocery, or crockery businesses. Subscribers paid a yearly fee, and agents sent Tappan twice-yearly write-ups on the character, liquidity, and worth of local businesses, likewise alerting the main office to problems. Others began to realize the value of Tappan's services—that paying him was a wise investment—and signed on. The good idea did not go unnoticed. Competitors appeared in 1842 offering something that Tappan lacked—southern coverage. As the economy started to improve in 1844, Tappan ventured into that region and soon arranged for southern correspondents to dispatch reports to a colleague so they would not be embarrassed sending them to the self-proclaimed abolitionist. By 1846, the Mercantile Agency had some 700 correspondents scattered around the country, and Lewis brought in Arthur as a partner. The business turned out to be a great success. Lewis left the firm at the end of the decade, and Arthur stayed until he was bought out in 1854. In 1859, Robert Graham Dun took over the agency, and the firm was eventually renamed Dun & Bradstreet.[15]

The economy finally started to revive when British credit was loosened, and European nations sought American crops following their local agricultural failures. Hone's finances likewise became more secure. His mill (located up the Hudson) was rebuilt, and at the start of 1844 he wrote, "Trade is returning into its own channels, commerce reviving, and confidence gaining strength." He especially appreciated the success of the Delaware & Hudson coal mine, which produced 1.2 million tons the previous year, turning it into the largest private corporation in the nation.[16]

* * *

One thing that constantly replenished the city's economy was the arrival of immigrants—as an example, Alexander Turney Stewart, the son of Scotch-Irish parents. Stewart was born in Lisburn, Ireland, on October 12, 1803. His father died soon afterward, and his mother, Margaret, remarried and came to the United States. Raised on his grandparents' farm, Stewart studied classics at the Belfast Academical Institute. With $500 and money from his grandfather's estate, he headed to New York in the spring of 1818. Once in the city he moved in with his mother and tutored at Isaac N. Bragg's academy on Roosevelt Street.[17]

Stewart dreamed of opening a dry goods firm, and during the winter of 1822–23 sailed back to Ireland and bought assorted Irish linens, laces, and dress trimmings. Then, on September 1, 1823, the 19-year-old Stewart opened a shop at 283 Broadway, just north of City Hall Park and Astor and Hone's homes in the then-fashionable residential part of town. This was far from the center of the traditional dry goods trade area, which was, as we've seen, on Pearl Street. But on that late summer day, the young merchant ran an ad in the New York *Daily Advertiser* to alert readers of his "New Dry Goods Store." There customers would find "wholesale and retail, a general assortment of fresh and seasonable DRY GOODS; a choice assortment of Irish Linens, Lawns, French Cambrics, Damasks, Diaper." Stewart went on to describe how the goods "will be sold on reasonable terms."[18]

It proved to be an inauspicious start in a small, $375-a-year shop, with a large front room and walls so thin that Stewart could hear his neighbors. In fact, after placing that ad, Stewart started a practice of not hanging a sign out front with the belief that those who wanted to buy from him knew the location of his shop. He worked 14 to 18 hours a day, and acted as the store's salesman, bookkeeper, and stock clerk. For a new businessman, credit could be especially hard to come by, so Stewart preferred to buy what he had money for. After establishing his business, he stopped by Arthur Tappan's store to purchase some goods. "Tappan had just received a small invoice of silks, which he had imported," recalled merchant Nathaniel Hubbard. "Mr. Stewart . . . took from the case what he had paid for on account, and . . . called in a day or two and paid the balance due and took the remainder of the silk." Stewart also bought for cash at auctions, thus earning a tidy 2 percent discount, and sought out "sample lots," small and less expensive assorted goods. He had married Cornelia Mitchell Clinch, the daughter of a ship chandler, soon after opening the shop. At night in their home, the couple went through the heaped-together lots. The goods were not always of the best quality, and they redressed and smoothed out gloves and pressed lace. Stewart then neatly arranged them on the shop's shelves, offering them for low fixed prices that he would not deviate from.[19]

Business did not always run smoothly. About two years after Stewart opened his shop, he had a large note due. Lacking the cash to pay it, the merchant took a chance, blanketing the city with handbills to let people know that he was offering his entire stock below wholesale prices. Soon "the little shop was crowded with suspicious and half-believing persons in search of bargains," wrote the journalist Matthew Smith. Stewart quickly sold out and was able to pay what he owed. With the money left over, he bought new supplies.

As the business grew, he hired clerks. In the 1820s and 1830s it was an accepted practice to pay higher wages to those who brought in the most profits. To do this, clerks sometimes switched cheaper goods for more expensive merchandise. Stewart wanted none of this. He believed that being straightforward with customers was not only the right thing to do, but good for business. Merchant Richard Lathers recalled how Stewart once overheard a salesman "inform an old lady that the calico there before them cost twenty-five cents a yard, but that he would sell it to her at twenty cents. Pleased with the reduction, the old lady purchased the dress pattern and retired." Stewart told the salesman, who argued that this was common practice, never to do it again.

As Stewart's reputation and business grew, he moved to a new and larger store on Broadway between Chambers and Warren Streets. When his business outgrew that, he moved to a yet bigger Astor-built building at 257 Broadway, between Murray and Warren Streets.[20] Like Tappan, Stewart avoided outlandish claims. He took seriously his motto, "Ten per cent and no lies!" Customers liked the one-price policy. And to keep good relations with his clientele, Stewart would often add something extra to their purchase, such as a ribbon. He also allowed returns and gave reasonable cash refunds. And at the end of the season, he slashed prices to clear off his shelves, an uncommon policy back when dry goods merchants who refused to part with an item for less than they paid lived by the axiom, "Sell and repent!"

Ever attuned to the needs of his customers, Stewart instituted an "open door" policy, whereby customers were left alone to browse. Most stores practiced the "closed door" approach, and a staff member always followed the customer. "The farmers soon came to know that when they made their periodic visits to the city, they could buy all the finery which their wives and daughters wanted, without the slightest fear of having their innocence imposed upon," wrote *Chambers's Journal*. "The Irish servant-girl . . . was satisfied that when she entered Stewart's store she would get the value of her money as well as if she were a lady." Business grew, and Stewart became an American citizen in November 1834.

There was money to be made in the expanding field of dry goods. In 1818 Henry Brooks had started a men's clothes store on Cherry Streets. His sons took it over after his death in 1833, and it became Brooks Brothers. In 1825 Aaron Arnold, who had immigrated from England, opened a store on Pine Street. There he sold English and Asian silks, woolens, shawls, and lace, taking on his British countryman James Constable as a partner in 1842 and forming Arnold Constable. In 1826, the British-born Samuel Lord and George Washington Taylor started their Lord & Taylor shop and sold silks, shawls, and hosiery. As businesses catered to the needs of women, clothes fueled New York's economy. "Broadway might be taken for a French street, where it was the fashion for very smart ladies to promenade," observed English novelist Frances Trollope. "The dress is entirely French; not an article (except perhaps the cotton stockings) must be English, on pain of being stigmatized as out of the fashion."[21]

* * *

A number of entrepreneurs and inventors meanwhile tried out new ideas, hoping that they might turn a profit. Samuel F. B. Morse came up with a way to transmit electrical signals in order to communicate over long distances. In January 1838, from his space in New York University's Washington Square building, he gave a private demonstration of his telegraph, sending the message: "Attention the Universe by kingdoms right wheel."

In the post–Great Fire era particularly, insurance proved be a good investment. The amount of life insurance increased 16 times from 1840 to 1860. Astor's brother Henry had been director of the Mechanics Insurance Company, and in the early 1830s Astor, Hone, and others became stockholders in the newly incorporated New York Life Insurance and Trust Company. Like Hone, John Jacob Astor saw a business opportunity and invested in fire insurance companies. Hone, as we've seen, was involved with the Eagle Fire Company. His brother John sat on the insurance firm's board in 1808, and Philip joined in 1811, serving there for three decades. Hone was also the first and last president of the American Mutual Insurance Company, which he helped organize in 1843. Trustees included Strong's uncle Benjamin. Fireman Morris Franklin and some friends bought stock in the Nautilus Life Insurance Company in 1841. Eight years later the firm renamed itself the New York Life Insurance Company. The growth of such insurance and banking firms helped law offices like Strong's firm, Strong, Bidwell & Strong, count as clients the Bank of America, the Neptune Insurance Company, the Seamen's Bank for Savings, and the Merchants' Exchange Company.

Meanwhile, of course, New York's rivers brought in and dispatched shiploads of goods. Throughout the 1830s, steamboats crowded the Hudson, cruising north to places like Albany and Troy. Ferries carried passengers.

Cornelius Vanderbilt had started his own ferry business at 16, and soon became one of the most successful ferry owners, running lines across and up the Hudson and between New York, the South, and New England. New York's waterfront was a bustling place of business, as ships arrived from Europe, Asia, and South America. Fishing skiffs, packet ships, ferries, barks, and tugboats skimmed the water, carrying people and goods from far and wide. In 1860 Whitman would write of "The countless masts, the white shore-steamers, the lighters, the ferry-boats, the black sea-steamers well-model'd." Vessels lined the shorelines as masts, furled sails, and spider webbing of riggings cast shadows on both the Hudson and the East River shorelines. "From this point up," wrote author Nathaniel Parker Willis of a stretch along the Hudson, "extends a line of ships, rubbing against the pier the fearless noses that have nudged the poles and the tropics, and been breathed on by spice islands and icebergs." These ships brought so many goods that throughout the day, workers guided drays and carts from waterway piers and down streets to businesses.[22]

By 1840, New York had 417 commercial houses dealing with trade between Europe, Asia, and Latin America, and 918 for domestic goods. The prosperous China trade, which Astor got out of in the mid-1830s, as we've seen, was big business. Merchants shipped furs and opium to China, and they returned with silk, tea, and porcelain. When the future Central Park designer and architect Frederick Law Olmsted first arrived in town in August 1840 from Hartford at the age of 18, he found work as an apprentice clerk at Benkard & Hutton. Part of his job included boarding ships for his dry goods and French silk importer to take inventory. He wrote his brother John, "The business is such that I am engaged from morning to night without ceasing." He soon tired of the work, and in 1843 decided to set out on a Pacific adventure. He shipped out on the *Ronaldson*, a bark belonging to the tea importer Gordon & Talbot. The 20-week trip to Canton turned out to be anything but an adventure. For $12 a month, Olmsted scrubbed decks, manned the watch, tarred the rigging, and got seasick. Fortunately for Olmsted, the captain learned that the young man could draw, made him a clerk, and had him copy sea charts. Once the *Ronaldson* unloaded its cargo in Canton, the crew waited for their tea shipment. Unfortunately, Olmsted contracted typhoid and only briefly saw the port city before returning home and starting a new career altogether.[23]

As trade grew, new wharves stretched out, and more ships streamed in. In 1853 over 4,000 ships arrived in New York, and by 1860 the city's ports commanded three-quarters of America's ocean steam tonnage. New York's main mercantile and shipping houses made a brisk business trading with all parts of the world. Hone's friends, brothers Gardiner and Samuel Howland, founded one of the biggest, G.G. & S.S. Howland. Their nephew, William Aspinwall, joined the firm as a clerk and became a partner in 1832, after which the elder Howlands retired. The firm now known as Howland & Aspinwall carried on extensive trade in Europe and Hong Kong and Canton, but specialized in Latin America and West Indies trade.[24]

All this business meant that ships were needed. The ring of water around the island made it a natural place to construct vessels, and by the time of the Great Fire, Manhattan had developed into the nation's largest shipbuilder. Much of the work occurred on the East River, which proved more condu-cive to shipbuilding than the Hudson. The river—actually a tidal estuary—connects the bay and the Long Island Sound. The waterway is protected from prevailing westerly winds, and there it was easier for sailing ships to get un-derway. And unlike the Hudson, the shallower East River is not as beset by ice floes.

Shipyards sprung up along the shores, their sites stretching for a mile from Corlear's Hook—which juts into the East River just south of where the Williamsburg Bridge now touches Manhattan—to 13th Street. The smell of tar and pitch filled the air, and the builders were surrounded by assorted sail makers, blacksmiths, and machine-engine manufacturers. The city's loca-tion likewise was ideal for getting ship timber, with wood coming down the Hudson from upstate New York, and up from New Jersey, as well as brought in by canals from the hinterlands: red cedar and locust from the Chesapeake Bay, pitch pine from the Carolinas and Georgia, and live oak from Georgia and Florida.

Steamers and large ships could take a few years to build, and crafts in var-ious stages of completion filled yards, from packets, pilot boats, and clippers, as well as schooners, periaugers—a shallow-drafted boat that was well suited for smaller waterways—side-wheel steamers, two-masted brigs, three- or more-masted barks, and warships. Some of the main yards were William H. Webb, Jacob A. Westervelt, Brown & Bell, and Smith & Dimon. Smith & Dimon, whose shipyard was on 4th Street, built packet ships, steamboats, and the Greek frigate *Liberator*. In 1833 they completed the brig *Philip Hone* for G.G. & S.S. Howland. Christened on July 6, the *Courier and Enquirer* noted that the square rigger had both a "handsome cabin and steerage accommodations," and it set sail on August 6. The ship focused on the firm's South America trade. In 1836 it sailed from New York to Valparaíso, Chile, stopping in Rio de Janeiro, Brazil, and Lima, Peru, carrying such assorted goods as 150 bales of paper shipped by Brown, Brothers &. Co., two cases of machinery from Thomas Irvin & Co., with Howland & Aspinwall sending out everything from gingham to codfish. The following year it carried for Howland & Aspinwall sugar, coffee, Spanish brandy, 60,000 silver dollar coins, 4,876 dry Lima hides, and 5,000 California hides, to Rio de Janeiro, Valparaíso, and Callao, Peru.[25]

Many ships slipped from East River docks into the water and headed for the seven seas. In 1845 Smith & Dimon built the 750-ton *Rainbow* for Howland & Aspinwall. Designed by the naval architect John Willis Griffiths, the *Rainbow* was a new breed of clipper ship, with an extended bow and a full midsection. Following its launching, it set new records for sailing to Hong Kong and back.

While good money could be made in shipping, it was a perilous business, as Astor had learned in 1811 when his fur-trading ship *Tonquin* was seized by local natives on the west coast of Vancouver Island in British Columbia and blown up. The *Philip Hone* endured an attempted mutiny in 1836. Twelve years later, the crew of *Philip Hone* found themselves caught in a severe hurricane that lasted for 18 hours and blew away its balance reefed trysail and stove bulwarks. And many ships sank. The *Rainbow* left New York in 1848 on its fifth voyage. As it headed around South America's Cape Horn it vanished. In July 1850, another ship, the *Elizabeth,* was caught in a gale and ran aground on Fire Island, with celebrated journalist and essayist Margaret Fuller, her husband Giovanni Ossoli, and their 22-month-old son Angelo perishing in the shipwreck.[26]

And there was cotton, the country's leading export. New York's position along the eastern seaboard made it a major player in the cotton trade. *De Bow's Review* estimated that prior to the Civil War, New York businessmen received 40¢ for every dollar spent on southern cotton. And southern businessmen not only shipped a lot of cotton through the city, but received loans from New York banks and coverage from New York insurance firms. Because of this, Bennett's *Herald* noted how southerners "are received with great hospitality." Businessmen and their families filled city hotels, boarding houses, and inns, attended theaters, dined in restaurants, and browsed in shops. As future mayor Fernando Wood would note, "The South is our best customer. She pays the best prices, and pays promptly."

Like many other merchants, Alexander Stewart sold to southerners. And while he might have respected Arthur Tappan's business practices, when it came to clients he distanced himself from the older merchant's hardline abolitionist stance. In November 1835 the *Herald* told of a Georgia lady who visited Stewart's. The woman was laden down with emerald and ruby rings, and the shopman set before her large and beautiful shawls. "They are indeed, Madam, the very best French shawls ever imported into New York by *Arthur Tappan*," he explained. When the lady heard the merchant's name she dropped the item to the floor, and exclaimed, "Take them away—take them away. I would not buy a shawl imported by Arthur Tappan, if it were to save me from perdition." She then pulled off one of her gloves, tore it and stomped on it. The next day the *Herald* ran a "Correction," stating that the incident did not take place at Stewart's: "They never buy goods of Arthur Tappan," and "recommended all lovely southern ladies to patronize" Stewart's store.[27]

Stewart's large and growing shop hired many young clerks and was seen as a good place to learn about business. He honed his staff and rewarded and advanced those who showed promise. The photographer Mathew Brady started there selling jewelry. Cyrus W. Field, who would eventually lay the Atlantic cable, began as an errand boy, arriving at the store between six and seven in the morning. When he became clerk, he worked from 8:15 until the evening. "I always made it a point to be there before the partners came and never to leave before the partners left," he recalled. "My ambition was to make myself a thoroughly good merchant." The place likewise became famous as a magnet for handsome clerks, whom Stewart hired after noticing female customers flirting with the men. The *New York Evening Chronicle* wrote how the good-looking staff would wax on the quality of silks, lace, and French muslins, and how the business was "a perfect cage or menagerie of Adonises."

Yet while Matthew Smith wrote that Stewart could be "genial, pleasant, affable," he could also be an exacting boss, a "cold, glassy, stern" employer who proved shrill to those he found disfavor with. If workers showed up late, misdirected a bundle, or gave the wrong change, they had to pay a 25¢ fine. The money went to a charity of the clerks' choice. Stewart's staff called him the General, and they knew to keep their distance from their commanding officer's ire. Once Stewart spotted one of his long-time salesmen sitting and reading a paper during store hours. Stewart fired the man. The man figured that Stewart would forget the incident and returned to work the following day. But when Stewart noticed the salesman, he ordered him out of the store.

The man became so enraged that he punched Stewart and knocked out some of his teeth.[28]

Despite Stewart's sternness with his own employees, customers appreciated his regular sales. This was especially true during economic downturns like the Panic of 1837. Stewart reduced his stock by selling at cost. At the time, he took in more than $5,000 each day. He then used the money to buy new stocks at a discount, picking up silks for 60 percent less than the cost. And, seeking other ways to save money, he hired merchants and agents in Europe, dispatching a partner to Europe in 1845 to establish branch offices. The firm eventually had agents in England, Scotland, Ireland, France, and Germany, as well as commissionaires as far afield as India.

With success, Stewart set out to improve his social standing. In the mid-1830s he and Cornelia bought a four-story brick home at 7 St. Mark's Place, then a fashionable location. The couple also had a pew nearby at the upscale St. Mark's Church in-the-Bowery. He and Cornelia tried to start a family, but their son John died soon after his 1834 birth. Four years later, Cornelia lost another child. Both were buried at St. Mark's. In 1842 the couple settled into a home on Depau Row on Bleecker Street.[29]

* * *

The business shift that came at the time of the Great Fire and the opening of Astor House had changed the character of Broadway. Stewart's store stood above and safely away from where the fire had burned. As development migrated north, businessmen moved into the City Hall area, which became a mecca of hotels, entertainment, and shops. By then, Pearl Street was losing its dry-goods prestige, and the *Herald* noted that "Broadway is moving up town. From St. Paul's down to Trinity, both sides of Broadway form only an extension of Wall street; it is equally as full of business. . . ." Soon Stewart added 20 feet of depth to his store and then a third, fourth, and fifth floor, making it one of the largest wholesale shops in the city.

The town brimmed as visitors arrived via the railroad or by carriages and then spent hours along the main street and side roads visiting shops like Stewart's, Tiffany, Young & Ellis, Lafayette Bazaar, James Beck & Co., and Hearn Brothers. They also went to see St. Paul's Chapel—where George Washington had worshipped—City Hall, the Mercantile Library, the Astor House, and the American Bible Society. The more adventurous headed to Barnum's American Museum, a spot that the following decade

Englishwoman Isabella Bird noted was filled with "a great deal that is spurious and contemptible" as well as "a collection of horrors or monstrosities."[30]

The spine of Broadway teemed with people, a thoroughfare that Herman Melville in *Bartleby, the Scrivener* recalled as a stretch filled with "the bright silks and sparkling faces I had seen that day, in gala trim, swan-like sailing down the Mississippi of Broadway." When Charles Dickens gazed on the roadway in 1842, he amazed at "the great promenade and thoroughfare" and asked, "was there ever such a sunny street as this Broadway! The pavement stones are polished with the tread of feet until they shine again; the red bricks of the houses might be yet in the dry, hot kilns; and the roofs of those omnibuses look as though, if water were poured on them, they would hiss and smoke, and smell like half-quenched fires."

With so many people streaming by his shop, Stewart started to dream big. In 1842, already worth $200,000, he came up with an idea that revolutionized business. He decided to build a store like no other, a place where under one roof customers could find all they needed. Such an all-encompassing dry goods store was a radical idea. Stewart decided to set it on Chambers Street on the east side of Broadway, and bought the site. Others scoffed at the notion of setting a shop on the eastern side of Broadway. Unlike the desirable western "Dollar Side," the eastern "Shilling Side" received the long, hot afternoon sun. "The mercantile community, and sensible men generally, looked upon his investment as an insane act," wrote Smith. No one had also ever built so large a business. The closest thing to it was the New York Arcade, a sky-lit corridor with 40 stores that ran parallel to Broadway, between Maiden Lane and John Street. As Stewart's new store went up, its architecture started to attract notice. Edgar Allan Poe's *Broadway Journal* predicted that the store would be "an ornament to the city when it is finished, and as a place of business we believe without a parallel in the world."[31]

8

Covering the Waterfront

The day before Alexander Stewart opened his revolutionary new store in September 1846, he rode home on the stagecoach and overheard other passengers chatting about it. Some praised his new venture as bold and innovative. However, nearly everyone commented on how he had unfortunately placed the structure on the less attractive "shilling side" of Broadway. Some even called it "Stewart's Folly." On the morning of the 21st, the businessman rose early and braced himself for the day ahead. He had been trying to think of ways to ensure success. He even contemplated making a big show of the unveiling by dressing up 25 African American men in fine livery and having them carry customers on sedan chairs across Broadway. He was prepared to try everything to bring in shoppers, and nearly wept at the thought that no one would come.

When Stewart arrived at Broadway and Chambers Street, however, he saw the police straining to control a surging crowd. The *New York Herald* observed that "the scene at that hour and throughout the day, was the most exciting imaginable." A thousand people an hour streamed though Stewart's store. And when the afternoon came and the sun arched away from the East River toward the Hudson River, its rays illuminated the building's white Tuckahoe marble exterior. In one blazing moment the naysayers saw the brilliance of Stewart's vision, and raised retailers—often contemptuously called "mongers"—to the level of merchants. His store quickly earned the name "the Marble Palace."[1]

Stewart's was the first big retail store in America, with merchandise divided into unique departments. Designed in the Palazzo style by the architects Joseph Trench and John Snook, it also proved to be a seminal work of architecture—an Italian renaissance palace with a riotous façade of columns, flat and gabled windows, and a crowning balustrade. The building made the Greek Revival, post-and-lintel commercial structures, such as the one Ithiel Town had introduced for Arthur Tappan's store 17 years earlier, seem quaint by comparison.

Stewart's Marble Palace inaugurated a look that quickly became the *de rigueur* style for those with money and power. The building proved revolutionary in other ways, too. It had a four-story-high and 70-foot-wide skylight-topped atrium, a central court whose creation ushered in a vogue for rotundas. And the structure, with its large plate-glass windows, was a new concept in New York, where shops traditionally featured small glazed windows. While Philip Hone found the windows "a most extraordinary, and I think useless, piece of extravagance," that could easily "be shivered by a boy's marble or a snow-ball," there was a sound business reason for such massive panes. Stewart's windows allowed light to stream in and show off his interior with its curly maple and mahogany counters, gas-lit chandeliers, and its capitals, all of which symbolized the marriage of commerce and luxury.[2]

The store, run by 100 or so clerks, overflowed with $600,000 worth of stock, from inexpensive pins to pricey shawls. "A lady on a journey, who passes a couple of days in the city, can find every article that she wants for her wardrobe at a reasonable price," wrote Matthew Smith. Women streamed into Stewart's Ladies' Parlor with its full-length Parisian mirrors, to view the country's earliest fashion shows. Sales at the Marble Palace proved brisk.[3]

With the Great Fire a receding memory and the Panic of 1837 fully behind the city, it had become an age for flaunting money, and Stewart catered to the wealthy who sat in their carriages as salesman brought out to the vehicles the store's goods to show them. Soon, though, even Stewart's grand palace proved too small. He needed to expand, and bought the adjoining property. For the enlargement, Trench & Snook added a fifth floor and stretched the length of the building the entire way from Chambers to Reade Street. Here the advantage of the Renaissance style showed its superiority over Greek Revival. For while the latter was inflexible and difficult to extend, the former allowed for practical, cost-efficient, and seamless enlargement through the repetition of forms. The Marble Palace became, according to *Harper's*, "a keynote, a model," making the view up Broadway mesmerizing. "There is, in its way, no finer street effect than the view of Stewart's building seen on a clear, blue, brilliant day. . . . It rises out of the sea of green foliage in the City Hall Park, a white marble cliff, sharply drawn against the sky."[4]

* * *

The growing mercantile royalty quickly copied Stewart and built their own marble palaces. In 1848 the inventor and builder James Bogardus fashioned cast iron into architectural pieces to remodel Dr. John Milhau's brick-fronted pharmacy on Broadway. Iron could be formed into any shape, and the easy reproduction of forms made designing simpler. In the process, Bogardus revolutionized construction by allowing workers to cast and then cart pieces to the construction site where crews bolted them in place. With it, buildings became standardized. More importantly, cast iron allowed architects to build solidly without using up much ground-level space, as masonry structures required. Foundries started to churn out doors, shutters, and windows. These firms flourished along the rivers, fueled by barges of pig iron along with coal from Maryland, Virginia, and Pennsylvania. Some, like the Novelty Iron Works facility on the East River at 13th Street, were enormous facilities. Novelty covered five acres, and by the 1850s employed 1,200 workers. In 1860 the city's 539 iron works, employing 10,600 workers, turned out everything from building parts and nails to printing presses. Walt Whitman noted of the factories, how their "chimneys burning high and glaringly into the night, Casting their flicker of black, contrasted with wild red and yellow light over the tops of houses, and down into the clefts of streets."[5]

When Harper & Brothers wanted a new building, Bogardus constructed one for them on Franklin Square, putting up a web of Corinthian columns, arches, piers, and sculptured plaques. In 1854 the Gilsey Building rose on Broadway and Cortlandt Street, a Venetian palazzo with pieces manufactured by Daniel Badger's Architectural Iron Works. Badger's designers offered a variety of facades for clients and architects to select from. He produced the greatest cast-iron structure of the era, architect John P. Gaynor's Haughwout Building on Broadway, a five-story Venetian-style fantasy complete with an elevator by the inventor Elisha Otis.

New York was growing faster than all the other cities in the nation. At the end of the 1840s, the city was responsible for half the U.S. imports, and a third of the exports left from there. Stewart had a lot to do with this. By the mid-1850s, he paid the highest duties of any importer in New York. Expanded businesses meant a need for more white-collar workers and professionals. There were lots of places for them to work, with 130 brokerage houses on Wall and William Streets in 1856, as well as 90 insurance companies, 75 banks, and headquarters for steamship, mining, and railroad companies employing clerks, accountants, and copyists. By that point, 215,000 of the city's 630,000 people were gainfully employed. Some 30 percent of them belonged to the middle class, which included small merchants, architects, engineers, shopkeepers, clergy, and doctors.

With more buildings and more traffic, others seeking space ventured further and further north on Broadway and along the side streets. City streets, which were traditionally lit by oil, were starting to be illuminated with gas. In the 1820s the New York Gas Light Company had set up lights on Broadway. The arrival of better lighting allowed later business hours. In 1830 the Manhattan Gas Light Company put lamps above Canal Street. By 1851, Dr. Joel Ross would comment, "Gas is now considered almost indispensable in the city." The following year, the Board of Aldermen reported that there were 6,696 gaslights in the city. By 1856 New York had 10,500 street lamps.[6]

New York was growing at a tremendous pace. After 1840 the city outpaced the state, the region, and the nation. In 1840 the city's population of 312,710 made up 4.6 percent of the Northeast and 1.8 percent of the country's total population of 17,063,353; in 1860, at 813,669, it had reached 7.7 percent of the Northeast's and 2.58 percent of the nation's 31,443,321. Change came faster and faster with the arrival of fresh water, gas lighting, transportation, heating, cooking stoves, and ice boxes. By the eve of the Civil War, New York and the surrounding ten counties contained 1.5 million people, linked by horse cars, steam railroads, and ferries. Henry Ward Beecher, brother of Harriet Beecher Stowe and a prominent abolitionist, enjoyed the view of New York Bay from his back window, where the pastor of Plymouth Church in Brooklyn Heights witnessed a "great city with a thousand shining eyes, couched down, but always watching, always murmuring, night and day, like some huge, muttering behemoth, waiting for its prey in the reeds by the seashore."[7]

One drawn irresistibly to the urban behemoth was 17-year-old Samuel Clemens. He found employment at the publisher John A. Gray & Green's on Cliff Street, where the *Knickerbocker*, the *Choral Advocate*, the *Jewish Chronicle*, and other publications were printed. "I have a pretty good view of the city," he wrote his mother in 1853 of what he could see from the publisher's fifth-floor window. "You have everything in the shape of water craft, from a fishing smack to the steamships and men-of-war; but packed so closely together for miles, that when close to them you can scarcely distinguish one from another."

Like the shorelines, the roadways became crowded, building-lined canyons. As business expanded and stores opened, pedestrians, newsboys, window shoppers, housewives, businessmen, dandies, speculators, clerks, merchants, and customers packed the streets. So much activity brought not only inconveniences but also hazards. In 1839 the *New York Mirror* listed some of the perils and nuisances on the streets, from "running at large of hogs," "throwing all rubbish into the street," "the villainous noise made by the milkmen," "allowing wheelbarrows and handcarts on the side-walk," "dogs running at large," "awning-posts on narrow side-walks," and "street-beggars by the thousand; hand organ and monkey, singing girls."[8]

People, vehicles, and public transports jammed the streets. The resourceful Clemens figured out a simple way to make it to the other side of the street. "To *cross* Broadway is the rub," he told his mother, "but once across, it is—*the rub* for two or three squares. My plan . . . is to get into the crowd; and when I get in, I am borne, and rubbed, and crowded along, and need scarcely trouble myself about using my own legs; and when I get out, it seems like I had been pulled to pieces and very badly put together again." The hatter John Nicholas Genin had a more practical solution for the congestion. He simply built a bridge over Broadway so that people could cross to his shop.

And it wasn't only Broadway suffering from crushing crowds. People jammed places like the discount shopping district on the Bowery, Grand, Canal, and Catherine Streets, and in Chatham Square, with their sidewalk booksellers, pawnbrokers, old clothes shops, auction houses, silversmiths, jewelers, and shoe stores.[9]

* * *

To deal with the increase in foot and vehicle traffic into the city, there was a growing need for hotels. The Astor House, as we've seen, had set the bar high for what people could expect, and as more money flowed in, developers strove to top the land baron with a slew of hotels appearing in the late 1840s and 1850s. Delmonico's opened a hotel on lower Broadway in 1846 to replace their lodging destroyed in an 1845 fire. Set near the Battery, it featured views of the river and the bay. The hotel expanded in 1847, with a spacious dining room and guest rooms that the *New York Evening Post* reported was "fitted up with the most elegant furniture." In 1848 the Irving House Hotel opened opposite Stewart's Marble Palace. With a staff of 150, it had room for 500 guests, bridal suites, a smoking room, and a bar, along with a barber, a wig maker, and a gentlemen's as well as a ladies' dining room.

In 1849 the Union Place Hotel appeared on Broadway and 14th Street. In 1851 the Clarendon Hotel opened on 18th Street. Designed by the architect (and George Templeton Strong Columbia classmate) James Renwick, it had velvet carpets, lace curtains, rosewood furniture, and marble basins, and was heated by steam. Around that time, Renwick's Lafarge House hotel on Broadway and Bleecker Street opened. In 1853 the Everett House started greeting guests at Fourth Avenue and 17th Street. On the northwest corner of Broadway and Spring stood the Prescott House. The Albion Hotel rose on Broadway, as did Renwick's St. Denis Hotel.[10]

Then, in the early 1850s, the brownstone-clad Metropolitan Hotel opened, standing on part of where Niblo's Garden once spread out. Designed by John Snook and Joseph Trench, architects of the Marble Palace, it cost nearly a million dollars and had sky parlors from which ladies could observe guests below. The marble-faced St. Nicholas Hotel, by Snook and Griffith Thomas, appeared in 1853 on Broadway between Broome and Spring Streets. It had an impressively long main entrance with a portico with four Corinthian columns, housed up to 800 guests, and had ceiling frescoes, walnut wainscoting, gas chandeliers, hot running water, a bridal chamber, and a lobby telegraph.

By 1854 the city had 45 hotels. They offered many their first introduction to such luxuries as gas lights. To keep up with the competition, the Astor House updated its interior. In 1853 the hotel unveiled its Astor House Exchange, an elliptical-shaped glass and iron court. Designed by Bogardus, it had a gushing fountain, sported a frescoed ceiling, and was lit by four chandeliers along with 34 gas burners. But more competition for Astor House was on the way, for the truly grand Fifth Avenue Hotel opened on 23rd Street in 1859. Designed by Griffith Thomas and William Washburn, the six-story marble building cost $2 million to build, had private bathrooms, 400 employees, along with a passenger elevator built by Otis Tufts .[11]

Food preparation also boomed in the city. In the early 19th century few places offered a sit-down place to get a bite to eat. There were spots like Cato's Tavern. Located in the distant north on 54th Street, Cato Alexander's place was a popular spot frequented by Hone as well as the Beekmans, Van Cortlandts, and others. Another early watering hole was William Niblo's Bank Coffee House, which opened in 1814 on William Street and in 1823 advertised a special four-course meal where diners could choose from such fare as green turtle soup, bald eagle, bear, owl, raccoon, and pudding pies, tarts, and jellies.[12]

By 1846 the city could boast of 123 eating houses and refectories, with 17 of them on Broadway. Delmonico's, which opened its first restaurant on William Street in 1827, was one of the more popular restaurants in the city. Their building, which was called the "Citadel" because of its rounded corner, catered to merchants and others from the nearby Stock Exchange and banks. While Hone was initially disappointed in the fare, when he went back in 1837 he found it much improved. That same year, Strong wrote how there he "drank some of the only good chocolate I ever tasted." Editor James Watson Webb enjoyed Delmonico's pastries, and regulars included Stewart, journalists like Nathaniel Parker Willis, and theater owner James Wallack. The place was especially popular with French and German merchants, and welcomed such visiting dignitaries as Charles-Louis-Napoléon Bonaparte, who would become Napoleon III.

Oysters remained a New York staple, and oyster harvesting developed into a big business. Ellis Island, as well as Bedloe's Island (current day Liberty Island) and a few smaller ones, were each originally known as Oyster Islands. Joseph Corre advertised in 1788 that he sold pickled oysters as well as soup and other foods for ship captains. In 1828 William Parker advertised "his Old Established Stand" on Broadway where he offered "Oysters Stewed, Fried, or in the Shell, and Refreshments of every kind served up at the shortest notice, and on the most reasonable terms."[13]

The East River oysters were the largest and fattest, used for roasting and eaten on the half shell. City Island oysters were a particular favorite. Oysters were brought in from Staten Island. As harvesters exhausted traditional beds by the early 19th century, watermen started to transplant small "seed" and larval "set" from Virginia. Others came in from New Jersey, Long Island, Delaware, Virginia, Rhode Island, and Massachusetts. By the 1850s, oyster harvesting was one of the region's main businesses. Oyster stands could be found all along the city's streets, with sellers crying out such enticements as:

> Here's your fat, good tasted oysters,
> Yorkbank oysters, large and small;
> With such a great variety,
> I'm sure to please you all.[14]

Oysters were enjoyed for meals and snacks. Strong recalled stopping with others at a stall at Fulton Market in the fall of 1855 and enjoying "some very special roast oysters." Canal Street had so many oyster cellars that people could opt for the Canal Street Plan, which was all one could eat for 6¢. Saloons and restaurants employed a vast number of workers who prepared dishes. One businessman had 15 to 20 men just to shuck oysters. Some oysters were so large they needed to be quartered. Charles Mackay, who edited the *Illustrated London News*, was amazed to see "oysters as large as a lady's hand," the dishes prepared in a variety of ways, "pickled, stewed, baked, roasted, fried, and scalloped; oysters made into soups, patties, and puddings; oysters with condiments and without condiments; oysters for breakfast, dinner, and supper; oysters without stint or limit."[15]

The most popular spot for oysters, without question, was oyster restaurateur Thomas Downing's place at 3 Broad Street. Downing was a gregarious host. Set near the Custom House, the Merchants' Exchange, and major banks, his place was decorated with chandeliers and damask curtains. Merchant Abram Dayton recalled how, "Leading politicians also made it headquarters, dropping in to have a chat while enjoying their half-dozen Saddle Rocks or Blue Points." Downstairs at Downing's stood three large vaults to hold his stock, kept fresh by a spring that flowed under his building. It allowed him to serve a lot of oysters, plain, as well as such dishes as oyster pie and turkey stuffed with oysters, which was roasted over a large gridiron of oak shavings.[16]

The African American restaurateur regularly advertised his mollusks and other offerings, as in July 1838 when he let people know of an "Extraordinary Turtle" that was caught at St. Simons Island, Georgia. The creature was on view until it was turned into a meal. And he happily crowed in 1855, "Take Notice!—I have got as good an oyster as I ever had . . . such as Saddle rocks, East rivers, Shrewsburies." And besides his ads, to show off his wares, Downing would prove the superiority of his oysters by entering and winning competitions. For instance, he won a Diploma in 1839 at the Twelfth Annual Fair of the American Institute at Niblo's Garden for his jarred pickled oyster. And at a competition at the Astor House for stewed terrapin, Downing beat out chefs from Washington, Baltimore, Philadelphia, and New York.

Downing's devoted clientele was a who's-who of the New York business elite. Ship captains especially liked Downing because he paid top price for their catch and treated them well when they afterward dined at his restaurant. Charles Dickens visited, as did Lord Morpeth, as well as the sharp-tongued James Gordon Bennett. The restaurateur regularly catered parties, opening a place for families and private gatherings at 245 Broadway. He even packed up a special supply of oysters for Queen Victoria, who in return sent him a gold chronometer watch. Downing made a good living. Downing's son George followed in his footsteps and opened his own establishment on Broadway before hanging out a shingle in Rhode Island.[17]

The city's eating houses were primarily but not exclusively for men. Wives accompanied their husbands to places like Delmonico's, and *Putnam's* reported in 1853 how women were also "solacing themselves with fricandeaus,

NEW YORK.

Plate 1 The Collect Pond once stretched next to Bayard's Mount. By the early 19th century the Collect was filled in and the hill leveled.

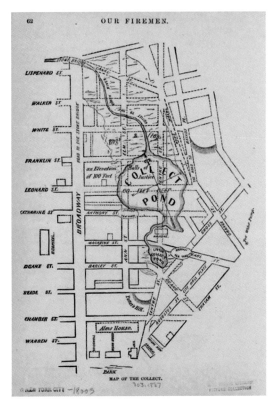

Plate 2 Laying to the north of Chambers Street, the Collect Pond (alongside the Little Collect) once served as a source of water for New Yorkers.

Plate 3 Lispenard's Meadow, a swampy land filled with marshes, snakes and bullfrogs, used to cover the area now known as Tribeca.

Plate 4 Philip Hone served as mayor of New York for one year in the late 1820s, and his diary offers an essential chronicle of the city's growth before and after the Great Fire.

Plate 5 Philip Hone's home (on the right) stood opposite City Hall Park, a residence Merchant John Pintard said allowed the former mayor to live "in the genteelest style of any man in our city."

Plate 6 Mayor Hone christened Washington Military Parade Ground—current day Washington Square Park—on the site of a burial ground for the poor and plague victims.

Plate 7 Italian artists Nicolino Calyo arrived in the city just months before the Great Fire of 1835, and from Brooklyn Heights painted one of his scenes of the conflagration.

HANINGTON'S DIORAMIC REPRESENTATION OF THE

GREAT FIRE in NEW YORK Dec. 16—17 1835.

Now exhibiting with other moving dioramic scenes, at the AMERICAN MUSEUM every evening.

Plate 8 Soon after the Great Fire, William and Henry Hanington unveiled their depiction of the blaze, a moving diorama accompanied by flashing lights, the sound of rattling fire engines and the shouts of citizens.

Plate 9 The ruins of the South Reformed Dutch Church following the Great Fire.

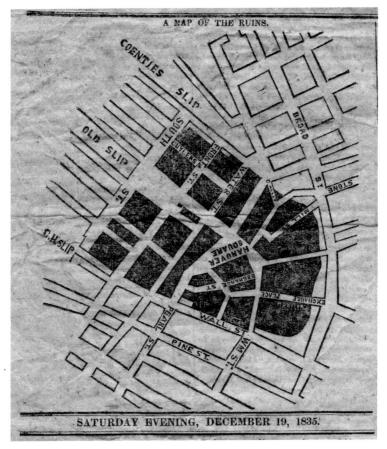

Plate 10 Papers like the *New York Sun* ran maps and illustrations showing the extent of the fire, and the *Sun* ran its presses round the clock to meet demand for news of the devastation.

Mr. Hamblain as Red Riven

Plate 11 Theater impresario Thomas Hamblin managed the
Bowery Theatre from 1830 until his death in 1853.

NEW YORK THEATRE
Erected 1826_ Front on BOWERY 75 feet_ Depth 170 feet.

103. NEW YORK THEATRE / Erected
1826 — Front on BOWERY 75 feet—Depth

Plate 12 Ithiel Town designed the first Bowery Theatre in 1826, and when Thomas Hamblin became owner of the second theatre on the spot, he turned it into a center of entertainment for both the common man and woman.

Plate 13 John Jacob Astor arrived in the city in 1784, started out in the fur trade and soon began buying up large tracts of Manhattan properties.

Plate 14 The Astor House hotel (on the right) opened in 1836, and proved so revolutionary that *New York Herald* editor James Gordon Bennett told his staff, "Anyone who can pay two dollars a day for a room must be important."

Plate 15 Farmhouses, as with this one on West 84th where Edgar Allan Poe once lived, dotted northern Manhattan. But the creation of the streets meant that many structures became stranded and needed to be moved or demolished.

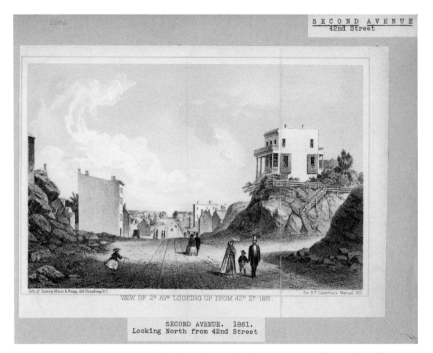

Plate 16 The Commissioners' Plan of 1811 laid out New York's grid, and as you can see from this view of Second Avenue and 42nd Street, it disregarded what was stood in the way.

SOUTH ST. from MAIDEN LANE.

Henry I. Megarey New York.

Plate 17 Ships lined South Street Seaport and other parts of Manhattan's shoreline, turning the city into what Walt Whitman called "mast-hemm'd Manhattan."

Plate 18 Trinity Church, seen here in 1830, would soon be demolished and replaced in 1846 by Richard Upjohn's grand Gothic Revival sanctuary.

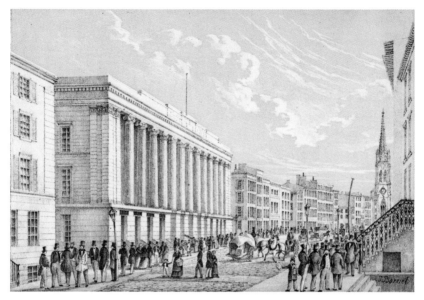

Plate 19 Following the Merchants' Exchange destruction in 1835, Isaiah Rogers created an even more resplendent replacement.

STEWART BUILDING, 1850
BROADWAY NORTH FROM CHAMBERS STREET

Plate 20 Alexander Stewart's Marble Palace opened on Broadway and Chambers Street in 1846 and revolutionized the way Americans shopped.

Plate 21 Walt Whitman arrived in New York just prior to the Great Fire, and as a journalist tramped along the streets, writing about the goings on around town.

Plate 22 Alexander Jackson Davis, Ithiel Town and James Dakin's New York University building opened on Washington Square in 1837.

Plate 23 A stereoscopic view of Jacob Wrey Mould's All Souls' Unitarian Church, its bands of colored stones and bricks earned the building the nickname Church of the Holy Zebra.

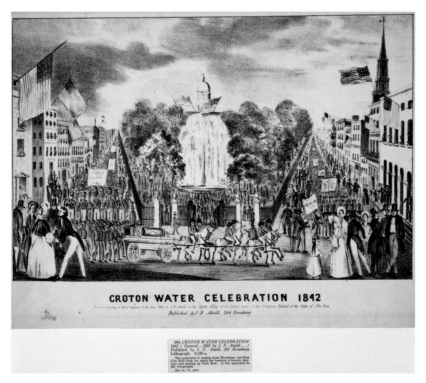

Plate 24 New Yorkers threw a huge celebration to mark the 1842 arrival of fresh water via the Croton Aqueduct.

Plate 25 The Murray Hill Distributing Reservoir stood on Fifth Avenue and 42nd Street on the spot where the New York Public Library now welcomes readers.

Plate 26 An 1849 view of Manhattan from the steeple of St. Paul's Chapel, with Barnum's American Museum lower left and Richard Upjohn's recently opened Trinity Church rising in the background right.

meringues and ices at Thompson's, Taylor's, or Weller's." Taylor's Saloon on Franklin and Broadway was especially popular, touting itself as the largest and most elegant restaurant in the world. It was created by architects Thomas and Son and opened in 1853. Isabella Bird noted how the spot "combines Eastern magnificence with Parisian taste." It had two grand entrances, marble tiled floors, and marble counters, and was filled with crimson and gold upholstered chairs and sofas. The main room was long and high, with marble floors and featuring a maze of frescoes, mirrors, carvings, and marble pillars. There were also two grand conservatories, a cut-glass fountain, ceilings ornamented with gilding and scroll work, and decorated with bronze and gilt statuary.[18]

All the restaurants were made possible by the easy availability of food. Supplies came to the city from Long Island, upstate New York, New Jersey, and Connecticut farms, and by way of the Erie Canal. And improved transportation meant that perishables could more easily make it to market. The arrival of the railroad ended cattle herding to the city, and New York became the nation's main cattle market, with merchants selling livestock from as far away as Missouri and Texas. Public markets were the main source of such goods. Places like the Catharine, Franklin, and Fulton Markets offered everything from eggs, milk, and meat to tomatoes, peas, beans, cabbage, asparagus, carrots, peaches, cherries, melons, pineapples, oranges, apples, bananas, butter, Indian corn, watermelons, cranberries, and blueberries.

James Fenimore Cooper was amazed at the wide variety of fowls, including, "grouse, canvas-backs, brants, plover, wild turkeys" for sale, as well as 70 to 80 varieties of seafood, from shad and mackerel to mussels and cockles. There were salmon, turtles, green lobsters, halibut, perch, sea and striped bass, and cod. The English businessman James Boardman marveled at how the lobsters and oysters "are often very large; the former, including the claws, sometimes measuring three feet in length, and the circumference of the shell of the latter as much as eighteen inches."[19]

* * *

While money was to be made in New York from all this business and activity, most of the wealth was held by a few. By 1845, 1 percent of the citizens possessed half the wealth, and the top 4 percent controlled four-fifths of the money. The following year, Moses Beach published a new edition of his *The Wealth and Biography of the Wealthy Citizens of the City of New York*. He filled the volume with brief bios of those worth at least $100,000, along with a small handful who belonged to a new and growing class of entrepreneurs called "millionaires." There were ten in the mid-1840s. John Jacob Astor topped the list at $25 million. The family of Stephen Van Rensselaer stood at $10 million, and besides their huge tracts of upstate land they "owned hundreds of lots in New York." William Astor, who had already inherited a sizable fortune when his uncle Henry died in 1833, was worth $5 million. Beach wrote that Stephen Whitney, who had started as a grocer, was worth $5 million, noting that his "investments in real estate many years ago have doubled his fortune." Peter Schermerhorn stood at $2.5 million. Alexander Stewart, who had arrived in the city with $500 to launch his business, was worth $2 million by 1855. Even Mary Okill, who ran a boarding school for young ladies, was listed as worth $250,000. In 1860 the city could claim 115 millionaires.[20]

The discovery of gold in Coloma, California, in January 1848 further fanned this wealth. Later that year, the *Journal of Commerce* reprinted a letter from Monterey, California, with the writer commenting that there was so much gold, "people are running over the country and picking it out of the earth here and there, just as a thousand hogs, let loose in a forest, would root up ground nuts." The claim was clearly exaggerated, but didn't prevent people rushing west, causing California's population to soar from 14,000 in 1848 to some 250,000 in 1852. Talk of gold was everywhere. "Gold! Gold! The California fever is increasing in violence; thousands are going, among whom are many young men of our best families," wrote Hone. Sons of such well-off families headed off as did others from Europe, South America, and Asia. "The frenzy continues to increase every day," George Templeton Strong noted. "It seems as if the Atlantic Coast was to be depopulated, such swarms of people are leaving it for the new El Dorado."

To get to California, some took the perilous route around Cape Horn, braving the deadly waves and frigid temperatures at the southern tip of the continent. Others sailed down to Panama and Nicaragua, crossed overland and by canoe—which brought with it the possibility of contracting malaria, Yellow Fever, and cholera—and then continued by ship up the West Coast. To help people across the Central American isthmus, Cornelius Vanderbilt launched his Accessory Transit Company. Meanwhile, tens of thousands trekked by way of North America, taking wagons, oxen, mules, and horses across Nebraska and heading into Wyoming, Idaho, and then Nevada before reaching California. It was a dangerous route, mainly due to illnesses.[21]

Ellen Strong's brother John hoped to make his fortune as a merchant out there. George Templeton Strong went with his father-in-law, Samuel Ruggles, to Howland & Aspinwall to help arrange John's accommodations once he arrived in San Francisco. John then headed out in April 1849, traveling overland with lawyer and family friend George Gibbs, who joined his brother Alfred—an officer in the Mounted Rifle Regiment—which went to take control of the Army post at Fort Vancouver, Washington. Once out west, Ruggles made his way down to San Francisco. He had become sick during the trip but recovered, and in the Bay City formed a partnership with others to establish a business at Marysville. Unfortunately, the weather was miserably wet, and along the way Ruggles suffered from diarrhea and possibly contracted scrofulous. Ruggles came down with dysentery, became delirious, and died on May 6, 1850. He was buried at sea.

While firms like Wells Fargo & Co. handled the movement of gold and other commodities, those heading to California needed clothing, firearms, and supplies. According to Hone: "the papers are filled with advertisements of vessels. . . . Tailors, hatters, grocers, provision merchants, hardware men, and others are employed night and day in fitting out the adventurers." And those bringing out supplies then brought back the sought-after mineral. In October 1848 Fernando Wood dispatched the barque *John W. Cater* to California to cash in, filling his ship with a wide assortment of fancy and general goods, from Cavendish tobacco and Russian hemp rope to playing cards.[22] The brig *Philip Hone* got underway for the "gold region" on January 27, 1849, docking in San Francisco on August 9, adding its 49 passengers to the 62,000 who would arrive by ship between the spring of 1849 and the spring of 1850. Many who headed there immediately searched for claims.

Once in California, some crews lashed their vessels to piers and abandoned their ships. In July 1850 the *Daily Alta California* ran a list of hundreds of ships abandoned in the port of San Francisco. Vessels were then turned into saloons, hotels, even a jail. The *Philip Hone* became a storehouse, and ads ran regularly in the paper touting its availability, "surrounded by deep water, free from fire risk, and accessible at all times by dray or scow." Eventually, the *Philip Hone*, like so many other ships, was scuttled, its bronze and brass fixtures sold off and its timber used to build homes. Smith & Dimon's once proud brig was soon turned into landfill, and now lies buried near Green, Union, and Battery Streets, much as the old ships the Dutch and British once sailed have become a part of Manhattan's shoreline.[23]

The arrival of California gold—$603,000 worth of gold coin and dust were aboard the steamship *Empire City* in September 1849—further spurred New York's economy. In 1849 over 3,000 ships from 150 foreign ports sailed into Whitman's "mast-hemm'd Manhattan." This was triple the amount in 1835. Additional ships were needed, and the 1855 census listed 31 shipbuilders in New York, Brooklyn, and Williamsburg. Launchings of square-rigger, side-wheel steamboats, clipper ships, schooners, and packet ships for the coastal and ocean trade were grand events. On the morning of January 28, 1850, Hone headed down to the christening of three steam vessels. The first was the *New World* at the shipyard of William H. Brown on East 12th Street. Hone wrote that as soon as she touched water, all her machinery "was set in motion; the wheels revolving, the smoke ascending, and the steam whizzing with its usual vivacity." The crowd then rushed to the Novelty Iron Works' yard. There, an 800-ton steamer, the *Boston*, slipped into the water. Soon after that "the *Arctic* began to move slowly and gracefully, heralded by the shouts of the immense multitude."[24]

Throughout New York's harbor, construction continued at a furious clip; workers filled the shoreline and extended the land, and new docks and piers stretched into the rivers. In 1850 there were 60 piers, wharves, docks, and slips on the East River and at least 50 on the Hudson. There was soon a need for more dock space, and construction started across the river in Brooklyn, where developers transformed marshes and built docks and warehouses.

New York was by far the largest manufacturer in the nation. Prosperity also meant additional smaller producers, and in the 1850s more buildings went up for light industry. Between 1840 and 1860 investment in manufacturing rose nearly 550 percent, and from 1855 to 1860 the value of industrial products went up 60 percent. Much increase was fueled by the 1842 arrival of fresh water from the Croton Reservoir, which manufacturers used for production and for steam. In the early 1850s the city was the main producer of clothes, made possible by the availability of tens of thousands of immigrants and their families who toiled away cheaply. By 1860 New York was the largest sugar refining area and a major center of machine building.[25]

* * *

With so much activity, businessmen needed to know what was going on. Papers ran news, social notices, crime reports, gossip, accounts of slave conspiracies, and literature, along with ads for everything from ship dockings to auctions for house sales. In 1828, the city had more than a dozen daily papers, along with assorted semi-weeklies and weeklies. As already noted, five years later the *New York Sun*, the first successful penny paper, appeared. Soon after, the Philadelphia *Public Ledger* noted how such inexpensive publications placed the news "within reach of the very poorest." The popularity of penny papers was a boon for some publishers, and they became a font of sensation-alizing news, a development that the *New York Commercial Advertiser* called "that last and most efficient invention of Satan."

Bennett unveiled his *Herald* in 1835, and the editor quickly displayed his preternatural sense of what people wanted to be informed about. He covered crime, the courts, and news about Wall Street and the city's finances in a manner that lay readers could understand. His beat reporters ferreted out local news, and Bennett launched boats to intercept ships before they docked to learn of news, stationed reporters in Albany and Washington, hired foreign correspondents, and used carrier pigeons.[26]

A fast and witty writer, Bennett's style, flourishes, contents, and independence when covering stories helped sell papers. On June 25, 1845, the *Herald* ran the first full-page image ever to appear in a daily when it covered Andrew Jackson's funeral. The illustration was topped with a portrait of the former president, followed by detailed images of the clergy, former president Martin Van Buren, General Winfield Scott, military guards and their horses, the city's Common Council, benevolent societies, and fluttering flags. Bennett, who had once worked for South Carolina's *Charleston Courier*, was pro-slavery. He gathered news from across the South and published critical articles about abolitionists and quacks (which he equated). In the 1830s, the *Herald* had a circulation of 15,000, reaching 400,000 by the time of the Civil War, which made it the nation's most successful newspaper. His stance on slavery and his ability to sell papers did not sit well with his competitors. The *New York Times'* Henry Raymond called Bennett "Satanic." Raymond even ran a cartoon of a horned Bennett holding a bag of brimstone.[27]

While his paper was phenomenally successful, Bennett lacked tact. He seemed to take pleasure in attacking competitors and anyone he disliked, lashing out with abandon at those like P.T. Barnum and Thomas Hamblin, both of whom retaliated in kind. Soon after founding his paper, Bennett noted of Hone, "we don't like the man, and yet we can't tell why. Can any one else tell?" Bennett's manner appalled his competition and their readership. In 1838 he scorched the *Journal of Commerce* for complaining about there being too "much adultery, fornication, seduction and concubinage existing amongst actors and actresses," and used it as an opportunity to lambaste the clergy. Bennett held special scorn for the Catholic Church, writing that the city's Catholic hierarchy should "come forth from the darkness folly, and superstition of the tenth century. We live in the nineteenth."[28]

For many, his comments and scandal-mongering went too far. In 1840 Bennett's competition launched what they called "a Great Moral War" and organized an economic boycott of the *Herald*. The effort was led by the *New York Evening Signal*'s Park Benjamin, the *New York Evening Star*'s Mordecai Noah, and the *Morning Courier and New-York Enquirer*'s Webb. Bennett's opponents were also joined by business leaders as well as the clergy. Perhaps unsurprisingly, the attacks only emboldened the editor, who wrote that the "holy combination" of his detractors confined themselves "to their natural weapons of lies, falsehood, folly, passion, stupidity, and bad grammar. As yet they only murder English." On the same page he censured Benjamin with a half column of insults, calling him everything from "Profligate adventurer," "Scoundrel Pen," and "Convict from the state prison," to "Blaspheme the Savior and Creator" and "Plague and pestilence." He appended to the end of the list some choice names for Noah, calling him a "Rogue," "Pickpocket," "Falsehood," and "Turkey Buzzard." In April 1842 Hone observed that Bennett "lives by lying." That same month, Walt Whitman had especially choice words for the editor, calling him in the *New York Aurora* "a midnight ghoul, preying on rottenness and repulsive filth." The attacks did affect the *Herald*'s circulation, yet nothing would crimp the editor's style.[29]

To fill their pages, papers needed news, and they needed it fast. After Congress passed a $30,000 appropriating bill in 1843, Samuel Morse ran a telegraph line from Baltimore to Washington, completing it in May 1844. Backers followed, and he started the Magnetic Telegraph Company with service from New York to Philadelphia. Soon after, a lead pipe was laid across the East River to connect Manhattan and Brooklyn by telegraph. Railroads used telegraphs starting in the 1850s, and the technology soon linked police stations. Newspapers greatly benefited from the new technology. During the Mexican-American War, which started in 1846, the *Herald*, the *Sun*, the *New York Tribune*, the *Journal of Commerce*, the *Courier and Enquirer*, and the *Express* shared information on the war as well as from Washington, and the group became known as the Associated Press. By 1849 New York boasted of 88 newspapers; by 1857 there were 104, along with numerous African American papers.

Book publishing also grew. Harper & Brothers had become the largest publisher in the country. In 1851 it brought out Herman Melville's *Moby-Dick* in three volumes. Reviews in America were not kind, and only 3,200 copies were sold in Melville's lifetime. Harriet Beecher Stowe's *Uncle Tom's Cabin*, published a year later in book form by John P. Jewett, sold nearly as many copies on its first day. It would energize the abolitionist movement and went on to be second only to the Bible in the number of copies sold in the 19th century. In 1847, inventor Richard Hoe patented the rotary press, and in the 1840s and 1850s the city became the center of printing and lithography, keeping illustrators like Thomas Nast busy at places like *Frank Leslie's Illustrated Newspaper* and the *New York Illustrated News*. In 1857, New York had more than 100 publishers. Some put out adventure stories and thrillers, while magazine publishers churned out issues on subjects as wide-ranging as women's fashion, culture, politics, science, and—this being New York—banking.[30]

9

Quenching a City's Thirst

There is a certain irony that the island Walt Whitman described as "encircled by many swift tides and sparkling waters" also lacked a reliable supply of drinkable water. From the time of the first arrival of the Dutch in the early 17th century, there were attempts to find a dependable source of water for both household use and for fighting fires. Every effort failed. But all that changed during the summer of 1842. At 3:30 on the morning of July 4, Fayette B. Tower inspected the newly constructed 35-acre receiving reservoir that stretched from 79th to 86th Streets. The assistant engineer of the Croton Aqueduct checked the depth of the water, and by 5:00 AM he had made it down to the Murray Hill Distributing Reservoir at Fifth Avenue and 42nd Street. There he updated his boss, John Bloomfield Jervis, on what he had seen.

Jervis' staff had kept busy in the meantime. Tower recalled that their chief had carefully "arranged his corps and made his movements by means of his officers with all the circumspection and tact of a Napoléon." Then, at "an hour when the morning guns had aroused but few from their dreamy slumbers, and even yet the rays of the sun had gilded the city domes," Tower headed to the top of the 24-million-gallon reservoir. There, along the parapet of the looming Egyptian style granite tub, which looked as if it had been pilfered by the French general from Egypt's Valley of Kings, Tower marveled as water from the upstate Croton Reservoir coursed in. He remembered being transfixed by "the first gush of the waters as they entered the bottom and wandered about as if each particle had consciousness, and would choose for itself a resting place in this palace towards which it had made a pilgrimage."

There was something appropriate about the water from the Croton River flowing south into New York on the Fourth of July, for its arrival marked a long-awaited Day of Independence for this city of more than 310,000. New Yorkers desperately needed a supply to draw on. Not only did the city require a vast amount for drinking and cooking, but also to combat the fires that ravaged the town, to stoke the engines of its growing industries, wash down its streets, flush away its filth and diseases, and generally make the city a more livable and desirable metropolis.[1]

* * *

The search for water on Manhattan went back centuries. When the Lenapes inhabited the land, they drew water from the ponds, streams, and springs. After the Dutch arrived and established New Amsterdam at the southern edge of the island in the 1620s, settlers likewise tapped the available sources. But, a harbinger of things to come, the lack of a reliable supply doomed their tiny outpost when the English colonel Richard Nicolls sailed into the harbor in 1664 with four of the Duke of York's warships. With minimal water in the fort, Dutch Director-General Petrus Stuyvesant had no choice but to relinquish control. Aware of what had befallen the Dutch, the anointed governor Nicolls of the newly rechristened New York sought water, writing in 1667, "I am very proud of a well in the fort which I cause[d] to be made . . . beyond the Imagination of the Dutch, who would [not] beleeve it till they saw it finisht, which produces very good water."

Nicolls' dig created the city's first public well. Others followed. Yet being so close to the shore, the water at Manhattan's lower end proved briny and of limited quantity. When Peter Kalm, a member of the Swedish Royal Academy of Sciences, visited the city in 1748, he wrote, "This want of good water lies heavy upon the horses of the strangers that come to this place; for they do not like to drink the water from the wells in the town."[2]

In addition, New York lacked a sewage system to take away its waste. So, while the English learned of the errors of the Dutch and dug wells, they didn't seem to heed the problems their conquered European compatriots had faced, and continued to foul their streets by dumping garbage into the small Dutch-made canals. After they had ruined these watercourses, they simply covered the streams and turned them into roadways like Broad and Beaver Streets. Such cosmetic changes proved inadequate. Backyard privies overflowed, and the night soil workers who carted off vats of human filth to the Hudson and East Rivers often spilled the contents along the way. Meanwhile, waste from teams of horses, herds of cattle, packs of dogs, and droves of pigs further soiled the town. All this pollution seeped into the wells and brought with it disease.

There was therefore a great need for safe water. Those who had limited funds had no option other than to use the water from the city wells. New Yorkers with means could obtain the finer liquid that flowed from the

Tea Water pump. Located near the Collect Pond—to the east of current-day Foley Square—the pump drew from the same sources as the pond, and made, as its name noted, a proper cup of tea. Other entrepreneurs meanwhile drew on different local spots to the north, and carted down the water.

Attempts continued to find better water. In April 1774 the Dublin-born engineer Christopher Colles proposed "to Erect a Reservoir, and to Convey Water thro' the Several Streets of this City." His New-York Water Works sought to dig a well alongside the Collect, raise the water by a wood-burning-powered steam engine, store it in a one-million-gallon reservoir, and pipe the liquid through 14 miles of hollowed pine logs. But when the American Revolution started, Colles and his wife fled New York, and the system fell into disuse.

Little changed during the seven-year British occupation of the city. Major General Valentine Jones forbade the throwing of "filth, carbage [sic], or dirt" into the Collect. After the British left in 1783, the city grew, pollution continued unabated, and the quality of water in the Collect declined. In 1785 a concerned citizen wrote the New-York Journal to note how some didn't even care to quaff Tea Water. The cause, he said, could easily be traced to the Collect, which by then had become popular "with whites, and blacks, washing their cloths, blankets, and things too nauseous to mention, all their sudds and filth are emptied into this pond, besides dead dogs, cats, &c. thrown in daily." Despite his and others' complaints, Tea Water owners continued daily to pump out 14,000 gallons in the winter and double that in the warmer weather. Yet as tanners and other industries set up shop near the Collect, they further befouled it by dumping carcasses in the water. Slowly the pond became, in the words of the New York Commercial Advertiser in 1798, "a shocking hole, where all impure things center together and engender the worst of unwholesome productions."[3]

Disease was a constant concern for New Yorkers. Yellow Fever had raced through the city during that summer of 1798, and eventually took the lives of 1,524 people, more than 4 percent of the population. In response, Dr. Joseph Browne, Aaron Burr's brother-in-law, looked into the feasibility of supplying the city with water and suggested tapping the Bronx River to the north, pointing out that it "will afford a copious supply of pure and wholesome Water." Such a source would "prevent the rise and spreading of putrid disease" and could be used to combat fire, which "may be reckoned the greatest calamity, to which Cities are subject." He also called for a massive one-million-gallon reservoir to ensure a sizable supply.

To bring this about, Burr, who had gotten involved, proposed the creation of the Manhattan Company. He and his associates formed a committee made up of both Democratic-Republicans and Federalists. The group included Alexander Hamilton. At the time, the future duelists remained on good social good terms. But Burr had scant interest in running a public utility, laying pipes in the streets, distributing water, or watching out for the health and welfare of his neighbors. What he and his cohorts really wanted was to form a bank, deal in real estate, and sell insurance.[4]

At the time, the city had only one state-approved bank, the Bank of New York, which Hamilton and his Federalist allies had formed in 1784. While Burr said the planned corporation solely cared about water, the company's charter contained a clause that allowed "said company to employ all such surplus capital, as may belong or accrue to the said company in the purchase of public or other stock, or in any other monied transactions or operations." The company, which would evolve into Chase Manhattan Bank and then into JP Morgan Chase & Co., offered public stock in April 1799. Both Federalists and Democratic-Republicans invested.

The Manhattan Company quickly scotched plans to tap the Bronx River. Instead they announced that they would draw water from the much-derided Collect. On Chambers Street, near the pond, the directors erected a reservoir with an imposing Doric portico topped with a relief of the Greek Titan Oceanus. But instead of the sea-sized tank that had been proposed, one capable of holding a million gallons, it only accommodated 132,600 gallons. They similarly decided to forgo iron pipes, with Browne calling for the use of long yellow or white pine logs. The company then laid the water lines in the streets, and using pumps powered by horses, raised the water and charged private houses $5 a year, and more if the building had additional fireplaces.

Burr left the board by 1802, and the firm had relatively free rein for its operations. It didn't have to supply water for street cleaning, nor repair the roads after they put in the pipes. Often customers received no supply whatever. One *New York Evening Post* subscriber complained how he had "not had a drop of water itself for nine weeks." And worst of all, the water offered proved to be of poor quality. In 1805, a city committee examined the nearby Collect and noted how it was "filled with the bodies of dead animals, and dangerous to the health of the Citizens in its vicinity."[5]

Calls continued for the cleaning the Collect, and work began on draining it and the nearby Lispenard's Meadow. The city still did little to seek a more reliable group to supply water from purer sources. People therefore sought home remedies to make what they had more palatable. When Swedish Baron Axel Leonhard Klinkowström arrived in the United States in 1818, he noted how "the water in New York is usually mixed with some French brandy or gin to make it safe to drink. Otherwise cider is a common drink." One Dr. Lewis Feuchtwanger sold "Groening's Lemon Syrup," which he recommended be added to water for a refreshing drink. Some simply avoided the water altogether, preferring alcohol.

Despite the additives and alternatives, New York's water quality continued to decline. In April 1824, the prominent doctor David Hosack, along with other physicians, published a report attacking the Manhattan Company's supply, calling it unhealthy and noting that it "is frequently productive of diseases of the stomach and bowels . . . and other complaints of the kidneys." Brewers in 1831 even warned the Common Council that the quality of their beer was "rapidly depreciating." That same year, doctors, chemists, and scientists at the Lyceum of Natural History of the City of New York noted how some well water mixed with lime and other substances from graveyards "communicates a ropy appearance to the water and the water from such wells becomes, in warm weather, very offensive in the course of a few hours."[6]

Some tried to cleanse what they had. In 1826, the New York Mirror had suggested that "a few ounces of soda will soften a hogshead of the hardest water." In 1833, readers of the Evening Post learned of Parkes's Patent Portable Filters, that would make the city's "Filthy fluid . . . PURE and BRILLIANT." In 1835, G. Wade offered a device made up of two separate jars, "the one containing the filtering media, being made to fit into the jar that receives the filtered water." Costing a pricey $8 to $14, it could process 15 to 30 gallons a day. For many, water from further north on the island seemed the only reasonable alternative. Some hotels spent a great deal for such distant liquids. The New York Evening Journal noted in 1830 about carts bringing water from the upper parts of the city and the suburbs, which, "although far from good, is much better than that obtained from wells in the city." To make it appear better, the New York Sun reported in 1834 how some distributors whitened their supplies with milk.[7]

Though the water found on the lower island was considered undrinkable, some still probed the area with deeper borings. In the later 1820s, tanner Jacob Lorillard decided to draw water from the area near his shop where Beekman's Swamp once stretched. He hired a well digger, who drilled down 128 feet and tapped into what he believed to be a mineral spring. Chemist George Chilton analyzed the water and determined that its contents "produces a brilliant and sparkling effervescence." Lorillard then touted the water from "Jacob's Well" for its special medicinal qualities. Hoping to capitalize on his find, he built a Moorish-style building on the site. Soon New Yorkers flocked there, paying sixpence for a drink. The water spot stayed popular until people realized that the water's "special something" came from old boot and tan bark extracts that had leached through the soil.[8]

The Manhattan Company only supplied a fraction of the population, and, fearing the loss of their water monopoly, the firm set out to upgrade the service. In the fall of 1821 they reported that the system had undergone significant repairs and that they had added additional pipes so that now there was "an abundant supply of Water, in every part of the city where the pipes are laid." A few years later they claimed further improvements. During the summer of 1828, the company started replacing the wooden pipes with iron mains. Yet, despite their efforts, the water stayed foul, with journalist Asa Greene writing that it sported a "peculiar hue and taste," causing most citizens to shy away from the supply. In 1831, Alderman Samuel Stevens complained how the Manhattan Company had not "complied with the conditions of their Charter" and called for repealing the agreement with the group.[9]

* * *

As the city expanded northward, officials started contemplating ways to obtain a larger and more reliable water supply. In 1821 the Common Council looked into diverting some of the Bronx River into the Harlem River, and pumping the water to a reservoir in Manhattan. Some people called for tapping ponds in Westchester County and the Housatonic River in Connecticut, and connecting the Saw Mill River with the Bronx River. Yet in 1824, the *Evening Post* reported how the city had still done nothing about finding a better water supply, commenting how "year after year is allowed to pass without a single step being taken to obtain the necessary supply."

It wasn't just foul water and limited supplies that was the problem. In fire-prone New York, the Manhattan Company was, amazingly, not required to supply water to firemen. They did, though, let them tap the pipes if they plugged the holes, and soon allowed for the installation of wooden hydrants. To help the fire companies, the city constructed rain-fed cisterns. New York soon had about 40 of these, but they only held about 100 hogsheads— or 6,300 gallons—each. In March 1829, the city's Committee on the Fire Department completed an octagon-shape stone reservoir on 13th Street that was filled by a steam engine. Despite its size, the system's water pressure proved inadequate.[10]

This ongoing lack of water contributed to the high losses from fires, and a situation that, as we've seen, early on spurred the growth of fire insurance companies like Hone's Eagle Fire Company. And then, of course, disease—much brought about by the city's fetid water and minimal sanitation—seemed to be endlessly tormenting New Yorkers. The city was filthy, yet medical professionals had no real idea what caused sickness or how to treat their patients. Because of this, citizens suffered through regular plagues, from smallpox in the 17th century to Yellow Fever starting in the 18th century. In January 1820, Governor DeWitt Clinton commented on the fever and how "it is sufficient to observe that all unite in recommending the utmost attention to the purification of our cities." He advised that "the establishment of public baths and common sewers will have a most salutary influence" on health, and called for bringing in "pure and wholesome water." And while the *Evening Post* reported in the early 1830s that New York had more "commodious and luxuriously arranged baths" than any other American city—with salt water, vapor, medicated, and shower baths—what it had was woefully insufficient to keep the community clean and healthy.

If the mosquito-spread Yellow Fever wasn't bad enough, a new and more deadly water-borne scourge, cholera, lapped over Manhattan's shores starting in the summer of 1832. The disease cut a wide swath through New York and indeed the entire country, preying on both the wealthy and the poor, the healthy and the sick. The city tried to cope with the illness, and many fingered the water and air as the main culprits. Washington Irving noted to *New York American* editor Charles King on August 9 that "the prevalence of other maladies in our city may be owing to the nature of the water we drink, which is nearly as important to health as the air we breathe." By the time the plague abated, 3,513 New Yorkers, nearly 2 percent of the population, had perished.[11]

Other cities grappled with the same problems. Philadelphia attempted to deal with the need for pure water by starting construction in 1799 on the Centre Square Water Works, and then building the Fairmount Water Works. By 1818, that city had some 32 miles of pipes. When cholera arrived in the City of Brotherly Love in 1832, only 935 Philadelphians died. New York's water commissioners believed the only way to explain this difference was that "Philadelphia is supplied with abundance of pure and wholesome water . . . while New-York is entirely destitute of the means for effecting any of these purposes."

Cholera became the impetus to change. Myndert Van Schaick, who had married John Hone's daughter Elizabeth, served as an alderman when cholera arrived in 1832. Unlike many others, this representative from the Fifth Ward and treasurer of the Board of Health didn't flee the city. As he monitored the disease's deadly progress, he and other like-minded leaders became determined to end the Manhattan Company's monopoly. In October, the Board of Aldermen's Committee on Fire and Water passed a resolution to look into getting pure water for the city. Then, on November 10, they appointed Governor Clinton's son, Colonel DeWitt Clinton Jr.—a civil engineer who did surveys for the Army Corps of Topographical Engineers—to find the most feasible source.[12]

Colonel Clinton looked north, dispatching engineers to look at the Bronx River, Rye Ponds, the Bryam River, and other sources. He soon recommended using the Croton River, 40 miles to the north in Westchester County. Bringing water from afar was not a new idea. In ancient Mesopotamia, the Sumerians formed reservoirs and built canals to tap the Tigris and Euphrates Rivers. The Egyptians likewise drew water from the Nile River via canals. Sennacherib, the 8th-century BCE king of Assyria, sought to create gardens with fruit and exotic trees in his capital of Nineveh. He tapped springs and streams and had his engineers construct the 59-mile-long Khinis canal. And in 312 BCE Roman statesman Appius Claudius Caecus started work on the empire's first aqueduct, an elaborate infrastructure project that would continue to AD 226—more than five hundred years—and supply the empire's urban centers.

In February 1833, the city asked Major David Bates Douglass to create an aqueduct. That summer, Douglass set out with a team to survey Westchester and figure out the best way to funnel the water south. The New Jersey–born engineer and former member of the Army Corps of Engineers arrived with high qualifications. He had served as chief engineer of Morris Canal, and surveyed the route for the Brooklyn and Jamaica Railroad. On May 2, 1834, Governor William Marcy signed "An Act to Provide for Supplying the City of New York with Pure and Wholesome Water." But since the grand project to bring the water from the Croton and build a reservoir was projected to cost $4.15 million—as well as an additional $1.262 million to lay pipes—the plan would first require approval of the city's inhabitants.

Public projects were not the norm at the time. The financing of the Erie Canal, however, made it easier for the city to justify such a project.

Commissioners set out to show that the expense was a wise investment from every point of view, including health. Dr. Nathaniel Shurtleff, a member of the Boston Medical Association, reported that the water from the city wells "is in a degree unwholesome, predisposing some to calculous and others to bilious disorders." And Dr. Lemuel Shattuck commented that the water's odor caused those entering New York "to hold his breath, or make use of some perfume to break off the disagreeable smell."

It was less the disagreeable stench than the deadly threat that would change people's minds. In 1834 cholera returned, killing 971. Moreover, in that year alone, 110 devastating blazes tore through the city. "The very great destruction of property by the late fires, owing mainly to the want of a full supply of water, are urgent considerations for a prompt action," wrote the commissioners.[13]

Work needed to start quickly, since the local supply was drying up, with the Committee on Fire and Water reporting in March 1835 that "The removal of the hills north of 13th street, and the building of sewers in that neighborhood have reduced the supply of the public well from 20,000 gallons a day to about 6,000." Supporters printed and distributed 2,500 copies of the water commissioners' report. Newspapers meanwhile ran abridged versions of the commissioners' remarks. Resistance proved especially strong in Westchester, where property owners feared for the confiscation of their property. Resident Theodorus C. Van Wyck even drove into town to distribute handbills attacking the plan. The city set the water vote for April 14 to 16, 1835. Hoping for an advantage at the polls, the Board of Assistants treated voters to some 400 gallons of Croton water so they could sample the product. In the end, citizens voted overwhelmingly—17,330 to 5,963—in favor of the plan. The following month, the city issued Water Stock, and on June 2 Douglass got to work.[14]

* * *

The Great Fire was the final straw, pushing even the most skeptical to change their minds. On December 21, 1835, five days after the fire, the *Commercial Advertiser* urged that the new water project "must be accomplished and that without delay." Douglass' engineers prepared land maps. He recommended a closed masonry gravity system, and the commissioners told him to draw up specifications for the aqueduct and put them under contract. The team started designing some of the structures, but work progressed slowly. Ten months after the Great Fire and 18 months after the vote, no ground had been broken, let alone a final route decided for the aqueduct. The *New York Herald* in October 1836 complained, "Not a shovel full of earth has yet been taken." Impatient with Douglass' inaction, the commissioners looked for a replacement engineer. Chairman and former mayor Stephen Allen tapped John Jervis, an engineer who had worked on the Erie Canal and intimately understood the requirements and problems that came with building large projects. On October 11, 1836, Jervis replaced Douglass as chief engineer.[15]

Jervis was a self-taught engineer, a "Practical Man," who knew what to do through hard experience. Born in Huntington, New York, on December 14, 1795, he was the oldest of seven children. The Jervises moved three years later to Rome, New York, where John worked at his father's sawmill and helped clear land, finishing school at age 15. The family belonged to the local Congregational church, where Jervis became imbued with a strong religious fervor. He would also fall under the sway of the revivalist Charles Grandison Finney, a charismatic preacher who was one of the main leaders of the Second Great Awakening, a religious revival movement that had been sweeping the United States since the late 18th century. While Jervis was a somewhat lonely and emotionally restrained man, he believed in the value of hard work, and when in 1817 the engineer Benjamin Wright asked the senior Jervis to help clear terrain for the Erie Canal, the younger Jervis eagerly signed up for the work crew, noting years later, "Having been brought up in a new country, I had acquired a very handy use of the axe."

While he labored, Jervis became intrigued by the surveying equipment that was being used, particularly by the "target man" who occupied, as Jervis later wrote, "the first step in the science of engineering. On reflection it appeared to me I could do that service if I could have a little practice."[16] As with the field of architecture, engineers simply learned on the job. Jervis quickly did. He became a target man, and rose through the ranks, conducting levels, working as a stone weigher, and learning how to read plans for everything from culverts to waste weirs. He also studied books on mechanics and natural philosophy. Meticulous, industrious, and exceptionally honest, Jervis endeared himself to those he worked with. Soon he became a resident engineer of a 17-mile section of the canal. In 1823 he became superintendent of a 50-mile stretch. By the time he left that project, Jervis could survey, draw maps and profiles, manage construction, make repairs, and write up estimates.

The Erie Canal opened in 1825, and that year Jervis became Wright's principal assistant engineer on Philip Hone's Delaware & Hudson Canal

Company. There Jervis organized the work, oversaw the construction, and filled in for Wright when he was away. When Wright resigned in 1827, Jervis took over. He stayed at the Delaware & Hudson until the spring of 1830, and continued in an advisory role for another year. He became the chief engineer of the Mohawk & Hudson Railway, as well as the Schenectady and Saratoga Railroad, served as chief engineer of the Chenango Canal, and worked as a division chief on the enlargement of the Erie Canal.

After Jervis had replaced Douglass, work on the Croton aqueduct moved quickly. He had maps, working plans, and drawings made up, selected materials, and analyzed alternative plans and routes to see which might be cheaper. Jervis dutifully watched over expenses and made the office run efficiently. Most importantly, he established workmanship standards. He designed a brick-lined aqueduct that had a high arched roof nearly eight and a half feet high and almost seven and a half feet wide. He set 33 ventilators along the run for air circulation, six waste weirs to purge the line of excess water, and 114 stone culverts so the aqueduct would not block streams and other bodies of water, and planned the system's conduits, protection walls, and embankments.

Jervis also turned his attention to designing the Croton Dam, which formed a 400-acre reservoir above Ossining. Throughout he insisted on durability. And while he eschewed frills and ornamentation—believing they were not only expensive but also masked potential problems—he insisted on quality. For instance, the engineer demanded that instead of using the quick lime that Douglass called for, they should use more durable hydraulic cement lime. Though the commissioners balked at the additional expense— $250,000—they eventually went along with his recommendation.[17]

To manage this massive project—nearly 40 miles in length, traveling parallel to the Hudson River—Jervis sought out staff on whom he could rely. He brought with him his assistant from the Delaware & Hudson, Horatio Allen, as well as Allen's assistant Fayette Tower, who during his five years on the Croton team would famously document its progress through letters and illustrations. And, as someone who worked his own way up the ranks through hard work and practical smarts, Jervis advanced those who showed promise.

Jervis divided the line into four sections, each stretching about 10 miles long. He then split up each part, creating nearly 100 subdivisions. The engineering squad was formed into four teams with a resident engineer, a first and second assistant, one or two rodmen and axmen, as well as one or two workers. Specifications were soon ready, and on February 28, 1837, the commissioners placed ads in newspapers for sealed bids for the first division's 23 sections, the area running from the Croton Dam down to the village of Sing Sing. Investors quickly snapped up the initial stock offering, and contractors signed on. Fortunately, all this occurred just prior to the Panic of 1837. Funding was thus in place for the system right when the economy slowed to a crawl. So while the nation's businesses shut down, banks closed, and people lost their jobs, work on the Croton system got underway.

Not everyone appreciated the huge project. Many Westchester residents voiced their outrage, and, as happened when John Randel surveyed the city for the 1811 Commissioners' Plan, stakes marking the line regularly vanished. Landowners like Pierre Van Cortlandt threatened crews with trespass, and residents verbally abused and assaulted surveyors. Locals also attacked the plan. Led by landowner Van Wyck, they petitioned the state legislature in March 1837, claiming that the commissioners were unfairly "invading the historic manor of Cortlandt and the County of Westchester." Those who agreed to part with their land demanded exorbitant prices. The commissioners ended up paying out, for instance, more than $100 an acre for some of the Van Cortlandt land, noting how much of it "is steep side-hill, and entirely unfit for cultivation." At the same time, speculators with an eye for a healthy profit bought up land along the route, even splitting properties into smaller lots in the hope of extracting higher appraisals. For those unwilling to sell, the city started the slow process of condemnation.

In the end, New York ended up having to spend a fortune for 813 acres of land, stretching from the Croton River down to the city.[18] But at last the work could begin.

10

The Croton River Flows into the City

Just seven months after becoming chief engineer in October 1836, John Jervis happily reported how "Young & Scott broke ground on Section 20" on May 16, 1837, and construction started on the Croton Aqueduct. Section 20 made up a strip of the line that included the Sing-Sing Kill Aqueduct Bridge in Ossining. Andrew Young's work impressed Jervis, and the engineer wrote how its "well dressed stone masonry, laid in hydraulic cement" with an 88-foot arched span "did not settle over of ¾ of an inch, and has not changed since. This I consider a very small settlement for so large an arch."

Meanwhile, in Manhattan, the laying of pipes in the streets began. By June, 390 workers labored away on the system, many happy for the work during the deepening depression. In September, more sections went under contract. That month the city acquired 37 acres for the Yorkville Receiving Reservoir, evicting the African American community that had occupied York Hill on the east side of what would become Central Park. Some of the residents most likely settled in the black community of Seneca Village just to the west. The city also got hold of the land for the Murray Hill Distributing Reservoir on Fifth Avenue and 42nd Street. By late that year, the *New York Evening Post* reported that more than 25 miles were under contract, with 1,200 men working.

Jervis worked tirelessly, touring the aqueduct's progress every week or two. Resident engineers meanwhile oversaw their individual lines, and made sure contractors did what was required of them. And if the work did not pass muster, the engineer could demand it be fixed before paying for the job.[1] Some complained about the slowness of construction; others commented that it seemed to be on course. In November 1837, the *Hudson River Chronicle* wrote that in several tunnels "the blasters are already nearly two hundred feet beyond day light." Two months later, one of their reporters visited a tunnel and noted that it ran 52 feet below the surface and already covered 335 feet.

The work proved hard and dangerous. In December 1837, an explosion killed worker Daniel Harrington and severely injured two others. Another accident occurred the next day, when a worker "laying down a short train of powder, imprudently applied a match" and was killed. Contractor Young had his skull fractured in June 1838 when a piece of a blasted rock struck him. Flying debris sometimes hit homes in Westchester.[2]

Landowners displeased by the intrusion not only made life difficult for the surveyors and engineers, but also for the laborers. Locals objected to the families of what they disparagingly called "Shanty Irish." Washington Irving, who moved to Tarrytown in 1835, griped about their presence, commenting how "a colony of Patlanders have been encamped about this place all winter, forming a kind of Patsylvania, in the midst of a 'wiltherness.'" In language reminiscent of the Headless Horseman from his "The Legend of Sleepy Hollow," Irving wrote of how some became convinced that the Westchester woods brimmed with "misshapen monsters whisking about their paths; sometimes resembling men, sometimes boys, sometimes horses, but invariably without heads." The occasionally riotous nature of the workers caused locals to complain. Many viewed the area, as one account had it, as "unsafe and imprudent for a respectable female to walk on, or near, or along where said aqueduct is constructing."[3]

Locals opposed the arrival of the workers, and water commissioners blamed residents for instigating much of the resulting friction. While rules prevented contractors from selling liquor to the men, no such restrictions existed for these same locals. Seeking to capitalize on the presence of so many paid laborers, some turned their farmhouses into taverns and set up what Irving called "whiskey establishments." As the commissioners noted: "the love of lucre has induced certain individuals . . . to open places of resort for the laborers, where this *enemy of man* may be obtained, in any quantity for money."

And while workers appreciated the employment, many chafed at the sparse accommodations and the paltry pay. The contractors overcharged them for food. One contractor refused to listen to growing demands for a raise, and the men quit "in a body, and proceeded along the line of the aqueduct in a tumultuous manner." Others joined, and soon several hundred men headed south. When they reached Mount Pleasant, the magistrate stopped the marchers. Around the same time, another contractor fired two of his men and was then beaten with clubs and stones.[4] Wages fluctuated, and in April 1840 contractors again refused workers' demands for a raise. A mass of club-bearing workers "turned out, and marching down from Westchester to Harlem prevented others from working," wrote Philip Hone, "and committed some acts of violence upon the workers." As they advanced, they drove fellow carpenters and masons from their work, broke mortar boxes, set loose horses, and threatened to whip foremen and contractors. Soon 1,000 men gathered in Manhattanville and said that if they didn't receive a raise, they would destroy the works. Mayor Isaac Varian called out the militia to quell the rioting. About 150 or so then made their way as far as 42nd Street and tried to interfere with workers constructing the Murray Hill Distributing Reservoir. The men did find some sympathy in the pages of the *Evening Post*, which wrote that their treatment by the contractors was "atrociously unjust and oppressive." There continued to be strikes and work shut-downs, but operations restarted as managers threatened laborers, and the police arrested ringleaders.

In addition to those Upstaters who opposed the project, some in New York worried that it would cost the city too much. A few even considered selling their property so as not to be burdened with additional taxes. Calmer minds prevailed. "It was currently reported of one large holder of real estate that he said to his friends he would sell his property," recalled Jervis. Before he did, though, the man "concluded he would first have a consultation with John J. Astor, whose opinion on real estate he highly valued." Jervis reported that the man talked with Astor, and that the land baron argued, "we can hardly spend too much for a good supply of good water." Mr. Astor's "cool treatment of the subject induced the property holder to hold on to his real estate."[5]

One of biggest challenges Jervis faced involved bringing water across the Harlem River to the northern part of Manhattan. Commissioners debated whether he should build something simple and practical, or embrace architectural splendor and construct a regal span. The frugally minded engineer calculated that a tunnel would come in at $636,738, and the larger High Bridge would cost $838,613. Jervis pushed for the less expensive route. Nonetheless, the commissioners opted for the bridge, and Jervis dutifully designed a grand span, one that would have suited the Romans. While working on the bridge in May 1839, his wife Cynthia gave birth to a daughter. But the child died within a few hours, and his wife passed away five days later. Heartbroken, Jervis poured himself into his work, and then at the urging of his family married Eliza Coates the following year.

By the start of 1840, the masonry conduit ran down New York's western edge, and pipes were laid; the dam and the Croton Lake reservoir neared completion. Early January 1841 proved cold, and a heavy snow fell. On January 5 the snow started to melt, followed by two days of rain. By the 7th, water swelled behind the Croton Dam. Aware of the impending danger, the son of a contractor set out at one in the morning on his horse and, blowing a horn, warned those downriver of the impending danger. "The water rose to within a few inches of the top of the embankment, and made a passage between the frozen and unfrozen earth," wrote Jervis of the unfolding disaster. The breaking water created such force that, as the commissioners noted, "the protection wall gave no resistance."

After the dam broke, water coursed for four miles, carried off the gatehouse, swept away orchards, skidded along boulders, uprooted fences, and wiped out roads and bridges. On its destructive trip it took with it a house as well as a gristmill, along with the tenants' houses, barns, and bridge. Workers—along with women and children—had to climb trees for safety. The accident caused a fortune in damages, and because of it Jervis was forced to replace the earthen embankment with a stone one. It included a spillway and surge pool at the base, a design that would become the standard form for such structures.[6]

Work meanwhile progressed on the Murray Hill Distributing Reservoir at Fifth Avenue and 42nd Street. Designed by Jervis and James Renwick, its massive granite walls tapered to the top. Hone visited there in October 1841. A contractor showed him and a companion around the four-acre site, and told them how the water would come from the 35-acre reservoir in Yorkville by way of "double rows of enormous iron pipes." Hone commented how the fresh water offered would give a boost to the anti-saloon "temperance teetotallers." As work neared completion, assistant engineer Fayette Tower wrote his mother in December about how they "have finished the big 'Tea Pot' with which we can fill the cups of the citizens of N.Y."[7]

Soon the watercourse was ready to start its run into New York City. To make sure all was well with the route, on June 8, 1842, Jervis and a number of commissioners set out on a three-day inspection tour. The men started at the Croton River and followed the length of the aqueduct, both above and below the surface. Then, early on the 22nd, the commissioners opened the aqueduct gates at the new Croton Lake, and Jervis, the commissioners, and the assistant engineers embarked on a second trip, this one aboard *The Croton Maid of Croton Lake*. As the water coursed into the aqueduct, the 16-foot-long wooden skiff slipped along the current. The boat coursed faster than expected. Soon the crew pulled into Sing-Sing. They took a break and then headed to the waste gates at Mill River, arriving at 3:00 PM. Then they set off for Yonkers, pulling in at 10:30. The men started again in the morning, arriving at the Harlem River at one in the afternoon. From there, they portaged over the land to the Yorkville Reservoir.

On the 27th, water flowed into the 150-million-gallon Yorkville Reservoir. The gently sloped sides of the man-made lake stretched from Sixth to Seventh Avenue and from 79th to 86th Streets. "When it was known in New York that the waters of the Croton were actually beginning to pour into the receiving reservoir at Yorkville, an immense crowd gathered," wrote Governor William Seward. Fifteen to twenty thousand people soon swarmed the area, arriving by trains, cabs, omnibuses, and carriages. Seward, Mayor Robert Morris, congressmen, members of the Common Council, and others came to witness the spectacle. "The Corporation made an affair of the arrival of the waters, troops were ordered out, a salute of thirty-four guns, being the number of miles the water had traveled to reach us, fired," wrote Hone.[8]

Flags fluttered, and Samuel Stevens, the chairman of the Board of Water Commissioners, presented the boat, *The Croton Maid of Croton Lake*, to the Fire Department, telling them, "We give her to you as emblematical of the capacity of the Aqueduct to introduce an abundant supply of water for the great object of your organization—the extinguishment of fires." Even the 78-year-old Astor showed up. "I was introduced to him and took his hand," observed Tower. "His head was bent forward beneath the weight of years and being introduced to one of the contractors for building the reservoir, he turned up one eye toward him and remarked 'I think you ought to make *money* here.'"[9]

Then on July 4, 25,000 flocked to the streets around the Murray Hill Distributing Reservoir. People climbed the stairs to the iron-railed parapet, and a huge cheer went up as citizens watched the water flow in. A few days later, Jervis had the effluent gates opened and water gushed into the city's water mains. A week later, Hone and his family went up to see the reservoirs and rejoiced at seeing the "clear, sweet, soft water . . . flowing in copiously."[10]

Officials planned a grand celebration in October. The fete set off on the 14th, and New Yorkers treated it like a national holiday. Crowds gathered to witness a party on the scale of the one that had taken place for the opening of the Erie Canal in 1825. "Never saw the street so crowded," reported George Templeton Strong. To launch the festivities, a 100-cannon salute was fired, church bells rang, and ships in the ports and in harbor unfurled their national colors. Flowers draped windows, cornices, and balconies, and flags stretched across Broadway and fluttered from City Hall and the Carlton, President, and Howard Hotels, as well as from Niblo's Garden, and Barnum's American Museum.[11]

Thousands lined the streets, crammed onto church steps and climbing trees and awning posts to get a better view of the celebratory parade. Others craned their necks from windows, balconies, and doorsteps; youngsters shot off firecrackers and popguns. Fayette Tower found a space on top of one of Broadway's highest buildings. The street "was full to the very house tops," he wrote, and it was "our brilliant day of the celebration." But when the engineers and contractors heard that Jervis had been told he must walk the processional route instead of riding in one of the carriages, they threatened to boycott the festivities. Governor Seward immediately invited the engineer to sit up front with him. As martial and other music played, troops and all the carriages carrying dignitaries and honored guests, including mayors from other cities and foreign diplomats, set off.[12]

Fire Chief Cornelius Anderson led some 3,000 New York firemen, including one Zophar Mills, who served as one of the assistant marshals. Fire companies from Philadelphia, Connecticut, New Jersey, and Long Island turned out to show their support, and all marched alongside their polished engines bedecked with flags, banners, ribbons, and flowers. And, as a reminder of the sort of destruction they hoped to prevent in the future, two of the banners—that of the Chatham Engine Co. No. 2 and the Forrest Engine Company No. 3—displayed views of the burning of the Bowery Theatre. Workers from the aqueduct and soldiers marched along or sat in large, horse-drawn trucks. Members of various trades, such as ironworkers, millers, and bakers, took part in the parade. Children representing Croton Lake water sprites filled another float. One float even carried Benjamin Franklin's printing press. The *New York Commercial Advertiser*'s William Leete Stone supervised as printers ran off and tossed out copies of "The Croton Ode" by journalist George Pope Morris, whose most famous work was "Woodman! Spare That Tree!"

Unlike regular New York public holidays, there were no liquor booths along the parade route, and most grog shops stayed shut. Contingents of temperance society members from such groups as the Manhattan Temperance Society, the Bloomingdale Temperance Society, and the Maine Temperance Society marched. One cart carrying ice sported the label, "An Original Croton Cooler." The Cold Spring Temperance Society had a blue silk banner proclaiming, "Turn; drink of the pure fountain of life, come with us and be free." Another group hoisted a banner bearing an image of an overturned liquor decanter and the inscription, "Right side up!"

The whole procession took seven hours to wend the seven miles from the Battery at the southern tip of the island to Union Square, and then down the Bowery to City Hall. There, celebrants listened to speeches, and Stevens talked of how "the water is of a pure and transparent character," will "protect our city from the awful conflagrations," and will ensure that a destructive blaze on the scale of the Great Fire of 1835 "shall never be repeated." He also reminded them how citizens would become "more temperate," because "we shall now no longer afford the apology for mixing brandy and rum with water—that of making it drinkable." Officials then christened the City Hall fountain, its center jet shooting water 50 feet into the air. As it did, 200 male and women members of the New York Sacred Music Society sang out Morris's Ode:

> Water leaps as if delighted,
> While her conquered foes retire!
> Pale Contagion flies affrighted
> With the baffled demon, Fire!
> Safety dwells in her dominions,
> Health and Beauty with her move,
> And entwine their circling pinions
> In a sisterhood of love.[13]

After the ceremony, hundreds feasted at City Hall on cold collation and quaffed Croton water and lemonade. Candles flickered in the windows at the Astor House as fireworks lit up the night sky. At a ball given at Washington Hall, Governor Seward toasted how "today the pure mountain-stream gushes through its streets and sparkles in its squares."

Now, with his work completed, Tower agonized over what to do next, writing his sister-in-law, "Where then shall I go? I fear this work has spoiled me; for I can scarcely condescend to go begging for employment among the paltry railroads, since I have seen this noble work start from the designs upon paper, and stand forth in the beauty and grandeur of construction."[14]

* * *

As the *New York Tribune* observed, "The Croton Water is good," assuring New Yorkers that they "will find it richly worth its cost." Generally, New Yorkers agreed. Lydia Maria Child, who edited the *National Anti-Slavery*

Standard—and two years later would pen "Thanksgiving Day," which begins with the line, "Over the river and through the wood"—exclaimed about the "clean, sweet, abundant water!" After visiting the fountains in the Park and Union Square, she wrote, "My soul jumped, and clapped its hands, rejoicing in exceeding beauty."[15]

For many the arrival of water meant a boom in business. Even before water flowed into the city, plumber Abraham Brower ran an ad in the *Evening Post*, offering his services to install pipes and faucets for "the Lovers of Pure and Wholesome water." Houses for sale also advertised water as an amenity, with a three-story brick home on Beach Street coming complete with "a convenient kitchen with Croton Water." As the *Evening Post* noted, "No one can witness the arrangements for health, refreshment and convenience which the introduction of the Croton water has enabled builders to introduce into the houses they are erecting, without being satisfied that the benefits of that great enterprise are not yet fully appreciated." The only group it didn't help, obviously, was the independent water suppliers. And while the Manhattan Company focused on its core banking business, it still held on to its wells for fear that if it gave them up, that would forfeit their charter.[16]

In the end, Croton cost $13 million, $8 million more than initially budgeted. At nearly twice the price of the Erie Canal, this was simply a colossal amount of money. The price of the system worried many. To help pay for it, the Croton board charged homeowners a yearly fee—$10 for a two-story house, $12 for a three—while boarding houses paid $10 to $20 and livery stables $5 per stall. People complained about the amount they had to pay for hookups. Those who had the water, though, received a reduced premium rate from the Firemen's Insurance Company.

With water flowing into homes, residences receiving water not only benefited from the fresh supply but also gained bragging rights by installing water closets and sinks. The Strong family put one in their Greenwich Street home. The 23-year-old George Templeton—who at the time lived in a rear building at the house and planned a bathroom for his space—channeled Samuel Taylor Coleridge's 1816 poem "Kubla Khan" when he wrote:

> In Greenwich Street did G.T.S.
> A stately backbuilding decree,
> Where clear the Croton Water ran
> Through pipes impervious to man—
> Up to the third stor*ie*.

Strong tried out his newly installed bathroom that July, and crowed that it was "a great luxury—worth the cost of the whole building."[17]

In May 1844, Edgar Allan Poe recommended to readers of the *Columbia Spy* that they should go to see the Distributing Reservoir, telling them, "The prospect from the walk around the reservoir is particularly beautiful." By then, the system south of 42nd Street consisted of 150 miles of pipes, supplying 600 water hydrants and 1,500 fire hydrants. To pay for it, a total of $92,626 was raised by the fees to customers. Croton commissioners wanted to make sure that people paid for what they used. P.T. Barnum had opened his American Museum in 1842, and one of his displays included a small model of Niagara Falls. While the showman touted "the Grand and Sublime Exhibition of the stupendous FALLS OF NIAGARA!" he admitted that it was "small potatoes." Yet one day the water board summoned Barnum and told the showman that his $25-a-year water bill was too low. "We cannot furnish water for your Niagara Falls without large extra compensation." The master huckster smiled, and as he described the actual size of the exhibit, his explanation met with a "hearty burst of laughter from the Commissioners."[18]

Yet, though businesses and those with money got running water, many New Yorkers could not afford the cost. Renters quickly learned that many landlords refused to cover the price of installation, forcing their tenants to continue using the public wells. The *Commercial Advertiser* observed in 1845 that it didn't help that the pumps were unequally distributed, with some streets containing "superabundant hydrants, in others not half enough." And how, in the uptown Sixteenth Ward, "there are neither pumps nor hydrants." In 1846, most of the city still lacked water.

For those who could not bring water into their homes and hook up baths, businesses supplied the service. In 1842 Rabineau's new Hot and Cold Salt Water Bath on Desbrosses Street offered a large swimming bath and private baths, as well as "Ladies Baths, with a pure sweeping run of water" at the Battery. Yet such places catered to those with enough to pay the price of admission, and from the start, the *New York Spectator* implored that, "There ought to be public baths, open to everybody at a trifling charge or not charge at all." Improvements slowly appeared. In 1860, the *New York Times* reported that nine years earlier "a number of benevolent gentlemen" started the People's Washing and Bathing Establishment on Mott Street near Grand with a place to wash, dry, and iron clothes.[19]

At the start, people commented about the quality of the unfiltered water. Some complained about the "embryo, the spawn of the fish, &c. putrid slime and decayed vegetable matter" in the liquid. A leather factory on Ferry Street reported finding the remains of an eel that had washed through the system. Disregarding such talk, the water board insisted that the supply offered the purest and healthiest liquid around—"No person need to be afraid of Croton water." Nonetheless, to play it safe, the commissioners had wire meshes placed over the entry pipes to ensure that only water washed into the system.

Work meanwhile continued on the High Bridge, with water flowing across the Harlem River through low-placed pipes. Strong visited the construction site in October 1847 and wrote how a "Very great piece of work is the bridge." The 1,450-foot-long span was finally finished the following year. Its monumental arches proved to be the most costly parts of the system. *Harper's* wrote about "its interminable line of lofty marble piers and arches every where, from far and near, charming the eye as the tales of fairy land delight the fancy." More importantly, the bridge increased the system's pressure. And it quickly became a popular weekend destination for many wanting to get out of the city to enjoy the views and head over to nearby restaurants and beer gardens.[20]

* * *

Croton revolutionized New York and spurred its continued growth, as water flowed to homes, businesses, even fountains at hotels, such as the one in the Astor House courtyard and on top of Barnum's. When the Irving House Hotel opened in 1848, it boasted of water closets and baths throughout, with all rooms, even the ones at the top, supplied with Croton Water. The city's population continued to rise with the water pressure. As he looked north from the parapet of the Murray Hill reservoir in 1849, Whitman noted "these immense stretches of vacant ground below, will be covered with houses; the paved streets will clatter with innumerable carts and resound to deafening cries; and the promenaders here will look down upon them, perhaps, and away 'up town,' toward the quieter and more fashionable quarters, and see great changes."

Not surprisingly, and perhaps inevitably, people started to take the water for granted. New Yorkers used 12 million gallons a day in 1842. By the following May, the Croton Aqueduct Board reported how many of the city's 1,400 fire hydrants were "continually unclosed and made to flow by persons wholly unauthorized thereto." Such waste lowered pressure and hampered the work of firemen. In July 1844, the city passed an ordinance fining those who watered streets and sidewalks from 8:00 AM to 7:00 PM. Two years later the board again complained of the waste "from the hydrants, day and night, was so excessive." As the *Tribune* commented that August, "The demand for water is so great [during] the present hot weather that it is found impossible to keep up the supply in the distributing basins as fast as it is taken out." By 1850, the city was tapping 40 million gallons a day. Officials were worried. Fire Chief Alfred Carson issued a dire warning that the city needed to expand the system or would not have enough water to fight fires.[21]

The water's health benefits, though, became clear from the start. "The introduction of the Croton water exercised an important and most salutary influence upon the pestilence," wrote Dr. William Buel in the *New-York Journal of Medicine, and Collateral Sciences* when comparing the cholera epidemic of 1832 with the one that arrived in 1849. Because of the system, "the intensity of the epidemic influence seems to have been somewhat more dilute in one respect in 1849 than in 1832." And because of the growing conviction that it prevented sickness, tens of thousands of new customers signed up to receive Croton water. Yet while those opposed to alcohol consumption hoped that the water would cause people to exchange the evil "Devil's Brew" for pure "Adam's Ale," they unhappily learned that it instead supplied breweries with a reliable supply to make beer.[22]

Hoping to make sure that the system ran efficiently, the Croton Water Board in 1842 was placed under the care of five commissioners, with John Lawrence as president. Whichever political party was in control of the government reaped political spoils, and in January 1848 a Whig board took over, giving Hone the presidency and earning him $1,500 a year. But in April 1849, Hone had to give up the position when the system became the Croton Aqueduct Department .

Given growing demand for water, the city started to work on a larger receiving reservoir. By April 1857, the water board reported that the system had 225 miles of street pipes and mains, with 54,000 buildings receiving water, including 531 bakeries, 340 barber shops, 5,711 rum bars, 60 breweries, 22 distilleries, 34 bathing establishments, 120 factories, 384 fountains, 115 hotels, 162 refectories, 17 laundries, 24 packing houses, 147 slaughterhouses, 101 horse troughs, 41 soap factories, 467 steam engines, 11 sugar refineries, and 10,834 water closets. As Whitman observed, more than just the comfort of getting "an abundant supply of clean, sweet, soft, wholesome water," the water meant a chance to "save this half-wooden city from ruinous conflagrations. Say, you heroic dare-devils who man the engines, how often have you been balked and dismayed, less by the furious flames than by the absence of water to put them out?"[23]

11

The Power of the Fire Engines

The arrival of Croton water in 1842 not only gave the city potable water, it supplied the firemen with a reliable source to fight the flames. It was hoped that an accessible water supply would make the city safer. Yet blazes still flared up. Sadly—somewhat incredibly—the Bowery Theatre caught fire for the fourth time on April 25, 1845, two and a half years after the Croton celebration. As the cast and crew rescued the wardrobe and scenery, engines and hose companies rushed there and, according to the *New York Herald,* "set the invaluable Croton at full liberty." George Templeton Strong ran over, too: "Before I was two blocks from Broadway, the smoke was suffocating and blinding," he reported. As he watched, aghast, he saw "a flicker of deep red flame streaming up under the cornice in the rear, and subsiding again, then another and another, and at last it caught on the roof, one or two dazzling little streams of fire ran like lightning along the cornices, and in one minute the whole area of the building was a mere furnace, sending high up into the air such a mass of intense raging flame as I never saw before."

As it burned, the Empire and Southwark engine companies tried to stop it from spreading to the adjoining building, and others rescued horses from the stables on Elizabeth Street. While they fought the blaze, the *Herald* observed how people were "dashing chairs, tables, beds &c., through the windows, not waiting to open them, but throwing them through the frames, smashing the articles to pieces in their fall." Forty minutes after the discovery of the fire, the interior of the Bowery collapsed in upon itself. Thomas Hamblin did not have insurance for his theater, and as he watched the theater crumble, he bemoaned, "There go the labors of seven years!"

Philip Hone, who laid the cornerstone for the first theater in 1826, noted how "This great tinder-box, the gigantic Loco-foco match of New York, was destroyed last evening by fire." He wondered whether it was "the voice of fate," discouraging anyone from building "another temple of the drama on the forbidden ground." Hone was wrong, however, for even as the men were extinguishing the fire, Hamblin proclaimed, "We are not dead yet boys!" Indeed, the following day the impresario had crews start cleaning out the site, and he made plans for a new house. Even his arch-nemesis James Gordon Bennett felt sympathy for him, writing in the *Herald*, "With the recent sad calamity on his shoulders, the poor man is indeed to be pitied; and therefore we say let by-gones be by-gones, and are willing to lend him any aid in our power."[1]

Three months later, the new Croton Aqueduct system received a serious test. The summer of 1845 proved to be brutally hot. Early in the morning of July 19, a fire broke out at J.L. Vandoren's sperm-oil store on New Street. The merchant's business stood on a narrow alley lined with wooden buildings occupied by cooper and carpenter shops. The flames fed on the dry staves, hoops, pine boxes, and shavings inside, and spread quickly. Half-dressed residents fled into the streets. The fire soon reached the Broad Street warehouse of Crocker & Warren, which happened to contain 336,000 pounds of saltpeter. While the firemen arrived quickly, events spiraled out of control. "Some gentleman near us shouted out, 'Run for your lives, No. 22, the building is full of gunpowder,'" recalled Garret B. Lane, foreman of Engine Company No. 22. "We started, and by the time we had proceeded about thirty yards the first explosion took place. In about two seconds afterwards the second explosion went off. The air was filled with bricks, rafters, beams, and showers of fireballs of saltpeter." Firemen Augustus Cowdrey of Engine Company No. 42 and David Van Winkle with Engine Company No. 5 were outside when it exploded. The blast propelled Van Winkle across the street. He landed with just a few injuries. Search crews never found Cowdrey's body.[2]

The explosion occurred not far from the Strongs' home, and George Templeton recalled how it "shook the house like an earthquake and must have blown me out of bed." He threw on some clothes and rushed to see the blaze. Broad Street featured some of the finest stores in the city, and Hone recalled that they "were instantly overthrown; the flames were communicated in every direction." It reminded him, of course, of the Great Fire almost a decade earlier. "[T]he progress of the flames was so rapid, and its approach so unexpected, that scarcely anything was saved." The fire spread to Broadway, toward Bowling Green, and neared the recently opened Merchants' Exchange. Marines helped the firemen pump their engines, citizens emptied fountains and poured water on roofs, while store owners covered windows with wet blankets.

By 11:00 AM, the firemen had gotten the blaze under control. The smoke cleared to reveal a smoldering ruin of blackened brick, burned rafters, and charred goods. The air of lower Manhattan reeked of burning spirits and oil. People frantically dug through rubble looking for relatives and friends. Four firemen, as well as 26 citizens, died. While not as destructive as the 1835 fire—which scorched some of the same streets—it took with it 345 buildings, as well as 14,000 bales of cotton, 20,000 chests of tea, 1,500 boxes of brown sugar, 100,000 pounds of fleece, 100 casks of nutmeg, 15,000 boxes of Malaga raisins, and 300 cases of Bordeaux prunes.[3]

As in 1835, people piled goods in the streets. Citizens assessed the damage, and some voiced the need to ban the storage of combustibles like gunpowder, saltpeter, salt of tartar, and sulfur in the populated sections of the city. There was also discussion of limiting wood in buildings and requiring the use of tin roofs, iron shutters, and metal doors. Losses from the fire added up to about $5 million (approximately $175 million today), a quarter of that of the 1835 blaze. It cost the Eagle Fire Company, of which Hone had been a director until January, nearly half a million dollars. He had also recently helped found the American Mutual Insurance Company. As that firm's president, he noted how the office was "all in confusion," and he was there until late that evening "cancelling fire and marine policies. . . . Fortune is against me. I must submit. The Lord's will be done!"

While what became known in some circles as the other Great Fire wiped out American Mutual and brought physical, personal, and financial damage to many, the Croton water supply proved its worth, providing "a great facility for the extinguishment of fire," observed the *New York Evening Post*. The paper also noted that even had the fire continued, "we doubt whether the water would have been completely exhausted."[4]

Work progressed quickly to rebuild all the damage. Meanwhile, Hamblin's new Bowery—the fifth—opened on August 4, less than four months after the previous theater had burned. John M. Trimble, who had been a carpenter for the theater, designed a new space fronted by four large fluted columns. Edgar Allan Poe's the *Broadway Journal* said that "its general arrangements are excellent. The stage is capacious, and well appointed," though the paper felt that the theater's lack of color on the paneling in the boxes and the gallery gave the house a "Quakerish air." The theater first staged performances of *The Sleeping Beauty* and *Charles II*, and the paper noted how "The theatre has been crowded every night since its opening."[5]

* * *

Croton Reservoir or no, fire proved to be a constant threat, as it had been from the city's founding. Buildings contained a deadly combination of wood, foul chimneys, lamps, and chain smokers. To combat the plague of fires, the Dutch had started fire patrols in 1648. The British conquered the colony in 1664, and in the early 1700s officials required homeowners to keep three-gallon leather buckets ready so they could form lines to convey water from the wells and the rivers to the flames. The city acquired its first two fire engines in 1731. But these London-built, sidestroke machines were hulking contraptions. Their long bars required some 20 men to pump, in order to maintain pressure to shoot a steady stream. Six years later, the colony's General Assembly called for the formation of a volunteer fire department.[6]

At the start of the American Revolution, New Yorkers worried that the city might fall to the British. American general Nathanael Greene even suggested torching the city. British general William Howe easily routed the revolutionaries from Brooklyn in August 1776, forcing George Washington and his men to flee to Manhattan. Howe followed, landing at Kip's Bay on the East River and driving the Patriots to the northern part of the island. On September 21, a fire broke out at the Fighting Cocks Tavern near the island's southern tip. Fierce winds whipped up the flames. Loyalists racing out to fight the blaze found fire bells missing, equipment destroyed, and water buckets damaged.

The fire raged for 10 hours. By the time it stopped, it had destroyed more than 500 buildings in a mile-long stretch of the city. Washington had watched the sky glow from his headquarters in Harlem Heights, and two weeks later wrote his cousin, Lund Washington, "Providence—or some good honest Fellow, has done more for us than we were disposed to do for ourselves, as near One fourth of the City is supposed to be consumed." Thousands living in the city found themselves homeless. Three hundred people sought shelter in the almshouse. Others constructed tarp-roofed homes in an area at the foot of Broad Street in the southeast part of town that was dubbed "Canvas Town." The British tried to prevent a repeat of the blaze, but in August 1778 another fire broke out along the East River, destroying more than 60 houses and several businesses.[7]

The United States and Britain signed a peace treaty in September 1783, and New Yorkers regained control of their town on November 25. Still, by what became known as Excavation Day, the fires and seven years of British occupation had all but ruined the town. Citizens returned and rebuilt, and on February 15, 1786, the Common Council called for the formation of a new fire department with five engineers, 274 men, 15 engine companies, and two hook-and-ladder companies. In 1792, firemen insisted on running the department and elected delegates to the administrative board. The men were exempt from military service. And as they organized, they created their own companies, which would become entrenched, fiercely independent, and entitled fraternal groups that lasted through the Civil War.

In the early days of the nation, many of the city's elites, artisans, and tradesmen joined the department. Sons often followed their fathers into service. John and Nicholas Roosevelt and brewer Peter Rutgers belonged to the first fire companies. George Templeton Strong's uncle Benjamin joined the force in 1791. Mayor Daniel Tiemann served, as did future mayors like Charles Gunther. There were many others, from Harper & Brothers publisher Fletcher Harper to restaurateurs Siro, Lorenzo, and Charles Delmonico.

Vigorous support for the department was necessary, as over the years New York continued to endure blazes both small and devastating. Papers routinely covered them, regularly running such headlines as "Another Destructive Fire!" "Terrible Conflagration!" and "Most Alarming Fire!" followed by detailed accounts of the blaze, the names of the victims, what went up in smoke, and who did or didn't have insurance. Forty-eight buildings burned in the Coffee House Slip fire on December 9, 1796. Forty-one were lost on December 18, 1804. And more than 100 houses were destroyed on May 19, 1811, after a fast-moving fire left 150 families homeless.

The lack of a proper water supply prior to Croton hindered efforts, of course, and the Manhattan Company stayed woefully unresponsive when it came to assisting the city. As a result, one could not live in New York without being affected by fires. When John Pintard's office at the Exchange Building burned down on April 27, 1826, he was left "totally prostrate." In August 1829, Hone complained how "Scarcely a night passes without our citizens being awakened by the cry of 'Fire!'" Between 1825 and 1829, there were 443 fires in the city.[8]

Interest in fires could be a full-time obsession for those like Strong who were mesmerized by them. In January 1840, he left his office at 7:30 PM and came upon a fire on Water Street. He watched it for a while, but didn't stay because he viewed those gathered there as a disreputable crowd, and there was "so much hustling and swearing and rowdying going forward." As he walked uptown he came upon a fire burning on South Street, which produced "quite a showy affair." Then, at three in the morning, he noted how he was awakened by "a furious alarm of fire." He quickly dressed and rushed over. When he got there, the fire, disappointingly, was out, "but the cinders were showering down like a snow-storm in Pandemonium or a 'sulphur shower.'"

Visitors often commented on the city's continuous blazes. In 1842, a Mrs. Felton wrote of her visit to the city and how, "From the flat roof of our residence, one evening, I saw three fires at the same time; two of them appeared to be of considerable magnitude; the other was only an oil and turpentine store." William Ross, writing around the same time in the *Architectural Magazine*, commented that alarms rang so frequently that "the rule is, if the alarm is given during the night, to put the hand on the wall at the head of the bed, and, if it feels rather warm, to get up; but, if otherwise, to turn about and go to sleep again."[9]

* * *

As the century progressed, the makeup of the fire department changed. In September 1850—15 years after the Great Fire of 1835 and five after the 1845 one—nearly 2,000 men were in the department's 34 engine companies, 47 hose companies, nine hook-and-ladder companies, and three hydrant companies. Most were not from patrician backgrounds. These post–Jacksonian era men saw themselves as a new breed of American, by-their-bootstraps journeymen, artisans, office workers, and laborers who felt beholden to no one. Man of the people and future congressman Mike Walsh served, as did future Tammany Hall boss William Tweed, along with nativist leaders like the ominously named William "Bill the Butcher" Poole and boxer Tom Hyer. With increased immigration, Irish membership of the force rose from 11.9 percent in 1840 to 37.8 percent in 1860.

Since fires were a constant threat, getting the word out was a priority. In the 17th century, the Dutch group called the Prowlers roamed the streets with rattles, bells, buckets, hooks, and ladders, and sounded the alarm. Sextons also alerted people. As the 19th-century journalist Asa Greene noted, being a church bell ringer in such a combustible town could be exhausting work. James Fenimore Cooper commented how once word was out, "The cry is sounded by boys and repeated by the firemen themselves, for a minute or two, and then a few or more bells, according to the degree of the danger." During his 1842 visit, Charles Dickens noted, unhappily, the city's "intolerable tolling of great bells."[10]

To spot fires quicker, the city started building bell towers. City Hall had one in its cupola, manned by a watchman 24 hours a day. When he saw flames, he would ring the bell and use a light to direct firemen to the blaze. As Lady Emmeline Stuart-Wortley wrote in 1851, "The sound can be heard from one end of the city to the other, and is almost instantaneously responded to by a

hundred others in every direction. The number of strokes indicates the particular ward." As the men rushed to the flames, they relied on "The Firemen's
Guide," a detailed street map that showed them the locations of hydrants and
cisterns. The system proved far from foolproof, and sometimes the authorities had to dispatch messengers to redirect the men.[11]

Whatever their shortcomings in training, firemen committed themselves
zealously to their calling. One of the best on the force was Zophar Mills.
When a blaze broke out during his wedding, he found himself tempted
to bolt. Afterwards he told fellow fireman William Hampton that "he was
praying for the parson to cut it short so that he might help the boys at the
fire." Happily for Mills—but perhaps not his bride—before breakfast the next
morning, "there was another fire, and I went to that."

The men found battling blazes intoxicating. Young men and fire—as Walt
Whitman rhapsodized:

> O, the fireman's joys!
> I hear the alarm at dead of night,
> I hear bells, shouts! I pass the crowd; I run!
> The sight of the flames maddens me with pleasure!

For the men, it was all a matter of waiting for the call. "The hours passed pleas-
antly and innocently," recalled fireman James Tyler in 1878 of how the men
lounged in the firehouse. "Not infrequently were these sittings interrupted
by shaking at the door, and the cry of 'Turn out here!' 'Fire! Fire!'" It didn't
matter what they were doing when an alarm rang. In the 1850s, P.T. Barnum
staged an extravaganza called *The Patriots of '76*. Having noticed how well
the crew of Lady Washington Engine Company marched in parades, he convinced its members to appear in his show as Continental soldiers, Hessians,
Indians, and even Molly Pitcher, a hero of the 1778 Battle of Monmouth
Court House in New Jersey. During the opening performance, the call for a
fire rang out, and the 30 costumed-clad cast members rushed from the stage
to their engines.[12]

Once near a fire, the men set their engines alongside the closest hydrant. If
it burned far from the water, other engines helped, sometimes getting water
from as far away as the river. As the firemen worked, the foreman would yell
directions through his speaking trumpet: "Work her lively, lads!" "You don't
half work," "Now you've got her!" recalled Tyler, as "twenty partially stripped
men, (ten on a side) manning the brakes of a short-stroke engine and dashing

her down, at the rate of sixty or seventy strokes a minute, some with their hair floating about their faces at every stroke." After just a minute or two, others relieved the men, as the work was "so violent and exhausting." While some doused the building and covered neighboring structures with wet blankets, others ran through doors or threw up ladders to search for people and save belongings.[13]

Fires did not discriminate. Both the wealthy and the poor suffered losses and death. John Jacob Astor lost his home near Hell Gate on July 7, 1816, when a fire started in a crack in his chimney, spread up to the garret, and burned down the house. That December, a fire ripped through dozens of homes and stores on Water and Front Streets as well as Burling Slip, where George Washington Strong's office was nearly destroyed. The upper part of Astor's City Hotel caught fire in late April 1833, on the same day as the funeral of Astor's brother Henry. As Hone noted, "I attended this afternoon the funeral of Henry Astor, whose body was committed to the earth in one part of the city while the ruins of his brother's splendid hotel were smoking in another." Former mayor James Harper's family publishing business on Cliff Street burned down in December 1853 after a plumber carelessly threw a match into a basin of camphene, which was used to clean ink from rollers in the press room.[14]

* * *

Theaters, as we've seen abundantly with the Bowery, seemed especially prone. Astor's Park Theatre burned down in May 1820, and again in 1848. General Charles Sandford ran both the Lafayette Theatre and the Mount Pitt Circus; they both burned in 1829. The National Theatre went up in flames in September 1839, the new National in May 1841, and Niblo's Theatre in September 1846. Tripler Hall, which was also known as Metropolitan Hall, burned down in January 1854.

Fires turned into grim street theater, featuring a vast cast of characters and neck-craning audiences. In 1847 Whitman wrote for the Brooklyn *Daily Eagle* about the aftermath of a blaze that destroyed a dozen uptown middle-class houses: "The most pitiful thing in the whole affair was the sight of shivering women, their eyes red with tears, and many of them dashing wildly though the crowd, in search, no doubt, of some member of their family, who, for what they knew, might be burned in the smoking ruins near by."

Entertaining or not, such scenes presented dangers for the firemen. While crews battled a fire on Park Place in 1832, the roof caved in, trapping Brass

Back Engine Company foreman Morris Franklin. Miraculously, Fire Chief James Gulick rushed up and pulled him free. Franklin's burns confined him to bed for a month and a half. The following year, Gulick was fighting a fire on Gold Street when he fell from a shed. Though seriously injured, he continued his work. Then, in 1834, he was at a blaze on South Street. The store's floor gave way and he tumbled into the cellar. Buried up to his neck in the debris, his arms and legs were burned. Fortunately, assistant engineer Edward Hoffmire and William Hopson pulled him out.[15]

The threat of death loomed over those in the volunteer company. On April 25, 1854, a massive fire broke out at the William T. Jennings & Co. clothing store on Broadway across from City Hall Park. As the fire bells rang, fireman Andrew Schenck with Hook and Ladder No. 1 was at the home of his fiancée. She urged him not to go, but he promised that it would be the last one. It was a large blaze, and as Engine Company No. 42 sprayed the upper floors, the cold water hit a glowing iron arch at the rear of the building. The metal cracked, the rear wall collapsed, and the floors crumbled, burying more than 20 men, including Schenck.

The department honored their lost brothers with somber processions. One of the largest services was held for those who died at the Jennings fire. The firehouses that lost men marched to their homes to gather their bodies. Hearses assembled at City Hall, and firemen marched six abreast through streets jammed with spectators. As the procession advanced, there could be heard the dull, heavy tolling of the City Hall bell and the measured ringing of church bells. Along the route, homeowners dressed their buildings in black. The Astor House hung long streamers of crepe from its flagpole, which was set at half-mast. The coffins were then taken across to Brooklyn and brought to Green-Wood Cemetery.

* * *

The department evolved into a power in life and city politics. Their strength had already become evident during the aftermath of the Great Fire. Because of the vastness of that blaze, the lack of water, and the subzero weather, the fire had been the most destructive in New York's history. Some directed their anger toward the firefighters, and as we've seen, Gulick was fired in May 1836. The backlash over his sacking was immediate. The men refused to embrace the new chief John Riker. In September they staged a mass resignation, with 608 of the 1,365 firemen quitting. Suspicious fires started to break out, and equipment was destroyed. On September 24, an early-morning fire in the basement of the Church of the Nativity on Avenue D and 4th Streets spread to neighboring houses. A number of firemen refused to help, and according to the *New York Sun* they "taunted and derided those who were exerting themselves to extinguish the fire."[16]

The firemen formed what they called the Resigned Firemen's Association, which set out to secure Gulick a new job. The Whigs and the Native American Party placed him on its ballot for City Register. On October 14, they held a large meeting at Howard House on Broadway, where they received the support of a number of prominent figures. Despite the fact that Gulick was backed by anti-Catholic nativist groups, his supporters handed out handbills at St. Patrick's on Mulberry Street following Sunday services. The papers reminded the Catholic congregants how Gulick had prevented the loss of their church in June 1835, just half a year before the Great Fire: "Who Saved the Cathedral? James Gulick. Vote for him for Register." That November, the former chief easily beat his Tammany Hall opponent. In December, during a special election for the New York State Assembly, Morris Franklin won a seat while running on the Whig line. In the spring of 1837, the firemen brought about Riker's expulsion. Cornelius Anderson became the new chief engineer. By then, quite a few of those who had quit the previous fall had rejoined the force.

Many felt this was an outrageous use of power. In January 1840 the *Herald* called on the Common Council to make a "complete purification and re-organization of the Fire Department." Bennett called for the dismissal of bad eggs, and demanded, in his usual overstated way, that "the riotous ruffians be shot down like so many mad dogs, as pests to the community, whose deaths are a common blessing." The *Herald* also demanded the formation of a professionalized and salaried fire department. Many agreed with the need for a change. "From all I've seen of fires of late," observed George Templeton Strong that February, "I'm fully convinced that our fire department is utterly and shamefully incompetent." Strong thought it was a miracle that "half the city don't burn up." He predicted that it might still happen and that then "they'll get to work to reform in earnest."[17]

Throughout, the firemen themselves resisted change. They considered it manly to pull their own engines, only reluctantly using horses during the cholera plague in 1832, given that so many members were out ill. The objection to horses continued into the 1840s. But changes slowly started. The Exempt Firemen's Company was formed, made up of a number of men who had long served on the force. The group had two steam engines and one large hand-engine to help with what Zophar Mills called "Cases of the greatest emergency." And after Chief Alfred Carson took over in 1848, he issued badges to firemen and had telegraphs linked to bell towers. Looking to reduce their losses, insurance companies set up their own fire patrol, with the men walking the streets in search of blazes.[18]

Yet, while the department could be a thorn in the side of those governing the city, to many citizens the members were seen as Olympian heroes. Whitman praised those he referred to as "Roman gladiators" and wondered "whether any city in the world can turn out a more manly set of young fellows." New Yorkers were quite grateful for their work. In January 1827, when Charles Gilfert ran the Bowery Theatre, he held a Fire Department benefit with a performance that included *Life in New York, or Firemen on Duty* and the farce *Fire & Water*. In early 1832, donations were collected from Eagle insurance, Supply Engine Company No. 1, and the wardens of the Fourteenth Ward to buy a silver trumpet for Gulick. After the 1833 fire, during which Gulick became injured by falling from the shed, those on Gold Street printed a "Card of Thanks" in the *Evening Post*, noting that "they cannot pass over the present occasion to express their admiration of the skill displayed by James Gulick, Esq."

These demigods were further enshrined in the character of Mose in Benjamin Baker's short sketch "Mose the Fire B'hoy." The fireman-turned-playwright followed it up with his 1848 play *A Glance at New York*, as well as subsequent Mose plays like *Mose in a Muss* and *Mose in China*. Baker, who worked with Engine Company No. 15, intimately understood the life of the firemen. He fashioned his Mose partly on Paul Bunyan and partly on a big-hearted, rabble-rousing leader of the Bowery B'hoys. Mose could not only down prodigious amounts of beer and gorge on oysters and beef, he was devoted to his girlfriend Lize and assisted clueless out-of-towners.[19]

* * *

From the very early days in New York, firemen had stature, especially in the eyes of the city's boys. When William Tweed was young, he dreamed of becoming one. Tweed's family hailed from Keslo, a town southeast of Edinburgh on the River Tweed in Scotland. His great-grandfather had left in the mid-1700s, settling in the area just to the east of Beekman's Swamp, halfway between the East River and City Hall. The Tweeds were blacksmiths, and Tweed's grandfather Phillip worked a forge on Rutgers Street. His son Richard, Tweed's father, apprenticed to a chair-maker. He married Eliza

Magear, prospered, and opened a shop and home on Cherry Street. The couple had a number of children, with Bill appearing on April 3, 1823. The young Tweed liked to read, excelled at math, and attended public school on Chrystie Street.

The elder Tweed had a heart condition, and the family needed help, so at the age of 11 Bill learned the family trade, ran errands, and made deliveries.[20] Like so many young men at the time, Bill started an apprenticeship, laboring for Isaac Fryer, a Pearl Street saddler and hardware dealer. He satisfied his passion for the firehouses by listening for the jangling of the fire bells, and rushed out when he could to see the crews racing with their engines. As with other lads, Tweed got into regular fights, though soon "Little Bill" blossomed into "Big Bill," and those who crossed the strapping young man earned a thrashing. Tweed and other local boys belonged to a gang called the Cherry Hillers, and as the strongest of the lot, Tweed served as the leader. After working for one year at Fryer's business, Bill attended a boarding school in Elizabethtown, New Jersey. There he sharpened his math skills and learned accounting. A year later he started as a junior clerk with J. and G.C. Alexander, a tobacco merchant on Front Street. Tweed handled their books. At the same time, his father bought an interest in Daniel Berrien & Company, a brush company on Pearl Street. So when Bill finished his work at the tobacco office, he returned home to take care of Berrien's accounts. On September 18, 1844, the 21-year-old Tweed married his childhood friend Mary Jane Skaden. They wed at St. Stephen's Episcopal Church, moved into the top floor of the Skaden's Madison Street home, and started a family.

Having grown up in a strict Baptist home, Tweed cast his first vote for the publisher-turned-politician James Harper, who in 1844 ran for mayor on the nativist American Republican Party ticket and won. Like many others, Tweed gravitated toward fraternal organizations, and initially joined such groups as the Masons and the Odd Fellows. He especially liked to do things for his fellow members. In the fall of 1846, one of his lodge buddies got married. The man didn't host a party, so Tweed and others decided to give him "a splendid serenade," sending to his home a flautist and some singers. They followed this up with "Twenty Five instruments from the Fisherman Tin Horn to the Conk Shell, embracing drums . . . Trombone—accordion, dinner bells—Sleigh Bells—Tambourines, &c &c." Apparently they kept this up for an hour until the poor man "sent a messenger with a Flag of Truce suing for peace," which was not honored until he had paid "the invading army their expenses and a champagne Supper."[21]

Tweed became good at browbeating generosity from others, and being in a fraternal association gave him a chance to rub shoulders with prominent members and develop contacts. But while he prospered, Tweed had other things on his mind, mainly his love of fire companies. The group was the most visible and chummy organization around. And firehouse contacts could help those seeking financial, political, and social advancement. Tweed reveled in the fire company's welcoming, nurturing, and dramatic environment, and served with Fashion Hose No. 25, Oceana Hose No. 36, Fulton Engine Company No. 21, and Knickerbocker Engine No. 12.[22]

In 1848, Tweed and others hoped to form a new firehouse. They met at a local saloon on Hester Street and petitioned the Common Council. Engine Company No. 6 duly appeared in January 1849. The founders debated what to call their house. The Black Joke Engine Company had been disbanded in 1844, and the men discussed either continuing the company's name or calling themselves "Eureka," "Fredonia," or "Franklin." Tweed suggested naming it for Amerigo Vespucci, the Italian explorer from whom the nation derived its name. The group ended up settling on the Americus Engine Company, though likewise it was known boastfully as the "Big Six."

Americus' 75-member company hailed, appropriately, from a wide range of backgrounds—an amalgam of businessmen, clerks, artisans, shipyard workers, carpenters, printers, artists, and sign painters. They set up in the Black Joke's former Gouverneur Street headquarters, with the Little Six hose company housed next door. The company took as its symbol a snarling Bengal tiger. In July 1849, Tweed became assistant foreman. In August 1850, he rose to foreman. His men presented him with a silver trumpet and an engraved gold watch.

Belonging to an engine, hose, hook-and-ladder, or hydrant company meant being busy almost constantly. The city suffered 289 fires between August 1849 and August 1850. Fighting fires was only a small part of the fireman's life. The firehouse served as a place of camaraderie. Many recalled bonding as they debated politics, spun yarns, smoked penny cigars, sang such popular ballads as "Red Robin" and "The Angel's Whisper," and waited for an alarm. The firehouses likewise gathered together for grand parties, with Hamblin giving over the Bowery for free after 1830 for their annual ball. At a fête at the Apollo Hall on Broadway, Tweed showed up wearing a blue coat with brass buttons. One assistant foreman recalled he was "a tip-top dancer and never wanted a partner." The different houses likewise headed out for mostly friendly competitions, particularly water throwing matches and shooting parties, with the journalist Thomas Nichols writing that they marched "out of town, behind a band of music, to fire at a target." They were, in their way, militias. "Every company of firemen has its annual excursion."[23]

To best show off their house, they polished and pampered their machines, which they festooned with ornate insignias. Joseph Johnson of Big Six was an artist, and he painted Americus' engine panels. The house then displayed it at the American Institute Fair in Castle Garden, where it won a certificate. With their engines, the firemen gladly strutted. In the spring of 1851, Americus traveled to Philadelphia and Baltimore on their way to Washington, D.C. When they arrived in the capital, they made their way along Pennsylvania Avenue alongside their polished engine. For the display, Tweed donned a tall beaver hat with a white fireman's coat slung over his shoulder, and shouted orders through his silver trumpet. The company then headed to the White House, and Tweed introduced his men to President Millard Fillmore. When the company received a new Philadelphia-style double engine later that year, Tweed borrowed eight white horses, adorned them with silver harnesses, and carried a torch as he led his men at night through the main streets of the Seventh Ward.

Competition created rivalries. Firemen likewise loved racing other houses. Big Six and Engine Company No. 8 had bouts, and crowds gathered at Chatham Square to watch the two companies zip along the street. With so many young men rushing to combat a blaze, these matchups took on a Wild West quality. The men saw no reason to be low-key, for their activities counteracted the drabness of their work lives. The general rule was that the first company on the scene could claim the right to fight a blaze. Beating other houses proved almost as important as battling fires. Such a rough-and-tumble lifestyle suited those like Tweed. They would race through the streets, even hopping curbs and sidewalks and knocking into pedestrians to make sure they arrived first. As they pulled up, they might also cover hydrants with barrels to hinder their competition and then fight, ignoring the nearby burning buildings.[24]

Some battles turned vicious. On a Saturday evening in September 1841, an old grudge match broke out as Engine Companies No. 30 and No. 33 waited on the Bowery for No. 44. Knives were drawn, and several of the men were hurt. In 1846, Engine Company No. 12 was returning from a fire at the Astor House when they ran into Engine Company No. 8. The foreman of No. 12 knocked a man to the ground with his trumpet, and a man was injured when No. 12's engine ran over him. In June 1853, Engine Company No. 1 and

Hook and Ladder Company No. 8 were both returning from a fire in the fifth district, when they met up at Eighth Avenue and 37th Street. The *New York Times* reported that during the fight, one man received "a frightful wound with a dirk that penetrated to the fifth rib."

Besides the sometimes-brutal competition, there was the added problem of "runners," young unofficial volunteers who attached themselves to companies. Hone succinctly called such hangers-on "idlers and vagabonds." And while companies needed additional help—especially pulling the heavy engines—many of the runners simply fought other crews on the way to and from a fire in the hope of showing their worthiness. Volunteers sometimes raised false alarms and even started blazes, according to Asa Greene, "for the pleasure of running after, or helping to drag, the engines."[25]

And while a company's command might overlook bad behavior, the public didn't. In June 1824, the Common Council directed the chief engineer to order each fire company "to dispence with the services of the Volunteers." Their behavior didn't stop, and continued to attract the ire of officials. In December 1832, members of the Watch were told to check firehouses "to report whether the same is not occupied or frequented by boys at all hours of the night." Another directive was repeated in 1836, complaining of the "young men who appear at fires in the garb of Firemen, but over whom the Engineers have no control."

The companies had to likewise contend with the territoriality of gangs. As gangs grew in the 1820s and 1830s, some attacked firemen. In 1850, Chief Alfred Carson complained that gangs were making "deliberate and bloody attacks on our firemen . . . destroying the apparatus, and often by stratagem, pitting certain companies in collision with each other . . . and creating in every way, endless broil and confusion in the department." Sometimes the police stepped in, and sometimes they were aiders and abettors "of the fire-boy roughs." Attacks occurred frequently and could be severe. Carson reported that in August 1850, "a murderous gang of club rowdies, numbering about one hundred" set fire to several tar barrels on 32nd Street in order to draw Engine Company No. 19 there. As the firemen neared, "these demi-devils . . . suddenly emerged from their hiding places, and attacked the company with large stones and clubs, upset and broke the engine."[26]

And, occasionally, the problems sprang from the heads of the houses. Tweed wanted to lead Americus to greatness, or at least a position of dominance over the other houses. As a large man with a booming laugh, large fists, broad shoulders, solid head, wide face, and imposing nose, Tweed set out to prove that Americus was a company not to trifle with. This led to regular scuffles and outbursts. In September 1850, Chief Carson accused Tweed of overseeing an attack on Hose Company No. 31, using what Carson described as "boxes, barrels, and missiles of various kinds." The chief deemed such actions "dastardly and cowardly," and sought to expel Tweed from the force and have Big Six suspended for three months. But Tweed only earned a three-month suspension thanks to what Carson called "Mr. Tweed's disinterested friendship" toward Assistant Alderman Florence McCarthy, who in return for his help sported "sundry golden trinkets."[27]

Aldermen like McCarthy could make a good living through their friendships with firemen and others. Tweed understood that the perks of politics were much more appealing and profitable than the trappings of Americus and the fire department. It wasn't long before he started to make plans to depart from Americus and broaden his political horizons.

12

Firemen and Politics

In cities across time and throughout the world, politics and money rule. The ways in which patronage and the spoils system governed New York—as we'll see in the case of William Tweed—are, however, unique in their way, and on a scale larger or just more evident than most anywhere else. Of course everyone, from the connected to the aspirational, lobbied for a spot on the public payroll. Because of his various financial setbacks, Philip Hone, for example, continued to seek a federal posting. He and his daughter Catharine headed to Washington in 1849 to attend Zachary Taylor's March 5 inauguration and ball. In April, Hone received a commission as Naval Officer for the District of New York, earning him $5,000 a year. He noted how the position was not only "a highly responsible and honorable office," but "will afford me a convenient remuneration." The position also brought with it its own spoils system, and Hone made use of it. He appointed his nephew Isaac as auditor, and his son Robert as deputy auditor. "Enough *Hones* to supply one department, we should think," noted the *Hudson Gazette*. "But there is nothing like keeping it in the family."[1]

Nationally, the early 19th century witnessed a series of major shifts in political control. At the start of the century the Federalist Party, which Alexander Hamilton helped to form in the late 1700s, proved popular with merchants and businessmen. It lasted into the early 1800s. As that party faded, Hone, like many other conservatives, joined the Whig Party, which drew support from a coalition of bankers, factory owners, storekeepers, and clerks. They backed a national bank, favored high tariffs and modern financial markets, and pushed for internal improvements like canals and roads. Their opponents were the Democratic-Republicans, the party of Thomas Jefferson and James Madison, which would evolve into the Democratic Party at the time of Andrew Jackson. Jackson and his followers favored territorial expansion and, as we've seen, opposed the Second Bank of the United States.

Smaller short-lived third parties likewise appeared and disappeared during this period of unrest after the Era of Good Feelings. The Anti-Masonic Party, for example, fixated on the idea that secret fraternal orders of

Masons conspired to take control of the nation. As that group declined in the early 1830s, many of its members joined the Whigs. The abolitionist Liberty Party emerged in 1840. Some of its followers soon joined with anti-slavery Democrats and "Conscience" Whigs and formed the Free Soil Party in the late 1840s.

A pronounced nativist, anti-immigrant streak ran through American politics, then as now. Many viewed Catholic immigrants in particular as a corrupting threat to Protestant America. They agreed with the *American Republican* newspaper that because of their influx—mainly Catholics from places like Ireland—"public morals have become degenerated, pauperism and crime unendurably abundant, and religion and morality little better than words." Such xenophobia increased following the Panic of 1837. As the economy shrank, nativist parties surged in popularity, in New York and elsewhere.[2] The American Republican Party, which was formed in the 1840s, was a prime example of such a political organization. In New York they backed publisher James Harper and supported his reformist, anti-immigrant platform during the 1844 mayoral election. Harper promised to root out patronage and corruption, and called for law and order, sobriety, tax cuts, and a 21-year naturalization period to ensure the proper assimilation of foreigners. He won office but lasted only one term. The more enduring and popular nativist group was the Know Nothing Party, which flourished in the 1850s, earning its name from the policy that when someone asked a member about the group he would respond, "I know nothing." As the *Know Nothing Almanac and True Americans' Manual* proclaimed, the group was "for light, liberty, education, and absolute freedom of conscience, with a strong dash of devotion to one's native soil."[3]

All this jostling for control resonated in New York, where Tammany Hall was the most powerful political organization. The Society of St. Tammany, or the Columbian Order, had started in the late 1780s as a patriotic political and social club geared toward craftsmen. John and Philip Hone were early members. The group adopted as their namesake Tamanend, the legendary 17th-century Lenni-Lenape chief. They adopted pseudo-Indian customs, called members "braves" and "warriors," referred to leaders as "sachems," and consisted of 13 "tribes." They even christened their hall "the Wigwam." On paper the organization was non-political, but in the early 1800s they formed the General Committee of Tammany Hall, their political wing, which was closely linked to the Democratic Party. The Jeffersonian group opposed the aristocratic trappings of Hamilton's Federalists. They supported expanded suffrage and, starting in the 1820s, began to court workers, anti-bankers, and merchants with ties to the South. They also fought nativist policies and helped immigrants gain citizenship, which meant they could tally more votes at election time. Patronage was key to their operations. To further expand their base, Tammany's "Ward Heelers" found work for members.[4]

But, while growing to become a powerful political presence in New York, Tammany was far from monolithic. There was constant infighting, and the group struggled to keep its disparate factions in check. One offshoot was the Workingmen's Party. Begun in the late 1820s, it focused on the needs of the "Workies," craftsmen and journeymen, and advocated male suffrage, shorter hours, and better educational opportunities. In the 1830s some of Tammany's members formed the Equal Rights Party. They opposed monopolies, banks, and tariffs, called for a 10-hour workday, and sought immigrant support. They assumed the name "Locofocos" when at an 1835 Tammany nominating meeting their opponents shut off the gaslights. To continue the gathering, those assembled struck Loco Foco friction matches to illuminate the space. While Locofocos membership dropped after 1840, Tammany acknowledged their issues and started to support some of their reforms, including impartial juries and the end of licensed monopolies. Splintering of Tammany would become especially visible during the 1840s over the issue of slavery.

There were continuous struggles not only in the halls of Tammany but on the streets of New York, amplified by those who actively sought to control the vote for their own purposes. Many of those who worked to help their parties were known as "Sporting Men," who liked to gamble, took easy offense, and loved to drink and fight. Those among them who harbored political aspirations found ways to align themselves with one of the political parties so as to gain power and money. One of them was Captain Isaiah Rynders. The journalist Thomas Nichols called the Shakespeare-quoting Rynders "a lithe, dark, handsome man" who possessed "a knowing smile, and a sharp look altogether." Rynders had earned his bars on a sloop that ferried goods along the Hudson River. He was pro-slavery and spent some time in the South, arriving in New York City shortly after the 1837 Panic. Rynders was a bruiser and, sensing that the Democratic Party needed to galvanize support during the 1844 presidential election, set out to create his own power base and formed the Empire Club. Made up of a thuggish collection of ruffians, thieves, and gamblers, the Empire Club went to Whig and other parties' meetings to drown out speakers with catcalls and hisses and pelt them with cabbages, carrots, and worse.[5]

In the 1844 election, the Democrat former Tennessee governor James Polk ran against the Whig former Kentucky senator Henry Clay. Polk owned slaves and demanded the annexation of Texas, which many saw as a way to add an additional slave state to the Union. He also insisted that the United States obtain from the British control over the territory of what is today Idaho, Oregon, and Washington, as well as much of British Columbia, an area located up to latitude 54°40′ north. The night before the election, Rynders mounted a white horse and led a procession of pro-Polk New York Democrats carrying torches and, according to Nichols, shouting "never ending hurrahs for Polk and Dallas, Texas, Oregon, Fifty-four-forty or fight."

The efforts of Rynders and others proved successful at blocking the opposition's vote while also using "repeaters" who made early-and-often visits to the polls. This reportedly resulted in nearly 10,000 more ballots cast than the number of eligible voters. Polk won the national election, and for his help, Rynders became a Tammany stalwart and earned a no-show job as a measurer in the New York Custom House. Polk's administration then brought about a huge expansion of American territory, with the annexation of Texas in 1845, negotiations with the British over the Oregon Territory, and the Mexican-American War, which added to the United States mostly land in present-day California, Arizona, Utah, Nevada, and New Mexico.[6]

Rynders was no outlier. Mike Walsh, who hailed from Youghal, Ireland, arrived in New York as a child, and would work as a correspondent for the *New York Aurora* where Walt Whitman was the editor. A scrapper whom the poet said was "imbued with the true blue American spirit," Walsh regularly criticized the Tammany sachems, and with friends from his Red Rover fire company started the Spartan Association, a Democratic splinter group that deemed the sachems "unprincipled blackguards."[7]

Walsh's group wielded their own form of rough politics, and attracted radical laborers. During Democrat Martin Van Buren's failed 1840 presidential run against Whig William Henry Harrison, Walsh's men raided the Whig headquarters. Walsh in 1843 co-founded *The Subterranean*, whose motto was "Independent in everything—neutral in nothing." The paper exposed the exploitation of workers, demanded shorter work days and free land for settlers, and supported anti-rent movements. His work made him a thorn in Tammany's side, and his fist-wielding form of politics helped him into the U.S. Congress.

Another kindred spirit to Rynders and Walsh was the Irish-born John Morrissey. Morrissey had made his way to the Five Points with the hopes of showing his muscle and taking on the prize fighter Charles "Dutch Charley" Duane. But when Morrissey arrived at the Rynders-owned saloon, Duane wasn't around, so he decided to challenge those present to a match. A group of men attacked him, and knocked him unconscious with a spittoon. Morrissey's gumption nonetheless impressed Rynders, who hired him as an Empire Club "shoulder hitter"—an enforcer unafraid to use brute force to make a point. Morrissey then headed to California, where he earned good money. When he returned to New York in the early 1850s he became a Tammany hero to the Irish and battler of the Know Nothings. In October 1853, Morrissey bested James "Yankee" Sullivan in a 37-round match in Boston Corners, New York, to become the boxing champion of America.

Morrissey meanwhile had a long-running feud with William "Bill the Butcher" Poole, a nativist butcher who had a stall at Washington Market. Poole, whose enemies noted that he possessed a "savage" disposition, was a pistol-packing, heavy-drinking brawler for the Know Nothings and orchestrated his cohorts in beating up Democratic opponents. In July 1854, Poole and Morrissey fought at the Amos Street dock. It turned out to be a quick battle, with Poole the winner. Others who aligned with Poole included Tom Hyer, a fellow butcher and prize fighter, who seemed to take pleasure in leading his gang on violent sprees, and in the late 1830s briefly landed in jail for attacking a number of brothels.

* * *

With so many literally battling for primacy, a growing economy, an exploding population, and an attendant rise in crime, local officials struggled to keep up. The politicians in Albany, which had become the state capital in 1797, generally ignored the city, and local reformers focused on the idea of small government, along with the needs of the wealthy and the middle class. The poor, immigrants, and the dispossessed relied on Tammany to fight for their interests. The organization saw them as a potent political force and as a source of recruits.

One obvious place of Tammany strength was the firehouse. That was where so many had their first taste of power and took their hesitant initial steps up the rungs of society and politics. At the start, William Tweed had not been tempted by the allure of Tammany. He had voted for publisher and nativist leader James Harper in his successful mayoral election as the American Republican Party candidate, and was happy with his situation. But he also saw how politics worked. Harper served just one lackluster term. He was ousted by the Tammany politician and sugar merchant William Havemeyer, and Harper's nativist party didn't carry a single of the city's wards. Tweed could see and appreciate the ways that Tammany wielded control. Seeking a grander and more lucrative platform from which to hold sway, he became a Democrat and slowly started his departure from the firehouse and into the bare-knuckle world of New York politics.

It turned out to be a smart move for him, and for Tammany, too. Tweed arrived with a number of useful connections aside from his firefighting background. He came from a successful family, was known around town, was good at making friends, temperate, an easy talker, and most importantly, knew how to endear himself to all classes of people. Though a large and imposing man, Tweed could be a subtle charmer with a large smile, firm handshake, twinkling blue eyes, and an uncanny memory for faces and names.

In the fall of 1850, Tweed accepted an invitation from Tammany to run as the Democratic candidate for the office of assistant alderman in the Seventh Ward. Tweed's first political venture did not pan out. Whig candidate Thomas Woodward beat him 1,428 to 1,381. While he lost the election, however, Tweed won was a lesson in politics. The following year he earned a new nomination for alderman. Knowing he required an advantage over his opponent, Tweed convinced a friend to enter the race as an independent. With the help of his Americus colleagues in getting out the vote, and with the pro-Temperance friend splitting the Whig vote, Tweed won the three-way contest by 47 votes.[8]

That year the Democrats grabbed a majority on the Common Council, and their dominance would allow Tweed to get a real education in patronage building. At the time the council consisted of 20 aldermen—who served a two-year term—and 20 assistant aldermen who served for one year. These men wielded considerable power. Aldermen appointed patrolmen and precinct commanders, served as justices on the Mayor's Court, where they heard cases dealing with polling-place violations, judged criminal court trials, and oversaw grand juries and licensed saloons. Most importantly, they doled out franchises.

On January 5, 1852, Mayor Ambrose Kingsland administered the oath to Tweed and the others, telling them that, "First in importance stand the financial concerns of the city" and that it needed to be governed "in the most economical and advantageous manner." The new aldermen then organized their board. Tweed joined the Law, Ferries and Repairs and Supplies committee, the Broadway Paving Committee, and worked on the special committee tasked with looking into finding a new spot for a potter's field.[9]

At the time, aldermen earned $4 for an hour's work at the special sessions, $4 for the general sessions, $3 or $4 as excise commissioners, $5 for an inquest, $3 or $4 as a supervisor, and $4 an hour as an alderman. Officeholders thus could make $25 to $30 a day, a hefty sum in the early 1850s. But politics could also be expensive, costing aldermen $3,000 to $8,000 to win office. "It is generally understood that this money is to be got back somehow," explained the New York Day Book. "An alderman buys the privilege of voting, or rather his vote, of the electors, at this enormous expense, expecting to sell it at a profit." Many politicians therefore sought to recoup their investments. And despite Mayor Kingsland's admonishment, this was something the new aldermen and assistant aldermen set out to do right away.[10]

The aldermen who took office in 1852 were far from the first to dip their hands into the public coffers. For some time, New York politicians had looked for ways to profit off their offices. And while not everyone in Tweed's class of 1852 qualified as a grifter, the group ushered in the most corrupt council the city had ever seen. Because of this, the aldermen earned the nickname the "Forty Thieves" for taking advantage of what Tammany leader George Washington Plunkitt would later (in 1905) term "Honest Graft." And with the city's phenomenal growth, the aldermen had a lot of ways to earn cash. An 1849 reform charter had reorganized the city's government to limit the power of the Common Council. Seeking to decentralize power, it created numerous executive departments dealing with everything from finance, street construction, the Croton Aqueduct Department, and inspectors, to prisons and the almshouse, law, fire, and police. The departments were popularly elected, and the various political parties battled for the spots, fielding long slates of candidates. Election ballots thus proved confusing at best, making it easier for party manipulation of power, jobs, and prestige. So instead of improving the system, the charter created a fractured government headed by a mayor who lacked true executive power and departments run by separately elected officials.

Tweed was a quick study who took note of everything, always showing up at events and sizing up his opposition. Along with mastery of parliamentary procedures, this allowed this savvy politician to assume a prominent role in the Common Council, controlling council meetings and consolidating power. Complaints about Tweed and this new band of aldermen emerged quickly. On February 7, a month after they took office, the New York Tribune commented how the aldermen were "seizing upon several large contracts for their hungry partisans." Hungry was right. Dining well soon became a popular pastime for the group (or at least putting in large bills for meals and pocketing the cash). In January and February 1852, 30 to 40 aldermen and assistant aldermen spent $1,053.88 for food and drink, as well as $248 for cigars, which came out to some 17 cigars per man per meal. And in February, they packed away—on paper at least—305.5 pounds of beef, 120 loaves of bread, 360 quarts of milk, and consumed large amounts of chicken, ham, oysters, eggs, venison, coffee, tea, and cake.[11]

On February 19, members of the Common Council headed out for a field trip to Randall's and Blackwell's Island to the north on the East River to look for a new site for a potter's field. On Blackwell's, the *New York Times* noted, the party of 60 had a "splendid dinner" along with lots of champagne. Nothing, though, was done about the choice of the cemetery. Even so, the men planned another excursion. When the aldermen finally chose a site for a new potter's field, they picked a 69-acre tract on Wards Island, paying the owner $103,450 for a patch of land that cost only $30,000. The aldermen then earned generous kickbacks. Getting around could also be profitable. Large bills were submitted for carriages, with Tweed claiming $438.50 over a 12-month period, which was 14 percent of the $3,090.25 charge by all 40 aldermen and assistant aldermen.[12]

As they jockeyed for position and money, the aldermen sought other ways to make cash. When profitable, they set prisoners free, for example, causing Mayor Kingsland that August to order captains of police not to discharge prisoners on authority of the aldermen or police magistrate "as a preventative to the outrages which are almost daily occurring." Their rapaciousness led to fights over profits. The *Tribune* commented on their approach to hiring, noting that when the Commissioner of Streets and Lamps "had the temerity to appoint lamplighters without asking the permission of certain Aldermen and Assistants" they undermined his authority and hired their own. And they "threatened a measure of usurpation which is of the most serious nature" by taking control of school funds "so that 'the party' shall have the sole benefit of its distribution."[13]

Besides eating, excursions, and appointments, the Forty Thieves took advantage of showy and expensive festivities. Senator Henry Clay died on June 29, 1852, and arrangements were made for a public procession as his body passed through town on the way to Kentucky. On the 30th, Tweed, who served on the Committee of Arrangements, delivered a speech for the senator, intoning that "Our whole country is again in tears!" Clay's body arrived on July 3. Cannons fired, black banners draped hotels and Tammany Hall, and 100,000 people lined the sidewalks. Thirty-one pallbearers, among them some of the city's most prominent citizens, accompanied the coffin. Clay's remains then headed to Albany, with dignitaries boarding the steamer *Santa Claus* to escort him north. For the trip, the aldermen charged a small fortune for cigars, wine, and other refreshments, as well as for flags and black-and-white bunting.[14]

There was a vast and steady amount of money that could be earned through city appropriations and contracts for such improvements as widening, paving, and extending streets; prison and school construction; streetcar and ferry franchises and selling real estate; not to mention issuing saloon licenses. As a result, the cost of running the city rose, with citizens seeing a 45 percent increase in the cost for lamps and gas and 70 percent for street cleaning. This didn't mean that the products and services New Yorkers received were any better. On the contrary, many contractors simply used inferior materials and pocketed the difference.

Aldermen even made money doing nothing, through what they called "Strike" legislation or "Cinch" bills. The men proposed bills that could cost companies, bankers, and businessmen money. The officials then received payments to kill the bills. At the time, the Common Council orchestrated shady land sales as they sold off profitable properties. For example, they leased a plot of land on Amos Street for 21 years for $610 a year, though the property was worth between $60,000 and $100,000. The Gansevoort Market along the Hudson was one of the city's most valuable bits of land. Bids came in for $225,000 and $300,000, but instead they accepted an offer of $160,000 from a buyer representing others. The aldermen then made away with somewhere between $40,000 to $75,000.

Not all members of the board were bad eggs. Some condemned their group's excesses. In September 1852, Aldermen Daniel Tiemann and John Boyce, along with Recorder Francis Tillou, submitted a report complaining about the costs of doing things, noting "the unlawful and unnecessary expenditure of the public moneys for entertainments, refreshments, and demonstrations of various kinds." But as the minority, they could do little to stop them.

To organize ferry lines from New York to Brooklyn, applicants had to shell out thousands of dollars, with the ferry from Wall Street to Montague Street in Brooklyn going to timber dealer Jacob "Jake" Sharp for $20,000 a year in rent. Railroads, which replaced what the *Tribune* called the "lumbering, clumsy, noisy, and inconvenient" omnibuses, proved especially profitable. There was a frenzy of applications and "a perfect swarm of schemes" for the aldermen to choose from. When the aldermen tried to take the Eighth Avenue Railroad franchise away from its original grantee and give it to another, the courts and the mayor stopped them. Despite that, the aldermen reportedly earned $40,000 in bribes. And they also made sure that their relatives got a cut of the deals. Tweed's father-in-law was one of eight who received the Second Avenue Railroad Company.[15]

Most of all, the Forty Thieves salivated over the idea of a Broadway railroad. As the city's main thoroughfare, Broadway was lined with shops, warehouses, hotels, and theaters. Pedestrians had such trouble crossing the street that some merchants hired liveried escorts to escort people to the other side. In July 1852, a petition to the Common Council from Jake Sharp, lawyer and future Tweed Ring member Peter Sweeney, as well as two dozen others requested the right to start a Broadway Railroad. This surface line, they said, would run from South Ferry to 59th Street. They also proposed to build a downtown depot, and noted that they would have a number of sleighs on hand for when it snowed.

Sharp's group promised that their plan would solve the congestion problem. It didn't bode well that he only proposed a $20 license fee per car, a miniscule amount. An overwhelming majority of Broadway landowners and tenants opposed the construction. Alexander Stewart and other merchants feared that the extra traffic would not only cut into their profitable carriage trade and harm real estate values, but adversely affect the character of the street. A public meeting was called in the hope of squelching Sharp's plan. Stewart made an offer for the franchise, saying he wouldn't charge more than 3¢ a passenger along with a per-car license fee of up to $1,000 a year. Others put forward their own ideas. Real estate tycoon Thomas Davies said he would pay the city 1¢ for every 5¢ made. Meanwhile, David H. Haight—who owned the St. Nicholas Hotel—and others, proposed to pay a yearly $10,000 license fee.

In the end there were some 50 applications. While many were fiscally better for the city, Sharp shelled out bribes, and not surprisingly, on November 19 Tweed and his colleagues granted him the franchise. The *Evening Post* commented on how the city was being fleeced, noting that "None of these grants are subjected to any scrutiny," and "none of them provoke any debate."[16]

The papers, the merchants, and the citizens of New York weren't the only ones up in arms about what was going on. Judge John Duer enjoined the Broadway project from going forward. The case then moved to the Court of Appeals. When the franchise's resolution arrived at Mayor Kingsland's office, Stewart and others paid him a visit. On December 18, Kingsland vetoed the franchise. The council promised to re-pass it; Stewart and the others brought a suit in the Superior Court. On December 27, Judge William Campbell issued a restraining order. Four days later, the *Tribune* commented on the board's "atrocity and rascality" and wondered if "part of this shameful plunder were ultimately to line the pockets of Bill Tweed?" It then quoted Tweed on how the board members "know the virtue of a $50 bill when it is wisely employed, and the echo that it will produce." The Court of Appeals sustained the superior court's decision, deeming the streetcar grant invalid. Stewart and others meanwhile lobbied Albany to transfer to the state legislature the power to grant franchises. Over the next two decades, Stewart spent a good deal of time and money to stop repeated attempts to build the Broadway line.[17]

The aldermen's reign took a severe toll on the city's coffers. In February 1853, City Comptroller Azariah C. Flagg noted the vast increase in expenditures in the city. He soberly reported that the new cost for city expenditures—$5,171,802.79, an increase of $1,791,391.74 over 1852—was just $640,197.21 "less than the aggregate annual expenditures, for the ordinary support of government, of the thirty-one states of this Union, including half a million for California."[18] In April 1853, the *Tribune* investigated the aldermen's financial grasping. The paper reported that during their time in office "they own more houses, lands, stocks, and other disposables than most any other forty men who have been grouped together since the days of Ali Baba." The paper then reported that quite a few aldermen held stock in the new Central Bank, with Tweed owning 120 shares.

Tweed meanwhile set his eyes on an even larger prize. While an alderman for less than a year, he decided to run for Congress. The Fifth Congressional District included both New York and Williamsburg, Brooklyn. Knowing that some people wanted a ferry linking the two cities, Tweed promised Democratic leaders that if they helped him secure the nomination he would make sure the ferry franchise passed. The nominating committee tied, and Tweed as the chairman cast the deciding vote, stating, "Tweedy never goes back on Tweedy—Tweedy goes for Tweed!" In the November election he beat his Whig opponent.[19]

Given that he still served as alderman through the end of 1853, Tweed availed himself of the power and perks of office. On July 14, 1853, along with President Franklin Pierce and Mayor Jacob Westervelt, he took part in the dedication of the Crystal Palace. And Tweed was one of those who voted on the choice of a major urban wonderland, casting his vote for the creation of Central Park. In December he checked into Washington's Willard Hotel, but came back to New York on the 7th to vote again for the Broadway Railroad. The *Tribune* noted that Tweed could be seen "hanging round the City Hall in the Park, taking his $4 per day from the municipal Treasury for services as Alderman, at the same time bleeding Uncle Sam $8 per diem for absenting himself from his congressional duties."[20]

Most of New York eagerly awaited the end of the reign of the Forty Thieves. The *Tribune* happily noted that month that "The last sands of the 'Forty Thieves' are nearly run." The prospect of the incoming reformers was a welcome change: "We expect them to sweep out of office every inefficient, knavish, loafing, drunken functionary . . . and fill their places with honest, capable energetic, faithful public servants." On December 31, the Forty Thieves' last day in power, they discussed other ways to clinch the Broadway Railroad. Tweed called for more money for a new Fireman's Hall, and said that the complaints about high taxes were not the fault of the council.

After their term ended, many of the aldermen were reported to have earned a lot of money. When Moses Beach brought out his 1855 edition of *The Wealth and Biography of Wealthy Citizens of the City of New York*, he reported that Tweed was "one of the few who manages to save something out of their salaries while holding office." With his earnings, the politician lived "in an elegant style in Rutgers Place" and he and his father were each worth $100,000.[21]

Washington proved very different from New York City for Tweed. He entered the same year as Mike Walsh, and as a junior congressman he possessed little power. He did not sponsor any significant bills, only sat on the Committee on Invalid Pensions, and voted for the Homestead bill. The issue at the front of national politics, however, was slavery. New York had close ties with the South, with many waterfront commission merchants working as factors for southern plantations. Southerners vacationed in the city, stayed at hotels, attended the theater, dined at restaurants, visited museums, shopped, and sent their children to city schools. The New York Democrats therefore saw no reason to oppose their southern colleagues when it came to issues dealing with slavery. When Tweed took the floor on May 10, 1854, he spoke about the Kansas-Nebraska Act, which sought to repeal the 1820 Missouri Compromise. There Tweed held to the party line. He called the Missouri Compromise "a flagrant wrong and gross injustice" against the Constitution, and how ending it would "endeavor to make the Union a political paradise."[22]

Overall, Tweed had little love for the life of a representative. He found his stay in the nation's capital disappointing. Others were not thrilled with him being there, either, and the *Times* commented of his "waning popularity." Tweed failed to be re-nominated for the next election. He returned to town and earned the nomination for his former alderman seat in the Seventh Ward. But in a four-way race, the *Times* wrote that the electorate "overawed the inspectors into decency," and Tweed came in second with 910 votes to Charles Fox's 1,043. Although the vote did not go Tweed's way, the election turned out to be a pivotal one for a dysfunctional city believing it needed a strong leader. That fall, merchant Fernando Wood won the office of mayor, and his time as chief executive would go on to transform that institution.

Now out of power, Tweed bided his time and redirected his efforts. By then, he and his wife, Mary, had a household full of children. In 1855 he received a spot on the Board of Education. It was a minor job at best, but became useful since it allowed him to earn kickbacks from the sale of textbooks, as well as on repair work and the purchase of furniture. Then, in 1856, he was made secretary at the Democratic Party's state convention in Syracuse and began planning his return to power.[23]

13

Corporation Pudding and Death

Not long after the arrival of western Europeans in the early 17th century, the settled part of lower Manhattan Island started to become a polluted place. While Dutch officials passed an ordinance that required the citizens of New Amsterdam "to keep the streets clean before his house or lot," residents generally ignored such laws. A 1657 report complained how "many burghers and inhabitants throw their rubbish, filth, ashes, dead animals and such like things into the public streets." People dumped slop on the ground, and, when it rained, it washed into buildings and poured into the town's streams which, along with waste from overflowing privies, then took it into the rivers.

In 1798 in the early years of the American republic, the *New York Commercial Advertiser* commented on the "stench which is exhaled from the heaps of filth" along the streets. Papers reported on the rancid vegetables, the dead rats, and the swirling flies, to no avail. In 1821 the *New York Evening Post* wrote how "Scarcely a street, particularly a wide one, but exhibits heaps of mud and dirt of the most offensive kind, raked up in the middle." So much soot, ash, and pulverized brick powder wafted through the air that the *New York Times* noted in March 1853 that for a New Yorker, "A good bath in the morning may serve for half an hour."[1]

The garbage piles—which the public nicknamed "Corporation Pudding"—were supposed to be cleared up by the Department of Street Cleaning. The contractors rarely did their job, however, and as the *Evening Post* reported in 1839, there was "not an ash cart or sweeper to be seen in any direction." Token attempts at cleanliness took place only as an election neared, when the sweepers became "as numerous as the locusts of Egypt" until the balloting "and then were immediately dismissed." And while workers removed very little, the records show that the non-effort did not come cheap. City officials attempted to legislate cleanliness, mandating in April 1849 that "No ashes, offals, vegetables or garbage" as well as "dross, cinders, shells, straw, shavings, dirt, filth or rubbish" could be left in the streets. Such rulings, though, had little effect. Because of the clutter, New York's streets proved hard to navigate. In March 1854, George Templeton Strong complained how "every crossing

[is] ankle deep with confluent filth. Even the sidewalks reek with greasy, slippery, semi-fluid nastiness."[2]

Adding to the nastiness was the mass of livestock in New York City. A number of citizens kept pigs at home over the years; one man housed 45 in his cellar and allowed them out each day. While the animals stank and soiled the streets, they also performed a valuable service by doing the only real street cleaning. Yet, so many roaming animals inevitably caused problems. In 1817 a hog frightened a horse, causing a man to be thrown from his gig. Animals rutted in both the impoverished Five Points and around the glitzy Astor House Hotel. In 1842 the *New York Tribune* reported that the city had 10,000 pigs living in the streets. Charles Dickens marveled how along Broadway one had to "Take care of the pigs."[3] Some captured and sold the loose animals to butchers. The city tried to clear up the problem with legislation and roundups. These latter had little effect, as citizens would sometimes band together to free their livestock. During August 1821, the *Evening Post* reported that marshals and constables gathered a great many hogs "in spite of all the opposition of broom-sticks and hot water."[4]

Another fixture of New York streets was the roaming dogs. In 1727 the Common Council discussed the "Very great Number of Mischievious Mastiffs Bull Dogs and Other useless Dogs" that attacked cows and made "the passage of the Inhabitants of this City upon their lawfull Occasions Very dangerous." Citizens feared hydrophobia—rabies. When a small girl in 1831 died from the disease, it set off a panic. Authorities passed an ordinance authorizing people to kill unleashed dogs, which resulted in a general massacre. In one season in the late 1840s, more than 3,500 dogs met an untimely end. The *Tribune*'s Horace Greeley editorialized that "dogs must die."

Some made good money from the situation. In 1849 Henry Boggs, whom the *Tribune* dubbed "the notorious Dog Killer," earned $3,000 to $4,000 for his work. "The annual bloody hunt" has some "revolting features," commented the paper. Young boys "went about the streets during the Summer, staggering under clubs as heavy as themselves, striking down and then horribly mangling with many blows every dog they encountered." The bounties likewise encouraged petnapping, and some dog killers even shipped in dogs by the boatload and killed them in the city to qualify for the fees.[5]

New York citizens had to contend with more than just small animals. A report from 1857 stated that the city had 22,540 horses, roughly half of them for pulling omnibuses, railcars, hacks, and milk wagons. Cattle were corralled in yards in the city and driven down streets. Occasionally, one would break loose and maim or kill pedestrians. In August 1851, Patrolman William Bell recalled being on duty when "a wild steer ran down Broadway, taking the sidewalk along the Park, knocking down every person." One elderly woman was "severely gored." Petitions called for the end to cattle herding, and in 1853 the Board of Aldermen prohibited daytime drives south of 42nd Street.

With so much filth, the citizens had to likewise contend with rats. James Boardman wrote in 1833 of "scarcely a building being entirely free from them." And James Fenimore Cooper's daughter Susan recalled that at their home on Beach Street in the early 1820s, "I remember distinctly their running over the bed in which I slept."[6]

All of this meant mounds of waste ripening in streets and yards. And since so many animals roamed the streets, there were also a lot of dead animals. Officer Bell reported on a pond of stagnant water at Avenue A and 17th Street filled with carcasses of dogs and other animals. City Inspector Henry G. Dunnel wrote to the Board of Aldermen in 1837 that 347 horses, nine cows, 1,418 swine, 1,182 dogs, 3,091 cats, and other dead creatures had been removed from streets, docks, slips, and other places.

Nuisances though they were, animals proved to be big business. Abattoirs were kept busy processing them, with blood spilling from the slaughterhouses into the streets. The amounts could be astounding. In 1853 the *Times* reported that in the month of May alone, 725 tons of blood and other offal, 44 tons of bones, and four tons of diseased and spoiled meats were removed from slaughterhouses. Fat-and-bone boilers collected carcasses, as well as kitchen refuse from hotels and boarding houses, all of which they melted down for the grease. Complaints abounded. In 1850, City Inspector Alfred W. White called for banning facilities where "the carrion of horses, and oxen, cows, hogs, rancid fat, bought or begged at the markets, are all thrown into the cauldrons and boiled."[7]

It was bad enough for the health of citizens that throughout the first half of the 19th century, New York streets were foul, the land polluted, and domesticated animals ran wild. In New York, even the milk from local dairies could be adulterated. Dubbed Swill Milk, it came from facilities where owners fed the cows distillery waste products. The product had a bluish color, and to make it appear palatable, dairies mixed in chalk, magnesia, stale eggs, molasses, and other substances. In 1848, Dr. Augustus K. Gardner investigated the massive Johnson's distillery on Tenth Avenue and 16th Street. The complex sat alongside sheds that housed thousands of dairy cows, and the animals were fed the distillery slop that Gardner deemed "rather offensive, with its peculiar, half sour, half spirituous odor." Gardner wrote how children who drank the milk became "afflicted with obstinate vomiting and purging, great loss of flesh, and extreme emaciation." Tuberculosis and brucellosis often contaminated such foul brew, and the liquid contributed to a high death rate of those under 10. Finally in 1862, the state legislature passed a "swill milk law," though it was rife with loopholes.[8]

* * *

Sanitary conditions were the main cause of the diseases that permeated all levels of 19th-century New York society. People suffered from cholera, smallpox, diphtheria, Scarlet Fever, and measles. Illness did not discriminate, striking the rich, the poor, the healthy, the young, the old, the righteous, and the immoral. Doctors had little if any concept of how to deal with sickness. One treatment was bloodletting. When Bernhard, Duke of Saxe-Weimar-Eisenach, was coming to New York in the mid-1820s, he woke one morning "with such a dreadful pain in my right side, that I could scarcely move in bed." He asked a companion for help, and the friend "opened a vein in my arm . . . gave me a purgative," tapped 16 ounces of blood, and spread a liniment on his side. "The pain had so much abated in the afternoon, that I could move with more ease." The duke was one of the lucky ones. Often such a "cure" became deadly. During the apoplexy that struck him just after the Great Fire, Dr. David Hosack lost the use of his arm and could not speak. Despite Hosack's belief that the widespread use of bleeding was unwise and warned against "the promiscuous use of the lancet," his son Alexander, who was also a doctor, bled him of 18 ounces of blood. Not surprisingly, "His symptoms increased," observed the younger Hosack, "his articulation became more indistinct, and finally unconsciousness and stupor came over him." The good doctor died a few days later.[9]

Like bloodletting, most treatments proved ineffective at best, barbarous at worst. They ran from blistering, applying caustic materials that irritated the flesh and caused fluids and pus to flow, spreading hot mustard and laying leeches on their skin, to purging with calomel, mercury chloride. Ads such as one from a Dr. John Loudon ran in the *Evening Post* in 1833, touting his single treatment for "gleets, ulcerated legs, salt rheum, leprosy, white swellings, and venereal ulcers, rheumatisms, blotches on the face, coughs, cancer and dropsy, and all diseases arising from impurity of the blood or the abuse of mercury."

With limited understanding of medicine or a sense of how to combat disease, plagues long wreaked havoc on New York. Yellow Fever was one of the first, arriving in the city in 1702. Caused by a flavivirus, the disease is contracted from the bite of a mosquito. It brings on headaches, aching joints, and vomiting, along with jaundiced skin, which give it its name. As the disease progresses, it can cause kidney failure, liver damage, bleeding, seizures, delirium, vomiting called "black vomit," coma, and death. When Yellow Fever reappeared in New York in the summer of 1798, it cut a deadly swath across the city. More than 700 people perished. The Scottish-born seedman Grant Thorburn recalled seeing "two small boys going along the streets selling coffins from a little hand-cart. They told me their father . . . and four journeymen made coffins night and day." To treat patients, the city erected hospitals. Dr. Hosack opposed harsh purges, calling instead for mild baths and good nursing as well as lots of liquids. When he became sick that year, he treated himself by washing his "limbs with cold vinegar and water" and drinking "toast water, common tea or a cup of balm or catmint tea." Others took more drastic measures. Commission merchant Richardson Underhill helped treat patients, purging those suffering from delirium by applying "hot applications of ashes, bricks, &c. wet with vinegar and spirits."[10]

As Yellow Fever deaths increased, health commissioners recommended disinfecting cellars with quick lime. Thousands meanwhile fled, with businessmen relocating to Greenwich Village. In September 1798, 954 people died. More than a dozen perished on Ann Street, including the blacksmith William Tompkins and his wife and son, the bricklayer John Ogden and his wife, and Philip Hone's parents. Hone recalled their passing 50 years later, noting it was part of "a great mortality," and how "I am ten years older than my father was at his death."[11]

Yellow Fever continued to appear, and the belief grew that the city had to do more to fight it. Merchant John Pintard began collecting mortality numbers in 1802, and in 1804 he became the city's first health inspector, setting out "to furnish data for reflection and calculation" that could make the fever "more controllable and less mortal." In 1805, the Common Council formed the first New York City Board of Health. To combat Yellow Fever, it prohibited foreign cotton and damaged coffee, instructing that "no dead animal shall be left exposed." It prohibited "pickled or salted beef" south of Lispenard's Meadow, forbade butchers from bringing to market "the head of any sheep or lamb," banned oysters as well as "undressed skins, hides, blubber," and stopped burials of victims in the populated parts of the city. As each wave of the disease passed through, people fled. When Yellow Fever struck in 1819, the Tontine Coffee House and such firms as J. & P. Hone & Co. auctioneers and Arthur Tappan & Co. set up shop in Greenwich Village.[12]

When another devastating wave hit in 1822, the city considered the area below City Hall as the "infected district." The *Evening Post* suggested "the acid fumigation" of the area. One citizen recommended that the Board of Health fire cannons loaded with black cartridge into the area. Glasgow businessman Peter Neilson, who arrived as the plague raged, noted how authorities ended up purifying the air "by strewing the infected district with quicklime and charcoal." Believing that bad air emanating from Trinity Churchyard graves contributed to the disease, Dr. Cornelius Roosa had his workers cover the churchyard with 52 casks worth of quicklime. They also spread quicklime at St. Paul's Chapel and the North Dutch Church.[13]

Nonetheless, the disease could not be stopped. That August, George Washington Strong's family left for Whitestone, Long Island. Strong's brother Benjamin sent four of his children to Oyster Bay, Long Island, and stayed behind at their home on Leonard Street. Later that month, James Hardie recorded that the city looked like "a town besieged." All day long, "one line of carts, containing boxes, merchandize and effects, were seen moving towards Greenwich Village and the upper parts of the city." Because so many had left, the city lacked enough firemen to battle blazes. Banks, the post office, and the Custom House all relocated to the north on the island. The *Evening Post* moved to a new building on Broadway between Spring and Prince Streets, next to the *New York Mercantile Advertiser* and the *New York Gazette*. Many "erected shanties" above Spring Street, and Neilson wrote how in Greenwich Village "hundreds of wooden houses were reared up in a twinkling." One clergyman told his congregation "that this pestilence was the effects of Divine vengeance" because of such wicked activities as "sabbath-breaking." Finally in early November, the epidemic subsided.[14]

Ten years later, in 1832, came the first visitation of cholera. The disease was historically isolated to India, though might have struck ancient Greece and Rome. It migrated out of the subcontinent in 1817, making its way to Europe. A second pandemic was set off in 1829, laying waste to Russia, Poland, and killing hundreds of thousands in western Europe.

The plague soon arrived in North America. "Every preparation is now making in the city for the expected pestilence," architect Thomas Wharton noted in his diary on June 19, 1832, "cleaning the streets and alleys, strewing the gutters with Chlorine of Lime, and the druggists busily occupied" making up prescriptions. The *Evening Post* recommended residents take constant sips of strained gruel, sago, or tapioca to protect themselves. The chemist Lewis Feuchtwanger sold a Cholera Lamp that spread "Perfumes, Scents, Essences, Aromatic Vinegar, Chloride of Soda and Lime" to purify the air. Reverend Benjamin Onderdonk meanwhile implored citizens to pray "in a truly devout and christian frame of mind, with deep repentance for your sins." And the Ready Made Coffin Warehouse informed citizens that they kept "constantly on hand an extensive assortment of COFFINS," made from mahogany, walnut, cherry.[15]

On June 25, 1832, a Mr. Fitzgerald, "a steady and temperate man" who came from Ireland and lived on Cherry Street, near the Tweed family home, became ill. He recovered, yet his children—Margaret, seven, and Jeremiah, four—died on the 27th. Two days later, his wife Mary became ill and died. The disease progressed quickly through the city. Dr. John Stearns, in a report to the Board of Health, recalled how one of his patients told him that "The attack was sudden & violent—his impression was that 'he fell as if knocked down with an ax.'"

People fled before the advancing disease. One hundred thousand people— half the city's population—left that summer. Most of the city still lived below 14th Street; many headed up to Murray Hill or Harlem Heights. Hone, his wife, Catharine, and their daughter Margaret traveled to the Rockaways. George Washington Strong took his family to Wilton, Connecticut. Carts, carriages, and people jammed the streets, and passengers packed ferries and settled in farmhouses and country homes outside of town. On July 3, the *Evening Post* noted, "Almost every steamboat which left New York yesterday was crowded with a dense mass of fugitives flying in alarm from the imaginary pestilence."[16]

In this age before germ theory and the study of microorganisms, no one had any concept of the origins of disease, and no idea how to treat illness. Most did sense the existence of a link between filth and sickness. James Fenimore Cooper and others believed that illness was due to "the Taint, corruption, or animalculæ in the air." Many believed that this "taint" was a miasma, a foul and poisonous presence in the atmosphere from particles of decaying organic matter. Others sensed that it was somehow transmittable between people. It was actually caused by a rod-shaped bacterium called *Vibrio cholerae*. Cholera spreads through water tainted by human waste, making its way to the small intestines. The toxin it produces brings on nausea, vomiting, leg cramps, and watery diarrhea called "rice water."

The blood pressure in its victims drops, their eyes assume a hollow, sunken look, and their skin wrinkles. Subsequent dehydration and circulatory collapse lead to cyanosis, giving the flesh a bluish hue, the reason the disease was bestowed the name "Blue Death."

Working with what they had, doctors did the best they could. The Board of Health set up cholera hospitals, turning the Hall of Records into a hospital and opening numerous others. Physicians searched for cures. The most widely used remedy was calomel, and when doctors saw that the patient developed pus-y gums—a sign of mercury poisoning—they believed that their cathartic procedure had succeeded. Dr. John Rhinelander, who worked at the Crosby Street hospital, recommended actively rubbing pulverized chalk on the flesh, and the inhalation of nitrous oxide gas.

On July 20 the Medical Council ran the following in several papers:

NOTICE . . .
BE TEMPERATE
in eating and drinking; avoid crude Vegetables and
Fruits; abstain from Cold Water, when heated; and
above all from
ARDENT SPIRITS;
and if habit have rendered it indispensable, take much
less than usual.
SLEEP AND CLOTHE WARM.
Avoid labour in the heat of day.
Do not sleep or sit in a draught of air, when heated
AVOID GETTING WET.
TAKE NO MEDICINES WITHOUT ADVICE.

Some doctors administered sulfuric ether, or offered French brandy, port, and herbs. They also applied mustard poultices, gave a powder of capsicum, immersed patients in icy water, inserted enemas, and plugged the rectum with beeswax and oilcloths to stop discharge. Those taking anti-cholera pills were advised that "using warm flannel next [to] the skin, will be a great means of preventing the individual from being seized by the pestilential disease." The Special Medical Council told Fire Chief James Gulick and his men that working at night "exposes them in a greater degree to an attack of the prevailing disease." The council advised them that if they got wet, they should keep moving until they returned home, then take off their clothes, get into bed, and only have a little warm gruel or barley water. Much of what was tried could be wrenching to the body. Reverend Charles Grandison Finney had just been installed at the Chatham Street Chapel when he "was seized with the cholera." As Finney would note, "The means used for my recovery, gave my system a terrible shock."[17]

While physicians and pharmacists tried to save people, the British travel writer Edward Thomas Coke commented how quacks "flocked into the city from all quarters" to take advantage of the sick, suggesting "hot-baths and cayenne pepper for every complaint." Broadsides promised miracle cures. In the *Cholera Bulletin,* sponsored by the Association of Physicians, an article outlined the full range of quackery. "In the foremost rank stand the Bleeders, then advance the Calomel Band, escorted by a troop of Opium foragers; here a file of Stimulators, and there a Tobacco brigade; here a company of Saline Aperients, and there again a guard of Leechers and Blisterers. The men of friction are in the van, and the rear is composed of the Icy legion."

Yet whatever doctors, citizens, or quacks tried had little real effect. Death came painfully and quickly. A young woman arrived at the Rivington Street Hospital: "Her voice was clear and distinct," reported the doctors. "In less than 20 *minutes she was a corpse.*" The minister Henry Dana Ward wrote to his father, Thomas, in Shrewsbury, Massachusetts, about a friend who "took the cholera bad." Ward and his wife, Abigail, were "very attentive to him," yet "in the morning we buried him cold in the grave."[18]

The lack of medical insight made many believe that cholera sprang from moral faults, excessive alcohol consumption, and poor living habits. Coke noted broadsides everywhere warning citizens to "Quit dram-drinking if you would not have the cholera." The *New York Mercury* commented on July 18 on a prostitute on Mott Street "who was decking herself before the glass at 1 o'clock yesterday, was carried away in a hearse at half past 3 o'clock." The devout, like the abolitionists Arthur and Lewis Tappan, believed that the fear of death and damnation would entice people to give up their dissolute ways and accept the Lord. Ministers preached that only the righteous could be saved. While churches shuttered, many clergymen stayed in town. The Catholic Church actively ministered to the physical and spiritual needs of citizens.

The worst suffering took place in the slums, which had limited sanitation and access to clean water. Hone wrote, "the mortality is principally among the wretched population about the Five Points and similar places." Pintard just as uncharitably noted that "Those sickened must be cured or die off, & being cheifly [sic] of the very scum of the city, the quicker despatch the sooner the malady will cease." When patients died, many were tossed into shallow graves in potter's fields. So many bodies filled the areas that grave diggers found it easier to simply dig large trenches. In untended parts of the city, corpses lay in gutters.[19]

Houses, offices, warehouses, and shops shuttered. "The public gardens and theatres were closed," Coke noted, with the Bowery Theatre's Thomas Hamblin advertising that he "deems it a duty to the Public at large" to close the theater "until the alarm now existing has subsided." Hamblin himself came down with the disease, and doctors bled him and administered laudanum. Some places stayed open. When a journalist from the *New York Mirror* visited the Richmond Hill Theater, he reported that while it was staging the comedy *Paul Pry*, he only found "one or two disreputable looking gentlemen" in the audience. When Jacob Woodhull, the theater's manager, became ill, a sick Hamblin climbed from his sickbed to host a benefit for him. Woodhull died on August 31. As traffic decreased and shipping dropped, the *Evening Post* wrote that the only activity being carried out in the city was "at the Hospitals, and among the medical faculty." Painter John Casilear wrote to Asher B. Durand, "There is no business doing here if I except those done by Cholera, Doctors, Undertakers, Coffin makers."[20]

A Committee to Provide Accommodations for the Destitute Poor evacuated some from their homes and set them up in shanties around town. Those remaining were advised against eating green apples, which was seen as "a most dangerous mistake." They were also told to avoid ardent spirits, and should instead have vegetable bitters, wormwood, chamomile, hoarhound, tansy, spearmint, and peppermint. "There were some who would not eat meat, and others who would not eat vegetables," wrote Coke, "some who would not drink any thing except water, and others who would only take 'anti-cholera,' as they termed brandy and port wine." James Riker Jr. and his family "scarcely ventured farther than the apothecary's opposite to obtain drugs, or to examine the daily report of deaths by cholera." Like others, Riker didn't know what to do. Then his grandmother took sick and died. His uncle, whom Riker called "an uncommonly rugged man," also passed away "that gloomy night." The family then packed up furniture and clothes and departed to Westchester. So many people abandoned the town that the *Evening Post* observed on August 6 that the usual pall of smoke that hung over New York had dissipated, and that "the buildings of the great metropolis appear with unusual clearness and distinctness." What smoke there was came from the bedding and clothes of the dead being burned.[21]

Social standing was no protection. Pillars of society, aldermen, doctors, clergymen, and businessmen perished. On August 1, Magdalen Astor

Bristed, the eldest child of John Jacob Astor, died. Theater critic William Dunlap wrote James Fenimore Cooper that "we begin to be reconciled to being killed." By the time the cholera had run its course in late August, 3,513 had perished. Even after returning to the city and finding "thousands of the refugees back in their home," the Hones took care of what they ate, believing that the disease could still be spread through food: "The peaches and melons in vain throw their fragrance around; we look at them, we sigh for their enjoyment—but we don't touch them." When the carnage passed, Pintard noted, "A few short weeks, cholera, like Yellow fever in its day, will be forgotten, except by the heart stricken who are left to mourn over departed friends & desolated families."[22]

* * *

Seventeen years later, cholera returned. The disease was first reported in New York in May 1849 on Orange Street. Philip Hone observed that it appeared in a part of town "where hundreds are crowded into a few wretched hovels," eating food that "a well-bred hog on a Westchester farm would turn up his snout at." An Irish laborer there developed cramps and started vomiting. Dr. Harriot reported finding him and two women "lying on a few filthy rags, on the half-decayed floor of a miserably damp and dark basement." To combat cholera's spread, the city banned the sale of fruit, vegetables, and fish from carts. Mayor Caleb Woodhull ordered the streets cleaned. On Orange Street, workers used Dr. Grant's Disinfecting Agent, whitewash, and Croton Water to scrub surfaces. Within a month, thousands of loads of manure and dirt were removed from the Fourth Ward east of City Hall, and the city hired 30 additional sweepers as well as a health inspector, opened hospitals, and closed bone, offal, and fat boilers.[23]

Despite their efforts, the disease's progress could not be impeded. At the start of June 1849, Hone noted that "The cholera increases, the weather is foggy, murky, and damp,—just such weather as produces and propagates this dreadful disease." Seeking to protect themselves, citizens stocked up on popular potions, sulfur pills and candies, tobacco-smoke enemas, aconite, and strychnine. "I've laid in a supply of camphor and paregoric, calomel, pepper, and mustard," George Templeton Strong wrote, "and am now waiting silently, 'hushed in grim repose' for the first symptom of diarrhea to let slip the dogs of war, to ravage my interior with calomel and opiates, and to scarify my outward man with mustard and cayenne."[24]

Editors like Horace Greeley filled columns with reports of the disease. James Gordon Bennett's *Herald* meanwhile observed how "Bad food—bad ventilation—bad effluvia—bad doctors—bad drugs" were swelling "our bills of mortality." Many believed that pigs spread the disease, and City Inspector Alfred White forced thousands of hogs uptown to less populous areas. As they trotted north, a nervous Greeley kept a close watch on the growing mass of animals near his Turtle Bay home, complaining that the beasts filled the air with "exhalations of the swinish multitude." Yet despite what Greeley, White and the Board of Health thought, the decrease in the number of roaming pigs downtown only meant the presence of fewer animals to clean up the ever-present garbage. And because inspectors shut down bone boilers, businessmen simply dumped horse and cattle carcasses into the river, where they remained, as White put it, "bloating and festering in the sun and heat, floating, with the ebb of the tide, out of the slips, and returning, with the flood."[25]

The weather was particularly oppressive. On July 12, "before we realized our danger," Greeley wrote that he and his wife Mary's young son Arthur Young had become ill. That day turned into "one of the hottest, as well as quite the longest, I have ever known." With no doctor available, the couple treated their child, whom they called Pickie, as best they knew how. Yet they could do nothing to "stay the fury of the epidemic." Pickie died, breaking Greeley's heart. "I knew that the Summer of my life was over, that the chill breath of its Autumn was at hand, and that my future course must be along the downhill of life." As he noted in his paper the following day, Pickie was but five years, three months, and 20 days old.[26]

Strong desperately sought a place out of town for his family, and sailed to West Point to reserve some rooms. As he headed home down the Hudson River on the 14th on the steamer *Roger Williams*, fellow passenger Alexander Robertson Wyckoff, who served as treasurer of the Hudson River Railroad Company, told him he did not feel well. Strong could see that he had trouble standing. There was no doctor onboard, so Strong placed Wyckoff in a cabin, gave him some brandy, and used his handkerchief to form a mustard plaster for his abdomen. Strong then treated him as best he could with some camphor that he had on him, as well as some opium-based laudanum that he found in the ship's bar. The camphor and opium treatment stopped Wyckoff's diarrhea. Yet soon after, "he began vomiting pailfuls." When the ship docked, Strong had Wyckoff carried to a carriage. The businessman then started to convulse. Fearing he might "die at any minute," Strong raced uptown. Yet while Wyckoff's condition seemed to improve, he died soon after. Strong then rushed his family to West Point.[27]

The day Wyckoff died, the city had 37 other reported cholera deaths, including the lawyer David B. Ogden and the cotton broker James Reyburn. Strong could not help but note how the disease was "the all-pervading subject." So many bodies piled up on Randall's Island that many did not receive proper burials. Hone was right when he wrote how "Poor New York has become a charnel house; people die daily of cholera to the number of two or three hundred."

The disease, which would take the lives of over 5,000 New Yorkers, proved especially deadly for the ill and the elderly. At 68, Hone suffered from gout, rheumatism, and lumbago. His health also had been weakened by an exhausting trip two years earlier to the Midwest. On September 1, the former mayor exhibited symptoms of the disease. His son Robert rushed him home to Great Jones Street. By then, Hone had severe chills, followed by a serious bout of diarrhea and vomiting, and his hands and face took on the dreaded bluish tint. His physician visited, and Hone recalled that "his treatment was judicious, and his tenderness and devotion touching to the extreme." Hone survived, as we might guess, and the press followed the former mayor's recovery, with the *Day Book* remarking that "the whole community will rejoice at this prolongation of the valuable life of one of the most respected and venerable citizens of New York."[28]

14

"A Burial Can Scarcely Take Place without Disturbing a Previous One"

Philip Hone, who is one of the main figures of this story—in some ways its narrator—was the 10th of 12 children born to his parents, Hester and Philip. He was also their third son named "Philip." Both previous Philips died before their first birthdays. In the Hone family, six of the children didn't reach the age of two. Just four of their children—Judith, John, Samuel, and Philip—made it to adulthood. Judith died soon after getting married in 1788, a passing that, Hone wrote, "left a cloud over my mother's mind which never passed away." Samuel died in 1816 at age 48. Philip Hone and his wife, Catharine, were considered lucky. They had seven children: Catharine, John, James, Margaret, Mary, Philip, and Robert. All but James—who died at three and a half months—lived to adulthood. Hone's brother John and his wife Joanna were less fortunate. They had 16 children, seven of whom died by age two.[1]

The high mortality affected both the wealthy and the poor, although of course higher in the latter, who had less access to proper sanitation and clean water. All this contributed to the fact that the average life expectancy in New York during the second decade of the 19th century stood at only 26.15 years. That figure didn't change much over time. In the third decade, it came to 24.36 years, the fourth decade 19.46 years, and the fifth decade 20.78 years. In some years deaths outpaced births. Numbers were only slightly better in places like Boston, where they were 27.75, 25.88, 22.72, and 21.43 years. Urban centers proved so deadly in the early 1850s that one physician reported that just living in New York meant that a citizen would lose "nineteen years, or nearly one-half of the proper term of his life."[2]

Childhood death touched all segments of society. George Templeton Strong was the first child of George and Eliza Strong. And while he went on to live until 55, his younger brother John Wells only survived until his second birthday.[3] Just five of John Jacob and Sarah Astor's children survived childhood. Arthur and Frances Tappan had eight children; all but Mary and Arthur lived to adulthood. Jane, the daughter of oysterman Thomas Downing and his wife, Rebecca, died while young. (When Rebecca passed in February 1851 at 49, her death received a rare mention of an African American woman in the newspaper.) John Turney, the son of merchant Alexander Stewart and his wife, Cornelia, died in 1834 at 20 days old. In 1838 they had a daughter who was stillborn. Engineer John Jervis's newborn daughter lived just a few short hours in 1839, and his wife, Cynthia, died five days later. Tammany boss William Tweed and his wife, Mary, lost two of their children at an early age. Central Park designer Frederick Law Olmsted and his wife, Mary, lost their son John Theodore, who died at two months from cholera infantum, an intestinal disturbance in infants.[4]

Grief was a constant in life. When Hone's daughter Mary died on November 13, 1840, he wrote, "My heart sinks within me, whenever any thoughts are concentrated on the greatest grief which has ever oppressed it." Hone's journal contains numerous mentions of the passing of friends. In September 1849 at age 64, he noted the death of Christopher Hughes and commented how "One by one these companions of my former pleasant days are dropping off, and I begin to feel like the solitary, leafless, weatherbeaten tree, on the sandy beach of Rockaway." Then on May 24, 1850, Hone's wife, Catharine, passed away, "died as angels live, peaceful, serene, sensible to the last moment, free from pain, and perfectly resigned to the will of God."[5]

Catharine's death so traumatized Hone that he did not attend her funeral. Former and current Columbia College presidents William Duer and Charles King, and others acted as her pallbearers at St. Mark's Church in-the-Bowery. Hone finally emerged from his home on May 30. By then, his own health had suffered, having already been severely weakened in 1849 by the cholera which almost took his life, as well as by an exhausting trip to Wisconsin two years before that. On his birthday in October 1850, he noted, "I am seventy years old; a mere wreck of what I was."

By the spring of 1851, Hone had filled nearly 28 volumes of his diary with some two million words, religiously chronicling his life, his family, and the changes in New York and the nation. On April 30 he commented that the most recent book only had four pages left, but he had not written anything because of his "continued unmitigated illness." Hone recalled how a few years earlier he and Catharine visited Brooklyn's Green-Wood Cemetery and were struck by the beauty and simplicity of the inscription on one of the monuments: "There is rest in Heaven." When he got home he started to write out his own epitaph, and wondered, "Has the time come?"

> The weary traveler on earth's dull road,
> The pilgrim fainting underneath life's load,
> The stout heart struggling 'gainst the adverse wave,
> And sinking, with no mortal arm to save,
> Finds hope and consolation in the blest decree
> Pronounced by angels' lips—"there's rest in heaven for thee."[6]

Philip Hone died five days later on May 5. He was 70 years old.

At the time of Hone's birth in 1780, New York City had fewer than 30,000 people. When he died, the number was more than 500,000. His passing was noted privately and publicly throughout the town. In his honor, City Hall, the Custom House, and other buildings flew flags at half-mast. Family, friends, and officials attended his funeral. Charles King gave a eulogy, and Hone's personal physician spoke, too, commenting on how Hone had spent three decades keeping a journal about the people and events in New York. His body was then laid in a crypt in the churchyard alongside Catharine.

Both local and national papers eulogized Hone. The *New York Evening Post* called him "a gentleman of polished and courteous manners, amiable character, and dignified address." The *New York Tribune* wrote, "His conduct, whether in the different public stations he has filled in the course of his profession, or the circle of private life, has invariably been marked by a generous and liberal spirit and a high sense of honor." Even James Gordon Bennett, who only sparingly lauded others and who took pleasure in attacking Hone in his paper, praised the former mayor, writing in the *New York Herald,* "In private life, Mr. Hone was much esteemed by his large circle of friends, as a gentleman of refined manners, amiable character, and benevolent disposition."[7]

By the 1850s, the generation of the Great Fire was beginning to fade. Thomas Hamblin's health was also declining. Yet despite the repeated fires and the strains from running a playhouse, he continued his administration of the Bowery Theatre. Throughout, he found himself weighed down by financial woes. Hamblin worked to spiff up the theater, adding new velvet seats. When there was a move to foreclose on the house, friends held benefits to raise money and keep him afloat. Just over a year after John Jacob Astor's 1848 death, Hamblin had rented and settled his family into the tycoon's home at 585 Broadway. In May 1852 he moved with his family to Broome Street. On November 30, Hamblin's friend, the actor Junius Booth, was heading toward Cincinnati when he died onboard the steamboat *J.S. Chenoweth.* Less than two weeks later, Hamblin was buffeted by another death, that of his friend the English bass singer Arthur Seguin. Hamblin served as one of Sequin's pallbearers. Soon after, he reportedly received a hefty offer of $350,000 for the Bowery. He turned it down. Then, on New Year's Eve, Hamblin suffered from a "brain fever," which could have been either cerebral meningitis or cerebral syphilis. He seemed to recover, but then had another attack a few days later. He died on January 8, 1853, at age 52.

The Bowery Theatre closed in Hamblin's honor, and at his funeral on the 11th, friends and associates gathered at his Broome Street home while some 1,000 "Bowery boys" crowded outside and quietly mourned. The grievers then accompanied Hamblin's body as part of a 56-carriage cortege that traveled down Broadway to South Ferry and across the river to Green-Wood Cemetery. In a rare bout of charity toward his constant foil, Bennett—who seemed to be softening in his older age—wrote in the *Herald* that "If the deceased had, in common with his kind, many frailties and weaknesses of character, they were redeemed in an eminent degree by many private though well acknowledged merits."[8]

Ten months later, on November 24, 1853, Strong's mother, Eliza, died at age 68. She was buried in Trinity Churchyard. Then on June 27, 1855, George Washington Strong died at age 72, and was set alongside his wife. "I find myself every morning expecting to see him in his accustomed place at the desk where he worked honestly, wisely, and untiringly for fifty years," George Templeton wrote in July of how he missed his father. "When I think of it as a fact that is indeed true, I feel like a child that has lost his way in the street."[9]

* * *

With so much death, New York had constant funerals. Churchyards, such as those at Trinity Church and St. Mark's Church in-the-Bowery, served as the traditional final resting places for many I have featured and quoted in this history. Yet, while some of the dead were buried in the yards of fine churches, the city's lax sanitary laws meant there were few rules regulating burials and the upkeep of even the wealthier sites. A number of citizens had always objected to the presence of cemeteries in populated areas. In 1822, Dr. Samuel Akerly had written how the grounds at Trinity appeared so crowded that "a burial can scarcely take place without disturbing a previous one." The smell from the site proved especially pungent, causing neighbors to write a petition.[10]

The poor had fewer choices when it came to burials, and many ended up in potter's fields alongside criminals and the vast tolls struck down by plagues. The term "potter's field" itself comes from a verse in the Book of Matthew in the New Testament: "And they consulted together and bought with them the potter's field, to bury strangers in." The city's first such strangers' burial ground opened in October 1794 on the site of the current-day Madison Square. Burials took place on the spot until 1797, when the city decided to establish a new field to the south in Greenwich Village. Alexander Hamilton and 56 other residents tried to stop the city from setting it there and petitioned the government, noting the expansion of the city and how in "the course of a few years the aforementioned field will be drawn within the precincts of the city and long remain a subject of nuisance and inconvenience to the Community." The city rejected their claim, and the site quickly became active when a wave of Yellow Fever stuck in 1798. One doctor commented how it was "known to you all to have been our Golgotha."

Residents of Greenwich Village had justifiably worried about the graveyard being set in their neighborhood. In 1819 one of them wrote the *Evening Post* about how plots contained up to a dozen coffins, with the area left open and "covered only by a few boards, (which are removable at the pleasure of all.)" And New Yorkers noted how a blue mist hovered over the land on hot days, and that the decomposing bodies leeched into the local water system. The site stopped receiving burials in the mid-1820s. In 1823, the land where Bryant Park now stands became a new potter's field. It closed in 1840 as New York set out to build the Murray Hill Distributing Reservoir, and the area on the western side became Reservoir Square. Another potter's field opened in 1825 between 48th and 52nd Streets west of Third Avenue.[11]

African Americans meanwhile had limited choice for where to bury their dead. In 1697, the city forbade Blacks from being buried in the city's public cemeteries, so they started holding funerals at the African Burial Ground near a ravine alongside the Collect Pond. It was closed in 1794. As they established their own congregations, Blacks also laid out their own churchyards. These likewise drew criticism. In 1807, neighbors of the African Methodist Episcopal Zion Church complained of the stench of the hundreds of bodies lying in a vault under the church.

The mass of ill-disposed bodies created a market for cadavers for medical schools. Those digging up the corpses were dubbed "Resurrectionists," stealing from places like the African Burial Ground and Trinity. The thievery led to a rampage that became known as the Doctors' Riot. In April 1788, citizens chased and assaulted doctors, ransacked their homes, and caused the deaths of as many as 20 people. The following year, "An Act to Prevent the Odious Practice of Digging Up and Removing for the Purpose of Dissection,

Dead Bodies Interred in Cemeteries or Burial Places" outlawed digging up graves. It did, though, allow for the study of the bodies of executed prisoners.

This did not close down the market for bodies and the efforts of resurrectionists. In 1809, officials dismissed the keeper of the potter's field, who allowed for the exhuming of remains. In 1833, authorities nabbed two men carrying a body out of a churchyard in the upper part of the town. They also arrested the physician who hired them. Those not caught could earn a few dollars per corpse. British author James S. Buckingham wrote in 1841, in his historical and statistical study of the United States, how "it was a common practice in New York, to ship off the bodies of dead negroes." These corpses "were put up in salt and brine, and packed in the same kind of casks as those in which salted provisions are exported."[12]

As land prices in New York rose, the dead were seen as lying in the way of progress. Bodies and coffins were built over, vaults demolished, and the remains moved to new sites or simply dumped in trash heaps or the rivers. As the *Evening Post* noted in 1833 on the cutting-through of streets: "Mountains and rocks, churches, and churchyards, full of the bones of the revered dead, all yield to their touch."[13]

The truncating and closing of cemeteries, the moving of bodies along with constant reinvention, was a regular event in the city in the first half of the 19th century. Hone had bemoaned in 1845 how "the very bones of our ancestors are not permitted to lie quiet a quarter of a century." When Chambers Street had been opened around 1792, the road went right through part of the African Burial Ground. At the turn of the century, the construction of Bancker Street sliced into part of Shearith Israel's Chatham Square cemetery. A few years later, Trinity bought the Lutheran Burial Ground at Broadway and Rector Street. As they prepared the site for Grace Church, workers carted away fragments of bones and coffins, which they then poured in the Hudson River. A letter writer in 1808 complained how workers digging a foundation on the site of the potter's field dug up "coffins and dead bodies which are disposed of in the most indecent and disrespectful manner." The laying of Second Avenue in 1815 went through the Methodist congregation's cemetery. Two years later, the creation of 1st Street did the same to St. Stephen's Church cemetery. Other defilements followed, from 6th Street taking over part of the potter's field and the widening of Nassau Street running through the vaults of the Middle Dutch Church, to the laying of 11th Street that cut off part of Shearith Israel's second cemetery.[14]

As workers sank awning posts at Broadway and Reade Streets in May 1829, they pulled bones from the African Burial Ground. The *New York Mirror* reported in 1840 how laborers shifted 2,000 to 3,000 bodies from the potter's field on 49th and 50th Streets for the building of the Harlem Railroad, writing of the hope that New York would move the bodies to any place "where one generation cannot dig up the dust of the one that preceded it, for the purpose of laying out new streets, or constructing new store-houses." In the early 1850s, Reverend Theodore Parker observed how at one building excavation, "a large quantity of human bones [were] thrown up by workmen." They belonged to African Americans who had fought and died in the Battle of Long Island, yet were summarily "carted off and emptied into the sea." When a section of Fourth Avenue and 50th Street was graded in 1857, workers stacked up old coffins. All along the area lay the bones of the deceased. The *Herald* reported macabrely how the matted and tangled hair of one female skeleton swayed in the wind. This led a writer to the *New York Times* to complain the following year how he could see "coffins, skulls and decayed bodies lying exposed," and how "Every Sunday crowds can be seen idly gazing at the decayed remains, and at intervals tossing the skulls and bones from one spot to another by way of amusement." The following month, in May 1858, the city had 3,000 graves exhumed and the contents shipped to Wards Island. And when the city expanded the Bowery in the mid-1850s, congregation Shearith Israel had to remove 256 graves from its Chatham Square cemetery and move the remains to its third cemetery, located on 21st Street just off Sixth Avenue.[15]

Despite the unrelenting demand for land, some successfully fought attempts to drive roads through churchyards. In 1832 Benjamin Wright—the Erie Canal and Delaware & Hudson Canal engineer—served as New York's street commissioner and surveyed the land so that Pine Street, on the east side of Trinity's churchyard, could connect to Albany Street on the west side. Two years later the city offered the congregation a sizeable sum for its strip of land. The church refused, and fought for two decades to stop the city from building the road. In 1852 Trinity erected the Soldiers' Monument in the street's proposed path. The towering Gothic memorial was dedicated to the Revolutionary War soldiers held captive by the British, and who were said to be buried in the yard. In December 1854 the city's Board of Councilmen voted 39 to 13 not to take the grounds, with the *Times* proclaiming, "Trinity Church Triumphant! . . . the churchyard is still saved."

Many had been agitating for some time to change where people buried their dead. Sanitary laws started to evolve, and as development marched northward, the city banned burials below Canal Street, and then 14th Street. Congregations meanwhile kept pace, moving their loved ones as they built new sanctuaries. In 1831 the New York Marble Cemetery, the city's first non-sectarian cemetery, opened for business. The place covered half an acre on Second Avenue between 2nd and 3rd Streets, and was laid out with over 150 underground vaults. George Washington Strong handled the conveyances, and Benjamin Strong and John Hone served as two of the first trustees, with Hone laid to rest there in 1832, followed in 1838 by his wife, Joanna. Dr. David Hosack was buried there in 1835, as was Wright in 1842 and his wife, Philomela, in 1835. Benjamin Strong's wife, Sarah, was buried there in 1843, and he joined her in 1851. The cemetery proved so successful that an-other nonsectarian resting place, the New York City Marble Cemetery, with 258 vaults, opened just to the east. President James Monroe, who was living at the Prince Street home of his daughter Maria, died on July 4, 1831. After a funeral service at St. Paul's Chapel, a procession brought him to New York Marble, where he was briefly interred before being moved across the street to New York City Marble, and eventually brought home to Virginia, where he lies today.[16]

Because of the lack of space, cemeteries had already started to appear outside the city. Designed by David Bates Douglass, who initiated the work on the Croton system, Green-Wood Cemetery—which has come up a number of times in this narrative—opened in Brooklyn in 1838. When George Templeton Strong visited there in July 1839, he found it "a most exceedingly beautiful place," and "where a man may lay down to his last nap without the anticipation of being turned out of his bed in the course of a year or so to make way for a street or a big store or something of that kind."

Trinity Church opened a cemetery and mausoleum far uptown on 155th Street and Broadway in 1842. After St. Thomas Episcopal Church burned down in 1851, John Jacob Astor and his relatives were reinterred there. The state's 1847 Rural Cemetery Act further restricted interment in Manhattan, and Brooklyn's Cypress Hills Cemetery soon started accepting burials. By 1851 the city forbade any and all burials below 86th Street unless they occurred in a private cemetery or vault. In 1856, the Brick Presbyterian Church sold its sanctuary and cemetery. Plans formed to widen Beekman Street. Thirteen vaults with some 100 graves lay in the path. The church set aside money for the moving of the bodies, and the court had Samuel Ruggles

look into the question of who held the rights to the bodies resting in cemeteries. Referee Ruggles's *An Examination of the Law of Burial* found that the
rights of the remains belong "exclusively to the next of kin." Soon after, the
church relocated to Fifth Avenue and 37th Street, and they transferred their
burials to Cypress Hills.[17]

* * *

By 1850, with overcrowded burial places, mounds of manure, and general
filthiness, the city had no choice but to look into ways to clean up New York.
Even with the Croton system in place as of 1842, the city still lacked a uniform
sewage infrastructure. Large homes or buildings generally had cesspools
or sinks. Better smaller houses might have privies, which were temporary
holding spots with tubs that could be taken out and emptied. And though
the city called for such structures to be constructed of stone, brick, or mortar,
people often used wood. They were also supposed to set privies far from a
pump or a well. That did not always happen. In poor neighborhoods, such
as the Five Points, overflowing waste washed into alleys, yards, and courts.
And even with Croton water, people continued to use private wells, which
were contaminated by the leeching of filth into the groundwater.[18] As George
Waring, who would later construct the drainage system in Central Park,
noted, with Croton in place "one would naturally suppose that intelligent citizens would have realized the importance of immediate action in the provision of an intelligent and comprehensive system of sewers." The opposite was
true. Most New Yorkers still relied on the old drains and sewers.[19]

The challenge was that as land to the north began to develop, there were
fewer places to dispose of waste. Night soil workers were supposed to dump
human waste above 14th Street. But that was often too far away, so after dark
they carted it to the rivers. "The general mode is to convey the material from
the yard to the street in open tubs," reported City Inspector John Griscom in
September 1842, two months after Croton water arrived; "these, in the open
street, are emptied into a large open box on the cart, and this box is left open
until it is filled from the tubs." When the box was filled it was covered but not
fastened, meaning that "a large portion of the contents of the box is jolted
out as the cart goes to its dumping place." And when the loads arrived at the
river, the laborers dumped it in the water, often without checking if a small
boat was below. Sometimes vessels were "either wholly or partially filled, and
instances are said to have occurred of their being carried to the bottom with
their unnatural load." And with so much disposed that way, "Some piers have

hence become nearly useless." In 1850 the *Evening Post* reported how more than 30 docks were "almost choked up with filth."[20]

Early sewers were essentially designed to carry off storm water, and generally ran down streets. The one on Canal Street was 16 feet wide. But the wider they were, the slower they flowed, and when they became stopped up, the heat from the sun caused the contents to rot. To deal with the problem, many people simply covered them over. Even so, they continued to become clogged, and if gas built up it could lead to explosions. As early as 1820, Dr. Hosack called for laying sewers to carry sewage to the river, and a water supply to flush the lines. Some places had basic systems. Property owners just needed to petition the Common Council for permission. The Astor House had a sewer that ran to the Hudson. The city also let some industries hook up to storm sewers, though it forbade tanners and slaughterhouses from doing so. Most building owners, though, resisted sewers and drains because of the cost. Ongoing development—the raising of low-lying lands, the razing of hills, and the filling and evening of the surface—only exacerbated the situation by stopping up natural drainage channels and leading to increased flooding.

Problems resulting from poor drainage were everywhere. The areas worst affected by such development lay in the Fourth and Sixth Wards to the east and north of City Hall, where some homes stood on top of the former Collect Pond and the surrounding marshes. The Sixth Ward's police station sat in the Hall of Detention and Justice. Popularly known as the Tombs, the massive building rose on the site of the vanished body of water. An 1832 "Reports of Hospital Physicians" determined that while the land was filled, "the soil must still retain its character as low and damp." Subterranean springs continued to flow into it, and the building filled with foul fumes. Captain Brennan noted in 1851 how, "The sleeping room for the men is not fit for any human being to sleep in."[21]

John Jervis, the creator of the Croton Aqueduct, early on had pushed for a uniform sewage system. But while at first the city avoided funding another expensive infrastructure system, it soon felt it had no other choice. Sewage plans and development progressed slowly, and when individual lines were built, there was no uniform plan like there had been for Croton. And with so much flowing into these lines, it led to flooding. Then, in 1849, the same year as the devastating cholera outbreak, the legislature authorized the municipal Croton Aqueduct Department to build a new system and to clean and repair sewers and underground drains. In October 1854, the Board of Aldermen passed an ordinance "which will compel all persons owning buildings on streets where sewers are laid, to connect with the same." By 1855 the department had installed 70 miles' worth. Two years later, the city had 138 miles in use. Despite the delays, New York was ahead of many other big cities. London didn't start working on their unified system until the end of that decade, and Boston not till the 1870s.[22]

But, as with the introduction of Croton water, the system largely benefited the wealthy, who could pay the $10 it cost to be hooked up. Most homes lacked such connections, and landlords refused to cover costs for poorer tenants. Even in streets where sewers ran, fewer than one in ten houses were connected. Construction contracts generally went to the lowest bidder, and much of the work was of poor quality. Inlets for allowing water in from the street were often crude, lacked proper grades, flowed slowly, and could not prevent mud, garbage, and dead animals from flowing in. Waste got trapped and rotted.

In 1858, Egbert Viele, who served as the first superintendent of Central Park and as president of the Board of Engineers of the Citizens' Association, decried how "one of the chief causes of mortality is to be found in the defective drainage of certain districts of the city, and furthermore, that this is an evil which is increasing as the city extends itself towards the northern portion of the island." In 1865 he expounded on the problems caused by waterways being cut up and buried. Believing that watercourses should be allowed to flow freely, he commented that it would be "folly," given that the city was built on them, to believe that "no water will find its way into the beds of its original streams."[23]

The creation of a uniform sewer system was a slow process. It would take until the turn of the 20th century for much of New York City to properly flush away a large amount of its filth.

15

A Southern City in the North

In early 1860, Thomas Downing had to appear in New York Supreme Court. Once there, the oyster king and restaurateur objected to being sworn in on the grounds that since the United States Supreme Court's 1857 Dred Scott ruling stated that African Americans did not qualify for citizenship, he had no rights as one and shouldn't be present. Judge Josiah Sutherland decided that for this purpose, "he might be considered a human being and a citizen." Soon after, Downing refused to give the census department the value of his property, arguing that because the federal government viewed him as chattel, and slaves cannot own property, he wasn't required to reveal his wealth.

An African American rarely and so vocally insisted on their rights in pre–Civil War New York, but Downing believed that he should make a stand. This was nothing new for him. Decades earlier, in December 1828 when he received a counterfeit bill as payment, he put an ad in the paper asking that "The young gentleman who passed a $5 note, on the Ontario Bank, for a supper of oysters last evening, is requested to call on the subscriber at No. 5 Broad st. and give a good note for the above, which is a forgery." Similarly, in June 1837, a customer tried to pay with a counterfeit $1 bill from the Bank of Vermont. Downing refused to let him leave until he paid with coins. The customer, irate, wrote to the *New York Herald* to complain about his treatment by a Black man: "How I wished I had him down in Virginia." James Gordon Bennett responded, "We rather think Downing was right. —Why should any man be compelled to take worthless paper money for his goods and wares?"[1]

Some of Downing's struggles turned violent. On December 30, 1840, he took the Harlem Railroad home from 14th Street. Two white women sat in the car when he entered. The driver Lucius Deleber and the conductor William Skirving told Downing to leave. He refused to budge. The men then grabbed Downing, beat and kicked him, bruising his legs, cutting his ears, and throwing him from the car. Downing sued the Harlem Railroad and the men, and the case went to trial in February. The defense insisted that while some Blacks had ridden inside the cars, the railroad's regulation stated that they could only ride on top of the vehicles. The defense also produced two witnesses who said that Downing had simply hurt himself when he struck a railing or doorpost. When the jury found the railroad men innocent, the audience broke out in a loud applause.

Such events did not deter Downing. In March 1850, he and Bradley Goodman catered a ball at the Chinese Assembly Room. The hosts expected 250 people, and promised Downing and Goodman 75¢ per guest. But a disturbance broke out at the outer door of the barroom, and many guests left. Despite having prepared all the food, Downing and Goodman only earned $40.50. They insisted on receiving the agreed-on payment, and after two trials, the court awarded them $166.97.[2]

Downing's success bothered many. In November 1850, John Smith, who ran a gin-and-oyster cellar on Canal Street, complained about Downing in a letter to the New York Tribune. Smith accused him of being a "notorious abolitionist" and noted that Downing had made the statement "that if he were seized and claimed as a slave, he would resist the aggressor unto blood." Smith also wrote how "there are many other oyster cellars in this city, kept by black men, who entertain the same heinous and destructive sentiments." He called for the city's papers to denounce Black men who believed in self-defense and for citizens to boycott their places.[3]

Then on September 24, 1855, Downing and a friend hopped onto an uptown Sixth Avenue Railroad at Park Place and Church Street. The moment they boarded, the conductor told them to leave. They didn't, and when the train pulled into Chambers Street, the conductor grabbed Downing by the shoulder. The restaurateur courteously tried to explain that they were rushing to deliver some letters. As he later recalled, "Two or three gentlemen who sat opposite us, told us to sit still, as the conductor had no right to put us out, as we had as much right to ride as they had." The support of white passengers did not sway the conductor, who threatened to call the police. "This I said was the very thing I wanted, as the officers were placed for the purpose of keeping peace, and he was disturbing me," he replied. The conductor looked at Downing and said, "Well, my orders are to put you out." When they pulled into Canal and Varick Streets, the conductor called for help, and others arrived. Downing still refused to budge, and the men stayed back because the restaurateur held a brass key, which they probably thought was a knife. "I don't leave this car till I get to the end of my journey," Downing said stoutly, while also trying to reason with them, explaining that they should take his card, and if he had broken the law they could easily find him.

The car started rolling again. One of the passengers sat next to Downing. "I will sit with you. I have known you for the last thirty years in Broad street." People along the street figured out what was happening, and some yelled, "Put him out." Others responded, "Stay in, Downing," and a shout arose, "Three cheers for DOWNING—Hurra, hurra, hurra!" When the car stopped again, a mob surrounded it and climbed onto the platform, making it hard to evict the restaurateur and his friend. The driver then decided not to stop if Downing rang the bell, regularly glancing back to see who had signaled to be let out. When Downing realized the driver's intent, he told the passenger next to him that he wanted to get off at 38th Street, asking, "Will you be kind enough to ring the bell for me?" As the train neared his destination, the gentleman signaled. When the driver saw a white man standing, he stopped the car. The man exited with Downing and his friend.

Papers covered the ruckus, with the *Evening Post* reporting how "Our venerable friend, Thomas Downing," a man who "is one of the most respectable and aged colored men in this city," experienced "an indignity at the hands of some of the conductors of the Sixth Avenue Railroad."[4]

Two months later, Downing received a warrant for his arrest "for non-appearance at Company Parade." The court had charged the wrong "Downing," and as a Black man he could not belong to the Third Regiment. Upon seeing the restaurant owner, the fine collector immediately cancelled the warrant. In response, a reporter with the *Evening Post* wrote a poem that begins "Have you heard how Thomas Downing— / Downing, publican, of Broad street / Downing, he whose famous oysters / Drawn from Chesapeake and South Side, / Lie upon his shilling saucers . . ." The poem goes on to recount the case of mistaken identity when this "black man, / Or a rather dark mulatto" was told he must go to prison.

> So this venerable man of color
> Went to court at once, and showed 'em
> That, at least at that time, they had
> The wrong passenger awakened.
>
> Saying, "Here I am before you,
> Black and old, as you may see, sir;
> Folks like me the law don't call on,
> And I don't see wherefore you should:
> But if you will choose me captain,
> I'll stick fast to color *sartin*,
> And I never will turn pale, sir.

The poem relates that the officer, realizing the error, dismissed him—
"Downing, 'one I owe you.'"

> Live contented with your trophies,
> Oyster-shells and fine-collectors.[5]

This treatment of one of New York's most successful businessmen, church vestryman, and member of the Odd Fellows and the Masons was nothing new. Yet, as the *Evening Post* noted, it mattered not at all to most people that his "private character is without reproach" or that he raised his sons to be educated and good businessmen, or even that he had amassed a fortune "as the keeper of a refectory which is frequented daily by throngs of the principal bankers and merchants of Wall and Broad street." To the city's train conductors and many of its citizens, Downing deserved nothing. New York and the American society at large saw no difference between a successful northern freeman and an enslaved plantation worker.

Downing was of course far from being the only African American treated that way. Responding to the incessant and appalling behavior of the railroads, the *Colored American* in June 1838 implored its readers to boycott the lines. "Cease giving your money to men, who forbear not to degrade you beneath the dogs. . . . Let us, for the time being, hold intercourse through the Mail, or go on foot."[6] Nor was Downing the only African American to fight back. On rare occasions, some received legal satisfaction for their grievances. On a Sunday afternoon in 1854, Elizabeth Jennings, along with friend Sarah Adams, boarded a Third Avenue car to get to Jennings' organist job at the First Colored American Congregationalist Church on East 6th Street. The train conductor told her that she had to take the following car for Blacks. That vehicle, though, was full, and the conductor told Jennings that if the passengers objected to her presence she would have to leave. Soon after, the conductor threw Adams off and then came for Jennings. "He took hold of me and I took hold of the window sash and held on, he pulled me until he broke my grasp," she said. Jennings was then "pulled and dragged" to the platform. "I screamed murder with all my voice. . . ." When a policeman arrived, he ejected Jennings.

Jennings sought to punish "those monsters in human form," and a group of African American leaders hired future president Chester A. Arthur, who belonged to the law firm of Culver, Parker & Arthur. At the trial, Judge William Rockwell instructed the jury that the company was liable for the acts of their agents, and "that colored persons, if sober, well-behaved, and free from disease, had the same rights as others." The jury ended up finding for Jennings, and the court awarded her $225.[7]

The city's commuter lines were just one of many places where African Americans experienced such indignities. They endured segregation, exclusion, and debasement at all levels of New York and American society—from work and housing to religion, health, and legal protection. In a nation sharply divided between states that allowed human bondage and those that didn't, most in this city with close economic ties to the South were deeply racist. Frances Trollope, who visited the United States in the 1820s, keenly observed of Americans, "you will see them with one hand hoisting the cap of liberty, and with the other flogging their slaves." During his visit to the United States in the early 1830s, the British travel writer Edward S. Abdy recalled how a Frenchman "was pelted with brickbats in the streets of New York, for merely speaking civilly to a woman of color belonging to the house in which he lodged." And while the city boasted of a growing number of hotels, all an African American could find in such a place was work in a kitchen or as a waiter. "He may cook every meal; he cannot eat one out of the kitchen," wrote Thomas Nichols. "He may stand behind the chair; he must not sit at the table."[8]

* * *

This state of the union existed from the time of New York's founding. Enslaved African Americans first arrived in 1626, soon after the Dutch established the colony of New Amsterdam. They were brought from Angola, Congo, and the island of São Tomé off the coast of Gabon, and life was precarious at best for them and all those in the small town. Enslaved people worked on the construction of Fort Amsterdam at the southern end of Manhattan Island. They cut timber and firewood, split palisades, cleared land, burned lime, and brought in the grain.

Defense of the small community became especially necessary following Director-General Willem Kieft's decision in 1643 to attack and slaughter members of the local native tribes. In response, the Lenape retaliated.[9] With Kieft's War raging, the Dutch hoped to create a buffer between the Indians and the settlers, and therefore granted land to some Blacks. The first eight acres went to Catalina Anthony, a widowed free Black. In 1644 the Council of New Netherland also responded to a petition by Paulo d'Angola, Manuel de Gerrit de Reus, Simon Congo, and eight others by giving them and their wives land and freedom "on the same footing as other Free people here in *New Netherland*." Nonetheless, the effects of Kieft's War proved devastating. By the time the strife ended in the summer of 1645, the natives had ravaged Dutch homes, destroyed crops, and killed citizens.

Soon, three dozen Black-owned farms stood between what is now Canal and 14th Streets. The area became known in the middle of the century as "Land of the Blacks" or "Negroes Land." Settlers lived in simple thatched and wood-roofed homes, raised livestock, and tended their fruit trees. When the Dutch surrendered to the Duke of York's forces in 1664, the Black population of the newly christened New York stood at a few hundred. The British imposed restrictions on them, so much so that by 1737, when they numbered 1,719 and made up a fifth of the population, the Black population had lost all their land.[10]

Such a racially and socially stratified society produced occasional paroxysms of terror. In April 1712, two dozen slaves sought retribution for their mistreatment. They gathered firearms, swords, knives, and hatchets, and burned one of their masters' houses. Governor Robert Hunter wrote how as people ran to put out the flames, "severall [of] the slaves fired and killed them." Hunter summoned soldiers from the fort, who rounded up the rebels. Of the more than 20 executed, "Some were burnt others hanged, one broke on the wheele, and one hung a live in chains in the town, so that there has been the most exemplary punishment inflicted that could be possibly thought of." In 1741, racial tensions were high in New York, partly from competition over jobs. A series of mysterious fires broke out. Some accused people they called Catholic saboteurs of seeking to free slaves. The authorities brought charges against 200 people, including some 20 whites. Despite the flimsiness of the evidence—including the testimony of a teenage Irish indentured servant who received a promised reward for naming names—the subsequent trial resembled the Salem witch trials of a half-century earlier. A crowd gathered to watch while as many as 30 Blacks were hanged and burned at stakes, and four whites were hanged.[11]

Throughout the 1700s and through the American Revolution, New Yorkers regularly bought and sold slaves. After independence, New York's state constitution gave the right to vote to every man who possessed £20 worth of property or rented a place that cost them at least 40 shillings. Yet while some African Americans qualified, many of those found themselves turned away at the polls.

Change, though, filled the air, and there was talk of ending slavery. In 1785 Alexander Hamilton, Aaron Burr, and others founded the New York Society for Promoting the Manumission of Slaves, and Protecting Such of Them as Have Been or May Be Liberated. Future chief justice of the Supreme Court John Jay served as the group's first president, writing that, "To contend for our own liberty, and to deny that blessing to others, involves an inconsistency not to be excused." In 1787, Congress passed the Northwest Ordinance, banning slavery in the territory that would become Ohio, Indiana, Illinois, Michigan, and Wisconsin.

Slavery started to decline, though in New York it took longer than in other parts of the Northeast. Vermont banned it outright in 1777. In the 1780s, Connecticut, New Hampshire, Pennsylvania, and Rhode Island enacted gradual emancipation laws, and in 1783 Massachusetts abolished it. In 1790, New York City was home to 2,369 enslaved people. In 1794, the federal government deemed it illegal to equip ships engaged in the slave trade for travel overseas. Then in 1799, New York State passed an act for the Gradual Emancipation of Blacks, stipulating that by July 4, 1827, those born after July 4, 1799 were free.[12]

The British banned the trade in enslaved people in 1807, but not slavery itself. The United States outlawed the importation of enslaved people the following year. That March, John Hone freed an enslaved man named George. Then on February 23, 1809, Philip Hone, then 28, freed an enslaved women in his household named Charlotte. Mayor DeWitt Clinton signed the conveyance, declaring that Hone "fully and absolutely manumit make free and set at liberty my Black Slave named Charlotte hereby willing and declaring that the said Charlotte shall and may at all time and times hereafter exercise hold and enjoy all and singular the liberties Rights privileges and immunities of a free Woman as fully to all intents and purposes as if she had been born free."[13]

Despite increasingly widespread abolitionary efforts, slavery grew in some parts of the country, spurred by increased cotton production made possible by the cotton gin. It did decline in New York, dropping to 1,686 slaves in 1810. In 1817, New York State passed full emancipation, though it would not take effect until 1827. At the time, even some Blacks owned enslaved people. By 1820, the number of enslaved in the city dropped to 518.[14]

Thomas Downing, as we've seen, has been one of the more important figures of this narrative and was certainly a major figure in New York history and in the fight to end slavery in the years between the Great Fire and the Civil War. Born in 1791 in Chincoteague, Accomack County, Virginia, his parents had been freed, and they had some land surrounded by ancient oaks. Downing recalled that their property had a pond with geese, and that they owned a cow, a rooster, and a dog named Rip. The Downing children raked for oysters and dug clams and gathered turtles. Thomas had learned to read, and during the War of 1812 he headed north with the American troops. He stopped in Philadelphia, where he learned how to prepare turtle, the basis for one of the dishes which attracted diners to his restaurant. He decided that making food would be a good way to earn a living. While there, he met and married Rebecca West. The couple arrived in New York in 1819.[15]

Downing started out with an oyster saloon on Pell Street, though by the late 1820s he had the place on Broad Street for which he became famous. He worked hard, waking at two each morning so he could row a skiff to New Jersey, where he tonged for oysters. Late at night, he would visit the docks to await the returning oyster boats, and even rowed out to vessels still in the harbor so he could scoop up the best specimens before the boats docked. Back on land, Downing would then bid with others for the rest of the haul. His Broad Street restaurant proved very profitable, and he soon took over the spaces on either side and even opened a branch on Broadway and Murray Street. The business, as we've seen, attracted New York elites. The Downings had five children: George, followed by twins Thomas and Henry, Jane, and Peter William.

Downing belonged to the top tier of successful Black New Yorkers. Henry Scott ran a ship chandlery and a warehouse, and was one of the city's largest picklers. Edward Clark's jewelry and catering business loaned silver, glasses, and other goods. Elizabeth Jennings' father, Thomas, was a clothier and the first African American with a patent for a dry-cleaning technique called "dry scouring." Katy Ferguson made a living as a cake baker, caterer, and cleaner of fine linen. Dr. James McCune Smith was America's first professionally trained African American physician. Patrick Henry Reason made a living as a fine engraver, creating the much-disseminated abolitionist image of a man-acled Black girl with the caption, "Am I not a sister?" And Cato Alexander ran a popular tavern.

By the 1830s, some African Americans prospered as carpenters, blacksmiths, sail-makers and shoemakers, as well as millers, barbers, plasterers, preachers, and pilots. But because the town had a limited number of Black craftsmen, few could hire apprentices and journeymen. Whites refused to train Blacks. This was a situation that African Free School teacher Charles Andrews decried, noting that when a young Black left school he

found "every avenue closed against him." Many found employment in me-
nial labor as common stewards, brick makers, whitewashers, rag pickers,
chimney sweeps, and coachmen. Others worked as waiters, laundresses,
chambermaids, servants, cooks, and porters, and sold fruits, vegetables, and
hot corn.[16]

Since so few opportunities existed, the New York Mission Society was
founded in 1812 to help many learn trades. Girls received training in household economics, boys in sail-making, cobbling, carpentering, tailoring, and
blacksmithing. Yet only a small percentage of Blacks were able to rise above
poverty. The 1850 census listed nearly 50,000 African American men over
age 15 in New York State. A mere 122 worked as barbers, 33 as butchers,
seven as clerks, nine as doctors, one as a gunsmith, four as lawyers, and
434 as mariners. This is compared to 888,680 white male workers over 15,
which included 1,610 barbers, 4,826 butchers, 26,562 clerks, 5,060 doctors,
500 gunsmiths, 4,263 lawyers, and 11,102 mariners. Competition for limited
work only increased as European immigrants flowed in. This became especially true following the Irish potato famine, which started in 1845, and the
German Revolution in 1848.[17]

African Americans also found themselves trapped in the middle of power
plays between political parties. At the time of the Revolution, many allied
themselves with the wealthy Federalists for whom they often worked. But as
that party withered in the early 19th century, the Democratic Party grew and
sought to expand white suffrage while reducing that of Blacks. At the time,
election restrictions were piled on, including, in 1811, a voting rule requiring
proof of a government-endorsed certificate of freedom. Then, in 1821 when a
state constitutional convention granted greater voting rights for 21-year-old
white men, it further cut off Black access to the ballot box by imposing a $250
property qualification as well as three-year residency. Yet, since the vast majority of African Americans were poor, voting was not even a possibility. Of
the 12,499 Blacks in New York County in 1826, only 60 paid taxes and a mere
16 qualified for the vote. In 1835 that number reached 68.[18]

Exercising the right to vote could be dangerous for the few who had it.
In 1849 election, the *Herald* chillingly reported the "amusing incident" of a
"negro hunt" during which a Black voter was chased by a group of B'hoys.
The poor man was forced to run "for his life, amidst shouts and yells, while
his pursuers chased him most vigorously, still keeping close on his track, till
at length he gave a short double round the corner of a street and 'earthed'
himself in a friendly house."

While Blacks and poor whites lived in the same areas of the city, and often interacted, they didn't attend the same schools, worship at the same churches, or frequent the same theaters and amusement areas. Many African Americans were forced to rent dank homes like those on top of the filled-in Collect Pond in a section of the Five Points called "Little Africa," or in the drained Lispenard's Meadow. Some lived in Black-only boarding houses. As the Irish moved into the Five Points, some African Americans settled in Greenwich Village, where they established a new "Little Africa." Those who tired of the conditions downtown headed north to less congested and more affordable areas. Some settled on the east side of what would become Central Park in a community called York Hill. Others moved to the west side of the future park in the 80s to an area that became known as Seneca Village.

As the July 4, 1827, day of New York's abolition approached, the African American community opted to hold off on its Independence-Day festivities till the 5th in order to avoid having to deal with whites using the holiday to commit violence. But on the 5th, 4,000 people reveled, watching a parade in which Grand Marshal Samuel Hardenburgh rode astride a milk-white steed. Others followed, many splendidly dressed in silk scarfs and carrying flags and banners. From the sidewalks women waved, some with West-Indian "gay bandanna handkerchiefs." A letter writer to the *New York Commercial Advertiser* noted how he heard the passing parade while having dinner, and "it appeared to me so commendable and orderly."[19]

Independence, though, changed little in the daily existence of city Blacks. Attempts nonetheless continued to expand the rights of African Americans. In 1837 Downing helped put together a petition to Albany to change the state constitution and end restrictions on voting. Two years later, he became vice president of the New York Association for the Political Evaluation and Improvement of the Colored People. An 1840 state convention called for assisting Blacks to "become possessors of the soil, inasmuch as that not only elevates them to the rights of freemen, but increases the political power in the State, in favor of our political and social elevation." The Downings, David Ruggles, and others also founded the American Reform Board of Disenfranchised Commissioners, which called for extending citizenship rights. During the 1846 New York constitutional convention, Horace Greeley advocated for the end to property qualifications. "I stood at the poll of the XIXth Ward of this city all one rainy, chill November day, peddling ballots for Equal Suffrage. I got many Whigs to take them, but not one Democrat," the editor recalled. Voters roundly defeated the equal suffrage amendment, 224,336 to 85,406.[20]

Bigotry made discrimination palatable and acceptable. Harassment of African Americans was endemic, with attacks focusing on successful Blacks. In January 1831, tavern owners George and Andrew Luke headed with others to Cato Alexander's tavern on East 54th Street. They brought with them chains, and once there, one of the women made believe she had fainted. As Alexander brought over smelling salts to help her, the gang attacked him and his pregnant wife, Eliza. While there, John Priest, one of the assailants, was wounded. He vowed revenge, proclaiming that "no such damn Negro should live." The group returned the next night, and as Alexander and his family hid, the attackers wrecked his business.

As with most other things, education for New York's African Americans was different than that for whites. The earliest benevolent school was the aforementioned New York African Free School. Opened in 1787 by the Manumission Society, it taught students how to read, write, and do math, as well as such topics as geography, astronomy, navigation, advanced composition, and knitting. Cornelius Davis—architect Alexander Jackson Davis's father—served as its first teacher. By the time the Marquis de Lafayette—the French nobleman who fought in the American Revolution—returned to the United States in 1824 and 1825 for one last look at the nation he helped create, the school boasted 700 students. Lafayette found it the "best disciplined and the most interesting school of children" he had seen. It was during that visit that 11-year-old James McCune Smith delivered a speech before their esteemed French visitor. Many other future Black leaders and abolitionists attended the African Free School. The Downing children did, as well as Reverends Samuel Cornish, Henry Highland Garnet, and Alexander Crummell, professor Charles Reason, his artist brother Patrick, and the actor Ira Aldridge. Getting there, though, could be difficult. George Downing had to fight white kids who tried to block his passage. And butcher boys from the Centre Street Market regularly set their dogs on students.[21]

These were the lucky ones. Education did not reach most. In 1830, Charles Andrews at the African Free School observed that the city had 1,800 school-age Black children, with only 620 going to African Free Schools and 100 to private ones. In 1834 the Free School was transferred to the control of the Public School Society, and in 1847 it became part of the public school system. The change caused attendance to drop. Not surprisingly, few places of higher education admitted Blacks. Even divinity schools stood closed to them. And while James McCune Smith graduated with honors from the African Free School and knew Latin and Greek, he couldn't gain admittance to a college in the United States. Fortunately, he had supporters and headed to the University of Glasgow in Scotland. Education changes slowly took place in New York. The Oneida Institute of Science and Industry in Whitesboro, New York, was the first college to enroll Blacks and whites on an equal basis. In 1848, the first Black student graduated from New York University. In 1849, New York Central College opened its doors in McGrawville and allowed Blacks to attend, and had African American professors.

At the same time, the Black community formed their own support groups. Some 50 such organizations appeared during the first half of the century, from fraternal societies to ladies' auxiliary organizations. The New York African Society for Mutual Relief assisted members if they became sick or couldn't work. The African Clarkson Association helped with the education of members. The Juvenile Daughters of Ruth carried out philanthropic work. There was likewise a serious interest in intellectual advancement and the establishment of cultural groups such as the New York Female Literary Society. In 1833, the Phoenix Society of the City of New York formed, "the object of which shall be to promote the improvement of the colored people in morals, literature, and the mechanic arts," and had such members as Downing, Hardenburgh, and Christopher Rush.[22]

Since Blacks found themselves segregated even in houses of worship, they established their own congregations. The Methodists were the first group from which Blacks separated. At the turn of the 19th century, members constructed the African Methodist Episcopal Zion Church on Church and Leonard Streets. Soon after, Blacks started to detach from the Episcopal church, and in 1818 built St. Philip's Church on Centre Street. The Black Baptists formed the Abyssinian Baptist Church. There were also Black Presbyterians and Congregationalists. And, as with all levels of African American society, these churches endured regular harassment and attacks. On New Year's Eve in 1827, a Callithumpian band—one of the discordant musical groups armed with whistles, pots, pans, and drums that often traveled the city at New Year's—went to an African American church on Elizabeth Street, beat congregants with sticks and ropes, broke the church's windows, wrecked the doors and seats, and even tried to pull down the building.[23]

* * *

The violence, routine as it was in New York, appalled some whites. Arthur and Lewis Tappan were among the main white advocates for equal rights for African Americans during the pre–Civil War period. Originally from Northampton, Massachusetts, they were the sons of a gold- and silver-smith who opened a general store there. The family lived simply, and the children grew up in a world of strict Congregationalist beliefs overseen by their mother. Born in May 1786, Arthur was the eighth of 11 children. Lewis arrived in May 1788. Early on, Arthur became imbued with an unusual compassion for others. As a child he grew fond of a neighboring enslaved woman named Lill. Lewis recalled how the children would receive from her "many kind words and bits of cake." Most of all, Lewis could not help but note that "her kindness to Arthur, and the affectionate regard he had for her, doubtless laid the foundation for the interest he ever after took in people of color."[24]

At the age of 14, Arthur started work as an apprentice at the Boston exporting store of Sewell and Salisbury. By age 21 he and Henry Sewell, the boss's nephew, headed to Portland, Maine, to start a dry goods store, and in 1809 they opened a business in Montreal. Tappan married the following year, and he and Frances would go on to have eight children. He soon settled in New York, where he founded Arthur Tappan & Company, offering everything from bales of broadcloths, cambric muslins, French silk, and men's leather gloves, to taffetas for umbrellas, assorted crockery, and cashmere. His firm sold goods throughout the country and was unusual for its standards and low prices, reflecting Arthur's religious exactitude. By the mid-1820s, Tappan & Co. had become the largest silk business in New York, and in 1826 the firm divided $131,000 between the partners. Lewis, who had married Susan Aspinwall, started a family, joined the firm in 1827, and worked as a silk jobber and credit manager. Soon the Pearl Street business handled $2 million a year in trade, and by the early 1830s Arthur had become quite wealthy.

The Tappans poured their earnings into assorted charities. The brothers had fallen under the sway of revivalist minister Charles Grandison Finney. The preacher held vast revival meetings in upstate New York, Delaware, and Pennsylvania, promoted reform issues, and opposed alcohol, prostitution, and, of course, slavery. The Tappans were so impressed by him that they urged him to come to New York. Finney hoped to preach at the Bowery Theatre, but it proved too expensive, so in the early 1830s the Tappans and others acquired the old Chatham Street Theater and converted the 2,000-seat space east of Broadway into the Chatham Street Chapel. Finney refused to offer communion to slaveholders.

The Tappan brothers viewed slavery as a sinful, ungodly system. They actively instilled abolitionist ideas through the *Journal of Commerce*. Many, though, did not care for Arthur's fervent and unbending beliefs. Some, like naval engineer Charles Haswell, called him "a zealous bigot of a pronounced type." And while some New Yorkers were repelled by his religious fanaticism, Tappan's extreme activities terrified southerners. Yet, when people stopped by Pearl Street in order to gaze upon this fearful, slavery-hating demon, they instead came across a simply dressed, grandfatherly looking character.

To spread the word about the evils of slavery and increase the number of messengers, Tappan became interested in the Lane Theological Seminary in Walnut Hills, Ohio. He convinced Lyman Beecher—one of the leaders of the Second Great Awakening—to become its president. Yet, when the trustees refused to take a stand on immediate emancipation, dozens of students left. Tappan then sent the bolting students money, and they established evening classes for adult African Americans. Tappan soon focused his philanthropic interests on the newly established Oberlin College, giving money for a new building. Largely because of his work, Blacks gained admittance to the school.[25]

* * *

By the 1830s America was deeply rent over the issue of slavery. Philip Hone had found himself uncomfortable with the fanaticism of both the abolitionists and slave holders. He feared upsetting business ties with the South, and felt that efforts to stop the institution would only destabilize the land. As a young man, George Templeton Strong regretted "the introduction of abolitionism into politics" during the election in 1838, writing that it "may play the devil with our institutions and which is at any rate a new force brought into the system, with an influence now almost inappreciable, but which may grow greater and greater till it brings the whole system into a state of discord and dissension, from which heaven preserve it!"

Reflecting the division, New York's press split over the issue of forced servitude. Charles King's *New York American* opposed the system, as did Greeley's *Tribune*, which railed how people were condemned "to unrequited labor by the terror or the application of the lash, and to sell children from the mother, the husband from the wife, in hopeless, life long separation." As we've seen, James Gordon Bennett had spent time in the South before coming to New York, and defended the institution in the pages of the *Herald*. Editor Mordecai Noah mocked African Americans in his *National Advocate*. James Watson Webb's *Morning Courier and New-York Enquirer* supported colonization—sending Blacks back to Africa—and saw abolitionists as "haberdashers of murderous negro tracts." As the Civil War approached, other publications that looked down on those who opposed slavery included Benjamin Wood's *New York Daily News* and the *New York Morning Express*. And despite the *Journal of Commerce*'s origins under Arthur Tappan, its subsequent owners supported slavery.[26]

African Americans continued to seek a larger voice in society through the press. In March 1827, Samuel Cornish and the Jamaican-born John Russwurm—one of the first Blacks to graduate from Bowdoin College—brought out the *Freedom's Journal*. The partners clearly stated their paper's aim from the start: "Daily slandered, we think that there ought to be some channel of communication between us and the public." The publication reported on the economy, literature, local news, slavery, and events in Africa. It stressed the need for education, ran poems and essays, advised readers to work hard, and covered kidnappings of both free African Americans and those who had escaped enslavement. At first, the *Freedom's Journal* supported immediate abolition. Yet after Cornish left, Russwurm switched the focus to colonization. The paper shut down in 1829. Cornish then started the anti-colonization *Rights of All*, which lasted less than a year, and in 1837 launched the *Weekly Advocate*. Later, the abolitionist-leaning paper changed its name to the *Colored American*.[27]

Some newspapers not only opposed slavery but called for more than just agitation. There was *The Anglo-African* newspaper and the *Ram's Horn*. In 1831, the reformer and editor Joshua Leavitt published the *New York Evangelist*, and later edited the *New York Emancipator*. The anti-slavery works of the Quaker poet and editor John Greenleaf Whittier spread the idea of abolition to a large audience, as did Lydia Maria Child, whose 1833 *An Appeal in Favor of That Class of Americans Called Africans* promoted emancipation, integration, and intermarriage. In 1841, Child started editing the *National Anti-Slavery Standard*. And of course, there was Frederick Douglass's *North Star*, soon to be renamed *Frederick Douglass' Paper*. Founded on December 3, 1847, Douglass set forth the paper's goals: "to hasten the day of freedom to our three million enslaved fellow-countrymen."[28]

None of the papers, though, matched the influence and intensity of the work of William Lloyd Garrison. The firebrand from Massachusetts attracted attention soon after arriving in Baltimore in 1829 to help Benjamin Lundy bring out the *Genius of Universal Emancipation*. Garrison viewed slavery as an abomination to God, and while there, branded a merchant a murderer for his involvement in the interstate slave trade. The authorities charged Garrison with libel and tossed him in jail. But incarceration could not silence Garrison, and from his cell he issued press releases and pamphlets. When Arthur Tappan learned what happened to Garrison, he sent him bail for the fine. Garrison headed back to Massachusetts. He saw himself as a prophet for change, and with seed money from Tappan founded *The Liberator*. That paper became his bully pulpit. In its first edition on January 1, 1831, Garrison fiercely proclaimed his aims: "I *will be* as harsh as truth, and as uncompromising as justice. . . . I am in earnest—I will not equivocate—I will not excuse—I will not retreat a single inch—And I WILL BE HEARD."[29]

Garrison abhorred violence. Yet the continued turmoil brought on by slave revolts only burnished his position as a Christian anarchist. For seven months after the *Liberator* appeared, the South was rocked by its deadliest slave uprising. Nat Turner believed that God directed him to lead a revolt in southeastern Virginia. On August 21, 1831, Turner and other enslaved men headed out to do what they believed to be the Lord's will. "The black men passed from house to house," wrote *Atlantic* writer Reverend Thomas Wentworth Higginson, who two decades later would become one of John Brown's financial supporters. "There was no gratuitous outrage beyond the death-blow itself, no insult, no mutilation; but in every house they entered, that blow fell on man, woman, and child,—nothing that had a white skin was spared." As they progressed, Turner and his followers grabbed muskets, axes, and scythes, and set out to devastate the town of Jerusalem. Soon they had taken some 55 lives. Whites' vengeance then descended. A North Carolina reporter wrote that 120 Blacks died in one day. Some were burned, maimed, and tortured. Turner was captured at the end of October and, before his execution, commented, "Was not Christ crucified?"

The violence of Turner's uprising caused many to shy away from abolitionism. But not Garrison, who wrote, "The first drops of blood, which are but the prelude to a deluge from the gathering clouds, have fallen." His words reached and inspired many, such as Angelina Emily Grimké, the daughter of John Faucheraud Grimké, a chief judge of the South Carolina Supreme Court. While Angelina and her older sister Sarah grew up in the lap of luxury, they abhorred the fact that their family owned hundreds of people. At the age of 13, Angelina refused confirmation, since the Episcopal Church supported slavery. Sarah abandoned South Carolina "to escape the sound of the lash and the shrieks of tortured victims" and headed to Philadelphia. Angelina joined her in 1829. The sisters became Quakers and joined the Philadelphia Female Anti-Slavery Society. Angelina first contacted Garrison in 1835, writing him that to end slavery, "Let us endeavor, then, to put on the *whole* armor of God, and, having done all, to stand ready for whatever is before us." Her words moved the editor—who published her letter that September.[30]

The following year, Grimké wrote her anti-slavery pamphlet *An Appeal to the Christian Women of the South* and implored women to "*overthrow* this horrible system of oppression and cruelty, licentiousness and wrong." The sisters lectured, speaking to tens of thousands of women as well as men about the evils of the trade. In 1838, Angelina married Theodore Weld, and next year they and Sarah published a book entitled *American Slavery as It Is: Testimony of a Thousand Witnesses*. It contained accounts they hoped would melt hearts, with articles on floggings, chains, branding, and maiming. The book had personal narratives, pieces on the "Privations of the Slaves," copies of ads for lost slaves, and even an account by a member of an Alabama church who said she wanted to "cut Arthur Tappan's throat from ear to ear." This encyclopedic compilation touched many and influenced Harriet Beecher Stowe when she wrote *Uncle Tom's Cabin*.[31]

Garrison likewise inspired Douglass, who called the *Liberator* "my meat and my drink." Douglass was born in February 1818 as a slave named Frederick Augustus Washington Bailey. He secretly organized a school for slaves, and after being discovered was placed under the slave-breaker Edward Covey, a man whose job it was to destroy the wills of those seen as rebellious. Instead of submitting to Covey, the teenage Douglass fought back, generally a fatal thing for a slave to do. Surprisingly, Covey did not retaliate. "The story that he had undertaken to whip a lad, and had been resisted, was, of itself, sufficient to damage him," wrote Douglass.

Hired out to another farmer, Douglass tried to escape in 1836, but was jailed and then sent to a Baltimore shipyard, where he learned to caulk. While there, he met housekeeper Anna Murray. In 1838, with money from Murray and papers from a free Black sailor, he fled to New York. "I was walking amid the hurrying throng, and gazing upon the dazzling wonders of Broadway," he recalled of his first taste of freedom. "The dreams of my childhood and the purposes of my manhood were now fulfilled." Still, Douglass was a fugitive in a potentially dangerous city, where Blacks were routinely snatched and never heard from again. Fortunately, a sailor found him sleeping on the wharves and brought him to David Ruggles' house. Soon after, Murray joined him, and Reverend James Pennington, who himself had escaped from slavery in 1827, married the couple. When Ruggles learned that Douglass was a trained caulker, he suggested he head to the whaling town of New Bedford. The newlyweds set off for a new life in New England.[32]

Douglass started to talk about his experiences at anti-slavery meetings and proved a mesmerizing speaker. Garrison heard him in 1841, and found him so impressive that he encouraged Douglass to become a traveling lecturer. In 1845 Douglass wrote *Narrative of the Life of Frederick Douglass, an American Slave*. Knowing that the book would reveal his identity and lead to his arrest, Douglass fled to Europe, staying there until friends purchased his liberty for $711.66. Douglass then settled in Rochester, New York, where he published his paper and helped escaping Blacks make their way to Canada.

Despite the 1827 emancipation, for the Black community New York was in many ways a southern town. Alexander Stewart learned that when, as we've seen, an outraged Georgia lady—"her bright brilliant eyes flashing fire enough to burn a city down"—found out that he bought silk from Arthur Tappan and stormed out of his Marble Palace. The city kept close links to the South. Lewis Tappan wrote of a New York window display of Bowie knives bearing the inscription "Death to Abolition." In 1847, future mayor Fernando Wood wrote to South Carolina senator John Calhoun that, "Many of my friends and myself have long ago determined that if this narrow spirit of fan[a]ticism continues at the North, and produces disunion, *our homes* will be found south of the Potomac, where true freedom, chivalry and honour characterise the people."[33]

The basis of this North–South link was cotton. Businessmen earned fortunes off the fibery plant. New York merchant houses had networks of agents spread throughout the South, and the city was the transit point between southern growers and English factories. Because of this, some New Yorkers became wealthy as the value of cotton exports went from nearly $4 million in 1822 to $12 million in 1860. The city also served as a conduit for a vast array of goods going south, from wheat and textiles to furniture. And because New York had become the center of urban American culture, southerners spent time in the city. A few even trekked out to Brooklyn's Plymouth Church to hear Lyman Beecher's son and Harriet Beecher Stowe's brother, Reverend Henry Ward Beecher, lambaste their home region. One visitor noted in 1854 how the minister called southerners "man-stealers," and observed, "we had the satisfaction of hearing ourselves prayed for as among those steeped in the guilt of slavery, as one of a numerous band of murderers and robbers."[34]

While the importation of enslaved people had been outlawed in 1808, it was still big business. Their value increased four times between 1800 and 1860. During those years, more than three-quarters of a million human beings were sold or transferred from eastern states to the Southwest through such ports as New York, Baltimore, and Portland. The New York Committee of Vigilance reported in 1837 that the city had many docked ships with "slaves illegally held, by captains and passengers . . . brought direct from the coast of Africa, others from the West Indies, South America, and other foreign ports." When the *Braman* anchored at the Brooklyn Navy Yard in 1856, Walt Whitman snuck onboard. Writing in *Life Illustrated*, he described its claustrophobic hold, where the captives "have been stowed, laid together 'spoon-fashion,' half lying, half sideways, and close in on another's laps, in ranges across the deck—to smother, groan, and perhaps to perish, in the hot pestilential atmosphere, during the passage across the Atlantic." Enforcement of laws banning such practices proved woefully inadequate. Human cargo arrived despite American and British naval ships cruising off Africa, Brazil, and Cuba in search of smugglers. Between 1845 and 1854, American courts heard only five cases of violation of the law.

Slave traders seemed to work with impunity. They established dummy corporations to hide their work, with Portuguese businessmen on Pearl Street outfitting up 30 to 40 slave ships a year. Contracts for slave vessels were agreed to in places like the Astor House, and Whitman told how ships could be acquired for $5,000, earning $135,000 after just a few trips. In July 1856, the *Herald* reported that 18 such ships had left the city during the previous three years. Three years later, the *Herald* wrote how "New York and Boston are the favorite ports, from the simple fact that in the bustle, the turmoil and whirl of trade, there is less risk of detection."[35] While those bringing in enslaved people tried to stay in the shadows, many sought to shine a light on what was going on in the city.

16

The Search for Freedom

By the mid-1850s, the nation lacked any clear consensus on what to do about slavery. Back when Missouri sought admission to the Union, there had been a move to stop the institution's growth. A compromise hammered out in 1820 allowed Missouri into the Union as a slave state, while admitting Maine as a free one. At the same time, what was known as the Missouri Compromise kept slavery out of the rest of the area of the Louisiana Purchase north of latitude 36° 30'. But the compromise and its marking of the borders of slavery only deepened the divide.

Many held strong beliefs on what to do about the African Americans in their midst, whether to continue their enslavement, promote a reverse colonization, provide for gradual abolition, call for immediate liberation, or start the full integration of African Americans into society. Even those supporting the most radical of ideas—to rid the land of the institution and give Blacks equal rights as Americans—realized they had to do more than enact laws to change people's thoughts. They had to transform hearts.

Colonization—the sending of Blacks back to Africa—seemed to some like a desirable solution, one that was first discussed prior to the Revolution. In 1787, British abolitionists set up Freetown in Sierra Leone, on Africa's western coast, as a safe port for free and enslaved British Blacks. Taking a cue from the British, the American Society for Colonizing the Free People of Color of the United States formed in 1816. In 1822, it established an outpost in Liberia southeast of Sierra Leone, and started sending Blacks there. In 1829, editor John Russwurm emigrated there and took over as editor of the *Liberia Herald.* After the Maryland State Colonization Society set up a colony at Cape Palmas in the south of Liberia, Russwurm became its governor in 1836.

African Americans like Thomas Downing and Dr. James McCune Smith dubbed the colonization society "a gigantic fraud," and roundly denounced as unconstitutional the appropriation of taxpayer money to the organization. While some like Arthur and Lewis Tappan at first supported the society, many soon realized its infeasibility. In 1832, William Lloyd Garrison founded the New England Anti-Slavery Society. Abolitionist sentiments strengthened the following year when the efforts of such English leaders as William Wilberforce and Thomas Clarkson helped bring about the Slavery Abolition Act of 1833, which ended slavery in most British colonies, South Africa, the Caribbean, and Canada.

Hoping for a similar success in the United States, a notice appeared in New York newspapers in September of that year, signed by several prominent abolitionists and calling a meeting at Clinton Hall for "The Friends of Immediate Abolition of Slavery in the United States." In response, William Leete Stone's colonization-supporting *New York Commercial Advertiser* published a notice imploring "All citizens who may feel disposed to manifest the true feeling of the state on the subject are requested to attend." Broadsides papered the town, advising all opponents of abolition to flock to the hall, and a meeting at Tammany Hall passed resolutions condemning the Tappan brothers, Garrison, and other abolitionists. Fearing trouble, the abolitionists shifted their gathering to Chatham Street Chapel. There, they formed a constitution for the New York City Anti-Slavery Society and left before their detractors appeared.[1]

In December 1833, supporters met in Philadelphia to create the American Anti-Slavery Society, with Arthur Tappan as president and his brother Lewis on the executive board. Garrison penned the Society's *Declaration of Sentiments*. The organization had relatively moderate platforms, calling for the end of slavery in the District of Columbia as well as the territories. By the late 1830s, the society claimed 250,000 members and gained the backing of such prominent African American leaders as Reverends Samuel Cornish, Theodore Wright, Peter Williams Jr., and Christopher Rush. Blacks also had their own organizations. In Philadelphia, in September 1830, they organized the American Society of Free Persons of Colour. And in 1836, Downing and others helped create the United Anti-Slavery Society of the City of New York.

Yet, despite increasing opposition to the institution of slavery, it continued to grow. From 1820 to 1850, the population of the United States rose from 9.6 million to 23.2 million, and the number of the enslaved doubled from 1.5 million to 3.2 million. Whatever their position on slavery, many Americans feared the mixing of the races. The concept of miscegenation, of amalgamation, terrified both polite and not-so-discreet society. *Morning Courier and New-York Enquirer* editor James Watson Webb and others saw the fusing of the races as the mongrelization of humanity and "disgustful in *our* society." Yet, contact and the mixing of the races was common in the city's working-class wards. Some rumored that Reverend Henry Ludlow married whites and Blacks at his Spring Street Presbyterian Church. And stories spread that abolitionists planned to marry their daughters off to Blacks, that Arthur Tappan had divorced his wife and married an African American, and that abolitionists had adopted Black children.[2]

These fears would give birth to disastrous consequences. On June 12, 1834, while on his way to St. John's Chapel overlooking St. John's Park, Arthur Tappan met Cornish. He invited the light-colored editor and minister to join him in his pew. And even though Reverend Samuel Cox's congregation considered itself socially liberal, the actual presence of Cornish with Tappan outraged members. It didn't help that Cox said that Christ was probably dark skinned like many Syrians, a comment that quite a few people around town found offensive.

The following month turned brutally hot. On the Fourth of July, an audience gathered at Chatham Street Chapel and listened to a mixed choir sing a hymn by John Greenleaf Whittier, a reading of the Declaration of Independence, and Lewis Tappan's reading of the Declaration of Sentiments of the American Anti-Slavery Society. A mob then surged in. They screamed and stamped and yelled, "Treason! Treason! Hurrah for the Union." The choir meanwhile struck up the last five stanzas of Whittier's hymn. This back and forth went on for about an hour. The following day, a parade marched through the streets to celebrate the end of slavery. Journalist Thomas Picton recalled how it "did much to excite animosity against the gaily clad processionists among the working people, operated upon by scheming demagogues." An argument also broke out at a hotel near the Bowery Theatre, where a butcher named Abraham Sentis was having a drink. Bowery stage manager George Farren, who was British, was there. "Damn the Yankees," he said, "they are a damned set of jackasses." Not surprisingly, Sentis took offense and confronted Farren over the insult, and Farren knocked him down.[3]

On the 7th, the *Commercial Advertiser* ran a patently false letter from a man named Bandy Pomp looking for a white wife: "I hab conquer all my prejudices, so dat I be willing to malgumate and jest as lib marry white woman as any." That same day, African Americans gathered at Chatham Street Chapel. The New York Sacred Music Society generally used the space on Mondays, but the group had subletted it. Society members, though, hadn't been informed of the change, and when they showed up they were not happy to find Blacks present. The African Americans refused to leave, and a fight broke out. One of the white leaders raised a chair over his head, but Reverend

Samuel Ringgold Ward wrote how someone "knocked him over with a well-aimed missile." Rioters, white and Black, broke the lamps, smashed the collection box, splintered chairs to make clubs, and tossed benches down from the gallery. When the police arrived, they arrested six men, all of them African American. Some whites soon made their way to City Hall Park "to act out their patriotism" by assaulting Blacks. When Alderman James Ferris tried to stop them, the mob knocked him down.[4]

The papers meanwhile further stirred things up. The *Commercial Advertiser* wrote that some Blacks were "threatening to burn the city." Lewis Tappan recalled how on the 8th, "A well dressed young man shook a cane or club over a young colored woman who lives in my family. . . . This, and the excitement, agitated the poor girl so much that she afterwards swooned and lay insensible half an hour." In the evening, the Moral Lyceum met at Clinton Hall, and the organization started to debate whether slavery should be abolished. A mob of 100 whites disrupted the meeting.

July 9, 1834, proved to be one of the hottest days of the year, with temperature topping 100 degrees. Handbills appeared around town warning, "Look Out for Kidnappers!" It was illustrated with a whip-wielding rider on a horse driving before him a Black man, as his wife and child tried to stop them. Whites assaulted Blacks on the streets. A mob swarmed over to the bookstore owned by the abolitionist Isaac Hopper. As the mob neared his shop, Hopper was advised to put up shutters, to which he responded, "I shall do no such thing." When the crowd arrived, Hopper stood his ground and simply glared at them. They then left and went to Chatham Street Chapel to confront the abolitionists. None were there, but they broke in anyway and were soon kicked out by the watch.[5]

By then, word of Farren's insult and his assault on Sentis had spread around town. Edwin Forrest was appearing at the Bowery Theatre in the tragedy *Metamora*, part of a benefit that Thomas Hamblin had planned for Farren. As the audience enjoyed his performance, 4,000 people, outraged by Farren's supposedly anti-American slight ("damn the Yankees") gathered on the street. Someone yelled, "To the Bowery," and the crowd massed to the theater. They broke in the front door, filled the boxes, climbed onto the stage, and kicked off the actors. Hamblin tried to calm the crowd by waving an American flag, but, as Hone noted, they pelted the theater owner "because the hand which held it was that of an Englishman." The invaders started to chant, "Forrest! The American Forrest!" They finally settled down when the actor spoke and got the performers to sing "Yankee Doodle" and the minstrel song "Zip Coon." Soon, Mayor Cornelius Lawrence and 100 members of the police force arrived, and the crowd left when they were told of Farren's sacking.

The mob then made their way to Lewis Tappan's home on Rose Street. The silk merchant knew what was coming and had whisked his family off to Harlem. Unlike Hopper's place, the crowd did not move on. "The house fell an easy prey to the fury of the rabble, who smashed in doors, demolished furniture, ejected looking-glasses and pictures, making a general wreck of its household contents," wrote Picton. As the hour-and-a-half rampage unfolded, one of the crowd realized that they were about to burn a portrait of George Washington. Someone shouted, "It is *Washington*—in the name of God don't burn Washington." Carrying the portrait before them, the crowd "marched slowly and deliberately from the scene of riot and disorder."[6]

By now, some felt that the mob had gone too far, and Mayor Lawrence was under pressure to suppress them. But the crowd had dispatched messengers to alert them of the approaching police. Hone had observed that "the mob had made so many points of attack that they completed in many instances their work of destruction before the police and military could be brought to the spot." On the 10th a cry went out, "To Dr. Cox's!" The *New York American* reported that as many as 200 men went to Reverend Cox's St. John's Chapel: "They then commenced pouring vollies of stones and brick bats into the windows, which are mostly shattered to pieces." After destroying the church's sanctuary, they headed for Cox's Charlton Street house. The cavalry tried to block their approach, but the horde threw up a barricade of carts and other materials to hem in the troops and their horses. They then attacked the troops with fence poles and paving stones as others wrecked the minister's home. The mob remained until midnight, and afterward a group of boys went to Zion Church and pelted it with stones.[7]

On the 11th, editor Charles King wrote in the *American* that the mob "should be fired upon." But the crowd—largely made up of laborers, journeymen, mechanics, and young workers—could not be stopped. That day they headed to Arthur Tappan's Pearl Street store. While the first floor had shutters protecting the windows, the crowd smashed the upper windows. They tried to break in by battering the front door with an awning post. As they rammed the door, Tappan's clerks waited inside. The merchant had armed them with 36 weapons and a supply of 500 ball cartridges, and directed his men, "Fire *low*. Shoot them in the legs, then they can't run!" But the mob never made it past the entrance and left when the police arrived.

The crowd moved off to attack Reverend Ludlow's Spring Street church, smashed the doors and windows, and wrecked the interior. The horde likewise destroyed the African Society for Mutual Relief hall and the African Baptist Church, and demolished St. Philip's Church. Rioters had advised white residents to place a light in their window so that, like the Israelite slaves in Egypt, the wilding plague would bypass their homes. "In this way," wrote the *Commercial Advertiser*, "the streets in the neighborhood of the Five Points, presented a brilliant appearance." When an African American woman set a light in her window, they pelted her with stones. A few fought back. Even so, 500 people fled their homes and cowered in the City Hall Park. Desperate to restore order, Mayor Lawrence swore in 1,000 special volunteers and constables and ordered them to shoot insurgents.[8]

The violence finally subsided on the 12th when the First Division of the New York State Artillery came out and patrolled the streets with the local militia and citizens. Mayor Lawrence issued a proclamation "enjoining all good citizens to refrain from mingling with any crowd which may assemble in the streets during the evening." The *New York Daily Advertiser* estimated that at least $20,000 in property had been damaged. This is likely a conservative estimate. Seven churches had been attacked, dozens of homes destroyed. Many feared additional violence, and citizens inundated the mayor with letters telling of rumored targets and requesting help. Downing lived on New Street near his restaurant, and noted that he "has been informed that an attack will be made on his house and requests the authority to interfere if it should be necessary."

New Yorkers generally blamed the abolitionists for the turmoil. To distance themselves from what happened, Arthur Tappan and John Rankin coauthored a handbill stating, "We entirely disclaim any desire to promote or encourage intermarriages between white and colored persons." The riots scared away some abolitionist supporters. Reverend Charles Grandison Finney soon left for Oberlin. Others became radicalized. Lewis Tappan meanwhile boarded up his house, letting Theodore Weld know that, "It is my wish that My house may remain this summer as it is, a silent Anti-Slavery preacher to the crowds who will flock to see it."[9]

* * *

The July 1834 riots were the outward sign of the violent forces growing in society, forces that would only increase in intensity over the next quarter of a century. In 1834 alone there had been the election disturbance, labor unrest, nativist–immigrant tensions, the return of cholera, and similar upheavals, not just in New York but in Philadelphia; Charlestown, Massachusetts; and other cities around the country. Undeterred, the following year the Tappans and the American Anti-Slavery Society launched a postal campaign to inundate the South with anti-slavery literature. Their campaign enraged southerners, who saw a link between the general unrest and the propaganda from "Tappan's emissaries." On July 29, a mob broke into the Charlestown post office and lit a bonfire with copies of such abolitionist publications as *The Emancipator* and the *Slave's Friend*. The following night, 3,000 people burned more material along with effigies of Arthur Tappan and Garrison.

Hate mail regularly arrived at the Tappans' shop. Thomas Aylethorpe from Montgomery, Alabama, sent Lewis a letter containing, according to one account, "a negro's ear cut off close to the head," and advised him to add it to his "collection." The Committee of Vigilance of the Parish of East Feliciana, Louisiana, meanwhile offered $50,000 if someone could deliver to them the "notorious abolitionist, Arthur Tappan." James Watson Webb wrote in his *Courier and Enquirer* that he believed that the abolitionists were "concocting a pandora's box of miseries for the whole country." Some of New York's press came to the abolitionist's defense. When the *Richmond Whig* paper called Tappan "The scoundrel who has set a whole country in a flame," *The American* responded that "there are arms enough ready to protect him." And even James Gordon Bennett's *New York Herald*—no friend to the abolitionist movement—stood up for Tappan, responding to southern papers' criticism that any talk of "abducting a free but foolish citizen"—"would lead to the most fatal consequences."[10] Lydia Maria Child wrote how "Private assassins from New Orleans are lurking at the corners of the streets, to stab Arthur Tappan." To play it safe, the anti-slavery society put planks on their doors for protection, and Brooklyn's mayor set up patrols around Tappan's house. Calls began for a boycott. Merchants in the South announced that they would no longer buy any silk from Tappan. When a delegation from New York's Chamber of Commerce asked him to halt his campaign, Tappan replied, "I WILL BE HUNG FIRST!"[11]

Tappan was far from the only target. Abolitionists in New York and across the nation endured regular attacks. In September 1835, arsonists torched the store where David Ruggles sold anti-slavery material. The following month, a crowd attacked the Boston Female Anti-Slavery Society while Garrison was speaking there. The mob looped a rope around the editor's waist and led him through the streets. Fortunately for Garrison, Mayor Theodore Lyman had him thrown in jail for his own protection. In November 1837, a pro-slavery mob attacked *The Observer* in Alton, Illinois, and killed publisher Elijah Lovejoy.

The hostility aimed at the Tappan brothers would only grow. In early 1839, a small Portuguese slaver, *Tecora*, arrived at Lomboko on the west coast of Africa. It took on board some 500 enslaved people and shipped them to Cuba. Since importing the enslaved was illegal, a number of the captives were falsely classified as Cuban-born and sold to José Ruiz and Pedro Montez. The men stowed the Africans on a two-masted coastal schooner called *La Amistad* and headed to a plantation near Porto Principe, Cuba. But three days out, the captives mutinied, killed the captain and cook, took Ruiz and Montez prisoners, and ordered them to steer the ship back to Africa. At night, though, the slavers, without the Africans realizing it, altered the ship's course. Weeks later they dropped anchor near the tip of Long Island. The mutineer's leader, Sengbe Pieh, who was called Joseph Cinqué, took a boat ashore with others in search of supplies and were captured by sailors from the Navy brig *Washington*.

A group of abolitionists including Lewis Tappan, Joshua Leavitt, and Simeon Jocelyn sought to aid the Africans and formed the Amistad Committee. Most of the Africans hailed from the Mende tribe, and on a ship anchored in New York, the group found someone who spoke Mende and could translate for them. The daring attempt to escape the *Amistad* attracted national attention—Hamblin staged a play, *The Black Schooner or, the Pirate Slaver Amistad*, at the Bowery—and Hone had observed how Cinqué "would be exalted into a hero instead of a pirate and murderer if his color was right." President Martin Van Buren, who feared losing pro-slavery support in the 1840 election, simply wanted the issue dealt with quickly and for the Africans to be shipped to Cuba.

As the case headed to the Supreme Court, Tappan's group convinced congressman and former president John Quincy Adams to defend the Africans. The defense argued that the uprising was done in the glorious spirit of revolution and freedom, and in March 1841 the high court voted to free the group. Plans were arranged to train the men as missionaries. Though they headed back to Africa to set up a mission, it did not all go as planned. While a few stayed and worked with the missionaries, most returned home, and Cinqué became a chief and, ironically, a trader in enslaved people. Even so, out of the work on the *Amistad*, the American Missionary Association was formed by merging a number of anti-slavery evangelical groups.[12]

A great deal of money was advanced on both sides of the battle over slavery in America. In addition to the Tappans' efforts, other prominent whites supported abolition. One was Gerrit Smith, the son of John Jacob Astor's friend and business partner Peter Smith. In the early 1830s, Smith and his wife attended a number of revival meetings and soon became committed abolitionists. Smith had inherited an estate worth $400,000, much of it in land. As one of the largest property holders in the state, Smith sought to give African Americans the land ownership they needed to qualify for suffrage. In 1846 he set out to distribute property to 3,000 people and, with the help of African American leaders, formed a Black enclave called Timbuctoo in North Elba in northern New York State. One who settled near Timbuctoo was John Brown. Born in Torrington, Connecticut, Brown saw the fight against slavery as a mission bestowed on him by God. He and his family lived on a 244-acre spread, sheltered runaway slaves, and they set out to teach the generally urbanite Blacks how to farm. While there, he got to know Smith, who would help form the so-called Secret Six, the group of wealthy abolitionists who would fund Brown's suicidal raid on Harpers Ferry in 1859.

* * *

Throughout this turbulent period, roughly between the Great Fire and the Civil War, African Americans both embraced freedom and lived in constant fear that they would be snatched away. It was relatively easy to capture both free Blacks and escaped slaves; the New York Committee of Vigilance for the Protection of the People of Color commented in 1837 how kidnapping had become "so extensive that no colored man is safe." Those who made their living capturing Blacks were called Blackbirders. Some, like Tobias Boudinot and his colleague Daniel Nash, belonged to what was called the "Kidnapping Club," a group that *The Emancipator* referred to as a "band of human hyænas." Such men generally met at places like a restaurant on Fulton Street called Sweet's to make their plans. All they needed to capture someone was an affidavit that the person was property. Such documents could be easily purchased, and then, with paid witnesses who swore to the City Recorder, officials sped trials along before the defendant obtained a lawyer.[13]

Some of those profiting from this were New York public officials. Horace Greeley, who in an editorial reported how slave traders simply "bribe a jury, another time their counsel or agents spirit away a vital witness," labeled the city's police chief George Matsell a slave catcher since he earned cash from bribes on fugitive cases. Boudinot was himself a city constable. And after

Tammany boss Isaiah Rynders worked for James Buchanan's 1856 presidential campaign, he earned the job of US marshal. His term in office coincided with an increase in fugitive arrests in the Southern District, which included New York City.[14]

The Committee of Vigilance reported in 1842 that they knew of 1,373 kidnappings in the city in the previous seven years. The constant threat of capture caused African American parents to keep their children off of the streets. Some resisted capture. All that was necessary, according to Frederick Douglass, was "A good revolver, a steady hand, and a determination to shoot down any man attempting to kidnap." Abductions had been going on for decades before the Civil War. In 1819, a riot broke out as 40 Blacks tried to save a man on Barclay Street as he was being taken to a steamboat. In November 1832, Boudinot seized two men and accused them of being Virginia runaways. When the prisoners passed between City Hall and Bridewell Prison, a mob tried to save them and attacked Boudinot and Officer Davis. The police, though, thwarted the rescue.[15] In October 1846, a young enslaved man from Georgia named George Kirk was found on the *Mobile*, a ship commanded by Captain Theodore Buckley. The skipper put him in chains, and when they arrived in New York, Kirk was placed in jail. A judge set Kirk free. Buckley obtained a warrant for Kirk's arrest, and the police went to retrieve him. Kirk fled. The abolitionist William Johnson was passing by when he spotted Kirk running. "I joined in the chase, with a Mr. Smith, of the *Tribune* staff, hoping to be of aid to the man if he was overtaken," he wrote. "He ran across the City Hall Park, through Beekman Street to Nassau Street, and then turned into Ann Street. By this time the pursuers were at his heels, and he bolted into a basement pie bakery and disappeared." The crowd demanded to know where the man was, and a worker replied that he didn't see anyone, and they should leave because it was a private business.

For a few days Kirk hid at the *National Anti-Slavery Standard*. The paper was edited by Sydney Howard Gay, a Massachusetts-born abolitionist who helped many slaves to escape. Hoping to ferry Kirk to safety, supporters nailed him up in a packing-box, which was carried out of the paper's office. But as the cart containing Kirk reached Broadway, the police broke it open and dragged Kirk to the Tombs. John Jay II, the grandson of the Supreme Court Justice, served as Kirk's counsel. The judge dismissed the charge against Kirk. His supporters still feared that another attempt to arrest him would be made, and Lydia Child and other abolitionists made their plans. The group got a carriage with a swift team of horses and slipped Kirk out a side entrance. By the time anyone realized what had happened, Kirk was a mile away. He soon made it safely to Canada.[16]

To raise money for their efforts, abolitionists held fairs, bazaars, bake sales, and craft fairs, at which they sold everything from quilts and linens to watercolor paintings and toys. As they tried with the anti-slavery postal campaign, they printed leaflets and graphic images of the plight of the enslaved. Reverend Henry Ward Beecher forcefully shoved the issue in the face of his Brooklyn congregants at Plymouth Church by conducting mock auctions. Slave owners would receive a bond for their property, and subscribers donated money to emancipate men, women, and children. Probably Beecher's most famous such sale was held in February 1860. Sally Maria "Pinky" Diggs was a nine-year-old girl who was one-sixteenth Black. Her master planned to sell her for $800. As a compromise, she was brought to Brooklyn to see if Beecher could raise money for her freedom. As Pinky stood at his side, Beecher roused his congregation, and collection plates filled with more than $1,000 in cash and jewelry. When it was over, Beecher plucked a ring from the pile, placed it on Pinky's finger, and told her, "Now remember that this is your freedom-ring."

Most enslaved people lacked such saviors. And despite laws seeking to stop them from fleeing, many could not fight their yearnings for freedom. For them, the path to freedom was the Underground Railroad, the secret system of routes for those escaping the South. Starting roughly in 1810 and continuing up until the Civil War, some 100,000 Blacks traveled north, making stops along the way in Pennsylvania, Massachusetts, Indiana, and New York. Many settled in the city, which became a haven for escaped Blacks. In 1850, the census listed a fifth of the 13,815 Blacks in New York as born in southern states, and 3,066 as mixed-race.[17]

Those fleeing captivity received help along their way. As one of the founders of the Railroad, Isaac Hopper's bookstore became a refuge. Thomas Downing sheltered runaways in the basement of his oyster house. The Tappans probably hid slaves in their Pearl Street office. Enslaved people were possibly hidden in the chamber below the Mutual Relief hall on Orange Street. Albro and Mary Lyons ran the Colored Seamen's Boarding House on Vandewater Street, and he and his wife not only fed more than 1,000 escapees but also disguised them. Dennis Harris's sugar refinery on Duane Street served as a safe house, as did the office of the *National Anti-Slavery Standard*, where Louis Napoleon, a porter in Gay's office, assisted new arrivals. Theodore Wright's First Colored Presbyterian Church, the Nassau Street offices of the American

Anti-Slavery Society, and Beecher's Plymouth Church—these likewise all served as refuges.

The Vigilance Committee did everything they could, and were driven by a simple aim: "To protect unoffending, defenceless, and endangered persons of color, by securing their rights as far as practicable." Founded in 1835, they checked vessels in the port, monitored the activities of slave agents and kidnappers, and helped arrested Blacks. In 1837 the committee reported that it had aided 335 escapees. David Ruggles, who worked as the group's secretary, arrived in New York as a teenager, making a living as a butter merchant and a grocer. In the early 1830s he established a bookshop on Lispenard Street, where he ran a library and sold anti-slavery material. He founded the *Mirror of Liberty* magazine and used his paper to name slave catchers, described missing Blacks, kept track of men and women thrown in jail, and gave evidence against those trying to retrieve enslaved people. To monitor slave agents, Ruggles also compiled a *Slaveholders Directory*. He would help at least 600 people, and because of his prominence, Ruggles, too, became a target of Blackbirders. He recalled how in December 1835, just after the Great Fire, "Several notorious slave-catchers made an attack upon the house in which I board, and attempted to force open the doors." The armed men made it through, and despite the fact that they ran at him "like hungry dogs," Ruggles somehow managed to escape.[18]

* * *

The Tappans and all those who sought to end slavery had long realized that the idea of freedom and the reality of bringing it about were different things. Some abolitionists like Garrison opposed taking part in the political system. Tappan, Leavitt, and others understood that they needed to be active to bring about legislation. In 1840 they met in Warsaw, New York, and formed the Liberty Party and nominated former slaveholder James Birney for president. In the election, Birney garnered just 7,000 votes. Four years later, however, Birney earned 62,000 votes and probably helped tip the election to the Democrat James Polk. When the election was held in 1848, Gerrit Smith served as the Liberty Party's nominee.

While the Liberty Party focused on issues of slavery, the fractious Democratic Party was divided over what to do about the institution. Democratic opponents of slavery in New York were dubbed Barnburners, earning their inflammatory name from the belief that they were like a farmer who set fire to his barn to get rid of rats. Meanwhile, Barnburners called their

more conservative, anti-abolitionist opponents "Hunkers." This group received its name from the idea that they "hunkered" or "hankered" for political office and were willing to abandon their principles to succeed.

The issue of slavery came to the fore with the Mexican-American War,
which started in 1846. When it was over in 1848, the United States had acquired 55 percent of Mexico—525,000 square miles, an area that would
include California, Nevada, Utah, New Mexico, Texas, and Arizona. The
question was whether these territories would be free or slave. That year's presidential election witnessed the formation of the Free Soil Party, which united
Liberty Party members, Conscience Whigs, and Barnburner Democrats. It
also attracted a wide range of merchants, farmers, and workers—including
Walt Whitman, who founded and edited the Brooklyn Weekly Freeman, editor William Cullen Bryant, and engineer John Jervis—who called for "free
soil, free speech, free labor, and free men." Free Soilers concerned themselves
with the rights of whites, feared African American competition, and opposed
the introduction of either slavery or free Blacks in the territories. At their
convention in Buffalo, they nominated Martin Van Buren as their presidential candidate. The former president only earned 291,501 votes at the polls.
The Democrat Lewis Cass won 1.22 million votes. Both lost to Whig Zachary
Taylor, who earned 1.36 million votes. Taylor would die in office of cholera in
1850 and be succeeded by Vice President Millard Fillmore.

When California sought statehood in 1849, Senator Henry Clay called
for admitting it as a free state while leaving the issue of slavery in the New
Mexico and Utah territories to be decided by popular sovereignty. Congress
enacted the Compromise of 1850 to resolve slavery differences. Instead of
putting to rest the issue, the compromise only enflamed it. It came with a
new Fugitive Slave Act, which required citizens to assist in the apprehension
of enslaved people and denied the accused a trial to determine their status.
The unjustness of the law stunned many. Lewis Tappan wrote that it "compels
every citizen of the free States to be a 'slave-catcher,'" and "leaves the freeman
at the North no alternative. HE MUST DISOBEY THE LAW."[19]

This wasn't the first such rule dealing with the issue of recapture. But
the new 1850 law galvanized abolitionist forces. George Downing joined
his father Thomas, Philip Bell, Doctor Smith, and others in forming the
Committee of Thirteen to fight the law. Just eight days after it took effect,
attorney Thomas Clare came to New York. He claimed that James Hamlet, a
porter on Water Street, had escaped from Baltimore and belonged to a certain Mary Brown. Clare had Hamlet clapped in irons, and once he arrived

back in Maryland, Brown let it be known that she would emancipate him for $800. George Downing and others raised the money. When Hamlet returned to the city in early October, "A great demonstration was made in the Park," wrote Tappan. "Four or five thousand citizens, white and colored, assembled at noon, to welcome him back to his family."[20]

In the November 1852 national elections, the Free Soil candidate John Hale earned even less support than Van Buren did in 1848, tallying just 155,210 votes, while Whig candidate General Winfield Scott earned 1.39 million votes. Democrat Franklin Pierce captured the White House with 1.6 million votes. The election represented the twilight of the Whig and Free Soil Parties. By the mid-1850s Free Soilers, anti-slavery Whigs, abolitionists, and others had joined the new Republican Party. The party emerged around such issues as internal improvements and opposition to the expansion of slavery.

Throughout, there were some articulate observers of the legal and political storm brewing in the nation. Harriet Beecher Stowe's *Uncle Tom's Cabin* became, as noted earlier, the most popular novel of its time and brought the evils of slavery into America's parlors. Whitman knew the institution of slavery well. As the grandson and great-grandson of slave owners in West Hills, New York, he came to believe that it was "a disgrace and a blot on the character of our republic, and on our boasted humanity!"[21]

John Jervis began penning anti-slavery pieces in September 1855. Under the *nom de plume* Hampden, he started his first "Freedom vs. Slavery" letter to the *New York Evening Post* by noting, "Slavery and freedom are antagonistic. It is impossible that they can harmonize." George Templeton Strong's view of the institution also continued to evolve. Earlier he had criticized slavery, but by 1856 attacked the institution for "the selling asunder of families, remediless cruelty and oppression, enforced concubinage, incest," and how "It practically demoralizes and degrades the whole community where it exists."[22]

An unlikely voice on the issue of slavery proved to be Frederick Law Olmsted, whose evolution reflected a national trend. At first the future designer of Central Park voiced support for the American Colonization Society. He soon favored gradual emancipation, and then evolved into a Free Soiler. Olmsted's childhood friend Charles Loring Brace worked hard to convert Olmsted to a more militant view. Brace even brought Garrison and the abolitionist preacher Theodore Parker to Olmsted's farm on Staten Island to discuss the issue. Olmsted's stance shifted, and he started coming out against the Fugitive Slave Act. He worked with the New England Emigrant Aid Society to set up anti-slavery settlements in Texas, and in 1854 helped raise money for Adolph Douai, who sought to purchase the San Antonio *Zeitung* after the publisher was threatened for his stand on slavery. Then, in 1855, Olmsted bought weapons for those battling slavery supporters in Kansas.

Brace knew Henry Raymond at the *New York Times*. The editor liked Olmsted's 1852 book *Walks and Talks of an American Farmer in England* and asked Olmsted to write a series of letters on the conditions of enslaved people. As Olmsted explained to a friend, he was perfect for the assignment since, "I represent pretty fairly the average sentiment of good thinking men on our side." He planned to "make a valuable book of observations on Southern Agriculture & general economy as affected by Slavery; the condition of the slaves—prospects—tendencies—& reliable understanding of the sentiments and hopes & fears of sensible planters & gentlemen that I should meet."[23] Setting out in December 1852, Olmsted headed through Washington and down to Louisiana. Along the way he met with slave owners, enslaved people, and those who had been freed, as well as African Americans who owned enslaved people themselves. His articles started to appear in the *Times* in mid-February 1853 under the byline "Yeoman." Olmsted wrote how in cities like Richmond, he saw well-dressed enslaved peoples, and on farms he came across others who were filthy and used for brute labor. He watched African American funerals, observed whites deliberately knocking into Blacks on sidewalks, and saw shops bearing signs for "Slave Dealers," where men went for $1,200 to $1,300, and young women for $800 to $1,000.

Olmsted's time in the South only sharpened his opposition to slavery. The *Times* ended up publishing dozens of his articles. Raymond then asked him to head out to Texas for additional reporting. This time, Olmsted took his brother John with him. They left in November 1853 and traveled as far as the Mexican border. Olmsted wrote respectfully of African Americans, noting, "It is our duty, as it is every man's in the world, to oppose Slavery, to weaken it, to destroy it." Once back on Staten Island, Olmsted started to put together three books on his travels. He based his first volume, *A Journey in the Seaboard States*, which came out in 1856, on his initial trip. Material from the first part of the second trip came out in 1857 as *A Journey Through Texas*, with his return trip appearing in 1860 as *A Journey in the Back Country*.[24]

* * *

However much their plight was the cause of so much violence and pain in the decades leading up to the Civil War, African Americans just wanted a chance to live freely and peacefully, to take care of their families, and to prosper. In 1824 cart-man John Whitehead and his wife, Elizabeth, bought some farmland in the northern part of Manhattan. The Whiteheads were white, and their land stretched from what is now Seventh to Eighth Avenues in the 80s, making up a small part of current-day Central Park. The following year they started selling off parcels of their property. The African American community, needing a place to feel safe and secure, started to purchase some of the Whiteheads' land. Bootblack Andrew Williams paid $125 for three lots. That same day, Epiphany Davis, an African Methodist Episcopal Zion Church trustee, picked up 12 lots for $578. AME Zion had been using the burial ground in Washington Square for its congregants. But since the city had started to transform that area in the 1820s to a residential neighborhood, the church bought six lots from the Whiteheads for a cemetery. Over the next three years, a few other African Americans purchased land. Between 1825 and 1832, the Whiteheads unloaded 50 lots, with half being purchased by Blacks.

This undeveloped part of New York soon became known as Seneca Village. The origin of the name is obscure. Possibly it was named after the Native American Seneca Nation that lived in upstate New York. It could have also been a tribute to Lucius Annaeus Seneca, the first-century Roman philosopher who called for the better treatment of slaves and whose *Seneca's Morals* was embraced by activists and abolitionists. And because of its isolation from town, the name might have been a reference to the country of Senegal in northwest Africa, a code word for the Underground Railroad. In any case, the community slowly grew, and it seems likely that refugees from the 1834 anti-abolitionist riots settled there. The village prospered, and a number of the residents were known to have assisted escaped slaves. Some of those who lived to the east in the African American village of York Hill moved to Seneca Village when they were displaced in the late 1830s by the construction of the reservoir for the Croton water system.

With its growing population, the village became the area's largest and most densely populated development, with three times as many people as other parts of the future parkland. This stable community offered a rare chance for Black land ownership. By 1855, half of the Black households in Seneca Village had property. And while fewer than 100 of the city's 12,000 African Americans could vote in the mid-1850s, ten hailed from the village. By 1855, at least 225 people called Seneca Village home. The tidy, middle-class community had 52 houses, along with barns and stables. Most residents had property worth $500, the majority of the men could read, and their children attended school. Some worked as grocers, coopers, waiters, cooks, sailors, preachers, and cart-men. Resident George Webster had more than $2,000 in property.

While the streets planned by the 1811 commissioners hadn't yet been built this far north, the village appears to have followed the grid. Seneca Village's Spring Street led to a natural spring, which probably served as the community's main water source. Some residents lived in simple cottages; others had homes that stood two stories tall. A few of the properties had large gardens. The *Times*, in July 1856, called it "a neat *little settlement*," and in August 1857 the *Tribune* noted that a "number of these have fine kitchen gardens, and some of the side-hill slopes are adorned with cabbage and melon-patches, with hills of corn and cucumbers, and beds of beets, parsnips, and other garden delicacies."[25]

Churches proved central to the lives of Black New Yorkers and to those in Seneca Village. The African Union Methodist Episcopal Church bought land there for a church in 1837, and nearby stood Colored School No. 3. St. Michael's Episcopal Church, located at Broadway and 100th Street, constructed All Angels' Church, Seneca's largest sanctuary. In 1853, AME Zion held a solemn ceremony in which they laid the cornerstone for a new building.

Irish residents started arriving in the area of Seneca Village in the 1840s, and soon a third of Seneca's inhabitants were Irish. Sara and Pat Plunkitt, who in 1842 gave birth to future Tammany boss George Washington Plunkitt, lived on the edge of the community on Nanny Goat Hill, a spot Plunkitt described as "twenty feet inside the Central Park wall at Eighty-fourth Street." Tammany leader Richard Croker, who arrived from Ireland in 1846 at age three, also spent time there. His father made a living as an itinerant veterinarian, taking care of livestock. Many of the community's Irish and German residents joined All Angels. They prayed in its large white frame building, and congregants were buried alongside each other in the cemetery.

Such racial peace was not destined to last. For this part of New York that these people called home lay directly in the path of the relentless development that had been heading north for decades. Unfortunately for the tiny Seneca Village, Mayor Fernando Wood, a friend to the American South, took office in 1855. By then, the juggernaut of development was pushing at the community's borders in the hope of transforming this land, which contained an African American refuge, into something quite different—a retreat for the whole city, and of course one created mainly for New York's white citizens.[26]

17

Creating Breathing Space

Seneca Village appeared doomed. It had developed into a thriving middle-class community, one where Blacks and whites lived peacefully together, and featured nice homes, numerous churches, and well-tended gardens. Yet many New Yorkers saw this semi-rural neighborhood as embodying the threat of the mingling of the races. And while the land's rocky terrain had caused some developers to view it as unpromising, by the 1850s city leaders began to see it differently. New York had become an unparalleled boomtown. Open space was vanishing, and what remained needed to be preserved. City officials had searched for some kind of urban retreat, and that's when they began to look at the patch of earth and rock between Seventh and Eighth Avenues, from 81st to 89th Streets, along with much of the surrounding land. Here was property that could fulfill a long-neglected civic need. With it they could redeem their metropolis, bring nature's grace back to Manhattan, and restore what the *New York Mirror* called "the lungs of the city."[1]

In a city where location meant everything, this need for open land was something new. Back in the late 18th century, in the days of Philip Hone's youth, and in the early 19th century when George Templeton Strong was growing up, New York was a small town, a community settled near wilds, a place of sylvan hills and valleys, of fleeting streams and dense marshes. City officials sought to bring order to New York with the regulation of the land. But while the 1811 Commissioners' Plan laid out the surface in a rational manner, it lacked the visionary quality of, for example, Georges-Eugène Haussmann's mid-19th-century layout for Paris. Instead, commissioners Gouverneur Morris, Simeon De Witt, and John Rutherfurd simply had surveyor John Randel map out the Lenape's primal land, laying it under a grid shaped like an elongated checkerboard. Randel's uniform streets and perpendicular avenues stretched across and up the undeveloped island.

To many early 19th-century New Yorkers, such a plan appeared at best wildly aspirational. But with the 1825 opening of the Erie Canal, and even more so in the aftermath of the Great Fire of 1835, the city began to expand at a mind-boggling speed. Hemmed in by rivers and only allowing northward growth, the city forced those expanding it to choke off watercourses, fill the marshes, and extend the shoreline. All was smoothed out and then overlaid with Randel's seemingly endless ribbons of streets, with the surveyor noting with satisfaction that his grid had encouraged "buying, selling, and improving real estate, on streets, avenues, and public squares." Developers then staked out building lots and covered the land with rows of homes and blocks of businesses. And with it, the undeveloped island through which John Jacob Astor had once ridden his horse quickly vanished. As the city became the nation's commercial center, breathing room was nearly impossible to find. In the space of just one generation, in a place where rural space once ruled, open space had become an afterthought.[2]

New York did have a few spaces, as we've seen. On Broadway at the southern foot of the city stood Bowling Green, the city's first official park. This small patch of green was laid out in 1733, and on that spot in 1770 the city set an equestrian statue of George III. But Great Britain and its king soon fell out of favor, and in July 1776, following the signing of the Declaration of Independence, an irate crowd toppled the gilded statue and beheaded their former monarch. In 1843, James Renwick unveiled a new fountain for the park. This, the architect's first completed work, was made with an irregular pile of rocks arranged to create a waterfall. Lit with colored lights, the enclosed green was made to contain deer, geese, and swans.

Nearby, at the base of the island, stretched the Battery. The area took its name from the group of cannons set up to protect the city. Following the evacuation of the British troops in 1783, the area was enlarged with landfill, planted with trees, and fenced in. It became a popular destination for strolling New Yorkers like George Washington, who lived nearby when the town served as the nation's first capital. In 1828, the *New York Gazette & General Advertiser* commented how "this pleasant spot, ornamented as it is with beautiful trees, grass and walks is not excelled in the world."[3]

Just off the Battery stood Southwest Battery. The fort was built between 1808 and 1811 on a manmade island. In 1824 the structure became an entertainment center called Castle Garden. New York's main open space was the City Hall Park. The park long served as a meeting place for promenaders, as well as a staging area for political rallies. Further uptown, in 1802, David Hosack founded the Elgin Botanic Garden on 20 acres. On the site of what is now Rockefeller Center, he raised native and exotic trees, plants, flowers, and shrubs, and maintained an elaborate herbarium with medicinal plants.

The commissioners' utilitarian 1811 grid did set aside proposed spaces for squares, markets, a reservoir, and parade grounds, such as Manhattan Square, Hamilton Square, Bloomingdale Square, Harlem Square, and Harlem Marsh. Unfortunately these designated areas only came to a mere 470 acres in total. Using more space for parks, commissioners believed, was not justified because the city blessedly had two rivers and abundant land to the north. As city surveyor William Bridges noted, "Certainly if the City of New-York were destined to stand on the side of a small stream, such as the Seine or the Thames, a great number of ample places might be needful; but those large arms of the sea which embrace Manhattan Island, render its situation, in regard to health and pleasure, as well as to the convenience of commerce, peculiarly felicitous."[4]

Yet, even after the commissioners planned for parks, spaces were scaled back, while a few others were added. In the mid-1820s, the Common Council and Mayor Hone transformed the potter's field in Greenwich Village into the Washington Military Parade Ground. Grass was planted, the old buttonwoods and elms were retained, and ailanthus trees were arranged along the walks. William Curr, who referred to himself as the "Gardener of New York" and would landscape Trinity and other cemeteries, created the first design for the park. In 1849 the Common Council called for gas lighting for the square. And in 1852, Curr added a bluestone fountain.

The planned 55-acre Market Place was slashed to 10.5 acres. Workers drained the swampland, and in 1834 the area that ran from Avenues A and B and from 7th to 10th Streets became Tompkins Square, named in honor of former governor Daniel Tompkins. In no time, elegant homes surrounded the park. The oval-shaped Union Square on 14th Street opened in July 1839. Curr did the plantings there, and a large fountain was added in 1842 when the Croton Aqueduct started flowing.

Not far away, Stuyvesant Square was laid out, standing on land that had been part of Dutch governor Petrus Stuyvesant's 17th-century *bouwerie*. His great-great-grandson Peter kept an eye on the encroaching development, and in 1842 he and his wife sold four acres of their Petersfield farm on Second Avenue between 15th and 17th Streets to the city for $5 so it could become a park. Stuyvesant hoped to have the area surrounded by a railing, writing that he wanted to "plant and improve such enclosure similar to the improvements made in Washington Square." In 1852, Curr designed a circular bluestone basin with water jets. The 44-square-block Grand Parade was supposed to stretch from Third to Seventh Avenues and 23rd to 34th Streets, but it shrunk to just seven acres. Workers covered Cedar Creek, and when the city opened the park in May 1847, officials named it Madison Square in honor of the fourth president. A cast-iron fence enclosed the space with its diamond-shaped foot paths, and Curr did the plantings. That same year, the land just to the west of the Murray Hill Distributing Reservoir in the lower 40s became Reservoir Square, current-day Bryant Park.[5]

As the city fiddled with plans over the first half of the 19th century, some founded their own residential squares. In the early 1800s, Trinity Church established Hudson Square on the boggy farmland next to Lispenard's Meadows. Bordered by Hudson, Varick, Beach, and Laight Streets, the park to the north of City Hall was transformed into ornamental grounds surrounded by an iron fence, and featuring horse chestnuts, catalpas, and cottonwoods. Only residents living on the square could gain access to the ground. The towering St. John's Chapel—Reverend Samuel Cox's church on Laight Street—on the park's east side bestowed upon the area the name St. John's Park. Elegant brick townhouses rose around the space and attracted the wealthy, including naval engineer John Ericsson (who, during the Civil War, would design the USS *Monitor*, a warship with the first rotating gun turret), shipping merchant Silas Holmes, and Arthur Tappan. Strong's father-in-law, Samuel Ruggles, created one of the most desirable and enduring residential squares. In 1831 he set aside lots uptown for Gramercy Park. And in the midst of his development, Ruggles planted a park that could only be used for the "benefit and enjoyment of the owners and occupants of sixty-six surrounding lots of land." That remains the case to this day.[6]

By the early 1850s, the city's 17 public squares made up less than 165 acres of land. Many were untended, and two-thirds of them were not laid out and were situated far from the mass of people. Early on, this lack of park space created a lively business for pleasure grounds—small urban retreats. Vauxhall Gardens, which opened in 1797 and initially stood on lower Broadway, moved in 1803 to the area between the Bowery and Broadway on land leased from Astor. Vauxhall, named after the London garden, featured summer entertainments and fireworks.[7]

William Niblo opened his eponymous garden in the mid-1820s on the northeast corner of Broadway and Prince Street. In 1835, P.T. Barnum displayed Joice Heth—the woman he claimed was the 161-year old nursemaid of George Washington—in Niblo's Garden, and he recalled how the site's alcoves "were tastefully decorated on the outside with festoons of lamps of variegated colors." Hoping to keep drawing crowds, Niblo reconfigured the grounds each year, serving food along with lemonade and ice creams, setting off firework displays, and offering a wide assortment of entertainment. Edwin Forrest performed there in 1839, and the place regularly staged circuses, productions of *Hamlet* and *King Lear*, comedy acts, military bands, lectures, and the Ravel Family, an acrobatic troupe "with their astonishing performance of the Cord Elastique." "Novelty after novelty is produced in quick succession," extolled the *Mirror*, "and all the arrangements, in-doors and out, are of the most admirable description."[8]

On lower Broadway stood Contoit's New York Garden. It opened in 1810 and was a popular spot where patrons enjoyed ice cream and desserts. Strong deemed the garden's strawberry ices to be "superlative." Richmond Hill house originally stood on Charlton Street east of Varick Street. Once the home of Aaron Burr, it was moved to Charlton and Varick in 1820 and transformed into a summer resort two years later. In the early 1830s it became an Italian Opera House and soon featured equestrian shows, dramas, melodramas, circuses, and operas. In July 1853, as we've seen, the Crystal Palace opened in the lower 40s on Reservoir Square, the site of a potter's field next to the Murray Hill Distributing Reservoir. The spot proved quite popular and spawned nearby businesses like Crystal Ice Cream Parlors, Crystal Stables, and Crystal Fruit Stalls. The Maze Garden opened in 1853. It sat on two acres alongside the reservoir and offered "cream, ices and other refreshment." Bellevue Gardens appeared in 1856. Stretching from 79th to 81st Streets on 11 acres on the East River, it staged musical entertainment. Finally, the Palace Garden started in the summer of 1858 on the north side of 14th Street with lamps, flowers, refreshments, fireworks, and balloon ascensions.

But with land at a premium, the days for many of these commercial gardens were numbered. In the mid-1820s, Astor cut Lafayette Place through Vauxhall Gardens and developed the western portion of land. A smaller Vauxhall Gardens continued for a while, but came down in 1855. Richmond Hill shut down in the late 1840s. While considered fireproof, the Crystal Palace of course spectacularly burned to the ground in October 1858. The Metropolitan Hotel opened in 1852 on the site of Niblo's. And the Palace Garden shuttered soon after the Civil War.[9]

As railroads, ferries, and steamboats linked the city with places like Coney Island, Astoria, Staten Island, New Jersey, and the countryside, those New Yorkers who could afford it flocked elsewhere. In March 1831, Hone took one of his many trips to Long Island to fish for trout. Soon Hone and dozens of others invested in the Marine Pavilion in Far Rockaway, Long

Island. Designed by Ithiel Town and Alexander Jackson Davis's partner James Dakin, the rambling three-story complex with its towering Grecian colonnade was set on a private beach and opened in 1834. There were bathing carriages to take guests to the water, a dining room tended by French chefs, and reading and billiards rooms. Hone and others had their own cottages, with the resort welcoming such notables as Henry Wadsworth Longfellow and Washington Irving. The Strong family visited there in September 1837, and George Templeton found it at the end of the season "almost deserted." The place soon lost customers to resorts farther away, such as Virginia Springs, Saratoga, and Newport, Rhode Island. Hoboken, across the Hudson River, likewise became a popular destination. Astor had a summer house there, and Hone liked to visit the town. In May 1838, Hone and his family took advantage of the fine weather and visited Elysian Fields with its landscaped gardens, fruit trees, and plants. "New walks have been laid out, the grounds beautifully arranged, the woods cleared," he marveled.

To find peace, some also headed to rural churchyards and suburban burial grounds where they strolled through sylvan surroundings. Landscape pioneer Andrew Jackson Downing commented how citizens visited places like Green-Wood in Brooklyn, Mount Auburn in Cambridge, Massachusetts, and Laurel Hill in Philadelphia because "these cemeteries are the only places in the country that can give an untravelled American any idea of the beauty of many of the public parks and gardens abroad."[10]

* * *

In the 1850s, New York was on its way to becoming a world metropolis, strengthened by its businesses, banks, merchant houses, streets, water aqueduct, railways, ferries, food markets, and housing. As midcentury approached, New York was a center of culture, with Columbia University, New York University, Cooper Union, the Astor Library, the Academy of Music, the National Academy of Design, and assorted theaters. Yet, many felt beset by the growing constraints and impositions of urban life, demanding cleaner streets, better housing, more reliable transportation, fairer wages, and more disciplined police officers and firemen. So, as the city transformed, a growing chorus of voices called for alternatives to pavement and bricks. In 1844, *New York Evening Post* editor William Cullen Bryant pitched the idea of "A New Public Park" with "an extensive pleasure ground for shade and recreation." Horace Greeley at the *New York Tribune* followed with a similar call, and the two papers ran occasional editorials for the need for open space.

They were not alone, A few years later, Mayor Caleb Woodhull complained how "all the public squares below forty second street, comprise only in the aggregate, about sixty three acres." And as more citizens made their way across the Atlantic for grand European tours, there was a growing sense of New York's inadequacy when compared to Old World centers. Citizens covetously desired to have a stately park like those in many British and continental cities, such as London's Regent's Park and Paris' Tuileries Garden, and yearned to show that New York could stand as an equal to other great cities. Bryant noted, after spending time in Europe in 1845, that it was "a cause of regret that in laying out New York, no preparation was made, while it was yet practicable, for a range of parks and public gardens." Even the American Medical Association, founded in 1847, commented two years later on, "the necessity for public squares" as one of "the most powerful correctives to a vitiated air within the reach of the inhabitants of a populous place."[11]

What they lobbied for proved a tall order, but the man who helped bring it to life was Andrew Jackson Downing. The fifth and youngest child of Eunice and Samuel—a wheelwright and nurseryman in Newburgh, New York—Downing was born on October 31, 1815. He finished school at the age of 16, and joined his brother Charles at the family's Botanic Garden and Nurseries business. The firm offered fruit and ornamental trees, flowering shrubs, roses, and herbs. As Downing immersed himself in the field, he became heavily influenced by the works of the British landscape designers Humphry Repton, who created such estates as Uppark in West Sussex, and John Claudius Loudon, who wrote such influential works as his 1838 *Arboretum et Fruticetum Britannicum*. Downing grew to believe in the superiority of picturesque landscape and architecture, and how "even in third-rate towns, like the Hague, there is a royal park of two hundred acres, filled with superb trees, rich turf, and broad pieces of water." More importantly, he saw that such public places were "salubrious and wholesome breathing places" where "all classes assemble under the shade of the same trees . . . the pleasant drawing-rooms of the whole population; where they gain health, good spirits, social enjoyment."

Downing was a new type of architect, a gifted writer who promoted his ideas through such books as his 1841 *A Treatise on the Theory and Practice of Landscape Gardening*, a volume for which Davis contributed the illustrations. Downing's tastes paralleled the Romantic Movement in literature and art. He stressed the sublime, advocated for public support for agricultural education, and became an early proponent of suburban communities linked to cities by public transportation. His 1842 *Cottage Residences* and his 1850 *The Architecture of Country Houses* were leagues ahead of the average builders' guides. These pattern books presented modest houses within landscape settings and were filled with architectural plans for Gothic, Romanesque, and Italianate style buildings by architects like Davis, Richard Upjohn, and Gervase Wheeler.[12]

In 1846 Downing founded *The Horticulturist*, a monthly devoted to rural art and taste. That publication stressed sensible design and the creation of village improvement societies, and likewise offered plans for homes, country churches, schools, carriage houses, even an octagon house and an iron-roofed vinery. Downing's writings became enormously popular. According to the Swedish reformer and advocate for women's rights Fredrika Bremer, Downing's works "are to be found every where, and nobody, whether he be rich or poor, builds a house or lays out a garden without consulting Downing's works."

For Downing, fresh air served as a restorative tonic to societal ills. And as with reform-minded evangelical leaders like Charles Grandison Finney and Arthur Tappan, who strenuously advocated for an end to prostitution and slavery, Downing saw the outdoors as a bulwark against disease, an alternative to the distractions of gambling, and as a shield against the weaknesses of intemperance. Through his articles in *The Horticulturist* he sought to address the need for large public spaces in America, writing that "What are called parks in New-York, are not even apologies for the thing; they are only squares, or paddocks." He began campaigning for such a place. "There is nothing laudable in having a piano-forte and mahogany chairs in the parlor," he wrote in an editorial in *The Horticulturist*, "where the streets outside are barren of shade trees, destitute of side-walks, and populous with pigs and geese." What better place, Downing foresaw, than a Democratic America "filled with all classes of society, partaking of the same pleasures, with as much zest as in any part of the world." New York, he believed, could afford to build such places, spots unfettered by the grid, places that looked as if God had personally set them down.[13]

Establishing such a wonderland needed to be done soon. In April 1851, Mayor Ambrose Kingsland submitted a proposal for a 160-acre park at Jones' Wood on the East River. Kingsland argued that undeveloped and inexpensive land like Jones' Wood could "be converted into a park," which "would secure the gratitude of thousands yet unborn for the blessings of pure air." Many liked the idea of Jones' Wood. Landscaper Curr commented that "the chief advantages of Jones' Wood is, that the trees are already planted, and its being available to the present generation at a small expense."[14]

Jones' Wood ran from Third Avenue to the East River and 66th to 75th Streets, and had been named for tavern-keeper John Jones. The land had been divided among his children. Daughter Sarah had married Peter Schermerhorn, and one of their sons, John, married Hone's daughter Mary in 1832. George and Ellen Strong visited the area for the first time in October 1853, and he found the grounds "very beautiful, and strangely intact for the latitude of Sixty-first Street." Whig state senator James Beekman pushed for the creation of a park there, and worked with his colleagues to acquire it. Some, though, questioned his self-interest since he and other wealthy citizens owned nearby property. "It is absurd to call the proposed New Park a People's Park," complained the *New York Sun*. In any case, the Joneses and the Schermerhorns refused to sell their property, and a bill was passed to acquire it by eminent domain. William Schermerhorn wrote Beekman plaintively about how they "only ask to be left in the undisturbed enjoyment of our property."[15] In August 1851, Downing thanked Mayor Kingsland "most heartily for his proposed new park," but wrote that 160 acres was too small and would be "only a child's playground." He instead called for a grander space covering at least 500 acres, a place big enough that New Yorkers could "forget, for a time the rattle of the pavements and the glare of brick walls."

Some started looking for a better location. A Special Committee on Public Parks compared setting Jones' Wood on the East Side and a park in the center of the island. The report noted how the city's burgeoning population could rise to several million people by the end of the century. The numbers, the committee stated, would "throng a place so limited as *Jones' Park*, but be very amply accommodated in *Central Park*, of nearly five times the extent." The committee called for a park stretching two and a half miles, from 59th to 106th Streets and Fifth to Eighth Avenues. Others agreed for the need for such an unprecedented-sized retreat. The central area's rocky surface and ravines meant that grading the land for streets would cost twice as much as the area was worth, making it less desirable for building and thus cheaper to acquire. This proved a plus in a real estate–obsessed city that only favored prime land. Central Park was quickly deemed the superior site. City developers touted it, since it would make their town look good. Croton supporters saw it as an ideal spot for an additional reservoir. Residents abutting the area viewed it as a way to improve their property values. Even the *Journal of Commerce*, which catered to the wealthy and fiscally conservative, grudgingly endorsed the choice.[16]

While discussion continued, Downing headed down to New York on July 28, 1852, on the steamship *Henry Clay* with his wife and relatives. As they travelled from Newburgh to New York, the ship started racing with a competitor's vessel, the *Armenia*. Passing near Yonkers, the *Henry Clay's* boiler overheated, the ship caught fire, and Downing and dozens of other passengers perished. His death at just 36 was a tragic blow to design and to America. The *Tribune* commented on the loss of "A man of genius" who was able to "feel the deficiencies and to know the needs of our domestic, and especially of our rural, architecture."[17]

Though Downing was gone, he had in just a few short years implanted the idea of a park in others. But to make such a place a reality, the city had to move quickly. For though the land above 40th Street was not yet fully gridded out, it was developing fast. People were attracted to the Upper East Side, settling there with the opening of the New York & Harlem Railroad and the Third Avenue line. The Upper West Side had started to develop, too, with the laying of the Croton Aqueduct and with the Hudson River Railroad allowing for easier access.

By 1855, some 60,000 people lived uptown, including 1,600 on land that would become Central Park. Unlike downtown, uptown New York had a higher rate of land ownership. Gardens filled the area, with residents raising crops and tending livestock. Some, like the musician Jupiter Zeus Hesser— composer of such works as "Go Warrior Go" and "Congress Grand March"— had a two-story home on Seventh Avenue and 100th Street with a plot he dubbed "Jupiterville." A few had orchards. The park's residents were mostly German and Irish, with more than 90 percent of them immigrants. A tenth owned small businesses, working as butchers and grocers. The vast majority held unskilled jobs as domestics, laborers, and rag pickers. Seneca Village, nestled along the western edge, was the largest and most densely settled section, with three times as many people per square block as elsewhere in the park. In 1847 the Sisters of Charity of St. Vincent de Paul bought an old frame house in the northeastern part of the eventual park, and by the 1850s built the Academy of Mount St. Vincent. A few dozen nuns lived there, offering higher education for women. In 1847 work started on a new State Arsenal on Fifth Avenue and 64th Street.[18]

With population growth, the area attracted businesses, including those that made carriages and coaches. There were also less regulated industries, such as ones that produced wax and paint, not to mention the even more noxious distillers, slaughterhouses, bone- and soap-boilers, and leather dressers, which had been driven by development from the lower part of the city. In the southeastern edge stood an area called "Pigtown" with its Irish hog keepers. The area even had gambling halls, dance houses, and illegal liquor places called *shebeens*, and provided a convenient place to stow stolen goods.

If the city wanted the land, it needed to buy it before the price increased. The *New York Times* feared that time was short: "The growth of the city is so rapid that it will soon overspread every feasible position, and its tenanted blocks will render it impracticable to convert the ground on which they will stand into lawn and leafy bower." Twenty-one landowners possessed half the park, with three families owning a fifth of the land. The creation of the park would thus mean an economic windfall for Alderman Joseph Britton, who had lots on Fifth Avenue and 82nd Street; Alderman S. Benson McGown, whose family owned land on the east side reaching from 97th Street to 106th Street; Alderman Asahel A. Denman; and those like Mayors Fernando Wood and Daniel Tiemann. As the *Times* pointed out, "The projected location of a Park [in] a given part of the City, is too potent a temptation to the avarice of land-owners."[19]

Plans moved ahead to make the retreat a reality. Now it was a matter of displacing the Irish, the Germans, bone-boilers, rag pickers, and pig keepers. And also, of course, the African Americans. Although Seneca Village was a stable community, Mayor Wood and the colonization-supporting Beekman abhorred its African American residents. Seneca residents were easily clumped together in the collective mind with the area's less seemly inhabitants. Such a mindset was abetted by Egbert L. Viele, the future park's chief engineer. Viele wrote that the area had served as a home for people "dwelling in rude huts of their own construction, and living off the refuse of the city, which they daily conveyed in small carts, chiefly drawn by dogs, from the lower part of the city through Fifth Avenue."[20]

On July 21, 1853, the legislature passed the Central Park Act, declaring the area "a public place." Residents of Seneca Village appear to have been unaware of the eminent domain bill; two weeks later, they gathered to break ground and lay the cornerstone of the new AME Zion Church building. The city finalized its plans for acquiring the land in 1855, and the state Supreme Court appointed commissioners to decide on the value of the park's more than 7,000 lots as well as the more than 300 structures owned by 561 landowners. By then the economy had slowed, and the Common Council sought to lop off more than half a mile on the park's southern end. But Mayor Wood vetoed the move, stating: "Let New-York follow up the noble spirit asserted so boldly in the introduction of the Croton Water."

As with others in the area, Seneca Village residents protested their land assessments. The commission, for instance, offered Andrew Williams $2,335 for the lots he had purchased in 1825 for $125. He filed a petition stating that the property on which he erected a two-story frame home was worth more. The city then paid him $3,500. When all the land was finally acquired in 1856, it ended up costing the city more than $5 million. And by taking so much property off the market, surrounding land values increased. Officials gave residents until February 1856 to evacuate.[21]

Wood had gotten the Common Council to hand the park commission to him and to Street Commissioner Joseph Taylor, entrusting them "with power to employ the necessary persons to execute the repeatedly expressed wishes of the people, and appropriating certain funds to carry out the provisions of the ordinance." Wood and Taylor formed a consulting committee with Washington Irving, George Bancroft, and others. Wood also appointed a special force called the Central Park Police. Overseen by Captain J.W. Bennett, it worked out of a station house near 86th Street. The men wore the same uniform as the City Police, but their gray hats sported the letters C.P.P. The police presence was needed, if only to stop people from stripping the area's plantings. The *Evening Post* reported how "Trees have been cut down and carried off, valuable plants stolen, and every species of plunder carried on by thieves."[22]

Now that he was in charge, Wood appointed Viele engineer-in-chief and told him to start work. Viele, a West Point graduate who had fought in the Mexican-American War and on the southwestern frontier, had started a civil engineering office in New York, worked as a topographical engineer for the state of New Jersey, and prepared an engineering report on New York Harbor. Work began in May 1856. On June 13, Viele sent out surveying teams to determine the various grades in the park. They plotted off the land in 50-foot sections, delineated the topography, surveyed the watercourses, and listed geological profiles. The study was completed just a few days later; Viele had long hoped to design the park and had already started his work.

Viele was concerned with proper drainage to prevent disease. In 1855 he had created a "Plan of Drainage for the Grounds of the Central Park," and complained how it was "a pestilential spot, where rank vegetation and miasmatic odors taint every breath of air." He also saw its potential. And despite

his extensive derision of the site, he called for retaining much of the topography, stating that, "The hills, the valleys and the streams, are nature's
pencilings on the surface of the earth, rivaling, in their pictured grace, the
most beautiful conceptions of the finite mind; to alter them, would be dese-
cration; to erase them, folly!"[23]

While work got underway, Republicans in Albany, wary of Wood's involvement, sought to wrestle control of the park from him. Wood had long been a
thorn in their side. They placed it under a state-appointed commission, and
in April 1857 established a Board of Commissioners with six Republicans,
four Democrats, and one Know Nothing. Almost all the board members
were wealthy gentlemen. Thankfully they were also municipally minded, and
saw themselves as public stewards.

Quite a few residents continued to live on the land, and soon an announcement was issued ordering those remaining to abandon the site. The police
then arrived, and, according to a park report, removed or demolished 300
dwellings as well as "several factories, and numerous 'swill-milk' and hog-
feeding establishments." Then, on September 15, many of the remaining
park-site buildings were sold. John Lloyd & Sons Auctioneers handled the
sale, and terms for the buildings were cash only. Once bought, the structures
needed to be taken away in 30 days. The only ones that remained were the
Academy of Mount St. Vincent building, the Wagstaff House, the Bogardus
House, the Armory House, the Arsenal and Powder House, and the Geary
and Stantial Houses. [24]

As work got underway, Viele's vision was immediately called into question. His plans included a cricket ground, drives, lakes, and a 50-acre parade ground, and to some these appeared uninspired at best. Architect
Calvert Vaux, for one, sniffed that Viele's design lacked an artistic concept
and a central idea, calling it quite simply the wrong thing for the site. Vaux
also felt "that it would be a disgrace to the City and to the memory of Mr.
Downing . . . to have [Viele's] plan carried out."[25] As a protégé of Downing,
Vaux was in a powerful position from which to agitate. Born in London on
December 20, 1824, he apprenticed with the Gothic Revival style architect
Lewis Nockalls Cottingham and joined the Architectural Association in
London. When Downing visited England in 1850 in search of an assistant,
he saw Vaux's "Design for a Baptistery" at an association show and asked
the young man to join him in Newburgh. Vaux was immediately taken by
Downing—whose "thoughts and observations were so apparent"—and
"without a fear I relinquished all and accompanied him." Vaux settled in

Newburgh at Downing's Bureau of Architecture. He oversaw construction projects and designed rustic-looking houses that melded with Downing's landscapes. Among the firm's plans were those for the grounds of the White House. The practice proved successful. Downing made Vaux a partner, and British architect Frederick Clarke Withers then joined them. With Downing's death, Vaux and Withers continued the work. In 1854, Vaux married Mary Swan McEntee, the sister of Hudson River painter Jervis McEntee, and soon became a U.S. citizen.

Realizing that more business could be found downriver, the Vauxes relocated to New York, where Vaux quickly established his practice. He was hardworking and focused. A friend said that he had a "kindly and unselfish disposition [that] endeared him to every one with whom he was closely associated." Vaux joined the Century Club, the Athenaeum Club, and the National Academy of Design. In 1857 he published his *Villas and Cottages* and helped found the American Institute of Architects. Vaux not only knew Central Park commissioner Charles Elliott—who had worked with Downing—but helped build a house for Commissioner John A.C. Gray.

Vaux argued against Viele's plan, and was far from reticent about sharing his complaints, noting that, "I discussed the subject not only with [the] commissioners but with any other interested persons who cared to listen to my remarks." He distributed copies of his *Villas and Cottages* and lectured Gray, Elliott, and others of the shortcomings of Viele's design. He both advocated for a new plan and proposed a design competition. His agitation worked, and the commissioners rejected Viele's plan.[26]

A change was in the works, and its full ramifications became clear in August 1857, when a search for a superintendent to oversee the workers and the police was undertaken.

18

A Rural Retreat in the Gridded City

As the Central Park commissioners made plans to find a new designer and superintendent, Frederick Law Olmsted headed to an inn in Morris Cove, Connecticut. He went to work on the manuscript for his *A Journey in the Back Country*, the third of his books dealing with his trip through the South. While sitting at one of the tea tables, he spotted Central Park commissioner Charles Elliott. The two men knew each other through Charles Loring Brace, with whom Elliott helped start the Children's Aid Society. As a progressive Free Soiler, Elliott admired Olmsted's writing on slavery and helped him acquire weapons for anti-slave settlers in Kansas. Besides having studied with Andrew Jackson Downing, Elliott worked as a landscaper and appreciated the importance of nature. He told Olmsted about the progress at Central Park and how they were hiring workers. As Olmsted recalled, "He added that at their next meeting they intended to elect a Superintendent."

Olmsted then asked what the duties were, and Elliott explained them, indicating "that the park shall be managed independently of politics." Olmsted agreed that good management would be critically important. Elliott then asked why Olmsted would not be himself interested in the job. "Till he asked the question," recalled Olmsted, "the possibility of my doing so had never occurred to me, though he probably suspected I was thinking of it." He remembered saying that were it offered, he would take it. "Nothing interested me in London like the parks, and yet I thought a great deal more might be made of them." Elliott told him that it wasn't a matter of appointment, but that if he got "to work," Olmsted stood a chance of getting the job. Olmsted asked if he was serious. Elliott replied that he was. His advice: "Go to New York and file an application; see the Commissioners and get your friends to back you." Olmsted said he would take the boat back to New York that very night. "If no serious objection occurs to me before morning, I'll do it."[1]

He indeed rushed back to New York, and the following day met with James Hamilton, with whom he was also involved in the Free Soil campaign. The former U.S. Attorney offered his help in applying for the position, and Olmsted then brought Commissioner John Gray a letter of introduction from Elliott. Meanwhile Parke Godwin, an editor at the *New York Evening Post* whom Olmsted knew from *Putnam's Monthly Magazine*, wrote to Commissioner Andrew Green: "Let me assure you, that I know no man in the country better qualified than he for such a place." On August 12, 1857 Olmsted applied for the superintendent job, noting, "For the past sixteen years my chief interest and occupation has been with those subjects, familiarity with which is most needed in this office." He supplemented his petition with many "weighty signatures," including those of Hamilton, Washington Irving, William Cullen Bryant, and Peter Cooper.[2]

Olmsted then went to meet with Egbert Viele, but the Central Park engineer-in-chief essentially ignored him. Olmsted finally had the chance to sit alongside him in a streetcar running back to the city. "I then had an opportunity to state on what grounds I had ventured to think that he would find me useful as an assistant in his work," Olmsted recalled. Viele replied that he would rather have a practical man. "I did not learn why I could not be regarded as a possibly practical man, but it was only too evident that the gate of hope was closed to me in that direction." Olmsted was mistaken. When the commission sat to consider his application, it voted in his favor, hiring him on September 11. Olmsted later learned that the desire for a "practical man" would "have defeated me had it not been for the autograph of Washington Irving on my papers. That turned the balance."[3]

* * *

The new superintendent was a strong-willed, energetic man. And while he had flitted from occupation to occupation, he had what would prove to be the talent and the vision needed for a project on the scale of Central Park. Born on April 26, 1822, Olmsted was the son of a prominent Hartford merchant who sold dry goods, silks, woolens, and carpeting. He had a younger brother, John, and when Olmsted was three, their mother died from an accidental overdose after swallowing laudanum for a toothache. Fourteen months later, his father remarried and had six more children.

Olmsted had a somewhat haphazard education, attending various grammar and boarding schools. He considered himself "strangely uneducated—miseducated." He embraced the outdoors, playing and hiking in the Connecticut Valley. "The happiest recollections of my early life are the walks and rides I had with my father and the drives with my father and [step-] mother in the woods and fields." He later noted how he had "a rare fondness for natural scenery" and his stepmother had "a strong love of nature."[4]

Out in the open, he started to see the natural world and gained a respect for the "enjoyment of scenery, and extraordinary opportunities for cultivating susceptibility to its power." One of Olmsted's childhood friends recalled him as "a vigorous, manly fellow, of medium height, solidly built with rather broad shoulders and a large well formed head." He read voraciously, and later recalled how Johann Georg Zimmermann's *Solitude* was the first book that made him think about natural beauty. He likewise became fascinated with 18th- and 19th-century British authors, and through Reverend William Gilpin's *Remarks on Forest Scenery* as well as Sir Uvedale Price's *Essay on the Picturesque* he learned about landscape gardening and the creation of scenic landscapes.[5]

Design was not Olmsted's obvious career. In pre–Civil War America, landscape architecture wasn't even a profession. Thankfully, Olmsted had the insight and passion, as well as the financial resources, to explore all he fancied. Following his ill-fated 1843 trip to China aboard the *Ronaldson*, Olmsted took up farming, working near Waterbury, Connecticut, and then in Camillus, New York. In early 1847, with money from his father— whom Olmsted recalled as "the kindest and most indulgent of fathers"— Olmsted set up a farm at Sachem's Head on Long Island Sound. That August, Downing's *The Horticulturist* printed Olmsted's first piece, a letter from him on "the culture of the quince." In October he headed back to Downing's nursery to buy apple and quince trees, and at the time met with Alexander Jackson Davis to discuss a new house. Olmsted soon sold the farm and bought another in Staten Island, settling there in March 1848 on a place he named Tosomock Farm. There, Olmsted grew crops and fruits and started a nursery. He also began to amass a library, picking up books at New York auctions.[6]

In the spring of 1850, Olmsted, his brother John, and Brace sailed to Europe for a six-month visit. The trio hiked across the British countryside, making their way through Wales, Scotland, and England. Olmsted was smitten by the landscape. They visited farms, and parks like the newly opened Birkenhead Park near Liverpool. Impressed by what he saw at Birkenhead, Olmsted wrote a piece for *The Horticulturist*. Signing it "Wayfarer," he noted how after just a few minutes in the park, "I was ready to admit that in democratic America, there was nothing to be thought of as comparable with this People's Garden." He was especially taken by how many park-goers came from "the common ranks," noting that "The poorest British peasant is as free to enjoy it in all its parts, as the British Queen."

From there the group headed to Ireland, France, Belgium, Holland, and Germany. As they traveled, Olmsted collected material and planned his book *Walks and Talks of an American Farmer in England*. The volume appeared in 1852, with Olmsted dedicating the second half to Downing, who had died in that boat accident in July, three months before its publication. At the end of that year Olmsted began his reporting tours of the South for the *New York Times*, and in 1855 he started at publisher Dix & Edwards, working as managing editor of its *Putnam's Monthly Magazine*. There he met such authors as Irving, Henry Wadsworth Longfellow, Ralph Waldo Emerson, and Harriet Beecher Stowe. In 1856 he returned to Europe, visiting Italy and central Europe, saw the new parks of Paris, and lived in and explored London and its parks.[7] So, by the time Olmsted applied for the Central Park superintendent's job, though only 35, he already had more than the essential experience to be a "practical man."

Olmsted started at the park in September 1857. Viele had one of his assistants, a Mr. Hawkin, show him around the work site, and Olmsted recalled that while they were "Striking across the hill into what is now the Ramble," they came across some men gathering and burning brushwood. A man sat smoking under a tree, and Hawkin introduced him to Olmsted, telling the man that he would now be taking orders from him. "All the men within hearing dropped their tools and looked at me," recalled Olmsted. " 'Oh! That's the man is it? Expect we shall be pushed up, now.' He laughed, and the men grinned."

This process was repeated as they passed among some 15 gangs or about 500 men doing the same thing, randomly collecting and burning brush— and just as dismissive of their new boss. Despite his greeting, Olmsted quickly made his presence known. He explored the land and organized the workers. His efforts suitably impressed the commissioners, and by October they gave him the right to not only hire 1,000 workers but to dismiss those not doing their job. In January his salary was raised, putting it on par with Viele's. Writing his father, Olmsted noted, "I have got the park into a capital discipline, a perfect system, working like a machine."[8]

By this point Calvert Vaux's agitation for a new design for the park had worked, and on October 13 the commissioners announced a public competition and called for proposals. This was the first significant landscape competition in the country. Applicants received a copy of Viele's topographical map and were told that their idea had to contain at least four cross streets, a parade ground, three playgrounds, a concert hall, an exhibition hall, flower garden, a skating lake, fountain, and tower. The plan had to be prepared with India ink and sepia, and needed to include a written description. The final work could not cost more than $1.5 million to build, and there would be prize money for the winners.

Vaux hoped to submit a proposal for the park. He admired Olmsted's *Walks and Talks* book—the two had met in Newburgh—and asked the superintendent "to cooperate with preparation of a competition design for Central Park." Olmsted agreed with Vaux that Viele's original proposal looked as if it had been "staked off . . . from plans which they have formed with a rule and pencil in a broker's office," and the two formed a partnership. They proved a well-matched pair. Olmsted knew the land well. And with the recent death of Downing, the slightly younger Vaux—whom Olmsted called "the most ingenious, industrious and indefatigable man in his profession"— was the nation's most capable landscape designer. The team set to work. After Olmsted spent his days overseeing the land, he and Vaux explored the future-park area, and then passed their evenings at Vaux's home at 136 East 18th Street, working on their idea. It was a truly collaborative effort. Vaux did more of the drafting, and made watercolors and sketches. Olmsted wrote up the report, figured out the budget, and worked on ideas for the terrain.[9]

Olmsted and Vaux set out to create a beautiful, harmonious park. To present this, they enlisted family and friends, including the English architect Jacob Wrey Mould and Vaux's brother-in-law the painter Jervis McEntee, to prepare the materials, delineate the scheme, and even draw trees and bushes on a drawing on which they worked, which was ten feet in length. Vaux's son Downing, named for the horticulturist, wrote that "there was a great deal of grass to be put in by the usual small dots and dashes, and it became the friendly thing for friendly callers to help on the work by joining in and 'adding some grass to Central Park.'" They even hired photographer Mathew Brady to take pictures of the site. They then set the material on a dozen illustrative boards with Brady's "before" images along with Vaux's and McEntee's "after" oil sketches, thus creating what they called "Effect Proposed" images.[10]

The competition deadline was April 1, 1858. Thirty-three submissions arrived from assorted park engineers, surveyors, gardeners, and a property clerk. Applicants sent in proposals that included buildings designed in styles ranging from Chinese to Italianate, all set within both naturalistic as well as formal landscapes. The assorted plans called for, among other things, a crystal palace, a pyramid, shooting galleries for cannons, a carousel, a horse racing course, museums, zoos, and bathing houses. One offered an ornate series of gardens with glades and arbors shaped like stars and spirals. Another left nature much as it was. Yet another suggested curving drives and a large equestrian parade ground.

Vaux and Olmsted were the last to hand in a proposal. They titled it the "Greensward Plan," since it contained large grass-covered areas. Because they believed that the natural scenery should take precedence, they didn't set many architectural works in their plan, but did include such essential features as playing fields, a large fountain, exhibition buildings or music hall, and a skating pond. It took the commission four weeks and nine rounds of votes, and the six Republicans and the Reform Democrat Andrew Green voted in favor of the partners, awarding the pair the $2,000 first prize on April 28.

A few days later the men split their winnings. With the competition over, Vaux hoped to head back to his practice, telling Olmsted that he could use their plan so long as he was given credit. Olmsted urged Vaux to stay and, in the end, Vaux agreed. The two men started planning their unprecedented undertaking.

* * *

On 750 acres in the rocky heart of Manhattan, Vaux and Olmsted envisioned a vast stretch of land which they planned to integrate into the expanding city while keeping it as a separate retreat. In the spirit of British designers who turned rural spaces into crafted landscapes, the partners set out to create something that would not only look natural but improve on nature, an antidote to the pressures of civilization. Central Park, they hoped, would smooth out the disparities of wealth and, as Olmsted noted, in the process "supply to the hundreds of thousands of tired workers . . . a specimen of God's handiwork." For Vaux it was as a "big art work of the Republic." What they conjured would prove to be magical, and in its way historical for it would allow the city to retain a reminder of what the land had once been. And Olmsted wrote how "Then the priceless value of the present picturesque outlines of the ground will be more distinctly perceived, and its adaptability for its purpose more fully recognized."

With Vaux and Olmsted now in charge, the Central Park Commissioners let Viele go. Olmsted became architect-in-chief. The commission meanwhile made Vaux Olmsted's assistant, earning a per diem. This distinction and division of responsibilities rankled Vaux, since he was more of the team's designer while Olmsted was the administrator. The split led to the popular misconception that the park was solely Olmsted's design. Samuel Parsons Jr., who oversaw the park from 1881 to 1911, noted that while Vaux was "the creative artist," Olmsted "was a leader of men, a man of magnetism and charm, a literary genius."[11]

Olmsted and Vaux divided the park into the upper and lower areas, separated by a reservoir. Olmsted noted that the northern section was left much as it was: "The horizon lines of the upper park are bold and sweeping and the slopes have great breadth in almost every aspect in which they may be contemplated." Because of that, he stipulated that "formal planting and architectural effects" should be avoided. For the southern area, which "is far more heterogeneous in its character, and will require a much more varied treatment," the partners believed that the rocky hillsides to the south of the reservoir were the "most important feature in its landscape" and should be preserved, to provide views as well as "to afford facilities for rest and leisurely contemplation upon the rising ground opposite."

Creating this man-made confection was no easy task and required focused planning. To do it, Olmsted set up house there. Olmsted's brother John had died in November 1857, and his widow, Mary, came to New York with her three children. Mayor Daniel Tiemann married Mary and Olmsted in a home in the park on Bogardus Hill—now Great Hill—on June 13, 1859. In the process, Olmsted became stepfather to his brother's children. The family settled in the Sisters of Charity's Mount St. Vincent building at 109th Street. The Vauxes and their children, meanwhile, lived in the nearby priest's residence.[12]

The massive undertaking required a reliable staff and labor crew. Vaux oversaw the architecture, and later had his title changed to Consulting Architect and earned a regular salary. He appointed Mould the associate architect. Mould—who had studied with the British architect Owen Jones—handled many structures in the park, from a bandstand to designing or supervising the construction of more than 40 bridges. As John Jervis did two decades earlier when he prepared the Croton system, Olmsted searched for reliable supervisors. For park superintending engineer he appointed William H. Grant. Below Grant spread out a hierarchical group of men who had learned their trade working on canals, water systems, and railroads—with an assistant engineer in charge of each of the park's sections.

The creation of the park coincided with the Panic of 1857. Businesses failed, banks stopped making specie payments, and people lost work. Job applications swamped Olmsted's office, and public officials pressured him to hire many who lacked qualifications. "I have heard a candidate for a magisterial office in the city addressing from my doorsteps a crowd of advice-bearers," he wrote, "telling them that I was bound to give them employment, and suggesting plainly, that, if I was slow about it, a rope round my neck might serve to lessen my reluctance to take good counsel." Some job seekers were aggressive in their tactics, finding their way to his house and breaking into the drawing-room "in their eagerness to deliver letters of advice." The threat of lynching wasn't idle. For several days, a mob carrying a banner proclaiming "Bread or Blood" surrounded Olmsted's office. On November 16 the crowd got unruly, and to keep the workers at bay, armed police set up artillery on Fifth Avenue. More came out the following days. Olmsted wasn't the only one so harassed. "I have seen a president of the Park Board surrounded by a mob of similar bearers of advice, in Union Square," he wrote.[13]

To reduce the crowds, it was announced that all those seeking work would receive notice at their homes. Olmsted hired the most qualified he could get, and under his watch the park soon became the largest employer in the city. Construction got underway, and by the end of 1858 some 2,300 men labored there, growing to 3,600 workers in September 1859. A fifth of those employed were artisans, with 30 blacksmiths, 300 cart-men, and 160 stonecutters. The Irish comprised three-quarters of the laborers. There were also gardeners and Italian craftsmen. Very few women found work. And since whites often walked off jobs if they had to work alongside African Americans, no Blacks found employment. With so large a work site, Olmsted insisted on constant oversight, and supervisors turned in daily progress reports. While he "rigidly discharged any man who failed to work industriously & to behave in a quiet & orderly manner," in general he found the workers of "the most perfect order, peace & good feeling preserved."[14]

Wielding shovels, axes, and pickaxes to dig ditches, fell trees, and uproot bushes, the workers tore down stone walls and broke up rocks. Steam engines drove derricks, horse teams pulled rollers to even out the land. Hundreds of men used horses to raise the grade of Fifth Avenue. In the process, they cut out 300,000 cubic yards of gneiss, ridges, and large boulders by means of 166 tons of gunpowder. Thousands of cartloads of loose stone were removed and used to build the park's outer wall. At the same time, the men made paving stones and carted in millions of bricks, tens of thousands of barrels of cement, and massive amounts of gravel and sand. The work could also be dangerous. Five men died during construction. While laboring in a bog on 79th Street, more than 20 workers came down with fever and suffered from hot and cold sweating fits. In preparation for this, Olmsted had established a sick-fund society that took care of the ill.

George Waring created a system to drain the low and swampy area. Crews dug ditches and lay clay pipes and tiles to open up clogged pools and streams. To form Sheep's Meadow—which was then called the Parade—they blasted out rocks on the west side in the 60s and filled up a stretch of boggy land with topsoil. Excavated clay went toward creating the beds of artificial lakes and streams. Meanwhile, work got underway in 1858 to fashion a new reservoir. Called "Lake of Manahatta," the 96-acre, billion-gallon body of water stretched from Fifth to Seventh Avenues and 86th to 96th Streets.

The park had 50 gardeners, most of them of German extraction, who were supervised by the Austrian landscaper Ignaz Pilat. Much had to be added to the area. "Nearly all the earth needed for the growth of the trees and shrubs south of Seventy-second Street had to be brought in from the outside," recalled Olmsted's cousin George Putnam, who spent the summer of 1859 working under Pilat. From 1859 to 1863, the men planted tens of thousands of trees and shrubs, shaped slopes, arranged boulders, and laid out lawns. And while former park inhabitants had cut down much of the area's trees and shrubbery, the site still contained maple, elm, sweet gum, poplars, and black walnut, as well as privets, mulberries, bayberry, alders, witch hazel, and sassafras. All offered the gardeners a wide selection to choose from.[15]

Central Park's focal point was to be the Ramble, a 36-acre spot in the 70s that Olmsted saw as a "wild garden" where visitors could wander through woods and plantings and discover nature. The woodland with its streams, meadows, pond, large exposed boulders, and bridges was to give the area a feel of the Adirondacks. Near to it sat Bethesda Terrace, a spot that Vaux viewed as an "open air hall of reception." It proved to be the most ambitious and formal part of the park. Vaux and Mould laid out a grand promenade leading toward it, and in 1858 set rows of young elms along the quarter-mile path. The promenade's northern point sweeps down a grand staircase, through a subterranean arcade covered with 16,000 colorful Minton tiles designed by Mould, and the walls sport trompe l'oeil paintings. The arcade, which the designers saw as a shelter from the weather, serves as a sort of open-air reception area. The brownstone carvings throughout the terrace reference the wilds with animals, nesting birds, plants, the seasons—and phases of the day with a rooster, owl, and a bat. All this leads to a 20-acre lake, which the partners fashioned on the site of a former swamp.

They also laid out three types of roads in the park: drives for carriages, bridle paths for horses, and walkways for strollers. And since traffic needed access across the park, they created curving routes as part of a relaxed grid that included transverse roads that required extensive excavations and the construction of bridges. Some of the roads were sunk below grade so that those in the park would not see passing traffic—in the same way that the British fashioned sunken fences, otherwise known as "Ha-Has." As Vaux and Olmsted noted, visitors would only see the park's "undulating outlines, and picturesque, rocky scenery," and would not notice the "coal carts and butchers' carts, dust carts and dung carts."[16]

Central Park became the nation's biggest public works project. As with the Croton system, it quickly went over budget. Commissioners complained about the cost of matériel, such as the stone for bridges. They preferred marble, while Vaux advocated for the more expensive bluestone. When Commissioner Andrew Green became park comptroller in late 1859, he set out to rein in overruns. Olmsted would complain how "Not a dollar, not a cent, is got from under his paw that is not wet with his blood & sweat." Such oversight was needed, for the budget soon reached $2 million, and in 1860 the state legislature had to raise an additional $2.5 million to cover new costs.[17]

* * *

With work progressing, rules and regulations for the park needed to be established. "A large part of the people of New York are ignorant of a park, properly so-called," Olmsted wrote to the commissioners. "They will need to be trained to the proper use of it." To make this possible, he organized the men dubbed "Sparrow Cops" who were tasked with supervising and educating the public. In March 1859, Olmsted presented the "Rules and Conditions of Service of the Central Park Keepers." Officers needed to stand tall, could not "receive or drink ardent spirits when on the Park." And to avoid malingering, "He shall not stand at one point or in one part of his beat more than five minutes at a time in conversation." Likewise, no commercial vehicles could enter the park, roads had set speed limits, and no grazing animals were allowed.

While construction moved at a fast clip, for the average New Yorker it seemed to be a long process. Residents hankered to get in. The first people to use the park were probably some 300 skaters who came to the lake on a Sunday in December 1858. The spot was fed by Croton Water, and the following week 10,000 showed up, and on Christmas Day even more. Soon hotel keepers set up tents and sold refreshments, vendors rented skates for 10¢ an hour, and poor boys could earn a few coins helping wealthy visitors put on their blades. Some women found secluded spots to skate, and clubs of Scottish curlers sporting plaid shawls came with their curling stones. As Olmsted had hoped, the spot quickly revealed its democratic qualities, with the *New York Herald* reporting that "Masters Richard and William from Fifth avenue in their furs, and plain Dick and Bill from avenues nearer the rivers, with bunting flying and joints and middle seams, were all mingled in joyful unity, forgetting the distinction of home in their enjoyment of a common patrimony—free air and free water."[18]

Besides being a talented architect, Jacob Mould was also an accomplished musician. He and others believed that sound should likewise be incorporated into the park's design, and convinced Olmsted and officials of the need for entertainment. The straw-hatted band leader Harvey B. Dodworth gave the inaugural concert on the Ramble on July 9, 1859. An audience of some 5,000 listened while the band performed the *Festmarsch* and chorus from *Tannhäuser*, and selections from *La Traviata*, *Robert le Diable*, and *Il Trovatore*. The regular concerts proved highly popular. There were printed programs, and hundreds of gentlemen and ladies on horseback and in carriages, as well as a crush of pedestrians, gathered to enjoy the music. They soon formalized the concerts, and Mould designed a Moorish-style confection for the players.

The *Herald* marveled how Central Park was having a healthy effect on society. Sunday, July 24, 1859, was a clear day. Liquor stores and groggeries were generally closed, and 10,000 to 15,000 citizens came to the park to enjoy some afternoon music. Most visitors were middle-class professionals who walked there or took public transportation. The area was seen as a safe place for young women for an outing. Olmsted marveled at the civilizing effect the place had—a "refining influence upon the most unfortunate and most lawless classes of the city—an influence favorable to courtesy, self-control, and temperance."[19]

Most who visited the spot had no idea of the amount of work it had taken to create it. When Horace Greeley came by for his first look, the editor was stunned by his sense that little had been done, reportedly saying, "Well, they have let it alone a good deal more than I thought they would!" George Templeton Strong went to the site with his son John and friend George Anthon in June 1859. Unlike Greeley, though, he noted the vast changes and how it "will be a feature of the city within five years and a lovely place in A.D. 1900, when its trees will have acquired dignity and appreciable diameters." As the trio toured, they could hear the construction blasting going on. They explored the Ramble, and Strong wrote how while much of it was finished, the lower part of the park was in a "most ragged condition: long lines of incomplete macadamization, 'lakes' without water, mounds of compost, piles of blasted stone, acres of what may be greensward hereafter but is now mere brown earth, groves of slender young transplanted maples and locusts, undecided between life and death."

Strong returned that September to look over the southern part and was pleased with the progress made. "The system and order and energy of the work are very creditable, considering especially the scale on which it's conducted." By the following May, he observed that, "The park below the reservoir begins to look intelligible. Unfinished still, and in process of manufacture, but shewing the outline now of what it is to be."[20]

Tens of thousands came for each new opening, and in 1860, 2.5 million visited the park. The place became a place to display one's horses and carriages. Bridle paths proved very popular, as did carriage rides. The *Herald* reported in November 1860 that it was not uncommon to find 3,000 to 4,000 people in the park in costly vehicles, everything from "the sulkey to the dashing four-in hand carriage." Those who couldn't afford such carriages could hire one for $1 to $2 an hour from livery stables. But since work wagons and carts were not allowed in the park even if taking families, the rules restricted the democratic tone that Olmsted had hoped to establish and kept some artisans and others away. And people were not allowed on the grass except for some areas on Saturday, a rule that discouraged workers from spreading out blankets and picnicking. The poor came less often, since a streetcar trip there was too expensive for them.[21]

Building the park proved exhausting, and Olmsted wrote his father in September 1859 that "I have been growing weaker & more deeply fatigued since I began with it." That month, Olmsted took a trip to Europe to recover. There he visited not only English and continental parks and estates, and studied the work of 18th-century garden designer Lancelot "Capability" Brown, but also familiarized himself with sewage and drainage systems, bought shrubs and trees, and hired a photographer to take reference photos for his future plans. On June 14, 1860, Mary gave birth to their first child, John Theodore. Then on August 6, the couple went out for a ride. Their horse bolted, and Olmsted was thrown from the carriage and broke his thigh in three places, leaving him with a slight limp. A worse blow occurred eight days later when John died from cholera infantum.[22]

Yet the park was growing and attracting notice. In early 1860, the German city of Hamburg donated a number of swans to the park, and others soon arrived from England. The illustrator and painter Winslow Homer created wood engravings for *Harper's Weekly*, and Nathaniel Currier and James Merritt Ives turned out lithographic scenes. But the big inaugural event was the visit to the United States of the Prince of Wales, Albert Edward. The future King Edward VII arrived in America in October 1860, slept at the White House, visited Mount Vernon, and was roundly wined and dined. In New York, a committee of some 400, including William Backhouse Astor, Peter Cooper, and Cornelius Vanderbilt, feted him. The 18-year-old prince stayed at the Fifth Avenue Hotel, and Wood showed him around town.

The park was part of the prince's itinerary, and a large crowd gathered at the Mall and the Ramble. Olmsted showed up with 200 park laborers. The royal visitor came to plant an English Oak, while Commissioner Green was to put in an American Elm. Not knowing how to plant a tree, the prince asked Green what to do, and later in life Green pleasurably recalled how he handed him a shovel and advised him to simply dig. As the prince prepared to leave, someone pointed Olmsted out for him. "He turned & bowed to me several times until he caught my attention and I returned his salute," recalled Olmsted. Wood hosted the prince at his home. Guests included former president Millard Fillmore, Archbishop John Hughes, and James Gordon Bennett. Dodworth's band supplied the music. From there, the prince visited the Institution for the Instruction of the Deaf and Dumb and attended a ball at the Academy of Music. George and Ellen Strong met him at the Academy. Strong shook his hand, and he then joked in his diary that, "I think of having my right-hand glove framed and glazed, with an appropriate inscription." The next night, over a hundred fire companies turned out carrying lamps and calcium lights for a torchlight parade in the royal's honor.[23]

While the Jones and Schermerhorn families retained their Jones' Wood property, they leased part of their land for a park. And though the area didn't become the retreat some had envisioned, people still flocked there. The working class felt more comfortable in Jones' Wood than in Central Park. There they could enjoy themselves without Olmsted's restrictions. They spread out on the picnic grounds, visited the dance pavilion, watched circus performances, played ten-pin and billiards, went on a balloon flight, rooted at boxing matches, showed off their marksmanship at the shooting galleries, took donkey rides, browsed through shops and tents offering sandwiches, cakes, pies, oysters, lobsters, beer, cheese, and sausages, and watched fireworks. In July 1859, Jones' Wood held a music festival, attracting thousands.

Yet the spot lacked the breath and sublime beauty of Vaux and Olmsted's Central Park creation. And following a fire that swept through and destroyed it in 1894, Jones' Wood became absorbed into the gridded development that had transformed so much of the city. That regimented street pattern would never find its way into Central Park, a sylvan retreat whose creation belied the impending turmoil that was about to enflame the United States.

19

A Melting Pot Boils Over

It all began when an Irish American reportedly overturned an old woman's apple stall at the corner of Pearl and Chatham Streets. Locals argued with the man, and a fight broke out between members of a nativist gang, the American Guards, and Irish American residents. The fight spilled across Chatham Square and into Cross Street. There, the battlers hurled rocks, bricks, and anything else they could pick up. "A great number of the combatants had broken heads and black eyes," reported the *New York American.*

Behind the fight were tensions from reports that Irish immigrants were seeking to form the O'Connell Guards, a local militia named in honor of the Irish nationalist leader Daniel O'Connell. Nativists saw this as an affront to the United States. For a number of days in June 1835, only six months before the Great Fire, fights raged in the Five Points. Rioters broke into homes and saloons, and some attempted to attack St. Patrick's Cathedral on Mulberry Street.[1]

Such brawls regularly broke out in the city over issues both slight and large. In February 1839, a tavern keeper invited friends and neighbors to celebrate the opening of his porter house—a bar that attracted sailors, laborers, and other workers—on Willett and Broome Streets. As his 40 guests danced and enjoyed themselves, some gang members who also were volunteers with Black Joke Engine Company No. 33 stopped by and asked for free drinks. The celebrants refused their request, and the men then tried to break down the door. As they struggled, one gang member pulled out a Bowie knife and stabbed a guest to death.

Gang fighting was a common source of violence in early- to mid-19th-century New York. On New Year's Eve 1839, members of the nativist Bowery Boys gang rampaged through the city's streets and forced their way into homes, smashing furniture. They then went to Valentine Mager's house of entertainment on Elizabeth Street. Mager's patrons were mainly German American, and danced and celebrated the New Year in what Philip Hone noted was "a decent orderly manner." The gang "proceeded to break the glasses and furniture, insult the females, and commit the most disgraceful excesses." Mager's friends drove away the rioters. But the gang returned with reinforcements, and Mager reported that one of his guests "was stabbed in the forehead, near the eye, with a dirk." Both sides pulled out pistols and guns, and someone shot "a hopeful butt-ender"—a man who hoped to join a fire house—who was attached to Hose Company No. 43.[2]

Groups such as the Bowery Boys, the Chichesters, the Kerryonians, the Forty Thieves, the Atlantic Guards, the Plug Uglies, and the True Blue Americans were omnipresent in New York, and their appeal was to offer young male members status, alcohol, and a chance to rebel against a system seemingly stacked against them. These proto–wise guys drew membership largely from apprentices or journeymen, those like the youthful William Tweed, who found more excitement running around with the Cherry Hillers than working in a musty workshop. Gang membership tended to increase during economic downturns. And with the shift in the economy and the transformation of trades, many realized that since they might never attain the title of Master, they could at least gain prestige by joining a gang.

Each such gang sported proud and sometimes ominous monikers. Many dressed in colorful and unusual garb. The Shirt Tails, naturally, kept their tops untucked. The Roach Guards wore baggy, blue-striped slacks. The Dead Rabbits sometimes carried a standard displaying a dead rabbit impaled on a spike. For the gangs, territorial borders became deadly flash points as members eagerly tumbled into battle wearing hobnail stomping boots and armed with everything from clubs and brickbats to bludgeons and pistols.

In New York, gang-related attacks and assaults broke out constantly. Fights, brawls, and rowdyism were a fact of life. More than just gangs were involved. In January 1836, when the editors of the *New York Sun* heard from the police that James Watson Webb at the *Morning Courier and New-York Enquirer* had threatened to attack them, they let it be known that he would find that the *Sun*'s staff had armed itself with a "brace of 'mahogany stock' pistols." And in late September 1845, the *New York Tribune* commented on a fight, writing that there was a "characteristic row at the Five Points between a parcel of drunken negroes, white men, women, watchmen."[3]

Elections were an especially fertile time for violence. Voting in pre–Civil War New York had long been a wild free-for-all. In November 1832, when Andrew Jackson ran against Henry Clay for the presidency, the *New York Evening Post* reported how "a gang of Anti-Jackson desperados of the Fourteenth Ward" caused a disturbance and, waving clubs, rushed to the Seventh Ward, "possessing themselves of the ballot-boxes, destroying them." In April 1834, a riot convulsed New York during its first mayoral election. A change in the New York State constitution expanded voting to most white adults, and for three days Whigs and Democrats attacked each other and destroyed opponents' ballot boxes. The polling led to the narrow victory of the Democrat and Tammany candidate Cornelius Lawrence, with the Whigs winning the majority of aldermen and assistant alderman seats. And in November 1849, no one was surprised by what the *New York Herald* called "little game of fisticuffs" that broke out at the polling place on Broadway in the First Ward. Or how, in the Sixth Ward, a large crowd had arrived early to watch the anticipated, as that paper put it, "Great fun, broken heads and rioting."[4]

* * *

Violence grew as it became politicized, and as government stopped being the patrician affair it was when Hone served as mayor in 1826. Ethnic, cultural, and social struggles rippled through the city, reflecting the tragic side of New York's extraordinary growth. As a sense of privilege expanded during the Age of Jackson, democratic impulses turned violent. Many felt a sense of entitlement, and they sought to demonstrate their rights with both their ballots and their fists. This led to a spike in violent encounters at polling places and in public gatherings such as in the city's theaters.

Polarization was evident in New York's Dickensian juxtaposition of grinding poverty and great wealth, of grime and polish, of want and entitlement. The city was a split between the best-of-times haves and the worst-of-times have-nots, between the politically sophisticated and the socially dispossessed. While each side existed in a world apart, living in proximity meant continuous friction. The rich supported such cultural institutions as the Astor Place Opera House, browsed in grand shops like the Marble Palace, attended openings at high-end theaters like the Park, and dined at Delmonico's. A growing working class frequented taverns, plays at the Bowery Theatre, oyster cellars, beer halls, and Punch and Judy shows.

No two characters represented polarized pre–Civil War New York society as much as actors William Macready and Edwin Forrest. Macready, the refined English Shakespearean, appealed to the elite. Philip Hone had considered Macready "a gentleman." Meanwhile, Forrest was Philadelphia-born and known for his bluster and swagger, always receiving thunderous applause from Bowery Theatre regulars. On seeing Forrest, British actress Fanny Kemble gushed a little, calling him "A mountain of a man!"[5]

Both Forrest and Macready arrived in New York in 1826 and quickly became adversaries on the stage, both in the United States and abroad. Their
rivalry intensified in the mid-1840s when an audience booed Forrest off a
British stage during a tour. He accused Macready of inciting the crowd
against him. In response, Forrest hissed at the British actor during one of his
Edinburgh performances of *Hamlet*. Believing that Macready and his fans
then maligned him, Forrest vowed that Macready would receive a like reception in the United States. The actor easily tapped into growing nation-
alism along with working-class resentment at the tastes of the ruling class.
While Americans welcomed some foreign entertainers like the Swedish
soprano Jenny Lind and the Norwegian violinist Ole Bull, and embraced
the English-born Thomas Hamblin and his Bowery Theatre, New York
theaters enjoyed a tradition of foreigner bashing. Plays presented the British
characters as shallow, foppish, and pompous buffoons alongside solid, self-
reliant Americans.[6]

In 1825 a rumor circulated that the British actor Edmund Kean had
insulted an audience in Boston. When he appeared in New York, the audience wouldn't allow him to act. Kean quickly ran a letter in the newspaper
stating that, "Whatever are my offences, I disclaim all intention of offering
any thing in shape of disrespect towards the inhabitants of NEW-YORK."
A riot erupted during Joshua Anderson's appearance at the Park in 1831 over
his supposedly negative comments about Americans, leading Hone to comment of the "deafening shouts of 'Off! Off! Go back to England!'" as well
as nights of attacks on the theater. During the 1834 anti-abolitionist riots, a
mob stormed the Bowery because its British stage manager George Farren
had reportedly disparaged Americans. The crowd only backed off when
Forrest calmed them down. In response, Hamblin renamed the theater the
American Theatre, Bowery. A month after the riot, Hamblin also announced
how the theater would "pursue more diligently than ever . . . the encourage-
ment and promotion of Native American Talent." And in 1848, the dancer
George Washington Smith refused to dance the "Polka Nationale" with Julia
Turnbull at the Bowery, explaining that he was scheduled to perform with
an Italian dancer Giovanna Ciocca. Turnbull spoke to the audience, saying
that Smith preferred to dance with "a foreigner." The audience started yelling,
"Native Talent!" and spent an hour breaking benches and chandeliers. As the
Brooklyn Evening Star noted, "Truly we are a great people!"[7]

Tensions thus proved high when Macready returned to America for a
tour in 1849. Newspapers lapped up and spat out the theatrical venom,

with the *New York Herald* proclaiming the opening rounds of "The Theatrical Prize-Fight." Forrest had criticized Macready in the press, and when the British actor performed in Cincinnati, someone threw a sheep carcass onto the stage. Things started to spin out of control that May as Macready wrapped up his tour at the Astor Place Opera House. Macready was scheduled to play Macbeth there, so Forrest opted on performing the same play at the Broadway Theatre to the south. Realizing that audiences would be flocking to his competition, Hamblin decided to put on the play at the Bowery with himself playing the lead, and his wife, Eliza, as Lady Macbeth.

Forrest's American followers could not stand the idea of the British actor strutting across a nearby stage. The novelist E.Z.C. Judson, who went by the name Ned Buntline, railed against Macready in his periodical *Ned Buntline's Own*, imploring readers to give Macready the same treatment Forrest had received in Britain. Captain Isaiah Rynders, whom we've seen was a firebrand, meanwhile distributed dozens of tickets to the Astor Place performance to Forrest loyalists and members of fire companies. Fearing trouble during the May 7 performance, Chief of Police George W. Matsell posted deputies in the house. Hone recalled how during the play, Macready "was saluted with a shower of missiles, rotten eggs, and other unsavory objects, with shouts and yells of the most abusive epithets." The actor exited the stage and planned to head home, and changed his mind only after Washington Irving, Herman Melville, and others wrote an open letter "requesting you to reconsider your decision."[8]

Macready agreed to give it one more go on the night of the 10th. Forrest was appearing again at the Broadway, this time as Spartacus in *The Gladiator*. And of course, Hamblin planned to strut the Bowery's stage as Macbeth. That evening, Forrest's followers decided that a more serious display of American anti-British sentiment needed to be made. Rynders printed handbills proclaiming, "WORKING MEN, SHALL AMERICANS OR ENGLISH RULE! IN THIS CITY?" and called on people to "STAND BY YOUR LAWFUL RIGHTS!" When Macready entered the Astor stage in the third act, it was, according to the *Tribune*, "the signal for a perfect storm of cheers, groans and hisses." Soon thousands encircled the building. Buntline waved a sword and egged on the crowd, which yelled, "Burn the damned den of the aristocracy." The mob hurled bricks and stones. "Volley after volley of large paving stones was discharged against the windows." The glass was, of course, "in a few moments, all smashed to atoms."

General Charles Sandford showed up with the state militia. And as the troops and the police massed, the crowd was warned to disperse. A man shouted, "Fire, if you dare take the life of a free-born American for a bloody British actor!" A warning volley was shot, and then the troops fired their weapons into the crowd, killing 22 and wounding 150. Many innocent bystanders died.

The outrage was immediate. A rally at City Hall attracted furious protesters, with state assemblyman Mike Walsh calling the killings an "atrocity." The group headed back toward Astor Place, and somehow soldiers, police, and special constables dispersed the crowd. After that, the Astor Place Opera House earned the nickname "Upper-Row House in Disaster Place" and the "Massacre Opera House." It never recovered from the assault.[9]

* * *

Isaiah Rynders and Mike Walsh were far from the first to tap into cultural, political, and racial tensions in a city that Walt Whitman called "the Gomorrah across the East river." New York had come to be seen, rightly, as a free-for-all and a violent place. Cock fighting was popular, and at places like Patsy Hearn's grogshop, men huddled around a pit and bet on how many rats trained terriers could kill. High- and low-class gambling houses began popping up around the city in the early 1830s. Lottery shops in 1830 sold $9 million worth of tickets. That form of gambling was outlawed soon after. But while lotteries were banned, citizens could still buy tickets from other states. Mayor Fernando Wood's brother Benjamin held southern monopolies to run these games of chance in the city. It brought in big money, and when a reformer named John Bradford wrote a letter to the *Tribune* about the dangers of gambling and implied that Wood was a culprit, Wood headed to his Beaver Street office and assaulted him with a cowhide.[10]

Benjamin and Fernando Wood (who was of course complicit), like many others with similar money-making schemes, were loath to let anyone interfere with their business. Gambling was hugely profitable, and to keep it from being banned meant controlling the seats of political power in New York. There were numerous ways to tap into that power. There was the firehouse— as we've seen with William Tweed—along with the police station. Just as importantly, there was the saloon. Over the course of the first half of the 19th century, drinking establishments served as social and political community centers, a place not just to have a drink but to organize and mobilize. The connection between politics and drinking was a close one. As the

British writer Frederick Marryat noted in 1839, "Americans can *fix* nothing, without a drink. If you meet, you drink; if you part, you drink; if you make acquaintance, you drink; if you close a bargain, you drink; they quarrel in their drink, and they make it up with a drink."[11] Drinking establishments catered to assorted social, political, and ethnic groups. There were the "three-cent" houses, also called porter houses. The more upscale taverns or saloons were called "six-cent" houses, and appealed to clerks as well as artisans and tradesmen. New York had so many places to down a dram that Chief Matsell reported in 1849 that New York possessed 3,814 licensed and 729 unlicensed ones.

The ambitious figured out how to earn enough to open a saloon and then use it to gain political standing. The link between liquor and politics proved so clear that in 1856, the *Tribune* reported how "Nearly *fifty*, or more than *one third*, of the polls in the city are located in Rum Shops. Some of these are among the worst places of the kind in the city, and offer the amplest facilities for stuffing, double-voting, destruction of boxes, false returns." A number of polls were likewise set in fire houses, and some complained that "rum elected their Presidents, rum made their Governors, and rum their officers of State."[12]

More than a few prominent leaders got their start in saloons. When Tweed and his mates set out to form the Americus Fire Company, they held their first meeting at the Vivaramble beer saloon. Rynders' saloon became the headquarters of his Empire Club. John Morrissey dispatched his intimidating "shoulder hitters" from his Belle of the Union Saloon and gambling house. William "Bill the Butcher" Poole opened a bar called the Bank Exchange Saloon, and from there orchestrated the efforts of nativist gangs. And Poole's like-minded pal Tom Hyer had the Branch saloon on the Bowery.

The chumminess between politically savvy barkeeps and politicians directly affected the administration of justice. By the mid-1850s, 15 percent of office-holding Democrats owned saloons, and as a further sign of the closeness, there were just 39 arrests for selling spirituous liquor without a license from mid-July 1845 through December 1850, despite the fact that there were more than 65,000 infractions for intoxication and disorderly conduct. If a criminal knew the right people, he could simply be released on the say-so of a politician, alderman, or a local magistrate, a practice that caused George Templeton Strong to observe in July 1852 that, "if some drunken ruffian is arrested, he's sure to be discharged by some justice or alderman, who feels that it won't do to lose the support of the particular gang to which he belongs." It didn't matter if the prisoner robbed a corner store or assaulted a fireman. This state of affairs made Fire Chief Alfred Carson lament in 1850 to the Board of Aldermen that even if the police arrested gang members for attacking firemen, they "were no sooner in prison than the Captains of Police, the Aldermen, and Judges of Police, would discharge them to commit fresh attacks on the firemen the following night."[13]

And while drinking holes could be convivial places and political head-quarters, they could also be places where rivals settled grudges. When former deputy keeper of the city prisoners Archibald Reynolds refused a drink at Carleton House from Rynders, Tom Burns, and saloon keeper Mike "the Mick" Murray, they knocked him down and beat him. Murray once had gotten into a fight with Patrick "Paudeen" McLaughlin, and while Hyer held McLaughlin down, Murray bit off a large part of his nose. In October 1851, the butchers Poole and Hyer entered Florence's Hotel. They then attacked barkeep Charles Owens, and according to the New York Times, "beat his face to a jelly." In the summer of 1853, Poole was at the Gem Saloon. Former policeman Lewis Baker then walked in. They had words, and Poole tried to gouge out his eyes.[14]

Not surprisingly, a saloon was where the demise of Poole took place. He and Morrissey had a bitter and long-running feud. They had sparred at Amos Street in July 1854, and Poole handily beat Morrissey in just a few minutes. Animosity between the two men simmered, and in February 1855 they collided at the recently opened Stanwix Hall. Morrissey had been drinking with friends when he saw Poole. Morrissey called him a cowardly son of a bitch, and Poole tarred him as a liar. Poole brandished his Colt five-shooter, and someone ran to get Morrissey a pepper-box pistol. The police stopped the fight, and Morrissey headed home. Poole, though, stayed, and soon some of Morrissey's pals, Baker, McLaughlin, and James Turner, confronted him. McLaughlin locked the doors, guns and knives came out. The two sides fought, and Baker shot Poole in the chest. The butcher clung to life at his Christopher Street home until March 8, reportedly proclaiming in his last breath, "I die a true American."

Editor Horace Greeley, for one, hoped that Poole's death would put "a check upon that rampant ruffianism." In fact, it only elevated the butcher to the status of nativist martyr. A quarter of a million people lined the streets and peered from windows during Poole's funeral procession. When his flag-draped coffin—with "I die a true American!" printed in silver on black velvet hanging from the hearse—reached Grand Street, hundreds of butchers removed their hats and kneeled. After the funeral in Brooklyn's Green-Wood Cemetery, the Poole Guards and Poole Light Guards returned to Manhattan. There, they were set upon by Morrissey along with members of Engine No. 36 and gang members from the Buttenders and Short Boys. In retaliation, the Poole Guards and Light Guards burned down No. 36's firehouse.[15]

* * *

The fighting in New York was aimed at gaining some kind of advantage, whether respect, prestige, money, power, revenge, or civic control. The tendrils of the city's politics stretched from City Hall to gang dens. Those in power doled out jobs—street sweepers, clerks, and of course, police officers. For those wanting to become a policeman, the backing of a politician was enough. Once hired, a policeman then needed to stay in the good graces of someone politically connected, very often a saloonkeeper. Policemen earned fees instead of a salary, and secured rewards for recovering goods instead of apprehending criminals. Because of this, they rarely shared information with their colleagues. "It is not customary for one officer to tell his business to another officer," noted one policeman in 1840. Throughout, little discipline was brought to bear on the officers. When dismissed for such infractions as falling asleep or drinking on duty, they generally found work in another ward under the protection of a different alderman, ward heeler, or—yet again—a saloonkeeper.[16]

In 1835, the year of the Great Fire, only seven people were killed or murdered. But with the explosive growth of the city came higher numbers. From July 1845 through December 1853, the police arrested 160 people for murder, 1,061 for assault with intent to kill, and 293 for threatening life. Unreported deaths were common.

New York City was becoming a dangerous place. Pickpockets and thieves prowled the streets and skulked around the docks. Whitman offered simple "Advice to Strangers": "Don't go wandering about the streets or parks unnecessarily in the evening," since "New York is one of the most crime-haunted and dangerous cities in Christendom." In 1832, to contain the growing criminal elements, a castle-like penitentiary had been built on Blackwell's Island in the East River. A few years later, a new jail went up on Centre Street. The Halls of Justice and House of Detention contained 148 cells. This imposing gray granite structure by architect John Haviland looked like it sprung from ancient Egypt, earning the nickname the Tombs. Its reputation was grim. Charles Dickens heard of an inmate there who was "half-eaten by the rats in an hour's time."[17]

A reliable police force was desperately needed. Yet calls for police reform long fell on deaf ears until the 1841 murder of Mary Cecilia Rogers. The young woman worked at a tobacco shop on Broadway and Liberty. She became a much-loved fixture, selling cigars and charming the likes of Washington Irving. On July 25, Rogers told her mother she planned to visit relatives in New Jersey. She never returned, and three days later her body was discovered floating in the Hudson River near Hoboken. Theories abounded on how "the Beautiful Cigar Girl" had died, from being kidnapped, killed by a gang, the victim of an ill-fated date or a botched abortion. The police never solved Rogers' death, and in 1842, Edgar Allan Poe wrote "The Mystery of Marie Rogêt" based on the case.

Rogers' murder brought some changes to the police force, which was widely perceived as inadequate to the task of solving it. While many Americans worried that an armed force might morph into a standing army that could suppress basic American freedoms, in 1845 the city established the "Day and Night Police." These men earned a salary and could not accept money or rewards without the permission of the mayor. Even so, applicants still secured their jobs through connections. And though they were becoming part of a more cohesive force, most continued to oppose reforms such as one that called for wearing uniforms and showing their copper badges.

* * *

Whatever its problems and issues, its reputation for corruption, lawlessness, and violence, immigrants flowed into New York looking for a new home. The earliest settlers were mostly Walloons, Belgium Huguenots fleeing religious persecution, who sailed aboard the *Nieu Nederlandt* to Manhattan Island in 1624. The Dutch trading post slowly filled with Dutch, English, Jews, French, and others. Two centuries later, political and social turmoil in Europe in the late 1840s forced thousands to leave France, Poland, and the Italian states. Equal numbers left Germany because industrialization cost them their jobs. Others fled their homelands to avoid military conscription. Jews departed because of crushing anti-Semitism, as well as restrictions on work and owning property. The Irish came in search of work and better opportunities. Then, in 1845, the spread of a water mold called "Late Blight" destroyed Ireland's potato crops and set off a famine. About one million people died, and more than a million emigrated.

While he might have dismissively written about the Irish, Hone assisted in raising money for famine relief in 1847. "There is a great movement in behalf of the suffering people of Ireland," he noted. He was made vice president of a massive benefit at the Broadway Tabernacle and collected $30,000. The town of Honesdale, the site where coal from Hone's Delaware & Hudson mine was loaded onto barges, even raised $1,000.

At the start of March, the Irish-born Alexander Stewart asked Hone to preside at the drawing of a lottery to help those from his homeland. By that month, the Relief Committee had received more than $50,000. Collections were made in churches, and Hone noted that "every denomination of Christians" were "united as one congregation in the brotherhood of charity." Stewart then loaded a ship with provisions and sent it to Ireland. For the return voyage, he brought young men and women to America.[18]

For the Irish and many others, the United States beckoned as a place for a new start. Shipping firms cashed in on those personal dreams, European discontent, and real fear, advertising passage in newspapers and distributing pamphlets that extolled the virtues of the New World. Many in Europe also received letters from relatives and friends who had already emigrated, which proclaimed the availability of land and work. Getting to America became easier with the introduction of regular packet ships, starting with the Black Ball Line in 1818. At the same time, the growth of trade and enticement for work increased with the opening of the Erie Canal and the laying of the railroads.

The prospect of going to America might have had appeal, yet it could be a harrowing voyage. While wealthier passengers secured good accommodations, most immigrants huddled in the unventilated "tween decks," a space between the upper and lower decks. This area might only have six feet clearance, few portholes and the bunks lay close together. And though ships took with them cows, sheep, pigs, and poultry, decent fare only went to cabin passengers. Those below received salted meat, bread, and scant other items. A doctor on a Liverpool passage noted in 1851 how passengers on his ship received just 5 pounds of oatmeal, 2½ pounds of biscuits, 1 pound of flour, 2 pounds of rice, ½ pound of sugar, ½ pound of molasses, and 2 ounces of tea per week. Because of this, many brought with them supplies that they kept in rat-resistant boxes. Not surprisingly, malnutrition was rife, and the doctor on the ship from Liverpool noted how the crew had to often pass around buckets of water and bags of biscuits to prevent starvation.

The air within the hull reeked, sanitation proved minimal, and diseases such as cholera, smallpox, dysentery, and typhus—commonly known as "ship fever," "jail fever," and "camp fever"—swept through vessels. Twenty percent of those on board died during passages, earning the crafts the nick-name Coffin Ships. Some ships went down, with one of the worst years being 1854 with the loss of the *Arctic, City of Philadelphia, City of Glasgow*, and the *New Era*, the latter leading to the deaths of 240 mostly German immigrants off the coast of New Jersey.[19]

After ships arrived, they docked in New York either on the Hudson or the East River, across in New Jersey, or on the Long Island Sound. When the *Henry Bliss* pulled in in 1843, after 56 days from Liverpool, the *Herald* reported on "Passengers in a state of starvation." The following decade, Isabella Bird watched as some 700 British emigrants arriving from that city disembarked following weeks at sea: "If they looked tearful, flurried, and anx-ious when they left Liverpool, they looked tearful, pallid, dirty, and squalid when they reached New York. . . . Many were deplorably emaciated, others looked vacant and stupefied."

Landings could be discombobulating for passengers. Once on shore, officials scrutinized the immigrants. Those who made it through expected to walk out onto gold-paved streets and into great wealth. Instead they were met by hucksters. These "Runners," agents for companies that took immigrants inland, approached them, spoke their native tongues, and offered tickets to places like Buffalo and Chicago that were either fake or sold for inflated rates. In 1848 more than 700 people worked as immigrant runners and agents, and journalist George Foster wrote that "many if not most of them [were] making large sums of money by deceiving, lying to, and swindling the poor Immigrants."[20] To try and stop such activities, the New York State Legislature created the Board of Commissioners of Emigration in 1847. It inspected ships, offered new arrivals useful advice, and told them of actual job opportu-nities. And when commissioners turned Castle Garden into a landing depot in 1855, immigrants could buy train tickets there from supervised firms, have their baggage properly weighed, pay appropriate porter fees, and learn about legitimate jobs and travel routes. Benevolent societies also helped. Some catered to compatriots from their foreign community with the St. George's Society (English), the St. Andrews' Society (Scotch), the Friendly Sons of St. Patrick (Irish), and the German Society disbursing advice on travel as well as offering assistance finding relatives.

While this was an improvement, it didn't completely stop the abuse. For beyond the confines of Castle Garden, hustlers employed by boarding houses continued to approach those making it out onto the streets. They touted reasonable rates for room and board and carted over luggage. Such places might charge three to four times the standard price, and demanded 50¢ to $3 for bedbug- and rat-infested spaces. The owners also made extra money at nearby stores and saloons, where, according to Foster, they offered "a few maggoty hams and shoulders, half-a-dozen bunches of lard candles melted into one, some strings of dried onions, a barrel of No. 3 mackerel, some pipes and tobacco." Families left such places as quickly as possible to find better rooms.[21]

* * *

Those who stayed in New York altered the city's ethnic makeup. In 1845, 236,567 city residents were native-born, and 134,656 were not. In 1855 the city had 307,444 native-born residents and 322,460 non-natives. In 1844, the nativist publication *American Republican* complained how the aliens "are more ignorant and more vicious and corrupt than the native inhabitants." And while many deemed those from the British Isles acceptable, they yanked up the welcome mat for others. The city's German population—which rose from 24,416 in 1845 to 97,572 in 1855—were viewed as particularly "other." They spoke a dark tongue and clustered in places like the Kleindeutschland neighborhood. And though the Irish were British and spoke lilting English, residents believed them to be an intemperate breed and worried as their numbers nearly doubled in a decade, going from 96,581 in 1845 to 175,735 in 1855.[22]

Because of this, it could be hard for immigrants to find work. Since they were often urban and educated, Germans more easily secured good positions. French Catholics experienced some barriers, but for many employers there was cachet to hiring the French. The Irish, though, hailed from an agricultural society and generally lacked urban skills. But men soon found spots in shipbuilding, furniture making, refining, clothing, metalworking, and public works, and by 1855 Irish men made up 87 percent of the city's foreign laborers. Homeowners generally preferred African American servants, whom they saw as more submissive than the Irish, and would run such ads as "No Irish need apply." Even so, Irish women still found positions. And once hired, many found a semblance of job security along with free board and lodging, earning as a chambermaid in a good house $5 to $6 a month. Others worked as seamstresses, dressmakers, shirt makers, and embroiderers. For extra money, some took in boarders and did laundry.[23]

Nonetheless, anti-Irish sentiment was widespread. Much of the opposition stemmed from competition for jobs. Many also believed that the Irish sought to undermine American democracy, their allegiance to the pope in Rome seen as a threat to the very core of Protestant America. Samuel F.B. Morse, who ran for mayor in 1836 for the Native American Party, warned of their nefarious ways, writing of "the fruits of *papal education!* of papal care of the bodies and minds of its children. Filthy and ragged in body, ignorant in mind, and but too often most debased in morals." Itinerant preachers dubbed "street angels" harangued against Catholics. Anti-Irish images were rife in society. The *Herald* in 1840 ran a farce in their paper with a prominent illustration entitled "Brilliant Bal Costume." It told of the "doings of dustmen— hackmen in high life" and featured an illustration of drunken revelers, and Satan drinking. Not one to forget one of his tormentees, Bennett inserted a dig at Hone, saying "he was dressed as a pie baker, was brought up before the devil, dressed as a judge, on a charge of putting dead dog's meat into pies."

People born in New York blamed the Irish for everything. Anti-immigrant tensions ran high in many cities in 1844. A series of fires aimed at the Irish neighborhoods ravaged parts of Philadelphia, and calls went out to destroy New York's Catholic sites. In response, armed parishioners massed in St. Patrick's Cathedral's churchyard on Mulberry Street to protect their sanctuary. Bishop John Hughes then visited Mayor Robert Morris, and when Morris asked if he feared "that some of your churches will be burned?" Hughes responded, "No, sir; but I am afraid that some of yours will be burned. We can protect our own. I come to warn you for your own good." Because of his bold stance, Hughes became a figure of hope for the Irish and derision to others. He actively organized his flock, built churches, and secured support for Catholic schools.[24]

With such a monolithic, large voting bloc to tap, Tammany had early on started courting Irish and other immigrants. They met docking ships and ran a "naturalization bureau" in Tammany Hall, which assisted with papers, granting the ability to vote years before they should have qualified. "The new comer," the Scottish poet and journalist Charles Mackay observed, could claim "the privilege before he had been a week on American soil." By recruiting the vote at the most basic local level, leaders like Rynders with his Empire Club, Walsh with his Spartans, and Morrissey got the newcomers to cast their ballots as they were told, with Hone commenting in 1835 that because of the vote, the Irish "make Presidents and Governors." Tammany, though, did not have a lock on the immigrant ballot. The Whigs, too, increased their ballot numbers by offering food, liquor, clothes, and money, and even tapped the alms house, shipped in prisoners from Blackwell's Island,

and brought in "floaters" from places like Albany to carry out voter fraud. In 1838, Whigs and Hone Club members were accused of giving money to 200 Philadelphians to get them to cast ballots.[25]

Clearly, election fraud was party-blind and would set the stage for the arrival of one of the city's most divisive mayors, as well as plant the seeds of its most corrupt political machine.

20

An Ungovernable Metropolis

New York's real estate continued to boom in the 1850s, and some New Yorkers settled in less-crowded uptown homes that boasted of running water, sewage connections, and gaslights. Most craftsmen, journeymen, and common laborers, though, struggled to relocate from downtown congestion. If they could find cheaper housing, such places were far away from their work. And since transportation proved dear, many had no choice but to stay where they were.

The shortage of housing drove landlords to transform attics, warehouses, and cellars into apartments, squeezing families into spaces that Walt Whitman noted were "not larger than properly-sized cupboards." Not only were buildings packed, some still had old privies and cesspools. The Association for Improving the Condition of the Poor reported how their inspector in 1853 found "Crazy old buildings—crowded rear tenements in filthy yards—dark, damp basements—leaky garrets, shops, out-houses, and stables converted into dwellings, though scarcely fit to shelter brutes." On Cherry Street he discovered a five-story tenement that contained more than 500 residents. As he observed, they were places where tenants "wash, cook, eat, sleep and die."[1]

The Five Points—which sat in the Sixth Ward, and was nicknamed the Bloody Sixth—was one of the worst areas. Bounded by the intersection of Anthony, Cross, and Orange Streets, *Hunt's Merchants' Magazine* reported that in 1850 the area contained 197,719 people per square mile. Visitors found the section so foul that in Solon Robinson's *Hot Corn: Life Scenes in New York Illustrated*, he warned that when going there you should "saturate your handkerchief with camphor, so that you can endure the horrid stench." Saloons, gambling dens, and dance halls packed a neighborhood that had become so notorious that even legendary frontiersman Davy Crockett had to get up his nerve before heading there, noting, "I thought I would rather risk myself in an Indian fight than venture among these creatures after night."[2]

* * *

The boom and the inequalities meant New York was a chaotic place, and much happened on the streets. A good many, native-born and immigrants, eked out a living as peddlers, their cries piercing the air as they sold baked pears, penny papers, roasted peanuts, oysters, locofoco matches, hot yams, socks, and toothpicks. Most residents did not appreciate what a reader of the *New York Tribune* described as the "incumbrances of sidewalks, the hawking, screaming" that went on, like the early morning cries for "Mee-ee-ee-ilk." Among the most famous hawkers were the Hot Corn girls, who called out "Here's your nice Hot Corn, smoking hot, smoking hot, just from the pot!" These young women sat for hours alongside their cedar buckets. The *Tribune* decried in 1853 the state of one such vendor: an "emaciated little girl about twelve years old, whose dirty frock was nearly the color of the rusty iron, and whose face, hands and feet, naturally white and delicate, were grimed with dirt until nearly of the same color."[3]

To survive, the poor pawned items, scavenged, and scooped food from broken dock-side barrels and crates. Girls made money sweeping roadways. Boys earned coins selling newspapers or shining shoes. And crowds of children constantly swarmed along the streets, causing George Templeton Strong to complain in July 1851 that, "On a rainy day such crews may be seen by dozens. They haunt every other crossing and skulk away together."[4]

Want filled the city, with masses of people struggling for basic survival. Editor Horace Greeley noted in 1845 that 50,000 New Yorkers "have not the means of a week's comfortable subsistence and know not where to obtain it." Poverty spawned tragedy. Greeley's *Tribune* reported in 1847 the scene of horror that officials found at 78 James Street: "There are, or were, seven of them, the parents and five children. The mother is dead, from the wet, and from hunger. Yesterday her corpse was lying, uncared for, in its rags on some wet straw scattered upon the floor in one corner, while the father and children were sick and moaning with hunger . . . in their abode, no fire, no food, no table, no shroud or coffin for their dead, no friends to console them!"[5]

As reputable work became scarce, many women found themselves forced into prostitution. One estimate is that at some periods in their lives, up to 10 percent of women ages 15 to 30 living in New York worked as prostitutes. The number of brothels went from 200 in the 1820s to 600 at the end of the Civil War. At one point, 27 of the 43 blocks around Paradise Square in the Five Points contained brothels, an area that the *New York Times* noted, "Every house was a brothel, and every brothel a hell."

Brothels clustered near theaters. The proximity made the entertainment centers convenient spots for meeting customers. Thomas Hamblin regularly visited Adeline Miller's brothel on Crosby Street. Miller was the mother of Bowery Theatre actresses Josephine Clifton and Louisa Missouri. The theater owner also spent time on Chapel Street in an establishment owned by Mary Gallagher, actress Naomi Vincent's mother. Like other houses, John Jacob Astor's Park Theater had an erotic third tier, an upper gallery where prostitutes freely solicited during performances. And the streets brimmed with them. In 1857, Dr. William W. Sanger, who the following decade wrote a history of prostitution, concluded that 7,860, or 2.2 percent of the female population at that point, were working as prostitutes in New York.[6]

Life for these women was precarious at best. Customers regularly assaulted the women, though only a small percentage of the crimes were reported. Occasionally the attacks captured the public's attention. Helen Jewett, who had lived in the City Hotel brothel, liked to attend the Bowery, and even sent a note to Hamblin praising his shows. She had been seeing Richard Robinson, a clerk. When Jewett realized that Robinson was also dating "a respectable young lady," she threatened to expose him. On the night of April 10, 1836, Robinson came by her rooms and demanded the return of his letters, watch, and other items. The *New York Herald* reported that Robinson then "drew from beneath his cloak the hatchet, and inflicted upon her head three blows." Afterward Robinson set fire to the room.

The murder shocked polite New York. Philip Hone called it "a most awful case of depravity." James Gordon Bennett had gotten into the room while it was still a crime scene, and his *Herald* filled columns about Jewett, calling the 23-year-old a "most beautiful girl." People were obsessed by the killing. Strong and his Columbia classmate Nathaniel Chittenden went to the crime scene a few days after her death, and thousands attended Robinson's trial. Hone had no doubts about Robinson's guilt, but observed, "it is to be feared that he will escape punishment" because of his "influential friends" and because Jewett was a prostitute. Hone was right. The jury deliberated for a mere 15 minutes before acquitting Robinson.[7]

* * *

Nineteenth-century New York lacked a social safety net for the poor and dispossessed. Some citizens tried to help others, starting early in the century. In 1801, Robert Randall bequeathed his 21-acre farm on Washington Square North to create a haven for "aged, decrepit, and worn-out sailors." Eventually it was decided that money from leases of the Greenwich Village property would be used for the construction of Sailors' Snug Harbor on Staten Island. Religious groups also performed charitable work. The American Tract Society, formed in 1825 with the financial help of Arthur Tappan, banker Moses Allen, and others, printed and distributed religious material, assisted people with clothes and rent money, and established mission stations.[8]

In 1831 Tappan and others formed the New York Magdalen Society. They hired moral reformer Reverend John Robert McDowall as chaplain and set up a "house of refuge" to teach "fallen" women useful trades. McDowall and his supporters headed into the Five Points, handing out tracts, "reading from the sacred Scriptures, and holding meetings for prayer and exhortation." To point out the need, the minister's *Magdalen Facts* presented statistics on prostitutes and their clients, reporting in 1833 that there were thousands of females in the city "Despoiled of character, bereft of friends, and excluded from the abodes of the virtuous."[9]

Others believed they could help the poor by promoting campaigns against such vices as gambling, Sabbath-breaking, and juvenile delinquency. The American Bible Society distributed Bibles to the poor, prison inmates, and the residents of houses of ill repute. In 1852 the Association for Improving the Condition of the Poor set up a public bath house. That same year, the Ladies' Home Missionary Society bought the Old Brewery building, a late-18th-century structure that housed hundreds of poor people in old vats converted into windowless cubicles. They demolished the structure and built the Five Points Mission, a school, and a bathing room.

Poverty was especially widespread among African Americans. The Female Missionary Society for the Poor of the City of New-York opened a church in the Bancker Street area in 1818 to minister to them. The *Herald* pointed out that "with the exception of the colored oyster merchant, [Thomas] Downing, and a few others," most of the city's 10,807 blacks in 1855 appeared in the census as "non-taxpayers." The Almshouse Department reported that of the Blacks in New York, 2,974, more than a quarter, were on the list of outdoor poor and received assistance either in the form of money or fuel.[10]

The key way to improve the life of the poor, white and Black, was through education. Yet school attendance was not compulsory, and some students only showed up for part of the year. In 1849 Police Chief George Matsell reported that over 2,000 of New York's children, or over 8 percent within 11 of the city's patrol districts, "never see the inside of a school-room." Many children worked or simply hung out in the streets, around hotels, at shipyards and wharves, committing petty crimes. Of the 16,000 criminals sent to the City Prison in 1851, a quarter of them were under 21, and 800 were under 15 years of age.[11]

One hero of the reform movement was Frances "Fanny" Wright. Dubbed the "Female Tom Paine," this charismatic Scottish feminist was a popular speaker who believed that democracy existed for all races, genders, and classes. With the Scottish-born utopian reformer Robert Dale Owen, she advocated for cooperative living, favored workers' organizations, called for taxpayer support for boarding schools for boys and girls, and discussed abolitionism and the formation of communal farms for former slaves. Another shining light in the fight to help poor children was Charles Loring Brace. A friend of Frederick Law Olmsted, Brace warned of the threat to the nation "from the existence of an ignorant, debased, permanently poor class, in the great cities." To combat this, Brace helped found the Children's Aid Society, and in 1854 that group set up the Newsboys' Lodging House with the aim of "the improvement and elevation of the vagrant and poor children of the streets." The society likewise had an industrial school for girls.[12]

Reformers also sought to end intemperance. Grog shops were found throughout parts of the city, and in 1830 Americans averaged more than seven gallons of liquor a year. In 1829, evangelists formed the New-York City Temperance Society, with Lewis Tappan in the leadership. The society soon had chapters throughout the wards. The New York Washington Temperance Society held meetings and offered alcohol-free amusement, dances, picnics, and concerts. In 1842 the *Tribune* called for the creation of Temperance Refreshment and Reading Rooms, where workers could relax and read newspapers and magazines and pass the time, "in the acquisition of useful knowledge, instead of habits of dissipation." And though yearly consumption declined, the *Herald* in 1849 felt that "All these attempts to eradicate the vice and crime of drunkenness have failed." A sign of this was that from mid-July 1845 through December 1850 the police arrested over 35,000 people for intoxication and nearly 30,000 for intoxication and disorderly conduct.[13]

* * *

To transform the city, more than do-gooders and private charities were needed. Spurred by the rapacious ways of William Tweed's Forty Thieves, the City Reform League formed in 1852. It sought to fight governmental corruption and set out "for the purpose of holding a strict surveillance over the actions of the Common Council." Reform League members included the industrialist Peter Cooper, publisher John Harper, and businessman Stephen Whitney. They forced the legislature to alter the city's government, and the Charter of 1853 abolished the 20-person Board of Assistant Aldermen and replaced it with an annually elected 60-member Board of Councilmen. The new council could not appoint judges, and the mayor, city recorder, and city judge were given oversight for the hiring of police officers. The granting of railway franchises along with ferry leases had to go to the highest bidder. Cooper and other civically minded leaders also demanded an independent judiciary and a strong mayor with a presidential-style veto.[14] Reformers didn't expect that their actions would have a direct effect on the mayor's office. Yet in New York, power, disorder, and violence were often allied with politics.

Fernando Wood sought a large slice of that power. The quandary for him was what path to take to gain it. Born in Philadelphia on June 14, 1812, Wood was one of seven children. His Quaker ancestors arrived in the United States in the 17th century, but he acquired his decidedly un-Quakerish given name because while pregnant with him, his mother Rebecca had read George Walker's *The Three Spaniards* and decided to name her child after its hero, Fernando de Coello, an adventurer whom one character describes as "a fiery-headed fellow." Wood's father sold cigars for a living and speculated in dry goods. The family moved frequently, heading to Kentucky, New Orleans, Havana, and Charleston before settling in New York in 1821. There, the senior Wood opened a tobacco store. That business failed, and he abandoned Rebecca and his children.[15]

Fernando Wood left school at 13 and learned the tobacco trade in Richmond. He then toured the South as an actor, and returned to New York in 1832 with his bride. Wood found work as a salesman and an accountant with an auctioneer named Varnum Shattuck. The auction house failed, yet with his wife's dowry, Wood opened a wine-and-cigar store on Pearl Street. It didn't last. He then borrowed money to start a chandlery shop to sell equipment and supplies for ships. But, like so many other businesses, it went under during the Panic of 1837. In 1838, Wood started a grog shop on Washington Street. That business shuttered in 1839.

As a struggling small-time merchant with large aspirations, Wood found politics attractive. He favored Jeffersonian-Jacksonian ideas, and in 1836 joined the Tammany Society. He became a member of the Young Men's Democratic-Republican General Committee and worked his way up Tammany's ranks. Like many other Democrats hurt by the financial panic, he was attracted to radical Locofocoism, which called for hard money and workers' rights. Charming and soft-spoken, Wood cut a smart-looking figure. Sharp-witted and self-assured, he seemed to possess boundless energy. Wood regularly took part in political rallies. Yet as work and politics consumed him, Wood neglected his marriage, and he and his wife divorced in July 1839.

In 1840 Wood attended his first Democratic National Convention, which nominated Martin Van Buren. Because of his work, Wood earned a spot on the Democratic ticket for Congress. Despite a small financial scandal in which he had been involved that was picked up in the press, Wood narrowly won the vote. Taking his seat in Washington in 1841, he actively enlarged his network. He became friendly with prominent southerners such as South Carolina senator John Calhoun, and a majority of time cast his vote with proslavery congressmen.

Like Tweed a few years later, Wood served just one lackluster term. His short stay, though, paid off. In April 1844, Calhoun became Secretary of State, and the following month appointed Wood dispatch agent at the Port of New York. It was a sinecure that involved sending dispatches abroad to counsels and minsters, as well as forwarding to officials in Washington reports arriving in New York. By then Wood had remarried, wedding Ann Richardson and starting a family. In the mid-1840s Wood revived his chandlery business. He had an office on South Street, leased ships, and became involved in the coastal trade as a shipping and commission merchant, mostly with the South. By 1847 he had eight ships. When gold was discovered in northern California in 1848, Wood, with the backing of his brother-in-law and others, outfitted the bark *John W. Cater*. The ship left for California with a wide assortment of goods and netted a $150,000 profit—a colossal sum. At the time, Fernando and his wife also invested in city real estate. They soon owned part of the Somerindyck farm, which yielded 110 city lots that stretched from Broadway to Riverside Drive, and from 76th to 78th Streets. They moved into and enlarged the Somerindyck house, named their estate Woodlawn, and used the land's increasing value as security to make other purchases in the city, as well as in Brooklyn and San Francisco. It was during this time that Wood reentered politics.

While Wood's pro-southern stance would have made him an ideal proslaver, he presented himself as a unifying Democratic moderate and worked to mend the party's rifts. For that he earned a shot at the mayor's office in 1850. Wood ran against the Whig sperm-oil merchant Ambrose Kingsland.

He politicked hard, spent lots of money, sought out the business and the immigrant vote, and secured endorsements from places like the *Herald*, which wrote that "We are satisfied that he will make a capital Mayor."[16]

As Wood campaigned, new and damning information emerged about him, an echo of the earlier financial scandal. It was revealed that he had cheated his partners on the *John W. Cater* shipment. To gain backing for that trip, Wood told his associates that he had received a letter from Navy agent Thomas O'Larkin advising that if he sent goods to miners he could make a lot of money. Based on that letter, his partners decided to invest in Wood's venture. But the O'Larkin letter proved a forgery. And while the *John W. Cater* shipment made, as we've seen, a large profit, Wood had produced fake vouchers and bills of sales, maintained that he had high costs, and shared less than he should have with his partners, who sued. The court made Wood pay some $13,000, causing Hone to quip, "Fernando Wood, instead of occupying the mayor's seat, ought to be on the rolls of the State Prison." Wood lost the election to Kingsland 22,546 to 17,973. The *New York Evening Post* noted how he "grossly overrated the influence of party organization, and as grossly underrated the importance of unimpeachable personal integrity in a candidate."[17]

* * *

With the election behind him, Wood turned his attention back to his business and his family. He sought to improve his image. He sent his children to private schools, and he and his wife joined St. Michael's Episcopal Church. In 1854 Wood decided to make another try for the mayor's office. Despite the danger of antagonizing immigrants, and to court the nativist vote, he quietly became a Know Nothing. When a report emerged that he had joined that party, he, like other party members, simply denied the claim. He also ignored reports about his past indiscretions, blithely stating, "The People will elect me Mayor though I should commit a murder in my family between this and the Election." Wood wasn't the only candidate with dubious qualifications. Retired dry goods merchant James Barker ran on the American Party ticket, and Strong observed that he "is accused of having set his store on fire in 1845 or 1846 in order to cheat an insurance company."

Isabella Bird was in town during the election, and noted that 10,000 Know Nothings had gathered in the Park, and as they left, a group of Irishmen called the Brigade fired at them. "For three days a dropping fire of musketry was continually to be heard in New York and Williamsburgh," she wrote. "I saw two dead bodies myself . . . both the side walks and the roadways were slippery with blood."[18] Wood won, taking in 19,993 votes to Barker's 18,553 and Reform candidate Wilson Hunt's 15,386.

By the end of 1854, though, the economy was in trouble. There were a series of business failures as firms and construction sites shut down, jobs dried up, and food prices rose. At Strong's Calvary Church, the congregation held a Thanksgiving meal of turkey and roast beef in the church's basement for Irish and German immigrant children attending the parish's Industrial School. Two weeks later, Strong reported on the cold, and "the hundreds or rather thousands of men with wives and children to be fed and kept warm, whom this cruel 'pressure' has thrown out of work." In the first three weeks of January 1855, the Five Points House of Industry fed its residents along with thousands of others. Thousands of unemployed took to the streets. Strikes broke out, and at mass meetings people demanded jobs. Alexander Stewart opened a soup kitchen in the basement of his Marble Palace.[19]

When Wood took office on January 1, 1855, he immediately presented himself as a reformist leader and as New York's savior. On his first day as mayor, he wrote to all the police captains and told them that they had to hold to "the most rigid adherence to the rules and regulations governing the Department," and that discipline "requires compliance with *every order.*" He likewise told the officers that they needed to report unclean streets, brothels, gambling dens, and a host of other nuisances. Wood's notion of reform seemed to involve "one-man rule," and he set out to create a strong executive office. He attacked the city charter, which he complained created "a complicated, many headed, ill-shaped and uncontrollable monster." Wood promised citizens better streets, public health regulations, a new City Hall, a Central Park, fiscal responsibility, and a cut in real estate taxes. The *New York Times* praised him for speaking "freely and frankly." Wood even placed a "Black Book" in City Hall, a volume where people could comment about everything from their neighbors and the government to lost cows and filthy markets. Heralding the age of the modern New York mayor, Wood took the job of mayor seriously, leaving his Woodlawn home early each day for the five-mile trip to City Hall. He also stayed in a home he had on 2nd Avenue near Astor Place, or at a hotel. All the while he answered letters, dealt with job seekers, and boasted publicly that the administration took no graft.[20]

Right after he took office, Wood called for enforcing Sunday laws and revoking the liquor licenses of those who did not comply. The effect was immediate. On Sunday, January 7, 1855, 235 public houses dispensed alcohol;

that number dropped to 180 a week later, and to 26 at the end of the month. Wood also sought to rid the city of brothels, gambling dens, and other public nuisances. His promotion of reform attracted the support of the city's elite. In mid-February, Strong commented that Wood was the first mayor in many years to "set himself seriously to the work of giving the civic administration a decent appearance of common honesty." At a March 21 meeting at the Broadway Tabernacle to deal with proposed changes to the police force, many of the city's wealthy and powerful came out to show their approval, from editors Horace Greeley and James Watson Webb to former mayor James Harper and developer Samuel Ruggles. They even called out a "three cheers" four times. Wood seemed to be making the right moves. The New York Temperance Society sang songs in his honor.[21]

But as the mayor made a show of taming saloons and other dens of iniquity, many such establishments simply reopened elsewhere, and the police conveniently left alone those who paid fees. Fashionable spots meanwhile remained untouched. In less than a year, support for Wood started to erode. He was accused of being dictatorial and engaging in partisan police appointments, and the *Times* reported how he discriminated against Whig officers. In November 1855, that paper questioned the sincerity of his moves, noting that, "The glowing stars in the brilliant constellation of our Mayor's inaugural promises have gradually waned and expired." And while Wood had pledged a reformist platform of good government, it became clear to many that he had little interest in improving the workings of the city. Moreover, like others in government, he sought to consolidate his position, selling favors and enriching himself with fees by doling out offices, franchises, and contracts.[22]

In spite of Wood's seemingly half-hearted efforts, temperance campaigners, not just in New York but nationwide, continued their efforts to curtail the availability of liquor. Back in 1851, a law banning the sale of liquor had passed in Maine. Soon a dozen more prohibitions took effect in other states. Such a bill passed the Whig-controlled New York State legislature in 1854, but Democratic governor Horatio Seymour vetoed it. Then on April 9, 1855, Albany passed the New-York Prohibitory Liquor Law: An Act for the Prevention of Intemperance, Pauperism and Crime. The legislation forbade the sale of domestically produced liquor. Not surprisingly, many, such as Tammany boss Isaiah Rynders, opposed the law: "I . . . drink what I like when I can get it," he boasted. "I thank God I have hitherto had what I want to eat, and as much as I needed to drink." The law was set to go into effect in July. Wood didn't care to enforce the law, so he had District Attorney A. Oakley Hall announce that from May 1 to July 4 there would be no restrictions on alcohol, and the police had been advised not to make arrests, since they could be charged with false arrest. The law was found unconstitutional in 1856.

Undeterred by his critics, Wood at the start of that year put forward an ambitious program to spur the still-slumping economy. He called for housing legislation to make healthier buildings, and established a corps of sanitary police. The mayor wanted to improve food quality, and called for the expansion of the Croton aqueduct system so that it could adequately supply water to the city's growing population. He proposed replacing old wharves and docks with stone ones, promised to force railroad companies to upgrade services, and insisted on a single commission to plan roadways and streets. The mayor said that tax money should be used to help create jobs, and called for the quick development of Central Park, which was in the works. And to make the city not only an economic powerhouse but a center of education, Wood proposed more free academies and a great city university. These all proved to be popular programs, and even with Wood's missteps, he was widely admired.[23]

Wood's 1856 run for reelection coincided with the presidential campaign between the Democrat James Buchanan, the Republican John C. Frémont, and the Know Nothing Millard Fillmore. The press churned up Wood's past with discussion of his tyrannical ways. The *Tribune* warned of the reelection of "this bold, bad man to the office he prostitutes and perverts." To show that he was serious about cleaning up the city, Wood that October had the police raid a "model artists" show, where they grabbed women performing an act of Venus rising from the sea, and dragged them out while still wearing their silk tights and transparent skirts.

So much of what Wood accomplished was made possible by his control of the police. New York's Municipal Police force had little choice but to do his bidding. Wood required policemen to donate to his reelection, and at a banquet at his home he made captains pay $15 to $25 toward the campaign. "I paid my $25 without a whimper to save my head," admitted one. In a single week the department contributed about $10,000 to Wood's war chest. Officers who showed a willingness to help could avoid their regular duties to do campaign work. If an officer did not pony up, he faced punishment or dismissal. Tammany meanwhile sped up naturalization so that new immigrants could supply more Democratic voters.[24]

Wood didn't just call on the police to back him up. He also sought the help of gangs such as the Dead Rabbits. Members of the gang, which was also known as the Mulberry Street Boys, worked as his eager foot soldiers in keeping order and using terror to gain power. As the *Tribune* wrote, their services were acquired for a price, "in secret conclave with the rowdy leaders, buying and selling the services of their gangs for so many dollars." During elections, gang members battled rivals, disrupted opposition meetings as their intimidating "shoulder hitters" assaulted and stoned voters, and destroyed ballot boxes. In the process, their loyal "repeater" voters cast needed ballots to ensure the election results their overlord desired.[25] Wood ran against the auctioneer Anthony J. Bleecker, a Republican, and the Know Nothing Isaac O. Barker. The Reform Democrat Party meanwhile put forward Judge James R. Whiting, and Alderman James S. Libby stood as an Independent Democrat.

Despite the hope of many, it was neither a fair nor a peaceful election. There were election-day fights galore. In the First Ward, the *Herald* reported how opposing sides came "armed with bludgeons, knives, and some few with pistols." When Charles Jonas, who worked at Hoppock & Mooney grocers, cast his ballot for Fillmore, Wood supporters tore up his ballot and gave him one for Buchanan and Wood. Jonas refused the paper, and they beat him and dragged him out of the building. Undeterred, Jonas returned to vote and was punched in the mouth. All the while, the police did nothing to stop the assault. The Sixth Ward was the scene of a wild brawl, with more than 20 gunshots and the wielding of knives, brickbats, axes, and clubs. The Frémont ticket box on Leonard Street was destroyed. The Seventh Ward had lots of black eyes and bloody noses. In the Eighth Ward, 400 people were prevented from voting. And there was a stabbing in the Eleventh Ward. When the election results were counted, Wood—who controlled the naming of vote counters and election inspectors—tallied 34,860 votes, compared to Barker's 25,209.[26]

* * *

The election was yet one more sign that New York was an ungovernable place, even given an autocrat like Wood. In April 1857, *Harper's Weekly* called it "a huge semi-barbarous metropolis . . . not well-governed nor ill-governed, but simply not governed at all."[27] This sense of an unhinged metropolis pushed the state to bring about the municipal revolution of 1857. The Republican-controlled state government in Albany sought to rein in Wood and the

Democratic-ruled city. As a result, a power struggle developed between Albany and Manhattan. Governor John Alsop King and the state legislature instituted various laws to force civic change, separate the administration of the city's government from local politics, limit the power of the wards and foreigners, end patronage, and create a more orderly administration. They began by amending the city charter and state-appointed commissions. On paper, the mayor's power appeared to grow—Wood was given control over the streets, for example, Croton, and the city inspectors department. At the same time, however, he lost a say over such areas as the fire and health department, and the almshouse. A series of significant city positions were now also decided by elections, further weakening the mayor's power.

Seeking to wrest the police from Wood, Albany in April 1857 passed the Metropolitan Police Act, which stripped Wood and local politicians of control over the force. In place of the Municipal Police, the state formed the new Metropolitan Police District, a consolidated department covering New York, Brooklyn, Staten Island, and Westchester County. And since most commissioner appointments came from Albany, the Republicans controlled the board. With just one seat on the board, Wood had limited say.

Not surprisingly, Wood opposed this power grab, challenging its constitutionality. He also told his Municipal officers not to acknowledge the new Metropolitans' authority. The court did not issue a permanent injunction. Hence, when the commission took effect, officers and patrolmen effectively had to decide whether to stay with the Municipals or throw their lot in with the Metropolitans. To make matters worse, Wood warned that Municipals who refused to obey him would lose their jobs. He simply filled spots with new loyal men. The *Times* lambasted his actions, writing how he placed on the force "the most notorious brawlers and ruffians in the whole City." One of his hires was saloonkeeper Mike Murray, who had bitten off Patrick "Paudeen" McLaughlin's nose. This bifurcated policing system meant that by the summer of 1857, 15 captains and 800 men sided with Wood, while seven captains and 300 men headed over to the state's camp. Rather than hurting Wood, the schism bolstered his image as a defender of home rule, portraying him as the heroic native David battling a brutish foreign Goliath.[28]

While many residents applauded Wood's actions, the city was ill prepared for the coming paroxysm of violence. Municipals told residents that the Metropolitans lacked authority, and the *Tribune* wrote how "brick-bats, stones, &c., have been frequently hurled at the members of the Metropolitan Police." On June 14, Metropolitan officers were escorting "a well-known loafer by the name of Tracy" to their station house. When the men reached Avenue C and 10th Street, a Municipal officer told the Metropolitans that they could not arrest the man. He then summoned bystanders to help free Tracy. But when more Metropolitans arrived, they arrested the Municipal officer. As they headed to the Metropolitan's station house, a Municipal policeman tried to rescue their officer. Thousands soon surrounded the Metropolitan station and threatened to burn it down. The spot was only saved when reinforcements arrived. An hour later, several hundred people attacked four Metropolitans on Avenue C, and one officer was stabbed with an ice pick.[29]

Amid all this turmoil, Street Commissioner Joseph S. Taylor died. The job of street commissioner was a plum patronage position, and Governor King appointed one of his own, Daniel Conover, to fill the spot. Wood meanwhile tapped Charles Devlin, who reportedly had donated a whopping $50,000 to the mayor. When Conover arrived at City Hall on the 16th to start work, Wood refused to swear him in. The mayor's Municipal officers then roughed up the would-be commissioner and tossed him out of the building. Undeterred, Conover obtained a warrant for Wood's arrest. Metropolitan Police Captain George Washington Walling and a force of 50 brought over the warrant. When Walling arrived, Wood looked at him and said, "I do not recognize you as an officer." Municipal Captain Abraham Ackerman and several of his men then rushed in, and Walling recalled how, "He and his men grabbed hold of me at Wood's order and forcibly ejected me from the office."[30]

By then, word of the struggle had spread, and a crowd gathered outside City Hall. The *Tribune* reported that there were at least 10,000 people "hooting" outside and acting "in the most savage manner. . . . We observed burly ruffians climbing the trees and tearing off huge limbs for clubs, while others gathered up stones and brickbats to use in the service of the Mayor." Like many others, Strong had completely lost faith in Wood, whom he referred to disparagingly as "Don Fernando," and would soon call him a "limb of Satan." When Strong learned of the stand-off he headed downtown with a friend. Once there, he observed how the Municipals were "being aided by their position and in greatly superior numerical force, and being backed by a miscellaneous assortment of suckers, soap-locks, Irishmen, and plug-uglies, officiating in a guerrilla capacity."

When the Metropolitans returned, several hundred Municipals, rowdies, and gang members attacked them. As they fought, Major General Charles Sandford and the Seventh Regiment happened to be marching down Broadway and rushed to aid the Metropolitans. They escorted the sheriff to Wood's office and arrested the intransigent city leader. Wood easily posted the $50,000 bail. When the Court of Appeals ruled on July 2 that the Metropolitans were the legitimate force, Wood was forced to disband his Municipals.[31]

All this occurred in the period leading up to the Fourth of July holiday, generally a boisterous time in New York. It didn't help that Wood refused to give the Metropolitans access to Municipal police stations and telegraphs. The change also happened on the day that the new state's Liquor Excise Law took effect. Despite the overturning of the New-York Prohibitory Liquor Law the previous year, temperance advocates had continued their agitation. They believed the new law would slash liquor consumption, cut down on crime, and transform New York into a godly place. This would be made possible by increasing the cost of licenses—ranging from $50 to $300—which made owning a saloon exorbitantly expensive. And to obtain such a license, barkeeps had to supply references, attesting to their civic virtuousness. The bars also needed to board visitors and close on election days and Sundays. Many resented the government's meddling with their drams of pleasure. Back in May 1857, the *Herald* questioned the school-marmish tone of temperance supporters: "The people of the rural districts want no end of prohibitory and coercive enactments. They daren't trust themselves alone with a loaded pistol, or a gin bottle, or a pretty girl, or a steam hammer without a good stout law to protect them and keep them in bounds."[32]

On July 3, as a group of Metropolitans were walking near the Bowery Theatre, a band of Wood-supporting Dead Rabbits attacked them. Officer Abraham Florentine Jr. ran into a bar, which happened to be controlled by the gang's archenemies the Bowery Boys. As Florentine entered, he yelled, "For God's sake lock the door or I'm a dead man!" The Bowery Boys barricaded the place. The Dead Rabbits heaved paving stones at it, as well as at a nearby coffee house where another officer hid. Outnumbered, the Bowery Boys fled out the back, but then returned with 300 members. The opposing gangs cobbled together barricades constructed of wagons, mattresses, barrels, kitchen tables, fire-hose carriages, lumber, and drays. Soon 1,000 people armed with knives, pistols, and stout cudgels battled it out along Bayard, Mulberry, and Elizabeth Streets, firing weapons, throwing stones, and swinging pickaxes. As the two sides surged back and forth, residents rained down candlesticks, dishes, oyster shells, and stones from their windows and roofs.

The fighting finally wound down when an officer and a Special Patrolman took off their badges, and, waving a white flag, went to the Dead Rabbits barricade on Mulberry Street and asked them to stop. The Dead Rabbits said they wouldn't until the Bowery Boys did. The officer told them that they had just left the Bowery Boys' side, and that the gang said they would desist if the Dead Rabbits would. The officers then repeated the feint at the Bowery Boys' barricade on Elizabeth Street. Both groups soon stood down. The riot took the lives of eight people, and at least 100 rioters and police suffered injuries. By the evening of the 5th, the Metropolitans and the militia had restored order.[33]

Turmoil continued to roil the city. On the 12th, resentment over the new liquor laws exploded in the German-immigrant neighborhood of Kleindeutschland after the police made an arrest on Avenue A and 4th Street. Several thousand residents taunted the officers. When reinforcements arrived, the residents threw brickbats. Police Captain Jedediah W. Hartt recalled how some of his men "were bleeding from the head." As they drove back the residents, a blacksmith who had nothing to do with the fight was killed. The next day Hartt met with residents at the house where the blacksmith's body lay, but had to flee when locals threw stones. That night locals lobbed more objects, and shot at two policemen. It took 400 officers, along with three National Guard regiments, to quell the violence.[34]

* * *

The police and gang rioting and fighting over the new police and liquor law crippled Mayor Wood's position. To further weaken him, the state had separated the federal and local election, and switched the mayoral election to take place in an odd year, making Wood run again that year for office. As he prepared for the election, the nation was plunged into the Panic of 1857. On August 24, the New York branch of the Ohio Life Insurance and Trust Company suspended payments, and soon the country's entire financial system started to tumble. In September, *Harper's Weekly* wrote how at the stock exchange, "prominent stocks fell eight or ten per cent in a day, and fortunes were made and lost between ten o'clock in the morning and four of the afternoon." The British withdrew capital from U.S. banks, and grain prices fell, railroads defaulted on debts, banks called in their loans, and land projects failed. The turmoil was further exacerbated by the September 12 sinking of the SS *Central America*, which was bringing tons of gold from San Francisco to Eastern banks.

New York soon had tens of thousands of people out of work. The Association for Improving the Condition of the Poor reported that "41,000 homeless, unsheltered poor, had, at different times, been lodged at night in the Station Houses." Women with baskets begged for food at kitchen doors. Lewis Tappan, who watched how the Panic of 1837 had crippled his brother Arthur's silk business, saw the downturn, as he did the Great Fire of 1835, as divinely orchestrated, writing, "God is chastising us. Let us amend our ways."[35] Strong closely followed events, reporting on the failures on "the bluest day yet" of some of the city's large firms like Bowen & McNamee, that "The Harpers have suspended," "The Central Bank of Brooklyn is swamped," and "There was a run on the Park Bank." On October 10 he noted how "People's faces in Wall Street look fearfully gaunt and desperate." Three days later he wrote, "the Bank of New York . . . our oldest bank had stopped." He couldn't help but exclaim on the 14th, "We have burst."[36]

While the Panic unfolded, Wood set out to help citizens through public works—not just the Central Park project but sewers, streets, and docks, and all "to be paid for from the public treasury." The mayor even suggested that the city distribute 50,000 barrels of flour and a similar amount of corn meal and potatoes to pay the workers. The Common Council ignored Wood's proposal, and the press attacked him. The *Times* accused the mayor of raising "the banner of the most fiery communism." Needing jobs, workers took to the streets carrying signs calling for "Work" and "*Arbeit*." Some seized bakers' wagons, and the police and the Marines rushed out to restore order. On November 10, Strong described a massive meeting in the Park, and how some three hundred policemen and around "one hundred and fifty United States soldiers from Governors Island and Marines were posted in the Custom-House and the adjoining Assay Office" to maintain order.[37]

In the election, conservatives and reformers put forward Peter Cooper's nephew-in-law Daniel Tiemann, a wealthy paint manufacturer calling for honest government. As an alderman at the time of the Forty Thieves, Tiemann was one of the board's rare voices of fiscal reason. The election saw marches, fights, and the destruction of ballot boxes. By the time the polls closed, Tiemann beat Wood 43,216 to 40,889. The *Tribune* praised the mayor-elect as "an honest and determined" man who will "clear the public service of a set of incomparable harpies, and to restore to the people of the city those rights of self-government of which they have long suffered themselves to be deprived." Strong could not mask his joy at the results, commenting that "The defeat of the Father of Dock Rats is a thing to be thankful for," though was also rueful that "so notorious and certified a cheat and swindler could get some 40,000 votes."[38]

Ousted from City Hall, Wood opened an office on Wall Street and managed his real estate. He paid $5,600 for a controlling share of the *New York Daily News* and gave his brother Benjamin the editorship. As Wood's star seemed to set, William Tweed's was rising again. In 1857, the state legislature established a new Board of Supervisors. The group was seen as a way to force good governance by auditing county expenditures, overseeing taxation and public improvements. The board was also empowered with appointing election inspectors. In order to make sure that the group properly monitored their efforts, they decided to balance its makeup with six Democratic and six Republican representatives. Being on the Board of Supervisors did not seem like such an important post. Even so, Democrats filled it with loyalists such as Tweed. Little did anyone realize what the ramifications would be.

This return to power proved to be quite a rebound for Tweed, who joyously celebrated his 35th birthday in April 1858 at a lavish dinner at the Westchester Hotel on the Bowery. That July, President James Monroe—who had died in New York on July 4, 1831, and was interred at the New York City Marble Cemetery—was disinterred for reburial in Richmond, Virginia. As church bells tolled, a horse-drawn procession took his coffin up Broadway. Tweed had the honor of being a part of the cortege, one that included Cooper, former mayor William Havemeyer, and editor Webb.

On September 5, 1859, Tweed gained admittance to the controlling hierarchy of the Tammany Society. At the time, the Board of Supervisors earned the power to register voters and pick election inspectors and supervisors. Choosing election inspectors was tantamount to deciding winners. All former Forty-Thiever Tweed needed to do to gain sway over the evenly divided board was to tilt one of the Republicans members to his side. That was done by giving the Republican Peter Voorhis $2,500. In return, Voorhis skipped a meeting to appoint election officials. Democrats thus filled 550 of the 609 slots with a list Tweed oversaw. Many of those picked ranged from saloonkeepers and gamblers to criminals.[39]

Whatever Tweed required to hold on to power, was what he sought. Yet, as he ensured Tammany's grip on the city's government, the state of the nation lost its hold on union, and America slipped ever closer to war.

21

The Approaching Storm

Even as the Civil War loomed on America's horizon, prosperity seemed to be on the march in New York. In May 1857, Columbia College sold its City Hall–area campus on Park Place and moved four miles north to Madison Avenue, between 49th and 50th Streets. They had taken over the Institution for the Instruction of the Deaf and Dumb, fixed up the old buildings, set up their chapel and library, and started classes. A year later, George Templeton Strong helped found a law school for his alma mater, and six years after that, a School of Mines (today the school's Earth and Environmental Engineering Department). Just a block away on Fifth Avenue, Strong's Columbia classmate, James Renwick, started construction on St. Patrick's Cathedral, the cornerstone of which was laid on August 15, 1858. The church, a monument of Gothic architecture, stood three miles north of its Mulberry Street predecessor. Many had dubbed Archbishop John Hughes' decision to move the church there "Hughes' Folly." Yet people had similarly scoffed at John Jacob Astor's decision to open his Astor House hotel in 1836, half a year after the Great Fire, on what then seemed the distant north. The cleric, like the land baron, proved prescient about where the future of the city lay. As the *New York Tribune* mused in 1856, "Where is up town? It is as difficult to answer as it is to locate that locomotive spot, the Far West."[1]

Beginning in the late 1850s, as we've seen, Central Park experienced its slow birth in the new uptown. Eventually stretching from 59th to 110th Streets, the 843-acre urban wonderland by Frederick Law Olmsted and Calvert Vaux dwarfed City Hall's nine-acre park. By then New York, now with a population of 800,000 souls, had arguably become the cultural, religious, educational, and mercantile center of the Western hemisphere, and, given its large number of newspapers and magazines, a major communications link between East and West. In 1854, Cyrus Field, with the help of Peter Cooper and others, set out to lay a cable across the Atlantic. They completed the work in August 1858, and Queen Victoria sent President James Buchanan the first message. At Niblo's Garden and other theaters, audiences and actors greeted the announcement of the transmission with cheers and the playing of "God

Save the Queen" and the "Star-Spangled Banner." A salvo of 100 guns was fired at sunrise in the City Hall Park, and a salute of 33 guns went off in the Battery. Church bells pealed throughout town, and factory bells and steam whistles joined in the chorus.

The city threw a celebratory parade, and among the participants was Olmsted, who along with others led a procession of Central Park and Reservoir men in carts and drays and a full brass band. The procession wended down to City Hall, where Mayor Daniel Tiemann reviewed the marchers. There were fireworks and bonfires, firemen marched in a torchlight parade, and businesses like Delmonico's, Genin's Hattery, P.T. Barnum's American Museum, and hotels like the Astor House set candles and gaslights in their windows. Unfortunately, sparks from the fireworks hit City Hall's cupola, and a fire broke out at midnight. The central fire alarm system was located inside the building, and there was therefore a delay in the call going out. When the firemen arrived, the spray from their hoses could not reach the top of the building "The scene, however, was magnificent," reported the *London Illustrated News.* "The statue of Justice, a familiar sight to all New Yorkers, stood wrapt for a length of time in the flames of the grand illumination, and serenely endured the fiery glow for more than an hour, until at length she was observed to totter and fall into the flames." The fire was finally extinguished, and the city and judicial records saved.[2]

The water system touted just a decade earlier for bringing pure water from upstate, helping the city expand and fight fires, had quickly become inadequate in a community growing at such a fast pace. The Croton Aqueduct supplied 12 million gallons a day in 1842; by 1850 it was delivering 40 million gallons. Seeking to improve service, work began on a new, larger reservoir in Central Park in April 1858.

By then, city buildings just a few decades old had become passé, as new institutions moved in and new structures went up. Philip Hone's palatial Great Jones Street home, which he had settled into in the late 1830s, was sold following his death in 1851. Purchased by the Empire City Bank, the institution was run by Elijah Purdy, one of William Tweed's future Ring cronies. The Astor Place Opera House, located a few blocks to the north, never recovered from the 1849 riot. Its contents were sold at auction in 1853, and Renwick turned the space into the new Clinton Hall. That year, the American Bible Society opened a new building nearby. Soon after, William Astor unveiled his father's library. Around the corner, Peter Cooper opened his Cooper Union for the Advancement of Science and Art in a building designed by Frederick Peterson. Just an avenue over on Broadway and 10th Street, architect John

Kellum began work on an Iron Palace department store for Alexander Stewart. On 14th Street and Irving Place, the Academy of Music, designed by Alexander Saeltzer, opened its doors in 1854. It could seat 4,600. Meanwhile in September 1860, Shearith Israel moved into a new Palladian style building designed by Robert Mook on 19th Street. The *Jewish Messenger* called it "probably the handsomest edifice of the kind in the United States." Into their old Crosby Street synagogue, Mayor Fernando Wood's brother Henry opened his Wood's Minstrel Hall.[3]

Following Thomas Hamblin's death in early 1853, his son William had taken over management of the Bowery Theatre. The audience greeted the young Hamblin with prolonged applause when he took to the stage on February 8 as Anthony in *Julius Caesar*. Following the show, he thanked everyone, telling them that he hoped never to "tarnish the dramatic fame of my father." Yet, as his father had known all too well, running a theater was hard, and he soon gave up the management of the Bowery. In 1854, after Thomas Hamblin's colleague Isaac Waldron bought the theater, Hamblin's eight children received $10,000 each, and Astor recouped the money the impresario owed him.[4]

In 1859 George L. Fox and James Lingard opened the New Bowery Theatre, located a few blocks from the old Bowery. Designed by old Bowery architect John Trimble, the New Bowery stood between Canal and Hester Streets. A third larger than the older structure—and the largest theater in the city—it had cast-iron columns and seated more than 4,000. The new interior was done up in a simple Grecian design with white-and-gold decoration and crimson seats, the ceiling painted by the Italian-born artist Giuseppe Guidicini, who had decorated the 1837 Calvin Pollard–built Bowery. Despite its classical demeanor, the new theater maintained its working-class appeal. The *New York Herald* noted how "The audience embraced all conditions of humanity. In the orchestra we noticed more than one *habitué* of the Broadway theatres, the pit was jammed with the democracy, unwashed and unterrified."

Then, in August 1860, theater manager George Wood took over the old Bowery, boasting on opening night how "The theatre has been entirely altered, improved and redecorated, and is now one of the most comfortable places of amusement in the City." The *New York Times* reported that it returned with a better quality of entertainment, noting that it staged Edward Bulwer-Lytton's *The Lady of Lyons* instead of its usual "blue fire melodrama."[5]

* * *

New York might be thriving, but the country was coming apart at the seams. The slavery divide—which Charles Dickens in 1842 had predicted would come to "a bloody end"—had grown much wider than when Olmsted toured the South for the *Times* in the early 1850s. In May 1854, Congress enacted the Kansas-Nebraska Act, which ended the geographic division set in place by the 1820 Missouri Compromise. Now popular sovereignty determined whether an incoming state would be free or slave, a move that only amplified division and tension over the issue of slavery.

That Fourth of July, the Massachusetts Anti-Slavery Society held a rally in Framingham, Massachusetts. Henry David Thoreau and abolitionists Sojourner Truth and Wendell Phillips were featured, but the main speaker was William Lloyd Garrison. "To-day, we are called to celebrate the seventy-eighth anniversary of American Independence," the *Liberator* editor told the gathered, as he looked out from the speakers' stand hung with flags bearing the names Kansas and Nebraska, along with an upside-down American banner that had been draped with black crepe. "In what spirit? With what purpose? To what end?" While the Declaration of Independence had stated that all men were created equal, thundered Garrison, "It is not a declaration of equality of property, bodily strength or beauty, intellectual or moral development, industrial or inventive powers, but equality of RIGHTS—not of one race, but of all races." As the audience called out "Amen!" Garrison lit a copy of the Fugitive Slave Act. He then held up the U.S. Constitution and also set it aflame as he proclaimed, "So perish all compromises with tyranny!" The only solution he announced for the current state was "A DISSOLUTION OF THE UNION."[6]

Just as Garrison had lit one of the founding documents, the political system it had created was on fire. The Kansas-Nebraska Act helped bring about the establishment of the Republican Party, and caused both supporters and opponents of slavery to flock to and send supplies into the territory. In 1855, Olmsted bought weapons for Major James B. Abbott for the struggle, amassing "a mountain howitzer . . . fifty rounds of canister and shell with time fuses; five hand grenades; fifty rockets and six swords." In February 1856, Reverend Henry Ward Beecher commented how the .52 caliber Sharps rifles were really a moral force, since each of the breech-loading weapons could do more there than 100 Bibles. The weapons flooded the area and soon became known as "Beecher's Bibles," a term bolstered by the fact that many of the weapons arrived in Kansas in crates marked "Books" and "Bibles."

One newcomer to the disputed territory was John Brown, who had settled in Timbuctoo in North Elba, the land set aside by Gerrit Smith in New York State for African American farmers. He joined his sons in Osawatomie, Kansas, and there became head of the local anti-slavery militia. As the conflict heated up, pro-slavers sacked the town of Lawrence on May 21, 1856. Then on the night of the 24th, Brown and his sons raided the cabins of the proslavery community of Pottawatomie Creek to the south of Lawrence. They hacked five pro-slavers to death, a savagery that earned Brown the name "Old Osawatomie Brown." On August 30, pro-slavers retaliated, killing Brown's son Frederick and four others, and burned Osawatomie.[7]

In the election of 1856, former president Millard Fillmore ran as a Know Nothing and the Republican Party put up its first national candidate, California senator John Frémont, while former Pennsylvania senator James Buchanan earned the Democratic nomination. Buchanan won and did little in the face of the intractable North–South divide. Many feared that there was to be no resolution to the problem of slavery. In March 1857, the Supreme Court ruled in the *Dred Scott v. John F.A. Sandford* case that Blacks were not citizens, causing William Cullen Bryant to write in the *New York Evening Post* that "Wherever our flag floats, it is the flag of slavery. If so, that flag should have the light of the stars and the streaks of running red erased from it; it should be dyed black and its devices should be the whip and the fetter."

At that time, the Radical Abolition Party, a successor to the Liberty Party, was founded, with Gerrit Smith as its presidential nominee. Smith felt that if slavery could not be peacefully stopped, a violent response needed to be made. The abolitionist not only donated money to the Kansas Free-State movement, he supported Brown, who continued his agitation, fighting along the border and making a raid into Missouri to free slaves. The spreading violence gave rise to the term "Bleeding Kansas." Smith, along with the like-minded abolitionists Reverend Thomas Wentworth Higginson, Reverend Theodore Parker, Dr. Samuel Gridley Howe—Julia Ward Howe's husband—businessman George Luther Stearns, and journalist Franklin Benjamin Sanborn formed a group called the Secret Six. They supplied funds to Brown to buy Sharps carbines and Colt revolvers, so he could incite a southern slave rebellion and unleash the wrath of God.[8]

As he planned his attack, Brown tried to enlist the support of Frederick Douglass. The two men had first met in 1847 in Springfield, Massachusetts. Douglass found Brown "in sympathy a black man, and is as deeply interested in our cause, as though his own soul had been pierced with the iron of slavery." In the summer of 1859, the two secretly met in Chambersburg, Pennsylvania. There Brown implored Douglass to join him in his quest to mass an Army of Emancipation, telling him, "When I strike, the bees will begin to swarm, and I want you to help hive them." Douglass felt the plan was quixotic, turned down the offer to join, and tried to convince Brown that he would be "going into a perfect steel trap, and that once in he would not get out alive."[9]

But Brown would not be stopped. On October 16, 1859, he, along with his sons Oliver, Watson, and Owen, five free Blacks, and more than a dozen others, headed across the Potomac River to Harpers Ferry, Virginia. The heavily armed band cut telegraph lines, seized the federal arsenal, and took hostages. They holed up in the engine house until Lieutenant Colonel Robert E. Lee and a company of Marines raided the building and freed the captives. During the battle, Brown was wounded and 10 of his party, including his sons Oliver and Watson, died, while Owen and others fled. A letter from Douglass was found on Brown, and upon hearing of Brown's failed attack, Douglass slipped into Canada and then sailed to England. Gerrit Smith was also implicated in the plan, and the governor of Virginia called for his arrest. In response, a local New York militia came out to protect him.

The state charged Brown with treason, inciting slave insurrection, and murder. Higginson collected money for Brown's defense, yet the jury in Charles Town quickly found the abolitionist guilty. In late November, the *Weekly Anglo-African* ran a letter from "the ladies of New York, Brooklyn and Williamsburg" to Brown's wife, Mary, to let her know "we desire to express our deep, undying gratitude to him who has given his life so freely to obtain for us our defrauded rights." At the December 2 execution, members of the Richmond Grays militia were stationed by the gallows to thwart any attempted rescue. One of the unit's new members was the actor John Wilkes Booth, Junius Brutus Booth's son.

As the execution took place, Lewis Tappan and others attended New York's Church of the Puritans to pray for Brown. Two days later Strong gushed about Brown's "simplicity and consistency," and how "Slavery has received no such blow in my time as his strangulation." Bryant simply noted that "history . . . will record his name among those of its martyrs and heroes."[10]

Mary Brown accompanied her husband's casket to North Elba, New York, for burial. Along the way they stopped in New York. George Anthon asked Strong to come along to view Brown's body, but the lawyer declined his friend's offer. So many supporters tried to see the martyred abolitionist that the police had to disperse the crowd. Several, including Anthon, managed to finally gain access, and Brown's coffin was opened so they could gaze on his face. Anthon obtained a lock of Brown's hair. Brown was buried in North Elba on the 8th, the same day that Mississippi congressman Reuben Davis warned that "a thousand John Browns, can invade us."

While many in New York came out in favor of Brown, the city, with all its southern ties, continued to be torn over the issue of slavery. An unsympathetic James Gordon Bennett wrote in the *Herald* of the abolitionist cause: "They do nothing but scold and rant and rave from morning till night; and they scold and rant and rave this year worse than they did last year." Local businessmen meanwhile feared for their southern trade. As the national rift widened, New Orleans' *De Bow's Review* wrote that if the supply of cotton ended, "the glory of New-York, like that of Babylon and Rome, would be numbered with the things that are past!"[11]

Fernando Wood had been meanwhile planning his return to power. Frozen out by Tammany, the ex-mayor formed his own political group, Mozart Hall, named for the hotel on Broadway and Bond Street where he held its founding meeting. Wood claimed that his Mozart Hall Democrats were the city's true Democrats. Determined to regain power, he distributed cash to gang leaders, attracted immigrants to his cause, and ran his own naturalization bureau. Wood fervently supported the South, and just days after Harpers Ferry warned those at a rally in New Rochelle of the effect of the loss of that trade: "What, in the meanwhile, will become of our great commercial interests so closely interwoven with Southern prosperity?" he asked. "The profit, the luxury, the comforts, the necessity, nay, even the very physical existence depending upon products only to be obtained by the continuance of slave labor and the prosperity of the slave master." Despite Tweed's sway over election officials, splits within the Democratic Party, support from workers and commercial men who appreciated Wood's southern sympathies, and the tireless work of his loyal band of shoulder hitters, Wood won the election, defeating Tammany candidate William Havemeyer and the Republican George Opdyke.[12]

As Wood headed back to City Hall, his wife, Ann, died in childbirth. Her funeral on December 12 attracted 5,000 people, a gathering that the *Times* called, "Probably the largest concourse of prominent citizens ever assembled at the funeral of a lady in the city." The ceremony turned out to be a rare sign of solidarity in a city caught up in political, social, and economic turmoil. Not only did the mayor's friends and associates show up, so did his opponents, members of Congress, the judiciary, those from both branches of the state legislature, as well as aldermen, councilmen, and police officers. Ann Wood was set in the family tomb in Trinity Cemetery. The *Times* reported that Mayor Wood was "low with the brain fever," adding that "There is no reliable evidence of the truth of the rumor, but the impression was quite general in public places."[13]

* * *

The fear that the South would secede from the Union over slavery continued to grow, and the *Herald* reported that many New York hotel owners had complained of a drop-off of southern business. In February 1860, Abraham Lincoln visited the city. The Illinois politician, who two years earlier made his famous "House Divided" speech on his belief that the nation had to make a choice to either keep or abolish slavery, stayed at the Astor House, visited the Five Points House of Industry, and had his photo taken by Mathew Brady. Lincoln had his eye on the presidency. Though a dark horse candidate, he had come to deliver a speech at Cooper Union, at which he announced his opposition to the spreading of slavery into the western territories. Introduced to the audience by the *Evening Post*'s William Cullen Bryant, with *Tribune* editor Horace Greeley and others on the stage, Lincoln implored the gathered, "Let us have faith that right makes might, and in that faith, let us, to the end, dare to do our duty as we understand it."

Lincoln's talk propelled him to national attention. That November, he ran against Democrat Stephen Douglas, Southern Democrat John Breckinridge, and Constitutional Union candidate John Bell for the White House. Four days before the election, Strong decided to cast his ballot for Lincoln, proclaiming, "I want to be able to remember that I voted right at this grave crisis." Others similarly felt that the moment had come to make a stand. P.T. Barnum had grown up as a Democrat and once owned enslaved people. However, when "secession threatened in 1860, I thought it was time for a 'new departure,' and I identified myself with the Republican party."[14]

Benjamin Wood meanwhile used his *New York Daily News* as a pulpit to support the slave economy and oppose freedom for African Americans. Similarly, the *Herald* warned Irish and German workers that "if Lincoln is elected . . . you will have to compete with the labor of four million emancipated negroes." Lincoln failed to carry New York City in the election, earning only 38 percent of the local vote. Yet upstate ballots helped him win the state's 35 Electoral College votes. Nationwide, Lincoln received 1.86 million votes, taking every northern state save New Jersey. He amassed 180 Electoral College votes, more than double what Breckinridge received. That same day, editor Wood, who likewise ran for office, won a congressional seat.[15]

With Lincoln as president-elect, southern states agitated for secession. Strong wrote, "I should welcome the prospect of vigorous war on Southern treason." He didn't have to wait long. As the Strong family prepared for Christmas, South Carolina seceded on December 20. Mississippi followed on January 9, 1861, Florida on the 10th, Alabama on the 11th, Georgia on the 19th, Louisiana on the 26th, soon to be joined by Texas, Virginia, Arkansas, North Carolina, and Tennessee.

The group formed the Confederate States of America. Yet it wasn't just South Carolina and like-minded states that wanted to be done with the Union. On January 7, 1861, Wood gave the mayor's annual message to the Common Council. He told the gathered that New York should likewise leave the union and form an independent state made up of Manhattan, Staten Island, and Long Island. Wood called his mini republic Tri-Insula—which in Latin means "three islands"—and said it would flourish. Its financial security would be made possible by its continued involvement in the cotton trade. And since New York collected two-thirds of the federal government's $64.6 million in taxes on imports, such a secession would prove financially prudent since "we could live free from taxes, and have cheap goods nearly duty free." By doing this, the city could likewise maintain its strong and close ties with the South. The *Tribune* responded that "Mr. Fernando Wood evidently wants to be a traitor; it is lack of courage only that makes him content with being a blackguard." The *World* called his speech a "monstrous and treasonable message."[16]

Wood's proposal went nowhere, and the federal government refused to accept southern disunion. Many became alarmed when the new Confederate government announced that it would not pay its debts to the North, causing panic in the business community. The loss of southern business drove 40,000 city businessmen to sign a petition to Congress imploring the government to compromise with the South. Nothing came of it.

After South Carolina seceded, President Buchanan refused to surrender Fort Sumter to that state's militia, and Union major Robert Anderson continued to command the Charleston fort. Confederate general Pierre Gustave Toutant Beauregard began a siege. That February, as war loomed, President-elect Lincoln came through New York and stayed at the Astor House, where a large crowd massed to see him. "Broadway crowded," Strong noted. He spied

Lincoln as he passed St. Thomas' Church, observing, "The great rail-splitter's face was visible to me for an instant, and seemed a keen, clear, honest face, not so ugly as his portraits." With so much secessionist discord in the air, Walt Whitman worried that among the thousands on the streets, "many an assassin's knife and pistol lurk'd in hip or breast pocket there, ready, soon as break and riot came."

Soon after Lincoln arrived in Washington for his inauguration, Captain William Skipworth docked his sloop *Motto* at Perry Street on the Hudson River. From his masthead, Skipworth hung an effigy of Lincoln, along with the sign, "Lincoln is dead and gone to h-ll." Skipworth said he would stab anyone who tried to remove the figure. The police arrested Skipworth, and a judge forced him to take down the effigy. Local boys, the *Times* reported, then "quickly tore it to pieces, scattering to the winds the straw and rags of which it was composed."[17]

Plate 27 New-York born lawyer George Templeton Strong's diary beautifully complements Philip Hone's take on their hometown, and chronicles the city during the Civil War.

Plate 28 Besides being famous as an architect, Alexander Jackson Davis created illustrations, as with this one of the Castle Garden restaurant and entertainment center.

Plate 29 In 1850 P.T. Barnum brought the Swedish soprano Jenny Lind to America, and her whirlwind tour proved popular and profitable.

Plate 30 Born on Cherry Street, William "Boss" Tweed would start his rise to power as the leader of a band of rapacious alderman dubbed the "Forty Thieves."

Plate 31 Lithographs by Nathaniel Currier and James Merritt Ives—like this one from their "The Life of a Fireman" series—sold well during the 19th century.

Plate 32 In 1849 William Tweed helped found Americus Engine Co. No. 6, and he and his colleagues pumped the engine's horizontal bars to build up pressure to shoot water.

Plate 33 The Crystal Palace by architects Charles Gildemeister and Georg J.B. Carstensen opened to great acclaim in 1853, and offered citizens a cornucopian exhibition of the arts and trade.

Plate 34 While many believed that the glass-and-iron Crystal Palace was fireproof, a blaze in 1858 fed off the pitch pine flooring, and in no time the structure melted and collapsed.

Plate 35 The rivalry between the British actor William Macready and the America Edwin Forrest led to a deadly riot at the Astor Place Opera House in May 1849, taking the lives of 22 people.

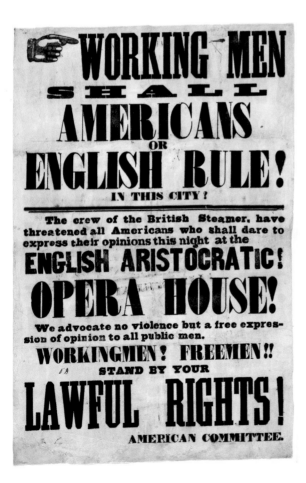

Plate 36 Political boss Isaiah Rynders and others stoked anger against British actor William Macready prior to his performance of *Macbeth* at the Astor Place Opera House.

Plate 37 Arthur Tappan made a fortune as a silk importer, and used his wealth to support such progressive causes as the fight against slavery.

Plate 38 New Yorkers loved their oysters, and along Canal Street one could opt for the Canal Street Plan, which was all you could eat for 6¢.

Plate 39 Diners craved the mollusks at Thomas Downing's oyster house, and he stored some of his tasty morsels in ceramic jars.

Plate 40 Slavery ended in New York State in 1827, and many African Americans hoping for freedom made their way to New York and elsewhere up north along the Underground Railroad.

PLYMOUTH CHURCH. REV. HENRY WARD BEECHER SELLING A SLAVE.

Plate 41 Minister Henry Ward Beecher held mock slave auctions at his Plymouth Church across the river in Brooklyn, raising money to free enslaved people.

Plate 42 A favorite spot for New Yorkers and her visitors was Barnum's American Museum, with its grand and sometimes spurious exhibitions.

Plate 43 In 1850, the Five Points, an impoverished and crowded section of the city, housed 197,719 people per square mile.

Plate 44 Mayor Fernando Wood proved to be one of the most powerful and divisive leaders of New York, and at the start of the Civil War called for New York's secession from the Union.

Plate 45 New York could be a violent place, and in 1857 a riot broke out between the Bowery Boys and the Dead Rabbits gangs, and soon 1,000 New Yorkers fought along the streets.

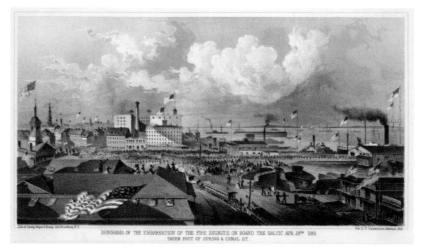

Plate 46 Following the April 1861 attack on Fort Sumter, New York firemen signed up for the First Fire Zouaves regiment, and fought that July at the First Battle of Bull Run.

Plate 47 George Templeton Strong's Union League Club organized the Twentieth Colored Infantry Regiment in 1864, and the men soon headed to war.

Plate 48 The architect Frederick Law Olmsted along with his partner Calvert Vaux designed Manhattan's Central Park, a priceless retreat in the heart of a hectic city.

VIEW IN CENTRAL PARK
Promenade looking South June 1858

Plate 49 To create Central Park, thousands of workers used pickaxes, steam engines and horse teams to shape the land, form ponds, and lay out walkways.

SKATING ON CENTRAL PARK, NEW YORK.

Plate 50 Ice skaters started showing up at the new Central Park in December 1858, and soon thousands arrived each week.

Maelstrom

Abraham Lincoln took the oath of office on March 4, 1861, and 39 days later General P.G.T. Beauregard commenced a bombardment of Fort Sumter. George Templeton Strong recalled the moment New York newspaper boys began yelling out the news: "Extry—a *Herald*! Got the bombardment of *Fort Sumter*!!!" Walt Whitman had just left a performance of Giuseppe Verdi's *A Masked Ball* when he heard the newsboys' cry. He bought a paper and read the issue as he stood outside the Metropolitan Hotel. Less than 34 hours after Beauregard started shelling the fort, Union major Robert Anderson and his soldiers surrendered.

Flags flew throughout New York. Strong commented a few days later how even "every cart horse decorated." On April 19, he and George Anthon watched the Seventh Regiment march by. Strong noted how "the roar of the crowd was grand and terrible. It drowned the brass of the regimental band." That day, Strong bought a flag and had a ship rigger hoist it on top of Trinity Church. As it rose, a crowd on Wall Street and Broadway cheered and chimes saluted it with "Hail Columbia," "Yankee Doodle," and the hymn "Old Hundred."[1]

Northern support for the South almost immediately evaporated, and many New Yorkers who had previously backed that region's interests joined the Union cause. Democrats like William Tweed and those in Tammany Hall who supported the struggle became known as "War Democrats." "Peace Democrats" couched their support of the federal government with talk of negotiation and reconciliation with the South, and the continuation of slavery. Fernando Wood was a leading Peace Democrat. He did call for a $1 million tax to raise money for the war effort, though his move caused Strong to refer to the mayor as a "cunning scoundrel," whose positions were designed to give "the least possible offence to his allies of the Southern Democracy." Peace Democrats became pejoratively known as Copperheads after the venomous snake.[2]

At the end of March, James Gordon Bennett had proclaimed, "The Lincoln administration is cowardly, mean and vicious, without the power to carry out its designs." When a mob threatened the *Herald*'s office, the staff unfurled the Stars and Stripes, a symbol of adherence to the Union. The *Herald* wasn't the only publication targeted. Pro-Union crowds massed at the *Day Book*, *Express*, and *Journal of Commerce*. *Frank Leslie's Illustrated News* quickly hung an American flag from their window. A mass of protestors then forced the New York Hotel as well as editors at the *Staats-Zeitung* and the *New York Demokrat* to do the same.

The *New York Daily News* proved more obstinate. Two hundred and fifty policemen had to rush over from various wards to protect Benjamin Wood's paper. Even as others felt forced to bow to popular sentiment, the mayor's brother held firm to his pro-southern beliefs, referring to the war as a "national fratricide." A federal grand jury would investigate the "traitorous" editorial leanings of such papers as the *News* and the *Day Book* and charged that these publications ran material "calculated to aid and comfort the enemy." The Board of Aldermen took away the *News*' designation as the official paper of the city, and the postmaster general forbade the paper from being sent through the mail. That summer Wood shut down his publication, and the following year wrote an anti-war novel, *Fort Lafayette; or, Love and Secession*.[3]

On April 15, Lincoln issued a proclamation requiring state militias to call up 75,000 troops on three-month enlistments. Right afterward, over dinner at his Washington Heights home, Bennett assured journalist Henry Villard—who had the ear of the president—that despite his previous editorials he would back the administration. The president also sent the Republican leader Thurlow Weed to see the publisher. Weed, thought Lincoln, had "considerable experience in belling cats." Over the next four years, Bennett would support the war effort as his paper covered the struggle, dispatching 63 war correspondents and spending half a million dollars. He even backed Lincoln's run for a second term in 1864.

At the start of the war, General Winfield Scott, a hero of the Mexican-American War, commanded the Army. Horace Greeley called for the military to take over the South, writing, "We mean to *conquer* them—not merely to defeat, but to *conquer*, to SUBJUGATE them—and we shall do this most mercifully, the more speedily we do it." "On to Richmond!" he proclaimed.[4]

After the initial shock to New York's economy, the city, like the nation, geared up for war. Indeed, the city was transformed into a military industrial juggernaut that stoked the Union's arsenal. Shipyards launched vessels. Ironworks forged everything from anchors and furnaces to boilers and engines. Gun-makers churned out weapons. Carriage-makers fashioned ambulances. Drug manufacturers produced drugs, bandages, and splints. To pay for the war, the federal government took out loans from Wall Street. And despite his pre-war support for the South, Alexander Stewart went on to make uniforms for Union soldiers, and served on the Union Defense Committee of the City of New York.

* * *

Most people believed it would be a quick war, and New York's men, in the words of Whitman, mobilized "To the drum-taps prompt":

> The new recruits, even boys—the old men show them how to wear their accoutrements—they buckle the straps carefully,
> Outdoors arming—indoors arming—the flash of the musket-barrels.[5]

Enlistment stations popped up around town, with various regiments preparing and veteran corps organizing. Frederick Law Olmsted put together a home-guard of 100 workers. Strong was myopic and not a good shot. However, that didn't prevent him from organizing the New York Rifle Corps. His corps ordered hundreds of Enfield rifles, and had a drillmaster train the men in Washington Military Parade Ground. Strong's brother-in-law, James Francis Ruggles, joined the Seventh Regiment as a sergeant. Philip Hone's great-nephew Joseph Howland received a commission as a colonel of the Sixteenth New York Volunteer Infantry. Tiffany & Co. made up flags for the regiment. Alexander Hamilton Jr.—James Alexander Hamilton's son—volunteered, and became a colonel and an aide to Major General John Ellis Wool. William Astor's son, John Jacob Astor III, earned a commission as a colonel and became an aide to General George McClellan. Bennett's son, James Gordon Bennett Jr., donated his schooner *Henrietta* to the Revenue Cutter Service, and Lincoln made him a third lieutenant. Egbert Viele received a commission as a brigadier general of volunteers. And Central Park's George Waring joined up and headed to Missouri as a colonel in the cavalry.

Colonel Elmer Ellsworth, a friend of Lincoln's, sought to raise a regiment and approached Fire Chief John Decker. Ellsworth wanted firemen-soldiers because he believed that they would make fine soldiers. "They are sleeping on a volcano at Washington," he wrote of the capital's precarious position, "and I want men who can go into a fight *now*." With the department's help, he formed the Eleventh New York Volunteer Infantry Regiment. Noah Farnham, who had been with Engine Co. 42, was made lieutenant colonel and the regiment's second in command. The men let citizens know that they had started a Committee of Subscriptions. Many firemen eagerly joined what became the Ellsworth Zouaves and the First Fire Zouaves. Zouaves were famed for their exotic, North African Franco-Algerian style uniforms, so Ellsworth saw to it that his men sported eye-catching blue trousers and red shirts, along with red fezzes or kepis.[6]

Congressman James Kerrigan meanwhile set up an office at the old Bowery and called for recruits for his Kerrigan Rangers battalion. On April 21 he signed up 600 men. Numerous actors enlisted for service, some joining the Lincoln Cavalry. New Bowery Theatre co-owner George Fox—who already belonged to the Eighth Regiment—served as a lieutenant. And Thomas Hamblin's son, Thomas, mustered in as a second lieutenant in Company G of the Life Guard. Many African Americans set out to serve. They even hired a hall, so they could train and drill. But Chief of Police John Kennedy told them to stop, and if they didn't he could not prevent them from being attacked. "They had no choice but to do as they were bidden," wrote Horace Greeley. When Governor Edwin Morgan received an offer for three regiments of Black troops, which the African American community said they would financially support, the governor turned them down.[7]

Camps for volunteers formed around town. Colonel John McGregor's Regiment had 800 men stationed in Central Park. The First Regiment Scott's Life Guard quartered at the old arsenal in Central Park, where they had 20 tailors busily altering and fitting garments for the men. When Mary Lincoln visited on May 17, she stopped by the Park barracks next to City Hall, and 2,000 soldiers lined up to welcome the First Lady. The Astor Infantry Regiment was stationed at Jones' Wood. Colonel Walter McChesney's Regiment had 850 men at Sandy Hook, along with 77 members of the Engineers' Corps. On and on it went: men bivouacked at places like Castle Garden and City Hall Park, and at the Division Armory on White and Elm Streets, where Hamblin was quartered.

New Yorkers trained for battle. Tammany Hall raised a regiment called the Tammany Jackson Guards, Forty-Second New York Infantry, which was headed by Grand Sachem William Kennedy. Not to be outdone, Mozart Hall formed the Mozart Regiment, which would attempt to distance themselves from Mayor Wood's anti-Union pronouncement—"we have no sympathy with his principles, no respect for his character, and hope the day is not far distant when such traitors will be shunned as lepers and outcasts."[8]

* * *

Men soon headed for war, some departing not long after Fort Sumter's surrender. On April 23, Strong wrote of seeing troops on Broadway, and how "The uniformed companies looked and marched well." The First Fire Zouaves received from the fire department white silk regimental colors with images of firefighting equipment and the slogan, "The Star Spangled Banner in triumph shall wave." Then, on the 29th, Strong watched as "the whole fire department" escorted them to the steamer to take them to Washington. Along the way they stopped at the Astor House, where they received a flag from Charlotte Astor, the wife of John Jacob Astor III. The Americus Fire Company and others sent them supplies, clothes, and food. In Washington, the firemen-turned-soldiers did some good. When a fire broke out at the Willard Hotel on May 9, the Zouaves broke into a firehouse to get an engine and put out the blaze. Unfortunately, they also carried on the unruly behavior that New York firemen had become notorious for. One of the men slaughtered a pig near the White House. A group of them also walked into a boot-maker's shop and made off with some shoes. "They have been ransacking the Capitol like so many rats," reported the *New York Times,* "breaking open doors, ripping cushions, and tearing up carpets, knocking down the guards, and chasing imaginary Secessionists through the streets—jumping on coaches, and going it, pell-mell."[9]

Soon enough, though, they had a hint of the brutal struggle they had signed up for. On the 24th while in Alexandria, Virginia, Ellsworth became the first northern officer to die in the war, shot by innkeeper James Jackson after he took down a Confederate flag at Marshall House on King Street. Corporal Francis Brownell then shot and bayonetted Jackson to death. Farnham, whom his men called "Pony" Farnham because of his short stature, took command of the regiment. More troops headed south. On July 16, Union general Irvin McDowell marshaled 35,000 men from Washington and set out to capture the Manassas, Virginia railroad junction. Securing it would give McDowell a vital approach to the Confederate's capital in Richmond. General Beauregard's 22,000 troops defended the spot. Some initial skirmishes broke out on the 18th, and on the 21st the North and South met at Bull Run, a small, meandering stream near Manassas. Northerners assumed the fight would be both the first and the last confrontation of the Civil War. There was so much excitement about it in Washington that both citizens and congressmen flocked there to see the clash, bringing with them opera glasses along with picnic baskets filled with sandwiches, oysters, wine, and champagne. Henry

Raymond arrived to cover the events for his *Times*, and Mathew Brady pulled up with two wagons full of camera equipment.

Soldiers showed up in good spirits, and according to Zouave lieutenant Edward Knox, Farnham's 950 men: "With cheers they moved briskly forward though the woods, singing and laughing and eager for the fight." The men ran "with a wild, wild yell, three cheers and a loud, fierce cry of 'Remember Ellsworth,' they dashed across the intervening space."

General McDowell ordered his troops across Sudley Springs Ford, and they initially forced the Confederates back to Henry Hill. Then General Joseph Johnston arrived with his 10,000 men, and General Thomas "Stonewall" Jackson came with his forces. The Confederates protected the rise as their artillery strafed the Union forces. The Fire Zouaves were some of the men sent to take the spot. Many were inexperienced 90-day recruits, and the Confederates forced them back. Knox recalled how the southerners assaulted the men with grape shot and canisters: "This continued for a long time, during which squad after squad was used up, man after man fell dead."

More advances failed to dislodge the Confederates, and by afternoon the southerners broke through the Union side, turning back the northern forces. Michigan senator Zachariah Chandler failed to stop the chaotic rout as soldiers yelled at the politicians, "Turn back, turn back, we're whipped." A Confederate shell hit Massachusetts senator Henry Wilson's buggy, and he escaped by mounting a stray mule. Brady lost all his glass-plate photos during the hasty retreat. As Union colonel Erasmus Keyes noted, "The road was filled with wagons, artillery, retreating cavalry and infantry in one confused mass."[10]

Four hundred sixty Union soldiers died during the First Battle of Manassas, or First Battle of Bull Run, with 1,124 wounded and 1,312 listed as missing or captured. Farnham was shot, dying three weeks later. He was one of the 24 Zouaves killed, not to mention the 46 wounded and 52 missing. Nineteen members of the Second Scott's Life Guards died there, 65 were wounded, and 54 missing. Hamblin was one of those captured. The Confederates had 387 killed and 1,582 wounded, and 13 reported missing or captured.[11]

The South gloated over and even exaggerated its success, with the *Raleigh Register* reporting: "It is said that their dead lay about in piles of ten, twelve, and sometimes even more, while the ground was literally covered with the slain in all directions." The article went on to say that "900 out of the 1,100 Pet Lambs [Fire Zouave], were slaughtered" and that other New York regiments "suffered terribly."

Hyperbole or not, Bull Run turned out to be a major and unexpected defeat for the Union. When Raymond made it to the telegraph office at 10 PM to send a news cable, he was "sun-burned, dusty, and hardly recognizable." His paper attacked the "certain reckless journals, whose senseless and incessant cry of 'Onward to Richmond,' has had this disastrous echo." And along the streets of New York, Abby Howland Woolsey wrote to her sister Eliza Woolsey Howland of some of the troop's arrival in the city: "I have just been up to the corner to see a sorry sight, the return of the Sixty-Ninth Regiment—oh, so shabby, so worn and weary—all sorts of hats and shirts and some with hardly any clothes at all, staggering along under their knapsacks which they should never have been allowed to carry up Broadway." And as the Fire Zouaves straggled home, many departed without the permission of their commanders. Their reputation became further tarnished when Captain John Vickers of the Seventeenth Regiment wrote to Mayor Wood that he "found in a pile of rubbish the Flags presented, by the City of New-York to the Fire Zouaves."[12]

Theater-owner Fox survived Bull Run unscathed. Like many others, he had only signed up for a 90-day enlistment. After he returned to New York on July 26, a large crowd greeted his regiment. The following day Fox appeared at the New Bowery, where he received a rousing welcome. He spoke to the audience, told them he was an "emigrant from Bull Run," and discussed the fight, paying tribute to the Zouaves. His partner James Lingard then came out and presented him with a gold medal. The following month the New Bowery staged Charles Gayler's *Bull Run; or, the Sacking of Fairfax Courthouse*, which was advertised as being written from details furnished by Fox.[13]

What many believed would be a brief and splendid war ended up being anything but. And conditions proved brutal for those captured. Hamblin had been shot in the left knee, and the Confederates deposited him in a shed, where he remained untreated for four days before being sent to Richmond's St. Mark's Hospital. Soon they moved Hamblin to Libby Prison. The building in Richmond, a three-story former tobacco warehouse, would become notorious for its squalid conditions. His captors then took him to the jail at Charleston. Confined in a small cell with four other men, Hamblin later wrote, "We were frequently locked up for days, and the only convenience for the relief of nature was a huge iron vessel, which stood in the corner, and which frequently remained unemptied for days. We were overwhelmed by vermin of all kinds." The men received condemned pork and rotten biscuits, and Hamblin had just a blanket on the floor and a block of wood for a pillow. At night, rats scurried over the prisoners.

From there the Confederates shuttled Hamblin between various prisons before he ended back at Libby Prison, where he stayed until his exchange in August 1862. "During the thirteen months of my imprisonment," he recalled. "I had only one imperfect suit of clothes part of which had been saturated with blood from my own wound and that of my friend Captain Hugh McQuaide, whom I had endeavored to assist on the field, where he was wounded." McQuaide had likewise been shot and captured at Bull Run. His left leg needed to be amputated. Infection nonetheless set in, and he died in Libby Prison the day after Christmas 1861.

By the time he returned to New York, Hamblin, whom his friend George Cooney had described as "much admired for his manly appearance & striking physique," suffered from fistula of the stomach—which allowed gastric fluids to seep through his stomach or intestines lining—and stricture of the bowels. When Cooney first saw his friend, he noted how "He was then evidently much enfeebled & impaired in health and strength." Hamblin, who had been promoted to first lieutenant during his captivity, was offered a commission as a captain, but couldn't accept the position because of his health, and received an honorable discharge.[14]

On August 17, 1861, hundreds came out for Farnham's funeral, viewing his remains at his father's home on West 38th Street. A procession made up of members of the Fire Zouaves, the Seventh Regiment, and relatives and friends then accompanied his body to Christ Church for a service. Afterward, his coffin was set on a train for burial in his hometown of New Haven. On the 29th, the Sixty-Ninth Regiment gathered in Jones' Wood for a picnic to raise money for the widows and orphans of soldiers. The outing attracted 50,000 people. There was dancing in parts of the woods along with wandering musicians like the Christy's Minstrels and Bryant's Minstrels. And James Magee in Philadelphia soon brought out the song "Ellsworth, the Gallant Zouave" about Ellsworth, with the stanza:

> Here's glory immortal to Ellsworth,
> And honor to Brownell the brave,
> Who avenged the foul death of his colonel,
> Like a true and a gallant Zouave.

The First Fire Zouaves reorganized, and a second regiment of Fire Zouaves was started, with many signing up to "avenge their brother firemen who fell so gloriously while in discharge of their duty at the battle of Bull's Run." Firemen paraded through the streets with fifes, drums, and a banner that read, "We have promised, and are ready."[15]

Early on, many New Yorkers called on Lincoln to abolish slavery. In March 1862, James Hamilton chaired an Emancipation Meeting at Cooper Union. He told the audience that the government should not only "crush out armed rebellion, but its malignant cause," a comment that earned long and uproarious cheering. Believing that the North needed to do it to save the nation, Greeley in August 1862 composed his impassioned "The Prayer of Twenty Millions," writing "that every hour of deference to Slavery is an hour of added and deepened peril to the Union."

Lincoln had avoided issuing an Emancipation Proclamation, hoping for a time where there might be some sign of Union success in the war. On September 22, five days after the Battle of Antietam, the bloodiest day in American history, the president issued his Preliminary Emancipation Proclamation. Then on January 1, 1863, he released the official one, declaring "that all persons held as slaves" within the rebellious states "are, and henceforward shall be free."[16]

Arthur and Lewis Tappan had long prayed for such a moment. By the start of the war, Arthur had already retired to New Haven, but Lewis was still busy with the American Missionary Association, which evolved from his work for the *Amistad* captives. The association had taken up the cause of African Americans coming into Union-occupied territories. It distributed food and clothing, opened schools and churches, and worked to help Blacks acquire land. On January 5, four days after Lincoln's proclamation, the 74-year-old Tappan spoke at the Emancipation Jubilee at Cooper Union. Most of the audience was Black, and the gathered sang "New John Brown Song" and other tunes. The following month, Strong, Olmsted, and others organized the Union League Club of New York. The club supported the Loyal Publication Society of New York and sought to counter what they saw as treasonous publications. To do this, members printed and distributed literature to fight the efforts of those like Samuel Morse, who headed up the Society for the Diffusion of Political Knowledge, which opposed Republican policies.[17]

* * *

The war seemed far off for many New Yorkers. In late 1861, merchant George Opdyke defeated Fernando Wood at the polls. Then on August 19, 1862, a vast stretch of citizens headed to Central Park to watch the first flow of water into the new Great Central Park Lake. Running from Fifth to Seventh Avenues and 86th to 96th Street and dubbed the Lake of Manahatta—as well as Manhattan Lake, and currently the Jacqueline Kennedy Onassis Reservoir—the *Times* wrote how the billion-gallon reservoir was "a graceful irregular shape, conforming somewhat to the irregularities of the ground." The site was six times the size of the earlier reservoir and could hold a 60-day supply of water. At three in the afternoon, with the playing of music and the firing of cannons, Chief Engineer Alfred Craven started filling the reservoir. It had started "in the time of profound peace," and was finished "in spite of the desolating war which has darkened so large a portion of the land."[18]

Stewart's new John Kellum–designed store opened at this time. His five-story cast-iron palace on Broadway and 10th Street cost a vast amount—estimates ran as high as $2.75 million. The Renaissance style building emulated and dwarfed Stewart's Chambers Street Marble Palace from 1846, and the merchant felt that its white arches looked like "puffs of white clouds." Throughout the town people attended plays like the revival of Lester Wallack's *Central Park* at his Wallack's Theatre. They could enjoy music at places like the Academy of Music, dine at such spots as Delmonico's, and have a drink at the Astor House Rotunda Bar. New Yorkers could also visit P.T. Barnum's American Museum. Ever attuned to the interests of his audience, the showman staged such plays as *Anderson, the Patriot Heart of Sumter*; displayed relics of the South, including slave shackles; had wax figures created of war heroes; and introduced two new Union-appropriate midget actors, Navy commodore Nutt and Army general Grant Jr.[19]

At the time, Barnum used his celebrity and that of actors to stage one of the grander weddings of the era, the February 10, 1863. nuptials of Tom Thumb to Lavinia Warren, whom Barnum advertised as the "Little Queen of Beauty." A grand event was held at Grace Church. Barnum touted it as "the biggest little thing that was ever known." Two thousand people attended the service, and the police strained to control the crowds that packed the sidewalk outside. Five thousand people then showed up at the Metropolitan Hotel reception. The newlyweds received such gifts as slippers from the actor Edwin Booth—brother of John Wilkes Booth—and a miniature silver horse and chariot from Tiffany & Co. On their honeymoon they went to the White House, where President Lincoln hosted them.[20]

It took a wartime exhibition to thrust the horrors of distant battlefields onto the streets of New York. In September 1862, just two days following the Battle of Antietam, Alexander Gardner visited the Sharpsburg, Maryland, field where 3,654 Americans had been killed in just one day. Gardner set up his stereo wet-plate camera to document the body-strewn lands, the burial crews, and the trenches in which they laid the men. The photographer worked for Brady, and when he returned to New York, Brady exhibited Gardner's work, hanging at his gallery a simple sign, "The Dead of Antietam." There, polite society saw possibly the first recorded images of war dead and could discern in Gardner's sharp images the faces of the men—fathers, sons, husbands, cousins, and neighbors. As the *Times* noted, "Mr. Brady has done something to bring home to us the terrible reality and earnestness of war. If he has not brought bodies and laid them in our dooryards and along the streets, he has done something very like it."[21]

* * *

Brady's show attracted both men and women, and the *Times* noted the distinct possibility that one of the women in the gallery might recognize a relative ready for mass grave burial: "For these trenches have a terror for a woman's heart that goes far to outweigh all the others that hover over the battle-field." As the war began to rip apart daily life, many New York women actively supported the war effort, which was unusual in a society with strict rules dictating what women could or could not do. Early on, Ellen Strong, Raymond's wife, Juliette, the spouses of doctors, and others gathered to make bandages and collect cloth and other supplies for the wounded. Groups formed in New York such as the New-York Ladies' Relief Union. In late April, Dr. Elizabeth Blackwell and her sister Dr. Emily Blackwell, who had founded the New York Infirmary for Indigent Women and Children, helped organize a meeting at Cooper Union and created the Women's Central Association of Relief for the Sick and Wounded of the Army. The *Herald* wrote of the "Spartan women . . . offering to place themselves in imminent perils of the battle-field . . . to attend to the wants of the bullet-stricken and sword-pierced soldier."[22]

The women's groups sought support for their efforts. Nonetheless, they didn't receive a welcoming response from official channels and reached out to private citizens. Reverend Henry Bellows, George Templeton Strong, and others agreed that more should be done to assist the troops. Much was needed, for the army had an inadequate medical infrastructure. Recalling the suffering of the British troops during the 1850s Crimean War and the work of the British Sanitary Commission, Bellows, along with others, went to Washington and on June 13, 1861, Lincoln established within the War Department the United States Sanitary Commission. The commission was empowered to oversee health conditions, with the inspectors relaying supplies to the field. It was the group under which the women's organizations would tirelessly work.

Meanwhile, despite the toll being taken by the war, work on the lower part of Central Park, which now stretched to 110th Street, was largely finished. Constant friction with Central Park commissioner Andrew Green caused Olmsted to want to quit his job. In June 1861, Olmsted took a leave of absence—Calvert Vaux would continue his work on the park—to become the Sanitary Commission's general secretary. Strong served as the organization's treasurer and was a member of its Standing Commission.

The commission quickly got to work, running an ad right after Bull Run: "IMMEDIATE DONATIONS WANTED OF ICE BY THE CARGO, WINE AND PURE SPIRITS, SHEETS AND SHEETING, FLANNEL AND TOWELING, MOSQUITO NETTING." Olmsted, who believed that the organization would strengthen the Union Army by ensuring the health of the soldiers, headed to Washington to inspect encampments. He found them disorganized, and members of the Army's Medical Bureau unhelpful. He therefore set out to reorganize it. Olmsted submitted his "Report on the Demoralization of the Volunteers," declaring that the army was lacking basics including medicine, food, and water. He also found "discipline, little better than a mob, which did not know its leaders."[23]

As he had done with Central Park, Olmsted structured the commission in a hierarchical system. He dispatched sanitary agents to visit army camps and review troops, checked on hospitals, and focused on such issues as water, rations, sickness, and death. To make sure that doctors and nurses received needed supplies, he established depots to bring materials to the front, with voluntary organizations—often those run by women—gathering donations of canned goods, blankets, bandages, and clothes. Strong, who regularly visited both battlefields and hospitals, commented on how Olmsted "works like a dog all day and sits up nearly all night."[24]

Since the Union Army didn't have a proper system to transport the wounded from distant battlefields to New York, Philadelphia, and Washington hospitals, Olmsted approached the Army's Quartermaster Corps, and received ships for the commission. During the 1862 Peninsula

Campaign, as General George McClellan's 100,000-man Army of the Potomac attempted to capture Richmond, Olmsted commanded the Hospital Transport Service's fleet from onboard the side-wheel steamer *Wilson Small*. His flotilla contained more than a dozen ships, including merchant vessels, steamboats, clippers, and those with shallow draft so they could slip up small tributaries. Besides the vessels, the commission's barges and wagons rushed medicine, fresh food, and clothing to military hospitals, field doctors, nurses, and orderlies, and whisked away the wounded.

Dr. Elizabeth Blackwell and others trained nurses. Eliza Howland and her sister Georgeanna Woolsey, along with Ellen Strong, were among the permanent nurses on Olmsted's transport ships during the campaign. George Strong reluctantly let Ellen go to war, but came to appreciate her work. There, she and the others toiled in crowded and hot hospitals, where they dressed wounds and watched over their patients. "*You can't conceive* what it is to stem the torrent of this disorder and utter want of organization," wrote Katharine Prescott Wormeley from onboard the *Wilson Small*. "To think or speak of the things we see would be fatal. No one must come here who cannot put away all feeling. Do all you can, and be a machine,—that's the way to act; the only way."[25]

Olmsted appreciated the dedication of the women: "They have all worked like heroes night and day. . . . I have never seen one of them flinch for a moment." As Ellen Strong was about to return to New York, Olmsted wrote about the women, "They beat the doctors all to pieces. I should have sunk the ships in despair before this if it hadn't been for their handiness and good nature."[26]

The Peninsula Campaign stretched from April through July 1862, and by the end of it the Sanitary Commission had cared for and moved some 8,000 wounded soldiers. Many headed to hospitals in Washington and New York. When they arrived in Manhattan they were brought to Bellevue Hospital, City Hospital, the Ladies' Hospital, the Park barracks, the old arsenal, Mother Jerome's Hospital, St. Luke's Hospital, the Jew's Hospital, and Central Park's Mount St. Vincent. Others went across the rivers to the Brooklyn Hospital and the Jersey City Hospital, as well as facilities on Davids Island, Bedloe's Island, Rikers Island, and Governors Island. Women volunteers would spend time at places like St. Luke's and the Jew's Hospital to care for the patients. Many of those who died were then buried in Brooklyn's Cypress Hill Cemetery, in an area that became known as the Union Grounds.[27]

Much was done on the home front to continue to support the organization. In 1864, Ellen Strong served as treasurer for the Ladies of the Metropolitan Fair, which raised money for the Sanitary Commission by organizing an exhibition in New York like the one at the Crystal Palace in the previous decade. The Metropolitan Fair contained displays of paintings by Albert Bierstadt and Thomas Cole, and audiences looked over a range of items, from floral arrangements to firefighting equipment. Importer William Aspinwall opened the doors to his private picture gallery with its Old Masters paintings. Those hoping to support the war effort could also catch Edwin Booth in the *Iron Chest*, go to the Old Bowery to see *Pomp of Cudjo's Cave*, enjoy food like steak and turtle soup at Delmonico's, and attend concerts. The fair raised more than $1.3 million. Alexander Stewart alone donated $10,000.

Individual New Yorkers likewise did all they could. When Whitman learned in late 1862 that his brother George, a lieutenant in the 51st New York, had been wounded at Fredericksburg, he went down to help him. The poet ended up staying to assist doctors tending to the wounded. He would write in *The Wound Dresser* how he started work on December 21 and spent the day at a makeshift hospital opposite Fredericksburg, one that "received only the worst cases. Outdoors, at the foot of a tree, within ten yards of the front of the house . . . I notice a heap of amputated feet, legs, arms, hands, etc.—about a load for a one-horse cart." Whitman would spend three years in Washington, D.C., working at assorted hospitals, tending to both Union and Confederate soldiers, writing how he "went among from eighty thousand to one hundred thousand of the wounded and sick, as sustainer of spirit and body in some slight degree, in their time of need."[28]

23

Ending the Deadly Embrace

As the war dragged on, the death toll rose, and the cost of basic necessities increased. This became especially hard for families, both in New York and across the nation, who were left without husbands, fathers, and brothers to provide for them. Fundraisers, like the one held in Jones' Wood following Bull Run, provided only limited help. Life proved especially difficult for the working class, which felt they had been called on to bear the brunt of the war's hardships. Then, in March 1863, arrived the National Enrollment Act. This military conscription law made all men ages 20 to 45 eligible for the draft if they were physically and mentally healthy, and were not the child of infirm parents, the only son of a widow, or a widower with dependent children.

The act angered many whites who resented being forced to fight a war to free African Americans. They found sympathy with Copperheads and newspapers like Benjamin Wood's *New York Daily News*—which started up publication again that May—as well as the *New York Weekly Day Book* and *New York Express*, which fanned the belief that whites would lose their jobs to emancipated slaves.

While the act called for drafting citizens, many avoided service. One simply needed to either find a replacement or pay $300. The wealthy could easily buy their way out. P.T. Barnum recalled how "I was too old to go to the field," and paid for four others to take his place. George Templeton Strong ended up giving $1,100 to Herman Henderman to be his substitute. The attorney wrote in his journal how he told the 22-year-old, who mustered in as a private in Company F of the Seventh New York Volunteer Infantry, "to write me if he found himself in the hospital or trouble, and that I would try to do what I properly could to help him." Henderman survived the war. The cost of finding a replacement, though, was way out of the reach of the average New Yorker, especially in a city grappling with wartime inflation. As one man wrote to the *New York Times*, "that 300-dollar law has made us nobodies, vagabonds and cast-outs of society, for whom nobody cares when we must go to war and be shot down."[1]

On July 4 at a rally at the Academy of Music, Governor Horatio Seymour railed against the new draft bill, reminding the audience that the "bloody, and treasonable, and revolutionary doctrine of public necessity can be proclaimed by a mob as well as by a Government." The drawing of names from a rotating drum dubbed the "Wheel of Misfortune" started on the 11th at the provost marshal's office on Third Avenue and 46th Street. According to the *New York Herald*, "On Saturday evening there was intense excitement in the neighborhood, and when the names of the conscripts were read there seemed to be a general determination to resist the law." The paper published the list of more than 1,200 names, and noted how "The fact that nearly all the men drafted were laborers and mechanics added fuel to the flame."[2]

As we've seen, firemen traditionally earned an exemption from military service. But John Masterson, a member of Black Joke Engine Co. No. 33—the second company to go by that name, having been organized in 1852—had his name picked. His compatriots resented the imposition, and on Monday the 13th raided the provost office, dumped turpentine on the floor, and burned down the building. Only after Fire Chief John Decker implored them to let the fire crew do their job did the Black Joke allow their colleagues to extinguish the flames.

The start of the draft came just a week after the Union scored a major victory at the Battle of Gettysburg, where northern troops turned back General Robert E. Lee's army. It was a critical moment, and the need for combat troops in Pennsylvania meant that General John Wool, who commanded the Department of the East, only had 550 men spread out in eight New York forts. There were not enough troops or police to handle the mass of people who poured out onto the streets to protest the draft. Laborers, shipyard workers, those from foundries, railroads, and machine shops marched against the law, and Strong watched in horror as more than 500 Irish day laborers, some carrying fence-palings, converged on two homes on Lexington Avenue and 45th Street. He heard that the building was either owned by a draft officer or that a wounded policeman had taken refuge inside: "After a while sporadic paving-stones began to fly at the windows, ladies and children emerged from the rear and had a rather hard scramble over a high board fence, and then scudded off across the open, Heaven knows whither." Strong watched as the men sacked the building, and then left. "I could endure the disgraceful, sickening sight no longer, and what could I *do*?"[3]

He did try to do something, for as the violence spread, Strong and Dr. Wolcott Gibbs begged for martial law to be declared. Mayor George

Opdyke maintained that it was up to General Wool, and the officer deferred responsibility to the mayor. Strong, Gibbs, and others then telegraphed President Lincoln for help. There was little he could do. Most of the Union's troops were still off in Pennsylvania.

Because of this, rioters had free run of the city. They attacked and burned buildings, broke into gun shops, stole goods and alcohol, assaulted the State Armory, tore up train tracks, cut down telegraph poles, and threw up barricades. Some ransacked Brooks Brothers, making off with clothing, boots, and shoes. Others torched places of moral reform like the Magdalene Asylum—which sheltered elderly prostitutes—and set the Five Points Mission on fire. The crowd burned the home of Colonel Robert Nugent, who ran the draft. They also sought to destroy the Fifth Avenue homes of the wealthy, yelling, "Down with the rich!"

Maria Lydig Daly, the wife of Judge Charles Daly, wrote how "Mrs. Hilton said she never saw such creatures, such gaunt-looking savage men and women and even little children armed with brickbats, stones, pokers, shovels and tongs, coal-scuttles, and even tin pans and bits of iron." The mob tried to tear down the home of Charles King—the former *New York American* editor who was then president of Columbia University—but two Catholic priests stopped them. They also raided Mayor Opdyke's Union Steam Works factory on Second Avenue and 22nd Street. A force fought them off, but had to abandon their efforts when the crowd stole weapons and set the building ablaze, killing 10 people. Despite Archbishop John Hughes' call for calm, the rioters wrecked two Protestant churches. Many feared that the mob might cut off the Croton water mains and destroy the gasworks. Soldiers set up cannons on Gramercy Park, and Strong, who lived by the park, played it safe by filling his bathtubs along with all the pots, kettles, and pails in the house with water.[4]

Not far away stood the 17th Street home of editor George Putnam. Edwin Booth's wife, Mary, had recently died, and the actor lived there with his young daughter Edwina, along with his mother, Mary, and sister Rosalie. Edwin's brother John Wilkes had also just arrived to visit after performing at Buffalo's Metropolitan Theatre. Edwin solidly backed the Union, and had had regular heated exchanges about the war with John, a fervent secessionist and slavery supporter. But as the riots started, the family worked together, and took into the home Adam Badeau, an officer on General Thomas Sherman's staff, who had been wounded at the Siege of Port Hudson, Louisiana. John not only helped Edwin carry Badeau inside, the officer recalled how both Edwin and

John "dressed my wounds, and tended me with the greatest care." John meanwhile headed out onto the streets to see what was happening and to search for household supplies. "Several times a day Wilkes went out to learn the situation, and when he returned reported it to us all: but he said not one word to indicate that he sympathized with the rioters, or with the cause that was their apparent instigation."[5]

The Metropolitan Police could not control the crowds lurching through the streets. One group assaulted Police Chief John Kennedy. "They beat him, dragged him through the streets by his head, pitched him into a horse-pond, rolled him in mud-gutters, dragged him through piles of filth indescribable," reported the New York Tribune. "All the time, kicks, blows, and cuffs innumerable were bestowed by those nearest to him. Those in the background reached over the stooping heads of their murderous colleagues in their front, and pitched stones, whole bricks, quantities of mud." The crowd left Kennedy for dead, and a contingent of police swept in and rescued him.[6]

Invalid troops—wounded and disabled soldiers who served on guard duty—attempted to quell the rioters, but the mob easily stripped them of their bayonets and assaulted and killed them with clubs, sticks, and swords. Those who managed to escape found themselves "hunted like dogs." Colonel Henry O'Brien, who in June had received the authority to reorganize Elmer Ellsworth's Eleventh New York Volunteer Infantry Regiment—the Fire Zouaves—used a howitzer to drive people from Second Avenue. It killed a woman and child. When the mob caught O'Brien, the Tribune reported how "every club that could be brought to bear; every brick or stone that could be thrown with true aim; every heel that could hit the head of the unfortunate man, was put into requisition." Women, men, and boys danced around his insensate body, and they only stopped to allow a priest to administer the last rites to the officer.[7]

As the mob rampaged, many focused their wrath on African Americans. A wire sent to Secretary of War Edwin Stanton reported how "Small mobs [are] chasing isolated negroes as hounds would chase a fox." While Booth hid Badeau's servant, Randall, in his cellar to protect him from those searching homes for Blacks, the fear of what the rioters might do to those harboring African Americans caused many not to shelter them. When Maria Daly's father realized that his family had hidden 15 African Americans in their home, he ordered them out. "We feared for our own block on account of the Negro tenements below MacDougal Street, where the Negroes were on the roof, singing psalms and having firearms." Blacks on Bleecker and Carmine Streets fought back against the attackers by hurling bricks they pulled from their chimneys. Mobs invaded and torched the house of abolitionists James and Abigail Gibbons—she was the daughter of the abolitionist Isaac Hopper—and gleefully focused on the residences of interracial couples. Some African Americans took refuge in police stations. Others fled on ferries out of the city, as did Albro Lyons' family, which, after trying to defend their Colored Seamen's Boarding House, had no choice but to escape to Williamsburg.[8]

The Longshoremen's Association demanded that "the colored people must and shall be driven to other parts of industry." At the docks, an Irish mob assaulted 200 African American longshoremen and destroyed nearby homes, dance halls, and brothels that catered to them. Rioters grabbed all those they could, drowned some people, lynched others, immolated and mutilated their bodies, and dragged them around the streets as onlookers cheered for Confederate president Jefferson Davis. On Seventh Avenue and 27th Street they broke into a home, grabbed 23-year-old Abraham Franklin, who worked as a coachman and belonged to the Zion African Church. They beat him and then hanged him as his mother watched. Franklin was miraculously still alive when the military came and drove the crowd away. But the troops had to continue battling others, and after they left, the crowd hanged Franklin again.[9]

A mob descended on the Colored Orphans Asylum at Fifth Avenue and 43rd Street. The building housed 233 children, who according to the institution's records "were quietly seated in their school-rooms, playing in the nursery, or reclining on a sick bed in the hospital, when an infuriated mob, consisting of several thousand men, women, and children, armed with clubs, brickbats, etc., advanced upon the Institution." They beat down the door with an axe. Superintendent William Davis and Head Matron Jane McClellan rushed the children out the back door, saving all of them.

The crowd ransacked the four-story building, took away beds, rugs, even baby clothes, and set the building ablaze. When Hook and Ladder Co. No. 2 came to fight the fire, they, too, were attacked. Despite the assault, the firemen continued to battle both the flames and the crowd. And when the marauders told them they would die if they did not leave, Fire Chief John Decker told their assailants that they "will have to pass over our dead bodies." One group of children became separated from the larger group, and members of Engine Co. 18, an Irishman named Paddy McCaffrey, and drivers from the 42nd Street crosstown bus line protected them and rushed the youngsters to a police precinct station house.[10]

The rioters set out to wreck pro-Union publications along Newspaper Row. Expecting an assault on his paper, editor Henry Raymond—who on the 14th ran the headline "Crush the Mob!"—distributed rifles to his *Times* staff, set Gatling guns on the building's roof, and manned one himself. Benjamin Wood joined Raymond at the newspaper office, standing at the door with a pistol, telling those seeking to attack: "Men, you know that the *Daily News* has always been with you for the maintenance of your rights, but it is not your right to destroy the property of your fellow citizens, and you shall not pass here while I am alive to prevent it." The crowd left the *Times* and attacked the *Tribune*. Horace Greeley's staff had set out bales of newspapers to block their way. Even so, the horde wrecked the office and were about to set it on fire when the police arrived. Wall Street was meanwhile well defended, with troops stationed by howitzers and the staff at the Custom House ready to lob bombs. Those at the Bank Note Company had prepared tubs of sulfuric acid to pour from windows, while some at the Sub Treasury cradled bottles of vitriol.[11]

Governor Seymour tried to quell the rioters, and went out with District Attorney A. Oakey Hall and William Tweed to say he would seek to postpone the draft. It was, though, the arrival of 6,000 troops who finally ended one of the worst outbreaks of urban unrest in American history. By then the days of turmoil had killed 119 people. Lincoln ended up reducing the city's draft quota from 26,000 to 12,000. The Common Council arranged $3 million to pay relief and bounties for citizens, with Tweed and his Board of Supervisors running the Exemption Committee, paying for substitutes for the poor and those with families.

Not surprisingly, the city's African American population plummeted after the riots, dropping from 12,574 in 1860 to 9,945 in 1865. While some New Yorkers had committed murder, many others abhorred what had happened. The Committee of Merchants for the Relief of Colored People, Suffering from the Late Riots raised some $40,000 for support, and worked with African American ministers like Henry Highland Garnet and Charles Bennett Ray, who visited victims' homes to see how they could assist them.

And, as a sign of their changed stance on African Americans, Strong, as well as many other New Yorkers, favored arming Black troops, asking that "God pardon our blindness" when it came to the issue of slavery. In March 1864—just eight months after the draft riots—Strong took special pride in seeing the appearance of the Twentieth Colored Infantry Regiment, which his Union League Club cofounded. More than 100,000 spectators gathered at Union Square, which, the *Times* reported, "was packed with a dense crowd of citizens, among whom were great numbers of the colored friends and relatives of the recruits." Wives, sisters, and daughters of Union League members waved from a platform ornamented with flags in front of the club, and Strong extolled, "Ethiopia marching down Broadway, armed, drilled, truculent, and elate."[12]

Black New Yorkers signed up for service, and others recruited soldiers, raised money, and gathered clothes for them and for freed slaves, forming the American Freedmen's Friend Society. Frederick Douglass, who had fled the United States following John Brown's capture, returned to the country in early 1860. In 1863 he helped recruit soldiers for the African American 54th Massachusetts Volunteer Infantry. His sons Charles and Lewis joined up.

* * *

On May 30, 1864, Sergeant William Anderson, who had joined the Twenty-Sixth Colored Infantry Regiment, was in Beaufort, South Carolina, and drowned while bathing. On June 17, Anderson's widow Ellen, dressed in mourning black, boarded the whites-only car of the Eighth Avenue Railroad. A conductor told her to leave. She told him she was "sick and wished to ride up home." She explained that she had lost her husband, and recalled how the conductor replied that "he did not care for me, or my husband either." When a policeman told her to disembark, she responded that she "had a right to ride there as well as any where else." Two conductors and an officer then grabbed her. "They got me off the seat; I got hold of the straps of the car and then they both pulled me and dragged me so that I was very sore, and they tore my hand and at last succeeded in dragging me into the street."

As the *New York Evening Post* noted, "she was black—that was her offence." Anderson sued the railroad and won. Police Commissioner Thomas Acton scolded the officer, saying, "It was rather his duty to have arrested the conductor than the woman." The director of the railroad likewise took the conductor to task. The company then desegregated its cars. The following week the Sixth Avenue line—the one which had expelled Thomas Downing nine years earlier—did the same.[13]

Besides the fear of African Americans taking jobs from whites, as the war went the North's way, those opposed to Lincoln and his policies spread the long-held beliefs that freeing the slaves would bring about an immediate blending of the races. Nowhere was this more blatantly portrayed in print in than the *New York World*. The paper opposed the president, who briefly shuttered the publication and had editor Manton Marble locked up after he ran a fabricated order claiming that Lincoln wanted to draft 500,000 men. As the 1864 election neared, the paper ran an attempt at a spoof, entitled the "Miscegenation Ball." It portrayed the Lincoln Central Campaign Club in New York hosting a party filled with Republican leaders furiously mixing with, dancing with, and kissing African American women.

However, anti-Lincoln publications, Peace Democrats, or southern forces could do little to stop the North's military's successes. General Philip Sheridan's forces ravaged the Shenandoah Valley in 1864. That September, General William Tecumseh Sherman's troops captured Atlanta and burned it, and then began their devastating March to the Sea. Desperate for a reversal of their military fortunes, the South set out to strike at the heart of New York with the hope that an attack would galvanize their supporters to rise to their cause.

One plan entailed dumping arsenic, strychnine, prussic acid, and other chemicals into the city's reservoir. Another called for wrecking the Croton Dam. Both would devastate the city, which was suffering from a prolonged drought. "Destroy this Dam and we deprive the city of its sole source of supply of water," wrote the southern spy Charles Dunham. "Water in New York would soon become as scarce and expensive as whiskey in Richmond. Thousands of poor devils who will otherwise be sent to the Yankee armies will be required to reconstruct the Dam—a work which it will require six months, and cost upwards of $5,000,000, to complete."[14]

Burning the city infamous for its fires, though, seemed simpler and more thorough, so in November a group of Confederates under the command of Lieutenant Colonel Robert Martin headed to New York to torch the town. The southern agents decided to target hotels and other public spaces, sought to capture the Sub Treasury, release the prisoners at Brooklyn's Fort Lafayette, and foment unrest in the city. They planned to attack on election day, November 8, but postponed their plot because their effort was uncovered. Lincoln won that election, defeating his former general George B. McClellan. In New York City, though, the president tallied just 36,765 votes, compared to McClellan's 73,666.

The Confederates then decided to burn the city on Evacuation Day, November 25, commemorating when New York was liberated from the British in 1783. Eight conspirators checked into three or four different hotels each, taking with them just a black satchel with an overcoat to make it appear that they had luggage. One of the men was 23-year-old John W. Headley.

After he arrived, the future secretary of state of Kentucky went to Washington Place in Greenwich Village and picked up a heavy leather valise with 12 dozen bottles. The glass vials contained Greek Fire, a combustible chemical mixture, which ignited when exposed to air. Headley lugged the case onto a downtown street car, and passengers noted the smell of rotten eggs, with one of them commenting, "There must be something dead in that valise." He then met up with his seven compatriots, and they divided up the four-ounce containers.[15]

Headley started his work at the Astor House Hotel. "After lighting the gas jet I hung the bedclothes loosely on the headboard and piled the chairs, drawers of the bureau and washstand on the bed." He went on to open the bottle of Greek Fire. "It blazed up instantly and the whole bed seemed to be in flames before I could get out. I locked the door and walked down the hall and stairway to the office, which was fairly crowded with people. I left the key at the office as usual and passed out."

Headley then went to the Everett House to continue his work. From there he looked over at the Astor House and noticed that "A bright light appeared within but there were no indications below of any alarm. After getting through at the Everett House I started to the United States Hotel, when the fire bells began to ring up town. I got through at the United States Hotel without trouble. . . . As I came back to Broadway it seemed that a hundred bells were ringing, great crowds were gathering on the street, and there was general consternation. I concluded to go and see how my fires were doing."

After one of Headley's fellow arsonists, Captain Robert Cobb Kennedy, set his fires, he stopped at a bar for a few drinks and then made his way to Barnum's American Museum. The building had attracted a crowd that day who came to see "The Tallest, Shortest and Fattest Specimens of Humanity Ever Seen." Once inside, Kennedy smashed a bottle of Greek Fire on the floor. Panic broke out. "People were coming out and down ladders from the second and third floor windows and the manager was crying out for help to get his animals out," noted Headley. "It looked like people were getting hurt running over each other in the stampede." As Headley made his way along the streets, he spotted Kennedy up ahead. "I closed up behind him and slapped him on the shoulder. He squatted and began to draw his pistol, but I laughed and he knew me. He laughed and said he ought to shoot me for giving him such a scare."[16]

That evening, the Booth brothers, Edwin, Junius Jr., and John, made their first and only joint stage performance. Advertised as "the three sons of the

Great Booth," they performed before 3,000 people at the Winter Garden Theatre on Broadway and 2nd Street, where they appeared in Shakespeare's *Julius Caesar*, which is of course all about political assassination. Edwin played Brutus, with Junius as Cassius and John as Mark Anthony. Edwin had arranged the show to raise money for a statue of Shakespeare for Central Park. The cornerstone for it had been laid that April, on the 300th anniversary of the Bard's birth. To prepare for the "Booth Benefit for the Shakespeare Statue Fund," John shaved his mustache. "The theater was crowded to suffocation, people standing in every available place," recalled the Booths' sister Asia Booth Clarke.

As the Booths performed, Confederate John Ashbrook set his fire in the neighboring Lafarge House hotel. "In the midst of the performance, there was a cry of fire," wrote Maria Daly. "Fortunately we did not know the extent of the danger." Edwin came on stage to tell the audience that while a fire had broken out at the Lafarge, it had been put out and they should stay calm. The show then continued. Meanwhile, fire crews easily quenched all the flames, which didn't spread because the Confederates had kept the windows and doors shut, cutting the fire off from extra oxygen.[17]

While the incendiaries failed, the Booth's Winter Garden performance proved a success. The brothers raised $4,000 for the Central Park statue, with the *Times* reporting that Edwin exhibited "a certain classic beauty and scholarly refinement," Junius a "vigorous execution," and John an "*élan* and fire which at times fairly electrified the audience and whirls them along with him." But at breakfast at Edwin's new home on 19th Street, talk turned to the previous night's fire. John argued that the attempt to burn the city was justified in response to what the North was doing to the South. When Edwin revealed that he had voted for the first time a few weeks earlier and cast a ballot for Lincoln, John became incensed. Edwin recalled how John then "declared his belief that Lincoln would be made king of America." Edwin branded his brother a rank secessionist and kicked him out of the house.[18]

The attempt to torch New York did not lead to a popular or spontaneous uprising. Captain Kennedy was one of those arrested, and hanged on March 25, 1865, at Fort Lafayette. He was the last Confederate soldier executed during the war. Nonetheless, he lived on at Barnum's American Museum, where the showman fashioned a wax figure of him for the very building he tried to torch.

The war finally ended two weeks later, on April 9, when Robert E. Lee surrendered to Ulysses S. Grant at Virginia's Appomattox Court House. Strong learned the news late that evening. "A series of vehement pulls at the front door bell slowly roused me to consciousness. . . . I made my way downstairs in my dressing-gown, half awake. . . . It was George C. Anthon come to announce the Surrender and that the rebel army . . . has ceased to exist. It can bother and perplex none but historians henceforth forever. It can never open fire again on loyal men or lend its powerful aid to any cause, good or bad. There is no such army any more. God be praised!"[19]

Coda

The Phoenix Takes Flight

On Friday, April 14, 1865, five days after the South surrendered, John Wilkes Booth shot Abraham Lincoln in Ford's Theatre in Washington. The president died the following day. New York—even though most of its citizens had not voted for Lincoln in either presidential election—started to grieve. When Walt Whitman walked up Broadway, he noted how, "All Broadway is black with mourning—the facades of the houses are festooned with black—great flags with wide heavy fringes of dead black, give a pensive effect—toward noon the sky darkened & it began to rain."[1]

George Templeton Strong traveled to Washington on the 18th, and the following day visited the White House, where Lincoln's coffin rested in the East Room. "I had a last glimpse of the honest face of our great and good President as we passed by," he wrote. "It was darker than in life, otherwise little changed." An honor guard then brought Lincoln's remains back to Springfield, Illinois, stopping in towns and cities along the way. On the 24th it arrived in New York. Alexander Stewart, William Tweed, Robert S. Hone, and others took part in the Committee of Arrangements. A hearse with six gray horses brought the president across Canal and down Broadway to City Hall, where hundreds of thousands of people lined the streets. Masses of citizens waited to pay their respects. On the 25th a cortege took Lincoln to the Hudson River Depot for his continued trip home. At the end of the procession marched African American freedmen. The following day, federal troops discovered Booth hiding in a tobacco barn near Port Royal, Virginia, and killed him.[2]

The four-year-long Civil War resulted in the death of more than 700,000 Americans, the destruction of the southern economy, and the leveling of many cities. New York emerged from the fratricide stronger, an undisputed international center of finance, industry, and culture. For many, the war was something they sought to put behind them. Strong had dinner at the Union League Club on May 22, and then spent an hour looking through a folio containing newspaper clippings from December 1860, which chronicled the lead-up to the war: "It seemed like reading the records of some remote age and of a people wholly unlike our own." The city of 1865 proved nothing like 1860. And it was a world away from the town that Strong grew up in, and even further from that of Philip Hone's youth. Hone had been born in 1780 during the British wartime occupation of New York in the American Revolution. When the first census was taken in 1790, New York had 33,131 people. When Strong was born in 1820 it stood at 123,706. By 1865, the city was home to 726,386 people.[3] In comparison, Boston, which had 43,298 people in 1820, had 192,264 people.

Slavery had ended in New York State in 1827. In December 1865 the 13th Amendment to the Constitution abolished it in the land. On July 6 of that year, Arthur Tappan, who spent a good part of his life and fortune battling the "peculiar institution," wrote to his brother Lewis that he rejoiced "to see the day of universal freedom in our country, and feel ready to say now, 'Lord, let thy servant depart in peace,' for I have seen the divine blessing resting on the efforts of thy servants for the poor slave." He died 17 days later in New Haven. Lewis died in Brooklyn in 1873. But there was still work to be done, with Frederick Douglass commenting in May 1865 that slavery would not be done away with "until the black man has the ballot." In July 1868, the 14th Amendment was ratified, granting citizenship to all persons "born or naturalized in the United States." This included former enslaved persons, and provided all citizens with "equal protection under the laws." Then in February 1870, the 15th Amendment stated that "The right of citizens of the United States to vote shall not be denied or abridged by the United States or by any State on account of race, color, or previous condition of servitude."

William Lloyd Garrison also believed his mission had succeeded, and shut down *The Liberator* on December 29, 1865, telling his readership, "Hail, year of jubilee!" Frederick Law Olmsted, who had resigned from the Sanitary Commission in September 1863 and gone to work at the massive Mariposa gold mining estate in the foothills of California's Sierra Nevada Mountains, returned east after the war. There he joined Garrison's son, Wendell Phillips Garrison, along with Edwin Godkin in publishing *The Nation*, which they saw as an heir to *The Liberator*, announcing in its prospectus: "*The Nation* will not be the organ of any party, sect or body. It will, on the contrary, make an earnest effort to bring to discussion of political and social questions a really critical spirit, and to wage war upon the vices of violence, exaggeration and misrepresentation by which so much of the political writing of the day is marred." In April 1866, restaurateur Thomas Downing died. The *New York Times* reported on both his passing and funeral, and the Chamber of Commerce closed for a day in his honor.[4]

At the time, Alexander Stewart's new Iron Palace on Broadway between 9th and 10th Streets was attracting vast crowds of customers. The establishment of his emporium helped spur the creation of what nearby became known as Ladies' Mile. The high-end shopping thoroughfare wended its way up Broadway, across 14th Street, over to Sixth Avenue, and then north to 23rd Street and east to Madison Square. The district became a retail hub of the city and would boast of such upscale businesses as Lord & Taylor, B. Altman, and Arnold Constable. And 11 blocks to the north, John Kellum built a Second Empire mansion for Stewart, a grand marble palace with a mansard roof that was set on a massive 100-foot-by-112-foot lot alongside the homes of John Jacob Astor II and William B. Astor II.[5]

Fernando Wood served in the House of Representatives from 1863 to 1865. In 1867 he returned to Congress, where the former Peace Democrat opposed Reconstruction efforts to help African Americans. He held office until his death at age 68 in 1881. William Tweed would continue his climb to citywide power and wealth. He would take on such roles as Grand Sachem of Tammany, president of the Board of Supervisors, and chairman of the Democratic Central Committee of New York County. And as commissioner of public works, he oversaw street openings. This let him know of development plans, so he and his cronies could buy up land where new streets and avenues were about to be created, thus allowing them to profit greatly. With so much control, he would become known as "Boss"—a title derived from the Dutch word *bass* for "master"—and was set on his way to running his infamous Ring.

What has become the most visible sign of Boss Tweed's ways sprouted in those years. On December 26, 1861, the cornerstone for the New York County Courthouse was laid on Chambers Street. The grand Italianate building designed by Kellum took some two decades to complete. Tweed purchased a marble quarry in Massachusetts, which supplied a large share of the courthouse's stone—and offered him vast kickbacks. And as work slowly progressed, nearly every contractor associated with its construction profited from vastly inflated payments. One day's worth of cabinetry work came out to $125,830.56. All this eventually ballooned the cost of what become infamously known as the Tweed Courthouse from the original $250,000 budget to some $12 million, with the *Times* reporting: "Just imagine the untiring industry, the wear and tear of muscle, the anxiety of mind, the weary days and the sleepless nights, that it must have cost the 'Boss' to procure all these sums of money and superintend their economical outlay, in order that the people might have a temple of justice." By the time that the *Times* in 1871 exposed evidence of his and his Ring's malfeasance and legal action was taken, they had drained the city of between $30 million and $200 million. Sentenced for his crimes, Tweed would die in the Ludlow Street jail in April 1878 at age 55.[6]

Years earlier, the proud volunteer fire department had given Tweed his springboard to power. Many had long hoped for an end to its rowdy ways. Fire Chief James Gulick had died in September 1861, and the companies, which he nobly led before and after the Great Fire of 1835, were phased out on March 30, 1865. Houses that generations of men loved, and which sported such grand and florid names as Excelsior, Americus, Oceanus, Black Joke, Live Oak, Niagara, Mazeppa, Cataract, Lafayette, Chatham, and Franklin were no more.

As a tribute to some of the men, Empire Engine Company No. 42 approached Trinity Church and asked permission to erect a monument to their house's comrades who "had been killed in battle or in the discharge of their duty as firemen." Strong served as a committee member at the church's meeting that looked over the request, and approved the monument. In March 1866, the company set an obelisk topped by an orb and surrounded by four posts close to the Broadway railings, with the *New York Sunday Mercury* calling the memorial "a neat marble monument." It honored those killed fighting fires, like Augustus Cowdrey who died on July 19, 1845, during the second Great Fire, and those who perished in the Civil War.[7]

In the place of the volunteer force, the state legislature—much as it did when it formed the Metropolitan Police District in 1857—created the Metropolitan Fire Brigade of New-York. The new professional force included Manhattan and Brooklyn, and christened its companies with prosaic-sounding names that started with Metropolitan Steam Engine No. 1. It had 579 members and could boast of three dozen engine companies, five hand engine companies, and 15 hook-and-ladder companies.[8]

Despite the organization of the new force, its horse-drawn engines, centralized command system, and fireboxes, blazes continued to ravage the town, most notably the one on July 13, 1865, that destroyed Barnum's American Museum. The morning show had already ended when the alarm sounded and smoke filled the structure. The staff uncaged many of the parrots, eagles, vultures, and hummingbirds so they could fly to safety. And a fireman saved

Ned the Learned Seal. But the monkeys, snakes, alligators, kangaroos, lions, and polar bears, along with two beluga whales in the basement tank, perished. People also threw objects out of the windows. While the waxed figures of Napoleon, Queen Victoria, and the hanged Confederate arsonist Robert Cobb Kennedy melted, someone succeeded in tossing the figure of Jefferson Davis onto the street. A crowd grabbed the deposed Confederate president's effigy and hanged it from a lamppost on Fulton near St. Paul's. As the *Times* noted, "Almost in the twinkling of an eye, the dirty, ill-shaped structure, filled with specimens so full of suggestion and merit, passed from our gaze, and its like cannot soon be seen again."

A severe drought was gripping the city, and Horace Greeley's *New York Tribune* went on to note that while "The Fire Department worked with great zeal and determination, and did all men could do to stay the progress of the flames," their efforts "were paralyzed for the want of water." The city had vastly grown since the Croton Aqueduct started bringing water to the city in 1842. The dearth of water proved to be a persistent problem, one that the paper pointed out continually. It also emphasized the need for larger water mains in the southern end of the town, the necessity of more reservoirs, as well as the overdue repair of the aqueduct. In 1866 work began on the 1.7-billion-gallon Boyd's Corner Reservoir in Putnam County to increase the city's supply.[9]

That fire cost P.T. Barnum $400,000, yet he only had $40,000 worth of insurance. He said he had enough to retire, and asked a few of his friends what he should do. Greeley told him, "If I were you, I would go fishing. I've been trying for thirty years to go fishing, and have never been able to do it." Barnum didn't in fact hang up his showman's hat. Knowing he had workers to help, he found a space at Broadway and Spring Street and sent his staff to Europe and Asia in search of new (and spurious) treasures, purchased a few museum collections, and reopened in the fall in a space with a 2,500-seat lecture hall decorated by Bowery Theatre artist Giuseppe Guidicini.

James Gordon Bennett wanted to build a new newspaper office on the burned Barnum site, and leased it from the showman. The *New York Herald* editor then sought to buy the spot. But when he struck the deal to purchase the land for $500,000, his 11-year lease money was still included, meaning Bennett found himself responsible for both the lease and sale costs. Barnum refused to refund the lease money to the man he had so easily duped with the Joice Heth story in 1836. He simply told Bennett's attorney that he had already spent the money and that "I don't make child's bargains." Bennett then refused to run Barnum's ads. Barnum in return got the city's theater owners to boycott the *Herald*, and for the next two years they only placed ads in his competitors' papers along with the statement, "This establishment does not advertise in the *New-York Herald*."[10]

Bennett retired in 1866, turning over his paper to his son, James Gordon Jr. That same year, following the death of his wife, Frances, William Cullen Bryant gave up daily oversight of the *New York Evening Post*. The following year, in a move he hoped would help heal the nation, Greeley sought to promote post-war reconciliation. Along with Gerrit Smith—the abolitionist who helped fund John Brown's raid on Harpers Ferry—and more than a dozen other Unionists, he raised $100,000 for a bond for the former Confederate Davis. Response to his action caused the *Tribune*'s circulation to dip by half. Greeley, though, accepted the loss, noting, "I was quite aware that what I did would be so represented as to alienate for a season some valued friends, and set against me the great mass of those who know little and think less. . . . So I went quietly on my way; and in due time the storm gave place to a calm."[11]

At the same time, turmoil continued to plague the Bowery Theatre. Managers George Fox and James Lingard had had a falling out over the New Bowery Theatre back in 1862. Lingard bought out Fox's share, and Fox took over the old Bowery, calling it Fox's Old Bowery Theatre. Then, on December 18, 1866, a fire started at the New Bowery just before five in the afternoon. "The fire raged fearfully, the flames apparently coming up from the basement, and emitting a heat so intense as to blister the doors, shutters, and crack the windows on the other side of the street," reported the *New York Sun*. The front of the building collapsed, as did the walls on Elizabeth and Hester Streets, and the wind blew flames down Elizabeth Street. Lingard had no insurance on the house, and, despite their differences, Fox ran benefits for Lingard, using 100 volunteers from the casts of the Old and the New Bowery. Four years later Lingard died, and Fox passed away in 1877. The old Bowery—the theater that originally opened in its first incarnation in 1826 in a building by Ithiel Town with a performance of Thomas Holcroft's *The Road to Ruin*—would miraculously survive for another half century, burning down for its fifth and final time in 1929.[12]

As it had with the fire department, the city overhauled how it dealt with health issues and plagues. Researchers had been searching for the cause of sicknesses. When cholera had returned to England in 1848, Dr. John Snow looked into the idea that a microorganism had contaminated the water and spread the disease. During an outbreak in the early 1850s, he studied the pattern of deaths around London, based on where people had drawn their water. By mapping the location of cholera cases, he showed that the disease originated from a specific street pump. When officials closed that pump, cases of cholera dropped. While a vaccine would not be produced until 1885, a basic understanding of the cause of the disease drove sanitary improvements in cities.

Many worked to bring such changes to New York. In 1864, the Citizens' Association of New York formed the Council of Hygiene and Public Health. The group sent out inspectors to report on the city's sanitary conditions, and systematically studied the link between sanitation and public health. The following year, the state empowered the Croton Aqueduct Department with the right to "devise and frame a plan of sewage and drainage for the whole city." The department began laying thousands of feet of lines. Then, as cholera neared the city again in 1866, the new Metropolitan Board of Health dispatched health officials to clean up yards, privies, and remove refuse, rotting carcasses, and manure. Street cleaners meanwhile scoured the roadways. All the work kept the cholera death toll to 1,137—under half of the 2,509 who died when the disease arrived in 1854, just over a fifth of those who perished in 1849, and a third of those who succumbed in 1832.

A move to improve housing likewise began. At the end of the war, the city had some 15,000 tenement houses. Many went up with scant regard for regulations. It was determined that 65 percent of New Yorkers lived in substandard housing, and the city enacted its first comprehensive housing law, the Tenement House Act of 1867. The law stipulated that buildings required a window or ventilator in sleeping rooms, as well as fire escapes, and "good and sufficient water-closets or privies." While the law proved weak and didn't really change the lives of most tenants, it was the start of decades' worth of efforts to improve conditions.[13]

* * *

During that year, the *Times* reported that the once stately St. John's Park, where Arthur Tappan and others lived, had become "filled up with cheap boarders; the fine old mansions are crammed with clerks, and tradesmen and mechanics, and the locality is so distinctively appropriated to these purposes as to be known chiefly as 'Hash-square.'" Trinity Church sold the land to the Hudson River Railroad Company for $400,000, and the *Times* predicted that in no time "its stately trees will give place to the bales and boxes that make up the vast freighting business."[14]

St. John's Chapel, where Tappan worshipped, miraculously survived the area's transformation. It stood alongside the rail yard until 1918, when the city demolished it as part of the widening of Varick Street. Much of such change to the island came about because of the building of surveyor John Randel's 1811 layout for the streets and avenues, which cut through the island's ponds, streams, marshes, hills, and farms. Randel's plan, though, just reached up to 155th Street, an area that in the early years of the century seemed so remote that the thought of running through streets appeared foolhardy. But within a few decades, development had rushed up the island. In 1860, the state formed the Washington Heights Commission, which surveyed the land above 155th Street. Frederick Law Olmsted and Calvert Vaux served as consultants, and starting in 1865, Andrew Haswell Green and his Central Park Commission oversaw the plans. They extended the streets. Unlike the commissioners in 1811, they also considered the area's topography. In the coming years, a modified grid that had more respect for Manhattan's landscape came into being in the north. As Green noted in November 1901, "It is the only portion where any trace of its pristine beauty remains undesecrated and unrazed by the levelling march of so-called 'public improvements.'"[15]

Others looked north, too. In 1892, Columbia University bought land in Manhattan's Morningside Heights. The following year the school chose Charles McKim at the architectural firm of McKim, Mead & White to design their stately new Beaux Arts campus, with the school moving from its 49th Street site to the 36-acre location in 1897. New York University—which had established itself on the 10-acre Washington Square Park in the 1830s— found Greenwich Village of the late 19th century too crowded. In 1895 it shifted its undergraduate and engineering colleges to a new 45-acre campus in the Bronx. The school, though, retained its Village site for graduate and professional training classes. Alexander Jackson Davis' Gothic citadel of learning was demolished, and a new, larger, Renaissance Revival building by Alfred Zucker went up. For their Bronx campus, they had McKim's partner, Stanford White, fashion the grounds overlooking the Harlem River with buildings of classical splendor. Both White and McKim, along with their partner William Mead, were spiritual heirs to Davis and Ithiel Town's fruitful collaboration, and major proponents of the City Beautiful Movement—with its idea of grand urban planning to improve the workings of cities—a design concept that would transform many metropolitan centers in the early 20th century.[16]

As Columbia and NYU settled into their new expansive spaces, Green saw the fruition of his vision for a greater New York. Starting in 1868, he had called for Manhattan's annexation of the Bronx, Brooklyn, Queens, and Staten Island. Six years later, New York took over the Bronx communities of Kingsbridge, Morrisania, and West Farms, and in the mid-1890s additional areas in the Bronx. By then, Green helped draft the Consolidation Law, and what was called Greater New York became a reality on January 1, 1898. "The end of the old New-York and the beginning of the greater city was marked last night by perhaps the biggest, nosiest and most hilarious New Year's Eve celebration that Manhattan Island has ever known," reported the *Tribune*. "The air was full of the din of hundreds of horns and thousands of shouts. The streets were full of a howling, pushing, shoving, hilarious multitude." There was a procession with mounted police, fire engines, colored floats, and bicyclists, and at the stroke of midnight, the city flag was raised to the top of the City Hall flagstaff, and singing societies performed "Auld Lang Syne."

At sunrise, a 100-gun salute was fired at Governors Island. Overnight the city went from a 65-square-mile to a 304-square-mile metropolis, its population leaping from some 1.8 million to 3.35 million, making it the second largest city in the world, after London. New York now sprawled across five boroughs with some 6,900 acres' worth of parks, 15 times more than set aside for New York in 1811. And the 843-acre Greensward Plan that Vaux and Olmsted had crafted in the spiritual center of New York had by then blossomed into something that people sorely relied on as a respite and popular destination.[17]

Novelist Edith Wharton, who was born in New York at the start of the Civil War, recalled, "One of the most depressing impressions of my childhood is my recollection of the intolerable ugliness of New York, of its untended streets and the narrow houses so lacking in external dignity, so crammed with smug and suffocating upholstery." Yet Wharton fondly recalled escaping the urban grittiness by heading to Vaux and Olmsted's Central Park for "a hunt for violets and hepaticas in the secluded dells of the Ramble."[18]

George Templeton Strong especially enjoyed his regular visits to the park after the Civil War, taking walks along its paths and drives with Ellen. He couldn't help but marvel at both the beauty of the spot and the vast changes wrought to his hometown. "Uptown this evening to Central Park," he wrote in July 1871. "With the growth of this city, my evening strolls have resumed their Northern or uptown direction. In old Greenwich Street days—1838–1848—they were up to 14th St. Now they are up to 79th & 80th St. This was a crystalline North West evening, & the sunset sky with a few horizontal bars of cloud shone chrysoprase beryl & sapphire—amber topaz & ruby. Entered the Park at 72nd St. and explored a new and lovely region in & around the Ramble."

For Ellen and George Strong, and so many other New Yorkers, the space proved to be what he called "a priceless acquisition." By preventing development in the land that became Central Park, the enforced absence of growth further spurred the expansion of the surrounding metropolis, as citizens sought to be close to a spot forever free of the city's unrelenting march of progress. It had, as Olmsted and Vaux had hoped, become a soothing ground that tempered the community's brasher urges, formed a gentler urban center, and established a vast and permanent escape from the frenetic pace of a metropolis seemingly never at peace.[19]

Notes

Preface: The Bowery Theatre Burns

1. "The horizon was lighted . . ." from *New York American* (*NYAM*), May 27, 1828; A line was formed . . ." from *NYAM*, June 3, 1828; "a pyramid of flame . . . from *New York Evening Post* (*NYEP*), May 27, 1828; "All out! . . ." from Augustine E. Costello, *Our Firemen: A History of the New York Fire Departments, Volunteer and Paid*, New York: Knickerbocker Press, 1997, p. 472.
2. "In no part of the world . . ." from *NYAM*, May 30, 1828; "The conclusion is irresistible . . ." from the Diary of Philip Hone manuscript (*PHD-MS*), May 27, 1828, New-York Historical Society; "Resolved . . ." from New York Association Papers, Minutes Book, Houghton Library, Harvard University, May 27, 1828.
3. "Doric simplicity . . ." from the *New-York Mirror, and Ladies' Literary Gazette* (*NYM*), August 23, 1828; "Immense Edifice . . ." from *PHD-MS*; "Certify without hesitation . . ." from *New-York Gazette & General Advertiser* (*NYGGA*), August 20, 1828.
4. "As pretty a theatre . . ." from Frances Trollope, *Domestic Manners of the Americans*, London: Whittaker, Treacher, & Co., 1832, pp. 270–271.

Introduction

1. "Rich mines" from *New York Commercial Advertiser* (*NYCA*), December 10, 1824; January 7, 1825, stock offering, Hagley Museum & Library, Wurts Family Papers, Series II, Box 2, Nos. 31–50½, 51–70; "The products of your . . ." from *Niles' Register*, August 6, 1825; "Mr. S. Pierce has fitted . . ." from *New York Farmer*, October 1833.
2. For New York's population in 1825, see Franklin B. Hough, *Census of the State of New York, for 1865*, Albany: Charles Van Benthuysen & Sons, 1867, p. XXIV. Drop in shipping rates, see Edwin G. Burrows and Mike Wallace, *Gotham: A History of New York City to 1898*, New York: Oxford University Press, 1999, p. 431.
3. For a grand and profoundly detailed overview of New York and US history, please read Burrows and Wallace, *Gotham*, cited above, as well as David S. Reynolds, *Waking Giant: America in the Age of Jackson*, New York: Harper Collins, 2008. Similarly, for a magisterial overview of all things New York, there is I.N. Phelps Stokes' grand six-volume *The Iconography of Manhattan Island: 1498–1909*, New York: Robert H. Dodd, 1915, as well as *The Encyclopedia of New York City*, Kenneth T. Jackson, editor, New Haven: Yale University Press, 2010. "The greatest commercial emporium . . ." from

Burrows and Wallace, *Gotham*, p. 427. For shipbuilding rates, see Robert Greenhalgh Albion, "Yankee Domination of New York Port, 1820–1865," *The New England Quarterly*, Oct., 1932, Vol. 5, No. 4, pp. 665–698, p. 683.

4. "It is only necessary . . ." from James Fenimore Cooper, *Notions of the Americans*, vol. I, Philadelphia: Carey, Lea, & Blanchard, 1835, pp. 112 & 123.

5. On auction house business, see Ira Cohen, "The Auction System in the Port of New York, 1817-1837," *The Business History Review*, vol. XLV, no. 4, Winter 1971, p. 495. The best source of information on Hone can be gleaned from his diary. The complete unpublished diary is housed at the New-York Historical Society (*PHD-MS*). There are abridged versions of the journal: Bayard Tuckerman, *Diary of Philip Hone*, New York: Dodd, Mead and Company, 1910 (*PHD-BT*), and Allan Nevins, *The Diary of Philip Hone: 1828-1851*, New York: Dodd, Mead and Company, 1927 (*PHD-AN*). Hone is regularly cited in books dealing with this era, and aspects of his life are covered in places like Herbert Kriedman, *New York's Philip Hone: Businessman-Politician-Patron of Arts and Letters*, New York: New York University PhD, 1965; Edward Pessen, "Philip Hone's Set: The Social World of the New York City Elite in the 'Age of Egalitarianism,'" *The New-York Historical Society Quarterly*, vol. LVI, October 1972, no. 4; "All kinds of Albany boards . . ." from *The New-York Gazette, and the Weekly Mercury*, July 5, 1773.

6. Catharine and Philip Hone were married at Trinity Church on October 1, 1801, by Minister Benjamin Moore (Trinity Church's database of baptisms, marriages and deaths); Tuckerman spells her first name Catherine while Nevins spells it Catharine. The Trinity register has it as Catharine, which is how it will be spelled here. Profits cited in *PHD-AN*, p. ix.

7. "Widely known . . ." from N.T. Hubbard, *Autobiography of N.T. Hubbard with Personal Reminiscences of New York City from 1798 to 1875*, New York: John F. Trow & Son, 1875, p. 48. Size of parks is based on those listed on the New York City Parks Department website; "In the gentlest style . . . " from John Pintard, *Letters from John Pintard to His Daughter, Eliza Noel Pintard Davidson*, vol. IV, New York: New-York Historical Society, 1941, p. 39.

8. Hone won the office of mayor on the eighth ballot, earning 13 votes to William Paulding's 11 and William P. Van Ness's one: *Minutes of the Common Council of the City of New York*, 1784–1831 (*MCC, 1784–1831*), vol. XV, p. 147. It wouldn't be until 1834 when the city would begin to hold popular elections for mayor.

9. "This spot which a few years . . ." from *NYCA*, June 19, 1826; "The path of a man-ager . . ." from *NYM*, June 24, 1826; "Is extremely grateful . . ." from *NYGGA*, October 24, 1826; "appeared in a most excellent . . . " from *NYM*, November 11, 1826.

10. Paulding, whom Hone replaced in 1826, was voted back into office on December 25, 1826, winning 14 to 11 (*MCC, 1784–1831*), vol. XV, p. 771. "Incomparably the best Mayor . . ." from *NYCA*, December 27, 1826; "Unsuspecting Phil . . ." from Bleecker, A., to Verplanck, GC, January 24, 1827, *N-YHS*, G.C. Verplanck Paper, Box 1, Folder 3, #104; "Dignified, impartial . . ." from *NYEP*, January 27, 1827; "I have occasion-ally . . ." from *PHD-BT*, April 6, 1829.

11. "Will hereafter . . ." from *NYEP*, October 18, 1831.

12. As with Hone's diary, the New-York Historical Society holds George Templeton Strong's journals. It was published in four volumes, *The Diary of George Templeton,* Allan Nevins and Milton Halsey Thomas editors, New York: Octagon Books, 1952 (*GTSD*). Strong's thoughts and musings offer a vivid picture of his life and the life of New York and the nation. His entire diary has been scanned in by the society, and can be accessed at: http://digitalcollections.nyhistory.org/islandora/object/nyhs%3Astr ong. For background on the firm his father, George Washington Strong, founded and which Strong joined after college, please see Deborah S. Gardner, *Cadwalader, Wickersham & Taft: A Bicentennial History, 1792–1992,* New York: Cadwalader, Wickersham & Taft, 1994. "Not at all effusive . . ." from George W. Strong, *Letters of George W. Strong,* New York: G.P. Putnam's Sons, 1922, p. 14. Strong's office and home locations are listed in Strong, *Letters of George W. Strong,* p. 13; George Washington Strong's partner, John Wells, died in September 1823. Strong's second son, named John Wells Strong, only lived from December 3, 1822, to December 14, 1824.

13. "The bustle in the streets . . ." from Timothy Dwight, *Travels in New-England and New-York,* vol. III, London: William Baynes and Son, 1823; "That would exert . . ." from Lewis Tappan, *The Life of Arthur Tappan,* New York: Hurd and Houghton and Co., 1870, p. 91. For background on newspapers, see Louis H. Fox, *New York City Newspapers, 1820–1850: A Bibliography,* Chicago: University of Chicago Press, pp. 3–7.

14. "We shall endeavor . . ." and "good tempered . . ." from *New York Herald* (*NYH*), May 6, 1835; "The days of Webb . . ." from *NYH,* May 11, 1836; "Brace of blockheads . . ." from *NYH,* May 16, 1835; "A descendant . . ." quoted in Jonathan D. Sarna, *Jacksonian Jew: The Two Worlds of Mordecai Noah,* New York: Holmes & Meier Publishers, 1981, p. 119; "Over the head . . ." from *PHD-BT,* April 20, 1831.

15. Number of buildings constructed in 1826, see *NYM,* January 13, 1827; "hill, hollows . . ." from *The Talisman,* 1830; "gaily painted . . ." from Tyrone Power, *Impressions of America, During the Years 1833, 1834, and 1835,* vol. I, London: Richard Bentley, 1836, p. 48.

16. "An honour . . ." from *NYM,* September 26, 1829; "There are very few . . ." from *NYGGA,* April 20, 1835.

17. On size of the fire department, see Lowell M. Limpus, *History of the New York Fire Department,* New York: E.P. Dutton, 1940, p. 134.

18. For wealth in the city, see Edward Pessen, *Riches, Class, and Power before the Civil War,* Lexington, MA: D.C. Heath and Company, 1973, p. 33. The number of eligible voters is cited in Amy Bridges, *A City in the Republic: Antebellum New York and the Origins of Machine Politics,* Cambridge: Cambridge University Press, 1984, p. 59.

19. "When suddenly . . ." from *PHD-AN,* April 10, 1834; "Let us fly . . ." and "Stop, for the love . . ." from the New York *Sun* (*NYS*), April 11, 1834. For election results, see Ralph J. Caliendo, *New York City Mayors: Part I: The Mayors before 1898,* Bloomington, IN: Xlibris, 2010, p. 399.

20. For the city's population in 1835, see Hough, *Census of the State of New York;* for 1865, p. XXV. On construction in 1834, *NYEP,* January 27, 1835. On purchase of the Stephen Allen home, *New York City Land Conveyances 1654–1851* (*NYCLC*), Grantees,

New York Public Library, D–H, p. 73, and from *Catalogue of the Library of the Late Thomas Jefferson McKee*, part VII, New York: Douglas Taylor & Co. 1903, p. 1272. Alexander Jackson Davis purchases, see Alexander Jackson Davis, Letterbook, 1821–1890, Scrapbook and Diary, Metropolitan Museum of Art, October 1835.

21. On New York insurance companies, see Dalit Baranoff, "Principals, Agents, and Control in the American Fire Insurance Industry, 1799–1872," *Business and Economic History*, Fall 1998, Vol. 27, No. 1, pp. 91–93.

22. Not to be confused with the current magazine founded by Harold Ross in 1925, the *New-Yorker* was established in 1834. Horace Greeley and Henry Raymond were editors. It lasted until 1841, and was succeeded by Greeley's New York *Tribune*. Hanington has also been spelled occasionally as Hannington, but the former is how they advertised themselves. "Citizens opposed to . . ." from *PHD-BT*, August 27, 1835. The reference to Comstock & Andrews and their scuttles is mentioned in *NYS*, December 22, 1835. Comstock & Andrews is the firm where the Great Fire of 1835 would start. Sale of the *Constellation Constitution* in *NYS*, December 8, 1835.

23. "Diabolical weather . . ." from *GTSD*, December 12, 1835; "A rough and penetrating . . ." from *NYCA*, December 12, 1835; "The coldest and most . . ." from *PHD-MS*, December 16, 1835; "You can by keeping it . . ." from *NYH*, December 21, 1835; "The bells were ringing . . ." from *PHD-MS*, December 16, 1835; "Had barely time . . ." from *NYAM*, December 16, 1835.

24. "The thermometer on my . . ." from *PHD-MS*, December 16, 1835; "We pity . . ." from *NYH*, December 17, 1835.

25. "Mr. Hart the celebrated . . ." from *NYCA*, December 16, 1835. Tweed at Knickerbocker is mentioned in Costello, *Our Firemen*, p. 160.

Chapter 1

1. "The coldest one we . . ." from William Stone, *History of New York City*, New York: Virtue & Yorston, 1872, p. 471; "Managed to force . . ." from Costello, *Our Firemen*, p. 453; Comstock & Andrews main address was 131 Pearl Street. The store ran through the block, with the back opening on Merchant Street, a short block that ran northwesterly and then angled into Pearl Street; "I was writing . . ." from *PHD-BT*, December 17, 1835; "We were all sitting . . ." from Letter Catherine Wynkoop to Margaret Silvester, December 17, 1835, NYHS, Misc. Silvester Papers.

2. "Immediately down" from *PHD-AN*, December 17, 1835; On Rogers & Co., from Joseph Scoville, *The Old Merchants of New York City*, New York: Carleton Publisher, 1864; "Fire! Fire!" from James W. Sheahan and George P. Upton, *The Great Conflagration, Chicago: Its Past, Present and Future*, Chicago: Union Publishing Co., 1871, p. 416.

3. "Those few of us . . ." and "A burning wall . . ." from Stone, *History of New York City*, pp. 471–472; "We got the engine . . ." from *The American Print Works vs. Cornelius W. Lawrence, Supreme Court of New Jersey*—Essex Circuit, October 1852,

New York: Collins, Bowne & Co., 1852 (*APW*), pp. 125–126. The case was held in 1847. Extensive depositions were taken from many of those who were at the fire, and the court found in former mayor Lawrence's favor; "Stop the fire . . ." from Costello, *Our Firemen*, p. 295.

4. "Fully fifty . . ." and "In a few minutes . . ." from Costello, *Our Firemen*, p. 453 and p. 295; "Never was there . . ." from *NYEP*, December 17, 1835; "Everything we took . . ." from *APW*, p. 141; "The fire is evidently . . ." from *GTSD*, December 16, 1835; "We immediately removed . . ." from Strong, *Letters of George W. Strong*, p. 142; "When I arrived . . ." from *PHD-AN*, December 17, 1835; "I at once . . ." from Hubbard, *Autobiography of N.T. Hubbard*, p. 139.

5. "Mr. Lambert . . ." from *GTSD*, December 16, 1835; "Considered out of . . ." from *PHD-AN*, December 17, 1835; "The church was built . . ." from *APW*, pp. 137–138; Garden Street was also called Exchange Place.

6. "What a sight . . ." from Stone, *History of New York City*, p. 474; "Close our eyes . . ." from Letter Wynkoop to Silvester; "Went on a straight . . ." from *APW*, p. 125; "Were devouring . . ." from Tappan, *The Life of Arthur Tappan*, p. 273.

7. "It was with difficulty . . ." from *New York Evangelist,* December 19, 1835; "An oven" from *NYS*, December 19, 1835; "All hands . . ." from Tappan, *The Life of Arthur Tappan*, p. 274; "Put on a warm . . ." from Stone, *History of New York City*, p. 471; "I went to work . . ." from *APW*, p. 114.

8. "Filled with piece goods . . ." from *NYCA*, December 17, 1835; "Some seventy-five . . ." from *APW*, p. 118; "There was accumulated . . ." from *New York Star*, quoted in *NYEP*, December 21, 1835.

9. "Nearly a hundred . . ." from *NYCA*, December 18, 1835; "A gust of flame . . ." from *NYS*, quoted in *Atkinson's Cabinet*, January 1, 1836; "Dissolved and mingled . . ." from Stone, *History of New York City*, p. 473.

10. "The bells ringing . . ." from *NYH*, December 16, 1835; "About 1,000 merchants . . ." from *NYH*, December 18, 1835; "If they would extinguish . . ." from Stone, *History of New York City*, p. 479; "The heat . . ." from Costello, *Our Firemen*, p. 442; "Stream reached the spot . . ." from Stone, p. 479; "That the firemen . . ." from *New York Star,* quoted in *Atkinson's Casket*, January 1, 1836.

11. "For salt . . ." from *APW*, p. 126; "Down like hail" from *APW*, p. 92; "I heard a great . . ." from *APW*, p. 123; "The hose was attached . . ." from *APW*, p. 23; "Lay like iron . . ." from *A Brief History Intended to Accompany the Beautifully Colored Views of the Destructive Fire in New-York, December 16 and 17, 1835*, Broadside by Lewis P. Clover; "Papa has not . . ." from *GTSD*, December 16, 1835; "Office became inevitable . . ." from Strong, *Letters of George W. Strong*, p. 142.

12. "There seemed . . ." from *APW,* p. 114; "Almost incapable . . ." from *PHD-AN*, December 17, 1835; "They commenced . . ." and "There were some trucks . . ." from *APW*, pp. 126–127.

13. "Some crossed their arms . . ." and "For what sum . . ." from Harriet Martineau, *Society in America*, vol. II, London: Saunders and Otley, 1837, pp. 267–268; Noise of wagons . . ." from Mary Pemberton Cady Sturges, *Reminiscences of a Long Life*, New York, F.E. Parrish and Company, 1894, pp. 163–164.

14. "As he passed . . ." from Scoville, *The Old Merchants of New York City*, pp. 52–53; "There in his gala . . ." from John F. Watson, *Annals and Occurrences of New York City and State, in the Olden Times*, Philadelphia: Henry F. Anners, 1846, p. 372; "I went in . . ." from *APW*, p. 88.

15. "The venerable pile . . ." from *Journal of Commerce*, December 18, 1835, quoted in William H. Hallock, *Life of Gerard Hallock, Thirty-Three Years Editor of the New York Journal of Commerce*, New York: Oakley, Mason & Co., 1869, p. 279; "Commenced performing upon . . ." from Stone, *History of New York City*, p. 179; "The bright gold . . ." from New York *Star*, quoted in *Atkinson's Casket*, January 1, 1836; the New-York Historical Society has a melted fragment of the bell; "Prepared us fully . . ." and "By this one feat . . ." from *Journal of Commerce*, December 18, 1835, quoted in Hallock, *Life of Gerald Hallock*, p. 279.

16. "He got water . . ." from *APW*, p. 119; "The rapid flames . . ." from Stone, *History of New York City*, p. 480; "A solid building," from *APW*, p. 106; "I went up . . ." from *APW*, p. 141; "We mounted the steps . . ." from *NYM*, March 19, 1836.

17. "The public gaze . . ." from Stone, *History of New York City*, p. 476; "Blazing light . . ." from *NYH*, December 21, 1835; "With a tremendous crash" from *NYS*, December 18, 1835; "Is there a surgeon . . ." from Stone, *History of New York City*, p. 479.

18. "The most awful . . ." from Costello, *Our Firemen*, p. 453; "People on all sides . . ." from Asa Greene, *A Glance at New York*, New York: A. Greene, 1837, p. 202.

19. "The agonizing cries . . ." and "My God . . ." from *NYCA*, December 19, 1835.

20. "The burning liquid . . . ," "a terrible . . . ," and "fired hogshead . . ." from Stone, *History of New York City*, pp. 473–474; "Flakes of fire" from *NYCA*, December 17, 1835.

21. "Poured down into . . ." from *NYEP*, December 21, 1835; "The ladders were frozen . . ." from James Hamilton, *Reminiscences of James Hamilton: or, Men and Events, at Home and Abroad, during Three Quarters of a Century*, New York: Charles Scribner & Co., 1869, p. 288; "Were incapable . . ." from *APW*, p. 105.

22. "No means existed . . ." from *APW*, p. 124; "I entertained . . ." from *APW*, p. 167.

23. "Long and tedious . . ." from *APW*, p. 168; "I went immediately . . ." and "get ready . . ." from *APW*, pp. 89–90.

24. "Found a stray boat . . ." from *APW*, p. 103; "There was a cart . . ." and "I got a piece . . ." from *APW*, pp. 146–147.

25. "I fastened one end . . ." from *APW*, p. 169; "All present . . ." from Hamilton, *Reminiscences*, p. 286; "The whole building . . ." from *APW*, p 148.

26. "It threw down . . ." from Hamilton, *Reminiscences*, p. 286; "I saw that the wall . . ." from *APW*, p. 148; "The men's fingers . . ." from *APW*, p. 99; "I was concerned . . ." from *APW*, p. 91.

27. "Clear the street . . ." from *APW*, p. 130; "It was consequentially . . ." from Hamilton, *Reminiscences*, p. 287; "I stood looking . . ." from *APW*, p. 130.

28. "Seeing that this would . . ." from Hamilton, *Reminiscences*, p. 287.

29. "After setting fire . . ." from Hamilton, *Reminiscences*, p. 287; "By blowing up . . ." from Wynkoop to Silvester, January 17, 1835; "Many of them . . ." from New York *Star*, quoted in *Atkinson's Casket*, January 1, 1836; "Actually stood up . . ." from Costello, *Our Firemen*, p. 442; "My cloak was stiff . . ." from Hamilton, *Reminiscence*, p. 288.

Chapter 2

1. "Heart rending..." from *NYH*, December 18, 1835.

2. "Opened upon New-York..." from C. Foster, *An Account of the Conflagration of the Principal Part of the First Ward of the City of New-York*, New York: C. Foster, 1835, p. 4. "Fatigued in body..." from *PHD-BT*, December 17, 1835; the Erie Canal cost $7 million to construct.

3. "Was hastened by . . ." from Stone, *History of New York City*, p. 480; "Had been seized..." from *PHD-BT*, December 18, 1835. On Hosack's treatment, see Alexander Eddy Hosack, *A Memoir of the Late David Hosack, M.D.*, 1861, p. 334.

4. "Forgive us our sins..." from *NYH*, December 17, 1835.

5. "Presents a splendid spectacle..." from *GTSD*, December 17, 1835.

6. "Were seen shivering..." from *NYH*, December 17, 1835; "From the corner..." from *NYH*, December 18, 1835.

7. "Nothing but flames . . ." from *NYH*, December 18, 1835; "For sundry . . ." from Watson, *Annals*, p. 379.

8. "As a guard . . ." from Isabella Field Judson, *Cyrus W. Field, His Life and Work*, New York: Harper & Brothers, 1896, p. 19; "Liberal supply..." from *NYS*, December 21, 1835; "Refreshments, consisting . . ." from *Proceedings of the Board of Aldermen (PBA)*, vol. XXIII, New York: Chas. King, 1843, p. 407; "It seems almost . . ." from Letter, Wynkoop to Silvester, December 17, 1835; "Most of my nearest..." from *PHD-BT*, December 17, 1835.

9. On Rogers & Co., Scoville, *The Old Merchants of New York City*, pp. 52–53; "Lies in a state..." from *PHD-BT*, December 22, 1835; "Down William Street..." from Sturges, *Reminiscences*, p. 165.

10. "Blankets, silks..." from *NYCA*, December 19, 1835; "Great piles..." Watson, *Annals*, p. 371; "In an awful . . ." from *NYH*, December 18, 1835; Papers' notices, *NYH*, December 19 & 21, 1835; *NYS*, December 19, 1835; *NYCA*, December 22, 1835.

11. "Carmen and porters..." from *NYCA*, December 17, 1835.

12. "This is truly..." from *PHD-BT*, December 19, 1835.

13. "To extend every..." from *NYS*, December 19, 1835.

14. "A rebuke . . ." quoted in Bertram Wyatt-Brown, *Lewis Tappan and the Evangelical War Against Slavery*, Cleveland: The Press of Case Western Reserve University, 1969, p. 168; "That *inordinate spirit* . . ." from William Augustus Muhlenberg, "The Rebuke of the Lord. A Sermon, Preached in the Chapel of the Institute at Flushing, L.I. on the Sunday After the Great Fire in New-York, on the 16th and 17th Dec. 1835, Jamaica: I.F. Jones, 1835, p. 6; "It almost made . . ." from Letter, Wynkoop to Silvester, December 17, 1835; "Derived all . . ." and "He has acted . . . " referenced and mentioned from *NYH*, December 19, 1835.

15. "The whole insurance . . ." from *Letters and Literary Memorials of Samuel J. Tilden*, edited by John Bigelow, vol. 1, New York: Harper & Brothers Publishers, 1908, p. 3; "Brother Joseph's..." from Strong, *Letters of George W. Strong*, p. 143; Losses Eagle Fire Company from Louis Geldert, *The Eagle Fire Company of New York*, New York, 1906,

p. 73; "I suffer directly . . ." from *PHD-BT*, December 17, 1835; "Who had invested . . ." from Strong, *Letters of George W. Strong*, p. 143.

16. "There was an evident . . ." from *PHD-BT*, December 17, 1835; "More than . . ." from Strong, *Letters of George W. Strong*, pp. 143 and 148.

17. "The recent . . ." from *PHD-BT*, December 25, 1835; "Was so much affected . . ." from *PHD-MS*, December 25, 1835; "Evil in the city . . ." from Watson, *Annals*, p. 375; "Two Indians . . ." from Joseph Jefferson, *The Autobiography of Joseph Jefferson*, London: T. Fisher Unwin, 1889, p. 13; "To a very crowded house . . ." from *NYS*, December 24, 1835.

18. "These splendid exhibitions . . ." from *NYS*, December 22, 1835.

19. "Arthur Tappan & Co . . ." from *NYEP*, December 17, 1835; "Rebuild immediately . . ." from Tappan, *The Life of Arthur Tappan*, pp. 274 and 276; "The solitary front wall . . ." from *NYH*, December 19, 1835; "Other fastenings . . ." from Tappan, *The Life of Arthur Tappan*, p. 277.

20. "It is gratifying . . ." from *PHD-AN*, December 19, 1835; "Not one of Gayler's . . ." from *NYEP*, February 6, 1836; "Wrought Iron Roofs . . . " from *NYEP*, December 19, 1835.

21. "To alter the route . . ." from *Proceedings of the Boards of Aldermen and Assistant Alderman and Approved by the Mayor: From May 19, 1835, to May 23, 1836*, vol. III, New York: Common Council, 1836 (*PBAAA*), p. 129; "Producing regular blocks . . ." from *Documents of the Board of Assistants of the City of New York*, vol. II, New York: 1836 (*DBAsst*), p. 572; "the click of trowels . . ." from *The American Monthly Magazine*, January 1836; "with all convenient dispatch . . ." from *NYEP*, December 19, 1835.

22. "Like a Phoenix . . ." from Sturges, *Reminiscences*, p. 166; Vinegar in inkstands from *NYS*, December 24, 1835; "Hereafter I shall . . ." from *NYH*, May 10, 1836; "Fragments of the real statue . . ." from *NYS*, January 20, 1836; "The ringing of the bells . . ." from *The Knickerbocker or New-York Monthly Magazine*, December 1836.

23. "Rents have advanced . . ." from Strong, *Letters of George W. Strong*, p. 144.

24. "Greater than . . ." from *PHD-AN*, February 23, 1836; "In a comparatively . . ." from N.T. Hubbard, *Autobiography*, p. 139.

25. The South Reformed Dutch Church congregation split following the fire. The South Reformed Dutch Church moved to Murray Street in 1837, and the Washington Square Reformed Dutch Church settled on the east side of Washington Square Military Parade Ground in 1840. "Wealthiest and oldest families . . ." from *NYM*, June 11, 1836. On Delmonico's, see Lately Thomas, *Delmonico's: A Century of Splendor*, Boston: Houghton Mifflin Company, 1967, pp. 25–28.

26. Michael Weinberg, "The Great New York City Fire of 1835," *The Transferware Collectors Club Bulletin*, 2010, Fall issue, Vol. XI, No. 3, pp. 12–14; "No exertion on their part . . ." from *NYEP*, December 19, 1835; "Many slanderous . . ." from *NYCA*, December 26, 1835.

27. "Stand aside . . ." From *Documents of the Board of Aldermen of the City of New York*, vol. II, New York, 1836 (*DBA*), p. 393; "In less than five . . ." from *NYCA*, May 5, 1836; "In such a city . . ." from May 7, 1836.

28. "The part of the city . . ." from *NYEP*, June 29, 1836; "The streets . . ." from Gabriel Furman, "How New York Used to Celebrate Independence Day," *The New-York Historical Society Quarterly Bulletin*, July 1937, vol. XXI, no. 3, p. 94.

29. "The Bowery may as well . . ." from *NYH*, August 27, 1836.

30. "The mighty tongues . . ." from *New-York Spirit of the Times*, October 1, 1836; "Greater splendor . . ." from *New York Express*, September 26, 1836, quoted in Thomas A. Bogar, *Thomas Hamblin and the Bowery Theatre: The New York Reign of "Blood and Thunder" Melodramas*, Providence: Palgrave, 2018, p. 148; Monies raised at benefits, from *NYEP*, October 4 & 11, 1836.

31. "The worst . . ." from *NYEP*, August 29, 1836; "Kill him . . ." from *NYH*, November 18, 1836.

32. "Eleven months . . ." from *NYEP*, November 11, 1836; "The Great Fire of 1835 and the Marketing of Disaster," New-York Historical Society, From the Stacks blog post, July 10, 2019; "It is just a year . . ." from *PHD-BT*, December 16, 1836; "will be between . . ." from *PHD-AN*, December 28, 1836; "I have great reason . . ." from *PHD-BT*, January 1, 1837.

Chapter 3

1. "Boarding by the week . . ." from *NYEP*, August 16, 1822.

2. "Looks poorly . . ." from *PHD-AN*, April 7, 1834.

3. "An ornament . . ." from *PHD-AN*, May 1, 1834; "Imparts a most . . ." from *NYM*, June 11, 1836.

4. "The whole house . . ." from William Chambers, *Things as They Are in America*, London: William and Robert Chambers, 1854, p. 181; "Anyone who can pay . . ." from Axel Madsen, *John Jacob Astor: America's First Millionaire*, New York: John Wiley & Sons, 2001, p. 251.

5. Eric W. Sanderson's *Mannahattan: A Natural History of New York City* (New York: Abrams, 2009) is an essential book for understanding what Manhattan looked like before the Dutch set foot on the island in the 1620s. Other useful guides to that time are George Everett Hill and George E. Waring Jr.'s "Old Wells and Water-Courses of the Island of Manhattan," part I & II, in *Historic New York: Being the First Series of the Half Moon Papers*, Maud Wilder Goodwin, Alice Carrington Royce and Ruth Putnam editors. New York: G.P. Putnam's Son, 1897; Issachar Cozzens Jr.'s *A Geological History of Manhattan or New York Island*, New York: W.E. Dean, 1843; and of course Stokes's six-volume *The Iconography of Manhattan Island*; while Paul Cohen and Robert T. Augustyn, *Manhattan in Maps, 1527–1995* (New York: Rizzoli, 1997) offers an excellent visual reference to the city's growth. The south part of the island had hickory groves, which were sought after to make bows and arrows; "Rose gradually . . ." from William Alexander Duer, *New-York as It Was, During the Latter Part of the Last Century*, New York: Stanford and Swords, 1849, p. 13; the Washingtons settled into 3 Cherry Street in the spring of 1789. The home was leased from Samuel

Osgood for $845 a year. It proved, though, too small for the president's household, and they moved in 1790 to the more centrally located 39 Broadway.

6. "We used to catch . . ." from the *New York Times* (*NYT*), October 10, 1897.

7. "A sweet and rural . . ." from Washington Irving, *A History of New York; From the Beginning of the World to the End of the Dutch Dynasty*, New York: C.S. Van Winkle, 1826, p. 202.

8. "Hoop-Net, Draw-net . . ." *Minutes of the Common Council of the City of New York, 1675 to 1776*, vol. IV, New York, Dodd, Mead and Company, 1905 (*MCC, 1675–1776*), May 28, 1734, p. 209.

9. Population above 14th Street, see Isaac Kendall, *The Growth of New York*, New York: George W. Wood, 1865, p. 11; "I cannot tell you . . ." from Pierre M. Irving, *The Life and Letters of Washington Irving*, vol. 2, New York: Putnam and Son, 1869; Peter Washington Irving to Pierre Irving, September 26, 1835, p. 301.

10. "An ill-laid out . . ." from *NYM*, November 2, 1833. For an excellent study on the plotting and altering of Manhattan and the laying out of Randel's plan, please see Hilary Ballon, editor, *The Greatest Grid: The Master Plan of Manhattan, 1811–2011*, New York: Museum of the City of New York and Columbia University Press, 2012. "To lay out streets . . ." passed April 3, 1807, from *Laws of the State of New-York*, vol. V, Albany: Websters and Skinner, 1809, p. 125; "An estimable old . . ." from Martha J. Lamb, *History of the City of New York: Its Origin, Rise and Progress*, vol. III, New York, 1896: Valentine's Manual, Inc., 1921, p. 572; "A city is to be . . ." from Andrew H. Green, *Communication to the Commissioners of the Central Park*, New York: Wm. C. Bryant & Co. 1866, p. 30.

11. "It may be a subject . . ." from William Bridges, *Map of the City of New-York and Island of Manhattan*, New York: T. & J. Swords, 1811, p. 30; "Streets cutting each other . . ." from *Sunday Dispatch*, November 25, 1849.

12. "The great principle . . ." from Clement C. Moore, *A Plain Statement, Addressed to the Proprietors of Real Estate, in the City and County of New-York*, New York: J. Eastburn and Co., 1818, p. 23. On Fifth Avenue, the city received title to the streets from Waverly Place to 13th Street in August 1824, 13th Street to 24th Street in May 1830, 21st Street to 42nd Street in October 1837, 42nd Street to 90th Street in April 1838; see Henry Collins Brown, *Fifth Avenue Old and New, 1824–1924*, New York: The Fifth Avenue Association, 1825, p. 20.

13. "Every high hill . . " from *The Talisman*, "Reminiscences of New-York" no. II, 1830; "Away up at the corner . . ." from *PHD-AN*, January 28, 1847.

14. For information on the life of John Jacob Astor, see Kenneth Wiggins Porter's *John Jacob Astor: Business Man*, Cambridge: Harvard University Press, volumes I & II, 1931; John Denis Haeger, *John Jacob Astor: Business and Finance in the Early Republic*, Detroit: Wayne State University Press, 1991; and Madsen, *John Jacob Astor*, which was cited earlier. "Soon after . . ." from James D. McCabe Jr., *Great Fortunes, and How They Were Made; of the Struggles and Triumphs of Our Self-Made Men*, Cincinnati: E. Hannaford & Company, 1872, p. 63.

15. On Astor business Haeger, *John Jacob Astor*, pp. 244–250; "He gives cash . . ." from *New-York Packet*, October 28, 1788.

16. For Astor's 1789 purchase on the Bowery and buying his home from Rufus and Mary King from *NYCLC* Grantees, p. 158; "A valuable . . " and "modern Croesus" from *PHD-BT*, March 29, 1848; On purchasing his home, Porter, *John Jacob Astor: Business Man*, vol. II, p. 942.

17. For land values see *Documents of the Board of Assistant Aldermen*, December 5, 1831, Document No. III, Appendix, p. iv, and Samuel Osgood, *New York in the Nineteenth Century*, New York: New-York Historical Society, 1867, p. 67. For construction rates, see Elizabeth Blackmar, *Manhattan for Rent, 1785–1850*, Ithaca: Cornell University Press, 1989, p. 276. Building heights, Burrows and Wallace, *Gotham*, p. 576. "It looks like . . ." from *PHD-BT*, May 1, 1839.

18. Purchase from Ludlow, from *NYCLC* Grantors, p. 145; "This little farm . . ." from Moses S. Beach, *The Wealth and Biography of the Wealthy Citizens of the City of New York*, New York: Sun Office, 1855, p. 13.

19. "Why Mr. Astor . . ." from James Parton, *Famous Americans of Recent Times*, Boston: Ticknor and Fields, 1867, p. 456.

20. "With chimnies . . ." from *New York Daily Advertiser* (*NYDA*), December 25, 1820; "Many of the old . . ." from *Architectural Magazine, and Journal of Improvement in Architecture, Building, and Furnishing*, October 1838. On lease rates see Haeger, *John Jacob Astor*, p. 258, and Porter, *John Jacob Astor: Business Man*, vol. II, p. 925.

21. On investments, see Haeger, *John Jacob Astor*, pp. 276–278.

22. "The appearance of sending . . ." from Trollope, *Domestic Manners of the Americans*, p. 199. The city's population stood at 312,710 the following year. "Never knew . . ." from *GTSD*, May 1, 1844; "Pull down . . ." from *NYM*, May 15, 1841; "The pulling down . . ." from *PHD-AN*, May 21, 1839; "Overturn . . ." from *PHD-AN*, April 7, 1845.

Chapter 4

1. "Ancient grounds . . ." from *PHD-AN*, September 5, 1835; "Where to go . . ." from *PHD-AN*, March 12, 1836; "One of the best . . ." from *PHD-AN*, November 21, 1836; "I would not . . ." from *PHD-BT*, January 1, 1838; "Catharine is happy . . ." cited in *PHD-AN* on p. 295 at the start of 1838; "In a few weeks . . ." from *PHD-AN*, May 1, 1839.

2. Edward K. Spann's *The New Metropolis: New York City, 1840–1857*, New York: Columbia University Press, 1981) offers a wonderfully detailed view of New York in the years leading up to the Civil War. "In one year . . ." from *NYM*, April 9, 1836; "From present . . ." from *NYM*, May 11, 1839.

3. "There is no more . . ." from Strong, *Letters of George W. Strong*, p. 146.

4. For Strong's college awards, *NYCA*, October 4, 1838; "Clear and very . . ." from *GTSD*, October 4, 1838; "Goths are they . . ." from *GTSD*, March 16, 1844.

5. "From 1825 . . ." from Hamilton, *Reminiscences*, p. 66; "Take a survey . . ." from *Colored American*, July 15, 1837; "Every foot . . ." from *Colored American*, July 22, 1837; on African American real estate, see *NYTR*, March 8, 1859.

6. "And in which . . ." from *PHD-AN*, April 26, 1847; "Of all the curses . . ." from *The Subterranean*, February 13, 1847.

7. On stages see George Rogers Taylor, "The Beginnings of Mass Transportation in Urban America: Part I," *The Smithsonian Journal of History*, vol. 1, no. 2, Summer 1966, pp. 35–50; Burrows and Wallace, *Gotham*, p. 565; Edward Ruggles, *A Picture of New-York in 1846; with a Short Account of Places in Its Vicinity*, New-York: C.S. Francis & Co., 1846, p. 96; and Kenneth T. Jackson, *Crabgrass Frontier: The Suburbanization of the United States*, New York: Oxford University Press, 1987, pp. 34 & 41. "They are unfit . . ." from *NYGGA*, March 28, 1835.

8. "Dangerous to the personal . . ." from *NYCA*, February 16, 1833; "The multitudinous . . ." from *PHD-AN*, September 23, 1835.

9. "It occurred to me . . ." from *PHD-BT*, May 24, 1844; "Let us level . . ." and "Stay your hand . . ." from Walt Whitman, *The Uncollected Poetry and Prose of Walt Whitman*, vol. I, Emory Holloway, editor, Gloucester: Peter Smith, 1972, pp. 93 and 96; "The fatal enemy . . ." from *Harper's New Monthly Magazine*, July 1854.

10. "Nothing is respected . . ." from Richard Lathers, *Reminiscences of Richard Lathers: Sixty Years of a Busy Life in South Carolina, Massachusetts and New York*, Alvan F. Sanborn, editor, New York: The Grafton Press, 1907, p. 37; "Church spires . . ." from Kendall, *The Growth of New York*, p. 26.

11. "Are doomed . . ." from Edgar Allan Poe, *Doings of Gotham*, Pottisville, Penn.: Jacob E. Spannuth, 1929, pp. 25–26; "Rapidly covering . . ." and "For any purpose . . ." from *NYEP*, April 3, 1846; "Tell those 'hack'-men . . ." from *The Knickerbocker*, February 1849; "The crown . . ." from Kendall, *The Growth of New York*, p. 25.

12. "Must necessarily . . ." from Brooklyn *Star*, quoted in Jackson, *Crabgrass Frontier*, p. 27; Population of Brooklyn, see *The Encyclopedia of New York City*, p. 170; "Is to be found . . ." from Walt Whitman, *I Sit and Look Out: Editorials from the Brooklyn Daily Times*, New York: AMS Press, Inc., 1966, p. 145; "In one of those palace . . ." from Bird, *The Englishwoman in America*, p. 376.

13. "The general air . . ." from Matthew Hale Smith, *Bulls and Bears of New York*; "Small army . . ." and "from the dwellings . . ." from *The Continental Monthly*, August 1862; "Bible . . ." from James McCabe, *Great Fortunes*, p. 89; "From the dwelling . . ."; Astor investments and earnings from Porter, *John Jacob Astor: Business Man*, vol. II, p. 928, and Haeger, *John Jacob Astor*, p. 259.

14. "A rather shy . . ." from Julia Ward Howe, *Reminiscences, 1819–1899*, New York: Houghton, Mifflin and Company, 1899, pp. 73–74; "Every inch . . ." from Smith, *Bulls and Bears of New York*, p. 102.

15. "He was very fond . . ." from Howe, *Reminiscences*, pp. 74–75.

16. "Splendid crowd . . ." from *PHD-BT*, December 15, 1846; "It was very cold . . ." from Matthew Hale Smith, *Sunshine and Shadow in New York*, Hartford: J.B. Burr and Company, 1869, p. 124.

17. "Your son . . ." from McCabe, *Great Fortunes*, p. 93.

18. "Could I begin . . ." from Smith, *Sunshine and Shadow*, p. 117; "I am broken up . . ." from Porter, *John Jacob Astor*, Vol. II, p. 1259; "He sat at . . ." from *PHD-AN*, October 9, 1844.

19. "The doors thrown . . ." from *NYH*, April 2, 1848; "It is said . . ." from James Fenimore Cooper, *Correspondence of James Fenimore Cooper*, vol. II, New Haven: Yale University Press, 1922, p. 588.

20. "A suitable building . . ." from *NYH*, April 5, 1848.

21. "The whole day . . ." from *NYEP*, January 10, 1854; "The pauper . . ." from *The United States Magazine of Science, Art, Manufacturers, Agriculture, Commerce*, October 1855; "In its details . . ." from Charles Mackay, *Life and Liberty in America: or, Sketches of a Tour in the United States and Canada in 1857-8*, New York: Harper & Brothers, 1859, p. 16.

22. "Pull-down . . ." from Whitman, *Uncollected Poetry*, vol. 1, p. 92; "Newly excavated . . ." from *GTSD*, April 3, 1859; "This was done . . ." from *NYT*, October 10, 1897; Population New York in 1860, see Hough, *Census of the State of New York, for 1865*, p. XXV.

Chapter 5

1. "The Bostonians . . ." from *GTSD*, February 4, 1842; "With which you . . ." and "I need not . . ." from *The Letters of Charles Dickens*, vol. III, *1842–1843*, Madeline House, Graham Storey, Kathleen Tillotson, editors, Oxford: Clarendon Press, 1974, p. 25.

2. "One thing we . . ." from Philadelphia *Public Ledger*, February 15, 1842.

3. "Unsightly . . ." from *New York Tribune* (*NYTR*), February 9, 1842; "The great man . . ." from *PHD-BT*, February 15, 1842; "I am afraid . . ." from Margaret Armstrong, *Five Generations: Life and Letters of an American Family, 1750–1900*, New York: Harper & Brothers, 1930, pp. 298–299.

4. "Cheers, then . . ." from Thomas Nichols, *Forty Years of American Life*, vol. I, London: John Maxwell and Company, 1864, p. 289; "My dear sir . . ." from Brooklyn *Daily Eagle*, February 15, 1842; "The greatest affair . . ." from *PHD-BT*, February 15, 1842; "Benefit of the American . . ." from *NYEP*, February 14, 1842; "His tickets of admission . . ." from *Dramatic Mirror*, February 19, 1842.

5. "A large collation . . ." June 8, 1842; "Money making . . ." from *Letters of Charles Dickens*, p. 625; "A most wicked . . ." from *The Letters of Charles Dickens*, vol. III, p. 327; "Mr. Dickens has . . ." from *PHD-BT*, November 14, 1842; "Clever, light stuff . . ." from *GTSD*, November 8, 1842.

6. "There is a language . . ." C. Clement Moore, *Poems*, New York: Bartlett & Welford, 1844, pp. 135–136.

7. For a sense of New York's architecture in the years before the Civil War, see M. Christine Boyer, *Manhattan Manners: Architecture and Style, 1850–1900*, New York: Rizzoli, 1985; Ellen W. Kramer, "A Contemporary Description of New York City and Its Public Architecture c. 1850," *Journal of the Society of Architectural Historians*, vol. 27, no. 4, December 1968, pp. 264–280; and Talbot Hamlin, *Greek Revival Architecture in America*, New York, Dover Publications, 1944.

8. On Town's bridge, Letter Patent for Improvement on bridges, 1820, 1835, Ithiel Town Papers, Group no. 499, Box 1, folder no. 4, Yale University Manuscript Collection; "His services . . ." from *NYEP*, November 1, 1825.

9. Alexander Jackson Davis's life and career and partnership with Ithiel Town can be learned about though Edna Donnell, "A.J. Davis and the Gothic Revival," *Metropolitan Museum Studies*, vol. 5, no. 2, September 1936, and Amelia Peck, editor, *Alexander Jackson Davis: American Architect, 1803–1892*, New York: Rizzoli, 1992. Cornelius was previously married to Mary. She died in 1801. He then married Julia Jackson, and besides Alexander they had Martha Ann, Hetty Cornelia, and Edwin Randolph. "Mind [was] formed . . ." and "First study of Stuart's . . ." quoted in Peck, *Alexander Jackson Davis*, pp. 17–18.

10. "Every thing is Greek . . ." from *The Architectural Magazine, and Journal*, January 1835; "Superb edifice . . ." from *PHD-AN*, November 17, 1841.

11. "A Large proportion . . ." from *Brother Jonathan*, May 20, 1843.

12. "Too magnificent . . ." quoted in Luther S. Harris, *Around Washington Square: An Illustrated History of Greenwich Village*, Baltimore: The Johns Hopkins University Press, 2003, p. 84. Some sources cite Seth Geer as the architect of Colonnade Row. Morrison H. Heckscher in his "Building the Empire City: Architects and Architecture," in *Art and the Empire City, 1825–1861*, edited by Catherine Hoover Voorsanger and John K. Howat, New Haven, Yale University Press, 2000, p. 179, states that Davis's Daybook indicates that Geer paid him well for the designs.

13. Number of buildings erected in 1828 is cited in Heckscher, "Building the Empire City," p. 176; "A handsome fence . . ." from *NYEP*, May 10, 1828.

14. "The fashionable end . . ." from *NYH*, May 19, 1835.

15. "One era . . ." from *GTSD*, May 13, 1848.

16. "Most reckless . . ." from *GTSD*, May 25, 1849; "Furniture will soon . . ." from *GTSD*, September 21, 1849; "The organ . . ." from *GTSD*, September 28, 1849; "The great metropolis . . ." from *The Knickerbocker*, October 1848.

17. Statistics on school attendance cited in Burrows and Wallace, *Gotham*, p. 501; "Every attention . . ." from *The Christian Journal, and Literary Register*, May 1823.

18. On the Stonecutters Riot, *NYCA*, October 27 and 28, 1834.

19. On opening of Fifth Avenue, see Burrows and Wallace, *Gotham*, p. 580; On construction numbers see Blackmar, *Manhattan for Rent*, p. 276; For land values see Osgood, Samuel, *New York in the Nineteenth Century*, p. 67.

20. "Is, indeed, a palace . . ." from *PHD-BT*, February 3, 1849.

21. "Greece has fallen . . ." from *Putnam's*, February 1853; "Has an air . . ." from *United States Magazine*, November 1847. For background on the Italianate style, see Charles Lockwood, "The Italianate Dwelling House in New York City," *Journal of the Society of Architectural Historians*, vol. 31, no. 2, May 1973, pp. 145–151.

22. "Are more like . . ." from Chambers, *Things as They Are in America*, p. 177; "Few of our churches . . ." from *NYM*, August 23, 1834; "Beautiful,—and majestic . . ." from Brooklyn *Daily Eagle*, March 30, 1846.

23. "With gay . . ." from *PHD-AN*, February 5, 1846; "Universal genius . . ." from *GTSD*, January 3, 1858.

24. "Every man who builds..." from *NYTR*, September 21, 1848.
25. "Occasionally half ruins..." from C. Astor Bristed, *The Upper Ten Thousand: Sketches of American Society*, New York: Stringer & Townsend, 1852, p. 42; "It may be stated..." and "Simply a place..." quoted in Walt Whitman, *New York Dissected: A Sheaf of Recently Discovered Newspaper Articles by the Author of "Leaves of Grass,"* Emory Holloway and Ralph Adimari, editors, New York: Rufus Rockwell Wilson, 1936, pp. 93, 96; "The first thing..." from Bristed, *The Upper Ten Thousand*, p. 37; "Miss Ellen Ruggles..." from *GTSD*, January 26, 1848; On rate of intermarriage from Burrows and Wallace, *Gotham*, p. 723; "Could not have made..." from *PHD-AN*, February 7, 1832.
26. "On New Year's..." from Bird, *The Englishwoman in America*, p. 374; "A choice lot of Oysters..." from *NYTR*, December 28, 1841; "We had 139 callers..." from Brown, *Valentine's Manual of Old New York*, vol. IV, p. 28; "Poets, historians..." from Bird, *The Englishwoman in America*, p. 371.
27. "My family contributed..." from *PHD-AN*, February 28, 1840.
28. "The chaos of nuns..." from *GTSD*, March 2, 1854; "Several fashionable..." from *NYH*, July 17, 1839.
29. "Gave me a shocking..." from *GTSD*, December 7, 1847; Background on the assorted clubs discussed in Pessen, "Philip Hone's Set."
30. "The Beaver..." from the New York *Evangelist*, May 9, 1835.
31. "A Devonshire duke..." from John W. Francis, *Old New York; or Reminiscences of the Past Sixty Years*, New York, Charles Roe, 1858, p. 295; "Shall Truth..." from *PHD-AN*, December 25, 1838.

Chapter 6

1. "Filled with guests..." from *Columbian Magazine* July 1846.
2. "Where I intend living..." from Kenneth Silverman, *Edgar A. Poe: Mournful and Never-Ending Remembrance*, New York: Harper Collins, 1991, p. 219; "Very cordial..." from Walt Whitman, *Complete Prose Works*, Philadelphia: David McKay, 1982, p. 17.
3. "Mr. Plumbe..." from Ruggles, *A Picture of New-York in 1846*, p. 112; "There is hardly..." from William Bobo, *Glimpses of New-York City by a South Carolinian*, Charleston: J.J. McCarter, 1852, p. 120; "The very fine..." from *New World*, April 19, 1845.
4. "Held a large..." from Walt Whitman, *Complete Prose Works*, New York: D. Appleton and Company, 1910, p. 427; "Discharge of apples..." from Washington Irving, *Letters of Jonathan Oldstyle, Gent.*, New York: William H. Clayton, 1824, p. 17.
5. "Very finished..." from *GTSD*, October 7, 1848; "Conception of his..." from *GTSD*, October 17, 1848.
6. Bowery is an Anglicization of the Dutch *bouwerie*, farm. There were numerous large farms above the small town of New Amsterdam, and the path that linked the different

properties would become known as Bowery Lane and eventually evolved into just "the Bowery."

7. For detailed background on the first decade of the Bowery Theatre, please see Theodore Junior Shank, *The Bowery Theatre, 1826–1836*, Dissertation Stanford University, 1956. For the life of Thomas Hamblin, see Bogar, *Thomas Hamblin and the Bowery Theatre*, which was cited earlier. "A large, shapely . . ." from Walt Whitman, *November Boughs*, Philadelphia: David McKay, 1888, p. 89. According to Bogar, Hamblin's christening middle name was Souness. It was later incorrectly listed as Sowerby, a name used by his half-brother Frank.

8. "Handsomest in the city . . ." from *NYM*, August 20, 1836; "The Home of Satan . . ." quoted in Charles Burnham and Mary Ann Jensen, "New York's Vanished Theatres," *Princeton University Library Chronicle*, vol. 44, no. 2, Winter 1983, p. 89; "The realm of orange-peel . . ." from *NYTR*, March 12, 1855; "Throw not the pearl . . ." from *NYM*, June 1, 1839; "No act of my . . ." from *PHD-AN*, October 15, 1838.

9. "News-boys . . ." from Smith, *Sunshine and Shadow*, p. 215; "Vent in a perfect . . ." from *Spirit of the Times*, February 6, 1847; "A wider range . . ." from *NYM*, April 28, 1838. On week's gross for *Last Days of Pompeii*, see Bogar, *Thomas Hamblin and the Bowery Theatre*, p. 129.

10. "Gorgeous decorations . . ." from L. Maria Child, *Letters from New-York*, first and second series, London: F. Pitman, 1879, p. 344.

11. "He fancied that . . ." from *NYT*, June 19, 1887. While Hamblin could not remarry, Elizabeth could, and she wed actor James S. Charles. "An inflammation . . ." from *The New Yorker*, June 23, 1838.

12. "Lively, agreeable . . ." from *PHD-AN*, July 12, 1843.

13. "Will this splendid . . ." from *PHD-BT*, November 5, 1833; "Beautiful, proud . . ." from Whitman, *New York Dissected*, p. 19.

14. The pianist and music historian Vera Brodsky Lawrence created a detailed three-volume analysis of Strong and music: Vera Brodsky Lawrence, *Strong on Music: The New York Music Scene in the Days of George Templeton Strong*, Chicago: University of Chicago Press, 1995). "Most perfectly . . ." quoted in Lawrence, *Strong on Music*, vol. I, p. 157; "The music is vile . . ." from *GTSD*, June 25, 1851; "The louder . . ." from *GTSD*, September 1, 1851; "I'm still tingling . . ." from *GTSD*, December 1, 1858.

15. "The greatest musical . . ." from P.T. Barnum, *The Life of P.T. Barnum*, New York: Redfield, 1855, p. 297; "Spontaneous outbreak . . ." from *GTSD*, September 2, 1850.

16. "Tears ran down . . ." Brown, *Valentine's Manual of Old New York*, no. 4, p. 17; "Has secured . . ." from *PHD-BT*, September 17, 1850.

17. "The negro . . ." from Thomas L. Nichols, *Forty Years of American Life*, vol. II, London: John Maxwell and Company, 1864, p. 229; "An obscure portion . . ." from *Ira Aldridge: The African Roscius*, edited by Bernth Lindfors, Rochester: University of Rochester Press, 2007, p. 13; "The proprietors . . ." from *Quarterly Anti-Slavery Magazine*, July 1837.

18. "The efforts of the dramatist . . ." from *NYTR*, November 15, 1853.

19. "Listened with delight . . ." from N.M. Ludlow, *Dramatic Life as I Found It*, Saint Louis: G.I. Jones and Company, 1880, p. 392; "Was on everybody's . . ." from R.W.B. Lewis and Nancy Lewis, *American Characters*, New Haven: Yale University Press, 1999; "Is made to . . ." from *PHD-AN*, September 4, 1837.

20. "Company of Ethopian . . ." from New York *Atlas*, May 30, 1852; "The good is mixed . . ." from *PHD-AN*, November 15, 1841.

21. Slavery had been outlawed in New York in 1827. It was essentially finished in Pennsylvania, where it was gradually being abolished since 1780. By 1810 the state had 795 slaves, and 64 in 1840. In Kentucky, slavery was only done away by the Civil War. Barnum found Heth in Pennsylvania, where she was the property of Kentuckian R.W. Lindsay. Since buying slaves was not allowed there, Barnum appears to have leased Heth. "The most astonishing . . ." and "She retains . . ." from *NYS*, August 22, 1835; "One of the most . . ." from *NYS*, February 26, 1836; "Joice Heth . . ." from *NYH*, February 27, 1836.

22. "The greatest . . ." from Charles Dickens, *American Notes,* London: Hazell, Watson & Viney, Ltd, 1842, p. 119.

23. "One of the wonders . . ." from *PHD-BT*, December 4, 1839.

24. "The likeness is . . ." quoted in *PHD-AN*, 1842, p. 590.

25. "Mr. Hone is no . . ." from *NYEP*, May 6, 1826.

26. On Hanington's in the *NYS*, January 23, 1837.

27. "A perfect fairy . . ." from Albert Bigelow Paine, *Mark Twain: A Biography*, Vol. I, Harper & Brothers, 1929, p. 95; "The interior lit . . ." from *GTSD*, September 24, 1853.

28. "Accumulation of coffee . . ." from G.G. Foster, *Fifteen Minutes Around New York*, New York: De Witt & Davenport, 1854, p. 11; "Burned up . . ." from *GTSD*, October 5, 1858.

Chapter 7

1. On Hamblin and Medina, see Bogar, *Thomas Hamblin and the Bowery Theatre*, p. 155. "In his own . . ." from *NYH*, January 18, 1837; "Against the Hamblin gang . . ." *NYH*, February 25, 1837.

2. On state of the economy, see *The Wall Street Journal*, November 10, 2008, and *Commentary Magazine*, November 2008. On Samuel Swartwout thievery, see U.S. Customs and Border Protection website for "Did You Know . . . Samuel Swartwout Skimmed Staggering Sums?" "The most disastrous . . ." and "is too much . . ." from *PHD-BT*, March 4, 1837.

3. On Bread Riot, *NYH*, and *NYCA*, February 14, 1837, and *NYS*, February 6, 1837; "Bread, Meat . . ." and "Fellow-citizens . . ." from *NYCA*, February 14, 1837; "The Usual . . ." from *GTSD*, February 14, 1837; "Bread, bread . . ." from *NYH*, February 14, 1837.

4. "Came down with . . ." from *PHD-AN*, March 14, 1837; "Word was passed . . ." from *NYCA*, March 18, 1837; "The great crisis . . ." from *PHD-AN*, March 17, 1837; "The

distress . . ." from *Morning Courier and New-York Enquirer* (*MCNYE*), April 25, 1837; "Terrible lot of failures . . ." from *GTSD*, April 12, 1837.

5. "The business of the . . ." from *PHD-AN*, March 17, 1837: "Philip Hone . . ." from *GTSD*, April 22, 1837; "Ruin here . . ." from *GTSD* April 27, 1837; "A petition . . ." from *MCNYE*, April 25, 1837.

6. "Utter ruin" from *GTSD*, May 6, 1837; On species withdrawn, see Burrows and Wallace, *Gotham*, p. 613; "The press . . ." from *PHD-BT*, May 10, 1837; On rise of prices, Burrows and Wallace, *Gotham*, p. 609; "Never yet . . ." from *PHD-AN*, February 18, 1837.

7. "To a fearful amount . . ." from *PHD-AN*, March 4, 1837; "Arthur Tappan . . ." from *GTSD*, May 1, 1837; On Tappan's debt, Bertram Wyatt-Brown, "God and Dun & Bradstreet, 1841–1851," *The Business History Review*, vol. 40, Winter 1966, p. 434; "Heavy suspensions . . ." from *NYCA*, May 3, 1837. On loan from Bank of the United States, see Tappan, *The Life of Arthur Tappan*, p. 280.

8. On real estate values, see Osgood, *New York in the Nineteenth Century*, p. 67; "A deadly calm . . ." from *PHD-AN*, May 26, 1837; On August Belmont and Astor's purchases, Burrows and Wallace, *Gotham*, pp. 638–639.

9. "Go to the theatres . . ." from Frederick Marryat, *Diary in America with Remarks on Its Institutions*, vol. 1, London: Longman, Orme, Brown, Green, & Longmans, 1839, p. 46 and pp. 53–54; "Humble endeavors . . ." from *MCNYE*, quoted in the Albany *Evening Journal*, May 18, 1837.

10. "It is almost incredible . . ." from *PHD-BT*, September 4, 1837; Fire at the Bowery Theatre, *NYEP*, February 19, 1838; "One of the best . . ." from Walt Whitman, *Walt Whitman of the New York Aurora: Editor at Twenty-Two*, edited by Joseph Jay Rubin and Charles H. Brown, Westport, Conn.: Greenwood Press, 1950, p. 18; "Poor Tom Hamblin . . ." from *NYH*, August 30, 1837; "Inflammation of . . ." from *The New Yorker*, June 23, 1838; "The best actress . . ." from *The Ladies' Companion*, May 1842.

11. On Panic, see Burrows & Wallace, *Gotham*, pp. 616–618; "Money uncome-at-able . . ." from *PHB-BT*, August 2, 1839.

12. For land values, see Osgood, *New York in the Nineteenth Century*, p. 67; "The saddest proof . . ." from *PHD-AN*, March 7, 1840; "Departed this life . . ." from *NYEP*, September 6, 1841; On Matteawan fire, see *Hudson River Chronicle*, June 29, 1841; "Rents are fifty . . ." from *PHD-AN*, February 1, 1843. David Comstock and Robert Andrews, whose business Comstock & Andrews was the site of the start of the Great Fire of 1835, went out of business in 1842.

13. On development of the Mercantile Agency see Wyatt-Brown, "God and Dun & Bradstreet," pp. 432–450; "In prosperous times . . ." from Wyatt-Brown, *Lewis Tappan*, p. 229.

14. "The great prejudice . . . " from Edward E. Dunbar, *Statement of the Controversy Between Lewis Tappan and Edward E. Dunbar*, New York, 1846, p. 23; "To act as a spy" and "New clap-trap" quoted in Wyatt-Brown, "God and Dun & Bradstreet," p. 440.

15. On Mercantile customers, see Wyatt-Brown, "God and Dun & Bradstreet," p. 440; "Trade is returning . . ." from *PHD-BT*, quoted p. 204.

16. "Trade is returning . . ." from the start of January 1844, quote in *PHD-AN*, pp. 682–683. The mine shipped 1.2 million tons of coal in 1843 from its three Pennsylvania mining districts, Schuylkill, Leigh, and Lackawanna; see *Annual Report of the Board of Managers of the Delaware and Hudson Canal Co., to the Stockholders, for the Year 1844*, New York: Nathan Lane, 1845, p. 7. The mines were consistently producing more coal, with 112,083 tons in 1829, 557,780 tons in 1835 and 826,049 tons in 1840.

17. For background on the life and career of Alexander Stewart, please see: Stephen N. Elias, *Alexander T. Stewart: The Forgotten Merchant Prince*, Westport, Conn.: Praeger, 1992, and Harry Resseguie, "Alexander Turney Stewart and the Development of the Department Store, 1823–1876," *Business History Review*, vol. 39, no. 3m Autumn 1965, pp. 301–322.

18. "New Dry Goods Store" from *NYDA*, September 1, 1823.

19. On his first store, see Elias, *Alexander T. Stewart*, p. 15. "Tappan had just . . ." from Hubbard, *Autobiography*, p. 9.

20. "The little shop . . ." from Smith, *Bulls and Bears of New York*, pp. 191–192; "Inform an old lady . . ." from Lathers, *Reminiscences*, p. 45.

21. Richard Kurin, *The Smithsonian's History of America in 101 Objects*, New York: Penguin Books, 2013, p. 182; "The farmer soon . . ." from *Chambers's Journal,* June 17, 1876; "Broadway might be taken . . ." from Trollope, *Domestic Manners of the Americans,* p. 201.

22. On growth of insurance companies, see Spann, *The New Metropolis*, p. 209. "The countless masts . . ." from Walt Whitman, *The Complete Writings of Walt Whitman*, New York: G.P. Putnam's Sons, 1902, p. 256; "From this point . . ." from N. Parker Willis, *Rural Letters and Other Records of Thought at Leisure*, New York: Baker and Scribner, 1849, p. 240.

23. On commercial houses, see Burrows and Wallace, *Gotham*, p. 436. "The business is such . . ." from Letter Frederick Law Olmsted to John Olmsted, August 29, 1840, Papers of Frederick Law Olmsted, Library of Congress, Container 4.

24. Shipping in 1853, see *NYT*, January 2, 1854. For a history of the New York port and shipping, please see Robert Greenhalgh Albion, *The Rise of New York Port (1815–1860)*, Boston: Northeastern University Press, 1984.

25. On *Philip Hone*'s christening, see *MCNYE*, July 6, 1833; "Handsome cabin . . ." from *MCNYE*, January 16, 1849. Ship logs and cargo for the *Philip Hone* are part of the Comstock Family Papers, Harvard, Baker Library Historical Collections. For a sense of construction along the waterfront, see *NYEP*, October 9, 1847.

26. For conviction of mutineer Henry Grant, see *Army and Navy Chronicle*, December 29, 1836. For a report on the 1848 hurricane, see Glasgow *Herald*, December 1, 1848.

27. On profits from cotton, reference in *NYT*, January 6, 2011; "Are received . . ." from *NYH*, September 24, 1835; "The South . . ." quoted in Jerome Mushkat, *Fernando Wood: A Political Biography*, Kent, Ohio: Kent State University, 1990 p. 94; "They are indeed . . ." from *NYH*, November 16, 1835; "They never buy . . ." from *NYH*, November 17, 1835.

28. "I always made . . ." from Judson, *Cyrus W. Field* p. 18; "A perfect cage . . ." from New York *Evening Chronicle*, May 23, 1837; "Genial, pleasant . . ." from Smith, *Bulls and Bears of New York*, p. 199.

29. On Stewart's earnings, Elias, *Alexander T. Stewart*, p. 33.

30. "Broadway is moving . . ." from *NYH*, September 5, 1835; "A great deal . . ." from Bird, *The Englishwoman in America*, pp. 354–355.

31. "The bright silk . . ." from Herman Melville, *Billy Budd and Other Stories*, New York: Penguin Classics, 1986, p. 23; "The great promenade . . ." from Dickens, *American Notes*, pp. 105–106. Stewart's wealth in 1842 can be found in Moses Beach, *Wealth and Wealthy Citizens of New York City*, New York: The Sun Office, 1842, p. 6. "The mercantile community . . ." from Smith, *Bulls and Bears of New York*, p. 188; the New York arcade opened in 1827; "The store will be an ornament . . ." from *Broadway Journal*, March 22, 1845.

Chapter 8

1. "The scene . . ." from *NYH*, September 22, 1846.

2. "A most extraordinary . . ." from *PHD-BT*, September 10, 1846.

3. "A lady . . ." from Smith, *Sunshine and Shadow.* p. 838. Revenues for the store are from Resseguie, "Alexander Turney Stewart and the Development of the Department Store," p. 320.

4. "A key-note . . ." from *Harper's*, July 1854.

5. On iron works, see Burrows and Wallace, *Gotham*, p. 663. "Chimneys burning high . . ." from Walt Whitman, *Leaves of Grass*, New York: Smith & McDougal, 1872, pp. 193–194.

6. On industry and commercial numbers, see Spann, *The New Metropolis*, p. 244. "Gas is now . . ." from Ross, *What I Saw in New-York*, p. 226. For number of gaslights, see *PBA*, vol. XLV, p. 14, and *NYT*, October 1, 1856.

7. On growth of population, see Spann, *The New Metropolis*, p. 178, and Hough, *Census of the State of New York for 1865*, p. xxv. "Great city . . ." from Henry Ward Beecher, *Star Papers; or, Experiences of Art and Nature*, New York: J.B. Ford and Company, 1873, p. 214.

8. "I have a pretty . . ." from Minnie M. Brashear, *Mark Twain: Son of Missouri*, Chapel Hill: The University of North Carolina Press, 1934, p. 156; "Running at large . . ." from *NYM*, July 13, 1839.

9. "To *cross* Broadway . . ." from Brashear, *Mark Twain: Son of Missouri*, p. 157.

10. "Fitted up with . . ." from *NYEP*, June 29, 1847.

11. On number of hotels, see Spann, *The New Metropolis*, p. 99.

12. Niblo's long menu ran in *NYEP*, February 11, 1823; Sykes' ad in *NYEP*, August 12, 1822.

13. For number of eating houses and refectories see Ruggles, *A Picture of New-York in 1846*, p. 80. "Drank some . . ." from *GTSD*, October 6, 1837; "Oysters Stewed . . ." from *Freedom's Journal*, July 4, 1828.

14. For oyster sales, see Spann, *The New Metropolis*, p. 122. "Here's your fat . . ." from Knickerbocker, *The Cries of New-York*, New-York: S. King, 1830, p. 10.

15. "Some very special . . ." from *GTSD*, October 28, 1855; "Oysters as large . . ." from Mackay, *Life and Liberty in America*, p. 23.

16. "Leading politicians . . ." from Abram C. Dayton, *Last Days of Knickerbocker Life in New York*, New York: G.P. Putnam's Sons, 1897, p. 129.

17. "Extraordinary turtle . . ." from *NYEP*, July 25, 1838; "Take Notice! . . ." from *NYH*, February 21, 1855. For Downing's win at the American Institute, see *NYEP*, December 31, 1839.

18. "Solacing themselves . . ." from *Putnam's*, April 1853; "Combines Eastern magnificence . . ." from Bird, *The Englishwoman in America*, p. 353.

19. "Grouse, canvas-backs . . ." from Cooper, *Notions of the Americans*, p. 136; "Are often very . . ." from James Boardman, *America, and the Americans*, London: Longman, Rees, Orme, Brown, Green, & Longman, 1833, p. 87.

20. On the wealthiest in the city, see Pessen, *Riches, Class, and Power Before the Civil War*, p. 35. "Owned hundreds of lots . . ." and "Investments in real estate . . ." from Moses Beach, *The Wealth and Biography of the Wealthy Citizens of the City of New York*, New York: The Sun Office, 1846, p. 40.

21. "People are running . . ." The August 29, 1848, letter was run in the *Journal of Commerce* and then reprinted in the *NYTR*, December 11, 1848. "Gold! Gold!" from *PHD-AN*, January 29, 1849; "The frenzy continues . . ." from *GTSD*, January 29, 1849.

22. "The papers are filled . . ." from *PHF-AT*, January 26, 1849. Cargo of the *John W. Cater* available on Maritime Heritage Project of San Francisco site, Merchant Ships in Port, March 1849, 1846–1899.

23. "The gold region . . ." from *NYH*, December 13, 1848; "Surrounded by . . ." from *Daily Alta California*, October 4, 1851. On the location of the final resting place of the *Philip Hone*, see *San Francisco Waterfront: Report of Historical Cultural Resources*, San Francisco Wastewater Management Program, December 1977. There is also a map at the San Francisco Maritime Museum listing the location of numerous sunken ships including the *Philip Hone*. There are likewise many sunken ships below Manhattan Island, going back to the early 17th century. In late 1613, Dutch explorer Adriaen Block was preparing to return to Holland when his ship *Tyger* (*Tiger*) was accidently set on fire and abandoned. Block built a new ship called the *Onrust* (*Restless*). The settlement of New Amsterdam was established the following decade. The *Tyger* was discovered below Dey and Greenwich Street on the southern end of Manhattan in 1916 during the construction of the Interborough Rapid Transit system.

24. Hone mentioned the $603,000 figure in *PHD-AN*, September 14, 1849. Number of ships mentioned in Burrows and Wallace, *Gotham*, p. 653. "Mast-hemm'd Manhattan . . ." from Whitman, *Leaves of Grass*, p. 196. For number of shipyard workers, see Albion, *The Rise of New York Port (1815–1860)*, p. 300. "Was set in motion . . ." from *PHD-AN*, January 28, 1850.

25. On growth of manufacturing, see Spann, *The New Metropolis*, p. 403.

26. "Within reach . . ." from Philadelphia *Public Ledger*, March 25, 1836; "That last and most . . ." from *NYCA*, February 14, 1837.

27. On *Herald* circulation, see *Barron's*, June 29, 2013. "Satanic . . ." from *NYT*, December 11, 1861.

28. "We don't like . . ." from *NYH*, January 14, 1836; "Much adultery . . ." quoted in *NYH*, July 13, 1838; "Come forth . . ." quoted in James L. Crouthamel, "The Newspaper Revolution in New York, 1830-1860," *New York History*, vol. 45, no. 2, April 1964, p. 97.

29. "Holy combination . . ." and "profligate," etc. from *NYH*, June 2, 1840; "Lives by lying . . ." from *PHD BT*, April 4, 1842; "A midnight ghoul . . ." from Whitman, *Walt Whitman of the New York Aurora*, p. 115.

30. On publications and publishers in the city in 1849 and 1857, see Spann, *The New Metropolis*, p. 407. On number of publishers in the city in 1857, see Burrows and Wallace, *Gotham*, p. 682.

Chapter 9

1. "Encircled by many . . ." from Walt Whitman, *Complete Prose Works: Specimen Days and Collect, November Boughs and Good Bye My Fancy*, Boston: Small, Maynard & Company, 1901, p. 506; "Arranged his corps . . ." from Letter Fayette Tower to Helen Phelps, July 8, 1842, John Wolcott Phelps Papers, New York Public Library.

2. For background on New York's long and tortured search for a reliable water source, there are some very good histories: Nelson Manfred Blake, *Water for the Cities, A History of the Urban Water Supply Problem in the United States*: Syracuse, N.Y.: Syracuse University Press, 1956; Diane Galusha, *Liquid Assets: A History of New York City's Water System*, Fleischmanns, NY: Purple Mountain Press, 1999; Gerard T. Koeppel, *Water for Gotham: A History*, Princeton: Princeton University Press, 2000; and Edward Wegmann, *The Water-Supply of the City of New York, 1658–1895*, New York: John Wiley & Sons, 1896. "I am very proud . . ." quoted in Stokes, *Iconography of Manhattan Island*, vol. 4, p. 262; "This want . . ." from Peter Kalm, *Travels into North America*, vol. I, Warrington: William Eyers, 1790, pp. 237, 252.

3. "To Erect a Reservoir . . ." from *MCC, 1675–1776*, Vol. VIII, pp. 26–27; "Filth, carbage [sic], or dirt" quoted in John Duffy, *A History of Public Health in New York City 1625–1866*, New York: Russell Sage Foundation, 1968, p. 76; "With whites, and blacks . . ." from the *New York Journal*, August 25, 1785; "A shocking hole . . ." from *NYCA*, September 5, 1798.

4. Deaths from Yellow Fever in 1798 cited in Duffy, *A History of Public Health in New York City*, p. 109. "Will afford a copious . . ." from *Proceedings of the Corporation of New-York, on Supplying the City with Pure and Wholesome Water*, New York: John Furman, 1799, p. iii and p. 12.

5. "Said company to employ . . ." from *Laws of the State of New-York*, vol. II, Albany: Webster and Skinner, 1807, p. 374. On Manhattan Company reservoir, see Duffy, *A History of Public Health in New York City*, p. 207. "Not had . . ." from *NYEP*, July 26, 1803; "Filled with the bodies . . ." from *MCC, 1784–1831*, vol. III, New York: City of New York, 1917, p. 719.

6. "The water in New York . . ." from Axel Leonhard Klinkowström, *Baron Klinkowström's America 1818–1820*, Evanston, IL: Northwestern University Press, 1952, p. 69; "Groening's Lemon Syrup" mentioned in *NYCA*, July 9, 1834; "Is frequently . . ." from *Certificates, Relative to Manhattan Water, in New-York*, 1824, p. 1; "Rapidly depreciating . . ." from *NYEP*, February 18, 1831; "Communicates a ropy . . ." from *Communication from the Lyceum of Natural History of the City of New York to the New York Common Council*, February 22, 1831, p. 8.

7. "A few ounces . . ." from *NYM*, July 1, 1826; "Filthy fluid . . ." from *NYEP*, May 20, 1833; "The one containing . . ." from *NYS*, May 14, 1835; "Although far from . . ." from *New York Evening Journal*, August 16, 1830.

8. "Produces a brilliant . . ." from *New York Gazette*, July 1827.

9. "An abundant supply . . ." from *National Advocate*, October 27, 1821; "A peculiar . . ." from Greene, *A Glance at New York*, p. 181; "Complied with the conditions . . ." from *MCC, 1784–1831*, vol. XIX, New York: City of New York, 1917, p. 459.

10. On New York's reservoir supply in the late 1820s, see *MCC, 1784–1831*, vol. XVII, p. 723; "Year after year . . ." from *NYEP*, August 7, 1824.

11. "It is sufficient . . ." from *The Speeches of the Different Governors, to the Legislature of the State of New-York*, Albany: J.B. Steenbergh, 1825, p. 173; "Commodious and luxuriously . . ." from *NYEP*, April 24, 1833; "The prevalence . . ." from Washington Irving, *Letters*, vol. II, *1823–1838*, Ralph M. Aderman, Herbert L. Kleinfield, and Jenifer S. Banks, editors, Boston: Twayne, 1979, p. 714. On death stats for New York, *Summary of Vital Statistics 2017 of the City of New York*, New York: Department of Health and Mental Hygiene, 2019.

12. "Philadelphia is supplied . . ." from *Report of the Commissioners Under an Act of the Legislature of This State, May 2, 1834, Relative to Supplying the City of New-York with Pure and Wholesome Water*, February 1835, New York: W.B. Townsend, 1835, p. 401.

13. "Is in a degree . . . ," "To hold his . . . ," and "The very great . . ." from *Report of the Commissioners Under an Act of the Legislature of This State, passed May 2, 1834, Relative to Supplying the City of New-York with Pure and Wholesome Water*, New York: W.B. Townsend, 1835, pp. 399–403. For death rate, see *Summary of Vital Statistics 2017 of the City of New York*; for number of fires, see Richard B. Calhoun, *From Community to Metropolis: Fire Protection in New York City, 1790–1875*, PhD Dissertation, Columbia University, 1973, p. 348. The amount insurance companies had to pay out is from *Report of the Commissioners*, p. 524, and "The very great . . ." from p. 400.

14. "The removal of the hills . . ." from *DBA*, Vol. I, 1835, pp. 520–521; "The undertaking . . ." from *NYCA*, March 21, 1835. On outcome of the vote, see Koeppel, *Water for Gotham*, p. 171.

15. "Must be accomplished . . ." *NYCA*, December 21, 1835; "Not a shovel . . ." from *NYH*, October 14, 1836.

16. For background on John Jervis, as well as "Having been brought up . . ." and "The first step . . ." from John Jervis, *The Reminiscences of John B. Jervis: Engineer of the Old Croton*, Neal FitzSimons, ed., Syracuse, N.Y.: Syracuse University Press, 1971, pp. 25–27. Further early history can be found in Larry D. Lankton, "The 'Practicable'

Engineer: John B. Jervis and the Old Croton Aqueduct," Chicago: Public Works Historical Society, 1977, pp. 3–18.

17. For information on the plans for the Croton Aqueduct, see F. Daniel Larkin, *John B. Jervis: An American Engineering Pioneer*, Ames: Iowa State University Press, 1990, pp. 63–65.

18. On the start of the construction of the Croton Aqueduct, see Lankton, "The 'Practicable' Engineer," pp. 18–24; Larkin, *John B. Jervis*, pp. 60–63; Koeppel, *Water for Gotham*, pp. 189–209. "Invading the historic . . ." and the cost of buying the land can be found in *The Old Croton Aqueduct: Rural Resources Meet Urban Needs*, Yonkers: Hudson River Museum of Westchester, 1992, pp. 40 and 44. "Is steep side-hill . . ." from *DBA*, vol. IV, p. 99.

Chapter 10

1. "Young & Scott broke . . ." from John Bloomfield Jervis, Papers, Jervis Library, Box 2, Monthly Report, May 31, 1837; "Well dressed stone . . ." and "did not settle . . ." from John B. Jervis, *Description of the Croton Aqueduct*, New York: Slamm and Guion, 1842, pp. 15 & 19. On Jervis's relationship with Cynthia, see Larkin, *John B. Jervis*, p. 103.

2. "The blasters . . . " from *Hudson River Chronicle*, November 14, 1837; "Laying down . . ." from *Hudson River Chronicle*, December 19, 1837. On Young's accident, see the Baltimore *Sun*, July 2, 1838.

3. "A colony of Patlanders . . ." from *The Knickerbocker*, April 1840; "Unsafe and imprudent . . ." from *DBA*, vol. IV, Document #55, January 2, 1838, p. 356.

4. "The love of lucre . . ." from *DBA*, vol. V, July 2, 1838, p. 58; On pay rates and "In a body . . ." from *DBA*, vol. V, July 2, 1838, p. 57.

5. "Turned out . . ." from *PHD-AN*, April 7, 1840; "Atrociously unjust . . ." from *NYEP*, April 7, 1840; "It was currently . . ." from Jervis, *The Reminiscences of John B. Jervis*, p. 152.

6. On different costs to build High Bridge, see Blake, *Water for the Cities*, p. 156. "The water rose . . ." from Jervis, *Reminiscences*, p. 133; "The protection wall . . ." from *DBA*, Vol. VII, p. 533; cost of the accident, cited in Koeppel, *Water for Gotham*, p. 265.

7. "Double rows . . ." from *PHD-BT*, October 28, 1841; "Have finished . . ." quoted in Koeppel, *Water for Gotham*, from p. 272.

8. The trip along the length of the system is discussed in Koeppel, *Water for Gotham*, p. 273. "When it was known . . ." from Frederick Seward, *William H. Seward: An Autobiography from 1801 to 1834*, New York: Derby and Miller, 1891, p. 610; "The Corporation made . . ." from *PHD-AN*, June 29, 1842.

9. "We give her to you . . ." from *NYTR*, June 28, 1842; "I was introduced . . ." quoted in Koeppel, *Water for Gotham*, p. 275.

10. "Clear, sweet . . ." from *PHD-AN*, July 12, 1842. In June 1881, use of the Murray Hill Reservoir was discontinued, and in May 1884 the adjoining Reservoir Square, which

stood above a former potter's field, was renamed Bryant Park. Then, on May 23, 1895, trustees of the Astor and Lenox Libraries and the Tilden Trust agreed to consolidate their collections. Razing of the reservoir started in 1899 and was completed two years later. In 1902 the cornerstone for the new library was laid, and the structure on Fifth Avenue by John Carrère and Thomas Hastings was dedicated on May 23, 1911. For dates on the changes to the site, see Stokes, *The Iconography of Manhattan Island*, vol. V, pp. 1977, 1985, 2021, 2036.

11. "Never saw the street so crowded . . ." from *GTSD*, October 14, 1842.

12. "Was full to . . ." from Letter, Fayette Tower to John Wolcott Phelps, October 18, 1842, John Wolcott Phelps Papers, NYPL.

13. "The water is of a pure . . ." from *NYCA*, October 15, 1842. The Croton Ode is in *The Universalist Union*, vol. 7, New York: Universalist Union Press, 1842, p. 795.

14. Today the pure . . ." from Seward, *Autobiography*, p. 625; "Where then shall . . ." from Letter Fayette Tower to Helen Phelps, August 4, 1842, John Wolcott Phelps Papers, NYPL.

15. "The Croton Water . . ." from *NYTR*, September 17, 1842; "Clean, sweet . . ." from L. Maria Child, *Letters from New-York*, New York: C.S. Francis & Co., 1845, p. 212.

16. "The Lovers . . ." from *NYEP*, June 14, 1842; "A convenient kitchen . . ." from *NYCA*, February 13, 1843; "No one can witness . . ." *NYEP*, April 3, 1846.

17. Cost of Croton system, see Lankton, "The 'Practicable' Engineer," p. 29. Price for gaining access to the water listed in an ad from the Croton Aqueduct Department, *NYEP*, June 14, 1842; "Increased comfort . . ." from Fayette B. Tower, *Illustrations of the Croton Aqueduct*, New York: Wiley and Putnam, 1845, p. 150; "In Greenwich Street . . ." from *GTSD*, May 17, 1843; "A great luxury . . ." from *GTSD*, July 9, 1843.

18. "The prospect from . . ." from *Columbia Spy*, May 27, 1844. For extent, revenues, and the number of homes and businesses receiving the water, see *NYEP*, June 26, 1844. "The Grand and Sublime . . ." from *NYH*, January 30, 1842; "Small potatoes . . ." from P.T. Barnum, *The Autobiography of P.T. Barnum*, London: Ward and Lock, 1855, pp. 86–87.

19. "Superabundant hydrants . . ." from *NYCA*, March 7, 1845; "Ladies Baths . . ." from *NYEP*, June 14, 1842; "There ought to be . . ." *New York Spectator*, June 29, 1842; "A number . . ." from *NYT*, January 28, 1860.

20. "Embryo, the spawn . . ." from *NYTR*, August 15, 1846; "No person need . . ." from *NYTR*, August 14, 1846; "Very great piece . . ." from *GTSD*, October 29, 1847; "Its interminable line . . ." from *Harper's*, December 1860.

21. For population in 1840 and 1850, see Hough, *Census of the State of New York, for 1865*, p. xxv. "These immense stretches . . ." from *New York Sunday Dispatch*, November 25, 1849. For water usage, see Wegmann, *The Water Supply of the City of New York*, p. 107. "Continually unclosed . . ." from *DBA*, part I, vol. X, May 29, 1843, p. 51; "From the hydrants . . ." from *DBA*, vol. XIII, document No. 7, June 22, 1846; "The demand for water . . ." from *NYTR*, August 7, 1846.

22. "The introduction of the Croton . . ." from *New-York Journal of Medicine and Collateral Sciences*, vol. IV, New York: R.F. Hudson, 1850, pp. 15–16.

23. On the extent of the Croton system and number of customers in 1857, see *NYTR*, April 4, 1857. "An abundant supply . . ." from Whitman, *The Uncollected Poetry and Prose of Walt Whitman*, pp. 254–255.

Chapter 11

1. "Set the invaluable . . ." and "dashing chairs . . ." from *NYH*, April 26, 1845; "Before I was two blocks . . ." from *GTSD*, April 25, 1845; "There goes . . ." and "We are not dead . . ." from George P. Little, *The Fireman's Own Book*, Boston: Dillingham and Bragg, 1860, p. 220; "This great tinder-box . . ." from *PHD-MS*, April 25, 1845; "With the recent . . ." from *NYH*, April 28, 1845.
2. "Some gentleman near . . ." and "The concussion . . ." from *NYH*, July 22, 1845.
3. "Shook the house . . ." from *GTSD*, July 19, 1845; "Were instantly overthrown . . ." from *PHD-BT*, July 19, 1845. The *Herald* ran lists of some of the goods lost on July 22, 1845.
4. "All in confusion . . ." from *PHD-AN*, July 19, 1845; "A great facility . . ." from *NYEP*, July 22, 1845.
5. "It's general arrangement . . ." from *Broadway Journal*, August 16, 1845.
6. There are numerous excellent books dealing with the history of New York's fire department. Augustine Costello's *Our Firemen*, cited earlier, is a lovingly encyclopedic collection of material on the department and the men. For more recent works, see Richard B. Calhoun, *From Community to Metropolis*, cited earlier; Kenneth Holcomb Dunshee, *As You Pass By*, New York: Hastings House, 1952; and Terry Golway, *So Others Might Live: A History of New York's Bravest, the FDNY from 1700 to the Present*, New York: Basic Books, 2002.
7. "Providence—or some . . ." from George Washington to Lund Washington, October 6, 1776, Founders Online, the National Historical Publications and Records Commission.
8. On the size of the force in 1786, see *MCC, 1784–1831*, vol. I, pp. 200–203. "Totally prostrate . . ." from Pintard, *Letters from John Pintard*, vol. II, p. 260; "Scarcely a night . . ." from *PHD-AN*, August 4, 1829. Number of fires cited in Calhoun, *From Community to Metropolis*, p. 348.
9. "So much hustling . . ." and "A furious alarm . . ." from *GTSD*, January 27, 1840; "From the flat . . ." from Mrs. Felton, *American Life: A Narrative of Two Years' City and Country Residence in the United States*, London: Simpkin, Marshall, and Co., 1842, p. 52; "The rule is . . ." from *Architectural Magazine, and Journal of Improvement In Architecture, Building, and Furnishing*, November 1835.
10. Size of the department was stated in Chief Engineer Alfred Carson's report, which was reproduced in the *NYH*, September 6, 1850. On Irish membership in the force, see Calhoun, *From Community to Metropolis*, p. 144. "The cry is sounded . . ." from Cooper, *Notions of the Americans*, p. 307; "Intolerable tolling . . ." from Dickens, *American Notes*, p. 121.

11. "The sound can . . ." from Lady Emmeline Stuart-Wortley, *Travels in the United States, etc. During 1849 and 1850,* New York: Harper & Brothers, 1851, p. 149.

12. "He was praying . . ." from *NYH,* March 4, 1887; "There was another . . . " from George W. Sheldon, *The Story of the Volunteer Fire Department of the City of New York,* New York: Harper & Brothers, 1882, p. 20; "O, the fireman's . . ." from *Walt Whitman and the Leaves of Grass, an Introduction,* London: Watts & Co., 1905, p. 13; "The hours passed . . ." from James Tyler, *Reminiscences of the V.F.D.: From "Fire-Laddie to Supe,"* Bay Ridge: James H. Barr, 1878, p. 5.

13. "Work her lively . . ." from Tyler, *Reminiscences of the V.F.D.* p. 4; "O, the fireman's joys!" from W.H. Trimble, *Walt Whitman and the Leaves of Grass, an Introduction,* London: Watts & Co., 1905, p. 13.

14. "I attended this afternoon . . ." from *PHD-AN,* April 25, 1833.

15. "The most pitiful . . ." from Whitman, *The Uncollected Poetry and Prose of Walt Whitman,* 1972, p. 154.

16. On mass resignation, see Calhoun, *From Community to Metropolis,* p. 241. "Taunted and derided . . ." from *NYS,* September 26, 1836.

17. "Who Saved the Cathedral? . . ." from Sheldon, *The Story of the Volunteer Fire Department of the City of New York,* p. 328; "Complete purification . . ." and "The riotous ruffians . . ." from *NYH,* January 13, 1840; "From all I've seen . . ." from *GTSD,* February 3, 1840.

18. "Cases of the greatest emergency . . ." from Costello, *Our Firemen,* p. 446; "Where the smoke . . ." from Dunshee, *As You Pass By,* p. 91.

19. "Roman gladiators . . ." from Whitman, *Walt Whitman of the New York Aurora,* p. 36; "They cannot pass . . ." from *NYEP,* April 29, 1833.

20. For background on Boss William Tweed, please see Kenneth D. Ackerman, *Boss Tweed: The Rise and Fall of the Corrupt Pol Who Conceived the Soul of Modern New York,* New York: Carroll & Graf Publishers, 2005; Alexander B. Callow Jr., *The Tweed Ring,* New York: Oxford University Press, 1966; Leo Hershkowitz, *Tweed's New York: Another Look,* Garden City: Anchor Press, 1977; and Denis Tilden Lynch, *"Boss" Tweed: The Story of a Grim Generation,* New York: Boni and Liveright, 1927.

21. "A splendid serenade . . ." from Letter, William Tweed to Henry L. Davis, October 1, 1846, *NYHS,* William Tweed Miscellaneous Mss., Letters 1846–1857.

22. On firehouses Tweed belonged to, see Costello, *Our Firemen,* p. 458.

23. On fires 1849–1850 see *DBA,* vol. XVII, pt. 2, p. 920. "A tip-top dancer . . ." from *NYH,* April 13, 1878; "Out of town . . ." from Nichols, *Forty Years of American Life,* vol. II, p. 230.

24. On rivalry between Big Six and No. 8, see Sheldon, *The Story of the Volunteer Fire Department of the City of New York,* p. 106.

25. "A frightful wound . . ." from *NYT,* June 8, 1853; "Idlers and vagabonds . . ." from *PHD-AN,* March 23, 1833; "For the pleasure . . ." from Greene, *A Glance at New York,* p. 198.

26. "To dispence with . . ." from *MCC, 1784–1831,* vol. XIII, p. 774; "To report whether . . ." from *A Compilation of the Laws of the State of New York,* New York: McSpedon & Baker, 1855, p. 204. "Young men who appear . . ." from *PBA,* Vol. X, 1836 (*PBA*), p. 172;

"Deliberate and bloody . . ." and "a murderous gang . . ." from *DBA*, vol. XVII, pt. 2, pp. 929–930; "Of the fire-boy . . ." from Junius Henri Browne, *The Great Metropolis; A Mirror of New York*, Hartford, Conn.: American Publishing Co., 1869, p. 561.

27. "Boxes, barrels . . ." from *DBA*, vol. XVII, pt. 2, p. 945; "Mr. Tweed's disinterested . . ." from *NYH*, September 6, 1850.

Chapter 12

1. "A highly responsible . . ." from *PHD-AN*, quoted on p. 366; "Enough *Hones* . . ." from *Hudson Gazette*, quoted in Brooklyn *Daily Eagle*, May 15, 1849.
2. "Public morals . . ." quoted in Golway, *So Others Might Live*, p. 79.
3. "For light . . ." from *The Know Nothing Almanac and True Americans' Manual for 1855*, New York: De Witt & Davenport, 1855, p. 7.
4. For background on Tammany Hall, please see Oliver E. Allen, *The Tiger: The Rise and Fall of Tammany Hall*, Reading, Mass.: Addison-Wesley Publishing, 1993.
5. "A lithe, dark . . ." from Nichols, *Forty Years of American Life*, vol. II, p. 317.
6. "Never ending . . ." from Nichols, *Forty Years of American Life*, p. 318. The United States conquered 525,000 square miles of territory at the end of the war.
7. "Imbued with the true . . ." from New York *Aurora*, April 9, 1842.
8. Havemeyer versus Harper election results in *NYEP*, April 25, 1845; 1851 election results in *NYT*, November 6, 1851. Tweed received 1,381 to Webb's 1,334. The vote for Blackmer was not listed. The *Times* had only recently started publication, its first issue appearing on September 18.
9. "First in importance . . ." *PBA*, vol. XLV, p. 9. The proceedings lists their committees.
10. On rates earned by aldermen, please see *NYTR*, March 12, 1852. "It is generally understood . . ." from *New York Day Book*, July 17, 1852.
11. "Seizing upon several . . ." from *NYTR*, February 7, 1852. The aldermen's dining bills were reported in the *NYTR*, on March 12, 1852, and April 29, 1852.
12. "Splendid dinner . . ." from *NYT*, February 21, 1852. The purchase of Wards Island is reported in the *NYT*, April 22, 1852. Lynch in *"Boss" Tweed* states that the land was only worth $30,000; for carriage costs, p. 68; see also *Annual Report of the Comptroller of the City of New York, of the Receipts and Expenditures of the Corporation, for the Year 1852*, New York: McSpedon & Baker, 1853, p. 57.
13. "As a preventative . . ." from *NYEP*, August 30, 1852; "Had the temerity . . ." from *NYTR* February 7, 1852.
14. "Our whole country . . ." from *Report of the Committee of Arrangements of the Common Council of New York of the Obsequies in Memory of Hon. Henry Clay*, New York: McSpedon & Baker, 1852, p. 14. Charges for the *Santa Claus* and the July 4 fireworks are referenced in Allen, *The Tiger*, p. 61. The United States had 31 states at that point.
15. On increase in expenditures, see Spann, *The New Metropolis*, p. 300. On paying $610 for property worth $60,000 to $100,000, see *NYTR*, March 1, 1853. Sale of

the Gansevoort Market is cited at Allen, *The Tiger*, p. 61. "The unlawful . . ." from *Proceedings of the Board of Supervisors of the City and County of New York for 1852*, New York: McSpedon & Baker, 1852, pp. 244–245. For rates of bribes, see Allen, *The Tiger*, p. 61. "Lumbering, clumsy . . ." from *NYTR*, October 5, 1852. For bribes for Gansevoort and the Eighth Avenue line, see Spann, *The New Metropolis*, pp. 300–301.

16. For efforts to secure the Broadway line, see Harry James Carman, *The Street Surfaces Railway Franchises of New York City*, PhD Dissertation, Columbia University, 1919, pp. 78–84, and Elias, *Alexander T. Stewart*, pp. 144–145. "None of these grants . . ." from *NYEP*, November 23, 1852.

17. "Atrocity and rascality . . ." and "Know the virtue . . ." from *NYTR*, December 31, 1852.

18. Expenditures for the city, and "Less than the aggregate . . ." from *Annual Report of the Comptroller of the City of New York, of the Receipts and Expenditures of the Corporation for the Year 1852*, New York: McSpedon & Baker, 1853, p. 21.

19. "They own more houses . . ." from *NYTR*, April 21, 1853; "Tweedy never goes back . . ." from *NYS*, April 13, 1878. Tweed beat Hoxie 5,476 to 4,241. Election results in *NYT*, November 5, 1852. Joseph Morton was also running for the office, and on November 1, 1852, the *Tribune* warned that a vote for Morton just takes it away from Hoxie, and Tweed "may very well offer to pay Morton's election expenses in consideration of the aid and comfort the payee is rendering the payer." Morton received 768 votes, and Tweed beat Hoxie by only 235 votes.

20. "Hanging round . . ." from *NYTR*, December 23, 1853.

21. "The last sands . . ." from *NYTR*, December 23, 1853; "One of the few . . ." from Beach, *The Wealth and Biography of the Wealthy Citizens of the City of New York*, p. 13.

22. "A flagrant wrong . . ." from *The Congressional Globe: The Debates, Proceedings, and Laws of the First Session of the Third-Third Congress*, vol. XXVIII—Part II, Washington: John C. Rives, 1854, p. 1155; "Waning popularity . . ." from *NYT*, May 10, 1854.

23. "Overawed the inspectors into decency . . ." from *NYT*, April 13, 1878. Vote count reported in *NYT*, November 11, 1854.

Chapter 13

1. "To keep the streets . . ." from *The Records of New Amsterdam, From 1653 to 1674 Anno Domini*, vol. I, New York: Knickerbocker Press, 1897, February 20, 1657, p. 31; "Stench which is exhaled . . ." from *NYCA*, August 21, 1798; "Scarcely a street . . ." from *NYEP*, April 3, 1821; "A good bath . . ." from *NYT*, March 29, 1853.

2. "Not an ash cart . . ." from *NYEP*, March 18, 1839. The city expended a lot of money. For the year ending May 15, 1848, the city spent $55,798.82 to sweep the streets, $48,356.67 to cart manure, and $80,843 to haul off ash and garbage and load it onto vessels. For cost expended to clean the streets, see *DBA*, vol. XVI, p. 14. "No ashes, offals . . ." from *DBA*, vol. XV, April 2, 1849, p. 1029; "Every crossing . . ." from *GTSD*, March 10, 1854.

3. On the population of pigs in New York, see *NYTR*, September 17, 1842. "Take care of the pigs..." from Dickens, *American Notes*, 1996, p. 113.

4. "In spite of all..." *NYEP*, August 4, 1821.

5. "Very great Number..." from *MCC, 1675–1776*, vol. III, p. 407; "Dogs must die..." from *NYTR*, May 23, 1855. On slaughter of dogs, see *DBA*, vol. III, p. 26. "The notorious..." from *NYTR*, October 3, 1849.

6. For number of horses in the city, see *Francis's New Guide to the Cities of New-York and Brooklyn, and the Vicinity*, New York: C.S. Francis & Co., 1857, p. 124. "A wild steer..." from Sean Wilentz, "Crime, Poverty and the Streets of New York City: The Diary of William H. Bell 1850–51," *History Workshop*, no. 7, Spring 1979, p. 152. "Scarcely a building..." from Boardman, *America, and the Americans*, p. 338; "I remember distinctly..." from Cooper, *Correspondence of James Fenimore Cooper*, vol. I, p. 53.

7. On the amount of dead animals along the streets, see *DBA*, vol. V, p. 289. On amount removed from the streets in May 1853, see *NYT*, June 8, 1853. "The carrion of horses..." from *Annual Report of the City Inspector of the Number of Deaths and Interments in the City of New York During the Year 1849*, New York: McSpedon & Baker, 1850, p. 508.

8. "Rather offensive..." from *The Transactions of the New York Academy of Medicine*, vol. I, New York: S.S. & W. Wood, 1857, 34. Death rate cited in Spann, *The New Metropolis*, p. 123. The "Act to Prevent the Adulteration of Milk, and Prevent the Traffic in Impure Milk" passed April 23, 1862, and those convicted received a fine of at least $50 and possible imprisonment. Passage reported in the Brooklyn *Evening Star*, June 2, 1862.

9. "With such a dreadful..." from Bernhard, Duke of Saxe-Weimar Eisenach, *Travels Through North America. During the Years 1825 and 1826*, vol. 1, Philadelphia: Carey, Lea & Carey, 1828, p. 109; "The promiscuous use..." from *The Medical Repository*, vol. I, New York: T. & J. Swords, 1804, p. 225; "His symptoms increased..." from Hosack, *A Memoir of the Late David Hosack, M.D.*, p. 334.

10. "Gleets, ulcerated legs..." from *NYEP*, May 20, 1833; "Two small boys..." from Grant Thorburn, *Forty Years' Residence in America*, London: James Fraser, 1836, p. 72; "limbs with..." from David Hosack, *Lectures on the Theory and Practice of Physic*, Philadelphia: Herman Hooker, 1836, p. 259; "Hot applications of ashes..." from James Hardie, *An Account of the Malignant Fever, Lately Prevalent in the City of New-York*, New York: Hurtin and McFarlane, 1799, p. 23.

11. On deaths in September and on Ann Street, see Hardie, *An Account of the Malignant Fever*, p. 12. "A great mortality..." *PHD-AN*, September 13, 1848.

12. Yellow Fever deaths in 1798, see Duffy, *A History of Public Health in New York City*, p. 109. "To furnish data..." from *Documents Relating to the Board of Health*, New York: James Cheetham, 1806, p. 12; "No dead animal..." from James Hardie, *An Account of the Malignant Fever, Which Prevailed in the City of New-York, During the Autumn of 1805*, New York: Southwick & Hardcastle, 1805, pp. 115 and 30.

13. "The acid fumigation..." from *NYEP*, August 26, 1822; "By strewing the infected..." from Peter Neilson, *Recollections of a Six Years' Residence in the United States of America*, Glasgow: David Robertson, 1830, p. 120. On Dr. Roosa's efforts, see

F.D. Allen, *Documents and Facts, Showing the Fatal Effects of Interments in Populous Cities*, New York: F.D. Allen, 1822, p. 9.

14. "A town besieged . . ." from James Hardie, *An Account of the Yellow Fever, which Occurred in the City of New-York, in the Year 1822*, New York: Samuel Marks, 1822, p. 42; "Hundreds of wooden . . ." and "That this pestilence . . ." from Neilson, *Recollections of a Six Years' Residence in the United States of America*, p. 117.

15. For background on cholera in New York, see Duffy, *A History of Public Health in New York City 1625–1866*, already cited, and Charles E. Rosenberg, *The Cholera Years: The United States in 1832, 1849 and 1866*, Chicago: The University of Chicago Press, 1962. "Every preparation . . ." from Thomas K. Wharton Diary, Manuscripts Department, New York Public Library, June 19, 1832; "Perfumes, Scents, Essences . . ." from *MCNYE*, June 16, 1832; "In a truly devout . . ." from *MCNYE*, June 18, 1832; "Constantly on hand . . ." from *MCNYE*, June 16, 1832.

16. "A steady . . ." from *Reports of Hospital Physicians, and Other Documents in Relation to the Epidemic of Cholera of 1832*, New York: G. & C. & H. Carvill, 1832, p. 9; "The attack was sudden . . ." from letter from Dr. John Stearns, July 19, 1832, New York Municipal Archives, Health (Cholera Epidemic), July 1832, Box 2; "Almost every steamboat . . ." from *NYEP*, July 3, 1832.

17. "The Taint . . . " from Cooper, *Notions of the Americans*, vol. 1, p. 115. Notice from the Medical Council appeared in *NYEP*, July 20, 1832. "Using warm flannel . . ." from *MCNYE*, July 11, 1832; "Exposes them . . ." from *NYEP*, July 20, 1832; "Was seized . . ." from Charles Grandison Finney, *Memoirs of Rev. Charles G. Finney*, New York: A.S. Barnes & Company, 1876, p. 320.

18. "Flocked into the city . . ." from E.T. Coke, *A Subaltern's Furlough: Descriptive of Scenes in Various Parts of the United States, Upper and Lower Canada, New Brunswick, and Nova Scotia*, London: Saunders and Otley, 1833, p. 163; "In the foremost . . ." from the *Cholera Bulletin*, July 23, 1832; "Her voice . . ." from J. Mauran, Thomas H. Webb, and Samuel Boyd Tobey, *Remarks on the Cholera, Embracing Facts and Observations Collected at New-York*, Providence: W. Marshall and Co., 1832, p. 24; "Took the cholera . . ." from Letter, Henry Dana Ward to Thomas W. Ward, September 5, 1832, Henry Dana Ward Letters, American Antiquarian Society, Box 5, Folder 8.

19. "Quit dram-drinking . . ." from Coke, *A Subaltern's Furlough*, p. 165; "Who was decking . . ." from *New York Mercury*, July 18, 1832; "The mortality . . ." quoted *PHD-AN*, p. 73; "Those sickened . . ." from Pintard, *Letters from John Pintard*, vol. IV, p. 75.

20. "The public gardens . . ." from Coke, *A Subaltern's Furlough*, p. 161; "Deems it a duty . . ." from *NYAM*, July 10, 1832; "One or two . . ." from *NYM*, August 11, 1832; "At the Hospitals . . ." from *NYEP*, July 23, 1832; "There is no business . . ." from Letter, July 28, 1832, John Casilear to Asher B. Durand, Asher B. Durand Papers, Manuscript Department, NYPL.

21. "A most dangerous . . ." from *NYEP*, August 14, 1832; "There were some . . ." from Coke, *A Subaltern's Furlough*, p. 165; "Scarcely ventured farther . . ." from James Riker Jr., *Autobiographical Reminiscences*, June 1832, Riker, James, NYHS; "The buildings . . ." from *NYEP*, August 6, 1832.

22. The death of Magdalen Astor Bristed by cholera was referenced by John Pintard on August 2, 1832, in Pintard, *Letters from John Pintard*, vol. IV, p. 80. "We begin to be reconciled . . ." from Cooper, Correspondence of James Fenimore Cooper, vol. I, p. 277. On death stats see *Summary of Vital Statistics 2017 of the City of New York*. "Thousands of refugees . . ." from *PHD-AN*, August 27, 1832; "A few short weeks . . ." from Pintard, *Letters from John Pintard*, vol. IV, p. 90.

23. "Where hundreds . . ." from *PHD-AN*, July 28, 1849; "Lying on a few . . ." from *The New-York Journal of Medicine, and the Collateral Sciences*, vol. III, New York: Daniel Fanshaw, 1849, p. 96. The amount cleaned from the streets reported in *NYTR*, May 18, 1849.

24. "The cholera increases . . ." from *PHD-BT*, June 1, 1849; "I've laid in . . ." from *GTSD*, June 4, 1849.

25. "Bad food . . ." from *NYH*, July 27, 1849; "Exhalations of the swinish . . ." from Horace Greeley, *Recollections of a Busy Life*, New York: J.B. Ford and Company, 1868, p. 428; "Bloating and festering . . ." from *DBA*, Vol. XVIII, part 1, p. 509.

26. "Before we realized . . ." from Greeley, *Recollections of a Busy Life*, p. 428. Arthur "Pickie" Greeley's death notice appeared in *NYEP*, July 13, 1849.

27. "He began vomiting . . ." from *GTSD*, July 14, 1849. On death of Wyckoff and others that day, see *NYH*, July 16 and 17, 1849.

28. "The all-pervading subject . . ." from *GTSD*, July 26, 1849; "Poor New York . . ." from *PHD-AN*, July 28, 1849; "His treatment . . ." quoted in *PHD-AN*, p. 374; "The whole community . . ." quoted in *PHD-AN*, p. 374. On death stats see *Summary of Vital Statistics 2017 of the City of New York*.

Chapter 14

1. "Left a cloud . . ." from *PHD-AN*, September 30, 1844. For Hone family genealogy, see Stuyvesant Fish, *Anthon Genealogy*, 1930, pp. 86–90. It is possible Philip and Catherine had more than seven children. James was born in January 13, 1818, and died April 1818. In Trinity Church's database of baptisms, marriages, and deaths, a Mr. Hone is listed as burying a three-month-old in October 1805 (the Hones married in 1801). At the time, there were three Hones, John, Philip, and Samuel, listed in the city in *Longworth's American Almanack, New-York Register, and City Directory*, New York: Old Established Directory Office, 1805, p. 276. It would not have been John's child, because he and Joanna had daughter Ann on June 6, 1805. She would marry Reverend James Mathews. Samuel is listed as a baker. There is also a stillborn child of Philip Hone's, who is listed on May 14, 1810.

2. On life expectancy, see *Hunt's Merchants' Magazine and Commercial Review*, October 1852, p. 417. "Nineteen years . . ." from *DBA*, vol. XIX, p. 468.

3. For Strong family genealogy, see Benjamin W. Dwight, *The History of the Descendants of Elder John Strong of Northampton, Mass.*, vol. I, Albany: Joel Munsell, 1871, pp. 633–635.

4. Astor family genealogy, see Cuyler Reynolds, *Genealogical and Family History of Southern New York and the Hudson River Valley*, vol. III, New York: Lewis Historical Publishing Company, 1914, pp. 1259–1262. Tappan family genealogy, see Daniel Langdon Tappan, *Tappan-Toppan Genealogy: Ancestors and Descendants of Abraham Toppan of Newbury, Massachusetts, 1606–1672*, Arlington, Mass.: 1915, pp. 37–40. Downing family genealogy, see S.A.M. Washington, *George Thomas Downing: Sketch of His Life and Times*, Newport: The Milne Printery, 1910, p. 3. For Stewart family genealogy see Elias, *Alexander T. Stewart*, p. 145. For Jervis history, see Larkin, *John B. Jervis*, p. 103. For Tweed family, see Hershkowitz, *Tweed's New York*, p. 5. For Olmsted family, see Henry King Olmsted, *Genealogy of the Olmsted Family in America*, New York: A.T. De La Mare Printing, 1912, pp. 106–110.

5. On death of Mary, "My heart sinks within me..." from *PHD-AN*, November 16, 1840; "One by one..." from *PHD-AN*, September 19, 1849; "Died as angels..." from *PHD-BT*, May 24, 1850.

6. "I am seventy years old..." from *PHD-BT*, October 25, 1850; "Continued unmitigated illness" and epitaph from *PHD-AN*, April 30, 1851.

7. "A gentleman of polished..." from *NYEP*, May 5, 1851; "His conduct..." from *NYTR*, May 6, 1851; "In private life..." from *NYH*, May 6, 1851.

8. On offer to purchase the Bowery, *Baltimore Sun*, January 11, 1853; On Hamblin's funeral, please see Bogar, *Thomas Hamblin and the Bowery Theatre*, 265–267; "If the deceased..." and Hamblin's funeral, from *NYH*, January 10, 1853.

9. "I find myself..." from *GTSD*, July 10, 1855.

10. "A burial can scarcely..." from Allen, *Documents and Facts, Showing the Fatal Effects of Interments in Populous Cities*, pp. 8 and 21.

11. "And they consulted" from Book of Matthew 27:7; "The course of a few..." from Petition to the Mayor, Aldermen, and Commonalty of the City of New York, April 24, 1797, Founders Online, National Archives; "Known to you..." from Francis, *Old New York; or Reminiscences of the Past Sixty Years*, p. 25; "Covered only by..." from *NYEP*, July 27, 1819.

12. On firing of McKenzie, see Duffy, *A History of Public Health in New York City*, p. 240; On nabbing of grave robbers, see *NYEP*, March 12, 1833; p. 240. "It was a common practice..." from J.S. Buckingham, *America, Historical, Statistic, and Descriptive*, vol. I, London: Fisher, Son, & Co., 1841, p. 159.

13. "Mountains and rocks..." from *NYEP*, January 26, 1833.

14. "The very bones..." from *PHD-BT*, April 7, 1845. The New York *Gazetteer & General Advertiser* on February 25, 1833, chronicles quite a few of the cemeteries that were cut through and destroyed. "Coffins and dead bodies..." from *L'Oracle and Daily Advertiser*, July 25, 1808. On Shearith Israel, see Rosalie S. Phillips, "A Burial Place for the Jewish Nation Forever," *Publications of the American Jewish Historical Society*, No. 18, 1909, p. 120.

15. "Where one generation..." from *NYM*, June 13, 1840; "A large quantity..." from William C. Nell, *The Colored Patriots of the American Revolution*, Boston: Robert F. Wallcut, 1855, p. 151. On potter's field, *NYT*, June 9, 1858, and "Coffins, skulls..." from *NYT*, April 21, 1858.

16. "Trinity Church Triumphant!..." from *NYT*, December 19, 1854.
17. "A most exceedingly..." from *GTSD*, July 27, 1839; "Exclusively to the next..." from Shepherd Knapp, *A History of the Brick Presbyterian Church in the City of New York*, New York: Brick Presbyterian Church, 1909, p. 268.
18. For information on the development of the city's sanitation system, please see Duffy, *A History of Public Health in New York City, 1625–1866* which was cited earlier, and Joanne Abel Goldman, *Building New York's Sewers: Developing Mechanisms of Urban Management*, West Lafayette: Purdue University Press, 1997.
19. "One would naturally..." from George E. Waring, *Report on the Social Statistics of Cities*, Pt. I, Washington, D.C.: Government Printing Office, 1886, p. 570.
20. "The general mode..." from *DBA*, vol. IX, pp. 164–167; "Almost choked..." from *NYEP*, August 5, 1850.
21. "The soil must..." from *Reports of Hospital Physicians*, p. 13; "The sleeping room..." from *DBA*, vol. XIX, pt. 1, p. 108.
22. "Which will compel..." from *PBA*, vol. LVI, 1854; 70 miles cited in Spann, *The New Metropolis*, p. 133; 138 miles cited in *NYTR*, April 4, 1857.
23. "One of the chief..." from *Documents of the Senate of the State of New-York, 1859*, vol. II, Albany: Charles Van Benthuysen, 1869, p. 209; "Folly..." from *Report of the Council of Hygiene and Public Health of the Citizens' Association of New York upon the Sanitary Condition of the City*, New York: D. Appleton and Company, 1865, p. 206.

Chapter 15

1. "He might be considered..." from *NYEP*, March 19, 1860; "The young gentleman..." from *NYEP*, December 12, 1828; "How I wished..." from *NYH*, June 12, 1837.
2. Downing's case was covered by the *NYCA*, December 31, 1840, *The Colored American*, January 16 and February 20, 1841, and the *Journal of Commerce (JOC)*, February 26, 1841. On Downing winning case, *NYTR*, February 20, 1852.
3. "Notorious abolitionist..." from *NYTR*, November 13, 1850.
4. "Two or three..." and Downing's ordeal on the Sixth Avenue Train, see *NYEP*, September 25, 1855. "Our venerable friend..." from *NYEP*, September 25, 1855.
5. "Have you heard..." *NYEP*, November 28, 1855.
6. "Private character..." from *NYEP*, September 25, 1855; "Cease giving your money..." from *Colored American*, June 30, 1838.
7. "He took hold..." from *NYTR*, July 19, 1854; "Those monsters..." from *Pacific Appeal*, May 16, 1863; "That colored persons..." and the trial, see *NYTR*, February 23, 1855. In 2007, the city named part of Park Row near City Hall Park, a spot not far from where Jennings refused to exit the streetcar, "Elizabeth Jennings Place."
8. "You will see..." from Trollope, *Domestic Manners of the Americans*, p. 180; "Was pelted..." from E.S. Abdy, *Journal of a Residence and Tour in the United States of North America*, vol. I, London: John Murray, 1835, p. 301; "He may cook..." from Nichols, *Forty Years of American Life*, vol. II, p. 229.

9. For background on African American New York, please see Leslie M. Alexander, *African or American? Black Identity and Political Activism in New York City, 1784–1861*, Urbana: University of Illinois Press, 2008; Berlin and Harris, *Slavery in New York*, cited above: The New-York Historical Society, 2005; Paul A. Gilje, *The Road to Mobocracy*, Chapel Hill: University of North Carolina Press, 1987; Leo H. Hirsch Jr., "The Free Negro in New York," *Journal of Negro History*, vol. 16, no. 4, October 1931, pp. 415–453; Leo H. Hirsch Jr., "The Slave in New York," *Journal of Negro History*, vol. 16, no. 4, October 1931, pp. 383–414; Graham Russell Hodges, *Root & Branch: African Americans in New York & New Jersey, 1613–1863*, Chapel Hill: University of North Carolina Press, 1999.

10. "On the same footing . . ." from E.B. O'Callaghan, *Laws and Ordinances of New Netherland, 1638–1674*, Albany: Weed, Parsons and Company, 1868, p. 36. In 1737, the city had 8,666 people, 1,737 of whom were Black; see *Slavery in New York*, edited by Ira Berlin and Leslie M. Harris, New York: The New-York Historical Society, 2005, p. 60.

11. "Severall [of] the slaves . . ." from John Romeyn Brodhead, E.B. O'Callaghan editor, *Documents Relative to the Colonial History of the State of New-York*: Procured in Holland, England, and France, vol. V, Albany: Weed, Parsons and Company, 1887, p. 341.

12. "To contend for . . ." from John Jay, *The Correspondence and Public Papers of John Jay*, vol. III, *1782–1793*, New York: G.P. Putnam's Sons, 1891, p. 185. Number of slaves 1790 from Hirsch, "The Slave in New York," p. 391.

13. "Fully and absolutely . . ." from *NYCLC*, Deeds V. Liber 82, 1809, vol. 26, p. 180.

14. Slavery in 1810 and 1820, please see Hirsch, "The Slave in New York," p. 392.

15. For Thomas Downing's history, please see *AME Church Review*, April 1887; S.A.M. Washington, *George Thomas Downing: Sketch of His Life and Times*, Newport: The Milne Printery, 1910; John H. Hewitt, *Protest and Progress: New York's First Black Episcopal Church Fights Racism*, New York: Garland Publishing, 2000.

16. On Downing's family, see Washington, *George Thomas Downing*, p. 3. For information on Black businesses, see Martin Robison Delany, *The Condition, Elevation, Emigration, and Destiny of the Colored People of the United States*, New York: Arno Press and the New York Times, 1968, pp. 102–124; "Every avenue . . ." from Mary White Ovington, *Half a Man: The Status of the Negro in New York*, New York: Longmans, Green, and Co., 1911, p. 26.

17. On African American and white employment in 1850, see Arnett G. Lindsay, "The Economic Condition of the Negroes of New York Prior to 1861," *Journal of Negro History*, vol. 6, no. 3, April 1921, p. 198, and *Statistical View of the United States, Compendium of the Seventh Census*, New York: Norman Ross Publishing, 1990, p. 119.

18. On African American voter rolls, see Rhoda Golden Freeman, *The Free Negro in New York City in the Era Before the Civil War*, PhD dissertation, Columbia University, 1966, pp. 122–123.

19. "Amusing incident . . ." from *NYH*, November 7, 1849; "Gay bandanna . . ." from Rev. Henry Highland Garnet, *A Memorial Discourse*, Philadelphia: Joseph M. Wilson, 1865, p. 24; "It appeared to me . . ." from *NYCA*, July 6, 1827.

20. "Become possessors . . ." from *Proceedings of the Black State Conventions, 1840–1865*, vol. I, Philip S. Foner and George E. Walker, editors, Philadelphia: Temple University Press, 1979, p. 10; "I stood at the poll . . ." from Horace Greeley, *Mr. Greeley's Record on the Question of Amnesty and Reconstruction from the Hour of Gen. Lee's Surrender*, June 1, 1872, p. 21. For vote numbers, see *NYTR*, November 25, 1846.

21. "No such damn Negro . . ." quoted in Michael Kaplan, "New York City Tavern Violence and the Creation of a Working-Class Male Identity," *Journal of the Early Republic*, vol. 15, no. 4, Winter 1995, p. 607. School attendance in 1824, see Hirsch, "The Free Negro in New York," p. 429. "Best disciplined . . ." from Charles C. Andrews, *The History of the New-York African Free-Schools*, New York: Mahlon Day, 1830, p. 51. Marquis de Lafayette toured the United States from August 1824 to September 1825, his last visit to the nation he helped form. New York threw a grand parade, with the *New York American* reporting on August 17, 1824, that "the whole city was in a bustle," and throughout the city, "the ringing of bells, the roar of cannon, and the display of the National flag at all the public places, and on board the shipping, proclaimed that it was a day of joy in which all were anxious to partake." Lafayette then traveled around the country, laid the cornerstone at Bunker Hill, and visited the White House, Mount Vernon, and Yorktown, Va.

22. For African American school attendance numbers, see Andrews, *The History of the New-York African Free-Schools*, p. 113. "The object of which . . ." from *The Liberator*, June 29, 1833.

23. For Callithumpian attack, see *NYCA*, January 3 and 4, 1828.

24. For background on the life of Arthur and Lewis Tappan, see Tappan, *The Life of Arthur Tappan*, cited earlier, and Eugene Portlette Southall, "Arthur Tappan and the Anti-Slavery Movement," *Journal of Negro History*, vol. 15, no. 2, April 1930; "Many kind words . . ." from Tappan, *The Life of Arthur Tappan*, p. 198.

25. For Tappan profits in 1826, see Smith, *Bulls and Bears of New York*, p. 483; Susan Aspinwall Tappan died in 1853, and Lewis soon after married Sarah Jackson Davis. "A zealous bigot . . ." from Charles H. Haswell, *Reminiscences of New York by an Octogenarian (1816 to 1860)*, New York: Harper & Brothers, 1896, p. 189.

26. "The introduction of abolitionism . . ." from *GTSD*, November 5, 1838; "A national sin . . ." from *GTSD*, December 20, 1842; "To unrequited labor . . ." from *NYTR*, July 4, 1846; "Haberdashers of murderous . . ." from *MCNYE*, March 20, 1833.

27. "Daily slandered . . ." from *Freedom's Journal*, March 16, 1827.

28. "To hasten the day . . ." quoted in Charles H. Wesley, "The Negroes of New York in the Emancipation Movement," *Journal of Negro History*, vol. 24, no. 1, January 1939, p. 96.

29. "I *will be* as harsh . . ." from *The Liberator*, January 1, 1831.

30. "The black men . . ." and "Was not Christ crucified?" reprinted in *The Atlantic*, March 2012; "The first drops . . ." from *The Liberator*, September 3, 1831; "To escape the sound . . ." from Theodore Dwight Weld, Angelina Grimké, and Sarah Grimké, *American Slavery As It Is: Testimony of a Thousand Witnesses*, New York: The

American Anti-Slavery Society, 1839, p. 22; "Let us endeavor . . ." from *The Liberator*, September 19, 1835.

31. "*Overthrow* this horrible . . ." from *The Anti-Slavery Examiner*, September 1836; "Cut Arthur Tappan's throat . . ." from Weld, *American Slavery as It Is*, p. 47.

32. For Douglass' life, see Frederick Douglass, *My Bondage and My Freedom*, New York: Miller, Orton & Co., 1857, and Frederick Douglass, *Narrative of the Life of Frederick Douglass, an American Slave*, London: H.G. Collins, 1851. "My meat . . ." from Douglass, *Narrative of the Life of Frederick Douglass*, p. 103; "The story that he had . . ." from Douglass, *My Bondage and My Freedom*, p. 247; "I was walking . . ." from Douglass, *My Bondage and My Freedom*, p. 336.

33. "Her bright brilliant eyes . . ." from *NYH*, November 16, 1835; "Many of my friends . . ." from Clyde N. Wilson and Shirley Bright Cook, *The Papers of John C. Calhoun*, vol. XXIV, *1846–1847*, University of South Carolina Press, 1998, p. 468.

34. On cotton export, see Berlin and Harris, *Slavery in New York*, p. 272. "Man-stealers . . ." from *Southern Literary Messenger*, January 1854.

35. For number of slaves sold and transferred, see Smithsonian, *The Civil War: A Visual History*, New York: DK Publishing, 2001, p. 22. "Slaves illegally held . . ." from *The First Annual Report of the New York Committee of Vigilance, for the Year 1837*, New York: Piercy & Reed, 1837, p. 31; "Have been stowed . . ." and profits for slave trading, see Whitman, *New York Dissected*, pp. 110 and 114. On Portuguese traders, see Hodges, *Root & Branch*, p. 257. "New York and Boston . . ." from *NYH*, August 15, 1859.

Chapter 16

1. "A gigantic fraud . . ." from *Proceedings of the Black State Conventions*, vol. 1, p. 87; "The Friends of Immediate . . ." from *NYEP*, September 28, 1833; "All citizens who . . ." quoted in Southall, "Arthur Tappan and the Anti-Slavery Movement," pp. 190–191.

2. For population numbers, see Reynolds, *Waking Giant*, p. 181; "Disgustful in *our* . . ." from *MCNYE*, October 30, 1833.

3. Tappan appears to have only lived at St. John's Park until the early 1830s. He is listed in *Longworth's New York Register* on Beach near Varick in 1827, yet in their 1833–1834 directory, his home is listed as being in Brooklyn. "Treason! Treason! . . ." from *The Liberator*, July 12, 1834; "Did much to excite . . ." from Thomas Picton, *Rose Street: Its Past, Present and Future*, New York: Russell Brothers, 1873, pp. 13–14; "Damn the Yankees . . ." from *NYS*, July 8, 1834.

4. "I hab conquer . . ." from *NYCA*, July 7, 1834; "Knocked him over . . ." from Samuel Ringgold Ward, *Autobiography of a Fugitive Negro: His Anti-Slavery Labors in the United States, Canada, & England*, Chicago: Johnson Publishing Company Inc., 1970, p. 47; "To act out . . ." from *NYS*, July 7, 1834.

5. "Threatening to burn . . ." from *NYCA*, July 8, 1834; "A well dressed . . ." from *Letters of Theodore Dwight Weld, Angelina Grimké Weld, and Sarah Grimké, 1822–1844*, edited

by Gilbert H. Barnes and Dwight L. Dumond, Gloucester: Peter Smith, 1965, p. 154; "I shall do..." from Maria L. Child, *Isaac T. Hopper: A True Life*, Boston: John P. Jewett & Co., 1853, p. 315.

6. "Because the hand..." from *PHD-BT*, July 10, 1834; "The house fell..." from Picton, *Rose Street*, p. 14; "It is *Washington*..." from *NYAM*, July 11, 1834.

7. "The mob had made..." from *PHD-AN*, July 12, 1834; "They then commenced..." from *NYAM*, July 11, 1834.

8. "Should be fired..." *NYAM*, July 11, 1834; "Fire *low*..." from Tappan, *The Life of Arthur Tappan*, p. 284; "In this way..." from *NYCA*, July 12, 1834.

9. "Enjoining all good citizens..." from *Mercantile Advertiser & New York Advocate*, July 12, 1834; "Has been informed..." from NYHS, New York City Riots, 1834, Misc. Mss., July 12, 1834; "We entirely disclaim..." from *NYAM*, July 14, 1834; "It is my wish..." from *Letters of Theodore Dwight Weld*, p. 155.

10. On death stats, see *Summary of Vital Statistics 2017 of the City of New York*. That same year, 233 people died of smallpox. "A negro's..." from *Slavery and the Internal Slave Trade in the United States of North America*, Executive Committee of the American Anti-Slavery Society, London: Thomas Ward and Co., 1841, p. 117; "Notorious abolitionist..." from *NYCA*, November 7, 1835; "Concocting a pandora's..." from *MCNYE*, October 1, 1835; "The scoundrel..." quoted in *NYAM*, with the "That there are..." being the *American*'s response, September 14, 1835; "Abducting a..." from *NYH*, September 21, 1835.

11. "Private assassins..." from Lydia Maria Child, *Letters of Lydia Maria Child*, Boston: Houghton Mifflin and Company, 1882, p. 15; "I WILL BE..." from Tappan, *The Life of Arthur Tappan*, p. 269.

12. "Would be exalted..." from *PHD-BT*, August 31, 1839.

13. "So extensive..." from *First Annual Report of the New York Committee of Vigilance*, p. 7; "band of human hyænas..." from *Emancipator*, March 12, 1840.

14. "Bribe a jury..." from *NYTR*, June 22, 1861.

15. Vigilance Committee report on kidnapping cited in Freeman, *The Free Negro in New York City in the Era Before the Civil War*, p. 70. "A good revolver..." from *Frederick Douglass' Newspaper*, June 9, 1854.

16. "I joined in the chase..." from Willis Fletcher Johnson, *History of the State of New York Political and Governmental*, vol. II, Syracuse: The Syracuse Press, 1922, pp. 288-290.

17. "Now remember..." from William C. Beecher, Samuel Scoville, and Mrs. Henry Ward Beecher, *A Biography of Rev. Henry Ward Beecher*, New York: Charles L. Webster & Company, 1888, p. 296. For African American population in New York in 1850, see *Statistical View of the United States*, p. 80.

18. For background on Underground Railroad sites, see Tom Calarco, *The Underground Railroad in the Adirondack Region*, Jefferson, N.C.: McFarland & Company, Inc., 2004, pp. 180-181. "To protect unoffending...," "Several notorious slave-catchers...," and the number saved, from *First Annual Report of the New York Committee of Vigilance*, pp. 4, 75, and 83.

19. Election results for 1848 from the Library of Congress Resource Guide. "Compels every citizen..." from Lewis Tappan, *The Fugitive Slave Bill: Its History and*

Unconstitutionality: With an Account of the Seizure and Enslavement of James Hamlet and His Subsequent Restoration to Liberty, New York: William Harned, 1850, pp. 20–21.

20. Election results for 1852 from the Library of Congress Resource Guide; "A great demonstration . . ." from Tappan, *The Fugitive Slave Bill*, p. 36.

21. "A disgrace . . ." from Whitman, *The Uncollected Poetry and Prose of Walt Whitman*, vol. I, p. 106.

22. "Slavery and freedom . . ." quoted in John B. Jervis, *Letters Addressed to the Friends of Freedom and the Union*, New York: Wm. C. Bryant & Co., 1856, p. 3; "The selling asunder . . ." from *GTSD*, August 5, 1856.

23. For background on Olmsted's views on slavery, see Witold Rybczynski, *A Clearing in the Distance: Frederick Law Olmsted and America in the Nineteenth Century*, New York: Scribner, 1999. "I represent pretty . . ." from Frederick Law Olmsted, *The Papers of Frederick Law Olmsted*: vol. II, *Slavery and the South, 1852–1857*, Charles E. Beveridge, Charles Capen McLaughlin, and David Schuyler, editors, Baltimore: Johns Hopkins University Press, 1983, p. 83.

24. "It is our duty . . ." from *NYT*, February 13, 1854.

25. For background on the settlement and building of Seneca Village, please see Roy Rosenzweig and Elizabeth Blackmar, *The Park and the People: A History of Central Park*, Ithaca: Cornell University Press, 1992, and Alexander, *African or American?*, pp. 154–173; "A neat *little* . . ." from *NYT*, July 9, 1856; "Number of these . . ." from *NYTR*, August 14, 1857.

26. "Twenty feet inside . . ." from *NYT*, July 7, 1924.

Chapter 17

1. "The lungs . . ." from *NYM*, July 23, 1842.

2. "Buying, selling . . ." from *Manual of the Corporation of the City of New-York*, D.T. Valentine, New York: Edmund Jones & Co., 1864, p. 848.

3. "This pleasant spot . . ." from *NYGGA*, June 16, 1828.

4. The city eventually filled in the water between the shore and Castle Garden (now called Castle Clinton), connecting the island to Manhattan. "Certainly if the City . . ." from Bridges, *Map of the City of New-York and Island of Manhattan*, pp. 25–26.

5. The parks laid out by William Curr are mentioned in *NYH*, June 26, 1853; On the reduction in size of parks, see *Documents of the Assembly of the State of New York*, Albany: Oliver A. Quayle, 1904, pp. 142–144. "Plant and improve . . ." from New York *Legal Observer*, November 19, 1842.

6. "Benefit and enjoyment . . ." from John B. Pine, *The Story of Gramercy Park: 1831–1921*, New York: Gramercy Park Association, 1921, p. 5.

7. On the number of parks and acreage see Rosenzweig and Blackmar, *The Park and the People*, p. 19.

8. On the various pleasure gardens around the city, please see Boyer, *Manhattan Manners*, pp. 10–15. "Were tastefully decorated . . ." from Barnum, *The Life of P.T.*

Barnum, p. 152; "With their astonishing . . ." from *MCNYE*, July 15, 1839; "Novelty after novelty . . ." from *NYM*, June 13, 1840.

9. "Superlative . . ." from *GTSD*, June 10, 1842; "Cream, ices . . ." from *NYT*, June 30, 1853.

10. On the Marine Pavilion, see *Philadelphia National Gazette*, June 5, 1834. "Almost deserted . . ." from *GTSD*, September 16, 1837; the complex burned down in June 1864. "New walks . . ." from *PHD-BT*, May 31, 1838; "These cemeteries . . ." from A.J. Downing, *Rural Essays*, New York: Leavitt & Allen, 1857, p. 144.

11. "A New Public Park . . ." from *NYEP*, July 3, 1844; "All the public squares . . ." from *DBA*, vol. XVII, part 1, p. 13; "A cause of regret . . ." from *NYEP*, July 22, 1845; "The necessity for public squares . . ." from *The Transactions of the American Medical Association*, vol. II, Philadelphia: T.K. and P.G. Collins, 1849, p. 438.

12. "Even in third-rate . . ." from Downing, *Rural Essays*, p. 140.

13. "Are to be found . . ." from Fredrika Bremer, *The Homes of the New World: Impressions of America*, vol. I, New York: Harper & Brothers, 1853, p. 46; "What are called parks . . ." and "filled with all classes . . ." from Downing, *Rural Essays*, pp. 485, 237, and 143; "There is nothing . . ." from *The Horticulturist*, June 1850.

14. "Would secure . . ." quoted in Clarence Cook, *A Description of the New York Central Park*, New York: F.J. Huntington and Co., 1869, p. 18; "The chief advantages . . ." from *NYH*, June 26, 1853.

15. "Very beautiful . . ." from *GTSD*, October 16, 1853; "It is absurd . . ." from *NYS*, June 28, 1851; "Only ask to be . . ." from NYHS, Beekman Family Papers, Box 2, Folder 9, Letter, W. Schermerhorn to James Beekman, December 18, 1852.

16. "Most heartily . . ." from Downing, *Rural Essays*, p. 149; "Throng a place . . ." from *First Annual Report on the Improvement of the Central Park, New York*, New York: Chas. W. Baker, 1857, p. 141.

17. "A man of genius . . ." from *NYTR*, July 31, 1852.

18. For population of the park at this time as well as the makeup of the residents, see Rosenzweig and Blackmar, *The Park and the People*, pp. 60–65.

19. "The growth of the city . . ." from *NYT*, May 21, 1852. For those who owned real estate in and around the park, see Rosenzweig and Blackmar, *The Park and the People*, pp. 47 and 78. "The projected . . ." from *NYT*, June 21, 1853.

20. "Dwelling in rude huts . . ." from James Grant Wilson, *The Memorial History of the City of New-York*, vol. IV, New York: New-York History Company, 1893, p. 556.

21. On cost of the park, see Morrison H. Heckscher, *Creating Central Park*, New York: Metropolitan Museum of Art, 2008, p. 17, and Rosenzweig and Blackmar, *The Park and the People*, pp. 87–90. "Let New-York . . ." from *NYT*, March 24, 1855. All told, the 843-acre final park cost $7.4 million. The following decade, the United States paid $7.2 million for Alaska. The 2007 restoration of the Bethesda Terrace Arcade was budgeted at $7 million.

22. "With power to employ . . ." *Transactions of the American Society of Landscape Architects, From Its Inception in 1899 to the End of 1908*, Harold A. Caparn, James Sturgis Pray, and Downing Vaux, editors, Harrisburg, Penn., J. Horace McFarland Company, N.D., p. 108; "Trees have been cut . . ." from *NYEP*, May 31, 1856.

23. "A pestilential . . ." and "The hills . . ." from *First Annual Report on the Improvement of the Central Park*, pp. 12 and 37.

24. "Several factories . . ." from *First Annual Report on the Improvement of the Central Park*, p. 35.
25. For background on the life of Calvert Vaux, see William Alex, *Calvert Vaux: Architect & Planner*, New York: Ink, Inc., 1994, and Francis R. Kowsky, *Country, Park & City: The Architecture and Life of Calvert Vaux*, New York: Oxford University Press, 2003; "That it would . . ." quoted in Alex, *Calvert Vaux*, p. 11.
26. "Thoughts and observations . . ." and "Kindly and unselfish . . ." from Kowsky, *Country, Park & City*, pp. 11 and 138; "I discussed . . ." from Alex, *Calvert Vaux*, p. 11.

Chapter 18

1. Olmsted's conversation with Charles Elliott is recounted in *Landscape Architecture*, July 1912, "The Beginning of Central Park, New York: A Fragment of Autobiography of the Late Frederick Law Olmsted," pp. 156–157.
2. For a history of Olmsted's life, see Rybczynski, *A Clearing in the Distance*. "Let me assure you . . ." and "For the past sixteen . . ." from Olmsted, *The Papers of Frederick Law Olmsted*: vol. III, pp. 201 and 76.
3. "I then had an opportunity . . ." and "Have defeated . . ." from *Landscape Architecture*, July 1912.
4. "Strangely uneducated . . ." from Frederick Law Olmsted, *Landscape Architect, 1822-1903*, edited Frederick Law Olmsted Jr. and Theodora Kimball, New York: G. P. Putnam's Sons, 1922, p. 69.
5. "Enjoyment of scenery . . ." from *Century Illustrated Magazine*, October 1893; "A vigorous . . ." quoted in Rybczynski, *A Clearing in the Distance*, p. 19.
6. "The kindest . . ." from Olmsted, *Landscape Architect*, p. 80.
7. "I was ready . . ." from *The Horticulturist and Journal of Rural Art and Rural Taste*, May 1, 1851.
8. For background on the building of Central Park, please see Rosenzweig and Blackmar, *The Park and the People*, and Heckscher, *Creating Central Park*, both cited earlier. "Striking across the hill . . ." and the following on how Olmsted was greeted by the crews, from *Landscape Architecture*, July 1912; "I have got the park . . ." from Olmsted, *The Papers of Frederick Law Olmsted*: vol. III, p. 113.
9. "To cooperate . . ." quoted in Heckscher, *Creating Central Park*, p. 26; "Staked off . . ." from Frederick Law Olmsted, "Public Parks and the Enlargement of Towns," American Social Science Association, Cambridge, Massachusetts, 1870, p. 14; quoted in Burrows and Wallace, *Gotham*, p. 794; "The most ingenious . . ." from Frederick Law Olmsted to Paul Dana, Frederick Law Olmsted Papers, Library of Congress, March 12, 1891.
10. "There was a great . . ." from *Transactions of the American Society of Landscape Architects*, p. 81.
11. The park was originally slated for 750 acres. It was soon after enlarged to 843, which is its current size. "Supply to the hundreds . . ." and "Then the priceless . . ." from Olmsted, *The Papers of Frederick Law Olmsted*, vol. III, p. 196; "Big art work . . ." from Olmsted, *The Papers of Frederick Law Olmsted*, vol. V, p. 385; "The creative artist . . ."

from Samuel Parsons Jr., *The Art of Landscape Architecture*, Amherst: University of Massachusetts Press, 2009, p. xxiii.

12. "The horizon lines . . ." Olmsted, *The Papers of Frederick Law Olmsted*, vol. III, p. 119.

13. "I have heard . . ." and "I have seen . . ." from Frederick Law Olmsted, *The Spoils of the Park*, February 1882, p. 29.

14. On size and makeup of crews in the park see Rosenzweig and Blackmar, *The Park and the People*, pp. 170–176, and Rybczynski, *A Clearing in the Distance*, pp. 174–175. "Rigidly discharged . . ." from Olmsted, *The Papers of Frederick Law Olmsted:* vol. III, p. 286.

15. For amount of matériel used, see Rosenzweig and Blackmar, *The Park and the People*, p. 150; "Nearly all the earth . . ." from George Haven Putnam, *Memories of My Youth, 1844–1865*, New York: G.P. Putnam's Sons, 1914, p. 87.

16. "Undulating outlines . . ." from Olmsted, *The Papers of Frederick Law Olmsted*, vol. III, p. 196.

17. Green, who has been called "The Father of Central Park," was a commissioner from 1857 to 1871, as well as serving as its president and comptroller. Many considered him to be very stingy with money for the park, and Olmsted and Vaux certainly saw him that way. "Not a dollar . . ." from Olmsted, *The Papers of Frederick Law Olmsted*, vol. III, p. 324. For the increasing cost of the park, see Rybczynski, *A Clearing in the Distance*, p. 184.

18. "A large part . . ." from Frederick Law Olmsted, *Forty Years of Landscape Architecture: Central Park*, edited by Frederick Law Olmsted Jr. and Theodora Kimball, Cambridge: MIT Press, 1973, p. 58; "Rules and Conditions . . ." from Olmsted, *The Papers of Frederick Law Olmsted:* vol. III, pp. 219–220; "Masters Richard . . ." from *NYH*, December 27, 1858.

19. Concert was reported on in the *NYT*, July 11, 1859. "Refining influence . . ." from Olmsted, *Public Parks and the Enlargement of Town*, p. 34.

20. "Well, they have . . ." from Cook, *A Description of the New York Central Park*, p. 110; "Will be a feature . . ." from *GTSD*, June 11, 1859; "The system . . ." from *GTSD*, September 2, 1859; "The park below . . ." from *GTSD*, May 28, 1860.

21. "The sulkey . . ." from *NYH*, November 21, 1860.

22. "I have been growing . . ." from Olmsted, *The Papers of Frederick Law Olmsted*, vol. III, p. 230.

23. On Green telling the prince how to plant a tree, see *Documents of the Assembly of the State of New York*, p. 156. "He turned & bowed . . ." from Olmsted, *The Papers of Frederick Law Olmsted*, vol. III, p. 275; "I think of having . . ." from *GTSD*, October 13, 1860. On torchlight parade, please see *NYT*, October 13, 1860.

Chapter 19

1. "A great number . . ." from *NYAM*, June 22, 1835.

2. The attack on the Willett Street porterhouse from the *New York Express*, copied in the *Long Island Star*, February 25, 1839. The attack on Valentine Mager's place was

covered in the *NYH*, January 5, 1840. "A decent orderly manner . . ." from *PHD-AN*, January 1, 1840.

3. "Brace of 'mahogany' . . ." from *NYS*, January 22, 1836; "Characteristic row . . ." from *NYTR*, September 22, 1845.

4. "Anti-Jackson . . ." from *NYEP*, November 8, 1832; "Little game of fisticuffs . . ." from *NYH*, November 7, 1849.

5. "A gentleman . . ." from *PHD-AN*, May 8, 1849; "A mountain of a man . . ." from Charles T. Congdon, *Reminiscences of a Journalist*, Boston: James R. Osgood and Company, 1880, p. 190.

6. Forrest first appeared in New York on June 23, 1826, at the Park Theatre as Othello in the Shakespeare play. Macready's New York debut, also at the Park, was on October 2, 1826 as Virginius in James Sheridan Knowles' *Tragedy of Virginius*.

7. "Whatever are my offences . . ." from *NYEP*, November 16, 1825; "Deafening shouts . . ." quote from *PHD-AN*, p. 49; "Pursue more diligently . . ." from *NYAM*, August 6, 1834; "Truly we are . . ." from *Brooklyn Evening Star*, August 17, 1848.

8. "The Theatrical Prize-Fight . . ." from *NYH*, April 5, 1849; "Was saluted . . ." from *PHD-BT*, May 8, 1849; "Requesting you . . ." from *NYH*, May 9, 1849.

9. "The signal for . . ." from *NYTR*, May 11, 1849; "Burn the damned . . ." from *NYH*, May 12, 1849; "Volley after volley . . ." from Diary of Edward Neufville Tailer, May 9, 1849, Journal 5, NYHS; "Fire, if you dare . . ." from J.T. Headley, *The Great Riots of New York, 1712–1873*, New York: E.B. Treat, 1873, p. 124.

10. "The Gomorrah . . ." from *Brooklyn Daily Eagle*, November 27, 1891. Wood's attack on Bradford was reported by the *Brooklyn Daily Eagle*, June 19, 1856.

11. "Americans can *fix* . . ." from Marryat, *A Diary in America*, p. 124.

12. On types of drinking establishments, see Kaplan, "New York City Tavern Violence and the Creation of a Working-Class Male Identity," p. 598. Police Chief Matsell's report is in *DBA*, vol. XV, p. 1109. "The honest fellow . . ." quoted in Helen F. Mulvey, "New York City in 1859: A Letter from Richard O'Gorman to William Smith O'Brien," *New York History*, vol. 34, no. 1, January 1953, p. 89; "Nearly *fifty* . . ." from *NYTR*, November 1, 1856; "Rum elected their Presidents . . ." from *NYT*, October 4, 1853.

13. On Democratic office holders owning bars, please see Paul O. Weinbaum, "Temperance, Politics, and the New York City Riots of 1857," *New-York Historical Society Quarterly*, vol. LIX, no. 3, July 1975, p. 267. For arrest numbers 1845–1850, see A.E. Costello, *Our Police Protectors: History of the New York Police*, New York: 1865, p. 116. At the same time, there were 11,347 arrests for vagrancy, "If some drunken . . ." from *GTSD*, July 2, 1852; "Were no sooner . . ." from *DBA*, vol. XVII, pt. 2, p. 930.

14. "Beat his face . . ." from *NYT*, October 23, 1851.

15. "A check upon . . ." from *NYTR*, March 9, 1855. The funeral, the attack on the engine company, and the burning down of fire house reported in *National Police Gazette*, October 30, 1880. Baker's two murder trials ended in hung juries.

16. "It is not customary . . ." from *NYCA*, May 9, 1840.

17. On number of those killed or murdered in 1835, see Edwin Williams, *The New-York Annual Register for the Year of Our Lord 1836*, New York: Edwin Williams, 1836, p. 322. For crime rates 1845 to 1853, see *DBA*, Vol. XXI, pt. 1, pp. 336–337. "Advice

to Strangers . . ." from Whitman, *New York Dissected*, p. 140; "Half-eaten . . ." from Dickens, *American Notes*, p. 121.

18. "There is a great . . ." from *PHD-AN*, February 12, 1847; "Every denomination . . ." from *PHD-AN*, March 1, 1847.

19. The letter from the doctor aboard the ship from Liverpool is in *NYT*, October 15, 1851.

20. "Passengers in a state . . ." from *NYH*, December 11, 1843; "If they looked . . ." from Bird, *The Englishwoman in America*, p. 380. Number of runners and "Many if not most . . ." from George G. Foster, *New York in Slices: By an Experienced Carver*, New York: W.F. Burgess, 1849, p. 84.

21. The *Herald* reported on June 15, 1851, how the previous night Mike Murray and others took 150 German immigrants by steamboat to boarding houses in Brooklyn. "A few maggoty . . ." from Foster, *New York in Slices*, p. 85.

22. For population numbers 1845–1850, see Ira Rosenwaike, *Population History of New York City*, Syracuse: Syracuse University Press, 1972, p. 42. "Are more ignorant . . ." from *American Republican*, August 10, 1844.

23. For earnings of men and women at the times, see Robert Ernst, *Immigrant Life in New York City: 1825–1863*, Port Washington, N.Y., 1949, pp. 67–69.

24. "The fruits of *papal* . . ." from Samuel F.B. Morse, *Foreign Conspiracy against the Liberties of the United States*, New York: Leavitt, Lord & Co. 1835, p. 168; "Brilliant Bal Costume . . ." from *NYH*, March 5, 1840; "That some of your churches . . ." from Henry Athanasius Brann, *Most Reverend John Hughes, First Archbishop of New York*, Dodd, Mead and Company, 1892, p. 97.

25. "The new comer . . ." from Mackay, *Life and Liberty in America*, p. 114; "Make Presidents . . ." from *PHD-BT*, December 17, 1835. On illegal voting, see Ernst, *Immigrant Life in New York City*, p. 162.

Chapter 20

1. "Not larger than . . ." from Whitman, *New York Dissected*, p. 99; "Crazy old buildings . . ." from *First Report of a Committee on the Sanitary Condition of the Laboring Classes*, Association for Improving the Condition of the Poor, New York: John F. Trow, 1853, pp. 7–8.

2. For a detailed look at the Five Points, please see Tyler Anbinder, *Five Points: The 19th-Century New York City Neighborhood that Invented Tap Dance, Stole Elections, and Became the World's Most Notorious Slum*, New York: The Free Press, 2001. Anthony, Cross, and Orange Streets would soon be renamed Baxter, Worth, and Clark Streets. The population density of the Sixth Ward comes from *Hunt's Merchants' Magazine and Commercial Review*, October 1852, p. 412; "Saturate your handkerchief . . ." from Solon Robinson, *Hot Corn: Life Scenes in New York Illustrated*, New York: De Witt and Davenport, 1854, p. 70; "I thought I would . . ." from David Crockett, *The Life of David*

Crockett: The Original Humorist and Irrepressible Backwoodsman, New York: A.L. Burt, 1902, p. 185.

3. "Incumbrances of sidewalks . . ." from *NYTR*, July 18, 1843; "Here's your nice . . ." and "Emaciated little girl . . ." from *NYTR*, August 5, 1853.

4. "On a rainy day . . ." from *GTSD*, July 7, 1851.

5. "Have not . . ." from *NYTR*, January 28, 1845; "There are, or were . . ." from *NYTR*, March 31, 1847.

6. For number of women working as prostitutes, see *Encyclopedia of Prostitution and Sex Work*, vol. I, edited by Melissa Hope Ditmore, Westport: Greenwood Press, 2006, p. 331. For concentration of brothels around Paradise Square, see Burrows and Wallace, *Gotham*, p. 534. "Every house . . ." from *NYT*, November 19, 1852. On number of prostitutes in 1857, see William W. Sanger, *The History of Prostitution: Its Extent, Causes, and Effects Throughout the World*, New York: Harper & Brothers, 1869, p. 584. New York's population in 1855 stood at 629,904 and the 320,194 women made up 51 percent of the population. Total population rose to 813,669 in 1860. Female population would therefore be at about 357,682 in 1857; Sanger concluded there were 7,860 prostitutes working, which comes to 2.2 percent.

7. "A respectable young lady . . . ," "drew from beneath . . . ," and "most beautiful . . ." from *NYH*, April 12, 1836; "A most awful . . ." and "It is to be feared . . ." from *PHD-AN*, April 11 and June 4, 1836.

8. "Aged, decrepit . . ." from Snug Harbor Cultural Center & Botanical Garden website.

9. "Reading from the sacred . . ." from John Robert McDowall, *Memoir and Select Remains of the Late Rev. John R. M'Dowall, the Martyr of the Seventh Commandment, in the Nineteenth Century*, New York: Leavitt, Lord, & Co., 1838, p. 194; "Despoiled of character . . ." from *McDowall's Journal*, January 1833.

10. "With the exception . . ." from *NYH*, April 1, 1860. Census and assistance numbers reported in *NYH*, April 1, 1860.

11. "Never see the inside . . ." from *DBA*, vol. XXVII, pt. 1, p. 58. On childhood delinquency, *Children & Youth in America: A Documentary History*, vol. I, *1600–1865*, Robert H. Bremner, editor, American Public Health Association, 1970, p. 756. For childhood crime and incarceration rates, see Spann, *The New Metropolis*, p. 263. The US census puts the city's population in 1850, a year after Matsell's report, at 501,732. There were 98,314 school-age children between five and 15, which comes to 19.5 percent of the population. The 11 police districts (which correspond to the wards) contained 144,334 people. Using that same percentage would mean there were 28,145 school-age children in those districts. Matsell said there were 2,343 children not going to school, which comes to 8.3 percent of that population.

12. "From the existence . . ." and "the improvement . . ." from *Second Annual Report of the Children's Aid Society*, February 1855, New York: M.B. Wynkoop, 1855, p. 3.

13. "In the acquisition . . ." from *NYTR*, February 11, 1842; "All these attempts . . ." from *NYH*, July 9, 1849. For arrest rates, see *DBA*, Vol. XVIII, part 1, p. 555.

14. "For the purpose . . ." from *NYT*, September 20, 1852.

15. For an in-depth study on Fernando Wood's life and career, please see Jerome Mushkat's *Fernando Wood*, which was cited earlier. "A fiery-headed fellow . . ." from George Walker, *The Three Spaniards, A Romance*, vol. I, New York: 1801, p. 76.

16. On Wood's rise, see Mushkat, *Fernando Wood*, pp. 16–26; Wood's wife's name has been listed as both Ann and Anna, but her tombstone spells it Ann. "We are satisfied . . ." from *NYH*, October 20, 1850.

17. "Fernando Wood, instead . . ." from *PHD-AN*, October 16, 1850; for election results, see Caliendo, *New York City Mayors*, p. 401. "Grossly overrated . . ." from *NYEP*, November 7, 1850.

18. "The People will elect . . ." from M.R. Werner, *Tammany Hall*, New York: Greenwood Press, 1968, p. 74; "Is accused . . ." from *GTSD*, November 6, 1854; "For three days . . ." from Bird, *The Englishwoman in America*, p. 385.

19. For election results, see Caliendo, *New York City Mayors*, p. 402. "The hundreds . . ." from *GTSD*, December 13, 1854. On the Five Points House feeding the hungry, see Carroll S. Rosenberg, "Protestants and Five Pointers: The Five Points House of Industry," *New-York Historical Society Quarterly*, vol. 48, no. 4, October 1964, p. 340.

20. "The most rigid . . ." from E. Hutchinson, *A Model Mayor: Early Life, Congressional Career, and Triumphant Municipal Administration of Hon. Fernando Wood*, New York: American Family Publication, 1855, p. 59. "A complicated . . ." from Donald MacLeod, *Biography of Hon. Fernando Wood*, New York: O.F. Parsons, 1856, p. 161; "Freely and frankly . . ." from *NYT*, January 3, 1855.

21. Drop in number of public houses open on Sundays, see *NYTR*, February 1, 1855. "Set himself . . ." from *GTSD*, February 14, 1855.

22. "The glowing stars . . ." from *NYT*, November 15, 1855.

23. "I . . . drink . . ." from *NYTR*, April 28, 1855.

24. "This bold . . ." from *NYTR*, October 18, 1856; "I paid my $25 . . ." from *NYTR*, October 20, 1856.

25. Mention that the Dead Rabbits were also known as the Mulberry Street Boys, from *NYH*, July 7, 1857. "In secret conclave . . ." from *NYTR*, March 1, 1855.

26. "Armed with bludgeons . . ." from *NYH*, November 5, 1856. Election results, Caliendo, *New York City Mayors*, p. 402.

27. "A huge semi-barbarous . . ." from *Harper's*, April 11, 1857.

28. "The most notorious . . ." from *NYT*, April 14, 1857. On the split in the police force, see Lynch, *"Boss" Tweed: The Story of a Grim Generation*, pp. 185–187. On the struggle over liquor, see Weinbaum, "Temperance, Politics, and the New York City Riots of 1857," pp. 246–258.

29. "Brick-bats, stones . . ." and "a well-known loafer . . ." from *NYTR*, June 15, 1857.

30. "I do not recognize . . ." from George W. Walling, *Recollections of a New York Chief of Police*, New York: Caxton Book Concern, 1887, p. 57.

31. "Hooting . . ." from *NYTR*, June 17, 1857; "A limb . . ." from *GTSD*, October 13, 1860; "Being aided by their . . ." *GTSD*, June 17, 1857.

32. "The people of the rural . . ." *NYH*, May 3, 1857.

33. On Bowery Boys–Dead Rabbits riot, see *NYTR*, July 6, 1857. "For God's sake . . ." from Lynch, *"Boss" Tweed*, p. 191.

34. "Were bleeding . . ." from *NYH*, July 17, 1857.
35. "Prominent stocks . . ." from *Harper's*, September 12, 1857, quoted in the *Brooklyn Daily Eagle*, September 15, 1857. 425 people perished when the SS *Central America* sank off the coast of South Carolina. The wreckage was discovered in 1988, 8,000 feet below the surface. "41,000 homeless . . ." from *The Fifteenth Annual Report of the New York Association for Improving the Condition of the Poor, for the Year 1858*, New York: John F. Trow, 1858, p. 29; "God is chastising . . ." from Wyatt-Brown, *Lewis Tappan and the Evangelical War Against Slavery*, p. 229.
36. "The bluest day . . ." and others from *GTSD*, October 9, 10, 13, and 14, 1857.
37. "To be paid . . ." from *Proceedings of the Board of Councilmen of the City of New York*, vol. LXVIII, New York: Charles W. Baker, 1857, pp. 910–911; "The banner . . ." from *NYT*, October 27, 1857; "One hundred . . ." from *GTSD*, November 10, 1857.
38. For election results Caliendo, *New York City Mayors*, p. 402. "An honest and determined . . ." from *NYTR*, December 3, 1857; "The defeat of the Father . . ." from *GTSD*, December 1, 1857.
39. Tweed's induction into Tammany, see Hershkowitz, *Tweed's New York*, p. 70. On election officials, see Callow, *The Tweed Ring*, p. 25.

Chapter 21

1. "Where is up town? . . ." from *NYTR*, June 17, 1856.
2. "The scene, however . . ." from *The Illustrated London News*, September 25, 1858.
3. On the sale of Philip Hone's home, see *Buffalo Courier*, December 2, 1851. It was announced in January 1853 that the Clinton Hall Association bought the Astor Place Opera House for $140,000; $75,000 was then spent to alter it. James Renwick Jr. was the architect. Information on the purchase and the modifications to the building can be found in *NYT*, January 22, 1853, and *NYH*, March 27, 1854. The Astor Library opened in January 1854. Soon it was enlarged to the north, and later extended even more to the north, with an attic added above the central section. Both the first enlargement by Griffith Thomas and the second by Thomas Stent were quite sensitive to Alexander Saeltzer's original design. "Probably the handsomest . . ." from *Jewish Messenger*, September 21, 1860.
4. "Tarnish the dramatic . . ." from *NYH*, February 11, 1853.
5. "The audience embraced . . ." from *NYH*, September 6, 1859; "The theatre has been . . ." from *NYT*, August 30, 1860; "Blue fire melodrama . . ." from *NYT*, August 31, 1860.
6. "A bloody end . . ." from Dickens, *American Notes*, p. 300; "To-day, we are called . . ." from Massachusetts Historical Society Collections online "No Slavery! Fourth of July!," https://www.masshist.org/database/431
7. "A mountain howitzer . . ." from Frederick Law Olmsted, *The Papers of Frederick Law Olmsted*, Vol. III, p. 370.
8. "Wherever our flag floats . . ." from *NYEP*, March 9, 1857.

9. "In sympathy . . ." quoted in Louis A. DeCaro Jr., *"Fire from the Midst of You": A Religious Life of John Brown*, New York: New York University Press, 2002, p. 41; "When I strike . . ." and "Going into . . ." quoted in David W. Blight, "Admiration and Ambivalence: Frederick Douglass and John Brown," The Gilder Lehrman Institute of American History.

10. "The ladies of New York . . ." from *Weekly Anglo-African*, December 3, 1859; "Simplicity and consistency . . ." from *GTSD*, December 4, 1859; "History . . . will record . . ." from *NYEP*, December 1, 1859.

11. "A thousand John Browns . . ." from *The Congressional Globe: The Debates, Proceedings, and Laws of the First Session of the Third-Sixth Congress*, vol. XXVIII, Washington: John C. Rives, 1860, p. 69; "They do nothing . . ." *NYH*, May 12, 1859; "The glory . . ." from *De Bow's Review*, vol. XXVI, 1859.

12. "What, in the meanwhile . . ." from *NYH*, October 20, 1859. Fernando Wood received 29,940 votes, William Havemeyer 26,913, and George Opdyke 21,417; see Caliendo, *New York City Mayors*, p. 402.

13. "Probably the largest . . ." and "Low with brain . . ." from *NYT*, December 13, 1859.

14. "Let us have faith . . ." from Abraham Lincoln Online, February 27, 1860; "I want to be able . . ." from *GTSD*, November 2, 1860; "Secession threatened . . ." from P.T. Barnum, *Struggles and Triumphs: or, Sixty Years' Recollections of P.T. Barnum*, Buffalo: Courier Company, 1889, p. 229.

15. "If Lincoln is elected . . ." from *NYH*, November 6, 1860. On Lincoln's vote in the city, see Burrows and Wallace, *Gotham*, p. 865. Nationally, Lincoln received 1.87 million votes and 180 Electoral College votes, to Breckinridge's 847,953 votes and 72 Electoral College votes.

16. "I should welcome . . ." from *GTSD*, December 15, 1860. On revenue rates, referenced in *NYT*, January 6, 2011. "We could live . . ." from *NYT*, January 8, 1861; "Mr. Fernando Wood evidently . . ." quoted in the *NYCA*, January 8, 1861; "Monstrous and treasonable . . ." quoted in the *NYCA*, January 8, 1861.

17. "Broadway crowded . . ." from *GTSD*, February 20, 1861; "Many an assassin's . . ." from Walt Whitman, *Specimen Days & Collect*, Philadelphia: Rees Welsh & Co., 1882–'83, p. 308; "Lincoln is dead and gone to h-ll . . ." from *NYT*, February 26, 1861.

Chapter 22

1. "Extry—a *Herald*! . . ." from *GTSD*, April 12, 1861; "every cart horse decorated . . ." from *GTSD*, April 18, 1861; "The roar . . ." from *GTSD*, April 19, 1861.

2. "Cunning scoundrel . . ." from *GTSD*, April 15, 1860.

3. "The Lincoln administration . . ." from *NYH*, March 31, 1861; "Calculated to aid . . ." quoted in James Melvin Lee, *History of American Journalism*, Boston: Houghton Mifflin Company, 1917, p. 316.

4. "Considerable experience . . ." from Thurlow Weed, *Autobiography of Thurlow Weed*, Harriet A. Weed editor, Boston, Houghton, Mifflin and Company, 1884, p. 616; "We mean to conquer . . ." from *NYTR*, May 1, 1861.

5. "To the drum-taps . . ." from Whitman, *Leaves of Grass*, p. 262.

6. "They are sleeping . . ." from Orville J. Victor, *Incidents and Anecdotes of the War: Together with Life Sketches of Eminent Leaders, and Narratives of the Most Memorable Battles of the Union*, New York: James Torrey, 1862, p. 94; Ad for the Ellsworth Zouaves: "The Zouave Regiment—Enlist for the War," *NYT*, April 22, 1861.

7. "They had no choice . . ." Horace Greeley, *The American Conflict: A History of the Great Rebellion in the United States of America, 1860–'65*, Hartford, Conn.: O.D. Case & Company, 1867, p. 515.

8. On Mary Lincoln's visit, *NYT*, May 18, 1861. The encampment and the training of the men are listed in *NYS*, April 30, 1861, and *NYT*, May 12, 13, and 18, 1861. "We have no sympathy . . ." from *Buffalo Commercial Advertiser*, April 13, 1863.

9. "The uniformed companies . . ." from *GTSD*, April 23, 1861; "the whole fire department . . ." from *GTSD*, April 29, 1861; "They have been . . ." from *NYT*, May 8, 1861.

10. Brownell received the Medal of Honor in 1877 for his actions. "With cheers . . ." from *NYT*, July 26, 1861; "Turn back . . ." from the United States Senate Art & History site; "The road was filled . . ." from National Park Service Series: The First Battle of Manassas.

11. The toll of the dead, wounded, and missing or captured is from the American Battlefield Trust website on Bull Run, First Manassas. The number of Zouaves and Second Scott's Life Guards who were killed, wounded, or missing is from the 11th Regiment as well as from the 38th Regiment, New York Volunteer Infantry Historical Sketches, in *Third Annual Report of the Bureau of Military Statistics of the State of New York*, Albany: C. Wendell, 1866. "It is said that their dead . . ." from *Raleigh Register*, July 27, 1861.

12. "Sun-burned . . ." from *NYT*, July 26, 1861; "Certain reckless journals . . ." from *NYT*, July 23, 1861; "I have just been . . ." from *Letters of a Family During the War for the Union: 1861–1865*, vol. I, private printing, 1899, p. 135; "Found in a pile . . ." from *NYT*, September 24, 1861. Following their return to New York, the Zouaves were seen as quite demoralized. That August, their regimental rolls listed 31 discharged, 24 killed, 103 wounded, 104 absent, 606 present, 20 in the hospital, and 43 in prison in Richmond.

13. "Emigrant from Bull Run," from *New York Clipper*, August 3, 1861.

14. "We were frequently . . ." and "During the thirteen . . ." from a letter from Thomas Hamblin, from June 30, 1888, contained in his Civil War Pension File, US National Archives & Records Administration, Can. No. 8974, Bundle 35; "Much admired . . ." from a July 25, 1888, statement by George W. Cooney, Thomas Hamblin Civil War Pension File.

15. Lyrics from sheet music, Song on the Death of Colonel Ellsworth, "The Gallant Zouave," J. Magee, Philadelphia, Pa., 1861. "So as to avenge . . ." from *NYT*, July 25, 1861.

16. "Crush out . . ." from *NYT*, March 7, 1862; "That every hour . . ." from *NYTR*, August 20, 1862. The Battle of Antietam saw the death of 2,108 Union and 1,546 Confederate soldiers. "That all persons . . ." from transcript on the National Archive's website.

17. The meeting was covered by *NYT*, January 6, 1863.

18. The 1861 election for mayor was a three-way race; George Opdyke (Republican) received 25,380 votes, Charles Godfrey Gunther (Tammany Democrat) 24,767, and Fernando Wood (Mozart Democrat) 24,167, from Caliendo, *New York City Mayors*, p. 402. "A graceful irregular shape . . ." from *NYT*, Aug. 20, 1862.

19. "Puffs of white clouds . . ." from *A History of Real Estate Buildings and Architecture in New York City*, New York: Record and Guide, 1898, p. 459.

20. "The biggest little . . ." from *NYT*, February 11, 1863.

21. "Mr. Brady . . ." from *NYT*, October 20, 1862.

22. "For these trenches . . ." from *NYT*, October 20, 1862; "Spartan women . . ." from *NYH*, May 3, 1861.

23. "IMMEDIATE DONATIONS . . ." from *NYT*, July 24, 1861; "Found discipline . . ." from *Documents of the U.S. Sanitary Commission*, vol. I, Numbers 1 to 60. New York: 1866, p. 104.

24. "Works like a dog . . ." from *GTSD*, January 26, 1863.

25. For efforts of the women on the ships, see L.P. Brockett and Mary C. Vaughan, *Woman's Work in the Civil War: A Record of Heroism, Patriotism and Patience*, Boston: Zeigler, McCurdy & Co., 1867, pp. 300–301 and 324. "*You can't conceive . . .*" from Katharine Prescott Wormeley, *The Other Side of War*, Boston: Ticknor and Company, 1889, p. 102.

26. "They have worked . . ." from Frederick Law Olmsted, *Hospital Transports: A Memoir of the Embarkation of the Sick and Wounded from the Peninsula of Virginia in the Summer of 1862*, Boston: Ticknor and Fields, 1863, p. 69; "They beat . . ." quoted in Nancy Scripture Garrison, *With Courage and Delicacy: Civil War on the Peninsula*, Mason City, Iowa: Savas Publishing Company, 1999, p. 104.

27. More than 3,000 Civil War veterans would be buried in Cypress Hills Cemetery. In 1870 the cemetery sold the section to the federal government, and it became the Cypress Hills National Cemetery.

28. "Received only the worst . . ." and "Went among from . . ." from Walt Whitman, *The Wound Dresser*, Boston: Small, Maynard & Company, 1898, pp. 22 and 44.

Chapter 23

1. "I was too old . . ." from Barnum, *Struggles and Triumphs*, p. 230; "To write to me . . ." from *GTSD*, August 29, 1864; "That 300-dollar law . . ." from *NYT*, July 15, 1863. On Strong and other exemptions, see *Prologue Magazine*, Winter 1994.

2. "Bloody and treasonable . . ." from *NYT*, July 6, 1863; On Saturday evening . . ." from *NYH*, July 14, 1863.

3. "After a while . . ." from *GTSD*, July 13, 1863.

4. "Mrs. Hilton . . ." from Maria Lydig Daly, *Diary of a Union Lady: 1861-1865*, New York: Funk & Wagnall's, 1962, p. 250.

5. "Dressed my wounds . . ." from *McClure's Magazine*, August 1893; "Several times . . ." from *Sunday Truth* (Buffalo), February 20, 1887.

6. "They beat him . . ." from *NYTR*, July 14, 1863. Chief Kennedy miraculously survived the assault.

7. "Hunted like dogs . . ." from *NYT*, July 14, 1863; "Every club . . ." from *NYTR*, July 16, 1863.

8. "Small mobs . . ." from *The War of the Rebellion: A Compilation of the Official Records of the Union and the Confederate Armies*, Washington, DC: Government Printing Office, 1889, pp. 886–887; "We feared . . ." from Daly, *Diary of a Union Lady*, p. 249.

9. "The colored people . . ." quoted in Iver Bernstein, *The New York City Draft Riots: The Significance for American Society and Politics in the Age of the Civil War*, New York: Oxford University Press, 1990, p. 27.

10. "Were quietly seated . . ." from *Fourth Annual Report of the Commissioners of Public Charities and Correction*, New York: Frank McElroy, 1864, pp. 188–189; "Will have to . . ." from Benson Lossing, *History of New York City*, vol. II, New York: Perine Engraving and Publishing Co., 1884, p. 467.

11. "Men, you know . . ." quoted in *States at War: A Reference Guide for New York in the Civil War*, vol. 2, Richard Miller, editor, Hanover, N.H.: University Press of New England, 2014, p. 63.

12. Population numbers come from Hirsch, "The Free Negro in New York," p. 415, and *NYT*, July 26, 2013. Similarly, *NYT*, July 26, 2013, cites the amount of money raised by The Committee of Merchants for the Relief of Colored People Suffering from the Late Riots. "God pardon . . ." from *GTSD*, February 24, 1864; "Was packed . . ." from *NYT*, March 6, 1864; "Ethiopia marching . . ." from *GTSD*, March 6, 1864.

13. "Sick and wished . . ." and "It was rather . . ." from *NYT*, June 30, 1864; "She was black . . ." from *NYEP*, June 20, 1864.

14. "Destroy this Dam . . ." from *The Protest of W.W. Cleary Against the Proclamation of President Johnson*, Toronto: Lovell and Gibson, 1865, p. 28.

15. On city election numbers for 1864, see *NYT*, November 22, 1864. Nationally, Lincoln won 2,220,846 popular votes with 212 Electoral College votes, to McClellan's 1,809,445 popular votes and 21 Electoral College votes; from Election Results for 1864 from the Library of Congress Resource Guide. "There must be something . . ." from John W. Headley, *Confederate Operations in Canada and New York*, New York: Neale Publishing Company, 1906, p. 272.

16. "After lighting . . ." and the rest of the description of the arson from Headley, *Confederate Operations in Canada and New York*, pp. 274–275; "The Tallest . . ." from *NYH*, November 25, 1864.

17. "The theater was crowded . . ." from Asia Booth Clarke, *The Elder and the Younger Booth*, Boston: James R. Osgood, 1882, p. 159; "In the midst . . ." from Daly, *Diary of a Union Lady*, p. 317.

18. "A certain classic . . ." from *NYT*, November 29, 1864; "Declared his belief . . ." from *The Century Illustrated Monthly Magazine*, October 1894.

19. Adam Badeau, whom Edwin and John Booth tended to during the Draft Riots, was on General Grant's staff, and witnessed Lee's surrender. "A series . . ." from *GTSD*, April 10, 1865.

Coda

1. "All Broadway is black . . ." from Gay Wilson Allen, *Walt Whitman*, New York: Grove Press, 1961, p. 96.

2. "I had a last . . ." from *GTSD*, April 19, 1865. Booth was shot by Sargent Thomas "Boston" Corbett, and, like Lincoln, would linger on till the following day when he died. Yet unlike the president, there was no grand funeral for him. Booth's body was buried at the Old Arsenal Penitentiary in Washington. Edwin Booth got permission from President Andrew Johnson in 1869 to disinter his brother, and placed John in an unmarked grave in the Booth's family plot in Baltimore's Green Mount Cemetery.

3. "It seemed like . . ." from *GTSD*, May 22, 1865. For population numbers of New Yorkers, see Hough, *Census of the State of New York, for 1865*, pp. XXIV–XXV. The United States Sanitary Commission ended its work on July 4, 1865. The following year Strong, Olmsted, Henry Bellows, and other USSC officers established the American Association for the Relief of the Misery of Battle Fields, which was a branch of the Comité International de Secours aux Militaires Blessés of Geneva, which was later known as the Red Cross.

4. "To see the day . . ." from Tappan, *The Life of Arthur Tappan*, p. 378; "Until the black . . ." from *NYT*, May 11, 1865; "Born or naturalized . . ." and "On account . . ." from the United States Constitution; "Hail, year of jubilee . . ." from *Liberator*, December 29, 1865; "*The Nation* . . ." from *The Nation*, July 6, 1865.

5. After Stewart opened the new Iron Palace, the Marble Palace on Chambers Street was used for wholesale; Stewart died on April 10, 1876.

6. Cost of cabinetry is cited in *NYT*, May 5, 1986. "Just imagine the untiring . . ." from *NYT*, May 11, 1871.

7. "Had been killed . . ." from Trinity Church's *Vestry Minutes*, September 26, 1865, pp. 101–102; "A neat marble monument . . ." from the *New York Sunday Mercury*, March 4, 1866.

8. On makeup of the new department, see *NYT*, November 3, 1865.

9. "Almost in the twinkling . . ." from *NYT*, July 14, 1865; "The Fire Department worked . . ." from *NYTR*, July 14, 1865.

10. "If I were you . . ." from *Harper's*, September 1865; "I don't make . . ." from Barnum, *Struggles and Triumphs*, p. 670. Barnum died on April 7, 1891.

11. Bennett died on June 1, 1872. "I was quite aware . . ." from Greeley, *Recollections of a Busy Life*, p. 416; Greeley died November 29, 1872.

12. "The fire raged . . ." from *NYS*, December 19, 1866. On New Bowery Benefits, see *NYTR*, December 28, 1866. On Lingard's death, see *Brooklyn Daily Eagle*, July 11, 1870.

13. "Devise and frame . . ." quoted in Goldman, *Building New York's Sewers*, p. 138. For deaths from cholera, see *Summary of Vital Statistics 2017 of the City of New York*. "Good and sufficient . . ." from Lawrence Veiller, *Tenement House Reform in New York, 1834–1900*, New York: Evening Post Job Printing House, 1900, p. 18.

14. "Filled up with cheap . . ." from *NYT*, March 9, 1867.

15. John Randel died in Albany in 1865. "It is the only . . ." from *Seventh Annual Report of the American Scenic and Historic Preservation Society*, Albany: J.B. Lyon Company, 1902, p. 86.

16. NYU was still officially called the University of the City of New York, though it was popularly known as New York University. In 1896 the school officially changed its name to New York University. Davis, thankfully, would not have to live to see his NYU building destroyed in 1894. He died on January 14, 1892. NYU faced severe financial problems, and in March 1973 sold the Bronx campus to New York's CUNY system. It became the Bronx Community College. NYU then focused its campus at its original home in Washington Square.

17. "The end of . . ." from *NYTR*, January 1, 1898. Park acreage in 1898 from nycgovparks. org, "A Timeline of New York City Department of Parks & Recreation History: Park Planning for Greater New York (1870–1898)."

18. "One of the most . . ." from Edith Wharton, *A Backward Glance*, New York: Charles Scribner's Sons, 1964, pp. 54–57. Vaux died on November 21, 1895. Olmsted lived to see the new century, dying on August 23, 1903.

19. "Uptown this evening . . ." from *GTSD-MS*, July 22, 1871. Strong returned to his legal practice following the war, but admitted on December 13, 1872, as he was retiring to become the comptroller at Trinity, that he "never got myself thoroughly into the legal harness again." He died of cancer on July 21, 1875, at his home on Gramercy Park. He was 55 years old. His 2,250-page diary was kept by his family, and in 1927 loaned to the museum of the American Red Cross in Washington, D.C., and would eventually come to the attention of Allan Nevins and Milton Halsey Thomas, who published it in 1952.

Selected Bibliography

Archives, Libraries, Collections, and Private Papers

American Antiquarian Society
    Henry Dana Ward Letters
Columbia University
Hagley Museum and Library
    Wurts Family Papers
Harvard University
    Houghton Library, New York Association Papers
    Baker Library, Comstock Family Papers
Jervis Public Library
    John Bloomfield Jervis Papers
Library of Congress
    Frederick Law Olmsted Papers
    Lewis Tappan Papers
Maritime Heritage Project, San Francisco
    Cargo of the *John W. Cater*
    Merchant Ships in Port
Metropolitan Museum of Art
    Alexander Jackson Davis Letterbook
National Canal Museum Archives
New York City Municipal Archives and Records Center
    Health (Cholera Epidemic) Papers, 1832
New-York Historical Society
    Beekman Family Papers
    Philip Hone diary manuscript (*PHD-MS*)
    New York City Riots Mss. file
    James Riker Jr., Autobiographical Reminiscences
    Silvester Papers
    Strong Family Papers
    George Templeton Strong diary manuscript (*GTSD-MS*)
    Edward Neufville Tailer Diary
    William Tweed Miscellaneous Letters
    G.C. Verplanck Papers
New York Public Library
    Alexander Jackson Davis Papers
    Asher B. Durand Papers
    New York City Land Conveyances, grantors and grantees, 1654–1851 (*NYCLC*)
    Thomas K. Wharton Diary
    John Wolcott Phelps Papers

New York University Special Collections
South Street Seaport Museum, Maritime Reference Library
Trinity Church Archives
    Database of baptisms, marriages and deaths, and Vestry Minutes
US National Archives & Records Administration
    Thomas Hamblin Civil War Pension and Military Service files
Wayne County Historical Society
Yale University Manuscript Collection
    Ithiel Town Papers

Newspapers and Periodicals

AME Church Review
American Heritage
The Anti-Slavery Examiner
Broadway Journal
Brooklyn Daily Eagle
Brooklyn Evening Star
Brother Jonathan
Century Illustrated Monthly Magazine
Chambers's Journal of Popular Literature, Science, and Art
The Cholera Bulletin
The Colored American
Columbia Spy
Daily Alta California
De Bow's Review and Industrial Resources, Statistics, etc.
The Emancipator
Frederick Douglass' Paper
Freedom's Journal
Harper's New Monthly Magazine
Horticulturist and Journal of Rural Art and Rural Taste
Hudson River Chronicle
Hunt's Merchants' Magazine and Commercial Review
The Knickerbocker or New-York Monthly Magazine
L'Oracle and Daily Advertiser
The Liberator
Life Illustrated
McDowall's Journal
McClure's Magazine
Mercantile Advertiser and New-York Advocate
Morning Courier and New-York Enquirer (MCNYE)
The National Advocate
New-York American (NYAM)
The New York Atlas
New York Aurora
New-York Commercial Advertiser (NYCA)

New-York Daily Advertiser (NYDA)
New York Day Book
New York Evening Chronicle
New-York Evening Journal
New-York Evening Post (NYEP)
The New-York Gazette & General Advertiser (NYGGA)
The New-York Gazette; and the Weekly Mercury
New-York Herald (NYH)
The New York Journal of Commerce (JOC)
The New-York Mirror, and Ladies' Literary Gazette (NYM)
The New-York Packet, and the American Advertiser
New-York Spectator
New-York Spirit of the Times
New York Star
New York Sun (NYS)
New York Sunday Dispatch
The New York Sunday Mercury
The New-York Times (NYT)
New-York Tribune (**NYTR**)
Niles Register
Putnam's Monthly Magazine of American Literature, Science and Art
United States Magazine and Democratic Review

Unpublished Dissertations, Theses, Papers, and Manuscripts

Calhoun, Richard B., *From Community to Metropolis: Fire Protection in New York City, 1790–1875*, PhD dissertation, Columbia University, 1973.

Carman, Harry James, *The Street Surface Railway Franchises of New York City*, PhD dissertation, Columbia University, 1919.

Freeman, Rhoda Golden, *The Free Negro in New York City in the Era Before the Civil War*, PhD dissertation, Columbia University, 1966.

Ginsberg, Stephen F., *The History of Fire Protection in New York City, 1800–1842*, PhD dissertation, New York University, 1968.

Kriedman, Herbert, *New York's Philip Hone: Businessman-Politician-Patron of Arts and Letters*, PhD dissertation, New York University, 1965.

Shank, Theodore, Jr., *The Bowery Theatre, 1826–1836*, Dissertation, Stanford University, 1956.

Trinity Church, *Vestry Minutes*, 1865.

Primary Sources

The American Print Works vs. Cornelius W. Lawrence, Supreme Court of New Jersey—Essex Circuit, Proceedings at the Trial of above entitled Cause, at Essex Circuit, October 1852, New York: Collins, Bowne & Co., 1852 (*APW*).

The Diary of Philip Hone, 1828–1851, edited by Allan Nevins, in two volumes, New York: Dodd, Mead and Company, 1927 (*PHD-AN*).

The Diary of Philip Hone, 1828–1851, edited by Bayard Tuckerman, New York: Dodd, Mead and Company, 1910 (*PHD-BT*).

The Diary of George Templeton Strong: Young Man in New York, 1835–1849, editors, Allan Nevins and Milton Halsey Thomas, New York: Octagon Books, 1974, in four volumes (*GTSD*).

Documents of the Board of Aldermen of the City of New York (DBA), various volumes.

Documents of the Board of Assistants of the City of New York (DBAsst), various volumes.

Longworth's American Almanac, New-York Register, and City Directory, New-York: Thomas Longworth, various years.

Minutes of the Common Council of the City of New York, 1675 to 1776, vol. IV, New York: Dodd, Mead and Company, 1905 (*MCC, 1675–1776*), various volumes.

Minutes of the Common Council of the City of New York, 1784–1831, New York: City of New York, 1917 (*MCC, 1784–1831*), various volumes.

Olmsted, Frederick Law, *The Papers of Frederick Law Olmsted: Slavery and the South*, various editors, vol. II, III, IV, Baltimore: Johns Hopkins University Press, 1983 to 1986.

Population of States and Counties of the United States: 1790 to 1990, from the Twenty-One Decennial Censuses, Washington, D.C.: Government Printing Office, 1996.

Proceedings of the Board of Aldermen of the City of New York, various years *(PBA)*.

Proceedings, Board of Aldermen and Assistant Aldermen of the City of New York (*PBAAA*), various years.

Proceedings of the Board of Councilmen of the City of New York, various years.

Trow's New York City Directory, New York: John F. Trow, various years.

Contemporary Accounts

Bird, Isabella Lucy, *The Englishwoman in America*, London: John Murray, 1856.

Boardman, James, *America, and the Americans*, London: Longman, Rees, Orme, Brown, Green, & Longman, 1833.

Bobo, William, *Glimpses of New-York City by a South Carolinian*, Charleston: J.J. McCarter, 1852.

Child, L. Maria, *Letters from New-York*, New York: C.S. Francis & Co., 1845.

Dickens, Charles, *American Notes*, London: Hazell, Watson & Viney, Ltd, 1842.

Greene, Asa, *A Glance at New York*, New York: A. Greene, 1837.

Hubbard, N.T., *Autobiography of N.T. Hubbard with Personal Reminiscences of New York City from 1798 to 1875*, New York: John F. Trow & Son, 1875.

Lathers, Richard, *Reminiscences of Richard Lathers: Sixty Years of a Busy Life in South Carolina, Massachusetts and New York*, Alvan F. Sanborn, editor, New York: The Grafton Press, 1907.

Still, Bayrd, *Mirror for Gotham*, New York: Fordham University Press, 1994.

Strong, George W., *Letters of George W. Strong*, New York: G.P. Putnam's Sons, 1922.

Trollope, Frances, *Domestic Manners of the Americans*, London: Whittaker, Treacher, & Co., 1832.

Whitman, Walt, *Complete Prose Works: Specimen Days and Collect, November Boughs and Good Bye My Fancy*, Boston: Small, Maynard & Company, 1901.

Whitman, Walt, *Complete Prose Works*, New York: D. Appleton and Company, 1910.

Secondary Sources

American and New York History

American National Biography, John A. Garraty & Mark C. Carnes, editors, New York: Oxford University Press, 1999, various volumes.

Browne, Junius Henri, *The Great Metropolis: A Mirror of New York*, Hartford: American Publishing Co., 1869.

Burrows, Edwin G., and Wallace, Mike, *Gotham: A History of New York City to 1898*, New York: Oxford University Press, 1999.

Cohen, Paul, and Augustyn, Robert T., *Manhattan in Maps, 1527–1995*, New York: Rizzoli, 1997.

Encyclopedia of African American History, Leslie M. Alexander and Walter C. Rucker, editors, Santa Barbara, Calif.: ABC-CLIO, 2010, various volumes.

The Encyclopedia of New York City, Kenneth T. Jackson, editor, New Haven: Yale University Press, 2010.

Reynolds, David S., *Waking Giant: America in the Age of Jackson*, New York: Harper Collins, 2008.

Spann, Edward K., *The New Metropolis: New York City, 1840–1857*, New York: Columbia University Press, 1981.

Stokes, I.N. Phelps, *The Iconography of Manhattan Island: 1498–1909*, New York: Robert H. Dodd, six volumes, 1915 to 1928.

Fires

Costello, Augustine E., *Our Firemen: A History of the New York Fire Departments, Volunteer and Paid*, New York: Knickerbocker Press, 1997.

Dunshee, Kenneth Holcomb, *As You Pass By*, New York: Hastings House, 1952.

Foster, C., *An Account of the Conflagration of the Principal Part of the First Ward of the City of New-York*, New York: C. Foster, 1835.

Golway, Terry, *So Others Might Live: A History of New York's Bravest: The FDNY from 1700 to the Present*, New York: Basic Books, 2002.

Hamilton, James, *Reminiscences of James Hamilton: or, Men and Events, at Home and Abroad, During Three Quarters of a Century*, New York: Charles Scribner & Co., 1869.

Limpus, Lowell M., *History of the New York Fire Department*, New York: E.P. Dutton, 1940.

Tyler, James, *Reminiscences of the V.F.D.: From "Fire-Laddie to Supe,"* Bay Ridge: James H. Barr, 1878.

Land Development

Ballon, Hilary, editor, *The Greatest Grid: The Master Plan of Manhattan, 1811–2011*, New York: Museum of the City of New York and Columbia University Press, 2012.

Blackmar, Elizabeth, *Manhattan for Rent, 1785-1850*, Ithaca: Cornell University Press, 1989.

Haeger, John Denis, *John Jacob Astor: Business and Finance in the Early Republic*, Detroit: Wayne State University Press, 1991.

Hill, George Everett, and Waring, George E., Jr., "Old Wells and Water-Courses of the Island of Manhattan," Part I & II, in *Historic New York: Being the First Series of the Half Moon Papers*, Maud Wilder Goodwin, Alice Carrington Royce and Ruth Putnam editors, New York: G.P. Putnam's Son, 1897.

Madsen, Axel, *John Jacob Astor: America's First Millionaire*, New York: John Wiley & Sons, 2001.

McCabe, James D., Jr., *Great Fortunes, and How They Were Made; of the Struggles and Triumphs of Our Self-Made Men*, Cincinnati: E. Hannaford & Company, 1872.

Porter, Kenneth Wiggins, *John Jacob Astor: Business Man*, volumes I & II, Cambridge: Harvard University Press, 1931.

Sanderson, Eric W., *Mannahatta: A Natural History of New York City*, New York: Abrams, 2009.

Culture

Barnum, P.T., *Struggles and Triumphs: or Sixty Years' Recollections of P.T. Barnum*, Buffalo: Courier Company, 1889.

Bogar, Thomas A., *Thomas Hamblin and the Bowery Theatre: The New York Reign of "Blood and Thunder" Melodramas*, Providence, 2018.

Boyer, M. Christine, *Manhattan Manners: Architecture and Style, 1850–1900*, New York: Rizzoli, 1985.

Donnell, Edna, "A.J. Davis and the Gothic Revival," *Metropolitan Museum Studies*, vol. 5, no. 2, September 1936, pp. 183–233.

Hamlin, Talbot, *Greek Revival Architecture in America*, New York: Dover Publications, 1944.

Harris, Luther S., *Around Washington Square: An Illustrated History of Greenwich Village*, Baltimore: The Johns Hopkins University Press, 2003.

Heckscher, Morrison H., "Building the Empire City: Architects and Architecture," in *Art and the Empire City, 1825–1861*, edited by Catherine Hoover Voorsanger and John K. Howat, New Haven, Conn.: Yale University Press, 2000, pp. 169–187.

Henderson, Mary C. *The City and the Theatre*, New York: Back Stage Books, 2004.

Kramer, Ellen, "Contemporary Descriptions of New York City and Its Public Architecture ca. 1850," *The Journal of the Society of Architectural Historians*, vol. 27, no. 4, December 1968, pp. 264–280.

Macmillan Encyclopedia of Architects, Adolf K. Placzek, editor, New York: The Free Press, 1982, various volumes.

Peck, Amelia, editor, *Alexander Jackson Davis: American Architect, 1803–1892*, New York: Rizzoli, 1992.

Commerce

Albion, Robert Greenhalgh, *The Rise of New York Port (1815–1860)*, Boston: Northeastern University Press, 1984.

Crouthamel, James L., "The Newspaper Revolution in New York, 1830–1860," *New York History*, vol. 45, no. 2, April 1964, pp. 92–113

Elias, Stephen N., *Alexander T. Stewart: The Forgotten Merchant Prince*, Westport: Praeger, 1992.

Fox, Louis, H., *New York City Newspapers, 1820–1850: A Bibliography*, Chicago: University of Chicago Press, 1927.

Gardner, Deborah S. *Cadwalader, Wickersham & Taft: A Bicentennial History, 1792–1992*, New York: Cadwalader, Wickersham & Taft, 1994.

Geldert, Louis, *The Eagle Fire Company of New York*, New York, 1906.

Resseguie, Harry, "Alexander Turney Stewart and the Development of the Department Store, 1823–1876," *Business History Review*, vol. 39, no. 3, Autumn, 1965, pp. 301–322.

Wyatt-Brown, Bertram, "God and Dun & Bradstreet, 1841–1851," *Business History Review*, vol. 40, Winter 1966, pp. 432–450.

Water and Sewage

Blake, Nelson Manfred, *Water for the Cities: A History of the Urban Water Supply Problem in the United States*: Syracuse, N.Y.: Syracuse University Press, 1956.

Jervis, John, *The Reminiscences of John B. Jervis: Engineer of the Old Croton*, Neal FitzSimons, editor, Syracuse: Syracuse University Press, 1971.

Galusha, Diane, *Liquid Assets: A History of New York City's Water System*, Fleischmanns, NY: Purple Mountain Press, 1999.

Goldman, Joanne Abel, *Building New York's Sewers: Developing Mechanisms of Urban Management*, West Lafayette: Purdue University Press, 1997.

Koeppel, Gerard T., *Water for Gotham: A History*, Princeton: Princeton University Press, 2000.

Lankton, Larry D., "The 'Practicable' Engineer: John B. Jervis and the Old Croton Aqueduct," Chicago: Public Works Historical Society, 1977.

Larkin, F. Daniel, *John B. Jervis: An American Engineering Pioneer*, Ames: Iowa State University Press, 1990.

Wegmann, Edward, *The Water-Supply of the City of New York, 1658–1895*, New York: John Wiley & Sons, 1896.

Crime & Disease

Anbinder, Tyler, *Five Points: The 19th-Century New York City Neighborhood That Invented Tap Dance, Stole Elections, and Became the World's Most Notorious Slum*, New York: The Free Press, 2001.

Duffy, John, *A History of Public Health in New York City 1625–1866*, New York: Russell Sage Foundation, 1968.

Ernst, Robert, *Immigrant Life in New York City: 1825–1863*, Port Washington: Ira J. Friendman, Inc., 1949.

Gilje, Paul A., *The Road to Mobocracy*, Chapel Hill: University of North Carolina Press, 1987.

Rosenberg, Charles E., *The Cholera Years: The United States in 1832, 1849 and 1866*, Chicago: The University of Chicago Press, 1962.

Weinbaum, Paul O., "Temperance, Politics, and the New York City Riots of 1857," *New-York Historical Society Quarterly*, vol. LIX, no. 3, July 1975, pp. 246–270.

African Americans

Alexander, Leslie M., *African or American? Black Identity and Political Activism in New York City, 1784–1861*, Urbana: University of Illinois Press, 2008.

Douglass, Frederick, *Narrative of the Life of Frederick Douglass, an American Slave*, London: H.G. Collins, 1851.

Foner, Eric, *Gateway to Freedom: The Hidden History of the Underground Railroad*, New York: W.W. Norton, 2015.

Gates, Henry Louis, and Higginbotham, Evelyn Brooks, editors, *African American National Biography*, New York: Oxford University Press, 2008, various volumes.

Hirsch, Leo H., Jr., "The Free Negro in New York," *Journal of Negro History*, vol. 16, no. 4, October 1931, pp. 415–453.

Hodges, Graham Russell, *Root & Branch: African Americans in New York & New Jersey, 1613–1863*, Chapel Hill: University of North Carolina Press, 1999.

Slavery in New York, edited by Ira Berlin and Leslie M. Harris, New York: The New-York Historical Society, 2005.

Tappan, Lewis, *The Life of Arthur Tappan*, New York: Hurd and Houghton and Co., 1870.

Wyatt-Brown Bertram, *Lewis Tappan and the Evangelical War Against Slavery*, Cleveland: The Press of Case Western Reserve University, 1969.

Washington, S.A.M., *George Thomas Downing: Sketch of His Life and Times*, Newport: The Milne Printery, 1910.

Central Park

Alex, William, *Calvert Vaux: Architect & Planner*, New York: Ink, Inc., 1994.

Heckscher, Morrison H., *Creating Central Park*, New York: The Metropolitan Museum of Art, 2008.

Kowsky, Francis R., *Country, Park & City: The Architecture and Life of Calvert Vaux*, New York: Oxford University Press, 2003.

Olmsted, Frederick Law, *Forty Years of Landscape Architecture: Central Park*, edited by Frederick Law Olmsted Jr. and Theodora Kimball, Cambridge: MIT Press, 1973.

Rosenzweig, Roy, and Blackmar, Elizabeth, *The Park and the People: A History of Central Park*, Ithaca: Cornell University Press, 1992.

Rybczynski, Witold, *A Clearing in the Distance: Frederick Law Olmsted and America in the Nineteenth Century*, New York: Scribner, 1999.

Politics

Ackerman, Kenneth D., *Boss Tweed: The Rise and Fall of the Corrupt Pol Who Conceived the Soul of Modern New York*, New York: Carroll & Graf Publishers, 2005.

Allen, Oliver E., *The Tiger: The Rise and Fall of Tammany Hall*, Reading, MA: Addison-Wesley, 1993.

Bridges, Amy, *A City in the Republic: Antebellum New York and the Origins of Machine Politics*, Cambridge: Cambridge University Press, 1984.

Callow, Alexander B., Jr., *The Tweed Ring*, New York: Oxford University Press, 1966.

Hershkowitz, Leo, *Tweed's New York: Another Look*, Garden City: Anchor Press, 1977.

Lynch, Denis Tilden, *"Boss" Tweed: The Story of a Grim Generation*, New York: Boni and Liveright, 1927.

Mushkat, Jerome, *Fernando Wood: A Political Biography*, Kent. Ohio: Kent State University Press, 1990.

Werner, M.R., *Tammany Hall*, New York: Greenwood Press, 1968.

The Civil War

American Battlefield Trust Website, https://www.battlefields.org/

Bernstein, Iver, *The New York City Draft Riots: The Significance for American Society and Politics in the Age of the Civil War*, New York: Oxford University Press, 1990.

Third Annual Report of the Bureau of Military Statistics of the State of New York, Albany: C. Wendell, 1866.

Illustration Credits

Frontispiece A map shewing the extent of the great fire which broke out about 9 O'clock on the night of the 16th December 1835, in the City of New-York, 1836, George Hayward, lithograph, Map Division, New York Public Library.

Plate 1 Collect Pond, Attributed to Archibald Robertson, 1798, The Edward W. C. Arnold Collection of New York Prints, Maps, and Pictures, Metropolitan Museum of Art

Plate 2 A view of Collect Pond and its vicinity in the City of New York in 1793: on which pond the first boat propelled by steam with paddle wheels or screw propellers was constructed by John Fitch, six years before Robert Fulton, Lionel Pincus and Princess Firyal Map Division, New York Public Library.

Plate 3 Sketch of Lispenard's Meadows, New York City, 1800, The Miriam and Ira D. Wallach Division of Art, Prints and Photographs: Print Collection, New York Public Library.

Plate 4 Attributed to Daniel Huntington, *Philip Hone (1780–1851)*, 1845–1850. Oil on canvas, 30 1/8 × 25 1/8 in. Purchase, art and Prosper Guerry Funds, New-York Historical Society, 1951.475.

Plate 5 Residence of Philip Hone Esq. and American Hotel, Broadway, The Miriam and Ira D. Wallach Division of Art, Prints and Photographs: Print Collection, New York Public Library.

Plate 6 Seventh Regiment on Review, Washington Square, New York, by Otto Boetticher, 1851, The Edward W. C. Arnold Collection of New York Prints, Maps, and Pictures, Bequest of Edward W. C. Arnold, 1954, Metropolitan Museum of Art.

Plate 7 Nicolino Calyo, *The Great Fire of 1835: View of New York City Taken from Brooklyn Heights on the Same Evening of the Fire*, ca.1835. Gouache on heavy paper, laid on Japanese paper, wrapped over board; 201/8 × 273/16 in. Purchase, New-York Historical Society,1935.167.

Plate 8 Hanington's Dioramic Representation of the Great Fire in New York, Dec. 16 and 17, 1835. Now Exhibiting with Other Moving Dioramic Scenes, at the American Museum Every Evening, H. Sewell, H. Sewell, 1836, The Edward W. C. Arnold Collection of New York Prints, Maps and Pictures, Bequest of Edward W. C. Arnold, 1954, Metropolitan Museum of Art.

Plate 9 View of the ruins after the Great Fire in New York, Dec. 16th & 17th, 1835. As seen from Exchange Place, 1835, Miriam and Ira D. Wallach Division of Art, Prints and Photographs Print Collection, *New York Public Library*.

Plate 10 "A Map of the Ruins," illustration from the Extra *Sun*, December 19, 1835. New-York Historical Society, 99239d.

Plate 11 Mr. Hamblain [Hamblin] as Red Riven, Billy Rose Theatre Division, New York Public Library.

Plate 12 Bowery Theatre, The Eno collection of New York City Views, New York Public Library.

Plate 13 John Jacob Astor, painting by Edward Dalton Marchant, 1836, New York Public Library.

Plate 14 St. Paul's Church, Barnum''s Museum, & Astor House, 1850, the Miriam and Ira D. Wallach Division of Art, Prints and Photographs: Print Collection, New York Public Library.

Plate 15 Brennan Farm House, 84th Street, n.d. half-tone photograph. PR 020, New-York Historical Society 84696d.

Plate 16 2nd Ave. and 42nd Street, Museum of the City of New York, X2012.61.27.39, MN164366.

Plate 17 South Street Seaport, c 1834, I. N. Phelps Stokes Collection of American Historical Prints, New York Public Library.

Plate 18 Broadway and Trinity Church 1830, I. N. Phelps Stokes Collection of American Historical Prints, New York Public Library.

Plate 19 Merchants' Exchange, The Miriam and Ira D. Wallach Division of Art, Prints and Photographs: Print Collection, New York Public Library.

Plate 20 Stewart Building, [Broadway between Chambers and Duane Streets]. 1850. PR 020, New-York Historical Society, 84551d.

Plate 21 Walt Whitman, 1853, Rare Book Division, New York Public Library.

Plate 22 New York University, 1850, I. N. Phelps Stokes Collection of American Historical Prints, New York Public Library.

Plate 23 All Souls' Unitarian Church, Stereograph, The Miriam and Ira D. Wallach Division of Art, Prints and Photographs: Photography Collection, New York Public Library.

Plate 24 The Croton Celebration, 1842, The Eno collection of New York City views, New York Public Library.

Plate 25 View of the Distributing Reservoir on Murray Hill, 1850, New York Public Library.

Plate 26 New York from the Steeple of St. Paul's Church, Looking East, South, and West, 1849, Henry A. Papprill, The Edward W. C. Arnold Collection of New York Prints, Maps and Pictures, Metropolitan Museum of Art.

Plate 27 George Templeton Strong, illustration from The Diary of George Templeton Strong. New-York Historical Society, 71367.

Plate 28 Castle Garden, Alexander Jackson Davis, The Miriam and Ira D. Wallach Division of Art, Prints and Photographs: Print Collection, New York Public Library.

Plate 29 Jenny Lind [as Amina in Bellini's] La sonnambula [graphic] / engraved by W.R. Mote after the original painting by J.W. Wright, Source Call Number: Art File L742 no. 1 (size XS), Used by permission of the Folger Shakespeare Library under a Creative Commons Attribution-ShareAlike 4.0 International License.

Plate 30 William Tweed, Hoxie Collection, Library of Congress.

Plate 31 The life of a fireman: the metropolitan system, Currier and Ives, Prints and Photographs Division, Library of Congress.

Plate 32 Americus Fire Engine No. 6., W. H. Van Tassell. Museum of the City of New York. 32.149.2.

Plate 33 Crystal Palace, 1853, The Eno collection of New York City views, New York Public Library.

Plate 34 Currier & Ives, The Miriam and Ira D. Wallach Division of Art, Prints and Photographs: Print Collection, New York Public Library,

Plate 35 Riot at the Astor-Place Opera-House, New York, (London?: s.n. 1849), Source Call Number: ART File N567.7 n. 2. Used by permission of the Folger Shakespeare Library under a Creative Commons Attribution-ShareAlike 4.0 International License.

Plate 36 Working men, shall Americans or English rule! In this city?/ American Committee, (1849 May 09), Source Call Number: 263-872b. Used by permission of the Folger Shakespeare Library under a Creative Commons Attribution-ShareAlike 4.0 International License.

Plate 37 *Arthur Tappan,* frontis illustration from *The Life of Arthur Tappan*, 1870. New-York Historical Society, 78647d.

Plate 38 Nicolino Calyo,*Oyster-Stand,*1840-1844. Watercolor, graphite, and gouache on paper, once bound into an album. 107/16 x 14¾ in. Thomas Jefferson Bryan Fund, New-York Historical Society, 1980.31.

Plate 39 A stoneware oyster jar from the Thomas Downing oyster house, ca. 1840, Object Number: 2019.52, Collection of the Smithsonian National Museum of African American History and Culture.

Plate 40 Fugitive slaves fleeing from slave catchers on horseback, 1849. Schomburg Center for Research in Black Culture, Manuscripts, Archives and Rare Books Division, New York Public Library.

Plate 41 Plymouth Church. Rev. Henry Ward Beecher selling a slave, 1897, Schomburg Center for Research in Black Culture, Manuscripts, Archives and Rare Books Division, New York Public Library.

Plate 42 Sleighing in New York, Thomas Benecke, engraver, 1855, the Miriam and Ira D. Wallach Division of Art, Prints and Photographs: Print Collection, New York Public Library

Plate 43 The Five Points, ca. 1827, Bequest of Mrs. Screven Lorillard (Alice Whitney), from the collection of Mrs. J. Insley Blair, 2016, Accession Number: 2016.797.17, Metropolitan Museum of Art.

Plate 44 Fernando Wood, 1860-1875, Brady-Handy photograph collection, Prints and Photographs Division, LC-BH83- 1814 [P&P], Library of Congress.

Plate 45 View from the "Dead Rabbit" barricade in Bayard Street, *Frank Leslie's Illustrated* newspaper, 1857, Prints and Photographs Division, AP2.L52 1857 (Case Y) [P&P], Library of Congress.

Plate 46 Panorama of the Embarkation of the Fire Zouaves on Board the Baltic Apr. 29th 1861, The Miriam and Ira D. Wallach Division of Art, Prints and Photographs: Print Collection, New York Public Library

Plate 47 Presentation of colors to the 20th U.S. Colored Infantry, Col. Bartram at the Union League Club House, N.Y., March 5, Emmet Collection of Manuscripts Etc. Relating to American History, New York Public Library

Plate 48 Frederick Law Olmsted, The Miriam and Ira D. Wallach Division of Art, Prints and Photographs: Print Collection, New York Public Library.

Plate 49 View in Central Park: Promenade looking south, June 1858, George Hayward, lithograph, The Miriam and Ira D. Wallach Division of Art, Prints and Photographs: Picture Collection, New York Public Library.

Plate 50 Skating in Central Park, New York, 1861, After Winslow Homer, lithograph, The Edward W. C. Arnold Collection of New York Prints, Maps and Pictures, No. 54.90.605, Metropolitan Museum of Art.

Index